IDENTITY
AND
LEADERSHIP
Informing Our Lives, Informing Our Practice

NASPA
Student Affairs Administrators
in Higher Education

IDENTITY
AND
LEADERSHIP

Informing Our Lives, Informing Our Practice

— EDITORS —

Alicia Fedelina Chávez & Ronni Sanlo

FOREWORD BY KEVIN KRUGER

NASPA
Student Affairs Administrators
in Higher Education

Identity and Leadership: Informing Our Lives, Informing Our Practice

Published by
NASPA–Student Affairs Administrators in Higher Education
111 K Street, NE
10th Floor
Washington, DC 20002
www.naspa.org

Additional copies may be purchased by contacting the NASPA publications department at 301-638-1749 or visiting http://bookstore.naspa.org.

Printed and bound in the United States of America

Library of Congress Cataloging-in-Publication Data

Identity and leadership : informing our lives, informing our practice / Alicia Fedelina Chavez and Ronni Sanlo, editors. -- First edition.
    pages cm
  ISBN 978-0-931654-83-1
  1. Student affairs services--United States--Administration. 2. Student affairs administrators--Professional relationships--United States. 3. Education, Higher--United States. 4. Educational leadership. 5. Social justice. I. Chavez, Alicia Fedelina. II. Sanlo, Ronni.
  LB2342.92.I43 2013
  378.1'60973--dc23
                        2012043479

FIRST EDITION

Contents

PART I
Intersections of Identity and Leadership

PART II
Voices of Identity and Leadership

PART III
Going Inward to Enhance Leadership

Foreword

In my career as a student affairs professional, I have been fortunate to have had occasions to contribute to a wide range of publications. However, none of these writing opportunities have had as much personal significance to me as being asked by Ronni Sanlo and Alicia Fedelina Chávez to write the foreword to *Identity and Leadership: Informing Our Lives, Informing Our Practice*.

Increasingly, we live in a fractious world where injustice is commonplace and often accepted. Remarks by public figures frequently reinforce decades-old perspectives based on bias, fear, and prejudice and threaten to undermine the social compact that is fundamental to advancing our society. However, as Nelson Mandela said, "Education is the most powerful weapon which you can use to change the world" (CNN, 2008, para. 7). The work of each of the authors in this text makes an important contribution to our collective scholarship. *Identity and Leadership* should be on the reading list for every graduate student and student affairs professional as we commit to creating an inclusive vision of student success.

My Own Journey

Lee Knefelkamp, Jamie Washington, Marylu McEwen, and Gwendolyn Jordan Dungy have all been critical teachers and mentors in the process of exploration of my own identity as a White man of privilege. Each, in their own way, has guided my understanding of the ways in which racism, sexism, and heterosexism have denied opportunities for others as well as favored and advantaged me. Thanks to these friends and mentors, I have come to understand my White male privilege as, what Peggy McIntosh (1988) called, an "invisible weightless knapsack of special provisions, assurances, tools, maps, guides, codebooks, passports, visas, clothes, compass, emergency gear, and blank checks" (pp. 2–3).

I have also come to understand that recognizing my own privilege is not about living a life of guilt and regret, but recognizing that I have access and opportunities not afforded to all. My personal challenge is to work toward using my power and influence to be responsible and responsive to the organizational changes necessary to widen the circle of privilege.

IDENTITY AND LEADERSHIP

As student affairs professionals, we must strive to develop a sense of empathy to guide our work with students and colleagues. As this book reminds us, we must learn about the lives, challenges, opportunities, and concerns of those whose identity experiences are different from our own. To do this, we must first conduct a personal inventory of our biases and privileges, and then we must be willing to listen with an open heart.

The essays contained in this book provide unique and candid access to the complexities of identity, oppression, and conceptions of leadership. We are fortunate to have the opportunity to hear the voices of these authors who are willing to share their stories.

Kevin Kruger
President
NASPA–Student Affairs Administrators in Higher Education

REFERENCES

CNN. (2008, June 26). Mandela in his own words. Retrieved from http://edition.cnn.com/2008/WORLD/africa/06/24/mandela.quotes/index.html

McIntosh, P. (1988). *White privilege and male privilege: A personal account of coming to see correspondences through work in women's studies.* Retrieved from ERIC database. (ED335262)

Preface

Welcome to this collection of identity and leadership essays. Our hope is that the courageous stories and insights of leaders in this volume will encourage you to more deeply consider the important manifestations of identity in your leadership practice as well as intersections of identity and leadership in the transformation of higher education for equity and social justice.

I will never forget the moment I felt a "becoming" as a Mestiza leader and the importance of humbly embracing my responsibilities as a mentor and activist. I was in my first days as a hall manager for a large residence hall at New Mexico State University in 1985. My name had just been added to my office door, and a young Navajo woman walked in and addressed me. I felt a jolt when she said, "You know, I never imagined myself as a leader, but seeing your name on this door makes me feel that perhaps I could be. Would you tell me what it means to be you and a leader at the same time?" From that moment, I began to delve deeply not only into the responsibilities I feel toward others because of who I am, but also into the fascinating question of how our multiple identities manifest in our leadership practice. I have written about identity and leadership on a number of occasions and always dreamed of asking other leaders to tell their stories of identity and leadership. I am humbled and forever grateful to the leaders who agreed to journey with us and courageously share their stories in this book.

In 1996, I served as national chair for the NASPA–Student Affairs Administrators in Higher Education Network for Educational Equity and Ethnic Diversity. At our first leadership meeting in Washington, D.C., I felt a common spirit with Ronni Sanlo, who was starting in her role as national chair for the Gay, Lesbian, and Bisexual Concerns Network. We came together, walked during many of our breaks, and spoke passionately about our lives, identities, and activist leadership on college campuses and beyond. When I felt it was time to pull together a volume of essays,

Ronni immediately came to mind as the person with whom I wanted to collaborate. She is to this day one of the wisest, most compassionate, and introspective leader activists I know. Thank you, Ronni, for our long-time friendship and collaboration.

Special thanks to Florence Marie Guido for allowing us to use one of her powerful and beautiful photos for the cover of this book. We chose this photo of a student flamenco dancer performing at the University of New Mexico– Taos for its power, beauty, and symbolism. Flamenco as an art form holds great strength and a stepping forward combined with beauty, gracefulness, and agility. These seemingly contradictory traits are critical in negotiating and applying our own identities as leaders transforming higher education for social justice. In addition, showing the back of this dancer symbolizes the many hidden identities we each carry and draw from in our leadership roles.

Alicia Fedelina Chávez
Taos, New Mexico
November 2012

Our life journeys do interesting things to and for us, usually when we are not paying attention. Little did I know that getting fired from a job I loved back in 1987 because I was a lesbian would kick-start a journey that would lead me to this day. Being painfully unemployed allowed me to be available to become an HIV epidemiologist in my home state of Florida at a time when few people wanted to work with patients with AIDS. The job came with education benefits, and I was able to expand on my bachelor's degree in music to earn a master's and then a doctorate in education, free of charge. Once completed, I was offered a job at the University of Michigan to direct the Lesbian and Gay Male Programs Office. Within six months, I became chair of the NASPA Region IV-East Gay, Lesbian,

Bisexual, and Transgendered Concerns Network (now the Gay, Lesbian, Bisexual, and Transgender Issues Knowledge Community); six months later, I became the network's national chair.

I do not know if I considered myself a leader back then. I just knew that there was work to be done and I was able to do it. My grandfather, a rabbi, always asked the age-old questions: "If not me, who? If not now, when?" Though I knew nothing about higher education hierarchy and protocol, I had the courage and a deep desire—perhaps a calling—to protect our gay, lesbian, bisexual, and transgender college students. Nothing more, nothing less.

One of the tremendous gifts of student affairs work is connecting with smart and passionate people. Alicia and I saw something in one another when we were national chairs of our respective NASPA networks in the mid-1990s. Alicia, I thank you from my heart for all that you do and have done for me through your friendship and for the profession through your scholarship. What a privilege it is to finally create this dream with you!

Our friendship and colleagueship has grown into a deep and warm connection that we also share with others. Many of the people we present to you in this book are among those folks. Over the years, we have wished and hoped and brainstormed, trying to decide the right vehicle for our collective hearts and stories. Together, we invite readers to join us in informing lives and practice through identity and leadership in academe. May you find experience, strength, and hope in the words you read here, and may your own leadership and identity become evident in every aspect of your life.

Ronni Sanlo
Palm Desert, California
November 2012

Introduction

Alicia Fedelina Chávez and Ronni Sanlo

As co-editors, we are very different from one another in visible and invisible ways. Our differences were evident from the first time we met. It was our differences that brought us together as fast and dear friends. Over time, we have shared deep talks and heartfelt passion for the work we do. Along with other tender colleagues, we have co-facilitated short as well as multiday workshops and contemplated a variety of publications. This book is the result of our deep shared desire to make a change in higher education through "talk-story," the sharing of hearts and words across the profession.

This book is a compilation of leadership reflection among experienced, novice, and emerging leaders in higher education. The intersection of identity with leadership is a mostly unexplored area of higher education and student affairs scholarship as well as the larger literature on leadership. We designed this book to be helpful to central administrators, student affairs professionals, and academic leaders at dean, chair, and program levels, as well as scholars, graduate faculty, graduate students, and student leaders.

ORGANIZATION OF THE BOOK

This book offers perspectives and guidance in leadership from a variety of identities including race/ethnicity, gender, sexuality, nationality/border, artistic, language, and ability/disability. It focuses specifically on higher education leadership and offers readers the opportunity to learn from higher education leaders about intersections of identity and leadership and to reflect through facilitated activities on their own identities in relation to leadership in higher education institutions, state higher education departments, and professional associations. The authors draw from their personal experiences to elucidate the very deep issues of making connections between identity and leadership and leading social justice and other efforts on college campuses.

Part I introduces our vision of identity and leadership in academe, some current literature, the role of stories in leadership and professional development, and why attention to intersections of identity and leadership is an important practice for leaders in higher education. We also provide an overview and author narratives that illustrate key insights from the leadership essays in Part II, with a special emphasis on intersections of identity, leadership, and social justice.

Part II, as the main part of the book, is divided into four sections. Each features essays from higher education leaders that examine how their specific identities manifest in their leadership practice and how they strive to lead authentically across differences from within these identities. Special emphasis is placed on intersections of identity with transformative leadership for social justice. These essays explore the importance and process of understanding our identities; how they emerge in our leadership practice; and their impact on serving the campus community, leading diverse populations, and transforming higher education for diversity, equity, and social justice.

Part III offers suggestions and guides for self-reflection, steps for analyzing and exploring identity, worksheets and facilitation guides for self-reflection, and implications of identity and practice among graduate students and those we lead. In this chapter, a guide to writing an Identity and Leadership Autobiography is presented for use in deep self-reflection and/or in facilitating introspection among professionals and graduate students.

PART I

Intersections of Identity and Leadership

Our Vision of Identity and Leadership in Academe

Ronni Sanlo and Alicia Fedelina Chávez

I dentity manifests in the way we lead, supervise, make decisions, persuade, form relationships, and negotiate the myriad responsibilities faced each day. As individual leaders, we practice within norms, assumptions, values, beliefs, and behaviors originating in our multiple identities. These identities influence transformative efforts, innovations, and limitations we experience as leaders. In addition, identity influences experiences and perceptions of power or lack thereof and affects how we think about and practice within power structures of colleges and universities.

This book offers experienced and emerging leaders a window into understanding deep intersections of identity and practice as well as guideposts for individual leadership development. Leaders from many levels and areas of higher education discuss intersections of some of their individual identities with everyday and transformative leadership practice. Identity and leadership reflection and self-analysis guides and activities are included to assist leaders and emerging leaders in developing greater self-knowledge and to become the transformative leaders needed in today's rapidly diversifying and globalizing higher education.

Transformative leadership for social justice by professionals with differing identities requires great individual authenticity, contemplative practice, humble dedication to ongoing learning, self-reflection, and a fierce passion to step forward for and with others (Chávez, 2009, 2010; Pope, Reynolds, & Mueller, 2004; Roper, 2005; Sanlo, 1998). Identity permeates everything we do as individuals (Birdwell-Bowles, 1998; Donovan,

2006). One of the great assets we as leaders bring to diverse campuses is our unique collection of identities from which we draw strength and innovation (Chávez, 2009; Ibarra, 2001; Valverde, 2008). This, however, can also be a barrier to our transformative efforts in understanding, influencing, and leading those who are different from us (Chávez, 2010; Roper, 2005). Developing stronger self-awareness about who we are and the identity origins of our leadership practices may assist us as individuals to draw from identity strengths, while minimizing limitations, increasing empathy toward others, and facilitating identity strengths in those around us. Transformative efforts are enhanced when leaders work to understand the influence of their identities on their leadership and on interactions with those holding different identities (Fried, 1995).

CURRENT LITERATURE

There is little written about intersections of identity and leadership in higher education practice. Most current literature focuses on corporate leadership at the international level, with some studies on gender. Sexuality, socioeconomic class, immigrant status, or disability and leadership are largely missing from the literature. This text goes beyond any single identity to illuminate ways in which a variety of identities manifest in leadership practice. In addition, it allows readers to learn about and compare ways in which a wide variety of identities manifest in many levels and types of leadership.

In higher education and educational leadership literature, books such as the edited collection of Dungy and Ellis (2011) offer a much needed focus on general competencies in higher education and student affairs leadership, yet an in-depth focus on identity and leadership is also needed as higher education continues to fall short of educating and retaining underserved populations of students, faculty, and staff. Although Pope, Reynolds, and Mueller (2004) discussed working across differences effectively in higher education, their emphasis was on student affairs generally and not specifically on leadership. This book takes a wide leadership perspective of higher education across areas including central, academic, student affairs, diversity, and library administration as well as levels of leadership responsibilities from entry level to the presidency.

Casting a wider net on leadership, Valverde (2008) focused on perspec-

Insights on Identity, Leadership, and Social Justice

Alicia Fedelina Chávez

The leaders featured in this book provide insights into the intersections of identity, leadership, and social justice. Each illuminates the reality that transformative efforts to promote equity and social justice are exceptionally complex and profoundly influenced by who we are, how we lead, and how we are perceived. Yet in some ways, each also makes clear that it is often straightforward ways of being, acts of transformative leadership, and stepping forward to protect and advocate that matter most in serving others and promoting social justice. In essence, we need to have courage and willingness to know ourselves and others, to continually learn and grow, and to lead pragmatically.

The following is a compilation of key insights from the essays in Part II. Some narratives clearly illustrate "ways of being"—characteristics, principles, values, beliefs, and ways of looking at higher education, ourselves, others, and transformative change efforts. Others are more about doing—ways of leading and working with others. This discussion of insights is grouped into these two larger aspects of leadership for social justice. A small amount of interpretation is offered with emphasis placed on illustrating through the narratives themselves. Author names and the pages on which their narrative quotes can be found are noted to assist readers in referring to related essays later in the book.

For these leaders, being and doing interact and integrate constantly in daily practice (see Figure 1 and Table 1). Ways of being are inherent qualities within the individuals and are likely to carry over into many aspects of leadership. Alternatively, ways of doing emerge from characteristic ways of being and from experience, learning, observing, and reflecting. Ways of being are often applied organically by these leaders to a variety of situations and evolve over time.

Figure I
Ways of Being and Doing: Leading for Social Justice

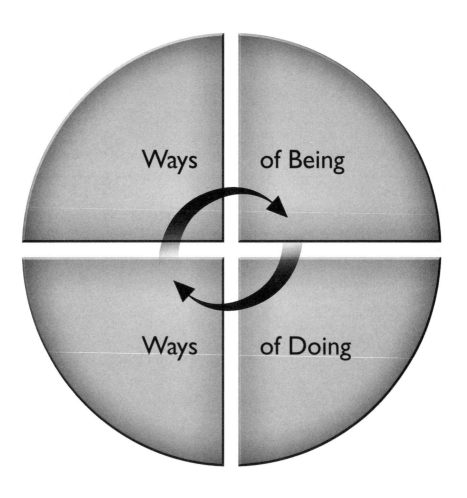

Table I
Insights on Identity, Leadership, and Social Justice

Ways of Being	Ways of Doing
Holding to strength, perseverance, and hope	Learning from, collaborating with, and cultivating gifts, uniqueness, and authenticity in others
Striving to know ourselves and continually grow and develop	Leading transformative change proactively and pragmatically
Acknowledging identity realities yet negotiating environments toward goals	Facilitating growth and trust in ourselves and others
Understanding the situational impact of our identities	Questioning ourselves, others, our professions, and our institutions in a respectful manner
Gaining empathy, determination, and skill from experiencing and/or observing oppression, injustice, and marginalization	Facilitating and maintaining safe environments for all
Shaping worldview and leadership by experiencing difference and oppression in some identities and privilege in others	Stepping forward to protect, serve, and advocate within and beyond our identity groups
Embracing responsibility for others, social justice leadership, and change	Mentoring and empowering ourselves and others as leaders and activists
Challenging our stereotypes and learning to understand and relate across differences	
Accepting discomfort, growth, chaos, and messiness as part of leadership and of social justice efforts	
Inherent interest in a diversity of people, ways of being, practice, and worldview	
Sharing openly who we are in service of others	
Imagining things differently and seeing potential	

WAYS OF BEING

Leader narrative falling under the theme "ways of being" consist of specific perspectives (such as those derived from experiencing oppression), ways of being in the world, sense of responsibility, and professional and personal characteristics. The leaders who penned these narratives all continually put themselves through a process of cultivating self-awareness. They are characterized by hope, strength, courage, determination, ingenuity, perseverance, and a willingness to stand forth and take on responsibility for transforming higher education toward greater equity and social justice. These qualities can be cultivated in any leader through introspection, observation, ongoing growth, learning, and a willingness to face discomfort and develop empathy in service to others.

Holding to Strength, Perseverance, and Hope

"I find that being a White female professor who has come from a background of poverty is not the weight that I had painted it to be but is instead an asset to students for whom I can be an example, a mentor, an ally, and an advocate."

—Marsha L. Baum (p. 91)

"As leaders, we are called in the midst of a broken heart and faded hopes to engage and reengage in right relationships while surrendering the outcome."

—Jean Chagnon (p. 122)

"Given that I am a member of the group in power, my perspective and leadership roles obligate me to advocate for others, while always recognizing that many of our students and colleagues pay a price for my privilege while I do so."

—Pete Englin (p. 74)

The overarching qualities in these essays are hope, strength, and perseverance toward a better higher education to serve students and benefit society. Each leader faces challenges and disappointment, many face persecution and oppression, some discuss privilege within their identities, and most acknowledge difficulties and heartbreak. Yet each emphasizes a belief that higher education can transform. We as leaders dedicate ourselves daily to guiding others in higher education toward greater service, equity, and social justice.

"I used my childhood experiences, discrimination, and racism as positive experiences. Those experiences allowed me to grow and mature into the person I am today."

—Alex Gonzalez (p. 206)

"The loss of trust and violation of belief I had in others nearly broke my purple heart and at the same time stoked the flames of my social justice consciousness based primarily on my socioeconomic experiences. Later, I would come to realize the power of this aspect of my narrative in enabling me to encourage and inspire others who face seemingly overwhelming odds and adversity."

—*Lea M. Jarnagin (p. 179)*

Shaping Worldview and Leadership by Experiencing Difference and Oppression in Some Identities and Privilege in Others

"For the first time, I could see that my identity as a lesbian woman not only affected but rather directly shaped my vision of leadership. I could see that leadership from the margin is different than leadership from the center. My identity as a lesbian woman affected the very questions I asked and the causes for which I advocated. It affected how people perceived me and how people responded to me or treated me. I also felt for the first time that being a lesbian woman often influenced how hard I had to work to accomplish my goals given people's differential perceptions of me."

—*Jean Chagnon (p. 119)*

"I spent the first half of my adult life trying to escape my upbringing and the second half capitalizing on it."

—*Elizabeth Hoffman (p. 252)*

"The first time I said the words, 'I am a very powerful individual,' I actually laughed out loud. . . . Based on my lived experience, 'powerful' was supposed to be 'White,' 'male,' and 'rich,' or powerful was 'bad' and 'untrustworthy.' Certainly, I, Luoluo Hong, was not powerful! . . . In addition, my privileged status as a heterosexual individual afforded me a degree of safety and freedom in the workplace that my gay, lesbian, and bisexual colleagues cannot automatically expect."

—*Luoluo Hong (pp. 45–47)*

In their essays, leaders make meaning of being shaped by experiencing oppression, marginalization, or difference (i.e., being the only one, the different one, the one whose behavior is outside the norm) of some identities and privilege from others. This is especially evident between visible and invisible identities and often serves as a catalyst for deep insight into and dedication to social justice. Many discussed the influence of contrasting experiences on their leadership practice and vision for higher education.

"Finally, after so many challenges and so much pain, I was able to integrate the history of my Jewish identity, the courage of my lesbian identity, and the wisdom of my educational identity. I remained as fearless and fierce as I was early on in my leadership experiences, but by now I knew how to move forward thoughtfully, intelligently, and inclusively."

—*Ronni Sanlo (p. 66)*

"The act of coming out has forced me to come to terms with my professional identity, my intellectual identity, my ethnicity, my spiritual identity, and all other aspects of my being."

—*Kevin T. Colaner (p. 156)*

Embracing Responsibility for Others, Social Justice Leadership, and Change

"Creating a learning environment that supports human connections, love, honesty, respect, truth, courage, wisdom, humility, and deep-lived consciousness perhaps will create a world that the student wants to be part of and contribute back to, rather than a world that bases self-worth on materialism and consumerism."

—*Miriam Garay (p. 128)*

"I believe the essence of leadership in higher education is to facilitate the success of every student and professional. . . . I explore intersections of leadership with values and worldview originating in my military and rural upbringing. These influences, interwoven with a drive toward social justice in education, mean for me a very pragmatic hope and practice of leadership for social justice."

—*Alicia Fedelina Chávez (p. 76)*

"It has been above all liberating, as I came to understand that my freedom to fully be myself can only occur if others also have that opportunity. In many situations, given my place and privilege, it is my obligation and responsibility to get out of my own way so that all can experience what I routinely take for granted."

—*Pete Englin (p. 69)*

Leaders write passionately about their sense of responsibility for others and for leading change in higher education especially to promote social justice. Often this sense of responsibility originates in early identities and experiences. Some express concern that all leaders do not utilize their positions and power to improve higher education and intervene when acts of social injustice occur.

"My identity compels me to be aware of and responsive to possible inequities I observe. My leadership is built on a commitment to giving voice to the voiceless and creating space for those who might otherwise be marginalized—values I acquired while observing the spirit-crushing impact invisibility and inaudibility had on my peers."

—*Larry D. Roper (p. 60)*

"Yet, nearly every day, I observe fellow senior administrators—regardless of their amalgamation of both privileged and subordinated identities—'give away' power (perhaps by waiting to see who applies for a job rather than actively recruiting a diverse pool of qualified candidates); fail to see the power they have to act or intervene (as in not speaking up when witnessing acts of workplace violence or social injustice); or disavow that they have any agency whatsoever in the organization (by asserting 'I am just a cog in the wheel on this machine'). I am angered and disappointed when power is squandered in these ways, yet I also understand why these behaviors occur."

—*Luoluo Hong (p. 48)*

"Her [my mother's] fear of my Americanization (the loss of Puerto Rican culture and values) was exacerbated whenever inequities between men and women were part of our conversations. . . . Those experiences frame the ferocity and passion with which I take on issues of oppression and gender equity."

—Marisa Rivera (p. 211)

Challenging Our Stereotypes and Learning to Understand and Relate Across Differences

"If I want to be respected as a thoughtful leader and accepted for who I am and what I bring to the conversation, I must look within myself and remember that a book cannot always be judged by its cover."

—Marisa Rivera (p. 212)

"The experience of openly acknowledging who I am has enabled me to accept and respect the diverse gifts of others more freely. It has allowed me to suspend judgment and seek understanding before acting on my initial observations of others."

—Kevin T. Colaner (p. 156)

"I share stories to illustrate my mistakes, particularly when I teach multicultural counseling, in hopes of reducing the isolation students often experience while learning challenging concepts about privilege and oppression."

—Susan Longerbeam (p. 189)

These leaders teach us that it is important to regularly question and challenge our assumptions and stereotypes about others. This way of being makes it possible to suspend judgment long enough to learn about others, find commonality, appreciate the benefit of differences, build relationships, and engage others in the work of higher education. This does not come easy, especially at first, yet is seen as essential to effective leadership, transformation of higher education, and advancing social justice.

"When I became a dean at Iowa State University, I had to learn the importance of racial and gender consciousness and the use of gender, racial, and ethnic political strategies the hard way."
—*Elizabeth Hoffman (p. 256)*

"Over subsequent years, a number of other experiences made it clear to me that I had developed negative subconscious beliefs about wealthy people. As I explored those feelings and beliefs further, I came to realize that during my early childhood the stories I heard of mistreatment my mother and grandmother experienced in homes of rich people for whom they worked led me to internalize the belief that affluent people were cruel."
—*Larry D. Roper (p. 56)*

"Deep biases that I could not justify initially were affecting my ability to connect, and I was disappointed in myself for it. While I do not know whether my discomfort was known, it certainly is a credit to many of my teammates, both from the United States and abroad, that over time our relationships grew and my capacity to be in new experiences with people who looked and sounded much different than me expanded tremendously. I came to cherish learning about other countries, cultures, and shared values and recognize that great people come from all over."
—*Pete Englin (p. 71)*

Accepting Discomfort, Growth, Chaos, and Messiness as Part of Leadership and Social Justice Efforts

"Social justice leadership requires a willingness to face discomfort for the benefit of others and a highly pragmatic approach to institutional change and individual advocacy and support."
—*Alicia Fedelina Chávez (pp. 76–77)*

"Inspiriting leadership requires tolerance for chaos in the service of freedom. I believe my role is to encourage environments in which it is safe to take risks and make mistakes. Although chaos can ensue from mistakes and the free flow of information (rather than information communicated through a hierarchy), it also creates an environment for enlivened, empowered, and energetic colleagues and students."

—*Susan Longerbeam (p. 191)*

"Losing Johnnie began my struggle with the reality that life and leadership requires of us a surrender that is both humbling and difficult—a surrendering to life in the face of uncertain and unpredictable outcomes. Surrender does not, however, give us permission to disengage. Rather, surrender is about letting go of the outcome while continuing to accept the invitation to stay engaged."

—*Jean Chagnon (p. 122)*

These leaders discuss needing to accept chaos, discomfort, and messiness when leading social justice efforts and for transformative leadership in general. They discuss the importance of continual growth and self-assessment as essential to leading in contexts of uncertainty. Many find this uncertainty and growth within intersections of their own and others' differing identities and see this interplay as essential to leadership development for social justice.

"I learned early on that bringing your vision to life is nearly impossible, but if you are willing to shift gears a bit along the way, surprising alternative solutions may present themselves. As a leader today, I still rely on creativity to resolve desperate situations because unexpected events always seem to occur in the middle of a project."

—*Mary Tafoya (p. 167)*

"Just because we possess or are given power does not mean we know how to use it. Only by living and leading at the intersections of our identities can we begin to understand ways in which we have agency in our lives and those of others."

—*Luoluo Hong (p. 48)*

analyze campus environments, facilitate growth in self and others, and face uncomfortable situations with a pragmatic, change orientation.

Learning From, Collaborating With, and Cultivating Gifts, Uniqueness, and Authenticity in Others

"As a child, I noticed at my church and in other situations that the level of one's education was not an appropriate measure of one's ability or intelligence. I had exposure to many people whom I considered wise, but who also had very little formal education. My current leadership is one that attempts to honor knowledge and ability, regardless of from where it comes."

—Larry D. Roper (p. 58)

"Asking for help is a sign of courage not weakness."

—Jody Donovan (p. 113)

"For example, while doing volunteer work in immigrant communities, I learned to judge people based on their values and actions, not their title, education, or the way they spoke. I saw individuals grow, taking on considerable responsibility because the person they worked for had confidence in them, encouraged them, mentored them, and inspired their commitment with vision and example."

—William V. Flores (p. 263)

These leaders proactively strive to cultivate others' abilities, learn from them, and collaborate in the transformation of higher education. In a variety of ways, we reach out to those in our organizations for ideas, support, and partnership. Leaders see difference and ability in others as an asset to be encouraged, valued, and drawn from in service to society. Many write of joy in working with and drawing out gifts in others.

"Leaders who value their followers and want to work collaboratively with them find ways to maximize the potential of each group member."

—Florence Marie Guido (p. 142)

"Those who have power can most afford to share it. When I am the decision maker, it is to the benefit of those I serve if I make an effort to consult with as many individuals as is possible and reasonable."
—*Luoluo Hong (p. 49)*

"I have a true fascination for others' gifts, especially when they differ from mine. Pointing out and encouraging others' abilities, sometimes ones they do not yet realize, is a favorite aspect of leading."
—*Alicia Fedelina Chávez (p. 77)*

Leading Transformative Change Proactively and Pragmatically

"My dad told me afterward, 'Remember, "No" is just a beginning point in negotiations. Never give up, especially if what they are doing is wrong. Find a different way of getting to "Yes".'"
—*William V. Flores (p. 261)*

"To effectively leverage my decision-making authority and influence, I must constantly be present in the moment, thoughtful, and self-critical—always scanning the organizational context and identifying ways in which power and privilege 'show up' in interpersonal and systemic dynamics and then ensuring that patterns of disempowerment and marginalization do not continue."
—*Luoluo Hong (p. 51)*

These individuals are highly pragmatic and proactive in their leadership strategies for transformational change in higher education. They show the importance of thinking beyond sensitivity and awareness levels of diversity development to determine what works in leading transformation. They often try different things until transformation has been achieved, refusing to give up in the face of setbacks, disappointment, resistance, or self-doubt. This includes encouraging personal growth, considering different perspectives, and transforming individual ways of leading.

"Growing up abroad brings many advantages beyond embracing diversity. I have developed a strong set of cultural skills. I have a global view of the world. . . . I am able to observe and understand people from cultures other than my own. I do not believe there is any one best way of being. I accept people for who they are. I am adaptable and flexible. I speak languages other than English."

—*Mark Emmons (p. 150)*

Stepping Forward to Protect, Serve, and Advocate Within and Beyond Our Identity Groups

"Along with perseverance, these realities gave me a strong urge to protect others from harm, from denial, and from having to endure pain."

—*Alex Gonzalez (p. 207)*

"To truly transform our communities and help them realize their full potential, however, we must teach ourselves and the next generation of citizens and leaders about the meaning of power, how to acknowledge our individual and collective power, and how to exercise that power in a manner that honors our human dignity and promotes social justice for all."

—*Luoluo Hong (p. 44)*

"I now believe it is insufficient for us as leaders to claim unawareness of the range of human sexuality, from the healthy to the abusive. An educated person should know enough to protect others, especially children, and all who may be vulnerable for reasons of identity and personal history."

—*Susan Longerbeam (p. 190)*

These individuals show a marked practice of stepping forward to protect. For many, this originates from personal experiences of harm by others. These leaders have developed effective practices for facing conflict, confronting harmful behaviors, developing their colleagues, and walking with others as they stand up for themselves. This is described by leaders as not only a choice to stand forth, but also a choice to develop ourselves in ways that allow us to do this effectively.

"I believe one of the most important things we can do to transform toward socially just environments is to stand up for ourselves as well as with others."

—Alicia Fedelina Chávez (p. 82)

"This tendency to be better able to understand and more likely to advocate for students like ourselves, if not recognized and consciously set aside, can disadvantage students who are not like us, making the diversity in backgrounds of faculty that much more important to ensure positive experiences for all students."

—Marsha L. Baum (p. 91)

"Even my choice of the type of institutions at which I have worked has been driven by my identity. Many times during my career, I had the option of pursuing employment at socially prestigious institutions; however, I have found myself drawn to institutions that serve working-class and underserved student populations."

—Larry D. Roper (p. 59)

Mentoring and Empowering Ourselves and Others as Leaders and Activists

"Throughout my career, I have been fortunate enough to find good mentors who encouraged my scholarship and who prodded me to consider administrative positions. Now, I encourage others to do the same, advising and mentoring them along the way."

—William V. Flores (p. 266)

"As a teacher and spiritual leader, it is my responsibility to integrate and create parallel studies that address students' majors and develop their inner lives by bringing conversation into the heart of teaching and making meaningful connections that foster positive values for social and organizational life."

—Miriam Garay (p. 129)

"Shifting from deficit- to strengths-based views of others is essential to social justice in higher education."

—Alicia Fedelina Chávez (p. 76)

Leaders characterize mentoring others as a powerful way to ripple out toward greater transformation and an important daily role for educators. Looking for and mentoring leadership skills and engagement in others is seen as essential to long-term and sustainable change. As some note, this is not always an easy activity and we must sustain through others' stages of development in the area of leadership and social justice work.

"Serving as a role model and mentor is a significant part of my responsibility as a transformative leader in higher education."

—Jody Donovan (p. 114)

"This dynamic emerges in others when I facilitate social justice education programs; those who develop newfound awareness about their privileged identities are far more likely to first experience shame and guilt than to recognize their capacity to do good and lead change."

—Luoluo Hong (p. 45)

PART II

*Voices of Identity
and Leadership*

We are pleased, honored, and humbled to present essays on identity and leadership from leaders across higher education. When we invited these respected leaders to join us in this journey, we knew they would provide deep and wise insights. We hoped they would share compelling narratives about intersections of identity and leadership and perhaps a few observations about leading social justice efforts. What we received went beyond our wildest hopes in the diversity of identities, incredible stories, and shared wisdom.

The essays are organized into four sections. In "Negotiating Complexities of Identity, Leadership, and Social Justice," leaders discuss unique interrelationships between multiple identities and leadership in general as well as leading specifically toward social justice in individual, group, and systemic or institutional transformation. In "Leading Through Invisible Identities," leaders discuss profound challenges and opportunities of leading from identities invisible to others. In "The Paradox of Intersecting Identities," leaders discuss challenges and contradictions inherent in negotiating multiple identities. Finally, in "Negotiating Professional and Personal Identities in Executive Leadership," leaders discuss the unique challenges of navigating multiple professional roles and personal identities in high-level leadership arenas, including leadership in the presidency, provost, as head of a national association, and as a state secretary of higher education.

Negotiating Complexities of Identity, Leadership, and Social Justice

In this section, leaders discuss unique interrelationships between multiple identities and leadership in general as well as with leadership specifically toward influencing social justice in individual, group, and systemic or institutional transformation.

How I Found My Titanium Ovaries

Living and Leading at the Intersections

Luoluo Hong

Luoluo (pronounced lō-lō) Hong's entire career has been passionately devoted to service in public health, social justice, and higher education. She serves as the vice chancellor for student affairs and associate professor at the University of Hawaiʻi at Hilo. She and her spouse are loving parents of three felines: Puck, Phoenix, and Kona. Luoluo can occasionally be found masquerading as a human warlock in World of Warcraft.

"When I dare to be powerful, to use my strength in the service of my vision, then it becomes less and less important whether I am afraid." (Lorde, 1997, p. 13)

One of the most compelling definitions of power I have encountered comes from Kofi Lomotey, who served on the faculty at Louisiana State University at the time he shared this concept: Power is the ability to define your own reality and have others believe it is their reality also. Similarly, Dworkin (1981) described the power of "naming" as the ability to "define experience, to articulate boundaries and values . . . to determine what can and cannot be expressed, to control perception itself" (p. 17). After becoming a rape survivor at age 18, I experienced firsthand what it means to be completely disempowered and dehumanized. I have spent much of my life since attempting to reclaim myself.

Both civil rights activism and social justice education seek to promote the equitable distribution of power and privilege so that all individuals, regardless of identity or background, may live in safe environments, have access to needed resources, and fully participate in shaping their lives and those of their families (Bell, 2007). To truly transform our communities and help them realize their full potential, however, we must teach ourselves and the next generation of citizens and leaders about the meaning of power, how to acknowledge our individual and collective power, and how to exercise that power in a manner that honors our human dignity and promotes social justice for all.

OVARIES? WHAT OVARIES? I THINK I'VE LOST MINE

Throughout childhood and most of adulthood, I recall many instances from the media highlighting the abuse and misuse of power. A lifelong fan of the book and film versions of *The Lord of the Rings*, I am fascinated by the representation of the "One Ring" as a source of absolute power that ultimately corrupts its bearer. The ring's power cannot be resisted—even by the most powerful wizard—and its innate evil is why the hero Frodo must embark on an epic journey to destroy it. Moving from fiction to reality, the recent case of former Pennsylvania State University assistant football coach Jerry Sandusky also provides insight into power. While Sandusky was convicted in June 2012 for multiple incidents of sexual abuse over nearly a decade, the earlier grand jury report (Pennsylvania Office of Attorney General, 2011) and subsequent news reports indicate that there were many others in positions of authority who knew or suspected what was occurring yet failed to intervene—and those who tried to intervene were driven from the institution.

Conversely, examples of power used responsibly and ethically are rarely showcased. Superheroes are a notable exception; however, their "powers" seem so fantastical that I could never see myself in them; they represent the world as it ought to be, rather than as it exists. As a result, I had a much clearer sense of how to use power over others to advance personal agendas, yet a more vague idea (until recently) about how to exercise power in collaboration with others to achieve collective goals.

Over time, I subconsciously came to equate powerful people with being unethical, immoral, and self-serving at worst, and targets of suspicion and mistrust at best. I consequently wanted to distance myself from power. This dynamic emerges in others when I facilitate social justice education programs; those who develop newfound awareness about their privileged identities are far more likely to first experience shame and guilt than to recognize their capacity to do good and lead change.

Students and colleagues may say something to this effect: "Gosh, I wish I was not White so that I would not have this power." Alternatively, they may retreat to disadvantaged aspects of their identity: "Well, I grew up poor even though I am a guy." They also ask how they can yield privilege or give it away. Yet, hope for societal change lies not in individuals disowning their power. In fact, failing to claim power that we each have—and not using it with care and compassion—is disingenuous and a disservice to ourselves and to our communities.

I HAVE OVARIES—AND I THINK I WILL KEEP THEM!

The first time I said the words, "I am a very powerful individual," I actually laughed out loud. I was in my mid-30s then and had just made a very difficult decision that set in motion both a chain reaction in the institution where I worked and in my own personal and professional journey. In my mind, I sounded ridiculous and pompous, yet I wondered why I had that visceral reaction. I was increasingly "owning" more of my personal power as I accepted myself as a senior student affairs officer and embraced the accompanying capacity to make a positive difference for students—a safer campus, a more inclusive and engaging learning environment, enhanced health services, increased access for those with financial need, the list goes on. Based on my lived experience, "powerful" was supposed to be "White," "male," and "rich," or powerful was "bad" and "untrustworthy." Certainly, I, Luoluo Hong, was not powerful!

I am the eldest daughter of Taiwanese immigrants. I was raised in a very traditional Chinese home, one in which children—daughters especially—were expected to defer meekly to the will of their parents. Today, I watch my PhD-educated sister raise her three children and express her desire to ensure that they "have a sense of their own agency" and I smile; this is so antithetical to our coming-of-age. To be a "good" Chinese daughter is to obey without question; it is to deny all personal goals and instead desire only to pursue what is best for one's family. While children inherently feel powerless in many ways relative to their parents—and rebellion against authority inevitably ensues during adolescence—my sense of subjugation and restriction of free will was especially pronounced relative to that of my peers. For example, my playmates were carefully screened as a child and I was not permitted to date until I was 21.

College was potentially a place for me to begin exploring my personal agency and empowerment, but that opportunity did not come to fruition. I was sexually assaulted by a fellow student during my freshmen year—before the media attention on date rape erupted—and that victimization only created a larger rift between who I could become and who I was. The perpetrator, based on things he said to me during the assault, singled me out both as a woman and as an Asian American. After several years of self-help, an amazing therapist during graduate school, and one suicide attempt, I transitioned from victim to survivor and went on to use the anger about the rape, my recommitment to life, and a new-found strength to move forward with a renewed soul. I did not know it then, but ingredients for my titanium ovaries had been discovered.

There is no doubt that "showing up" at work every day as an Asian American woman working in predominantly White institutions has exacted an emotional, physical, and spiritual toll. Even though I now work at an institution with no racial or ethnic majority, it is clear that prevailing patterns of privilege and marginalization that exist in broader U.S. society manifest themselves even here, especially because race is only one dimension of identity. One could argue that given my seeming professional success, I must have managed to overcome institutional sexism and racism; it is more accurate to say I overcompensated with an unquenchable work ethic, a seemingly endless supply of energy, and an extremely high degree of tenacity and conscientiousness—and, as a result, thrived despite disadvantages I experienced and benign discouragement I received throughout my career.

As a developing younger professional, I cannot recall any mentor who pointed me in the direction of senior administration. When I initiated the first steps toward this aspiration, I received feedback that it was "too soon" (even though younger colleagues had already advanced), that they "could not see me in that role" (was it because the model minority myth suggests that Asian Americans and Pacific Islanders [AAPIs] do not have what it takes to lead?), or that I was a "specialist" (in public health) while senior administration requires a generalist background (in a wide range of problems that ironically include excessive drinking, depression, interpersonal violence, and stress). I recognized "coded" language when I heard it. My experience is not unique; while AAPIs represent one of the fastest-growing populations entering college, they are disproportionately underrepresented at the level of provost and chancellor or president (Young, 2005).

For most of my life, my self-view was one of being disadvantaged, or—to borrow a phrase from social justice educator Jamie Washington (2010)—a member of the "one down" group. This perspective required that I see myself as an incomplete individual; while certainly my gender and ethnic identities are significant determinants of life experiences both in and out of the workplace, they also are not my only identities. By earning a doctorate and gradually advancing into a position of executive leadership, I shifted my socioeconomic status from working class as a child into one of privilege as an adult; while I had not inherited any wealth, I certainly had a stable source of sufficient income and a professional position that granted me access to decision-making tables and entry into certain spheres of influence—on campus and, to a certain degree, in the community. In addition, my privileged status as a heterosexual individual afforded me a degree of safety and freedom in the workplace that my gay, lesbian, and bisexual colleagues cannot automatically expect.

MY OVARIES ARE MADE OF TITANIUM!

From these places of being "one up" (Washington, 2010), I have been able to live and lead in ways that buffer the effects of subordination as a woman and person of color—although it does not make subordination right or acceptable. My leadership potential could not be fully realized until I recognized the intersectionality among my constructed identities of race, class, gender, sexual orientation, and so forth, thus allowing me to "get in touch" with my power. Johnson (2005) explained that because individuals belong to more than one social category—some dominant and some subordinate—it is possible for a person to be a member of a privileged group and yet not feel privileged; conversely, a person may be a member of a marginalized group yet not recognize this.

By virtue of the roles and responsibilities we bear, college and university administrators must hold ourselves to the highest standards when it comes to responsible and mindful use of our power. In considering the impact we have on thousands of students, we are powerful! Yet, nearly every day, I observe fellow senior administrators—regardless of their amalgamation of both privileged and subordinated identities—"give away" power (perhaps by waiting to see who applies for a job rather than actively recruiting a diverse pool of qualified candidates); fail to see the power they have to act or intervene (as in not speaking up when witnessing acts of workplace violence or social injustice); or disavow that they have any agency whatsoever in the organization (by asserting "I am just a cog in the wheel on this machine"). I am angered and disappointed when power is squandered in these ways, yet I also understand why these behaviors occur.

Just because we possess or are given power does not mean we know how to use it. Only by living and leading at the intersections of our identities can we begin to understand ways in which we have agency in our lives and those of others. As Wildman and Davis (2000) reminded us, "The presence of both the experience of privilege and the experience of subordination in differing aspects of our lives causes the experience to be blurred, further hiding the presence of privilege from our vocabulary and consciousness" (p. 56). No individual is ever completely powerless; this is certainly the case for those who have been able to secure a position as a higher education faculty or staff member or administrator.

You, Too, Can Have Ovaries of Titanium

I am still a learner myself, but in the short time I have been aware of my personal power, I have tried to leverage it purposefully and ethically. In reflecting on power and its potential both as a tool of destruction and instrument of creation, I make the following observations.

Those Who Have Power Can Most Afford to Share It

When I am the decision maker, it is to the benefit of those I serve if I make an effort to consult with as many individuals as is possible and reasonable. Higher education administrators are often afraid to ask the opinion of others when in the process of deciding—possibly because we are afraid others may contradict or criticize our viewpoint. However, when I have decision-making authority, I have nothing to lose by soliciting feedback and may possibly gain others' wisdom. As those in power, we owe it to those we serve to exercise due diligence in seeking information, carefully weighing various options, and then choosing a path that best achieves our desired goals. So often, administrators defer a decision because it is too difficult, too political, too controversial, or too stressful to choose—never understanding that failing to decide is actually a decision itself.

Those With Power Have the Ability to Create More Power

Many opponents of affirmative action fear that jobs are given to one group at the expense of another. This zero-sum view of advantage in U.S. society is a prevailing one and is a major reason why some individuals resist equal employment opportunity and other restorative justice initiatives. I find this conceptualization of power as a finite "pie," with only so many "pieces" to slice and serve to various groups, completely false. As a senior administrator, I am able to repeatedly create new avenues (or expand existing ones) to involve more students, staff, faculty, and other constituents in productive and generative activities on campus. By engaging and empowering more people in the development and enhancement of the organization, we are actually creating more power without requiring anybody to give up what power they already have.

When Exercising Power as a Leader With Marginalized Identities, Expect Resistance

Research on unconscious bias indicates that women pay a social penalty when placed in roles that require them to act in ways (e.g., be decisive, be strong) that are inconsistent with social expectations regarding their gender role (e.g., be nurturing, be warm) (Eagly & Karau, 2002). As has been observed about executive leadership, "Women face a . . . challenge: those viewed as tough and strong are also typically perceived as cold and unfeminine. Many experiments have found that women have trouble being perceived as both nice and competent" (Kristof, 2008, para. 14). Similar patterns of unconscious bias are identified relative to people of color (Moule, 2009). For example, AAPIs supposedly do not make waves and are satisfied to remain in roles that are behind the scenes—attributes incongruent with traditional leadership styles (Young, 2005). It is important to note that unconscious biases emerge among individuals regardless of their own gender, racial, or ethnic identity, and even when individuals view themselves as being free of prejudice (Women in Science and Engineering Leadership Institute, 2006).

Thus, while I may have been designated the institutional or positional authority, colleagues and subordinates are likely to challenge that authority. I must constantly strive to "prove" that I have the "right" to exercise authority inherent in my role—something I do not see my male or White (or older!) colleagues having to do as often. Further, I give up a certain amount of social capital each time I behave in a manner that is not "feminine" or "Asian" enough for others while fulfilling my duties as a senior administrator. For example, when I take appropriate action (including termination) to hold under- or nonperforming employees accountable, I have been accused of being heartless and unsupportive; male colleagues do so and they are regarded as decisive and strong.

When leading at the intersections of my identity, I in no way give up my "one down" identities, nor do I wish to: many of the cultural beliefs and values (e.g., honor, duty, and community) associated with my ethnic heritage inform and strengthen my practice of leadership. However, my "one up" identities can help me manage and cope with oppression or subtle disrespect I might encounter from those who are still operating within prescribed systems of institutionalized oppression and acting/reacting from unconscious biases. In addition, I find that identifying and connecting with allies when engaged in leadership work can help to mitigate impacts of this resistance.

Using One's Power Responsibly and Purposefully Is Challenging Work

To effectively leverage my decision-making authority and influence, I must constantly be present in the moment, thoughtful, and self-critical—always scanning the organizational context and identifying ways in which power and privilege manifest in interpersonal and systemic dynamics and then ensuring that patterns of disempowerment and marginalization do not continue. Having power also means I must accept responsibility for consequences of both my actions and inactions. These challenges are accompanied by the ongoing stress of having my authority routinely challenged as a woman of color. As a result, there are many times I do want to give that power away, yet I never really can; the power resides within us whether or not we choose to use it.

When power is judiciously used and tempered with integrity, inclusion, courage, and transparency, powerful people joining together to create powerful teams can generate positive, transformative outcomes for students. Ultimately, power is amoral and multipartial; it is the individuals wielding power who determine whether its use will maintain the status quo and all its existing social inequities or transform the communities in which we live and lead into ones of health and hope.

REFERENCES

Bell, L. A. (2007). Theoretical foundations for social justice education. In L. Bell, M. Adams, & P. Griffin (Eds.), *Teaching for diversity and social justice* (2nd ed.). New York, NY: Routledge.

Dworkin, A. (1981). *Pornography: Men possessing women.* London, England: Women's Press.

Eagly, A. H., & Karau, S. J. (2002). Role congruity theory of prejudice toward female leaders. *Psychological Review, 109,* 573–598. doi:10.1037/0033-295X.109.3.573

Johnson, A. G. (2005). *Privilege, power, and difference* (2nd ed.). New York, NY: McGraw-Hill.

Kristof, N. D. (2008, April 6). Our racist, sexist selves. *The New York Times.* Retrieved from http://www.nytimes.com/2008/04/06/opinion/06kristof.html?_r=1

Lorde, A. (1997). *The cancer journals* [Special ed.]. San Francisco, CA: Aunt Lute Books.

Moule, J. (2009). Understanding unconscious bias and unintentional racism. *Phi Delta Kappan, 90*(5), 320–326.

Pennsylvania Office of Attorney General, 33rd Statewide Investigating Grand Jury. (2011). Retrieved from http://www.attorneygeneral. gov/uploadedFiles/Press/Sandusky-Grand-Jury-Presentment.pdf

Washington, J. (2010, June 24). *Preparing for the future: Building competence for a socially just campus community.* Paper presented at Division of Student Affairs All-Staff Retreat, University of Hawai`i at Hilo, HA.

Wildman, S. M., & Davis, A. D. (2000). Language and silence: Making systems of privilege visible. In M. Adam, W. J. Blumenfeld, C. Castañeda, H. W. Hackman, M. L. Peters, & X. Zúñiga (Eds.), *Readings for diversity and social justice: An anthology on racism, antisemitism, sexism, heterosexism, ableism, and classism* (pp. 50–60). New York, NY: Routledge.

Women in Science and Engineering Leadership Institute, University of Wisconsin–Madison. (2006). Reviewing applicants: Research on bias and assumptions. Retrieved from http://wiseli.engr.wisc.edu/docs/BiasBrochure_2ndEd.pdf

Young, F. J. (2005, November 14). The committee of 100's Asian Pacific Americans (APAs) in higher education report card. Retrieved from http://www.committee100.org/initiatives/herc/C100_Higher_Ed_Report_Card.pdf

Living and Leading With Less Than Enough

Larry D. Roper

Larry D. Roper was born and raised in Akron, Ohio, and has served as vice provost for student affairs and professor of ethnic studies at Oregon State University since 1995. From May 2007 to September 2008, he served as interim dean of the College of Liberal Arts.

I was born in 1953, into a world of poverty and racial isolation. For the first 10 years of my life, I lived in my grandmother's two-bedroom house along with extended family that included my mother, father, grandmother, six siblings, and three cousins. Our home was crowded, chaotic, noisy, and characterized by busyness. Because of the number of people in the home, every conceivable space—including the basement—was used as spaces for children and adults to sleep. Everybody in the family shared a bed with another person; the youngest children slept more than two in a bed.

The home in which we lived was located in the inner city of Akron, Ohio, an industrial town known as the "Rubber Capital of the World." Low-income Black families populated the neighborhood; my elementary school was an all-Black school, as was my church. Everywhere I looked, I saw poverty.

As was the case for other families in our

neighborhood, my family struggled to make ends meet. My father was a tire builder for Goodyear Tire and Rubber Company, and my mother and grandmother both worked as domestics, cleaning the homes of and preparing meals for rich White families in the suburbs of Akron. Even with the three adults in the household working long hours, our family struggled significantly to make ends meet—we were often challenged to put enough food on the table to adequately feed everybody in the family; utilities were shut off frequently because of our inability to pay the gas or electric bill; our clothes were often ill-fitting and out of style; and missed meal cramps were a familiar feeling. The world into which I was born conditioned me to live with less than enough—not enough money, food, clothes, or space.

Even when my parents moved my siblings and me into our own rented home in the same neighborhood, we continued to experience the same dynamics as when we lived in my grandmother's home—we lived with less than enough. When I was 12 years old, my father died of a combination of lung cancer and the impacts of alcoholism, and my family was thrown even deeper into poverty. Members of my family and I learned the power of struggle and skills to survive under conditions of economic disadvantage; we also learned crucial lessons regarding psychological resilience and adaptability. While we struggled, we did not suffer. There was an emotional and psychological heaviness associated with the conditions under which we lived, but because of the spiritual dimensions of our lives there was lightness in our day-to-day interactions.

My identity and values were powerfully influenced by the conditions I experienced during my childhood. The circumstances of my family life, the neighborhood in which I lived, the church in which I was socialized, and the schools I attended provided me with a frame through which to view the world and the situations in which I found myself. I also acquired an orientation to how to navigate and be successful under conditions that are not designed for success; even in what appeared to be a dead-end world, possibilities were visible.

At the same time, my world felt disconnected from the larger world. While families having to survive on less than enough defined my inner-city world, the world beyond my neighborhood appeared to be more favored and characterized by families having more than enough—more than their fair share. From my vantage point, there were two kinds of people in the world—those with money and those without. In hindsight, this observation strikes me as odd, given the civil rights struggles that were taking place during my childhood. While race was the dominant social issue in the quest for equal rights for Black people, the dominant theme in my life was more about the scarcity of money. Even in a race-conscious society, I was more conscious of my economic situation than I was of my race.

DISCOVERING DIFFERENCES

While I was not aware of it at the time, during my childhood I developed strong feelings about the differences between those who appeared to have money and those who did not. I developed behaviors and attitudes regarding financial matters and those from more affluent backgrounds than my own. The attitudes and behaviors I adopted served me well on many occasions, but have also proven to be an obstacle at other times.

For example, I was fortunate to attend a small private college in Ohio for my undergraduate experience. I was able to attend college because of generous grants and scholarships; I took out student loans as well. The cost of attending college was more than my mother's annual income. Thus, college to me felt like an exclusive experience, and these were feelings with which I struggled mightily. My college experience represented the first time in my life that I was in a minority situation, as I found myself being both a racial minority and an economic minority. While I attended high school with Causcasian European Americans, prior to college I did not spend time in the presence of people from affluent backgrounds. The profile of my college was such that most of the students there were from financially well-off backgrounds. Thus, I found myself living in the residence hall and attending class with those whom I perceived to be "rich people," which represented my first experience living outside of my economic comfort zone.

My challenges regarding money and those who have money surfaced for me early in my freshman year and were most apparent in interactions with a fellow resident of my residence hall floor named Robert. Robert was from an affluent suburb of Buffalo, New York, and carried himself with an appearance of sophistication. Robert's typical wardrobe was a tweed jacket, khaki slacks, laundered and starched shirt, and a pipe. As relationships among members of my residence hall floor were initially being formed, my peers would refer to Robert as "Bob," and he would correct them and insist they call him Robert. Out of resentment, I developed the habit of referring to him as "Bobo." Most mornings when I encountered Robert, he would pleasantly greet me with, "Good morning, Larry." My typical response would be, "Morning, Bobo." He would often respond with, "Robert, please." On one occasion he confronted me and asked, "Why can't you call me Robert?" This confrontation both irritated and embarrassed me. I was irritated because I felt the force of what I believed to be his arrogance and desire to make me fit the constraints of his world. My embarrassment came from my awareness that I was behaving inconsistently with the value of respect for the dignity of others into which I was socialized as a child. The conversation that ensued between Robert and me was both direct and revealing. What became most apparent to me was the fact that the resentment I felt toward Robert was rooted in the fact that he was from a more economically privileged background. While he was sincere in his greeting for me each morning, instead of being able to hear, "Good morning, Larry," what I heard was "I have money and you do not." The conversation that morning compelled me to apologize to Robert and commit to him that from that point forward I would refer to him by his preferred name.

Over subsequent years, a number of other experiences made it clear to me that I had developed negative subconscious beliefs about wealthy people. As I explored those feelings and beliefs further, I came to realize that during my early childhood the stories I heard of mistreatment my mother and grandmother experienced in the homes of rich people for whom they worked led me to internalize the belief that affluent people were cruel. While I was never directly socialized into that belief, I certainly acquired that message from stories told in my home.

CONDITIONING SHOWS UP AT WORK

My experiences as a student affairs professional also helped me become more in touch with how other aspects of my childhood growing up in poverty influenced my identity and my performance as a leader. For example, because adults in my early life were often exhausted from the long hours they worked and stresses they were under, I grew up accustomed to not expressing my wants or needs. I learned to be personally and emotionally self-sufficient and to make the most of situations in which I found myself, even if the conditions did not match my hopes or expectations. Many times as a child I would not let my mother know when I was ill or had what might be an issue of medical concern. In one instance, I severely burned my finger and kept it to myself until more than a week later when the swelling and pain grew so serious that I needed to go to the emergency room to have my fingernail removed because of a developing infection. I also became very conscious of the fact that asking adults in my family for money created an uncomfortable situation for them—the response I typically received was an expression of a sincere desire to meet my need, but sorrow at the lack of money to do so. This type of response led me to not ask for money and to learn how to improvise as much as possible. These themes from my childhood created recurring challenges in my professional life.

My inability to ask for what I want or need from others often times puts me in situations where I am working under less than preferable conditions. I often find myself confronted with situations where I know others are willing and able to help and support me, but I cannot shake the belief that to ask for help will feel like an unnecessary imposition on the other person. At the same time, my hesitancy to ask for money is a characteristic of my leadership. This has proven to be problematic because one of the major responsibilities of my position as a senior student affairs officer is to advocate for and secure financial resources for my organization. I am vigilant in pushing back against these tendencies because they clearly do not serve my organization or me well. Nonetheless, I am aware that when I am in situations where I am advocating for additional resources, there is a part of me that feels like that child of poverty asking his mother for money.

While there are aspects of my identity as a child of poverty that create challenges for me, there are also strengths that come from my background. One attribute of my family situation was the expectation that everybody had a responsibility to contribute to the survival and success of the family. Every child, no matter the age, was expected to perform specific tasks. In my case, I was responsible for cooking most of the family's meals Monday through Friday and for going to the laundromat to wash the family's clothes. I was also socialized to believe that no matter how little we had, we were still responsible to help those who have less. Though my family was economically disadvantaged, there were always families in our neighborhood that appeared to be worse off than my family.

As a leader, I am committed to leading in a way that allows all members of our organization to contribute. I strongly believe everybody in the organization must share ownership for our survival and success of the Division of Student Affairs at Oregon State University. We employ a model of shared leadership that allows people to go beyond their traditional roles to contribute based on their ability. As a child, I noticed at my church and in other situations that the level of one's education was not an appropriate measure of one's ability or intelligence. I had exposure to many people whom I considered wise, but who also had very little formal education. My current leadership is one that attempts to honor knowledge and ability, regardless of from where it comes. My professional life has also been characterized by a commitment to service, both in my profession and in the community. My community involvements have particularly focused on serving those agencies that address the needs of the most socially vulnerable and most profoundly needy.

LEADERSHIP AND IDENTITY

My background of growing up with less than enough has had an acute impact on my identity and leadership. My experiences endowed me with a mindset that the absence of money should not and cannot be an impediment to my aspirations or those of my organization. The childhood conditions under which I lived oriented me to believe that no matter the circumstances, there are always possibilities for what can be achieved beyond what may seem possible in the moment. As a leader, I have consistently asserted that the financial conditions of the institution or organization should not define how we feel about ourselves as leaders; just as in my childhood, poor may have been what we were, it was not who we were.

I believe my upbringing equipped me with a high level of hopefulness and psychological resilience. I am not easily discouraged. Though I have the ability to recognize the level of difficulty associated with situations that confront me as a leader, my background instilled in me the inclination to look for the potential for success more so than the opportunities for failure. When the organization I am currently aligned with was confronted with extremely difficult budget situations that required us to cut in excess of 10% of our budget, I seized the opportunity to communicate a hopeful image of our organization's future. My general mindset, which was shaped by my early experience, is that the conditions I faced as a child were more dire and distressing than anything I have ever encountered and will likely encounter as an adult; if there was ever a time for me to feel despair it was when I was living under overwhelming circumstances over which I had no control. The only option I am willing to hold up for my organization, my co-leaders, and myself to consider is that we reside in hope.

Because of my perspective I have had to work very hard to be sensitive to those who perceive obstacles where I do not and whose personal history has not challenged them to sustain optimism in the face of difficult situations. I need to remember that my history of living in poverty sometimes causes me to downplay the necessity to advocate for financial resources needed by members of our organization; I have learned to manage my first reaction to others' requests for money.

The nature of my leadership position is such that I am frequently called upon to socialize with donors, trustees, and other stakeholders from affluent backgrounds. These situations bring out my insecurities from growing up in poverty. While I think I have become much better at managing myself in those situations, I know I am hardly ever my authentic self when in those social settings. Regardless of how much I have grown and matured, my identity as a child of poverty is a prominent feature in my interaction with the outer world. Even my choice of the type of institutions at which I have worked has been driven by my identity. Many times during my career, I had the option of pursuing employment at socially prestigious institutions; however, I have found myself drawn to institutions that serve working-class and underserved student populations. On some level, these institutional environments are probably safe for me.

THE STRENGTHS OF POVERTY

I feel strongly that my background growing up in poverty is an asset for me as a leader. While growing up, I learned the importance of utilizing all resources available to meet those challenges one must confront. I also learned that complaining about the circumstances of one's life is hardly ever productive, which enables me to model how to respond maturely to issues that arise in my leadership experience. At the same time, my childhood experiences gave me the ability to laugh at some of the absurd situations in which we found ourselves as a family. As a leader, I have come to embrace the importance of humor, even when we are confronted with matters that require serious attention. I believe it is important to bring lightness to my leadership, which means that I have a way of managing the psychological and emotional heaviness I might feel in such a way as to not burden others with my issues.

The values and lessons I learned from my family and community life are at the core of my identity as a leader. My identity compels me to be aware of and responsive to possible inequities I observe. My leadership is built on a commitment to giving voice to the voiceless and creating space for those who might otherwise be marginalized—values I acquired while observing the spirit-crushing impact invisibility and inaudibility had on my peers. In my adulthood, I feel it was a blessing for me to have the early life experiences that I had. I am certain my unique family circumstances provided me with a peculiar outlook and approach to leadership that allows me to bring distinct value to my leadership role, particularly during challenging times.

The world, our society, and our institutions are in need of healing, enlightenment, and the infusion of positive energy. The current leadership despair, created by economic conditions, that affects most organizations and our society has severely damaged the spirit of leaders and other members of our campus communities. If we are to ensure that our organizations are sustainable and have long and productive lives, we as leaders must be capable of nurturing success and generating hope—the restoration of hope is among the most fundamental of our leadership responsibilities. Members of our organizations are in need of relationships of care and opportunities to contribute. Our organizations require leaders who not only understand and feel the intensity of needs, but who are also resilient in the face of those powerful realities.

Our challenge as leaders is to work with others to construct an environment in which there is belief in the future. As unimaginable as it may seem, my childhood home environment and the faith that was instilled in me shaped my identity to have infinite belief in what the future might bring if one stays committed to a vision. While I grew up in an isolated world where I was conditioned to live with less than enough, I emerged from that experience with a perspective that allows me to look through a leadership lens that reveals that we often have more than enough. Through my eyes and in my heart I can see and I believe that our organizations have more than enough brilliance, energy, aspirations, commitment, hopefulness, and other positive characteristics to propel us toward higher achievement and greater productivity. That vision and belief is the gift I received from a childhood of poverty.

Lesbians and Jews and Education—Oh My!
A Tale of Intersecting Identities

Ronni Sanlo

Ronni Sanlo is the founding chair of the Consortium of Higher Education Lesbian Gay Bisexual Transgender Resource Professionals, and she is the originator of Lavender Graduation. She has served on the national boards of NASPA–Student Affairs Administrators in Higher Education and the Council for the Advancement of Standards in Higher Education. From activist to educator to retired mentor, Ronni's work has always been advocacy, service, and mentoring.

I was a pretty wild kid—undiagnosed but truly hyperactive—who was petrified that someone would discover my not-so-deep-but-very-dark secret. Lesbian. I did not know that particular word, but the concept smacked me hard when I reached puberty and immediately fell in love with Disney Mouseketeer Annette Funicello in 1958. That was not enough, of course: I developed ulcerative colitis that facilitated many uncooperative bodily functions. I was a psychological mess. I was only 11.

Too scared of my own body and heart and too afraid that either would give me away if I sat still for even a moment, I was leader of nearly everything in high school: outstanding student, outstanding musician, outstanding surfer, president of my sorority, and the highest-ranking female in my synagogue youth program.

The best little girl in the world syndrome. I kept busy so that no one—including myself—would notice my, uh, quirks.

I grew up in South Florida. My neighborhood of North Miami Beach was all Jewish and all White, an insulated community of people who looked and acted just like my family. However, at that time, throughout the rest of Miami, Jews, Blacks, and Catholics were openly prohibited from many locations, events, and hotels. The laws of restriction were alive and well, even in what appeared to be "liberal" Miami.

Too frightened to be different from my family, I married my college "default" date. I was so oblivious—so buried, really—in my dark, clueless closet that I totally missed Anita Bryant's "Save Our Children" campaign in 1977 that successfully repealed Miami's new gay rights laws. I missed it because I spent all my time and energy making babies, being supermom, and founding the Central Florida Community Band. I absolutely did not want to see anything concerning homosexuality. The colitis raged in my body.

Lesbian and Jewish

I came out as a lesbian two years later. I did not know the state of Florida had created its antigay parenting laws in honor of Bryant. On August 20, 1979, the court took my 3-year-old son and 6-year-old daughter away from me, giving full custody to their father—my now ex-husband. The anger, the rage, the stomach-churning all became fuel and thrust me immediately into activism and into leadership roles, roles for which I simply was not prepared. Yet within a period of 18 months, I founded two chapters of the National Organization for Women, became the executive director of the Florida Lesbian and Gay Civil Rights Task Force, was director of the Orlando Gay Center, and co-founded numerous other lesbian and gay organizations across the state. None of these positions offered leadership training, just dead ends during a burning-out and painful period of time. What I knew about leadership could almost fill a thimble. But I sure did know about identity.

As a Jewish kid at the Sabbath table, every Friday evening I learned about the history of the Jews. (Today, the brief Passover seder prayer in my home is *they tried to kill us, we won, let's eat.*) My grandfather, a rabbi, made sure his grandchildren knew and understood our devastating past as well as *tikkun olam*, the responsibility to change the world. He would frequently holler at us at the table: "If you don't do it, who will? If you don't do it now, then when?" He instilled the understanding of responsibility we had no choice but to own. It was our call and our responsibility to be leaders. But he never said how we were supposed to do that.

THE PAINFUL JOURNEY TO HIGHER EDUCATION

As a lesbian thrust into activism solely because I was deeply enraged at having lost my children, I had lofty goals but no understanding of how to be a leader. I was "the lesbian in charge" in Florida—the executive director of the Florida Lesbian and Gay Civil Rights Task Force. I had no idea what to do. I was hired because I was a fierce, fearless, willing warm body. I never took a class, received any mentoring or coaching, or had any skills regarding organizational development. What I had was a willingness to do the work while most of those who made up the lesbian, gay, bisexual, and transgender (LGBT) community in Florida were deeply, deeply closeted and totally invisible. In other words, I had an organization with no membership. The good news was I could do no wrong. The bad news was there was no oversight beyond a board of White gay men who were perfectly happy funding the organization as long as they did not have to be visible. As a result, I burned out within three years and buried myself in the Florida backwoods on the banks of the St. Johns River just west of Daytona Beach, surviving courtesy of unemployment compensation and food stamps.

After a stint of homelessness and living on the streets of Key West, Florida (I guess it could have been worse but it sure felt horrible back then), a friend found a job for me that paid a small salary and also provided a car. The next job—working for the state of Florida as the HIV epidemiologist—included educational benefits. Ironically, the state that took away my kids now provided my master's and doctorate at no cost to me.

My doctoral degree was in educational leadership and organizational development at the University of North Florida. When I began the program, I was assigned a mentor, Pritchy Smith, who was a Lakota Sioux and an early activist in social justice. Pritchy taught me about leadership, about leading with integrity, about leading from the heart. He also taught me what it meant to lead by serving as taught by the Greenleaf school of leadership. I read Max De Pree, Lee Bolman, Clarence Deal, and Stephen Covey. Finally, I was learning what it meant to be a leader and, more important, how to be an ethical leader.

I was hired by the University of Michigan as the LGBT office director in 1994, becoming a new professional in student affairs at the ripe old age of 47. Finally, after so many challenges and so much pain, I was able to integrate the history of my Jewish identity, the courage of my lesbian identity, and the wisdom of my educational identity. I remained as fearless and fierce as I was early on in my leadership experiences, but by now I knew how to move forward thoughtfully, intelligently, and inclusively. I knew my students needed a responsible adult to love and respect them. I had lost custody of my own children; I now had the privilege of caring for other people's children. While keeping students at the center of my focus, my leadership took me to places of advocacy, of speaking out for my LGBT students and all students to ensure they had a safe ride through our institutions.

A New Role

I retired from the University of California, Los Angeles, in 2010. While I retired sooner than many people in our field tend to do, I knew it was time. I had the incredible privilege of seeing my vision accomplished. I did what I set out to do in student affairs and higher education. It was time for me to do the responsible thing, to get out of the way of the young people behind me whose visions are far more broad than I could ever imagine. My role today is to support and mentor new professionals. It is a new role for me, a new identity that I cherish as much as any other I have ever had.

There is no doubt that I was called to do this work. *Tikkun olam.* I was indeed the change I wanted to see in the world, or at least in student affairs, and I look forward with great excitement to what the next generation will do with the work I began. My heart is full.

Learning to Serve, Learning to Lead With Privilege

Pete Englin

Pete Englin serves as director for the Department of Residence at Iowa State University following five years as dean of students. He has an adjunct faculty appointment in the Department of Educational Leadership and Policy Studies and is a member of NASPA–Student Affairs Administrators in Higher Education, the Association of College and University Housing Officers-International, and served as president of the Iowa Student Personnel Association.

The idea of being any kind of example in writing this essay has created significant dissonance for me. As a White heterosexual man, it is an ongoing journey of discovery to understand my privilege and the responsibility to others that comes with that privilege. To be tied with colleagues who also wrote essays is in many ways a great honor, but also a source of personal conflict as my life experiences tell me that their journeys to significant leadership roles have been vastly different and in many ways astonishing given the challenges.

So with some reluctance I accept this opportunity and own that at age 52 my learning continues. This opportunity has prompted me to revisit and reflect on how others experience me as the director of residence at Iowa State University. Much of that reflection also includes understanding how I was raised; how I was experienced in former roles as resident assistant, hall director, coordinator of residence life, associate dean of students, and dean of students; and the value of professional development experiences I received throughout my career. There are many lessons learned as I came to understand who I am and the impact on my service in leadership roles.

Those who have made a difference in my past and current learning have been the countless students and colleagues who were so caring and honest to have held up their "mirror," showing me who I am through their eyes and experiences. They typically did so not to hurt or indict me, but to show that my life experiences may have taught me in ways that are markedly different from their life experiences, so any assumptions that I have may or may not be valid.

A Strong Family Foundation

I am fortunate to have been raised in a family environment that allowed me to fundamentally embrace that I am imperfect, and to celebrate that imperfection because it is impossible to get it right all day and every day. This was not grounded in Christian ethic (I can count on one hand the number of times I attended church with my parents or brothers), though I believe in God and live life as a spiritual being. This was a journey shared with others, mostly in my young adult and adult life.

What my father, mother, and brothers did provide was a great support system that gave me a strong sense of self and a willingness to take risks. This allows me the ability to listen for messages about myself that do not "fit" or hurt, and often successfully hear these messages as growth opportunities rather than immediately rejecting them. I also believe this strong sense of self is informed by my privilege. I have grown up continually exposed to messages that affirm my value and place in the world.

My mom instilled in all of us a deep appreciation for education and a "can do" attitude, despite very modest means. We all shared in duties around the house and mom, a voracious reader, would encourage us to read often and well. She would start college at age 31, upon our move to the Minneapolis area. She completed an undergraduate degree in three years and then a master's degree in 13 months, while concurrently beginning her career as an elementary school teacher. The opportunities afforded to all of us were provided through education.

During my subsequent lifetime, constructive messages about or to me have often been subtle, but on a number of occasions have cut deeply as they challenged my core beliefs and attitudes. All have caused growth and reflection. I have learned to be more comfortable about inviting those messages and strive to behave in ways that convey to my students and colleagues that I truly mean the invitation. I admit I still become defensive if I do not trust the motivation behind the messages, but that is a part of my ongoing learning, as these messages convey their truth about the situation or the way my students and colleagues are experiencing me.

This journey was and is circuitous. Lessons come from many places, at odd times, and most often are unexpected. It has been above all liberating, as I came to understand my freedom to fully be myself can only occur if others also have that opportunity. In many situations, given my place and privilege, it is my obligation and responsibility to get out of my own way so that all can experience what I routinely take for granted. How I arrived at this juncture in my life follows.

I was born in 1959, the second of three boys at our small rental house in Lake Crystal, Minnesota, a half mile down a gravel road from the landfill for the city of Mankato. My dad, the only son of Swedish immigrants, was attending what was then known as Mankato State University on the GI Bill. He would soon become a teacher and move us to the town of Virginia, Minnesota, for a teaching job and complete a master's degree over a seven-year period. Mom, a high school graduate from South Dakota, stayed home with her two boys. Their third son would be born in 1962.

My own life was not without challenges that helped shape my character. I distinctly remember throughout elementary school heading out each recess hoping an even number of boys would show up on the east side of our playground area so I was guaranteed to get picked. While I was reasonably bright, I was not very athletic and this seemed to very much dictate who was in the popular group and who was marginalized. An odd number usually left me out, so I would hover at a distance watching to see the dynamics and hope to find a way to be included.

Affluence also played a large role in who was in the popular group and who was marginalized. In this west Minneapolis suburb, houses, cars, vacation locations, clothing, and other observable consumerism influenced who allowed you to be in their affinity group. As the son of a father who was a high school art teacher, I was left out more often than not due to a relative lack of resources. While I do not recall ever feeling poor, I did notice disparity in opportunities and the impact it had. By the time I reached high school, I developed a great group of friends with shared interests who supported each other.

While these events may seem insignificant in the grand scheme of society, as a young adult in college these situations provided me insight and understanding of how, on a greater scale, the world I lived in systemically marginalized so many who did not look like me. The challenges I faced were trivial and reasonably overcome through a strong sense of self and a great support system. However, as I entered higher education and started my career in student affairs, it quickly became apparent that so many others did not have these advantages. I came to realize the profound and positive consequences of being a White, heterosexual male who had a great support system and outstanding K–12 educational experiences.

College Opened My Mind and Heart

The saying "you don't know what you don't know" really hit home for me as I started college. When I arrived in the fall of 1977, my first impressions were that most everyone looked like me and had similar life experiences. This changed when I was invited to play college club soccer. There were no varsity programs at that time and participation was based on ability and interest. Very few high school programs existed so most players were from abroad. The culture I grew up in was vastly different from the immersion experience I encountered when I started playing soccer with people from around the world.

In the homogenous community in which I grew up, racist, sexist, and homophobic comments from people who looked like me were pervasive and relatively accepted as bad humor. I found myself struggling with the realization that I could not help but be nervous around my teammates because most were so different from me. I understood that I was making unjustified and unfounded negative assumptions about my teammates based on language, dress, and ethnicity. I had always enjoyed participating in sports, while not always the most proficient. Sharing my love for soccer with my teammates gave me motivation to stick through this questioning period but also caused me to self-question what kind of person I really was. Deep biases that I could not justify initially were affecting my ability to connect, and I was disappointed in myself for it. While I do not know whether my discomfort was known, it certainly is a credit to many of my teammates, both from the United States and abroad, that over time our relationships grew and my capacity to be in new experiences with people who looked and sounded much different than me expanded tremendously. I came to cherish learning about other countries, cultures, and shared values and recognize that great people come from all over.

These early experiences inform me greatly when I listen to traditional-age students. It is so important to learn what they do and do not know. With White students, I often find their life experience to-date parallels my own. They have had little to no interaction with people different from themselves. Their values often inform them they should care for all people but they lack the skills and opportunities to practice. As they learn, they can make hurtful and harmful assumptions about others. This learning comes at a cost to them and their fellow students who are not members of the dominant culture. I often connect back to my playground experiences where understanding being left out takes a toll. My college experiences taught me our learned biases can stop or impede building relationships. For our underrepresented or marginalized students, the dominant culture can so negatively affect their day-to-day sense of well-being, ability to learn, and opportunity to live fully as themselves.

PRIVILEGE BRINGS PERSONAL AND
PROFESSIONAL RESPONSIBILITY

Given how I present as White male, I often talk with White students about striving to suspend biases and take risks with fellow students rather than continue to perpetuate their uninformed history. With underrepresented students, I speak to the lack of experience and opportunities for many White students that causes them not to necessarily be bad people, but perhaps, instead, uninformed and short-sighted. This scenario played out early in my career when the Multicultural Action Group (MCAG), a residential-based leadership group comprised almost exclusively of American ethnic multicultural students, wanted a voting position on the senate, the residential governing board that was made up of elected leaders from each residence hall floor. Rarely did multicultural students run for floor leadership given the few numbers or, if they did run, were elected. However, the MCAG members wanted their voices to be heard at the senate level where decisions were being made that affected them. I do not recall as a student advisor ever being involved in a more honest yet contentious debate. It took place over many weeks during meetings that ran into the early morning hours and in many conversations outside formal meetings.

During this time I was criticized from all corners, some for not using my "power" to dictate to the senate to allow MCAG a vote and from some elected White students for not putting a stop to multicultural students wanting to work outside the existing election processes. After many hours of dialogue, the elected student senate came to understand experiences of the multicultural students and barriers to their participation in democratic processes. Multicultural students came to understand that systems have value and that White students could come to understand and act positively upon new information. The senate decided, in collaboration with MCAG leaders, that creating an executive position in the senate was the best way for voices of underrepresented students to be included in the decision-making process.

I learned post-conflict that my role in facilitating dialogue helped maintain trust with both groups but was affected by my being a White male. I also became acutely aware that had I been an advisor from another ethnicity, the entire dialogue would have been very different. Post-conflict discussions I had with leaders from both groups caused me to reflect on what the outcome might have been if I had been Black or Latino. I learned my privilege and subsequent status gave me an opportunity to advocate with White students about barriers to involvement for multicultural students without appearing to be self-serving. I learned I was at greater risk of losing credibility with multicultural students because I did not state that if the dialogue did not create a good alternative for MCAG, I would use my power to correct the senate. I did believe, given my own experience, that once majority students heard the issues, their sense of fairness would prevail, and it did. However, I am also very aware my privilege gave me that perspective.

These early opportunities to use my privilege to educate, inform, and create shared understanding have influenced my life and leadership greatly and prompted me to take risks and engage in issues of fairness. At the 1993 National Conference on Race and Ethnicity in American Higher Education (NCORE) in New Orleans, the first session I attended was held in a large ballroom where the facilitator asked for volunteers to role play White males resistant to affirmative action in a fishbowl exercise. When everyone looked at me, I realized there were only four White men in the entire audience, so I had the opportunity to role play. At the next break, no one would engage me except the White woman who also took part in the fishbowl exercise. While for only three days, the entire conference provided some immersion experience that gave me insight into what many students of color experience daily, for years on end, on predominately White campuses.

For a number of years, I presented a session titled "Should White Men Be Angry?" to student groups and at conferences, where larger societal issues around gender, ethnicity, sexual orientation, and systemic unfairness were discussed using facts and data. It became abundantly clear to attendees that White men were disproportionately advantaged in just about every corporate, educational, political, financial, and legislative system. While I never stated emphatically "no" to the question, attendees left with a clear answer. I also came to understand, as I did during the NCORE experience, that White men do not routinely attend these kinds of events or pay attention to information that highlights their privilege. It caused me to engage White men in a more direct and individual manner.

As a heterosexual male, I have had many conversations where people assumed I would be like-minded and disapproving regarding lesbian, gay, bisexual, and transgender (LGBT) community members, only to learn I believe that fully being yourself is a tremendous gift meant for everyone. The dialogue and relationship can be maintained as I try to bring greater understanding and acceptance, because my perspective does not appear to have a self-serving element. I am able to listen to hurtful and hateful language without feeling the same impact my LGBT friends and colleagues may experience, because of my privilege. I can afford to be more patient about maintaining relationships with those with whom I disagree, because it takes far less of a toll on me personally. I also regularly observe homophobic and heterosexist attitudes changing over time through new experiences and information, and I am encouraged that patience can be rewarded.

One of my earliest recollections of advocating involves an African American male colleague who routinely appeared to passively participate in a number of staff training activities. With arms crossed and little emotion showing on his face, he listened. As his supervisor, I often discussed with him the implications of the materials for our work, how what we learned shaped planning, and how what was being taught had cultural bias and yet would help him understand the predominately White male student body he would be serving. I was confronted at subsequent training activities by my counterparts on his apparent disengagement, and I asked them "have you ever visited with him about what he is experiencing?" They had not. I shared that I found he was very engaged, well-informed, and energized to apply what he was learning. They seemed unconvinced. When I shared the issue with him, his response was simple but profound: "They never gave me the sense they valued my opinion since they never asked, so I have not offered. I looked for them, as the leaders, to initiate."

On a policy level, I have had some success arguing for improved compensation and additional positions for areas where we have underrepresented and underserved students and staff. I did not present new arguments or issues, but I found that my privilege allowed me to be heard differently. There did not appear to be self-interest or advantage for me to hold these positions, so there was more time and scrutiny given by reasonable people who wished to do the right thing but were blinded by who was bringing the message rather than the content of the message.

I believe many of my life lessons and their impact on my leadership have been rooted in the social justice model. Our world will be better when all voices have a place to be heard and we work toward common, good solutions to challenges in society. I believe we will never arrive at a place of balance given our nature as human beings to work from our own self-interest, yet adhering to a concept of fairness as an end goal will create accountability to a perpetual dialogue. Those in power are not inclined to provide opportunities to others, especially those who do not look, think, or believe like them. Given that I am a member of the group in power, my perspective and leadership roles obligate me to advocate for others, while always recognizing that many of our students and colleagues pay a price for my privilege while I do so.

Military Brat and Sheep Herder's Granddaughter
Doing the Work That Needs Doing

Alicia Fedelina Chávez

Alicia Fedelina Chávez is associate professor of educational leadership at The University of New Mexico. She served as dean of students at the University of Wisconsin–Madison, executive campus director at the University of New Mexico–Taos, diversity development specialist at Iowa State University, and in a variety of leadership roles in student affairs.

I love country music, perhaps a signpost of my military and rural ranching childhood. The simple, heartfelt themes—honor, family, rural life, responsibility, simplicity, silliness, and hard work—in the lyrics often touch me deeply. Some of my best times in college were spent two-stepping across a rough wooden floor at barn dances. A colleague not long ago told me that I should keep this love to myself, and I was too stunned in the moment to respond. Why would I enjoy country music any less or try to hide my enjoyment of it any more than loving Spanish guitar, piano-scapes, Gregorian chant, or singing in my car at the top of my lungs to Alison Krauss, Robert Mirabal, k.d. lang, Robert Cray, Los Lobos, Trace Adkins, Alicia Keys, Third Day, Shakira, James Taylor, Maria Callas, Enya, or Sarah McLachlan?

Hierarchies of everyday things are markers of social and economic class. Put-downs, lookdowns, lesser expectations, and oppression are sometimes subtle, sometimes glaring, and harmful to professionals and students. Many on our campuses struggle to hide rural, urban, or suburban working- or poverty-based social and economic origins. These individuals often worry about how to dress, act, and access material and social necessities others take for granted (Adair & Dahlberg, 2003; Dews, 1995). I believe as leaders we must facilitate understanding of the strengths students, faculty, and staff bring from their origins and challenge our subtle assumptions and judgments about others' identities. Shifting from deficit- to strengths-based views of others is essential to social justice in higher education. For example, what strengths derive from having to work, save, and wait for much of what you want in life? How does the necessary perseverance of living with less than enough develop innovation, determination, and empathy for others' circumstances in students and professionals? How does growing up with 24-hour responsibility for living beings on a ranch influence the way we care for others in higher education?

My early context of life as a granddaughter of New Mexico sheep herders on the Chávez side of my family and cotton farmers on the Gonzales side, as a military dependent during my early years of childhood, and later as a sheep-ranching daughter causes me to see and interact with the world through some definite identity lenses as a leader. I tend not to assume getting something done requires funding, become overly protective against "predators at the door," think innovatively with scarce resources, roll up my sleeves through the messiness of all kinds of work, struggle with wealth and elitism, use formal honorifics to show respect, and feel most at home in rural places, community colleges, and land-grant universities.

I believe the essence of leadership in higher education is to facilitate the success of every student and professional. In earlier writing, I explored influences of gender, culture, and spirituality on my leadership (Chávez, 2001; Chávez, 2009; Chávez, 2010). In this essay, I explore intersections of leadership with values and worldview originating in my military and rural upbringing. These influences, interwoven with a drive toward equity in education, mean for me a very pragmatic hope and practice of leadership for social justice. Social justice leadership requires a willingness to face discomfort for the benefit of others and a highly pragmatic approach to institutional change and individual advocacy and support.

Duct Tape, Bailing Wire, and a Spoon—Innovating from Scratch

I get jazzed at the challenge of innovating with very little or even nothing. A friend of mine often says that a rural person can fix anything with duct tape, bailing wire, and a spoon. Most of my relatives have similar abilities. The most precious and sought after gifts in our large family are handmade. This originated from my parents urging us to give time and talent as well as having few available resources in our early years. I will always remember my mom sharing that we could not afford to buy many clothes but she would teach me how to sew and always keep a trunk full of cloth, patterns, and notions to create my own. I hold fond memories of imagining the possibilities in that trunk, vying for my turn on the family sewing machine, and finding inspiration in my three sisters' creativity and enthusiasm. Similarly, meals were creatively cooked from scratch, and though we were lucky to never go hungry, I learned later in life that many recipes I grew up with did not have the less expensive filler ingredients to stretch them for a family of eight. As a result, scarce resources tend to stimulate my creative juices and motivate me to find ways of meeting students' needs through local support, fundraising, innovation, collaboration, and creating a little at a time. In addition, I have a true fascination for others' gifts, especially when they differ from mine. Pointing out and encouraging others' abilities, sometimes ones they do not yet realize, is my favorite aspect of leading.

As executive campus director for a small, rural institution, I experienced a collegiate context with less funding than I ever thought possible. I soon learned to encourage hiring officers to search for applicants who were excited about the possibilities of doing great things with very little. This was in essence a critical professional skill within our campus reality. As a result, the culture of our institution evolved into one of simple ingenuity, collaboration, risk-taking, laughter, and perseverance. It became commonplace for staff and faculty to tease me with outrageous suggestions and see a dawning idea on my face originating in that very suggestion.

This often led to an incredulous, "Oh no, I was only kidding," and then we would laugh together as we discussed the possibilities. These practices began in some ways to privilege those from working-class backgrounds in campus hiring and promotion processes. Applicants from working-class backgrounds and professionals with experience in organizations such as CARE and Peace Corp often have well-developed abilities to serve others with few resources. I learned to draw out these skills and lead toward sustainable operations, equity, and hope for the future.

ELBOW GREASE, A CAN-DO ATTITUDE, AND PERSEVERANCE WILL GET YOU THERE

My father, a military officer called to lead all over the world and through many incredible circumstances, was fond of saying, "A good sergeant will get anything up a mountain with a winch, can-do-attitude, and lots of elbow grease" ("elbow grease" meaning hard, physical labor). Similarly on a ranch or farm, when something breaks down, there are rarely funds or access to ready-made solutions. My parents, grandparents, uncles, aunts, and siblings taught me there is always a way. My mom was fond of telling us to try many solutions, and if we did not know how to do something, we should observe, ask, or go to the library. Because of my cultural heritage as Mestiza (Spanish and Native American), it is natural for me to turn to elders and colleagues for collaborative thinking to get through tough dilemmas. In the first few months of a new position, I typically take everyone I can think of—from administrators to custodial staff, from students to parents—for coffee or tea and ask what they advise. Individuals are almost always surprised and honored and launch into wonderful ideas and expressions of hope and concern for students and our campus. My subsequent challenge is to facilitate widespread organizational culture and capacity toward solving anything that comes our way and embracing opportunities through hard work and perseverance. Collaboration, innovation, hard work, and valuing a diversity of contributions are especially critical in leading campuses toward equitably serving students from all backgrounds.

This same trait leads to another common leadership behavior for me. Individuals often approach me to ask for advocacy and advice on how to deal with situations of mistreatment, oppression, and/or discrimination. In addition to referring them to appropriate personnel for services and possible reporting of a grievance, I am very upfront with them, usually saying something like, "I would like to be able to tell you that this is the only time you will experience this kind of treatment. Sadly, you will probably experience similar behavior more than once, so let's talk about some ways you can prepare for, cope with, and negotiate this in the future." I always initially see a look of shock on the individual's face, and then a kind of resolve to persevere and relief at receiving assistance to develop pragmatic strategies.

TWENTY-FOUR HOUR DUTY—GUARDING AGAINST PREDATORS

One of my greatest strengths and weaknesses is a sense of the world from a 24-hour protective warrior stance. I believe this originates in being raised in a military family and within a larger clan of sheep herders as well as from surviving childhood trauma. In military and sheep herding families, there is always a readiness to protect, always a lookout in place to signal danger. My first reaction, and one I must often soothe, is a fierce protectiveness. Friends, colleagues, and students often refer to this as my "mother lion" stance, sharing that it is a bit frightening and a shocking contrast to my usual cheerful, approachable manner. For me, it is no different than the many times my sister stood up physically to protect me in school, perhaps because I was very small, perhaps just pragmatically accepting a responsibility to protect her younger sibling.

My Danish-American husband, who is six-foot-four and 270 pounds, on more than one occasion has stepped in front of me when we have been out in public and I saw a person being put-down or abused. I tend not to notice danger to myself as I step forward to protect. On one occasion while I was a residence hall director, I received a call from a very frightened student who said his father was on the way with a gun to kill him. I placed a quick call to campus police and then ran to the student's room, placing myself physically between the student and the gun pointed at his face, ordering the father to hand it over. Luckily, he did and backed down immediately.

My fierce warrior stance typically has that effect yet is not necessarily the safest or most effective means. Ironically, I am far from a physically courageous person under other circumstances. I do not have the fearless ability to serve in the military, fly a plane, or enjoy skiing like my family members. Nor is a protective stance always helpful to another's growth. I believe our job in higher education is to assist others to develop so they are more able to do for themselves when we are not around. Soothing this warrior and protector identity is one of my toughest challenges as a leader because my response to seeing someone in harm's way is often visceral and automatic. I must continually weigh situations to determine when it is helpful to stand up with someone, to protect, to advocate, or to lead campus change efforts. Though I have become more measured in response over time, I believe balancing my warrior protective stance will always be a challenge.

STRUGGLING WITH CONTRADICTIONS OF ELITISM

Even with pride common in military and sheep herding professions there is certain humility inherent in the work. Both deal heavily in the messiness, humble realities, and sometimes horrors of life at its basic survival levels. Growing up amidst military and sheep herding cultures taught me in some deep seated ways to distrust, avoid, and sometimes harshly judge wealth, elitism, and elite institutions. I turned away recruitment to several elite universities for both graduate degrees and several leadership positions, not wishing to have my name associated. I also experienced an extreme period of anxiety at becoming a PhD. I feared becoming Dr. Chávez would separate me in some indefinable way from those I love and make it more difficult to connect, to empathize, and to advocate with those facing oppression. I almost hyperventilated the night before my graduation; I was so concerned about this—not wanting to be part of a subculture of people who from my reality have often brought damage to those of low socioeconomic status, to rural people, to working-class people, to people of color. Yet as I challenged this assumption in myself and worked side-by-side with social justice activists from across socioeconomic status, I came to understand that we each bring privilege and empathy, sometimes working from an insider perspective and sometimes from an outsider perspective for social justice.

Working years ago at an institution with an enrollment of primarily upper-class students taught me profound lessons about fears, anxieties, and pressures experienced by many students from high socioeconomic levels. Large ratios of eating disorders, cutting incidences, and suicide attempts as well as a marked similarity in hair, dress, and demeanor hinted at underlying pressures. Some students revealed fears of being "dropped" socially, familially, or financially if they did not conform to tight social expectations. This fear was often accompanied by a visceral terror at the thought of facing a future without known resources and support. I began to feel true empathy knowing from my experience a certain freedom engendered by working my way through high school and college, knowing in my deepest self that I could fall back on simpler skills to waitress, do physical outdoor labor, or be a baker, knowing I would not starve. This freedom allowed me to leave a job suddenly when, as a department director, I was heavily pressured toward unethical recruitment practices with students of color. Within a week, I secured several jobs, including waitressing and caring for plants at a local greenhouse. Two weeks later, I convinced the director of residence life at the same institution to hire me for several temporary projects while I decided what to do next.

I still fight my own stereotypes about elite institutions and people from wealthy origins. I choose universities and colleges with large enrollments of low-income and first-generation students, feeling most comfortable and needed serving those from these origins. In these institutions, I often find those who speak a language of social and economic class I understand. Yet I am profoundly humbled and transformed by kind, social-justice-oriented professionals from all backgrounds and students finding their way regardless of social or economic origins.

HONORING WITH AUTHENTICITY

"Hold your head up, Mijita, we worship no one but God." These words were said with empathy and fierce protectiveness by my maternal grandmother long ago when I came home hurt by put-downs. These words and belief have played a large role in my life and leadership. I rarely feel intimidated by someone with a higher title, degree, or different expertise because I was taught we are all of great worth. My paternal grandfather was a sheep herder, a school janitor, and a state representative simultaneously to provide for his family and serve his community. Life in a sheep herding and military family taught me that honoring others with a constant, overt respect and authenticity is critical to working together especially across differences. I tend to take on very formal demeanor and words with others especially when we first meet. Formal demeanor, words, and titles often cross boundaries by letting someone else know you think highly of them from the beginning. Saying "Thank you, Ma'am," "I am honored to meet you," or "No Sir" to bus drivers, students, and presidents alike is a way to show esteem without subjugation. Doing so with kindness and openness to what I might learn from them is something I put to good use as a leader.

There is another side to honoring with authenticity. I am less likely to let others dishonor me for who I am, what I do, or what I believe. Even at the age of 50, I continue to experience treatment from others signaling that I am somehow less. I usually respond at first with discussion and if this does not work, I might follow with action through formal written requests or notifications. This has mixed results, yet I believe one of the most important things we can do to transform toward socially just environments is to stand up for ourselves as well as with others.

Doing the Work That Needs Doing

Recently, a pack of dogs savaged the little flock of sheep cared for by my extended family in Taos, New Mexico. Along with several siblings, I put on my boots and headed out to search cliffs, desert, and river for scattered, terrified, and injured sheep. I clambered around the cliffs, "gentled" a frightened ewe with soft words, helped my sister administer shots of penicillin to the wounded, and worked in tandem with family to return lost sheep to the safety of the barn. Life in sheep herding and military families requires constant willingness to roll up your sleeves and do whatever is needed—mucking stalls, helping neighbors, dropping other activities to respond in a crisis, and pitching in to help with a whole range of sometimes pleasant and sometimes incredibly unpleasant or even dangerous work. Some of the work in sheep herding, in the military, and in higher education is very fulfilling, like advising students, supporting sheep through lambing season, or knowing that your brother and father are out there doing their best in the military to keep us safe as a nation. Some is not so pleasant, like tending the wounded, standing up to someone with hatred or bigotry in their heart, or comforting someone experiencing terrible loss. I think of the matter-of-fact way my brother, a retired fighter pilot, often sends me off with a hug, saying, "Be brave." I know he is being funny, yet I take his words seriously all the same. To lead social justice transformation in higher education requires courage, discomfort, perseverance, ingenuity, and honor. At its heart, it is about standing up for ideals upon which this country and my family were founded.

Serving as a hall manager, assistant director, director, dean of students, senior executive campus leader, and now as a teacher and scholar-leader includes duties I love as well as duties requiring all my fortitude and courage. Over the years, I "gentled" people through or just after extreme trauma, offering comfort, first aid, reassurance, and help with immediate problem solving. I stood up for student rights to protest campus and societal issues. I rolled up my sleeves to quietly clean up vomit and blood spilled so that an area would not be hard on those who passed by before custodial staff came on duty. I stepped forward with others outside my own identities to advocate for their needs amidst resistance, anger, indifference, or disdain.

I continue to take on uncomfortable and messy kinds of social justice work. Through it all, I remember the courage and wisdom of my parents, grandparents, and siblings leading us through difficult times in our military and sheep herding family. As a result, it is natural for me to take on the messy, protective, innovative, and honorable roles of social justice leadership in higher education. Mostly, I just put on my boots and head out to see what needs doing.

References

Adair, V. C., & Dahlberg, S. L. (2003). *Reclaiming class: Women, poverty and the promise of higher education in America*. Philadelphia, PA: Temple University Press.

Chávez, A. F. (2001). Spirit and nature in everyday life: Reflections of a Mestiza in higher education. In M. Jablonski (Ed.), *The Implications of Student Spirituality for Student Affairs Practice* (New directions for student services, no. 95, pp. 69–79). San Francisco, CA: Jossey-Bass.

Chávez, A. F. (2009). Leading in the borderlands: Negotiating ethnic patriarchy for the benefit of students. *NASPA Journal About Women in Higher Education, 1*, 39–65.

Chávez, A. F. (2010). Women and minorities encouraged to apply: Challenges and opportunities of critical cultural feminist leadership in academe. In C. C. Robinson & P. Clardy (Eds.), *Tedious journeys: Autoethnography by women of color in academe* (pp. 173–194). New York, NY: Peter Lang.

Dews, C. L. (1995). *This fine place so far from home: Voices of academics from the working class*. Philadelphia, PA: Temple University Press.

An Imposter in Legal Education
Growing Up Poor, White, and Female

Marsha L. Baum

After almost 20 years in law librarianship, law school administration, and teaching, Marsha L. Baum moved to full-time law teaching in 2003 and is currently a professor of law at the University of New Mexico. While her main focus is on property law, her course in ethics has offered the most opportunity to explore the impact of her experiences as poor, White, and female.

As a full professor of law with tenure, I am afforded many options that were inconceivable when I was growing up. I spend my working life teaching and researching. I have opportunities and invitations to travel and speak at conferences around the world. Students rely on my expertise and seek mentoring from me. My credentials give me a level of credibility that allows me to influence program development and curricular change at the law school and university and in the community at large.

Most of the people with whom I share my work life, my students and colleagues, do not know of my past and probably assume that I share a background similar to most of theirs. Law students and law professors tend to be a homogeneous group—they generally come from a middle-class or higher socioeconomic status, have experienced similar life events as they were growing up, and have benefited from advantages provided by their well-off families.

However, there are those with lower socioeconomic class roots who attend law school despite the odds. I am one of those people. When I was growing up, I did not know any lawyers, let alone law professors. The thought of teaching law some day was not even in the running for possible vocation, although I was encouraged to be a teacher or a librarian by my public school teachers. My road to law school and legal education was focused on becoming a law librarian, a profession that integrated my fascination with the law as a subject and my love of libraries.

BORN FEMALE

I was born female. I am the middle of five children, four girls and one boy. It was clear to me growing up that the boy was the important child and that, if any one of the girls that preceded him had been a boy, our family would have been smaller. This clear understanding of the lesser importance of a female child could have made me decide not to use my abilities and to seek to be the "proper" female to gain attention; however, I instead focused all of my energies on pushing myself to excel in school where teachers recognized and rewarded students who were smart and who were willing to complete the work. This recognition moved me to honor society, college, graduate school, and law school with a specific goal that still fit within the parameters of acceptable female jobs, law librarian. I was still limiting myself based on gender norms until my career path was transformed, ironically by the birth of children, and placed me in the male-dominated profession of full-time law professor.

GROWING UP POOR

In addition to being born female, I had the disadvantage of living my young life in a family of low socioeconomic status. When I was growing up, we lived in a drafty, old farmhouse with no heat in the bedrooms and an old woodstove in the living room. Today, this sounds trendy; at the time, it was just cold. Getting ready for school in the morning included steeling myself to get out from under the warm covers and run as fast as I could to stand near the woodstove to keep warm and try to wake up.

My working-class parents struggled to raise five children on a few thousand dollars per year. The addition of child number five led to my mother entering the work force on a full-time basis, much to my father's displeasure. Mom worked nights and dad worked days. The older siblings took care of the younger siblings. Mom slept during the day while the older kids were in school and the two youngest ran wild around the house.

VALUES LEARNED IN A FAMILY OF WORKING POOR

Even in the midst of this financial angst, my parents still believed hard work would be rewarded, you did not accept charity, and work was the first priority. Values of independence and self-sufficiency, hard work, and the importance of not appearing to be different were learned through modeling of behavior and through practice from an early age. Independence and self-sufficiency were critical to pride of self in my family of working poor. You earned everything that you had through hard work; nothing would be handed to you.

Work was the first priority. Social relationships and friendships were secondary to being sure the work was done. Parties were big affairs that happened a few times a year, but only included family. Weekends and holidays were times to work at home, not times to relax. School work needed to be done, I guess, but I do not recall my parents ever asking if my homework was done or setting a time or a space to do it. The expectations and understanding for all of us was that we did our chores as part of a large family so we had a clean house and clean clothes and food to eat.

Chores included indoor work and outdoor work. Every Saturday, we were called out of bed to clean the house. Every spring, my sisters and brother and I would go out into the garden to pick up rocks. Our standing joke now is that the best crop we grew in our garden was rocks; there seemed to be an endless supply. When the pump for the well stopped working, we all helped to pull it up so my father could fix it. We did not hire people to do things; either we did it or it did not get done.

This focus on work has shown itself throughout my life. If I am not working, I am being lazy. I feel like I should be busy at all times and am generally completely overbooked. I have worked and gone to school my entire life. I take on publishing projects on top of committee work on top of teaching on top of family responsibilities. I am completely goal-oriented, looking for the next project before the current one is completed. I do not understand people who are not completely focused on work and sometimes resent their ability to ignore work and focus on fun.

If you look at my life now, you likely would not see that child who grew up in nonwelfare poverty, part of the working-class poor with two working parents and not enough healthy food to eat, wearing hand-me-down or homemade clothes, riding the bus to school, working in the garden to raise food. Yet, I still identify myself with that socioeconomic beginning—of meals consisting of potatoes and creamed corn, of waiting for the twice-yearly explorations of the boxes of clothes stored in the attic to get something "new" to wear, of teachers adopting me because I was smart and apparently seemed in need of some attention, of spending summers playing only with my brother and sister because we lived in a rural area with our nearest neighbor a half-mile away until I was old enough to be the babysitter for my younger siblings while mom and dad were at work.

VALUES FOSTERED BY GROWING UP FEMALE

The focus on work and achievement also is a product of my identity as female. By realizing that attention and hard work were rewarded in school and recognized with awards, my focus became academic achievement. Being female and smart can be a difficult and frustrating combination in the face of people who have biases without basis in fact or logic. In my small farming community, I struggled against the accepted societal rules and railed against assertions of male superiority and patriarchal society as the token feminist in my senior class in high school.

While there are difficulties in being a female law professor, with the occasional student who expects a female instructor to be "nicer" or more nurturing and forgiving about deadlines, I am able to offer both male and female students a perspective in the classroom male law professors cannot offer. Being female has given me years of responding to bias and learning to handle mistaken beliefs about female abilities and to prove those biases wrong. For female students in the law school classroom, having a female law professor allows them to see possibilities for themselves. For male students in the law school classroom, having a female law professor allows them to practice responding to females in authority as they will in the courtroom. By teaching business law courses and logic-based analysis, I am able to demonstrate that critical thinking skills and rationality are not the male province.

POOR AND FEMALE AT ODDS WITH THE PRIVILEGE OF BEING BORN WHITE

Being born White, however, gives me an element of privilege that is at odds with my status as a female and as someone from socioeconomic disadvantage. Because race can be such a powerful characteristic, people may make assumptions about White people's backgrounds and experiences that may not reflect the other characteristics that have had an impact on their lives. I am sure that I have had students in my classes who have an inaccurate picture of my background based on my race and who assume I had advantages growing up that led to my position in legal education. To some, White people cannot suffer disadvantage because race and ethnic origin give an advantage or disadvantage that cannot be countered by other characteristics. Some feminists would, of course, say the same about gender.

Although I can "clean up" well and play the part of an academic, I sometimes feel like I am an imposter in my position as a law professor. When I look around me at other faculty members, I see people who have attended Ivy League schools, whose parents were, at a minimum, middle class and college-educated, who traveled the world while they were young, who visited museums and attended concerts and plays put on by professionals, and who had dinner conversation about politics and news of the day. This life experience gives a leg up in academic life, with easy recognition and allusion to cultural and literary symbols, that I spent a large portion of my adult life trying to fake so I could fit in with professionals around me.

IMPACT OF POOR, WHITE, FEMALE ON ROLES IN LEGAL ACADEMIA

Along the road to becoming a law professor, my background and experiences as a poor White female played a significant role in various choices I made and paths I took to reach my current position. That background and experience continues to play a significant role in ways I perform my professional responsibilities and ways I interact with my peers and my students. Early in my career, those choices and decisions were focused on hiding my background and trying to fit in by never exposing my roots. Pretending seemed necessary to gain standing in the legal profession and in the legal academy, where credentials and upper-echelon attitudes and behaviors were the way to gain and maintain power and status.

As a consequence of this early socioeconomic disadvantage and my resulting feelings of being an imposter, becoming a leader in an educational institution has taken a great deal of emotional energy. Up until the last few years, I focused on proving and improving myself in all settings while trying to, if not hide, at least not advertise my background. But, as I arrived at midlife, I took a different tack and began sharing the truth of my earlier experiences with colleagues and students. This new focus and willingness to share my life with others, far from detracting from my credibility or harming my ability to create change as I feared it would, gives me the ability and confidence to attack problems such as lack of programs and opportunities in law schools for White students with disadvantaged backgrounds and lack of training on the impact of socioeconomic status on client understanding and ability to respond to their lawyers. I find myself offering examples from my own life in class that allow students to see that opportunities exist, even for so-called "poor White trash."

Within the last few years, I was encouraged by one of the editors of this book, who was an instructor in an education course I was taking to improve my teaching, to reflect deeply on my characteristics and the impact those characteristics have on my teaching and my leadership within legal education. That reflection allowed me to consider ways to use my early life experiences to benefit my students and my school. For law students who are first in their families to go to college or to law school, having someone at the front of the classroom who has a similar background can be empowering and comforting. Seeing that someone else has been in the same position they are in now and has "made it" allows them to be more open to the experiences of law school and less fearful that they do not belong.

The identity of poor White female into which I was born has an impact on my teaching and leadership in higher education in ways beyond serving as a role model for students from similar circumstances. I am identifying areas in which assumptions I make based on my background affect my students and their learning. For example, just as colleagues from upper-class families may have assumptions, expectations, and values that make it easier to understand and work with students like themselves, I have found it easier to relate to students who share my background. This tendency to be better able to understand and more likely to advocate for students like ourselves, if not recognized and consciously set aside, can disadvantage students who are not like us, making the diversity in backgrounds of faculty that much more important to ensure positive experiences for all students.

In addition, the law as a service profession requires practitioners who are able to relate to their clients' circumstances and offer advice and counsel that meets their needs, not the results that the lawyers think the clients should want. Since many law schools tend to admit students from a certain background and then tend to try to orient students toward a particular method of thinking, frequently legal education seems to be creating lawyers who look like the current population of lawyers, leaving those who are different from the norm of middle- or upper-class White males to fight an uphill battle in understanding the goals of legal education and the legal profession. This may result in female lawyers leaving large firms, not because they cannot do the work, but because they look different. And, those who did not grow up playing golf and tennis and did not embrace trappings of middle- and upper-class lawyers are at a disadvantage.

I find that being a White female professor who has come from a background of poverty is not the weight I had painted it to be but is instead an asset to students for whom I can be an example, a mentor, an ally, and an advocate. By examining this identity and the impact it has on my professional life, I am able to find ways to incorporate my learning into course offerings, faculty activities, administrative work, and interactions with students. Attending workshops such as one on allies for the lesbian, gay, bisexual, and transgender community on campus created an impetus for developing problems in my legal ethics course to require students to think about the impact of their assumptions on their dealings with clients. As a result of being willing to expose my early background to others, I was able to work more effectively with the law school faculty and administration to amend the admissions policy to include socioeconomic status as an aspect of applicant background to be considered in our holistic admissions process.

Being who I am led me through the constant struggle that resulted in my current status as a law school professor who now has the opportunity to influence student attitudes and offer a role model of a trained professional who just happens to be a White female from an economically disadvantaged background. Lawyers are viewed as powerful people; poor people and women are not. But the people who need to be served by the law are those who are without resources or power. Movements that attempt to aid those in need of assistance without providing lawyers who look like them or who can understand their concerns cannot provide the level of support and access to the justice system that these clients need. By offering hypotheticals about a diversity of populations, including those of the rural poor and women, I can help classroom discussion serve as a way for students to consider and question their own assumptions and values. By using my reflections on background and bringing my underlying assumptions about the importance of work and the need to be serious and focused to the surface, I have been able to comfortably relay my experiences to students.

In the past few years, I have used my experiences to work with others in my law school to adopt changes in the admission policy, help students consider client backgrounds and the ways in which those backgrounds may affect reactions to the law and to lawyers and to the court, and develop discussion points for class to encourage students to consider and challenge their own assumptions and values. The start of these efforts to change approaches in the law school came about with my own testing of underlying assumptions and values that resulted from my experiences as a poor White female. By sharing those experiences with my colleagues and my students and no longer pretending to share the same background as other law professors and lawyers, I am able to be more genuine in my discussions and to offer students more options for their own lives. With an understanding of the impact of our early experiences, we are better able to hear the message of diversity and to handle differences, not as barriers to communication and understanding, but as differences in experience and perspective that can result in more informed discussions. The opportunity to share rather than to hide one's true self is a way to open communication rather than to stifle it.

Leading With Integrity
Maintaining Authenticity in Senior Leadership Roles

Peter A. Hayashida

Peter A. Hayashida is vice chancellor for advancement at the University of California, Riverside (UCR), and president of the UCR Foundation. He served in leadership roles during 19 years at the University of California, Los Angeles, before joining UCR in 2009. He served for 10 years on the Los Angeles Gay and Lesbian Center Board of Directors.

I led a nomadic childhood. My military family lived in 10 different homes across three countries and six states before I graduated from high school. People often ask how I liked that lifestyle. "Compared to what?" I muse. It was the only childhood I had. It was happy, to be sure, but I do not have the experience of being born and raised in one place so I hardly feel qualified to contrast the relative merits of a stationary upbringing. What I do know is that this perpetual motion played a formative role in shaping my identity. I would come to experience my whole life through the prism of constant change, occasional uncertainty, and the importance of family.

WHERE I HAVE BEEN

Living in suburban Virginia, Georgia, or Kansas, it was easy to forget I was a racial minority until someone asked me why I bombed Pearl Harbor. This overt racism stimulated both confusion and embarrassment. How does one explain to fellow first-graders the absurdity that my parents were not even born when the "day that shall live in infamy" transpired? Or that in some cases, my family had probably immigrated to the United States from Japan before theirs did from Europe? I considered myself American, and I thought that was all that mattered. This is my earliest memory of two dawning realizations. I was different and, as a result, my life would probably be more complicated.

The second milestone in forming my psyche was something I consider to be an accident of genetics. I earned good grades, was well liked by my teachers, and was very good at standardized tests, but hopelessly uncoordinated. That is to say I was a quintessential nerd. At school after school in city after city, I stood out for all the wrong reasons. I would later see many of these traits as assets, but during adolescence they were the kiss of death.

The final pillar in defining my identity was coming out as a young gay man in high school. Having experienced blatant racism earlier in my life, in some perverse way I was better prepared for some of the challenges that would follow, but I did not realize then how essential my identity as a gay man would be later in life. Many were very supportive, but I quickly learned which of my friends I could truly trust.

WHERE I AM

Today, I am in my fifth career. I have been a business analyst, academic counselor, program and event manager, chief financial and operating officer, and fundraiser. How I approach my current role as vice chancellor for advancement at the University of California, Riverside, offers useful insights into how identity shapes and informs my leadership style, approach, and perspectives.

First, I am very conscious of ways in which my life experience leads me to actively crave and seek environments that are dynamic and diverse. As a leader, not only do I want to see different faces around me, I foster respectful disagreement and positive tension that lead to richer and more nuanced solutions to problems. The key to exploiting my desire for diversity lies in knowing myself, understanding my environment, and being vigilant about keeping the two aligned. Knowing self involves keen and sometimes painful self-awareness—my strengths and weaknesses, my fears and aspirations, and the comfortable balance of confidence and insecurity I have come to recognize in others who know what they are and are not good at.

Understanding my environment was critical as I embarked on organizational culture change at two different institutions. My professional field suffers from demographic imbalances. According to a survey by the Council for the Advancement and Support of Education (2011), we in educational advancement are two-thirds female and 90% White. How does one begin to address such systemic anomalies to create balance in building a team so, for example, alumni of color believe the institution values them and is committed to providing opportunities to all?

My approach is to be direct, seizing opportunities to describe my diversity goals and remind others of our collective responsibility to be good stewards of the profession. The solution is not to blame current leaders in the field for a bad situation, but to instill in ourselves a sense of mission to provide better circumstances for a new generation of professionals and ensure that we are constantly evolving and improving.

The second way in which my identity has shaped me as a leader concerns visibility and accessibility. When I was starting in my field at the University of California, Los Angeles, role models who superficially "looked" like me were conspicuously rare. I knew a straight, Asian American assistant vice chancellor. I knew a gay White assistant vice chancellor. On a campus of 36,000 students and 25,000 faculty and staff, none shared the same pair of racial and sexual orientation identities that I had. This led me to question whether I would be welcome among those ranks.

I was told as a young employee that I should stay away from advancement because "the gay thing" made alumni and donors uncomfortable. For better or worse, that train left the station more than a dozen years before I began this part of my career, so I came to a crossroads: Should I stay in higher education or find employment in the lesbian, gay, bisexual, and transgender (LGBT) community?

It was the Asian American assistant vice chancellor who challenged me to consider the impact I might make as an openly gay executive in higher education versus being a high-profile Asian American leader in the LGBT community. This question stimulated useful thought. I knew that while racism was alive and well everywhere, LGBT activism was progressive, and I felt it would not be long before Asian Americans established a stronger foothold among its top ranks. I was keenly aware as a young man in the early 1980s that stereotypes of Asians and Asian Americans—weak, passive, bookish, humorless—put me at a disadvantage in gay male social contexts where strength, virility, charm, and assertiveness drove success. But even a decade later, I saw early signs that the tides were shifting, and I felt sure progress was imminent.

I opted to stay in higher education, knowing this decision came with a responsibility to ensure that those who followed would not experience the same feelings of isolation, uncertainty, and disorientation that come with being the first or the only. It was my duty to pay it forward. A friend of mine describes some leaders from diverse backgrounds as wanting to be "the only chip in the cookie." That was not me.

I now spend time on campus, in the community, and out on the road simply being visible. Filmmaker Woody Allen is purported to have said, "Eighty percent of success is showing up." Certainly seeing an Asian American vice chancellor at a top-tier research university sends a message. On my campus, I am one of only a handful of non-White senior leaders, yet our student body is among the most racially diverse in the nation among research universities. As a result, I feel a sense of urgency to be present at activities that have no bearing on my professional success because others need to know that I am here, I am supportive, and that they, too, will pay it forward when it is their turn.

When asked about my weekend, I do not gender-switch pronouns to conceal my sexual orientation. My husband and I have spent 18 years building a beautiful, satisfying life together. Making him invisible would be disrespectful. In the relatively small and conservative community of Riverside, California, word travels fast. Those who want to know about my personal life ask. Those who do not want to know, do not ask. Interestingly, I cannot remember the last time I had to utter the words, "I am gay," but I suspect it was when I was in college. Living openly and confidently means that someone who spends any amount of time with me figures out my sexual orientation organically—as one might discover a new acquaintance has children, is Muslim, or lives with a disability. It is an integral part of my identity, like being male, Asian American, a military brat, from Hawai`i, or a son, brother, husband, or uncle.

By my example, I hope to provide a safe space for others to bring their whole selves to work. We all become stronger when each among us enjoys freedom from stigma and oppression. I consider that a duty of leadership if not one of its defining qualities. I do not believe one must experience prejudice or discrimination to have empathy, but in my case it has helped nurture a commitment to diversity and compassion for others.

Finally, my identity causes me to regularly question assumptions as a leader. Assumptions and stereotypes are not inherently negative and in some ways are unavoidable human coping mechanisms—we simply cannot meet every person in the world and form deep impressions of each. But there is danger in not recognizing stereotypes for what they are: heuristics that assist in interpreting reality, but not reality in and of themselves.

THE MANTLE OF LEADERSHIP

There are many perquisites of becoming a leader to be sure: higher self-esteem, increased control, satisfaction of service, and ability to influence organizational culture and outcomes. But leadership is not a position, a box on an organizational chart, or a corner office on a top floor. It is an intangible set of qualities that leads others to follow of their own accord, not by rote or out of fear but out of passion for a cause greater than themselves.

While it classically emanates from the top, leadership can come from anywhere in an organization. This is a lesson I learned early in my career as a result of another dimension of my identity. I have always been among the youngest incumbents of jobs at my level. This has caused me to rely more on persuasion than direction in accomplishing my objectives because I could not lean on decades of experience to make my case.

Paradoxically, this is a process I learned to appreciate from my ethnic heritage. Although Japan is a highly hierarchical society, directness is considered rude and presumptuous. I was taught early in life that finding ways to soften messages resulted in both sides "saving face" and outcomes that enjoyed greater buy-in. Although patience is not one of my virtues, conflict avoidance is ingrained in my psyche as a value. I will spend the rest of my life striking a balance between the relative value of outcome and process, yet my culture has proven to me that this is essential for my success.

As I reflect on who I am as a leader and how that relates to my identities, several inescapable conclusions emerge. First, experiencing prejudice at an early age amplified the value of achievement, already so prominent in Asian cultures. It is not enough for me to be good: I must strive to be the best—or certainly better than most. This attitude was not formed through external pressure from others, but rather is generated through internal narrative and manifests in work where the benefit sometimes outweighs the cost. That is, I continue to learn the painful lesson that good is sometimes good enough.

I also feel that my membership in multiple communities that have experienced historical oppression has left me with little tolerance for intolerance. When I encounter racism in the LGBT community or homophobia among people of color, it is hard to miss the irony. Yet it is human nature to cluster with others who are like us, so part of my job as a leader is to model behavior of reaching beyond my comfort zone in the bonds I form.

Today, I work on a very progressive campus in a conservative region of California. While I may not agree philosophically on a range of issues with some alumni, donors, neighbors, and colleagues, I cannot help but respect the passion and commitment they feel for their dogmas. I also grow and evolve as I learn about others who are different from me, so my value of diverse perspectives only grows as I age.

Finally, I believe my identity as a former military dependent instills in me its own set of values: fidelity, loyalty, industriousness, discipline, patriotism, and respect. All of these elements translate directly into my style as a leader, although I strive to resist the command-and-control approaches commonly found in such cultures. In practice, this causes me to value those who I perceive as loyal and disciplined, and work to model these characteristics myself.

Another leadership trait traceable to my roots in military communities is adaptability. When one has to relocate every year or two beginning before kindergarten, one learns a variety of valuable lessons early in life. I know that the world is filled with changes over which I have no control and the measure of my resilience is in how I respond to such shifts. I am a planner—there is no other way to move household goods efficiently than to detail every step—but I am also flexible because planning assumptions often change or are fluid.

I cherish this artifact of my childhood because I have witnessed that inability to process and react to change destroy individuals and organizations alike. I encourage my team to prepare for the worst, hope for the best, and be ready to improvise if the situation demands. It sounds so simple, but many people behave in ways that suggest they do not understand what has become for me a fundamental and driving philosophy of life. It is not the only philosophy, of course, nor is it necessarily right for anyone but me. However, if the alternative is whining about a lack of control over one's life, the choice seems clear: Develop a strategy that fits, implement it, test it, adjust it, and work to perfect it. Rinse and repeat.

A few words about authenticity. First, it is not absolute. I have many identities, and I strive to honor all of them, but sometimes I cannot do so simultaneously. There are moments when the competitive drive I feel as a male and the child of two first-generation college graduates comes in conflict with the respectful reserve my military and Asian cultures hold dear. At first blush, it would seem that any action in such a situation would serve one value and not the other.

Authenticity to me entails being true to self, and doing so requires accepting that "self" is a complex, layered, dynamic, and contextual construct. The decisions I make at work are not made using frameworks identical to those I use at home or in my volunteer board roles. That is neither good nor bad, although many would argue that one is not well-served interacting identically with one's spouse as one's coworkers. Instead, I would argue that authenticity requires developing self-awareness, defining one's values, maintaining consistent standards, and interacting with others in good faith.

SOCIAL JUSTICE

I often hear friends, colleagues, and social pundits bemoan the widening gulf between rich and poor. In fact, data from the U.S. Census Bureau (2010) on income distribution support that assertion, and access to resources is a compelling issue in contemporary society. There are myriad causes for this disparity, and the current economic crisis complicates an already tenuous landscape for society's most vulnerable members.

The question of how to address these inequalities is vexing and highlights fundamental tensions between classic American values. Serving those less fortunate, an integral precept of many faith traditions, is not mutually exclusive of the capitalist economy that has made "the American Dream" a reality for generations of immigrants. The notion that individuals can overcome poverty, discrimination, and limited access to quality education to achieve prosperity is akin to baseball and apple pie. Yet, to some extent, this zero-sum game leaves large segments of society struggling to eke out a basic existence.

So what exactly is the role of a leader in addressing social justice? A threshold function is to advocate for issues that often are not raised in global conversations in our nation's largest and most important organizations. Pay equity is only one element in this equation. How do organizations address the blending of generations, social classes, races, religions, and so forth to optimize outcomes for organizations, individuals, and society? Is this even the right hierarchy of masters? How do large institutions develop and disseminate best practices in the care and feeding of human capital to maximize employee satisfaction and organizational effectiveness? These questions lie at the heart of sound leadership.

At the end of the day, I am the leader I am because of the aggregate impact of my life experiences. I carry with me every day the devotion, commitment, perfectionism, and pride that were handed down through generations of ancestors both in Japan and in Hawai`i. I weave into leadership of my department the compassion, empathy, and openness that are benefits of having come to terms with my identity as a gay man. I enjoy the strength, decisiveness, and assertiveness that were taught to me as a young boy and continue to serve me well as a leader and team member.

But beyond those immutable characteristics, I also enjoy the adaptability, sociability, and agility I gained by being part of a military family that was constantly in motion. Perhaps the most important touchstone of identity for me is my affiliation with the University of California. As my employer for most of my adult life, my alma mater, and even for a time my home, the university has served as a source of inspiration, strong values, and community. My role as a leader is to make sure that the university is the kind of place that honors its heritage and makes the people of California proud of its world-class research and teaching enterprise—and to do so in ways that allow me to lead in alignment with my values, identity, and commitment to justice.

REFERENCES

Council for the Advancement and Support of Education. (2011). *2011/2012 CASE compensation survey*. Retrieved from http://www.case.org/Samples_Research_and_Tools/Benchmarking_and_Research/Surveys_and_Studies/CASE_Compensation_Survey.html

U.S. Census Bureau. (2010). *Income*. Retrieved from https://www.census.gov/hhes/www/income/data/inequality/middleclass.html

Leading Through Invisible Identities

In this section, leaders discuss profound challenges and opportunities of leading from identities invisible to others.

Leadership With a Traumatic Brain Injury and Beyond

Jody Donovan

Jody Donovan serves as dean of students at Colorado State University, where she also teaches in the student affairs in higher education graduate program. She has been a student affairs professional at large, public and small, private institutions. In every position, the highlight of her day is working with students.

"OK, Jody, can you name all the animals
that live in a zoo?"

"When getting dressed, what comes
first, shoes or socks?"

"Breathe from your diaphragm,
not your chest."

"Before you go grocery shopping, it is
important to remember to make a list of
things you need to purchase."

Less than a month after successfully defending my doctoral dissertation in 2006, I suffered a traumatic brain injury and was challenged by simple tasks of everyday living like those above. In this essay, I make meaning of my recovery and rehabilitation journey as it informs my identity and practice as a student affairs professional, spouse, mother, daughter, sister, friend, and colleague.

Life Before Head Injury

I am the daughter of educational privilege. All four of my grandparents possessed advanced degrees, my father earned his PhD before I was born and my mother worked on her two degrees while I was young and living at home. Intelligence, critical thinking, and a strong work ethic were highly valued in my family. I was taught I could achieve anything if I worked hard enough. My four siblings and I earned our parents' love and attention through hard work and good grades. Additional familial values were embedded in our upbringing:

- Never rest on your laurels, always strive to be better.
- If at first you do not succeed, it is because you did not try hard enough.
- Work before play, but there is always work to be done.
- No excuses and no whining—you control your destiny so get out of your own way.

In addition to my educational privilege, I grew up White, middle class, Protestant, heterosexual, and able-bodied. I am embarrassed to admit for the most part, I took these privileged identities for granted until I began my doctoral education. Immersing myself in the intellectual and emotional work of higher education, I was challenged and supported by faculty, colleagues, classmates, and mentors to further explore these identities. Through coursework, class discussions, and research, my lens was turned inward and outward, discovering the meaning of intersecting identities, privilege, and oppression. The work was exhilarating and exhausting. On October 13, 2006, I stood before family, friends, classmates, mentors, colleagues, and faculty and successfully defended my dissertation titled *Borders, Bridges, and Braiding: A Latino Family's Meaning Making of the First in the Family to Attend College* (Donovan, 2006). I was at the pinnacle of my intellectual capacity when my advisor, Florence Guido, introduced me as "Dr. Donovan" at the conclusion of the defense.

THE ACCIDENT

Merely three weeks later at the NASPA Region IV-West Conference in Breckenridge, Colorado, I joined colleagues, friends, and my two sons for a late-night sledding adventure on the ski slopes. On Friday, November 3, 2006, I was tired of being so serious and so focused on my academics, so I decided to cut loose and be silly for a change. The first run of the evening, my toboggan hit a rough patch and tipped, spilling me into the snow bank. I came to a complete stop on the side of my head, jamming my vertebrae into the base of my brain and breaking my glasses. I immediately knew something was wrong, but I did not want to ruin other people's fun. I could not turn my neck, my eyes were not working well together, and my head really hurt. The next morning, I had an extreme headache, incredible sensitivity to lights and noise, and could not put my thoughts into words. The closing brunch of the conference was a blur of noise, activity, and lights. We left the conference, drove down the mountain, and I went straight to bed, arguing that I would probably feel better after a good night's sleep. The next morning, my husband clearly knew something was wrong when I got lost walking less than five blocks to our church. He found me huddled on the curb, crying because I was so confused. We immediately went to the emergency room, and I was diagnosed with a severe concussion/moderate traumatic brain injury (TBI) and referred to a neurologist and the Center for Neurorehabilitation Services in Fort Collins, Colorado.

REHABILITATION TO RECOVERY

After extensive testing and evaluation, I was scheduled for five hours of integrated therapy per week at the center including:

- Occupational therapy: I worked on getting dressed, tying shoes, grocery shopping, cooking, budgeting, and making everyday life decisions.
- Physical therapy: My physical therapist worked on vertebrae that were shoved into the base of my brain, rib cage jammed into my upper body only allowing shallow breaths, and extremely tight

and knotted upper body muscles. Later in therapy, we worked on relearning how to run because my gate was choppy and awkward.

- Speech therapy: This was perhaps the worst experience emotionally because we worked on tedious exercises to help me find words when speaking, such as "describe a cup of coffee if you cannot remember the word 'coffee.'" Aphasia, or inability to find words, is a common result of TBI. *ABC World News Tonight* anchor Bob Woodruff suffered TBI when his convoy was hit by an improvised explosive device while embedded with the military in Iraq. He provided an accurate analogy related to aphasia: accessing your file cabinet that used to contain files of knowledge, but when you open the drawer, it's empty (Woodruff & Woodruff, 2007). I was challenged to stay optimistic when realizing I recently earned a PhD but could not describe my research, life's work, or even what I had for breakfast that morning.

- Neurotherapy: I spent hours completing various tests and assessments and was evaluated for depression and other mental health disorders resulting from my brain injury.

- Counseling therapy: I worked with a counselor to help me cope with frustration and the realization of a long-term disability. My husband and sons engaged in couples and family therapy to help us understand the impact of the injury on our relationships and, ultimately, to explore my new identity as a person with a disability.

I underwent 10 months of therapy, during which time I took three months of forced sick leave followed by six months of working 15 to 20 hours per week. Through the support and generosity of my supervisor and colleagues, I remained in my position as assistant to the vice president for student affairs at Colorado State University.

Therapy was grueling, but more punishing was my loss of identity as an intelligent, independent, hard-working student affairs professional. For the previous 19 years, I worked diligently to balance career with family life and most often, my career won. For the first time, I was forced to prioritize rest above work, self above others. My sense of self was lost as I struggled to discover who I was if I was not smart and high-achieving.

As I regained my capacity for speaking, problem solving, breathing, and running, I continued to struggle with extreme sensitivity to light and sound. I was easily distracted by noise and had trouble focusing and concentrating when trying to attend to multiple stimuli. My highly valued ability to multitask was no longer available, and my brain tired easily. Eventually, I was diagnosed with a long-term disability: Central Auditory Processing Disorder (CAPD). This diagnosis brought both peace of mind (I am not going crazy!) as well as frustration (I will forever be less than 100%!).

MY DISABILITY

To me, CAPD means that my brain gets overloaded with stimulation and shuts down. CAPD affects my ability to attend, understand, and remember when there is too much stimulation in the environment (American Speech-Language-Hearing Association, 2012). In reality, CAPD means no more loud concerts or action or 3D movies; needing ear plugs when there is talking or music playing while I am reading; and making a point to close my office door when I have to concentrate. I no longer get a "second wind" and cannot "push through" when I am tired. I have a low frustration tolerance when I cannot find a word or cannot express my thoughts. I mix up words and common phrases (which can bring about fits of uncontrollable laughter from my family). I must plan ahead, make lists, and cannot think on my feet like I used to. And lastly, serial, complex, multistage thinking continues to be challenging.

To others, CAPD means I am human. My family notices the deficits more than my friends and colleagues. My husband, sons, and siblings know when I am making decisions and compensating for my disability. They recognize nonverbal signs when I am struggling to find a word, trying to concentrate, or fighting my fatigue. My family has been an incredible support system, boosting me up when I am hard on myself and forcing me to rest when I hit my limit.

Because my disability is invisible, I spend most of my days interacting with colleagues, students, and community members who have no idea of my challenges or my rocky road to "recovery." I sometimes wonder if I am successfully "passing" as an able-minded and able-bodied person. Some-times I worry about my colleagues' judgment or assumptions about my abilities based on their knowledge or ignorance of my injury. Do others know why I stand outside of crowded receptions and meeting rooms prior to the beginning of programs, waiting for people to finally quiet down and settle into their chairs? Does anyone know how dependent I am on my "to-do list" and my whiteboard list of projects? When I restrict my eve-ning commitments, do others question my ability to represent Colorado State University? I ultimately realize this type of worry robs me of needed energy and focus. Instead, I need to embrace all of who I am, including my CAPD.

MAKING MEANING OF MY DISABILITY

My identity as a formerly able-minded and able-bodied individual dramati-cally affects my life, leadership, and practice. I own my disability rather than fight it. I wear my TBI label with pride because I fought hard to return to my current level of functioning. My brain injury was a gift because it slowed me down and forced me to rethink my priorities and how I live my life.

I am no longer solely defined by my job. I am multidimensional. I am a partner, mother, friend, daughter, sister, colleague, mentor, role model, neighbor, community activist, and volunteer. The quality of my out-of-work life is as important as the quality of my work life. I am valuable based on *who* I am, not *what* I am. I am more than the sum of my accomplish-ments. Sometimes I have to say, "No, I cannot/will not do that."

Being gentle with myself, forgiving my mistakes, being patient when I cannot find a word or do not operate at 100% are new-found behaviors that must be practiced and reinforced daily to become habits. It is a con-stant struggle to step back from old patterns of seeking additional work to feel a sense of accomplishment and instead, relish in a life well-lived.

Making meaning of my disability involves revisiting my familial mes-sages from youth. It is not realistic to believe I can achieve anything if I work hard enough. I have limits that are not eliminated through hard work. Sometimes when I do not succeed it is not due to a lack of effort, and I am not always in control of my destiny. Through therapy, I am learning the value of play, rest, and being comfortable with "good enough."

These lessons are translated through my work with undergraduate and graduate students, new professionals, and colleagues, as well as daily out-of-work interactions with friends and family. Everyone has a story. These stories may be visible or invisible, known or unknown. It is critical to refrain from judgment and, instead, listen for those stories. Demonstrating patience is key as individuals struggle with their challenges. It is my job to encourage, support, and be a cheerleader through the struggle. Asking for help is a sign of courage not weakness. We all have good days and bad days, but others cannot tell the difference without sharing in the experience. Effort does not always guarantee achievement. People are complex beings with value beyond their accomplishments. I learned that being is a lot harder than doing. It is up to all of us to celebrate others for who they are in addition to what they do. Lastly, it is important to not take one's gifts and talents for granted. Life can change in an instant and these gifts and talents may be forever gone. However, this change may bring about new opportunities for growth and fulfillment in different ways.

LEADING WITH A BRAIN INJURY AND BEYOND

Experiencing a traumatic brain injury at the age of 42 provided me with an opportunity to choose to lead a different life rather than give up and wallow in self-pity. My disability has become an integral part of my identity. I cannot stuff it in a closet or choose to leave it at home when I go to work. Just as I cannot separate who I am as a woman without also discussing my identity as a partner and mother, woven throughout is my identity as an individual living with TBI.

Transformative leadership acknowledges the intersection of all of our identities, empowering the expression of these identities, and celebrating the richness of life when our identities can exist without threat or degradation. I lead with an understanding that everyone has a story. My job is to listen and support story tellers to discover all of who they are including their gifts, talents, struggles, and areas for growth. As an advisor, mentor, faculty member, and colleague, I care about the whole person across the table from me. Tasks and responsibilities are important, but so are people.

My advisees quickly learn I will inquire about in- and out-of-class learning, leading, and living. It is critical for student affairs staff to self-author (Magolda, 2010) their lives as they help undergraduates do the same. Some want to gloss over challenges, or focus solely on accomplishments. Instead, I lift them up as examples for others struggling with making meaning of their identities or weighed down by society's prejudice and oppression. Staff across the university know about my story and refer students with TBI or other cognitive difficulties to me. Serving as a role model and mentor is a significant part of my responsibility as a transformative leader in higher education.

Yes, I am still a daughter of educational privilege, and I proudly continue that tradition of valuing education and intellectual capacity. However, I also wake up every morning to face life's challenges as a person recovering from a traumatic brain injury.

REFERENCES

American Speech-Language-Hearing Association. (2012). *(Central) Auditory Processing Disorder: Working group on auditory processing disorders.* Retrieved from http://www.asha.org/docs/html/TR2005-00043.html

Donovan, J. A. (2006). *Borders, bridges, and braiding: A Latino family's meaning making of the first in the family to attend college* (Unpublished doctoral dissertation). University of Northern Colorado, Greeley, CO.

Magolda, M. B. (2010). The interweaving of epistemological, intrapersonal, and interpersonal development in the evolution of self-authorship. In M. B. Magolda, E. F. Creamer, & P. S. Meszaros (Eds.), *Development and assessment of self-authorship* (pp. 25–43). Sterling, VA: Stylus.

Woodruff, R., & Woodruff, L. (2007). *In an instant: A family's journey of love and healing.* New York, NY: Random House.

My Journey as a Twin
A Relational Blueprint for Leadership

Jean Chagnon

Jean Chagnon, PhD, is a licensed psychologist in private practice who specializes in working with women who are survivors of trauma. While working in higher education for 15 years, she served as a staff psychologist, wellness center director, and associate dean. She was co-owner and managing partner of Counseling Psychologists of Woodbury, Minnesota, for eight years.

I t is November 23, 1991—a Sunday. I am in the second month of my internship at the counseling center at the University of Minnesota. My desk is covered with case files, articles, and training materials. I have come to my office to get through all the paperwork. I feel as if I need to get caught up so that I can make some space to get back to my dissertation. It is late afternoon and I head home, feeling good about what I have accomplished. Once again, I am hopeful that I might find time to work on my dissertation.

I get home and my partner says, "Sit down, your mom called." I can tell something is dreadfully wrong. "It's John . . . "

"He's dead," I interrupt.

"Yes, I'm sorry," she says.

I talk with my mom—he has taken his own life, he was in . . . the burial will be Friday . . . she's driving . . . will meet me. . . .

My mind is a blur. I feel the rug being pulled out from underneath me. I feel my world shake to its very core. I feel alone in the world for the very first time—ever. Johnnie is not just my brother, he is my twin brother. I have never known myself except in relation to him. We were conceived together, developed together, birthed together, played together, went to school together. Now he is gone, and I am hopelessly and desperately adrift without the core relationship that has defined me since the beginning of my worldly journey.

Being a twin is not an often discussed aspect of identity. Moreover, looking back it might seem that my identity as a woman, as a first-generation college student, and then ultimately as a lesbian woman shaped my experience of leadership more dramatically and noticeably than my identity as a twin. However, in the more than 20 years since that fateful day, I have come to understand that no other reality in my life, both by its presence and its brutally unexpected disappearance, has shaped me and how I see myself more dramatically or completely than the experience of being a twin. Being a twin and losing a twin created a blueprint for relationship building that I carry in every cell of my body. This blueprint informs and guides my approach to leadership more completely and fundamentally than any other aspect of my being. I believe this blueprint is a profound paradigm for leadership in the new millennium.

THE EARLY YEARS OF LEADERSHIP

I began my path through leadership early, as a young Girl Scout. I was immediately hooked by the activities and all-girl camaraderie and stayed with the organization from Brownies all the way through high school. My enthusiasm for the outdoors, my willingness to volunteer, and the support of many wonderful adult women led to many opportunities for me in Girl Scouting. I did everything from organizing trips with my peers to serving as an assistant leader, to being a unit leader at summer camp, to being on the board of directors for the local Girl Scout Council. These experiences taught me many proverbs about leadership—be the change you want to see; delegate and follow up; never do the work you can get 10 competent girls to do. Through these I developed a commitment to role modeling; came to understand that delegating is not the same as washing your hands of a situation; and finally realized that leadership is not about doing but about teaching, training, letting go, and not micromanaging.

I went from these formative experiences to an abundance of leadership opportunities during my undergraduate years—commuter student council, student program assistant, student government, resident assistant. People saw me as a leader, I acted as a leader, and I readily accepted the opportunities and stresses of leadership. However, I never really gave much thought to what it meant to be a leader or what my "style" of leadership was. To me, leaders were the people who volunteered or those who were asked and said yes. Leaders were the people who had your Girl Scout cookies or who you turned your permission slip in to or who came early and stayed late. They were the people who ran meetings, who got things done, who organized. I saw myself as a leader because I handed out cookies, collected permission slips, came early, stayed late, organized, ran meetings, and got things done. I did not think about leadership more deeply than that. I do remember, however, that I asked the director of the summer camp why I always seemed to get the hard-to-work-with children and staff members. She stated that it was because she saw that I treated them with respect while not allowing them to be inappropriate. I treated them like people and expected them to treat others that way. She obviously saw things about me as a leader that I was not aware of and had not considered.

As I pursued graduate academic training—first in business, then education, and ultimately psychology—I was presented with opportunities to think about leadership and then to examine issues related to identity. In the mid-1980s, leadership was mostly about management in the MBA program I attended. Management meant getting the correct number of widgets to the correct location on the correct day. We occasionally talked about management using leadership-oriented concepts such as ethics, or managing people, or the common good. Leadership and management were considered important and necessary bedfellows, but not synonymous. As such, my time in business school was not very much about what I would now consider leadership. I have no recollection of talking directly about leadership or leadership development during my master's in education program, also in the mid-1980s. We examined leadership indirectly through our exploration of development. In other words, the implication was that educational leadership was about creating academic environments that support and challenge young people in K–12 or postsecondary education to develop—intellectually, socially, and morally. Our educational institutions in the new millennium wrestle more directly and more intentionally with issues of leadership and leadership development as does the business community. However, all of that was after my time. I left academic training in both business and education—two arenas in which arguably leadership is essential for success—woefully underprepared and uneducated about what I would now consider essential elements of leadership.

My graduate training in psychology was my first opportunity to study issues of identity and identity development in depth. We explored models of ethnic, gender, and cultural identity development. We explored stereotypes regarding race, ethnicity, sexual orientation, disability, and so forth as they affect the client-therapist interaction. We examined how individuals from diverse backgrounds and various identities accessed or were limited in their access to health care. During this time, individuals from minority communities were beginning to exercise leadership within the profession advocating for changes and modifications in the way mental health services were delivered. These leaders challenged our profession to make adjustments, change our worldview, think differently, and ultimately provide more just and equitable services that accounted for identity as a significant and important variable.

As I was studying identity in the classroom, I was also continuing my service as a leader in the community. One semester, I served as the first graduate student assistant in the newly formed Office for Gay, Lesbian, and Bisexual Student Services at The Ohio State University. I had recently begun to identify as a lesbian woman and, as such, the job was an eye-opening experience. At the same time, I served as co-advisor of the South Area Black Student Association (SABSA)—an African American student association within residential life at Ohio State. My co-leader and I spent many hours guiding the leaders of SABSA as they processed conflict between SABSA and the lesbian, gay, bisexual, and transgender (LGBT) community and subsequently developed a response to gay and lesbian activism on campus. During this time, I thought about identity a lot—my identity, the identity of the LGBT community, the identity of subgroups within the LGBT community, and LGBT and African American identity. Despite having been a leader, having studied "leadership," having studied identity, and having been a leader in the midst of identity issues; I did not think about leadership and identity as related. Moreover, nobody mentored, guided, or coached me about identity and leadership during any of these experiences.

A LEADER IN THE PROFESSIONAL WORLD

Not until I entered the professional arena did issues of leadership and identity collide for me. At Iowa State University, I was "the" out lesbian member of the counseling center, using my voice to support LGBT students on campus. I was still the person who ran meetings, got things done, organized, and showed up on time. However, I now also saw leadership as advocacy to create more just and equitable access and policies. This advocacy got me in trouble at the counseling center and more broadly in the conservative Christian community in Iowa. This model of leadership as advocacy continued for me as I moved on to other positions in higher education over the next 10 years. In all of these positions, I was more inclined to advocate for and on behalf of students on the margins of the community—students with disabilities, first-generation students, LGBT students. I used my leadership skills, power of my position, my time, and my energy to advocate on behalf of students, faculty, and staff on the margins.

For the first time, I could see that my identity as a lesbian woman not only affected but rather directly shaped my vision of leadership. I could see that leadership from the margin is different than leadership from the center. My identity as a lesbian woman affected the very questions I asked and the causes for which I advocated. It affected how people perceived me and how people responded to me or treated me. I also felt for the first time that being a lesbian woman often influenced how hard I had to work to accomplish my goals given people's differential perceptions of me. I found all of this difficult and troubling having been a leader for many years and not having been aware of being limited by or treated differently because of my identity as a woman or even a lesbian woman. However, even more troubling was my growing awareness that the very core of my identity was often at odds with the institutions where I worked and the broader culture. It was this awareness that led me to understand how my experience of being a twin has always shaped my approach to leadership even when I was not aware that it did.

RELATIONAL LEADERSHIP

As anybody who has been pregnant can tell you, the process of making room in your body for another life that ultimately weighs somewhere around seven pounds is quite the interesting experience of stretching and accommodating. Obviously with two living, breathing beings both weighing around seven pounds, that process becomes even more interesting and fascinating. Johnnie and I, without any spoken words or conscious awareness, figured out how to make room for, accommodate, and mutually support each other in the relatively tiny womb space. On a biochemical, energetic, and spatial level, this is a compelling and fascinating dance between respecting the needs of the other while holding fast to one's own needs. I do not pretend to know how that actually worked. What I do know is that I have ingrained within me a unique experience of relationship.

Many times in life we are individually or collaboratively focused on a single goal. For example, in pregnancy, much of what the mother does is centered on achieving the singular goal of a healthy pregnancy—food, rest, fluids. If all goes well, this process moves along quite naturally. By contrast, Johnnie and I needed to figure out how to cooperate in the effort of two equally important though not identical goals—his growth and my growth. So often in today's world, one person's growth competes with or conflicts with another person's growth because we often operate from a zero sum paradigm. In a zero sum paradigm, more for me means less for you. As a twin, this was not an option. Rather without conscious thought or intention, we operated from an abundance paradigm where our mutual support produced mutual growth in an ever reinforcing circle of support and growth.

This circle of mutual support in the pursuit of multiple goals forms the fundamental aspect of what I call "right relationship." Right relationship is a way of encountering and being with someone else that is reciprocal, mutually respectful, and grounded in an abundance paradigm. This authentic and mutually empowering style of relationship invites each of us into deeper connection with ourselves, each other, and the world around us. In turn, right relationship creates the foundation for healing, for acts of justice, for moments of compassion. My experience of being a twin, I believe, created a foundation of right relationship from the moment of conception in ways that few other people in the world have the privilege of experiencing.

Only recently have I come to acknowledge that right relationship, surrender, and reengagement constitute my blueprint for leadership. As I look back on my years of leadership, I can see that more than my willingness to volunteer or show up or even to do the work, the thing that defined who I was as a leader was the relationship that I built with people and the impact of those relationships. As a Girl Scout leader, I treated every difficult child in my unit with respect while demanding their respect toward me and others. This relationship helped other children in my unit make friends with those they would previously have ignored or treated poorly. Likewise, the difficult children were able to feel included and supported in their camp experience, instead of in constant conflict. As a resident assistant, I focused on really knowing the students on my floor. I introduced myself, I met their parents, and I knew their other friends and romantic interests. I focused on the quality of my time with fellow residents, not the quantity. This high-quality time allowed me to negotiate challenges and conflicts throughout the year with grace and firmness. As the co-advisor to SABSA, my co-leader and I used our relationships with the leaders and members of that student group to push them beyond their initial reactions fueled by a zero-sum paradigm to reach a more just and compassionate response to LGBT students on campus. A commitment to relationship is not unique among women leaders. I do believe, however, that my immersion in the mutually reciprocal relationship of being a twin is unique. At the deepest level of my existence, I believe that mutual support yields mutual growth. This forms a foundation for right relationship for me that is, in my experience, quite unique.

Sadly, my experience of being a twin also forced me to deal with surrender in unique and profound ways. Because of the circumstances of life, Johnnie had fewer experiences of right relationship than I. The ravages of alcoholism and other difficult realities separated Johnnie from himself and from me. While our deep connection kept me painfully aware of his struggles, it did not allow me to reach him or to pull him out of those struggles. We all want to believe that our lives and our relationships have meaning and are important. We often make this evaluation based on the outcome of the relationship or our effort in the relationship. Did that student turn his life around and graduate? Did the institution adopt more inclusive and socially just policies? Losing Johnnie began my struggle with the reality that life and leadership requires of us a surrender that is both humbling and difficult—a surrendering to life in the face of uncertain and unpredictable outcomes. Surrender does not, however, give us permission to disengage. Rather, surrender is about letting go of the outcome while continuing to accept the invitation to stay engaged.

Many years ago during a National Public Radio interview, I heard the following: "We know our hearts will be broken, the question is whether or not they will be broken open." Another way to express that sentiment is the simple phrase "we are a people of hope." My heart broke and my hope faded on that day in November in ways I pray it never will again. Moreover, I pray that as leaders our hearts are not broken and our hopes do not fade as painfully and deeply as mine did with the loss of my brother. However, our hearts do get broken and our hopes do fade. The student we went the extra mile for—drops out. The staff person of difference that we took a chance on makes bad choices and must be let go. The institution we have committed our lives to still cannot see its way to enact domestic partner benefits. As leaders, we are called in the midst of a broken heart and faded hopes to engage and reengage in right relationships while surrendering the outcome.

Spiritual Efficacy, Learning, and Leadership Development

Miriam Garay

Miriam Garay is an educational advisor at the New Mexico Educational Opportunity Center and teaches for The University of New Mexico–Taos in personal computer applications and spiritual development for holistic health and healing arts. She is currently a doctoral student of transformative studies at the California Institute for Integral Studies.

It is 4 a.m., my mind is rested, and I pray to begin this day where I can be of service to those in need of help. I feel the cold air coming through the dirt-insulated roof of this old adobe house. The clay-tiled floor chills my bare feet. As I open the kitchen door, the crisp, high desert air fills my lungs and awakens my body. The dark New Mexico morning sky, with its abundance of stars, begins to exchange places with dawn's light. A police siren brings me out of meditation and I pray for the well-being of those involved in the distress. I close the door and feel the frigid air lingering on my pajamas as I prepare the ritual pot of coffee, a routine that provides a sense of place, love, and caring within my family.

As I enjoy my roasted dark coffee, I read about planned educational budget cuts for the humanities that will erode the value of these studies within higher education (University of Michigan, 2010). I wonder how the outcome will affect the students I counsel who are pursuing degrees in holistic health, psychology, or social work. Will the decrease in funding for the humanities also influence the acquisition of critical thinking and inquiry, which are vital skills for creating and maintaining healthy relationships and leadership skills?

In regard to being, living, and acting in leadership, Lao Tzu, a sixth-century philosopher and founder of Taoism, said, "Go to the people. Learn from them. Live with them. Start with what they know. Build with what they have. The best of leaders when the job is done, when the task is accomplished, the people will say we have done it ourselves" (Lao Tzu quotes, n.d., para. 1).

Having the ability to recognize and develop leadership skills is an ongoing process and necessary to support empowerment of others and to be an effective leader in the rich, diverse, and risky ever-changing world we live in.

LEADERSHIP

My sense of leadership arises primarily within the classroom, an environment where change and inspiration can direct a student toward fulfilling a desired goal. Astin and Astin (2001) stated that leaders are people of action who foster change and students are possible leaders. I have experienced many life transitions, and each allowed me an opportunity to reinvent myself and to be consciously aware of who I am in the world. When I see students graduate, I wonder if their collegiate education has prepared them to enter a workforce that is faced with economic crisis and into a world that is much more uncertain than 20 years ago. How comfortable will they be entering life transitions and becoming leaders of their own lives? Have we prepared them to be aware of their own authenticity and spirituality? Spiritual development is vital to everyone's health in body, mind, and spirit. It leads to having good moral character, establishing and sustaining healthy relationships with self and others, being environmentally conscious, finding meaning to life, and is a means to leadership development (Doohan, 2007).

In the process of making meaning of my life and spiritual development, I embrace all spiritual teachings that evolve my consciousness toward the inequities of societies, present state of our ecology, and paucity of spiritual pedagogy in higher education. My involvement in learning and practicing Native American Ojibwa teachings grounds and strengthens my sense of self. The sweat lodge ceremony that I facilitate and participate in allows me to step back from life's routine, go inward, and come out with gratitude and recognition that all of life is sacred. Every day I explore how to integrate this understanding and experience into life, counseling, school, and community with respect toward others' personal and cultural beliefs. Through self-reflection, dialogue with others, and spiritual practices, I reinforce the development of leadership principles I hope to exemplify. In search of spiritual happiness, I discovered purpose, concern for all my relations, and that to deny my spirit is to ignore an important aspect of being a leader. I share my story of personal transformation to support and encourage faculty and students to find spiritual efficacy in the many forms in which it can develop, and to inspire deep-lived consciousness, leadership, and community action.

SPIRITUAL EFFICACY

The psychological definition of observed self-efficacy is "people's beliefs about their capabilities to produce designated levels of performance that exercise influence over events that affect their lives" (Bandura, 1994, p. 71). The definitions of spiritual and spirituality invite various interpretations, which cannot be captured in any specific meaning because it is so personal and unique to each individual. My spirituality is a process of seeking personal authenticity and wholeness by gaining meaning, purpose, and direction in life through an open exploration of integrating relationships with self, others, and community. Having personal authenticity is essential to my academic leadership because it mirrors the values, strengths, and uniqueness that emerge from my search for identity and meaning of life. The following authors suggest that spirituality is influenced by self-assessment and by our lived cultures. Chickering, Dalton, and Stamm (2006) stated that "definitions of spirituality intimately interact with major vectors of human development: integrity, identity, autonomy, and interdependence, meaning, and purpose" (p. 9); and Eleanor Nesbitt (Erricker, Ota, & Erricker, 2001) conceived spirituality as "the developing relationship of the individual, within community, tradition, to that which is perceived to be—an ultimate concern, ultimate value, and ultimate truth" (p. 130). Nash and Murray (2010) defined spirituality as being "hard-wired into all humans, to ponder the imponderable, to ask the unanswerable questions about the meaning of life, especially omnipresent, unavoidable pain, suffering, and death—conditions that paradoxically coexist with life's unalloyed joys, pleasures, and satisfactions" (pp. 53–54). Palmer and Zajonc's (2010) definition of spirituality implies that it is "not always something good or something bad" and it is "the eternal human yearning to be connected with something larger than one's own ego" (p. 48). And Tisdell (2003) defined spirituality as it relates to her life, commitments, and purpose as an educator and to cultural relevance: "It means attending to what is culturally relevant to community members and honoring what is sacred to them in terms of academic knowledge, narrative writing, art, poetry, symbols, and ways of interacting" (p. 8).

I have come to realize that the closer I get to defining spirituality, the more it loses context; equally, the more I put it into context, the more the definition is lost. Wong Ping Ho (Erricker, Ota, & Erricker, 2001) categorized spirituality as being sensitive to "the awareness of one's awareness" and that "an attempted definition [of the spiritual] is not only futile but totally counter-productive because it is a characteristic of spirit and the spiritual that is the dynamic" (p. 170).

According to the Dalai Lama (Palmer & Zajonc, 2010), "ignorance is the root cause of suffering and genuine open-minded inquiry into the nature of reality can be of great benefit to humanity by dispelling ignorance" (p. 64). There is an unceasing inquiry in understanding my ignorance in maintaining open-mindful principles upon which I base leadership. Integration of self-efficacy and spirituality in my life presents opportunities for wholeness and service to others. It is a mixing of three interrelational and simultaneous processes that are not necessarily spontaneous but may occur over one's lifetime. They are the belief in a higher power or principle, finding connection and relationship with others, and self-reflection for the transformation and enrichment of one's own existence. I consider the relation of spiritual development and positive self-efficacy elemental to understanding life purpose and personal agency. Identification with these principles gives me a new perspective and vision to develop spiritual leadership and become a voice for social justice issues.

FACILITATING SPIRITUAL EFFICACY

In facilitating spiritual efficacy in the classroom or in student advisement at The University of New Mexico–Taos, it is necessary that I develop cultural sensitivity to the diverse student body, which consists of Latinos, Native Americans, African Americans, Anglos, and international students from the Middle East, Africa, and Asia. Finding common ground and connections among people and things is fundamental to developing spiritual pedagogy. This creates reciprocity between instructor/advisor and the student, and it includes the whole person—body, mind, spirit—and cognitive, emotional, and interactive aspects of learning and acquiring knowledge (Pigza & Welch, 2010).

Despite cultural differences, everyone is a channel for spiritual development. Culture, like spirituality, is difficult to define; both interact with an individual's social background and social influences, and grow and develop from relationships. Gergen (1999) provided a sense of how culture influences personal development and conveys what people have inherited over two millenniums of cultural influences out "of deliberation on and deliberation of the subjective self, our sense of being, reasoning, and choice-making individuals" (p. 6). Born as a woman of Latino descent, I live in a culture that devalues women and separates humans from nature. I spent years trying to understand and fit into a man's world. Fortunately, I was raised by a strong and independent single mother, who encouraged me to go beyond dominant culture's definition of what a woman could study or how a woman could work. I chose to be an independent woman, teaching computer science for major corporations and educational institutions that supported my success in the modern world.

A modern culture, according to Linda Whitehead (Flanagan & Jupp, 2007), is a culture whose goals are to remove the mystery of the world, to separate people from having significant relationships and "beliefs, customs, ritual, and ceremonies of a rural society and into a vast, anonymous, rationalized world of urban industrial society where human need is exchanged to meet the demands of capitalist production" (p. 116); a dominating culture that uses language and power to "control women, nature, children, animals, other men, their own bodies, their feeling and sensations" (Christ, 1997, p. 161). I became uncomfortable, then outraged and thirsty for freedom from this modern culture to which I had become accustomed. The disillusionment of my life prompted me to make a leap of faith and relocate from New York City to northern New Mexico. It was here that I found a spiritual connection with the land and its people. The land, people, and Spirit began to cultivate and strengthen my spiritual efficacy. I no longer focused on what I wanted to control and dominate, but on what engages our heads, hearts, and spirits.

Conveying my spirituality while remaining sensitive to other's beliefs requires awareness that any person of any age and culture is spiritual. I respect every individual and where they are in their life. Helping students to understand and nurture ethical and spiritual relationships and to be open to new perspectives is what I hope to create in the classroom. Is this not an important gift a college or university can give to a student? Creating a learning environment that supports human connections, love, honesty, respect, truth, courage, wisdom, humility, and deep-lived consciousness perhaps will create a world that the student wants to be part of and contribute back to, rather than a world that bases self-worth on materialism and consumerism.

SPIRITUAL LEADERSHIP

I imagine my connection to spirit as a creative strength that makes and sustains my life. It is what inspires me to flourish despite life's hardships. It is a leadership that values women and men and promotes interdependence, community, connection, and sharing. In a speech given by Donna Bivens (2004), the terms of dominance and leadership were presented regarding the question: What makes a good leader? Traditional beliefs of autonomy, hierarchy, domination, austerity, war, and death were the demands of leadership, and continue to be so. I envision a leadership that is celebratory of life, is expressive of spirituality and service-learning, and embodies awareness of an infinite presence in everyone; a leadership, as Bivens indicated, that is "measured not by our education or title or ideology but by our being true to our spirit and taking responsibility for that leadership day-to-day" (p. 1). When students walk into a classroom for the first time, they walk into uncertainty, unsure if the environment will be friendly or indifferent. To create a friendly and safe environment, I welcome all students into the classroom by stating my gratitude for their choosing to learn, grow, and empower their lives. By sharing my own story about finding the courage to overcome my fears of learning new pedagogies, I demonstrate a commonality with them. Though I am a teacher and leader, I am also a friend who is committed to helping students transform their lives in their pursuit of meaning and purpose.

Palmer and Zajonc (2010) discussed the renewed interest in the relationship of spirituality and higher education along with student's desire to "explore the values, meaning and purpose of their lives while at college" (p. 117). I concur with Palmer and Zajonc that students long for a classroom that is open to discussion and addresses "their inner or spiritual concerns thoughtfully and deeply" (p. 117), and to not separate leadership from life. Silencing their spiritual voice in favor of the academic can no longer be ignored (Dillard, Abdur-Rashid, & Tyson, 2000). Doohan (2007) supported this rising change toward an integrated and holistic leadership by indicating that:

> Contemporary studies stress the person or leader and their call to serve others and pursue a common vision that affects not just the working environment but personal, family, institutional, and social environments in an ever expanding influence of the dedicated leader. Leadership for those who are called to serve others is never static but always dynamic, growing and maturing through stages that enrich one's life as well as one's leadership. (p. 122)

As a teacher and spiritual leader, it is my responsibility to integrate and create parallel studies that address students' majors along with developing their inner lives by bringing conversation into the heart of teaching and making meaningful connections that foster positive values for social and organizational life. I created a spiritual development class called "Sacred Ceremony" in which participants from diverse backgrounds learn how to develop their lives through ritual, prayer, and ceremony. The class is centered on creating ritual and discussion of various methods to access the unconscious such as dream journals, meditation, divination, and prayer. Sharing self-reflections as a group promotes meaningful connections and unity. Discourse on the value of gratitude stimulates questions such as: Why do we see a lack of the exchange of gratitude in our society? Where do we start in showing gratitude? We are reminded that through the ritual of gratitude we begin to think about the spiritual needs of our families and self for social transformation. I am not only a teacher of this class; I am also a student in understanding the commitment it takes for self-development and appreciation of diversity.

COMMUNITY ACTION

As a citizen of the United States, I have taken for granted the abundance of goods and services available: the Internet, high-definition cable television, washing and drying machines, and microwave ovens, to name a few. Only a 10-minute drive away is Walmart, which is richly stocked with consumer items. Yet with all the conveniences, I still do not know my neighbor except for a rushed hello when we meet in one of the aisles. Has this modern way of living created a breakdown and less involvement within the community? How do we shift back from the global community to the local community? Last semester, I was amazed at how many of my students were unaware of the Occupy movement occurring in major cities. Discussing the movement in class, students were motivated to create presentations on social justice issues. The classroom became a forum for rekindling students' sense of community engagement that, like spirituality, is "characteristic of being relational by responding to human and community needs" (Welch & Koth, 2009, p. 6).

For two decades, I have worked with people who are struggling to learn how to survive hard times. I see my face in theirs, confused, in fear, and wanting direction to solve their problems. I am attentive to their stories about losing jobs, not having computer skills to meet requirements for employment, dropping out of school to support families after parents pass away, and how work is given precedence over education. What I learn comes from stories of others enlightening and transforming me as I witness their transformation. Their story is my own. I remember the mystic

Pierre Teilhard de Chardin's profound statement, "You are not a human being in search of a spiritual experience. You are a spiritual being immersed in a human experience" (Teilhard de Chardin quotes, n.d., para. 1), which brings light to understanding life purpose and personal agency. The kind of leadership I wish to share with others begins in me. I challenge myself to take responsibility to be true to my spirit in everyday leadership by checking in with my belief systems, being open to change, and living in integrity. Reawakening students' engagement can be paramount to their spiritual efficacy, their sense of place in the world, and their transformation. To discover self-identity creates awareness of responsibility for all relationships as part of becoming a whole human being and authentic leader. It is an invitation to collaborate with students and peers to challenge the complex problems of established belief systems and values affecting our creation of a holistic world.

REFERENCES

Astin, A., & Astin, H. (2001, January). *Principles of transformative leadership*. Retrieved October 22, 2012, from http://www.aahea.org/aahea/articles/transformative_leadership.htm

Bandura, A. (1994). Self-efficacy. In V. S. Ramachaudran (Ed.), *Encyclopedia of Human Behavior* (Vol. 4, pp. 71–81). New York, NY: Academic Press.

Bivens, D. (2004, March 11). What makes a good leader? Retrieved from http://www.thewtc.org/What_Is_SL.html

Chickering, A. W., Dalton, J. C., & Stamm, L. (2006). *Encouraging authenticity and spirituality in higher education*. San Francisco, CA: Jossey-Bass.

Christ, C. P. (1997). *Rebirth of the goddess: Finding meaning in feminist spirituality*. New York, NY: Routledge.

Dillard, C. B., Abdur-Rashid, D., & Tyson, C. A. (2000). My soul is a witness: Affirming pedagogies of the spirit. *International Journal of Qualitative Studies in Education, 13*(5), 447–462.

Doohan, L. (2007). *Spiritual leadership: The quest for integrity*. Mahwah, NJ: Paulist Press.

Erricker, J., Ota, C., & Erricker, C. (2001). *Spiritual education: Cultural, religious and social differences*. Brighton, England: Sussex Academic Press.

Flanagan, K., & Jupp, P. C. (Eds.). (2007). *A sociology of spirituality*. Surrey, England: Ashgate.

Gergen, K. R. (1999). *An invitation to social construction*. Thousand Oaks, CA: Sage.

Lao Tzu quotes. (n.d.). Retrieved from http://thinkexist.com/quotation/go-to-the-people-live-with-them-learn-from-them/348565.html

Nash, R. J., & Murray, M. C. (2010). *Helping college students find purpose: The campus guide to meaning-making*. San Francisco, CA: Jossey-Bass.

Palmer, P. J., & Zajonc, A. (2010). *The heart of higher education: A call to renewal*. San Francisco, CA: Jossey-Bass.

Pigza, J. M., & Welch, M. J. (2010, January). Spiritually engaged pedagogy: The possibility of spiritual development through social justice education. *Spirituality in Higher Education, V*(4). Retrieved from http://www.spirituality.ucla.edu/publications/newsletters/5/4/welch.php

Teilhard de Chardin quotes. (n.d.). Retrieved from http://thinkexist.com/quotation/you_are_not_a_human_being_in_search_of_a/257982.html

Tisdell, E. J. (2003). *Exploring spirituality and culture in adult and higher education.* San Francisco, CA: Jossey-Bass.

University of Michigan. (2010, February 8). 2011 federal budget has increases for science, education. *The University Record Online.* Retrieved from http://ur.umich.edu/0910/Feb08_10/744-2011-federal-budget-has-increases-for-science-education

Welch, M., & Koth, K. (2009, February). Spirituality and service-learning: Parallel frameworks for understanding students' spiritual development. *Spirituality in Higher Education,* 5(1), 1–9. Retrieved from http://www.spirituality.ucla.edu/docs/newsletters/5/Welch_Koth_Final.pdf

Learning Who I Am and How I Lead From a Proud South Texas Italian Woman

Florence Marie Guido

Florence Marie Guido's higher education leadership includes advisor to student organizations as a new professional, coordinator of a doctoral program, and an editorial board member of the *NASPA Journal.* Her formal roles subsume hall director, director of career planning and placement, dean of students, and faculty member. She currently serves as a full professor at the University of Northern Colorado in the Higher Education and Student Affairs Leadership program.

L osing my 84-year-old mother meant a loss of my innocence for good. I am still in shock. Not until mom died suddenly several months ago did I realize the immense extent of her influence on my identity, in my personal and professional lives. Mom's death also got me thinking about stories she told me, or those we lived, in the protection of the San Antonio neighborhood where I grew up. Without knowing it, she graciously modeled leadership (sometimes loudly, but mostly quietly) through her actions. In effect, this exceptional American woman with deep roots in Sicily taught me the gifts of my ancestry, including core values such as practicing rock-solid strength, standing unconditionally by blood relatives (Gambino, 1997; Mangione & Morreale, 1992), holding each other up, giving generously, and weaving fun and laughter throughout our lives. My mother's gifts formed my early identity and were passed tacitly to me through observation well into adulthood. Sixty years later, I see how they made me a better person and leader.

A quick portrait of mom frames her spirit. My mother was a "Southern Angel," the equivalent of opposites attracting, an oxymoron much like a "steel magnolia." Strong southern White women usually have a veracity that defies argument. In the midst of their character is a painfully truthful outside, a fierce weapon to behold, a warrior, a protector, a survivor, an activist. Often, these not-to-be-reckoned with women carry a soft, hidden inside, which is sweetened with angelic tenderness so gentle that comfort comes quickly to those in their wake. Add an ethnic Italian influence, where women traditionally are subservient to men, to this hard exterior, and the range of sounds dance on a continuum from verbal firecrackers to silent prayers.

In this essay, I tell stories of my mother's influence in my early life, her contributions to my identity formation, and how these experiences shape who I am as a higher education and student affairs faculty leader. With few exceptions, I focus on the values my mom instilled in me that resonate with my nearly 25 years of teaching graduate students. Along the way, I point out how values she lived and thought were important made an impact on my faculty role. Although my mother never worked outside the home for pay, what she said and how she lived her life are a part of who I am today and how I lead. In full self-disclosure, I realize that I am only choosing a certain perspective of my mom, as a complete picture might go in ways I am not ready to make public, not now, or maybe ever.

SOUTH TEXAN AND ITALIAN: A POTENT COMBINATION

Antoinette Varisco Guido, my mom, left a large and wonderful footprint with her tiny size four shoe. She was a lady who grew up with early 20th century southern "rules" (e.g., no wearing white until Easter; eat black-eyed peas for good luck on New Year's Day; fill Sunday brunch with grits, biscuits and honey, scrambled eggs, and venison sausage), as well as holding stereotypical beliefs of a tightly knit Italian immigrant family (e.g., family first no matter what; family babies are abundant; Italian food is always served at holidays, sometimes along with turkey and dressing; extended family comes together often). Putting family first is a characteristic of many families in the United States (Evans, Forney, Guido, Patton, & Renn, 2010; Guido-DiBrito & Chávez, 2003), and my Mediterranean roots were constantly exposed in the way my family lived.

Back in the day, mom wore 1950s and 1960s classic clothing. Draped in pencil skirt suits with a pill box hat like Jackie Kennedy, she wrapped herself in a mink stole smiling behind those big, white Hollywood-style sunglasses that made her seem eternally young. This woman, my mom, from a cotton farm in east central Texas devoured books like ice cream on a hot day, loved the life of the mind and exercised it daily, cooked some of the best food I have ever eaten, and appreciated the power of education and the arts to sustain and enrich life. My first model and mentor helped me navigate my identity in my youth and even now as I live on in her absence. Several years ago, mom gave me a ceramic angel with these words inscribed on it: "Someone to watch over you." Although it represents immense sentimentality, I do not have to look at the plaque to feel blessed by her every day of my life since I feel like she is always with me.

As one of her friends remarked in a note of condolence to the family, Toni was a "San Antonio TREASURE." Her willingness to connect with those in her purview led her deep into the local neighborhood community where she was president of the garden club and my kindergarten and parochial grade schools' parent-teacher association. She served on the board of directors for the San Antonio Symphony and the Texas A&M University College of Education, and joyfully was an unrelenting patron of the arts. She was active in the Ladies Golf Association until five years before she died and played bridge weekly with friends until the day before she died. Make no mistake, everyone she touched would have been less without her presence. At her funeral, I first learned that mom started the library at the parochial school I attended for eight years. She believed education was the key to success and unselfishly put her money toward college education for her grandchildren—all 12 of them. Her father had a sixth-grade education and she had a college degree. She was proud of it all. Being a southerner and Italian turned out to be a potent combination for mom (Guido, 2011).

CONNECTOR

Mom was a stranger to no one. One of her gifts was that she could strike up a conversation with anyone. When I had to rush dad's suit at the dry cleaners' drive-up window three days before her funeral, I told the woman who took his clothing that mom had passed away. Without skipping a beat, she turned to those working diligently in the store and shouted out, "Mrs. Guido died," as if everyone working there knew her and would suffer a loss for her passing. The woman turned to me and said, "We loved your mother. She was such a character."

My mother knew most of the individuals within her sphere of influence (Astin & Leland, 1991; Helgesen, 1995). Even though she may not have called all by name, she had individual relationships with each one. From my female cousins who felt strong affinity for my mother to the women she played golf and bridge with weekly to the women who cleaned the ladies locker room at the country club to the women she met at the gym, she added sheer delight to their day. She would ask about their family—children, husbands, mothers, fathers—all of them. She had a wealth of information in her head about who was related to whom in this big family of ours and in the city of San Antonio.

My mom connected with everyone and touched their lives in ways our family will never truly know. She could go anywhere, the grocery store, the beauty shop, the bank, the country club, or her favorite clothing store—even The Russian Tea Room in New York, the Tower of London in Britain, or the Coliseum in Rome—and strike up a conversation. She was a connector, which is a necessity for a leader, particularly one who understands the value of a helpful network (Allen & Cherrey, 2000). She loved people and they loved her, as evidenced at the rosary the night before her funeral. An hour was not enough to greet the several hundred people who came to stand in line to pay their respects to our family on a Monday night. The crowd included an elementary school classmate who was first in line, her hair dresser, a bank president, her facialist, her bridge friends, several architects, plumbers, and the list went on and on. Without her even being there, she was connecting us all over again with people who loved her.

One of my dearest friends once told me that I can work a room like no one else. As an introvert, she runs from crowds, so I imagine for her it is perplexing. As a flat-out but mellowing extrovert, I see it as saying hello to people I know and meeting people they know. I consider it a precious tool to keep connected with colleagues so my teaching stays fresh and to learn as much as I can about student affairs professionals who might hire the doctoral students who studied with me. Connecting plays a significant part in my leadership role in the doctoral program I teach in now and coordinated for several years. By tacitly mimicking some of the ways in which mom would connect with her world, I am able to connect with colleagues and the students my peers send me. My identity as a leader is based solidly on the idea of connecting people to one another for a single goal, and I learned this from my mother.

Visionary

When I look back at my life with mom, another kind of memory emerges. Over the years, I came to know what my mother did and did not like (and she always knew what she did and did not like). One Sunday morning when I was about 12, I came out of my room knowing I found the perfect outfit to wear to church. It was a perfectly pressed blue and red sailor dress with a huge white collar. I was right, she loved the dress, but she disliked the shoes. Sometimes I had the feeling I could never get it right from her perspective. If I am honest (and certainly she was at all times), I might have held it against her from time to time. I could not see how I could be the person she wanted me to be. In fact, I can remember her asking most of us: "Have you gained weight?" "Honey, don't you have a hair brush?" or, "You're going to wear that?"

But here is what I see now that she is gone. Mom was a perfectionist. It is not just that she had high standards, which is what I always thought. What I am now learning is that she was a visionary. She could see the world as it "could be." She knew what was possible and she could see the absolute best in all of us. She would not settle for any less, and she would not let us either. Mom was relentless in her desire to manifest the perfection she saw in each of us—everyone who loved her. Her (what I call) "visionary perfectionism" is why she sent all her grandchildren to college, graduated valedictorian of her high school at 15—college at 18 (Vassar College, she would always explain with immense pride)—and took on her children as her life's work. In hindsight, I marvel at that gift of hers: how she could always see the best of what was possible for each of us and herself. She refused to be complacent and settle for anything less than the fullest expression of her family's potential as people. She could see the sophistication, the refinement, the intellect in each of us, even when we did not.

Seeing the potential in people and organizations is helpful for any leader (Helgesen, 1990). Basically, what I do every day as a faculty member is to encourage the greatest potential of others. I do not always inspire in the way I had hoped because I sometimes challenge students in an unhelpful way—for example, by asking uninspiring questions like, "What were you thinking?" I try to be more gentle now, but unquestionably my reputation precedes me in the classroom. Sometimes awkwardly, but always with a determination to make it right, I find ways to meet students at their ability level. With as much support and challenge as I can possibly give, I guide, encourage, and lead them along their educational journey. I look at students developmentally, too, as I challenge them to reach what I can see is their full potential (Evans et al., 2010), not unlike mom and not unlike any good leader.

As the faculty member who crafted the focus of a master's and doctoral program in higher education and student affairs, I was proud to lead the program's shift from a spotlight only on college student personnel to a broader focus on student affairs in the context of higher education with an across-the-curriculum, integrated social justice perspective. In 2000, even with plenty of dissent and as the only full-time tenured program faculty member, I was able to envision and implement a vital graduate program that now boasts four tenure-track faculty and enrolls 50 master's and 50 doctoral students.

COLLABORATOR

It was always important to mom that we come together as a family—especially at holidays. She made Christmas holidays a spectacle when I was a child, and we helped mom make her vision of all that delights. As children and teenagers, my siblings and I all had to help make the Christmas meal. What an all-consuming event with a moist, 20-pound turkey; southern dressing highlighted by chicken gizzards; baked sweet potato casserole chock full of pecans and covered with melted marshmallows; trays of homemade lasagna featuring tiny meatballs; and my favorite, meatball soup, which required the same tiny pork and beef morsels. My friends who have helped me make the tasty meal for no fewer than 30 people know it takes hours to create the sauce and roll the tiny meatballs for the lasagna and soup. I made the lasagna only once for a class of students with no help and it never happened again.

Sitting in the kitchen at the two-sided booth adorned with red leather benches and a red tabletop is where our family ate breakfast and often prepared food for a big family meal. Having many people makes less effort of such monotonous toil, makes time advance more quickly, and gets those engaged in the task to focus more on their relationships. The intricate details of the coveted family recipe and its labor intensive preparation made fertile ground for learning about working with groups. In truth, it was in these early "work groups" as a kid that I learned about the power of many. Mom would always say, "Many hands make less work," and she was right. Her experience taught her that organizing people to work collaboratively gets the work done quicker, like when she enlisted her children to make the family lasagna recipe.

Working collaboratively translates well into teaching, learning, and leading (Allen & Cherry, 2000) students through their graduate careers. For the past 20 years, I have taught a doctoral core class in collaborative research. As a result of my childhood experience, I organize students in teams of four or five and lead them through substantive neophyte research in a semester. Rolling meatballs is like transcribing interview data and trying to make sense of it. Both take a long time, both contain some monotony in creating handmade products, and both prove the delight of completing work quicker through collaborative effort. My identity as a group member is still played out in my role as a leader who makes sure power is shared, all voices are heard, and transparency prevails (Guido-DiBrito, Nathan, Noteboom, & Fenty, 1997; Helgesen, 1995).

CONCLUSION

After mom's death, her most recent *Vassar Alumnae Directory* was delivered to the front door of my dad's house. My heart skipped a beat and a tear raced down my cheek as I realized I would never be able to look through it with her and identify the people she knew and talk joyfully about them. When I turned to the page that identified mom, she had proudly identified her occupation as 'homemaker.' Mom was more than a homemaker, though, and her light left a path for me to form my identity in ways that became road signs for my leadership. Her gifts laid the groundwork for me to be successful as a faculty member and teach my students to connect and work collaboratively with each other for richer outcomes. Leaders who value their followers and want to work collaboratively with them find ways to maximize the potential of each group member (Guido-DiBrito et al., 1997).

While losing my mom will remain one of my greatest losses, I gain some comfort in my memories and knowing she is with the angels now. It has also been a wonderful surprise because I discovered things about her I could never see when she was here. How she connected so effortlessly with everyone she encountered. How she stood for love in the family. How she could see the best of what was possible for each of us. How she collaborated in ways that brought the family together. How she refused to be complacent and settle for anything less than our maximum potential. Now that she is gone, it is easy to see how much like the moon she is, always there, silent, graceful, shining a divine light on me. A light that is here with me now more than ever. A light that helps me lead the way, as a connector and collaborator, down a path I can envision and put to practice daily thanks to a proud South Texas Italian woman.

REFERENCES

Allen, K. E., & Cherrey, C. (2000). *Systemic leadership: Enriching the meaning of our work*. Lanham, MD: University Press of America.

Astin, H. S., & Leland, C. (1991). *Women of influence, women of vision: A cross generational study of leaders and social change*. San Francisco, CA: Jossey-Bass.

Evans, N. J., Forney, D. S., Guido, F. M., Patton, L., & Renn, K. A. (2010). *Student development in college: Theory, research, and practice* (2nd ed.). San Francisco, CA: Jossey-Bass.

Gambino, R. (1997). *Blood of my blood: The dilemma of the Italian Americans*. Toronto, Canada: Guernica.

Guido, F. M. (2011). Life stories of the daughter of first-generation Italian immigrants: Gender, ethnicity, culture, and class intertwine to form an Italian American feminist. In P. A. Pasque & S. E. Nicholson (Eds.), *Empowering women in higher education and student affairs: Theory, research, narratives, and practice from feminist perspectives* (pp. 69–77). Sterling, VA: Stylus.

Guido-DiBrito, F., & Chávez, A. F. (2003). Understanding the ethnic self: Learning and teaching in a multicultural world. *Journal of Student Affairs, 12,* 11–21.

Guido-DiBrito, F., Nathan, L. E., Noteboom, P. A., & Fenty, J. E. (1997). Traditional and new paradigm leadership: The gender link. *Initiatives, 58*(1), 27–38.

Helgesen. S. (1990). *The female advantage: Women's ways of leadership*. New York, NY: Doubleday Currency.

Helgesen, S. (1995). *The web of inclusion: A new architecture for building great organizations*. New York, NY: Doubleday.

Mangione, J., & Morreale, B. (1992). *La storia: Five centuries of the Italian American experience*. New York, NY: HarperCollins.

Third Culture Kid
Tales of a Global Nomad

Mark Emmons

Mark Emmons is the planning and assessment officer for The University of New Mexico Libraries. His sense of identity and leadership have been profoundly influenced by his upbringing as a third culture kid raised in countries outside of the United States.

I n September 2006, I was invited to Veracruz, Mexico, to present a three-day workshop on teaching. As I sat on the tarmac in Albuquerque, I felt a mounting sense of excitement. I realized, except for a week in Toronto, it had been more than 10 years since I set foot outside of the United States. That so much time had passed without a trip abroad was a bit confounding since my early years left me with a deep-seated restlessness. Feelings of anticipation, exhilaration, and rightness were familiar from my childhood, when my family moved to a new country every two or three years.

I am a *third culture kid* (TCK), also known as a *global nomad*. My father was a diplomat for the United States, which means the majority of my childhood was spent in six foreign countries. I grew up in Colombia, Burundi, the Ivory Coast, and Argentina—all of this from the time I was in kindergarten through my junior year in high school. We always lived in local communities and I attended local (or at least colonial) schools until I reached high school. In total, I spent 8 of my first 16 years in other countries, followed by annual visits to Poland and France during my college years.

American sociologist Ruth Hill Useem introduced the concept of the TCK (Useem & Downie, 1976). Useem and her husband worked in India and raised their kids there on two occasions. She noticed that they were different from children who had been raised exclusively in the United States and decided to make it an area of study. In a series of articles summarizing her life's work, Useem (1999) found that TCKs love learning and are much more likely to complete higher education degrees. They are interested in helping others. They embrace diversity, especially as related to nationality, and do not necessarily feel an affinity for members of their own cultural group. They desire independence and are slow to commit themselves, preferring first to observe. They feel they can adapt to every environment but never quite fit in anywhere.

David C. Pollock and Ruth E. Van Reken (2009) extended Useem's work on TCKs, defining a third culture kid as:

> A person who has spent a significant part of his or her developmental years outside the parents' culture. The third culture kid builds relationships to all of the cultures, while not having full ownership in any. Although elements from each culture are assimilated into the third culture kid's life experience, the sense of belonging is in relationship to others of the same background. (p. 13)

They found three dichotomies in the typical TCK profile that provide advantages and challenges. First, TCKs benefit from an expanded worldview yet are challenged by confused loyalties in ideology and culture. Second, their lives are enhanced by a three-dimensional view of the world but they can be hurt by a painful view of reality influenced by their firsthand knowledge. Third, they gain from cross-cultural enrichment but are at times ignorant of their home cultures. Together, these dichotomies help shape adults who have a rich social worldview, but who are challenged in their personal lives by the different lens through which they see the world. I believe that more than any other factor, being a TCK has shaped who I am today.

EVERYWHERE AND NOWHERE

I did not fully realize the impact of growing up overseas on my identity until I returned to the United States to finish my senior year in high school and attend college. When I lived abroad, it was clear that I was a foreigner. I was rightly treated like someone different, someone who did not grow up in the country, someone who did not share the same cultural upbringing. As a foreigner, it was incumbent on me to learn the local language and ways. If my learning was incomplete, that was accepted as natural. But because I lived in local neighborhoods and attended local schools, it was also natural that the local culture influenced me and shaped my identity. As a result, I returned to the United States as a person who did not share the same experiences and culture as people who spent their entire childhoods in the United States.

When I first arrived at the University of California, Los Angeles, I lived in a residence hall on an all-male floor. I immediately became a part of a crew of young men who spent most of the time outside of the classroom together. In a pattern that would repeat itself in other environments over the next several years, I found myself at the margins of the group. I believe this was because I was different. They looked at me and saw a fellow American and expected me to be similar to them. When they saw subtle disparities in attitude, manner, and dress, they attributed them to my character, thinking me a bit strange and perhaps arrogant. I believe that it is this sense of otherness that is at the core of being a TCK.

Luckily, this otherness in TCKs is tempered by a strong ability to adapt. Growing up in other countries forced me to become a keen observer of people and culture. I look beyond surface traditions such as food and dress to learn deeper customs, norms, and mores. To this day, I tend to be an observer first and an actor second, joining in only after I have a sense of expectations.

The most significant impact being a global nomad has had on my identity is the dichotomy between otherness and adaptability. The most common trait Pollock (2009) found in his study of TCKs is that individuals feel they fit in everywhere and nowhere, and this is certainly true of me. I used to be somewhat of a chameleon, wanting to blend in perfectly with my surroundings. That only changed when I realized that the best way to have a sense of identity and belonging is to first be comfortable with myself.

FAMILY AND FRIENDS

Family and friends are the most important parts of my life. Though both values are directly attributable to the way I was raised, they came about for different reasons. When people ask me where I am from, I have to decide whether to give the short answer or the long answer. Most often, I give the short answer, which is that I am from California. If the person is familiar with California, I usually let them know that my home town is in San Rafael (in northern California) and that I spent nearly 20 years in Los Angeles. The long answer includes that my father was a diplomat and I lived in six countries outside of the United States while I was growing up; though I am American, I am fundamentally shaped by my experiences in other countries. I point to San Rafael as home because my parents were very careful to build roots there. They made sure we returned to the United States regularly and when we did, we returned to San Rafael to visit grandparents. Their home town became my home town. Though I have never gotten to know it well, I still feel I am home whenever I visit.

As I reflect back, I realize the real answer is that I am not from a place, but from a family. My immediate family of father, mother, and sister were my home. Although both my parents were only children, they each came from extended families. When my father joined the Foreign Service, we left extended families behind. Instead, we relied on each other for support and continuity in the form of the most basic nuclear family. For the most part, our interdependence was a very good thing as our parents were mostly positive influences and my sister and I became good friends. But the fact remains that for better or worse, my family was my primary influence. I carry that value today. My own family is the most important part of my life. My wife and two daughters take precedence over all else. In addition, over the years I welcomed my mother-in-law and two brothers-in-law into my home because I value family.

Friends are the other important part of my life. When I was growing up, I would leave my friends behind every two or three years—or they, as fellow nomads, would leave me behind. When I was young, I accepted this loss as a natural part of my life. I learned to make friends quickly and learned to leave. As I got older, I began to resent the leaving. I lost contact with friends from high school (though social networking websites like Facebook have made it possible to reconnect in recent years). Thus, when I made friends in college, I was determined to keep them. I now expect friendship to last forever. I am happy to say that my circle of friends stood the test of time, though I still mourn the one college friend who seemed content to let us drift apart.

EMBRACING DIVERSITY

Useem (1999) noted that TCKs do not necessarily feel an affinity for members of their cultural groups and are more likely to marry and make friends with people outside their cultural groups. This is true of me. My wife was born and raised in the Philippines and moved to the United States when she was 15 years old. When we met, I felt an immediate attraction and connection. Though we are different in many ways, we have now been happily married for over 25 years.

My closest friends are also quite diverse. None share my ethnic background. However, it is interesting to note that all are male and straight and highly educated, and most are close to me in age. I never thought even once about their backgrounds when making friends. I was instead interested in the kind of person they were, their ideas about the world, and the personal connection we made. Once again, I follow the TCK pattern of making friends outside of my cultural group.

I observe that some people who spend their entire lives in one country experience discomfort when interacting with people outside of their own culture. Instead of seeing an individual, they see a representative of a group and they either generalize about the person based on group characteristics or filter and judge the person based on their own experiences. I believe that growing up TCK breaks down these narrow ways of seeing people and leads to embracing diversity instead.

A COSMOPOLITAN VIEW

Growing up abroad brings many advantages beyond embracing diversity. I have developed a strong set of cultural skills. I have a global view of the world. As I mentioned earlier, I am able to observe and understand people from cultures other than my own. I do not believe there is any one best way of being. I accept people for who they are. I am adaptable and flexible. I speak languages other than English.

Strangely, I find these skills are not always valued in the United States. I tend to think of most Americans as insular when it comes to looking at the world and oddly satisfied with their insularity. What I see as narrow-mindedness, they proudly proclaim as the superior "American Way."

On the other hand, my cultural views may also have disadvantages. You may notice that I grouped all Americans into one big pot. This is because I have a tendency to view Americans as monolithic. I believe that growing up outside the United States has made me see more similarities among Americans than differences. For example, whereas people raised in the United States see race and ethnicity as colossal differentiating factors, I just see Americans. When I was asked to give a speech on multiculturalism for a job interview a number of years ago, I had to force myself to focus not just on international aspects of culture, but also to address issues of multiculturalism within the United States. I decided to sit down in a Los Angeles park and use my cultural skills to observe for several hours. I presented that park as a metaphor for multiculturalism during my interview (and yes, I did get the job). Since that time, I have come to distinguish and celebrate cultural differences within the larger framework of American society.

EDUCATION AND SERVICE

Useem (1999) noted that TCKs are much more likely to attain higher degrees and work in service and education professions. While both are true of me, I am not entirely sure why. I suspect that my desire to help arises from my experiences of being the "other." I know what it feels like to be the stranger in need of help. I am good at observing and listening to understand and anticipate service needs. I gain true joy from helping people.

Originally, I had no plans to enter education, but after a very brief career in the film industry I found myself working as an elementary school teacher before obtaining a master's degree so I could work as a librarian in colleges and universities. I am not sure why I resisted becoming an educator as it proved a perfect career for me. Not only do I like to help people, but I have always had a voracious curiosity about the world and a deep desire to learn. I am not sure this can be directly connected to growing up abroad, but I am sure it did not hurt.

LEADERSHIP AND THE THIRD CULTURE KID

Until very recently, my specialty as a librarian was to make sure that students graduated from college information literate, which is defined as the ability to find, evaluate, and ethically use information. At The University of New Mexico (UNM), my day-to-day work involved leading the library's information literacy program and teaching classes. I am now an administrator who values all of the roles the library plays in student success.

I believe that my background as a TCK has proven a great advantage in my career. Librarianship is a service profession, and one of my greatest strengths is the desire to help people that emerged directly from my experiences growing up abroad. My desire to serve has led me to adopt a philosophy of servant leadership in the context of a learning organization. I see my leadership role as one who serves employees so they can advance the mission of the library. My goal is to bring out the best in each person and to serve as a steward to the library. In my view, servant leadership is transformational. By transforming people in the organization, we transform the organization and people we serve.

Two examples from my days as coordinator of the information literacy program illustrate my philosophy. First, I wanted to enhance the library's freshman instruction programs by hiring a coordinator. I recruited a colleague to my department—after first sitting back and observing, naturally—because she was talented and interested. Her initial expectation was that I would tell her what to do. She was a bit taken aback when I, instead, gave her complete charge of the program. When I demonstrated that I was serious by providing her the resources and freedom she needed, she embraced the idea and created a vibrant and still growing program. Second,

I led a team of librarians who were responsible for teaching students how to conduct research. When we needed more librarians to teach in the expanding freshman instruction program, my supervisor mandated participation with limited success. I took a different approach. Most librarians come to the job with no teaching experience, and these librarians were no exception. I elected to offer ongoing teaching workshops designed to develop teaching skills among librarians. Over the course of my tenure, I was able to increase participation among librarians from a dozen to nearly forty by supporting their needs. I believe both examples are attributable to my genuine desire to serve employees in order that they might better serve our students.

I find that service and diversity go hand in hand. When I worked at Occidental College in Los Angeles, the students in the Peer Mentor Program in the Cultural Resource Center conducted a community resource mapping exercise to identify people and resources that would help them succeed in college. The center existed to foster a multicultural community by finding value in all individuals, groups, cultures, and perspectives. I am proud to say that I was the person they identified in the library. I believe that this was directly attributable to my desire to serve and my natural inclination to embrace diversity.

The adaptability I realized as a TCK has served me well. Though the library's mission and values have not changed in the more than two decades I have been a librarian, the environment has changed drastically, primarily because of the advent of computers and the Internet, but also due to issues of rising accountability and increasing diversity. While many librarians lamented the changes, I accepted them as natural and easily adapted. In addition, I believe servant leadership equips employees for change better than more autocratic leadership styles.

I truly believe that my background brought few disadvantages to my career, but I will address two issues. First, the fact that I like to observe before engaging can make me seem diffident, aloof, or even arrogant before people get to know me. I believe that I am well past that phase at UNM, but when I first arrived, I had some problems with colleagues. My mentor blamed this on the fact that many people did not know me, and he recommended I become involved more widely in the library. I took his advice, and my troubles disappeared very quickly. As an administrator and leader, observation before engagement has mixed results, with the potential for seeming indecisive offset by good decisions informed by scrutiny and thought.

The second issue is potentially more serious. As I mentioned before, I still have a tendency to believe that Americans are more alike than different, that the fact of being American overrides characteristics of race and ethnicity, which many people born and raised in the United States feel drive diversity. More than 30 years of living in the United States have tempered this idea only slightly, so it is possible that I might be blind to differences that are real and matter to the individual or the organization. Of most concern is the possibility that this blind spot might lead to a disparate impact in the workplace. I am aware of the possibility and do not believe I am guilty of any unintended discrimination, but it is difficult to demonstrate. The most visible example is hiring decisions, and I can say with confidence that the majority of the search committees on which I served over the years made their first offer to a candidate who is an ethnic minority. I would argue that my cultural sensitivity, though keyed more to international diversity, has been far more of an advantage than a disadvantage.

I have not yet had the opportunity to fully implement a servant leadership model as a positional leader because I have not yet served as a library dean. The academic libraries where I worked have all been vested in more authoritarian models of leadership. My ultimate goal as a librarian is to become a dean so I can see how my vision of a servant leader within a learning organization can transform the lives of both employees and students.

Conclusion

When we arrived in Veracruz, I realized how much I missed immersing myself in other cultures. We were only there for a short time, but I found that I quickly fell into the rhythms of observing and exploring. I found that I truly enjoyed interacting with my hosts in both the classroom and over meals. Though I was visiting Veracruz for the first time, it felt right to be there.

I feel blessed by my childhood. I believe that I was extremely fortunate to meet the people I met, to see the places I saw, and to be immersed in so many interesting and vibrant cultures. I have no doubt my experiences have had a major influence over who I am today—at home and at work—and for that I am thankful.

REFERENCES

Pollock, D. C., & Van Reken, R. E. (2009). *Third culture kids: Growing up among worlds*. Boston, MA: Nicholas Brealey.

Useem, R. H. (1999). TCK World proudly presents: Dr. Ruth Hill Useem, the sociologist/anthropologist who first coined the terms 'Third Culture Kid' ('TCK'). Retrieved from http://www.tckworld.com/useem/home.html

Useem, R. H., & Downie, R. D. (1976). Third-culture kids. *Today's Education, 65*(3), 103–105.

Coming Out and Coming to Terms
The Development of an Authentic Identity

Kevin T. Colaner

With more than 20 years of professional experience in student affairs administration, Kevin T. Colaner currently serves as associate vice president for student services at California State Polytechnic University, Pomona. In addition, he is an adjunct associate professor in the Rossier School of Education at the University of Southern California.

"Who are *you*?" said the Caterpillar. . . .

"I, I hardly know, Sir, just at present," Alice replied rather shyly, "at least I know who I was when I got up this morning, but I think I must have changed several times since then." (Carroll, 1865, Chapter 5)

Recently, a colleague told me, "We know people by stereotype and by reputation." To be honest, I take comfort in this truth. The stereotypes that surround me and the reputation I have acquired tend to fit nicely with the image of me that I want others to know. In writing this essay, I tried to get past these external measures to identify my core values regarding diversity and how these values are manifested in my actions. Through this process, I realized I have struggled for some time, through an

155

intense process of introspection, to provide a sense of unity between my public self and the intimate self that I do not share freely with others. In this regard, I have been trying to identify my "authentic self."

This struggle did not begin with the request to contribute to this book (though it has forced me to confront these issues from a new perspective and with new information). This struggle began as I first dealt with my sexual identity. Coming out is an endless journey of self-discovery. It is an ongoing process that does not end with a tearful letter to one's parents. When one "comes out" they come out with each new interaction and each new situation they encounter. The act of coming out has forced me to come to terms with my professional identity, my intellectual identity, my ethnicity, my spiritual identity, and all other aspects of my being.

This process has been overwhelming at times, forcing me to come to terms with who I am and summon the courage to share this knowledge with others. This experience allowed me, as a person who benefited from societal privileges afforded to White men, to experience the world from another perspective: that of the "other." By engaging in this process, I had to examine my strengths and weaknesses, my virtues and faults, and ask the world to accept me as I am. The experience of openly acknowledging who I am has enabled me to accept and respect the diverse gifts of others more freely. It has allowed me to suspend judgment and seek understanding before acting on my initial observations of others.

When I think about being an out and open professional, and often the first openly gay "fill in the blank," I think of all the times in my life when I actually was the first gay whatever, but no one knew it because fear and cowardice did not allow me to step up and out to be the leader I could and should have been. I believe one's identity is a combination of a number of socially constructed characteristics. These multiple identities include inherited and self-defined aspects such as race, ethnicity, gender, sexual orientation, and spirituality, as well as how one makes meaning and communicates that meaning in the world. I believe many of these characteristics are shaped by issues of privilege and power, and are dynamic in that they change over time. Erikson (1964) defined identity as the "ability to experience one's self as something that has continuity and sameness and to act accordingly" (p. 42). My own identity changed dramatically over my life as I moved physically, spiritually, and culturally away from the environment in which I was raised and grew into my own sense of self. My current identity challenge is to live a life of greater authenticity and consistency as Erikson described. This however, was not always the case.

Starting Out

> I'm an idea. I'm what you perceive me to be; but to me, I'm the sparkling water that cascades over the rocks and falls. I'm the reverberating crash of thunder and the quiet whisper of dawn. . . . To you I change, like day into night and winter in spring. To me I stay the same. Like water I grow deeper and broader, but what I am never changes. My experiences in life reflect through me and enhance me; yet they do not change me. They are like the wind which blows ripples on the placid water, or the rocks that cause its frothy foam. They enhance the water, yet do not change it.

This excerpt from an essay I wrote in fulfillment of an assignment for my freshman English composition course is instructive in that it portrays a level of self-confidence, and quite frankly grandeur, I do not recall possessing. It also shows significant ways in which my thinking changed with experience over time. My life began in mid-October somewhere near the middle of the day somewhere in the middle of Ohio. I was born the fifth of six children into a "mixed" marriage. My father was an Italian Catholic and my mother an Irish Catholic. That is about as mixed as it got in Ohio in the mid-1960s. I mention Catholic identity here not because of the role it plays in my life now, but because it was most certainly influential in how I became the man I am today, or more accurately, why it took me so long to become the man I am today.

I was never much like the rest of my siblings. I was the "different" one. I was what some in my family might describe as "creative"; more interested and successful in arts than in sports (although I dutifully ran track and cross country to fit in). I was active (some say overactive) during my early life as a "good Catholic." I was in a folk group, served as a Eucharistic minister, was active in teen retreats, and was even the Catholic campus minister early in my undergraduate career. While I loved (and still do love) my family and respected their strongly held beliefs, I longed to explore, to leave my humble background and venture out. It was not that I wanted to leave them as much as I wanted to find something else. In my heart I knew what that something was, but it would be years before I could accept that. I left home just days after my high school graduation.

MOVING OUT

I often think of something my mother told me when I was leaving home. She said, "The shortest road is not always the quickest." This simple truth has been very prophetic in my adult life; in fact, it just about describes my adult life. After spending a year in California, I ended up in Wilmington, North Carolina, where I attended university and began my career in student affairs.

My four years at the University of North Carolina Wilmington were a time of tremendous growth and learning for me. Yet, as I grew intellectually and excelled in my development as a leader, my personal development was an entirely different situation. I was a busy and hardworking student, traits I carry with me to this day. At any given time I was holding down two to three jobs in order to pay for my education. For a period of time, several people thought I was a twin because they noticed me working at several different places both on and off campus in the same day! However, my work schedule did not keep me from getting involved in campus life. From active involvement in Greek life, to campus service as an ambassador, to involvement in clubs and even student government, I was never at a loss for something to do. Whether I was trying to maintain my high grade point average to continue the "dues scholarship" provided by my fraternity, or advancing to at least the executive leadership team of every organization to which I belonged, I felt a constant pressure to excel. I wanted to guarantee that others would like me, and I felt if they knew what I knew about me, they would surely reject me.

Deep within my being, and years before I arrived on campus, I realized that I was attracted to other men. But this realization flew in the face of everything I had been taught was true, and good, and right. Acknowledgement of this truth, I believed, would result in complete alienation from my family, and it was most certainly nothing for me to be proud. I think I felt that if I just kept busy, kept working, kept making others happy, that they would not see my secret, or at the very least they, like me, would ignore it. This is not to say that I had a bad college experience, quite the contrary. I think I had a great college experience, mostly because of wonderful student affairs professionals who provided me numerous opportunities to grow, learn, and explore. They introduced me to a brilliant profession that matched my interests and skill set, and they (mostly without my knowledge) guided me to opportunity after opportunity to gain a broad and rich knowledge of the breadth and depth of what it means to work in student affairs. They helped me see my role in student affairs—as expressed in this excerpt from my graduate school application:

> I believe for one to be successful in working with college students, they must understand that students come to college with varied backgrounds and levels of maturity. It should be our goal to accept each student for who and what they are and help them to continue in their development in order to reach their fullest potential. College is also a place for students to try new things, establish values, and challenge beliefs. I feel that my role should be to help foster an environment which provides them with new perspectives from which to view their world and challenge them to expand as individuals.

While my rhetoric reflected an openness to explore, experiment, and challenge; my reality was very different. I cannot remember a single discussion during my entire undergraduate experience on the topic of my identity development.

Lately I have been questioning the role we, as student affairs professionals, play in helping students through difficult developmental challenges. How overt, how intrusive should we be? I wonder how my life could or would have been different if one of the many caring and talented student affairs professionals pulled me aside to talk about my personal and sexual development. If I had a gay role model to look up to and respect, would my life have been different or possibly better? I understand that no one can do the hard work for you and everyone must travel their own path; yet, I wonder, what if? What if someone had fostered an environment that provided me new perspectives from which to view my world and challenged me to expand as an individual? What if someone had been comfortable or confident enough to have a discussion with me about male sexuality and spirituality and being true to who I am?

Seeking different ways and truer answers—isn't that really our role? In assessing the development of our students, we need to ask ourselves, "What did that student learn from their interaction with me?" "In what observable ways did our program or service help that student to grow?" In order to truly influence students' development, we must be cognizant of our own development. Engaging in critical reflection on an ongoing basis is at the core of our development as professionals. Reflecting on our actions requires setting aside time. It requires us to stop doing for a few minutes and ask ourselves how are we doing, what are we doing, and why are we doing it? This requires difficult questions and even more difficult answers.

Coming Out

Coming out as a gay man has affected my life, both personal and professional, in a number of ways, but I can confidently say for the better. Personally, I was able to find someone to love completely, without fear or reservation. Professionally, I have been able to be more open, honest, and authentic in my interactions.

Coming out is seldom a painless or easy process. It is also an ongoing process that must be negotiated time and again. John C. Calhoun noted, "The interval between the decay of the old and the formation and establishment of the new constitutes a period of transition which must always necessarily be one of uncertainty, confusion, error, and wild and fierce fanaticism"(p. 90). This most certainly holds true for the coming out process and is evidenced in the less-than-tender response I received from one of my student affairs colleagues after I told her that I am gay. "I knew it! I knew it the minute I interviewed you!" she said. Granted, she was no longer my supervisor and we were friends and colleagues, but where had she been all those years I was struggling? Why was my authentic self such a taboo subject?

BEING OUT

Coming out is not a singular isolated occurrence, it is an ongoing activity. It happens every time I hire a new staff member, or meet a new faculty member, or speak before a new group of parents at orientation. I reason if my parents have come around and can deal with it any parent can. However, sharing something so personal about my life has an impact. It forces me to be more honest in general. It forces me to be more confident. And it forces me to look at everyone else in a more personal and open way. There was a time in my life and in my career when I would avoid personal questions. If someone I worked with seemed distant, I would convince myself not to take it personally. But since I have mustered the courage to come out and be who I am in my entirety, I no longer see the harm in tackling the personal. I am, after all, a person. I work and live with other people. By opening myself up and coming to terms with who I am, I am more open to acknowledging, understanding, and appreciating others.

In his book *The G Quotient: Why Gay Executives Are Excelling as Leaders . . . and What Every Manager Needs to Know* (2006), Kirk Snyder looked at the issue of being gay as more than a societal force and explored it as a business force. He revealed seven common leadership traits found among gay leaders in his study: inclusion, creativity, adaptability, connectivity, communication, intuition, and collaboration. These traits, he asserted, reflect a new paradigm of leadership. He found that in organizations under the direct leadership of noncloseted gay executives, an environment was created where employees cared more about their work, demonstrated deep commitment to professional excellence, and felt individually connected to advancing the success of the organization. Snyder posited (and I concur) that gay men have adapted to their surrounding environments in order to feel both physically and emotionally safe. This adaptability along with intuitive communication and creative problem solving are skills gay leaders have learned and developed during their careers.

Through the development of these skills, I learned to be more confident as a leader and more confident in allowing and nurturing others in their development as leaders. While coming out was not and is not easy, the vast amount of energy spent on hiding who I am and constantly trying to "pass" as something else could instead be better spent supporting my staff and improving our productivity. By accepting myself for who I am and acknowledging my minority status, I am better able to relate and appreciate others who represent minority populations or perspectives. By coming to terms with and valuing my own diversity, I am more accepting and appreciative of the diversity in others. I find I have a broader definition of diversity and seek out others with different worldviews, religious beliefs, skill sets, and backgrounds. By embracing my identity, I am more confident in building teams and surrounding myself with individuals who complement, and even challenge, my perspective.

Coming out is a powerful experience. It has allowed me to grow as a person and professional. It gives me the courage to engage in challenging and sometimes difficult conversations. I believe others can relate to me better because they see that I am comfortable being myself, and this creates an environment in which they, too, can be open about who they are and what they believe. Whether I am welcoming an incoming class of students or engaging an employee in a difficult conversation about personnel issues, I am more successful because the people with whom I am communicating are more open to my message because they have a sense of trust. They see my message is coming from a place of authenticity. I truly believe everyone would benefit from coming out. Imagine for a moment a reality where everyone with whom you interacted took the time to explore their life, their beliefs, their true feelings—and then professed those feelings and acted on them in an authentic manner. As I have noted earlier, we cannot do the difficult work for others, but like the Caterpillar in the story of *Alice in Wonderland* quoted at the beginning of this essay, we can engage our students and colleagues by asking the important question, "Who are *you?*"

References

Calhoun, J. C. (1851). *A disquisition on government and a discourse on the constitution and government of the United States.* Charleston, SC: General Assembly of the State of South Carolina.

Carroll, L. (1865). *Alice's adventures in wonderland.* London, England: MacMillan and Co.

Erikson, E. (1964). *Insight and responsibility.* New York, NY: Norton.

Snyder, K. (2006). *The G Quotient: Why gay executives are excelling as leaders . . . and what every manager needs to know.* San Francisco, CA: Jossey-Bass.

An Encompassing Artistic Practice

Mary Tafoya

Mary Tafoya has studied educational leadership and is an artist, writer, and instructional designer in Albuquerque, New Mexico. She coordinated a faculty development center for community college instructors and directed a mentoring program for American Indian science and technology majors. Currently, she works with a federal agency, developing distance learning training solutions.

When was it that I first realized God wanted me to be an artist? I was raised in a large Catholic family, and attended Catholic schools, so certainly I was trained to believe in a powerful Creator. But this was not God's power compelling me. I thought of God's will for me as a kind and generous gift. Now that I am older, I see that it is my nature to be an artist, as God intended, but also, I work hard to cultivate an artistic practice. While being an artist is not what I do as much as it is what I am, the evidence of that artistic self is in how I spend my time and what I make, as well as in how I approach things.

The same can be said about educational leadership—being a leader isn't what I do; it is a part of who I have become. The evidence of my values, beliefs, and approaches can be seen in what I do. In writing this essay, I sought to tease out the connections—the little lifelines of energy—between my artistic self and my leadership practice. I am grateful for this opportunity and hope that by integrating my creative strengths into my leadership approaches, I will become a better leader.

GROWING UP AND ART

Art-making has been my daily touchstone since grade school, when I first remember being identified by others as an artistic kid. Many significant events shaped my life, and not all of them have to do with my artistic self, exclusively. Yet as I look back, I can see my artistic self has been my refuge from trauma, my gateway into the world of work and the world of knowledge, an expression of spirit, and probably the most nutritious aspect of my cultural self.

I did not grow up with artists (or so I believed as a child), and I thought I had landed in Kentucky by mistake! Certainly, I would have to leave home to find excitement and adventure in my "true" family of other artists. The only museum in the region was on the campus of the local university. It smelled musty and the art seemed formal and formulaic, conducted according to some prescription I did not have the slightest desire to explore. Our church, on the other hand, was the most beautiful place I knew. It was a modern house of worship, with an altar backdrop of glittering mosaics and stained glass windows I thought of as adult coloring books, full of passion and deep meaning. Today I understand that real art feeds the soul, and soul feeds art. In that church, the light and the community of people made the colorful windows even brighter.

I liked to draw, sometimes with whatever was handy. The Avon lady would leave my mother samples of bright green eye shadow and hot pink lipstick, and she would give them to me. I had a large, old school desk in my room, complete with wrought iron fittings. Under the desk, where the wood was old and black, I drew on my secret chalkboard.

I remember concentrating on pencil sketches until my forehead was sweaty, struggling to make my drawings match my imagination, and then finally falling over on the couch or bed, exhausted and frustrated. One day I tried to draw a ballerina, but I could not get her face right. I erased over and over until I tore a hole in the paper. Out of desperation I reached for a magazine, cut out a picture of a woman's head, and glued it over the torn paper. I learned early on that bringing your vision to life is nearly impossible, but if you are willing to shift gears a bit along the way, surprising alternative solutions may present themselves. As a leader today, I still rely on creativity to resolve desperate situations because unexpected events always seem to occur in the middle of a project.

My fourth-grade teacher asked my classmates and me what we wanted to be when we grew up. The idea that we could be what we wanted had not occurred to me because I already knew what God wanted me to be. Some students did not know what they wanted to be. I felt sorry for them. Other students took it upon themselves to decide what they wanted to be, and I wondered if God was okay with that. I assumed God told all kids what they were going to be. Now I felt special, and I wanted to talk this over with my mother.

I explained what happened at school and said, "I think I want to be an artist." My mother (in a most uncharacteristic way), replied, "I think you have the creativity, but I don't think you have the talent." I was stunned. My stomach hit the floor, and I staggered up to my room, confused. How could my mother not know God's plan for me? Or was I mistaken?

A few days later, I visited our little branch library to find a new career. On a low shelf, I looked wistfully at the books about artists, and then I panned right, where I found an occupation called "archaeology." I learned that archaeologists study art from ancient cultures. I supposed since I could not be an artist, I would instead study to become someone who dug up their work. I took home a book about ancient Crete and was amazed to learn the Phoenician alphabet was almost the same as ours. Under my desk, I used the Avon lipsticks to write secret messages to my imaginary Cretan pen pal, a girl who leapt over bulls and decorated vases with extraordinary images of sea creatures. I learned my mother did not know everything, and in that separation, my inner artist grew stronger. Today, I lean on mentors and other wise leaders, but ultimately, I must follow my heart and trust myself to make decisions. When my inner artist is activated and I am connected to something I care about, I know I am on the right track.

ART AND SCHOOL, SCHOOL AND ART

As a teenager struggling to cope with an unhealthy family dynamic, I was impulsive and engaged in many risky behaviors. Being an artistic type in a conservative community, I felt isolated and longed to find people who understood me. Although I knew God's will for me was to be an artist, I had no clue how to become one, officially. Looking back on those painful and self-destructive teen years, I wonder if knowing God's plan for me kept me alive. I had plenty of friends who had no future, and I saw what that did to them. But knowing that I had a future, even if I did not know how to get there, pulled me through.

The importance of having this "gift of a future" has been confirmed over many summers working in precollege programs for teens. I see their discomfort when I ask where they will be in 10 years. Their bodies tense and their faces go blank. I tell them, "Believe me, you'll be around here somewhere and you'll be doing something. If you can choose what you'll be doing—what will you choose? What can you imagine yourselves doing?" And then I see their shoulders relax, and they start to think, and then they start to write. I can remember feeling that the future was a scary black hole. But my gift was having a sense that I would find something on the other side of it—an artistic life, where I would feel good about myself. Leading young people toward the future involves more than pointing out career choices. We must also help them to envision a future.

For a brief time, I worked at a small art studio owned by my high school art teacher. She was conservative and tenacious, and I would not call her a creative person. She had one rule—mix yellow ochre with everything. My short-term apprenticeship with her left me feeling stifled. I did encounter creative artists, but I did not recognize them until years later.

In those days, there was a great revival of traditional craft. Weavers were rediscovering and preserving natural dyes of Appalachia, and regional arts and crafts schools were burgeoning. My mother took me to artists' colonies such as Berea, in Kentucky, where they held a magical little rural arts and crafts fair. We walked up a trail through the woods, where quilters hung their blankets from clotheslines strung between the trees, and potters set out pitchers and mugs made from the same earth we walked on. There were whittlers and woodcarvers who made shining bowls out of huge burls of local woods. Today, I lean on these early impressions of artistic activity grounded in daily life, close to the natural environment.

After a year of college in Kentucky, I made my great escape to New Mexico to study fine arts. I was intimidated by people from overseas and cosmopolitan places like New York City. In eastern Kentucky, I was considered a city slicker, but here at the big state university, I was a hillbilly, and I felt unschooled. I did not yet recognize my strengths and talents, and my uniqueness embarrassed me. I tried hard to draw well, but inside I felt as though my mother's words were true—I did not have the talent to be an artist.

Today, I understand that it is perseverance and not talent that generates success over the long haul. Persistence, resilience, and a regular habit of practice make an artist. These qualities also make successful students and skillful leaders.

It took seven years to earn my BA because I worked and went to school part-time. I found work in a frame shop a welcome diversion from school. On the job, I met many local artists and learned from them how an artist lives and works. I listened to them talk about their art, outside the formal confines of the university.

I met an older artist who took me under his wing and introduced me to poets and musicians. He inspired me deeply at a time when I could have continued the self-destructive habits of my teen years. He was my first artist/mentor—the first person I met who was farther down the road I wanted to be on. He told me you can tell what you are supposed to do in life because whatever it is, it leaves you with more energy when you are done than when you started.

For me, that energizing calling would be teaching. I worked as a tutor in high school, and I felt recharged. At the university, I filled my electives with art education classes. Unlike the fine arts department, which was nationally acclaimed but left me feeling soulless and inadequate, art education courses were integrated with culture and community, infused with creativity and spirit. Here I reconnected with traditional crafts and learned to teach according to theories and practices that honor the whole person. My art education professors were themselves art practitioners, but unlike my fine arts teachers, they were trained in learning theory. I began to think of teaching as a craft, and my ongoing study of this craft would eventually carry me from a teacher of students to a trainer of college professors.

The art education seminars provided structure, wise mentors who understood the depths and breadth of art and soul, and a creative outlet through exploration of traditional craft materials. I felt as though I was starting my life over, from the beginning. Gradually, I gained a renewed energy and a new creative freedom. I spent hours spinning wool, roving it into yarn, and it calmed me. I copied East Indian miniature paintings, and I discovered the mysterious landscapes of Tibetan Buddhist art. I painted sunsets and took photographs of clouds. I was no longer a yellow ochre artist—the bright New Mexico skies had gotten under my skin.

After graduation, I worked as a graphic artist for a commercial printing company, where I met my husband. We walked the irrigation canals of our neighborhood, and I drew pictures of bare cottonwood trees in winter. I continued to paint and learned to decorate fabric. Through art, counseling, and a supportive relationship, I learned to heal what needed healing. Wherever we lived, I always had a little studio to call my own. I was not sharing my art with anyone, but I was engaged in art-making every day.

However, my day job was growing boring; I had learned all I could and most days were a grueling routine of monotonous deadlines. For an artist, monotony is like a little death. To overcome the boredom, I sometimes pretended I was explaining to someone else how to do my job. I began to think seriously about going back to school for a teaching certificate in art education, but before I could enroll, I learned about a job as a graphic arts instructor at a tribal college. I applied, got hired, and worked there for more than 20 years.

THE CRAFT OF TEACHING, THE ART OF LEADERSHIP

Early on, there were no graphic arts textbooks to speak of, so I was given free rein to develop my own curriculum. I discovered that I enjoyed the challenge and complexity of designing lessons with content that would be relevant to Native American students and would also build their technical skills in a logical sequence. My artistic self discovered an expanded environment in which to put my talents to work. I discovered that curriculum development takes creativity, and that teaching requires the same responsiveness as art-making—you have to maintain a balance between staying true to your original goals, while at the same time adjusting to unanticipated events along the way.

As my life became more stable and rewarding, I began to try things I would previously have been afraid to do. I submitted my work to shows, got accepted at a few national exhibitions, and even won a few awards. I also started writing articles for craft magazines. I began to receive invitations to teach and lecture across the country. I used my teaching skills to develop an art curriculum and began to mentor other artists in the same ways I encouraged high school students.

My artistic self led me around the world—figuratively—and educated me across many content areas. I rejected clerical courses in high school but when the opportunity came to earn more as a computer typesetter, I taught myself to type. This skill became my inroad to emerging computer graphics technologies and helped me qualify for my job at the college. I avoided science and math courses in high school, but through ceramics I learned the basics of chemistry. Studying beadwork and fiber arts, I became an anthropologist as I learned how those crafts are significant to people and cultures. It is challenging to apply this organic approach to learning in today's colleges as students are not usually allowed the time to follow a strand of inspiration wherever it leads them.

By embracing and giving voice to my artistic self, I survived and learned how to live and to lead. I make things almost every day, and when I am not making things, I am doodling in a journal. Art-making is spiritually centering for me, regardless of external recognition or monetary reward. I wish all of my students had a gift like mine in their lives; and in fact, many of them do. I believe that a good leader helps those they lead become true to themselves.

After several years teaching, I began training faculty in distance learning and the use of instructional technologies. In one of our faculty development courses, I learned that I am an intuitive thinker. I had always thought of intuition as something like a sixth sense, but I learned that in education it refers to global thinking. I see patterns, and I make connections between seemingly unrelated details. This is basically the mind of an artist, and this is how some psychologists define creative aptitude. I discovered I can see the whole picture, especially with regard to complex processes and organizational structures. I see the entire project in my mind, how it benefits each participant, how it responds to constraints and parameters, and how it will roll out over time. It is sometimes difficult to explain this to others. I want to say, "Trust me, I can see it all so clearly!" Fortunately, art-making gives me lots of practice bringing vision to fruition.

I was surprised at first to learn that not all instructors adapt well to change. Although I would not say that I thrive on change, I enjoy it, in portions. My creative self needs change in order to stay energized and engaged. With other more change-inhibited faculty, I have learned to adopt the role of available mentor, as they gradually adapt to new technologies and pedagogical approaches. I learned that professors, too, are adult learners who usually want to know "What good is this?" before they will invest in change. Responding to other people's rhythms is a bit like responding to an art project—every medium has its limitations, and so do people and organizations.

The artistic self is rich, deep, spontaneous, playful—and easily distracted! I might start in the morning tabulating surveys but by afternoon, I have created a digital photo album instead. It is good to wander, but it is also important for my artistic self to have a strict inner supervisor. I make lists of what I need to do, and I check off each task as I finish. If it is a particularly tedious day, I reward myself for tasks accomplished with things like downloading a free font or playing with a graphics program for half an hour. My inner artist is a tad self-centered.

Reflecting on my role as an educational leader, I realize that I thrive on creative energy and instinctively apply an artistic hand to projects and tasks. Being an artist is the card I was dealt. Integrating those skills and inclinations into my leadership style allows me to work with, not against myself.

My Purple Heart

Lea M. Jarnagin

Lea M. Jarnagin serves as the dean of students at California State University, Fullerton (CSUF), where she has served in a variety of leadership roles on campus since 1998. In addition to active involvement in NASPA, she serves as adjunct faculty in the CSUF Higher Education Program.

The color purple, which represents spirituality and a sacred place in my soul, brings me a sense of calm and powerful, feminine energy. The symbol of the heart signifies deep courage, caring, and compassion. Cumulatively, these two symbols shape who I am and how I serve others. Together, they comprise my purple heart. My leadership story offers insight into events that have transpired throughout my life, learning I have experienced and the meaning making I have gained along the way that illuminates the leader I am today. My story offers an explanation of how two important symbols in my life, the color purple and the heart, have come together to represent my leadership.

Why use the metaphor of the purple heart to symbolize my leadership style? I possess a deep love of the color purple; I use my intuition to lead from within, from my core. In other words, I lead from my heart, and I have come to understand how these two factors come together to give me strength beyond what I thought possible.

THE EARLY YEARS

As I have reflected on my life throughout the years, I have often wondered if I am supposed to be here. Surviving extraordinary experiences in my early childhood has led me to believe that indeed, I am. One of my earliest childhood memories involves walking alone along a small stream in a large, open field during the middle of winter at the age of five years old. I distinctly remember thinking "I have something special I am supposed to do with my life." I recall feeling confused because I had no idea what it was or why I was having the thought. However, somehow I knew that whatever it was, it would reveal itself eventually. This experience left an impression on me. It was more than a thought; I actually felt something physically in my body, as if a transformation took place along with the cognitive thought process. In his book *Leading Minds: An Anatomy of Leadership*, Howard Gardner (1995) described an inclination from early childhood for risk taking among future leaders and a personal understanding of the call to future leadership. This early identity-forming experience was the beginning of my understanding that I have a life's purpose larger than myself. That purpose would require accepting personal risk and finding courage to move forward despite fear of failure and lack of self confidence.

I was born with the viral form of spinal meningitis. At the age of 15 months, the virus activated and I became extremely ill. Rushed to the hospital with a 105°F temperature, I was placed into an isolation ward where I fell into a coma for the next 21 days. My mother retells the hysteria that swept the neighborhood as the bacterial form of the disease is highly contagious. A recent breakout of the disease at a nearby military base had already taken the lives of several individuals, including small children. Fortunately, I had the viral form of the disease; however, the next three weeks brought panic to my parents. Upon arriving at the hospital after work for her nightly visit, my mother found me absent from my ice-filled, padded oxygen tent in the isolation ward. She panicked at the thought of the worst happening, but the nurse led her down the hall to find me standing in a crib, smiling, bouncing up and down awaiting her arrival. Although I survived, the ordeal left my parents financially broken and we ultimately lost our home.

This early illness would have been enough; however, over the next few years I endured several additional potentially life-threatening injuries. Between the ages of 2 and 12, I was poisoned with liquid ant poison by my brother; fell out of the car during rush hour on a busy Southern California freeway off ramp and suffered a concussion; was hit in the mouth with a baseball bat (which finally stopped me from sucking my thumb, but 20 years later caused a cyst to grow in my face that would have to be surgically removed); and was hit in the head with a rock that nearly caused me to lose an eye. Later, during my teenage years, while attempting to use our 1926 kitchen stove, I made the mistake of leaving the gas on a second too long causing the antique appliance to blow up in my face. The accident burned off my eyelashes, eyebrows, and most of my hair. With no explanation for why my vision was not irreparably damaged, the doctor simply told my mother "she must be lucky."

For most of my life, I have accepted this simple explanation. However, as I aged and experienced greater insight into my life and the forces that shaped me, I began asking deeper questions about why I am the person I am today. The result has been a comforting, deeper understanding of the events that have unfolded over the past four decades of my life. The learning shaped my character and leadership capacity. In other words, my story of self-identity is the narrative that helps me think about and feel who I am, where I come from, and where I am headed (Gardner, 1995). Telling and retelling my story has become a powerful tool in leading myself and others.

SPIRITUALITY

At the age of 18 months, my mother took me to visit my great-grandmother. Terminally ill with breast cancer, my great-grandmother was Cherokee Indian from Tennessee and stood less than 5 feet tall. She was very proud of this and was angry when made to stand on a box for her wedding photo. She was a stalwart woman, no nonsense, with a work ethic that would put the strongest laborer to shame. Because I was her youngest great-grandchild, it was her wish to see me before she passed away. Unable to raise her arms at the time, my mother held me over my great-grandmother's chest so she could lay hands on me. As she rubbed my head, she spoke softly as if talking to herself. I believe that through her tender touch, she imbued upon me her spiritual blessing and strength of feminine leadership. I am comforted by the thought that she has served as my guardian angel ever since. It seems luck may not be entirely responsible for my being alive today. This very early experience serves as the beginning of the spiritual foundation of my life.

The connection of spirituality to feminine energy in my family has continued throughout my life. One of the most powerful experiences that shaped my understanding of inner strength took place at the age of 14. Stretched with the challenges of working two jobs, being a single mother, and addressing the substance abuse problems of my brother, my mother made the difficult decision of sending me against my will to live with my grandmother in another state. It was during the six months I lived with her that I discovered her favorite color was purple; not just any shade of purple, but the most intense, flamboyant shade of purple imaginable. I recall finding this extremely odd as it stood in direct opposition to her quiet, unassuming personality.

I am embarrassed to admit that watching my grandmother remain silent while her alcoholic husband filled our home with anger and rage led me to mistakenly assume she was weak. My judgment of her came in part from having grown up with an alcoholic stepfather until the age of 13. Walking on egg shells for fear of causing a problem and wondering why my mother did not do something to change our home into a happy one was all too fresh in my memory. Some 12 years later, as I dealt with the disappointments of my own failed marriage, I realized that strength comes in many forms. Inner strength to persevere, focusing on the necessities of living (Maslow's basic needs), and offering help to others when they need it the most (servant leadership) are qualities to be respected. Honoring those who have come before you is a call to give back the gifts you have received by lifting up and nourishing others (Astin & Leland, 1991). Humility and graciousness are admirable characteristics, and I consider myself fortunate to have gained these qualities from both my grandmother and my mother. In these two amazing role models I have connected to my own personal strength and committed to developing my inner leader so I may repay them by dedicating my life to helping others.

FEMININE ENERGY

It was not until my grandmother passed away in 1990 that I discovered my guiding color would soon become purple as well. My grandmother's final wish was for all in attendance at her funeral to wear her color. Owning nothing purple at the time, I purchased something to wear, and my mother wove purple flowers into my hair to honor her memory. Atop the Utah mountainside on the autumn afternoon of her service, I experienced a transformative spiritual moment that transcended the intellectual. I felt a physical change in my being that emanated outward as attested to by those who shared with me that I was "glowing"—a comment not typically made at a funeral. The experience, to put it simply, was profound. After going to the mountaintop (Gardner, 1995) to reflect on my thoughts and experience, I came to understand my transformation more clearly. The color of my grandmother, purple, had become the embodiment of the values, integrity and strength of character passed onto me by the history of strong women in my family. For perhaps the first time in my life, I realized the gifts of leadership I had been given by those who came before me: my great-grandmother, my grandmother, and my mother.

The loss of my grandmother enabled me to realize that although living with her may not have been my choice, it was her purposeful choices during those short six months that taught me important leadership lessons: to value personal integrity, strength, and dogged determination. These lessons, while learned without my realizing them at the time, have been captured in my love of the color purple gifted to me by my grandmother.

COURAGE

Growing up without a father, I looked primarily to my overburdened mother for clues to inform my understanding of relationships and personal boundaries. With four marriages and four divorces as examples, I learned what I would characterize as "please at any price." I also looked to myself and developed an unhealthy sense of independence that I would call "do what you want at any price." Despite my intuition screaming at me, I took many unwise risks, at times doggedly so, to prove myself and others wrong.

My first intimate relationship, which occurred during my mid-teenage years, is a perfect example of this dangerous combination of learning. My boyfriend was suffocating and overwhelmingly controlling, but I hid the reality of this abusive, two-and-a-half-year relationship from my mother and anyone who could help me. Lying about the circumstances of my daily life became a way of surviving, including blaming a broken wrist on a roller skating accident. After refusing to move to California and start my third new high school in yet another new state, my mother left me at the age of 17 in a small Midwest town to live my life with my abusive boyfriend and his family. The three weeks following her departure brought an intensity of loneliness and despair I had never known. I was in danger of losing the connection to the early identity forming experience of my youth in which my intuition told me my life would serve a larger purpose.

The heart is an amazingly tough muscle. Pumping continuously, it supplies oxygen and blood to our bodies and sustains our life force. Strong as it is, the heart can also be broken. Realizing that I put myself in harm's way out of my own stubbornness, I knew my purple heart was in danger of breaking beyond the point of repair. Knowing my purpose did not include living my life being controlled by someone else, something inside me fought its way to the surface and compelled me to do whatever it took to get out of there. It was my purple heart that helped me find the courage to physically escape the house and the humility to call my mom in California to ask for help. The leadership gifts of personal integrity, inner strength, and dogged determination imparted by the women in my family empowered me to find the courage to believe in my dreams of a future with a purpose.

Later, in my mid-20s, it was the transforming effect of education that ultimately empowered me to find the courage to leave my marriage and think freely how leadership would begin to take form in my life. Eight years in and out of the community college system allowed me to see that education was my ticket out of living my life through others. With no role models in my family to turn to, I filed for divorce and began my journey into higher education. Taking this leap started a legal process that resulted in the realization I had signed away my financial interest in our home and business without my knowledge about a year previously. Unknowingly duped, I found myself without financial resources or legal recourse after a nine-year relationship during which I worked full-time and put my husband through his undergraduate education. The loss of trust and violation of belief I had in others nearly broke my purple heart and at the same time stoked the flames of my social justice consciousness based primarily on my socioeconomic experiences. Later, I would come to realize the power of this aspect of my narrative in enabling me to encourage and inspire others who face seemingly overwhelming odds and adversity.

Today, when I engage with students and hear them struggle with their experience as first-generation college goers—lacking financial resources, academically underprepared, burdened with self-doubt—I share my story as a way of encouraging them. I tell them that I, too, had a dream of a college education as a path that would forever change my life. I share with them the story of my 10-year journey to achieving my bachelor's degree, the work-study jobs that helped me get there, and the voice of the first-generation student, the "little girl from the trailer park," who accompanied me during the late-night hours of homework. I reassure them they have within them the courage and self-determination to realize their dreams. By embodying my narrative, I reflect who I see them to be and encourage them to value their own learning.

Transformation

During the years I pursued my undergraduate degree, my relationship with my grandfather began to have a profound influence on my development as a leader. A 31-year veteran of the U.S. Air Force, my grandfather's humble beginnings as the eldest son of Tennessee potato farmers shaped his philosophy of hard work, humility, and what he called "intestinal fortitude." It was his belief in me that not only helped me succeed in my educational goals but also inspired my belief in the power of my purple heart to help others do the same. My grandfather's consistent communication of high expectations (no one owes you anything; if you want it, go out and get it) and unwavering belief in me provided inspirational motivation (Northouse, 2007). The more he encouraged me to persevere, the more committed I became to the vision of living life in service to others. His leadership cemented my commitment to servant leadership through transformational moments and the power of relationships. Although he passed in 2002, I think of him often and hear his words of encouragement and belief in me, which I impart to others with gratitude in my heart.

Ultimately, the coalescing of my dreams of helping others and the reality of finding a profession that fulfilled this personal destiny not only healed old wounds living in the dark corners of my heart, but also allowed me to envision the creative tension between my limits as an individual leader and the potential of education to dramatically impact the lives of students. As articulated by Parker J. Palmer (2000):

> If we are to live our lives fully and well, we must learn to embrace the opposites, to live in a creative tension between our limits and our potentials. We must honor our limitations in ways that do not distort our nature, and we must trust and use our gifts in ways that fulfill the potentials God gave us. (p. 55)

This vision of dedicating my life to honoring the gifts provided me and using those gifts to empower others shapes my leadership philosophy of working as a servant leader in my role as an educator.

Each time I receive a note from a former student or watch one of my current students succeed in overcoming an obstacle, my purple heart swells with pride. The smile on my face is psychic income more valuable than any title, position, or monetary reward. Moments such as these remind me of the reason I am alive—the larger purpose of why I am here. My purpose is to follow and lead others with care, compassion, and a never-ending commitment to continued learning. My gift of leadership is wrapped in a loving, caring purple heart that is capable of overcoming hardship and sharing compassion and wisdom gained from a life full of lessons. While some of the lessons have been difficult and required great courage, others have caused my heart to soar to heights far beyond what I ever imagined. In the end, I have come to understand that all lessons are invaluable as they comprise the leadership story. After all, life is a journey, not a destination.

References

Astin, H., & Leland, C. (1991). *Women of influence, women of vision: A cross-generational study of leaders and social change.* San Francisco, CA: Jossey-Bass.

Gardner, H. (1995). *Leading minds: An anatomy of leadership.* New York, NY: Basic Books.

Northouse, P. (2007). *Leadership: Theory and practice* (4th ed.). Thousand Oaks, CA: Sage Publications.

Palmer, P. (2000). *Let your life speak: Listening for the voice of vocation.* San Francisco, CA: Jossey-Bass.

The Paradox of
Intersecting Identities

In this section, leaders discuss challenges and contradictions inherent in negotiating multiple identities.

One Journey of Compassion
My Search for Inspiriting Leadership

Susan Longerbeam

Susan Longerbeam is associate professor at Northern Arizona University and leads the graduate program in student affairs where she developed the student affairs global learning initiative. Her research interests are in multicultural student success and in teaching to enhance student success. She previously served as co-director of student health services and interim dean of students at Oregon State University.

I was a college dropout. I crashed my sophomore year, a semester after returning from an immunization service tour in West Africa. During the service, I was attacked by a stranger who threatened to kill me. Unable to continue on the intellectual path I believed would "get me through," I yielded and returned to my family, accepted the emotions of grief, and began to heal. I identify as a survivor of assault. That summer service tour experience fundamentally changed my life, personality, and approach to leadership.

I have since adopted a fiercely compassionate kind of leadership, what I think of as "inspiriting," meaning to give energy and courage to others. I do not want others to feel anything like the complete surrender of life to someone else's control. Instead, I want to do my small part to make a difference in communities and individu-

185

als through encouraging (and giving energy to others, not taking energy from others). I want to encourage because I believe we are enlivened by leadership environments characterized by the freedom to take risks, be ourselves, and experience nurturance. In my core, I believe in leadership as inspiration. The primary way I attempt to inspirit is through compassion.

There are two parts of my identity that most influence my approach to leadership: survivor status and sexual orientation. In different ways, each identity gives me the experience of oppression and commitment to understand others' life experiences. I will begin by discussing my survivor status. The reactions from people at home to my traumatic, life-altering experience had a long-term influence, such that I tend not to tell the story. Those stereotyped reactions ("It happened when you were walking alone at night in the jungle?") taught me the visceral power of the U.S. race and gender narrative—a narrative I knew with the insight of a survivor's vigilance is deeply pernicious. That narrative continued the wounding and stood as a block to my healing.

Through that terror in being told and believing I would be killed on a lonely road one night, I was forced kicking and screaming into the realm of emotions, spirit, and compassion. Looking back, I am deeply grateful for the survivor's gift of letting go of perfectionism, control, and unilateral intellectualism—three impediments to inspiriting leadership, and a particular hazard for those of us, myself included, who are acculturated in comfortable middle-class Caucasian European American families. I let go because it was not possible to try for perfection or control while also in the deep pain of trauma. Intellectualism, trying to think my way to recovery, was making me worse. I had to let go. In my professional life these elements of control, perfectionism, and intellectualism devoid of spirit are hazards to offering inspiriting leadership to others. In order to encourage others, I try to exert more compassion, forgive more mistakes, and ease up considerably on control. In teaching, for example, when a student misses a course deadline, I ask him or her to suggest a new deadline, to which we then agree; thus, the student is keeping a commitment to himself or herself rather than to me, an external authority. Students routinely miss course deadlines (they almost never miss deadlines they choose for themselves) because their lives are complexly interwoven with intellectual, emotional, and spiritual dimensions. I learned to embrace emotional and spiritual dimensions of others' development in addition to intellectual ones, because I had to do this with myself to heal from trauma. I still struggle with the White privileged notion of a wish to control whether or not I am liked (not always conducive to leadership), but probably less than if I had not fought for my life, literally at the time of the incident and figuratively in the decades since.

COMPASSION THROUGH EMBRACING COMPLEXITY

Another aspect of my survivor status is embracing complexity and resisting dualism. My life continues to show itself more complex than my imagining. For instance, I ask myself, was being attacked a bad thing? Yes. Was it a good thing? Yes. How can both be true? Well, I could not be who I now am otherwise. I am a survivor because of a horrific and life-changing incident that informed my identity and gave me a sense of compassionate purpose for the rest of my life.

I try to remember to extend this notion of life's complexity to others. For instance, I tend to become skeptical and cautious about statements that feel reductive. Students in class recently discussed homophobia in religion, and one noted, "Mormons are the worst" (anti-Mormonism is disturbingly socially accepted in the Southwest United States). Rarely do I intervene, but on this occasion I said homophobia is painfully common and people who identify as Latter-day Saints (LDS) do not have a monopoly or corner on sentiments against those who are lesbian, gay, bisexual, and transgender. Later, a student who identifies as LDS wrote to me, "I just want you to know that for the first time in my entire academic career I felt like I had an advocate for tolerance of religious minorities (like members of my church)." That class day was a good day for me, because students, knowing my bisexual identity and my personal struggle, watched me wrestle with contradictions and complexities in the effort to inspirit each of them.

This ongoing realization of life's complexity informs me in different kinds of leadership situations, in teaching as above, and also in administrative roles. We can never know the whole of another person's experience. The best we can know is people are much more complex than we at first assume. I regularly fail to remember others' complexity, but I try to exert ever more compassion to inspirit others in a world of suffering. In my better moments, I remember life is hard for everyone. For instance, I struggle with leaders who seem self-absorbed, and though I remember the loneliness of leadership and its oppression, I feel critical of these leaders and constantly have to remind myself of their personal suffering. The close knowledge of suffering and vulnerability comes directly from my survivor identity. I strive to recognize that even when a student or colleague chooses not to share of their lives, there is a complex, tender history in each individual.

Coming Out and Negotiating Privacy

How does each of us decide whether to share of our complex lives, and if so how much? Especially now in this age of Internet openness, we negotiate our privacies anew each day. To what degree do we choose to come out about who we are? In how many settings do we decide whether to share of ourselves? And when we choose to share, to what degree do we risk others' assumptions about us, knowing they can never know our whole stories? In the digital age, we have a paradox of privacy; we want to hold onto and yet sometimes choose to relinquish privacy. The choice of either is a privilege, because not everyone enjoys the choice of whether or not to reveal themselves.

For many, whether to reveal racial identity is not a choice; whereas, my survivor and sexual identities are not readily apparent to others and so sharing them is my choice. My privilege is also in the ability to continually renegotiate these choices. Each of us has a vast complexity of identities. I try to remember that I will never know the whole of people's life experiences, and this remembering helps me be compassionate.

As a bisexual (bi) person, I have learned to continually negotiate coming out. Being bi, I embrace gender and sexual orientation as a continuum. Sexual orientation has influenced my leadership because it teaches me about oppression—and continually reminds me of each person's complexity. There are so many ways to be bi, and so many assumptions about those ways. How many times do we each come out—indeed about every aspect of our identities—and in how many ways? Coming out is not a one-time struggle; we come out over and over again in many contexts, such as I do every semester. As with any identity, there is no accurate way to tell a whole life at one time, even with close friends. But sharing our lives is a gift we give—here, see my life, learn what you can from it, live yours, intersect with other lives in loving ways. We will never know another's whole story. I try to remember the tough lessons and the hidden gifts of my sexual orientation are compassionate purpose—to give energy and courage, to inspirit where and when I am able.

I now understand the importance of telling stories to reduce others' isolation. Through an understanding of healing I will share my story. If you ask me about my bi identity, I will share my story. I strive for openness, service through compassion, and extending myself to others. These strivings are all part of understanding inspiriting leadership. Though there are times it may be easier to fold in, especially when I feel cautious, when I extend myself to others and open myself to their complex and multiple perspectives, then I meet my own expectations of leadership.

I share stories to illustrate my mistakes, particularly when I teach multicultural counseling, in hopes of reducing the isolation students often experience while learning challenging concepts about privilege and oppression. I explain that when we are pondering multiculturalism, we tend to make more micro-aggressive mistakes because race and culture are on our minds and we are sorting aloud through misinformation and bias. For instance, I share that I once confused two colleagues of Latino heritage, calling one by the other's name. When I acknowledged my mistake, the colleague graciously told me it was okay, and I responded that I regretted it and apologized again. The incident occurred in a public meeting. I share the story so students will know that although they are not alone in making multicultural mistakes, we each have the option to enrich relationships by embracing the possibilities inherent in acknowledging them.

INSPIRITING LEADERSHIP, SEXUAL AND GENDER IDENTITY, AND PRIVACY

I have lived with colleagues making assumptions about my sexuality—as an employee, a supervisor, and a peer. These wounds are deep and the harassment scarring. But as I remind students, if you live an honest life, people will come to know you over time. Try not to worry about the judgments others make of you. We each negotiate coming out over and over again, and you get to make your own choices about when and with whom to share your story.

However, no one's sexuality or gender identity should become a part of their working life against their choosing. Constructing sexual and gender identity are among the most private of human endeavors, and these identities are for the individual to share. Decisions about who we choose to love and how we identify our gender are personal. Taking those decisions away from someone is antithetical to inspiriting leadership. When individuals choose to share their sexual and gender identity with others, it is a gift of trust. But I have come to know that part of living an identity as a sexual minority means the relatively greater risk that our sexuality and gender identity will intrude on our working life because of homophobia.

I now believe it is insufficient for us as leaders to claim unawareness of the range of human sexuality, from the healthy to the abusive. An educated person should know enough to protect others, especially children and all who may be vulnerable for reasons of identity and personal history. In order to protect others, we as leaders should have a basic understanding of sexualities' misuses, healthy expressions, and intersections with gender, race, class, age, abilities, and other identities. The realm of sexuality is important in a discussion of inspiriting leadership because sexuality is a significant source of dispiriting others, from sexual harassment to sexual assault to homophobia. Our otherwise intuitive knowledge of abuse is sometimes occluded by discomfort, homophobia, or conflation—for example, between pedophilia and adult sexuality in the recent case at The Pennsylvania State University. When we conflate, we then fail to protect children because we do not see where real danger lies, or we fail to protect those with whom we work who have little organizational power. Understanding the range of human sexual and gender expression is an important dimension of inspiriting leadership.

FINDING INSPIRITING LEADERSHIP

My understanding of leadership arises out of the lessons of my identity. Being a survivor and a sexual minority taught me to strive to live openly, extend myself to others, and be compassionate about the range and complexity of human experience. These strivings are encapsulated in my notion of inspiriting leadership. When I meet my own expectations of leadership, I offer energy and courage to others. Finding inspiriting leadership and the spirit in my work is also gifted to me through many mentors and healers whom I sought and had the blessing to work with along the journey to compassionate purpose.

Inspiriting leadership requires tolerance for chaos in the service of freedom. I believe my role is to encourage environments in which it is safe to take risks and make mistakes. Although chaos can ensue from mistakes and the free flow of information (rather than information communicated through a hierarchy), it also creates an environment for enlivened, empowered, and energetic colleagues and students. I am surprised sometimes at the amount of hierarchy and control that still exists in the workplace. For example, when I walk into a meeting I can feel whether people are giving their full creative selves, or are holding back their gifts out of fear. Because I am saddened so much talent and greatness is squelched at work, I want to do my part to create inspiring, uplifting work and classroom settings.

Part of my understanding of inspiriting leadership is staying out of the way so creativity and brilliance can shine. I believe that in working with students and colleagues our role is to facilitate and offer structure (but not too much); whether we are teaching or supervising, we are leading. I believe we are partners along one another's journeys of growth and discovery. As an interim dean of students, I was a member of a team planning a diversity retreat. A well-known prospective keynote speaker was disrespectful to the administrative assistant arranging her travel itinerary. Through consultation among the planning team members, we decided to cancel the speaker. I asked the assistant to consider telling the speaker herself, so she could explain the ways in which the speaker's manner was inconsistent with our organizational civility values. She made the call and later said she was relieved by the opportunity to articulate her displeasure with the way she had been treated. This memory continues to remind me that leadership occasions energize others. I am moved by a student of Suheil Bushrui, a professor and interfaith scholar, who expressed his inspiriting, energizing leadership: "We caught his fire, so we gave it back to him" (S. Bushrui, personal communication, 2003).

Catching one another's fire can compensate for losses inherent in learning, which often requires the specific loss of a previous self, a self innocent of knowledge and insight. As a survivor, I have compassion for loss of self. Perry (1978) wrote about the need for teachers to acknowledge loss in the essay "Sharing in the Costs of Growth." A student spoke to the important difference this acknowledgement made in her increased courage and eagerness to learn: "Because he knew what I'd lost, I could stay with what I'd seen" (p. 271). Sometimes to encourage students I say to them:

> Everyone has a journey. Find yours and do not let anyone allow you to believe you are less. We all have a complex back-story; indeed, sometimes we are still discovering our own back story. Do not worry about grades, test scores, or money. You have a college degree; you are going to be fine. Focus instead on these things: be good to people, be respectful, challenge yourself, learn forever, and give of yourself to others and to communities and organizations. Choose to inspire rather than control. Above all, do not yield to shame. Everyone has shame; it is part of the human experience. But do not allow shame to make you be less of yourself in the world. We need you in all your humanness.

As I walk with students and colleagues, I try to remind myself that leadership entails creating environments of inspiration so we all become more human. I try for fierce compassion. In my core and out of my identity, I believe in inspiriting leadership.

REFERENCE

Perry, W. G. (1978). Sharing in the costs of growth. In C. A. Parker (Ed.), *Encouraging development in college students* (pp. 267–273). Minneapolis, MN: University of Minnesota Press.

Exploring Leadership From a Multicultural Background
Hawaiian, Chinese, and White Origins

Eleanor Radius

Eleanor Radius has served as leader and manager at Intel Corporation, as director of organizational learning at Central New Mexico Community College, and in various leadership roles in education. She currently works in research, deployment, and accountability for the Albuquerque Public School District where she collaborates to drive school improvement and turnaround efforts.

O n May 1, 1975, I had the honor of being crowned May Day queen at my elementary school in Honolulu, Hawai`i. May Day is the time of year that Hawaiians celebrate their culture by stringing together fresh flowers into beautiful leis. I remember the excitement and honor of being crowned queen. But at the young age of 7, I was unaware that Hawai`i was the only place where this might happen for me. The island's mix of people and cultures that blended together was all I knew at the time. I never really questioned how someone who looked like me could have been chosen as May Day queen. As the old adage states, beauty is in the eye of the beholder. I realized many years later that for me to be crowned as queen was unique to how I was viewed by the people of Hawai`i. After I left the island, the dominant culture of society imprinted on me that beauty came in the form of blond hair, blue eyes, and fair skin, characteristics of most of my classmates in New England. Hawai`i was the one place where the May Day queen could have long, dark-brown hair, golden skin, and almond-shaped eyes.

A MELTING POT OF CULTURES

Hawai`i is a unique place in that there is no ethnic majority group; instead, the population is made up of several groups of ethnic minorities. The state consists of a network of islands inhabited predominantly by Japanese, Filipino, Caucasian, Chinese, Vietnamese, Korean, Kanaka Maoli (full-blooded Hawaiians), and other Polynesian peoples. Each culture influences the overall culture of the island. About a quarter of the population today is mixed race or people having a blend of two or more ethnicities. Hawai`i is the U.S. state with the largest percentage of Asian people (39%), who function as the power majority. The different Asian races living in Hawai`i are relatively accepting of one another. For example, the Japanese get along with the Chinese and sometimes even marry one another. This type of union might be unheard of in Japan or China where races can harbor distinctions of superiority or prejudice against one another. Somehow in my home state of Hawai`i, Asian races and other ethnic groups are able to coexist. My early years were spent immersed in this melting pot of cultures. My father came from a Chinese immigrant family and my mother's family was heavily grounded in the values and beliefs of White Anglo-Saxon Protestants. My Chinese and Anglo ancestry earned me the label of *hoppa haoli*, which translates as half White, a term that carries a slightly derogatory connotation in Hawai`i.

My mother made sure we spoke proper English; hence, we were forbidden to speak in the island's slang, known as *pidgin*. No matter how strong her desire for us to encompass predominantly her culture, we still picked up the island's shared values and beliefs that blended into our family's culture. While the Asian and White cultures were the strongest influences for me, Hawaiian culture also influenced my identity formation and played a role in the development of my leadership qualities. In examining the blend of these three cultures—Chinese, Anglo, and Hawaiian—I conducted a self-exploration of my identity and the role it plays in my leadership. This self-awareness helped me better understand qualities of leadership I role model as an educational leader. As a part of my leadership practice, I continue to recognize my strengths and weaknesses. Three leadership values originating from my multicultural identity are: excellence, education and learning, and the Aloha Spirit.

EXCELLENCE

A strong sense of excellence was a value imprinted on me at a very young age. I remember distinctly high expectations from my mother and father, although they came from very different backgrounds. The message from my parents was clear: Do not settle for average or standard and always do your best. Both the Chinese and Anglo cultures reinforce an extremely strong work ethic that encompasses striving for excellence. This value is also part of Hawaiian culture and reinforced both in school and home. In Japanese school I learned about the concept of *kaizen,* or the belief that personal excellence is achieved by looking at and improving one thing daily. It is incremental change combined with a value of patience. This is how I learned to write in Japanese by practicing and making improvements each day. *Ke kela* is Hawaiian for excellence. The elders of Hawai`i choose to live by example and work toward bestowing excellence along with other Hawaiian values upon children. Excellence is a strong value on the island of Hawai`i, as it comes from several of the cultures blended together: the indigenous Hawaiian, Asian, and Anglo cultures.

In spring of 2006, I was recognized with Intel's Operations Excellence Award, which is given annually to four operations managers. Out of 80 front-line managers, I was nominated and received this award. It was an honor to know that my peers, engineers, and employees acknowledged and recognized my leadership skills.

The leadership behaviors that earned me this award were my uncompromising dedication to excellence, my unwillingness to accept average performance or rely on average solutions, and my innate desire to improve business processes. I led my team to envision and strive for improvements even if they caused uncomfortable change or challenged the status quo. I prioritized continuing to learn about manufacturing science, streamlining processes, and reducing waste. While others resisted change, I embraced the chance to spend time grappling with both theory and practice to understand the factory as a whole system. Based on my knowledge of manufacturing science, I knew we had to shift from an extremely tactical focus and learn how to balance it with strategic planning. To begin this work, we moved away from intrashift competition and figured out new ways to work together as a comprehensive team. This was easier to espouse than to execute, because each shift functioned as a competitor with a tendency to blame the others. I took the lead and began to share a vision of our area functioning as a whole, unified team.

EDUCATION AND LEARNING

For elementary school, I was fortunate to attend St. Andrew's Priory in Honolulu, Hawai`i. The school was founded in 1867 by Queen Emma Kaleleonalani, the wife of King Kamehameha IV. In the 1800s, it was revolutionary to create a school for young girls to gain a formal education.

The deep value of education and learning was a large part of the culture at school and at home. Education and learning were not viewed as activities that only occurred within the confines of a school building; instead, it was a life-long process not bound to a specific time or place. Life was seen as a compilation of experiences in which you learned about yourself and the world around you. The strongest imprint of education and learning for me came from Asian and Anglo cultures. In these cultures, getting a good education was integral to doing your part as a member of the greater society. It was given the utmost importance and became part of my identity as a young, Eurasian girl. Throughout my life, this strong value of continuous learning has helped me to develop my leadership practice.

As my father was fluent in Chinese, English, and German, I was frequently exposed to conversations in different languages, which influenced my love of learning new languages. In grade school, I attended Japanese school where I learned how to speak and write the language. In middle and high school, I studied French and Latin. During college, I decided to study abroad in Italy, and while living in Florence, I became fluent in Italian.

My year abroad in Europe was filled with learning about the early Renaissance, art history, Italian opera, as well as time to reflect on my culture, my country, and how Americans are viewed in other parts of the world. When you leave your homeland and live abroad it provides you with an experience that is optimal for gaining self-awareness. Learning a new language and culture provides you with new reference points. Being able to compare two cultures seems to make each one a little clearer. I used this time to explore my culture and decide how I wanted to be viewed in this world as I encountered people from other cultures. My desire to do this type of reflection was part of a strong value instilled in me through the blended cultures of Hawai`i, and I leveraged this value to develop my leadership.

My belief is that to be a transformational leader, I must continue to develop self-awareness, while learning from both successes and challenges. Over the years while working in business, government, and education, I learned that if a plan fails, it is best to analyze it to discover what went wrong and design solutions that avoid the same failure in the future. Rather than blaming others, which tends to be prevalent in workplace cultures across the United States, one can learn from mishaps through reflection and avoid repeating them. Instead of being destroyed by failure and never attempting anything new, I believe it is a leader's ability to learn and devise new ways to excel that further develops his or her leadership. This value is a strong part of who I am and has followed me into the field of education. I believe that to be a good leader, one must be a good teacher. And to be a good teacher, one must be a good learner. Leadership and learning go hand in hand.

ALOHA SPIRIT

For those who have not visited Hawai`i, it is more than a tourist destination where vacationers go to get a respite from the "rat race." While the island is an alluring sight to take in, to only revel in the physical beauty of its beaches, mountains, waterfalls, and sunsets would be a shame for these alone do not comprise the totality of its beauty. Oahu's inner beauty is present for the taking, but it is humble and sometimes overlooked. If you are willing and able to recognize its deep sense of spirit, you will absorb the indescribable feeling as it washes over you. The people of Hawai`i live there because of the deep sense of Aloha Spirit that permeates the islands. The Aloha Spirit encompasses the following values: *akahai*—kindness, expressed with tenderness; *lokahai*—unity, expressed with harmony; *'olu 'olu*—agreeableness, expressed with pleasantness; *ha 'aha 'a*—humility, expressed with modesty; and *ahonui*—patience, expressed with perseverance. It is said that people of Hawaiian blood, heart, and spirit who grew up in the island's splendor are immersed in *Aloha*. The belief is that Aloha Spirit rubs off on you after you swim in the surrounding *moana* (ocean), walk the *'aina* (land), eat the delicious foods, and inhale the sweet scents of exotic flowers, while living the local culture. As a native, Aloha Spirit was imprinted on me and is a part of my epistemology.

The Aloha Spirit is a philosophy shared as a gift from native Hawaiian people. It can be described as the coordination of mind and heart. It encompasses a deep sense of self allowing one to live with kindness, in balance with nature and others. This spirit has always allowed me to view family and community in a somewhat nontraditional way, connecting with people regardless of biological relationship. My view is diametrically opposed to the concept of American individualism. The way I connected it to my Anglo culture was through the deep sense of civic duty, to do your part to help society as a whole.

The Aloha Spirit has served me well as a manager and leader both within business and education. It helps me to look holistically at individuals and organizations. It is my belief that you cannot understand part of a person or system without understanding the whole. As a leader, I strive to engage people's whole selves, which includes their mind, body, and spirit. I have learned that this type of engagement can make work feel more fulfilling. I believe true rewards and fulfillment in life come when we can awaken peoples' sense of self and purpose, thus enabling them to do meaningful work that utilizes and capitalizes on their strengths.

Aloha Spirit is about unity, recognizing that we are all one and need to work together for collective good as opposed to battling against one another. Confucianism espouses that between two contending individuals there is truth on both sides. As a leader, I have seen many lengthy workplace battles, and this value helps me to gain perspectives of both sides. When having to make difficult decisions for a large group, I rely on this value to gain others' perspectives and to learn what motivates their thoughts and feelings, their hopes and fears. This helps me explain where my decision comes from and why it had to be made, in a manner that acknowledges their position.

IDENTITY AS AN EDUCATIONAL LEADER

The three values of excellence, education and learning, and Aloha Spirit form my identity and are integrated in my practice as an educational leader. The rich blend of cultures that influenced my identity formation is what defines me as multicultural. After two decades in the workforce, I have matured and I am more willing to bring my whole self into leadership. While this now seems natural to me, bringing nontraditional beliefs into the workplace can sometimes prevent one from upwardly mobile success in an organization. My belief is similar to that of Margaret Wheatley (2006) who posited that as humans we pay a great deal of attention to differences that seem to divide us, but our survival is dependent on our ability to learn how to participate in a web of relationships. Society can be viewed as a living system, and it is important to me to be authentic in these relationships even when not viewed favorably. Confucianism and Taoism are less concerned with finding the "truth" as opposed to finding the Tao—the way—to live in the world. These strong values that formed my identity also influenced greatly how I choose to live and lead in our world.

In my work experience within both the private and public sectors, I witness a phenomenon that sometimes occurs to leaders. When excessive pressure is exerted on leaders, they may naturally drop into survival mode. While in this mode others may perceive their behaviors as erratic, extreme, and noncompliant, which inevitably singles them out, and the larger population either pressures them out of their position or they opt out of the organization over time. As a leader, it is important to be self-aware—to understand your leadership values, where they originate from, and how they fit within the greater culture of the organization. Ideally, if you have done this type of reflection, when you encounter a situation in which your values clash with those held by others, you will be able to recognize it and avoid getting bogged down in lengthy, emotional showdowns that fester into win-lose power struggles. While you will not be able to avoid all emotional drains in the workplace, being aware of your values and recognizing when there is conflict can allow you to correct the course before disaster.

TRANSFORMING EDUCATION

As an educational leader, I strive to create a culture of learning, develop aligned systems of accountability, create outcomes-based models, enable instructional leadership to review and analyze data, and create continuous school improvement all in a manner that bolsters student learning outcomes. I believe in the importance of empowering leadership at all levels and spending time to develop leadership. I share my vision of everyone learning, teaching, and leading regardless of title or position. If we build a culture of life-long learning with teachers and instructional leaders who are reflective practitioners, I believe we can begin to transform education in our communities. I strive to ensure that teachers view themselves as leaders and empower their students to develop strengths and leadership. It is my belief that to be a good leader, one must be a good teacher and help in mentoring and developing the next generation of leaders. To be a good teacher, one must be a good learner who is engaged in self-reflection and personal growth. All of these skills are interconnected and are an integral part of leading people through transformational change. My sense is that to transform education, we must first transform people, who in turn will reform systems and policies that will lead to quality education for all.

REFERENCE

Wheatley, M. J. (2006). *Leadership and the new science: Discovering order in a chaotic world*. San Francisco, CA: Berrett-Koehler.

Shifting Between Worlds
Carrying Home on My Back

Alex Gonzalez

Alex Gonzalez served as associate director of scholarships, director of enrollment development, and is currently university registrar at The University of New Mexico. He was a member of many committees and task forces that addressed enrollment management, retention, graduation, and diversity. He also held a variety of leadership roles within NASPA–Student Affairs Administrators in Higher Education.

Because I, a Mestiza, continually walk out of one culture and into another, because I am in all cultures at the same time, alma entre dos mundos, tres, cuatro, me zumba la cabeza con lo contradictorio. Estoy norteada por todas las voces que me hablan simultaneamente ... a soul between two worlds, three, four. My head buzzes with the contradictory; I am disoriented by all the voices that talk to me simultaneously. (Anzaldúa, 2012, p. 99)

As a first-generation American Hispanic male, huge expectations were placed on me: do well in school, be the first in my family to attend college, and have a good job that goes beyond living paycheck to paycheck. I always felt these expectations were as if I was carrying a sack of onions on my back. I was constantly reminded by my family about great things I was expected to accomplish. My early life was not about enjoying the fruits of being a child but, rather, centered on reaching my dreams—and I was encouraged to dream big. But this was not the only sack of onions I was carrying on my back. My cultural upbringing living on the Texas–New Mexico–Mexico border brought strong beliefs in Catholicism, bilingualism, and Mexican customs and traditions. Being part of two cultures simultaneously made me feel like an alien in a dominant culture. I constantly struggled to understand who I was and how I fit into both cultures.

WALKING BETWEEN WORLDS

An imaginary line exists between two countries, stretching from the state of Texas to the edges of California. It divides a land into two parts, the United States and Mexico. These two countries are so close and yet very distinct, one a powerful nation and the other a third-world country. I spent 18 years jumping from one side to the other. I was born in El Paso, Texas, but raised in a small community in New Mexico, Sunland Park, minutes away from the Mexican border. My father came to the United States from Mexico as a young child when my grandparents decided to search for better opportunities. Both my father and mother graduated from high school but never attended college. My father was drafted during the Vietnam War and spent two years of his life in a foreign country. My mother was born in the United States from Mexican parents. Both my parents had blue-collar jobs and struggled to make ends meet for my brothers and me.

I distinctly remember a time while in the fifth grade having lunch with some friends and getting teased for being named Alexander. I never really liked my name but did not have a choice. As I moved onto junior high school, the teasing continued. Many students would ask me why my name was Alexander and not Alejandro. Knowing my background, the students were perplexed as to why I would be given an Anglo-American name. I never knew how to respond to them. My heritage was extremely important to me, and I was just as confused and started asking "Why?"

One day I built up the courage to ask my mother about my name. She said that my name was given to me in its form to help me have an easier life in the United States. She informed me of the many obstacles she and my father had to face while growing up with Spanish names. It was not easy to be of Mexican heritage growing up in times of discrimination and racism. While I understood their reasoning, I still was not satisfied. I felt that my Anglo name was denying me my heritage. I am extremely proud of who I am and where I come from, yet I struggled with how I fit into both cultures. To this day, I still get teased about my name.

FACING OBSTACLES, CREATING OPPORTUNITIES

The first obstacle I encountered in elementary school was learning how to speak English. Because my parents both worked, my grandparents raised my twin brother and me. They did not speak English, so my first language was Spanish. I worked extremely hard to pick up the English language and become fluent. I was afraid my Spanish accent would come forward when I spoke English. I practiced every day and it took me several years for my speech to lose the Spanish accent. I finally felt comfortable living in the dominant Anglo culture.

In order to be successful and attend college I felt I needed to be involved in high school clubs or organizations. For the most part, the Anglo students were the ones heavily involved in extracurricular activities even though the majority of the student body was Hispanic. I started hanging out with them and joined them for club meetings. I was entering a new identity and leaving my Mejicano behind. I really felt like I needed to do this to move forward and have a chance to attend college. I joined student government, the key club, and multiple honor societies. Joining these clubs gave me the opportunity to interact with a different type of student, a more affluent group of students. Being part of this new group of friends made me feel like a different person. I started feeling part of the dominant culture. I had broken through the wall that previously kept me apart.

When I was in high school, I always worried about my grades and was reminded about having a better life than my parents. I knew I wanted to go to college and I would be alone in this endeavor. My parents did not know anything about college and my high school counselor was too concerned with Anglo students and rarely helped me with the college application process. I spent 18 years living on the border and felt I needed to move away and experience a new location. During my senior year in high school, I met a recruiter from The University of New Mexico (UNM), and I started talking to her about my interest in attending UNM. She was excited to hear that and told me, "We need more Hispanic students at UNM, you would be a great addition to our school." I felt happy, someone wanted me. I convinced my brother to join me in this new adventure, and we both applied and were accepted to UNM. While we were both awarded scholarships to pay for our tuition, my parents, although excited for us, were unsure as to how they were going to pay for the rest of the expenses. They decided to use money our maternal grandmother left for us when she passed away.

I can still remember the day we moved into the residence hall as if it happened yesterday. My parents gave us a blessing, asking God to care for us. My mother started crying; her boys were leaving home and moving far away to attend college. I assured her things were going to be okay and we would call home every day. It was a very emotional farewell. We moved into the residence hall wing assigned to students who received scholarships. As my brother and I started to walk down the hall, we noticed we were the only two Hispanic students living in that wing. All the rest of the students were Anglo with the exception of one Native American student. I made friends with Anglo students in high school and thought this should not be a problem.

As the semester began, I would say hello to everyone as I walked down the hall but noticed none of them acknowledged me. I did not think much of this but then they started closing their doors as I walked toward my room. We were stunned by the lack of communication and unfriendliness from these students. Toward the middle of the semester, I overheard a couple of students say that my brother and I needed to stop speaking Spanish and speak English because we live in America. We decided to inform the resident advisor of the things I heard, and he told us to forget about it and not waste his time with petty things. Several weeks later as I walked back to my room after class, I noticed someone had cracked eggs on our door, the eggs still dripping down and eggshells on the floor. This infuriated me and I stormed to the resident advisor's room to complain. While he told me he thought it was a prank and he would get housekeeping to clean up the mess, I was not convinced that it was a joke.

Second semester came around and I noticed the students' behavior had not changed. I kept hearing them call my brother and me "wetbacks." One afternoon, I walked back to my room after class and noticed that the door, which should have been locked, was open. As I walked into the room I noticed water had been spilled all over our room, on our beds, our desks, our clothes, and TV. A note was taped to our TV that said, "Go back to where you came from, wetbacks." That day I felt like I was raped; everything I believed in and worked hard to achieve was taken away from me. We reported the incident to the resident advisor. No actions were ever taken, however, as the school could not pinpoint which student or students had done this. My brother and I felt betrayed by the system, and we decided to move out and move into an apartment off campus. This was the most difficult situation I had to face in being part of two different worlds. After this experience, however, I did not want to be part of the dominant culture any longer. All I wanted was my family.

Upon graduation, I originally intended to go to The University of Iowa for law school. At the same time, however, my mother was diagnosed with terminal cancer, and I felt I needed to stay close to home and be there for her and my family. I declined admission to law school and decided to look for a job on campus. I was lucky enough to get a job with the Scholarship Office. I was told I received this job because of my bilingual skills as no one in the office spoke Spanish. For once I felt that my heritage was useful in my life. The director retired within three years, and I was the next person in line to take over the leadership of the office. I was not hired as director of the office, confirming that my struggle to be part of two worlds would still follow me into my professional life. I was informed by the hiring officer that I still had to prove myself, and as Hispanics we need to work double the amount an Anglo person works. These comments sparked a flame inside me that started my work with social justice. The day I was denied the position, I decided I would go on to work extremely hard to help other Hispanics not be deprived of the opportunities they deserve. I also decided that would be the last day I would accept no for an answer. I worked hard for five years to prove that I can run an important office on campus, and I started creating relationships with Anglo male administrators. They noticed my work and dedication to the job, and I was finally promoted to associate director and then to my current role as registrar. I am thankful my experiences living on the border have allowed me to navigate through different worlds that helped me get to where I am today.

I remained in the higher education profession and decided that this is where I belong. I used my childhood experiences, discrimination, and racism as positive experiences. Those experiences allowed me to grow and mature into the person I am today. I still get teased once in a while about my name, Alexander, but I have learned to accept the things my parents did to better my ability to be successful in a dominant Anglo culture. From these painful experiences I want to protect students from being subjected to those feelings of loss, rape, and denial. Being denied a promotion and being told I was not qualified fueled my interest to fight for social justice. While we live in a world that is more understanding and welcoming of many different cultures, there is still much work that needs to be done. I am not afraid to speak up when needed and continue to use that ability to promote an agenda of justice and help the voiceless be heard. I value and treasure who I am and where I come from, a male born on the border who sacrificed many things to be where I am today, a Mexican American who is proud to be part of and embraces both worlds I live in, and an educator who helps students of all backgrounds attain their dreams of getting a college education.

CARRYING HOME ON MY BACK

As I consider the implications of this cultural aspect of myself on my leadership, I am reminded of Anzaldúa. She shared similar experiences while growing up on the border. "Yet in leaving home I did not lose touch with my origins because lo mexicano is in my system. I am a turtle, wherever I go I carry 'home' on my back" (Anzaldúa, 2012, p. 43). Her work helped me understand where I came from and how to navigate between two worlds. Like Anzaldúa, I will always carry home with me and home will never be forgotten.

There are three central elements I identify in my cultured self that I apply to my leadership and professional life. These elements are an ability to navigate through various worlds at once, a strong urge to protect, and the need to speak up.

The first element, the ability to navigate through various worlds at once, has been a strong focus in my life. For many years I struggled to live in two worlds and found a balance. Being born on the border brought strong Mexican beliefs and customs that define who I am. I could not ignore the fact that I also lived in a dominant Anglo country that at times conflicted with my beliefs and ways of doing things. I wanted to feel welcomed in the dominant culture but did not want to lose my Mexican identity, language, and customs. It is a struggle that has lasted for many years. Having to juggle two worlds could have turned out to be a limitation in my leadership abilities, but I realized I needed to use it as strength because navigating through academe is not an easy task.

Emotional, mental, and physical pain have been with me throughout my life. Whether it was working in the fields during hot summers or being called wetback and having my belongings drenched in water, all of these experiences taught me perseverance. Along with perseverance, these realities gave me a strong urge to protect others from harm, from denial, and from having to endure pain. I want to protect individuals from ever having to go through similar painful experiences. I constantly work to protect Hispanic students from being placed in uncomfortable situations.

My Hispanic culture also kept me from speaking up. I was constantly told to keep still and quiet anytime we visited friends or relatives. If I spoke up, my mother would pinch me. In my family we were to remain quiet and not move as visitors. So I went through my first 18 years being quiet and not speaking up. It was hard for me to speak up in class because of this early conditioning. When I came to college, I learned I needed to speak up if I wanted to be heard. I had to report the residence hall incidents; I had to speak to my professors if I was having difficulty understanding in class; and I had to speak up if I wanted to make friends. It took a lot of work for me to become comfortable speaking up. We need to be confident in ourselves, speak our minds, and be active participants.

Learning to speak up gave me the self-confidence I lacked while growing up in two worlds. Not because I was afraid but because I was taught to be silent. This self-confidence assisted me in accomplishing my goals, which included attaining a college education (undergraduate and graduate), working in a college setting, and moving up the ranks of administration toward a vice president position. I now feel comfortable speaking with and serving a diverse group of people. I am able to maximize my strengths by sharing my experiences and serving as an inspirational speaker. I decided to use my experiences to fight for social justice

I was born in two cultures and destined to navigate through various worlds at once. It has been a long road, but I learned many techniques to go from one world to another and still remain the same person in both worlds. Some goals for my continued journey in learning are to continue to be open-minded toward different people and backgrounds, to use my ability to speak up when necessary, and to be less protective. We must value diversity, and I hope I can be an inspiration to others as Anzaldúa inspired me to navigate through various worlds all at once.

References

Anzaldúa, G. (2012). *Borderlands, la frontera: The new Mestiza* (4th ed.). San Francisco, CA: Aunt Lute Books.

Windows, Cages, and Student Affairs
Lessons Learned About Fitting In and Breaking Out

Marisa Rivera

Marisa Rivera, PhD, is a lecturer and director of the Community College Leadership Program at Iowa State University. Her previous positions include associate dean of student affairs at Mount Mary College, adjunct faculty and assistant to the vice president for student affairs/director of special projects at Marquette University, and interim dean of students at Grand View University. She served as national coordinator for the Minority Undergraduate Fellows Program (now the NASPA Undergraduate Fellows Program).

I recently had the opportunity to return to the Williamsburg housing projects in Brooklyn, New York, where I lived until the age of 19. As I focused the camera to take a picture of what once was my bedroom window, a flurry of memories came rushing back. I could see the young girl resting her arms on the soft pillow and tears trickling down her cheeks as she spoke to God, pleading with Him to show her a way out. Back then my life was filled with sexual and physical abuse, self-mutilation, and an occasional bout with alcohol and valium. While there were times I laid in bed wanting to die, there was another part of me that fought to live and believed there was a world to conquer outside of Brooklyn.

Whether consciously or not, those experiences provided me with the tools necessary to

209

survive both academic and professional challenges and to be an effective leader and mentor. Most important, I am able to empathize with the students I serve while providing a little tough love when needed. The bottom line for me is to ensure that when a student leaves my office he or she never feels alone or unimportant.

CLASH OF IDENTITIES: CAN'T I BE PUERTO RICAN AND AMERICAN?

As a young girl, my family life was filled with contradictions, yet for Puerto Ricans there is usually one constant: religion. To the neighbors and congregation, we were pillars of our community and the epitome of a happy Puerto Rican family. However, pillars can have cracks in their foundation. Few people knew of my father's drunken rages or that my mother beat me. My mother was known as one of the best seamstresses in the Williamsburg community, and my father worked for an electronics company in New Jersey. As a result, we were financially secure for the 1970s and able to return to Puerto Rico at least once a year. I attended Catholic school, and we were first in our building to own a color television.

I recall staring out the window on Sunday afternoons watching my brother and his friends play whiffle ball in the courtyard. My mother always found a reason to keep me in the house when I was not in school or with family. My only view of the outside world was from my bedroom window. When I asked to join him, her response was always the same: It is inappropriate for young ladies to be outside unchaperoned.

I have always been proud to be Puerto Rican. However, the double standards between men and women espoused by family seemed unjust even to a 13 year old. When I pointed them out, my mother would respond by saying, *"Tu no entiendes como son las cosas para las mujeres!"* ("You don't understand how things are for women!") She would go on to say she was protecting *"el honor de la familia"* ("family honor"). My reply was always the same: Puerto Rican rules are one-sided; they favor men and oppress women.

At age 13, I did not understand civil rights, the women's movement, or social justice. However, the inequities between Puerto Rican women and men were obvious. Pointing out the inequities to my mother repeatedly led to being punished and served to tighten her hold on me because I was becoming *"una Americana"* ("Americanized"). She did not seem to understand the Americanization process began the day we all left Puerto Rico in 1961 and stepped off the plane at JFK International Airport. Her fear of my Americanization (the loss of Puerto Rican culture and values) was exacerbated whenever inequities between men and women were part of our conversations. This led to further tightening of the reigns and her decision that English was never to be spoken in our home. *"El ingles se deja para la escuela o la calle"* ("English is spoken in school or on the street"). Those experiences frame the ferocity and passion with which I take on issues of oppression and gender equity. More important, as an adult, I now have a greater understanding of the fear that drove my mother. New York was a land of wonderful opportunity for our family and it came with a high cost: The loss of our Puerto Ricaness, which was out of her control.

Do Not Judge a Book by its Cover

Growing up Puerto Rican in New York City I never thought about my fair complexion or hazel eyes. All I knew was that I was born in Puerto Rico, grew up in New York, and was accepted by my community of neighbors, family, and friends. The color of my skin was never fodder for conversation. When my children and I moved to the Midwest in 1990, we instantly became a subject of fascination exacerbated by my fluency in Spanish. Initially, I was offended and angry, wondering if I had made a mistake leaving the comforts of familiar surroundings. The people in my new community were confused by what they saw—I did not fit the images presented on television. Additionally, there were instances where my citizenship came into question: "Do you have a green card?" "Where did you learn to speak English so well?" Although frustrating, I soon realized my ignorance about life outside my corner of New York. After some soul searching, I came to understand the need to become a student of my new living environment (e.g., by adjusting to new vernacular—sucker and bubbler instead of lollypop and water fountain) and to set aside my biases (e.g., family values were just as strong for Midwesterners as they were for me). Although my adjustment to the Midwest was difficult, I learned a critical lesson that I carry with me still today: If I want to be respected as a thoughtful leader and accepted for who I am and what I bring to the conversation, I must look within myself and remember that a book cannot always be judged by its cover.

LIFE AND LEADERSHIP: IT IS ALL ABOUT RISK

Tenacity and persistence is what it takes to achieve your dreams. This is what I tell my students. It is not always about who is the smartest as much as it is about wanting something so much that you are willing to take risks and make sacrifices. In my case, I married at the age of 19 in order to leave home. While marriage created a different set of problems, I knew for a variety of reasons it would end in divorce and I would be free. Ten years and two children later, I filed for divorce, returned to school, and never looked back. The price of freedom was steep. It caused a tremendous amount of family drama, but I did not care. Divorcing my husband opened up the world to me in ways I never imagined.

The turning point in my life was the decision to return to school after dropping out 15 years earlier with a .75 grade point average. My original plan had been to pursue a two-year secretarial degree that would prepare me for a position as a school secretary with summers off. However, as I began to interact with university leaders, faculty, staff, and students, my self-image changed. I saw myself as a smart woman worthy of being in school. The first hint of this came after my first exam. It was a computer science test. I did not know how to study for it, but thankfully I had been invited into a study group. I earned 81%. Receiving that grade as well as the students in my study group motivated me to push myself harder, and I was determined to score in the 90s on the next test (which I did).

The people I met as a student were caring toward me and my children. They encouraged me to become involved in extracurricular activities, and although I felt I had nothing to offer, they were insistent. I was nervous and scared but agreed to become the student representative for faculty senate. The scent of power emanated throughout the boardroom, and the abundance of three piece suits indicated these people meant business. It was a surreal experience. It reinforced how sheltered I was and how little

I knew about life beyond my community. Education nourished my mind and soul and helped me find my voice.

Those experiences gave me a sense of belonging and impressed upon me the role of validation in the development of self-worth. They also played a critical role in my decision to pursue graduate school and gave me courage to leave New York City with two small children, two boxes of clothing, and $125 in my wallet. I look back at the decision to return to school as a rebirth. It is where I learned about the endless possibilities available through education. Today, the core of my leadership is based on the ability to take informed risks that will move the mission of my unit forward, while the foundation from the early days of my education manifests itself in the mentoring, time, and care I provide for students and colleagues.

WHAT EXACTLY DOES IT MEAN WHEN YOU ARE NO LONGER A "FIT?"

As with many who work in student affairs, I fell into my career serendipitously. The experiences I gained as a student worker and with student affairs staff members crystallized what my vocational path would be. My ultimate goal was to become a vice president for student affairs, and for a few years I was on track to meet that goal. However, my abilities and confidence were tested when I was asked to resign from my position because I was no longer a fit with the goals of the institution.

I was devastated. How did I get to this point? I kept replaying my job performance over and over again and wondered if I had been oblivious to the signs or if I chose to ignore them. After some soul searching and counsel from mentors, I came to accept that the warnings were clear, but I intentionally chose to disregard them. Perhaps it was disbelief that anyone thought my work performance was poor or my assumption that a good relationship with students would save my job. On paper, it was the perfect position. Everything I looked for—mission, vision, values—appeared to be a good fit personally and professionally. I believed this position would help me fine-tune my leadership skills, allow me to put more tools in my armamentarium, and propel me to the next level in my career. In my heart, though, I knew I did not belong there.

From the moment I arrived on campus, there were red flags. Within 14 months, 6 staff members were replaced. My first performance review, a 360 evaluation, was filled with negative and derogatory comments, many from colleagues I had not yet met nor collaborated with. Some of the comments questioned my professionalism and others degraded my character, ethnicity, and home town of New York City.

In my years as a professional, I had never felt so lost and alone. I knew I needed someone to talk to, but was ashamed. I wondered how the situation would reflect on me as a woman and as a Latina. I questioned what impact it would have on my future as a leader. Would I be perceived as an inept, emotional female leader? My confidence was waning, and I did not know who I could go to for counsel. In my desire to not appear vulnerable, it never occurred to me that others may have had similar experiences. I was at the end of my rope when I finally shared my concerns with two mentors. Both emphatically suggested I find another job as soon as possible. The writing was on the wall, they told me, as it was plain to see the institution no longer wanted me.

Initially, I heeded their advice and applied to other positions, received invitations to interview, and turned them down. Perhaps I thought if I tried harder everything would work out. Perhaps I saw it as failure and did not want to give up. Perhaps the shame and lack of political savvy impeded my understanding of the situation and hindered my ability to reach out for further counsel. Perhaps it was hubris. Regardless of the reasons, six months later I was unemployed. This experience destroyed me emotionally and led me to question whether I should continue my pursuit of leadership positions and if I belonged in higher education.

FINAL REFLECTIONS

Although I have moved on from those experiences to a fabulous job with a wonderful supervisor, the scars are a reminder of lessons learned. I learned the importance of developing a network of trusted friends and colleagues who care about me, have my best interest at heart, give me a gentle kick in the pants when I need it, and remind me (even if at the time I do not want to hear it) that there is always a silver lining to every bad experience. As a woman of color it is important to find other people of color who can teach you to translate the political landscape of the institution through a "colored" lens. I also learned when the writing on the wall is clear, there is nothing you can do to change it, and you need to move on sooner rather than later. In addition, the word "fit" is fluid; you can be a perfect fit one day and the next day you can be out. I now understand dreams can take a slight detour. As painful as the detour was, it gave me an opportunity to travel on a different path while picking up new skills. I believe I needed a reminder of my resilience and inner strength. As I approach the end of the detour, I am confident in my ability to guide the next generation of leaders with compassion, a sense of humor, and hope for the future.

How Family, Community, and Upbringing Influenced My Leadership Style

Vincent E. Vigil

Vincent E. Vigil is director for the Lesbian, Gay, Bisexual, and Transgender Resource Center at the University of Southern California (USC). He attended Whittier College for business administration and holds a master's degree in postsecondary administration and student affairs and a doctoral degree in education from the USC Rossier School of Education.

A s I reflect on my leadership style, it is important to acknowledge how my family and community shaped not only my character but more important my work ethic and leadership strengths. They taught me to be grateful for work opportunities and value every leadership responsibly. In my family, when someone complains about his or her job, a typical response is "Be grateful you have a job!" This candid response symbolizes my current work mentality because I remain grateful for every work position. No matter the job, the tasks, or the leadership responsibilities required, achieving success remains a major priority in my life.

MY EDUCATION AND WORK ETHIC

To attain a college degree was my first accomplished goal in life—I was the first in my family to graduate from college. This focus on education began my first day in prekindergarten and continued to when I completed my dissertation for my doctoral program. The importance of education was instilled through my community and family members; they stressed how education was the path for a better life. My determination combined with the importance of education was prominent as a teenager because work and education became a means to escape a dysfunctional life and make a better future for myself. As a result, I valued every job experience, from my work as a salesperson at the local mall when I was a teenager to graduate internships in my higher education program and even in my current position. I value every educational experience, and I continue to value every work and leadership experience. Every experience serves as a chapter in an encyclopedia I can refer to in future leadership roles.

LEARNING SHAPED MY VISION

It is important for leaders to focus on learning—learning that takes place through personal experiences and learning that occurs through organizational membership. In undergraduate business courses, I read Peter F. Senge (1990) and his concepts of learning organizations. His work taught me organizations can succeed and maintain a competitive advantage if they encourage learning. Methods to create a learning organization include professional development opportunities such as conferences, benchmarking studies, comparison studies, and so forth, yet leaders need to value their members' opinions and ideas. As a leader, these teachings have stayed with me throughout my career because I acknowledge that in order to stimulate innovation and growth in my organization, I must rely on its members. For example, student staff members had an idea for a first-year-experience program and outreach pamphlet for prospective students and together we refined these ideas, aligned them with a shared vision of the organization, and made them signature programs for the department. I never discourage ideas from organization members; if they are passionate and have an execution plan, I will assist to make the idea a reality. True accomplishment for a leader is seeing that members have learned something new and facilitated learning within the organization.

MY FAMILY'S ASPIRATIONS

Throughout my upbringing, I was taught to transform positive and negative life experiences—good times, bad times, and even ugly times—into valuable teachable moments in life that help maintain my focus. Looking back as an only child, from a single mother, and being raised in a working-class family, it is clear my upbringing taught me to persevere over challenges and be grateful my life was not as bad as that of my parents or grandparents. Although, my life was not privileged, it provided me more opportunities than family members before me. I realized this as my family expressed their hopes and dreams for me, to have a better life than they had. I felt an unspoken pressure to succeed and take advantage of all opportunities. As a leader, this morphed into ambition and confidence to succeed because I represented not only myself but also the hopes and dreams of my family.

An asset from my upbringing was learning how to manage a sparse budget. Growing up, my mom raised me on a strict budget. She knew how to stretch a dollar, often making crucial sacrifices on necessary items such as deciding whether to buy groceries or put gas in the car or even trying to muster enough funds to pay our electricity bill. To make harsh financial choices became my reality. Rather than being resentful, I learned how to spend money wisely, which is an exploitable leadership talent. This skill has benefited me when creating new programs and services with a limited budget. I know how to stretch my department's budget to produce valuable outcomes utilizing hard work and limited funds. A lack of funding will never get in the way of my goals or visions and, as a result, I have been able to create and maintain nationally acclaimed programs and services for an increasing student population without major budget increases.

LEARNING BUDGET MANAGEMENT FROM FINANCIAL HARDSHIPS

When I was a little boy, I dusted my grandmother's furniture for quarters. My grandmother was a waitress, and she would often have a jar of quarters from her tips. Later when I was about 15 years old, I continued cleaning tables, chairs, and floors at my elementary school through a city-sponsored summer youth program. I knew cleaning up after people was not my career ambition, but these jobs unconsciously formulated my strong work ethic and taught me that I must follow through on my commitments. It was not until junior high school that this work ethic became extremely beneficial as I focused on gaining acceptance into college, and it has remained a standard throughout my career. I do the task at hand regardless of how remedial it seems. If I am committed, the task will be completed.

PROBLEM-SOLVING TECHNIQUES

I strive to maintain a strong work ethic and approach each situation as a challenge to utilize my problem-solving techniques and an opportunity to showcase my leadership abilities. For example, my current leadership position is a position I created for myself. When I entered my institution for graduate studies, I noticed that lesbian, gay, bisexual, and transgender (LGBT) students lacked appropriate resources to succeed. I created graduate research projects detailing discrepancies and developed intervention strategies for LGBT inclusion on campus, which later led to the overall need for an LGBT department with a full-time director. My research, personal experiences, and determination proved that I could create and establish a new department. However, to create a new department was not an easy task. I applied my life experiences to this task and utilized skills I learned from my upbringing to make certain the department became a recognized national leader in LGBT student services.

MAINTAINING A STRONG WORK ETHIC

At times, I hear comments that my focused personality, strong work ethic, and ability to prioritize work responsibilities above my personal life are attributable to my Mexican American cultural background. Such commentaries are associated with stereotypical views about Mexican workers and how they may work for less, as witnessed when some politicians mention how immigrant Mexican workers are stealing jobs from Americans. I work hard. I stay late at work when needed, work through lunches, attend student programs on the weekends and weeknights, and reply promptly to student e-mails from my smartphone. I do this because I believe it is important to finish my responsibilities promptly. This type of mentality can put a damper on my work-life balance, but I remember how hard my family members had to work to get me to where I am today. I will not let their hard work and my hard work go unnoticed; rather, I will continue to prove to my family, myself, and others that I will succeed with my leadership responsibilities.

While growing up, my cousins, who were about the same age as me, were annoyed or even angry because I was viewed as the "perfect" child by my grandparents, aunts, and uncles. This expectation to be perfect became my goal throughout my adolescent years, and as a result, I maintained my focus on education rather than allowing family hardships to distract me. Some may diagnose me as a workaholic, but I prefer to be called ambitious.

As a teenager, I thought to myself: If I do not do it, then who will? My teenage years are when I took complete control of my entire life because my mother was distant; she was either busy working or voluntarily absent. I handled household chores like laundry, cleaning, preparing meals, and the dreadful lawn work. Days would pass without parental guidance, and I was often left on my own. Eventually, I moved in with my grandparents to escape an emotionally unstable living situation, and from that moment forward my ambition for success intensified. Rather than pity myself or become a wild child, my self-proclaimed independence motivated me to stay focused on the greater goal: college. Looking back, I created an intense focus on work and education to get into college but, more important, to avoid problems at home. This intensive work ethic did not end while in college, nor in graduate school, but became a part of my existence. It was no longer used as a coping mechanism but, rather, as a leadership attribute to complete large tasks on my own while balancing other personal and professional commitments. As illustrated when I was granted the task to create and establish LGBT student services for my entire institution, I attempted to balance these monumental responsibilities as a sole staff member and still maintain a personal work-life balance.

LET THE WORK SPEAK FOR ITSELF

My competitive nature motivates me to work to the best of my abilities to complete my goal. I may be that minority student you often read about in research articles, the person who beat the odds through perseverance and determination to break a cycle of despair to succeed in life through education. Do not base my leadership abilities on how I beat the odds but, rather, base it on the work that I do. It is my work that speaks for itself—nothing else. I prefer to let my work speak for itself and prove what I can accomplish regardless of accolades or recognitions as they will come in time if the work is good enough. My goal as a leader is to put forth the best of myself every day and in everything I do because I embody the hopes and dreams of my family. When I lead, I lead with the thoughts of my family's expectations on my shoulders along with the trials and tribulations of my personal life experiences. Every experience, either from books, research, or past experiences, serves as a building block to my leadership roles. Everyone has personal life experiences that shape them as leaders, and mine have made me the leader I am today.

Negotiating Professional and Personal Identities in Executive Leadership

In this section, leaders discuss the unique challenges of navigating multiple professional roles and personal identities in high-level leadership arenas, including leadership in the presidency, provost, as head of a national association, and as a state secretary of higher education.

Reflections on the Shifting Roles of Intersecting Identities

Gwendolyn Jordan Dungy

Gwendolyn Jordan Dungy is executive director emeritus of NASPA–Student Affairs Administrators in Higher Education. With more than 40 years of experience in higher education, she is a tireless advocate for students and consults regularly for colleges, universities, corporations, and government agencies.

I n 2011, I was en route to a reception at a conference in Georgia for which I was invited as a guest speaker. A group of White high-school-aged boys was coming on to the elevator when I exited. As I walked toward the lobby, one young man said very loudly, "Tanner, she's not ugly; that's just the way they look!" This was followed by guffaws as the elevator door closed, and all in the lobby looked up to see to whom the boys were referring. In stark contrast, at the reception I was repeatedly affirmed by individuals who commented on how nice I looked and how happy and honored all were that I was going to be a speaker.

WHEN AND WHERE I ENTER

As a Black woman, this episode reminds me of the title of Giddings' (1984) book *When and Where I Enter*. As with many others who are cognizant

225

of their multiple identities, which identity is most prominent in the perspective I take depends on when and where I enter. At the same time, I am aware that others will choose the lens through which they see and hear me. Regardless of the literature, wishful thinking, and positive survey results concerning the openness and accepting attitude of today's generation of young people, it seems that no matter when and where I enter, the debilitating and hateful vestiges of racial prejudice continue to be exercised and enjoyed.

Other than identifying as a racial minority—Black, in particular—I identify as heterosexual, married, a woman, a parent, a Christian, a Chicago West Sider, a first-generation college graduate, and from a family of what is euphemistically called the "working poor." Additionally, I chose to work in community colleges as a student affairs professional. All of these aspects of my identity create the physical and psychological composite of an extremely fortunate human being who served for more than 16 years as executive director of NASPA–Student Affairs Administrators in Higher Education, the leading association for the advancement, health, and sustainability of the student affairs profession.

When I am representing NASPA, I deliberately attempt to check my personal identities at the door and take on the role of advocate and spokesperson for student affairs and higher education even though my perspectives, the way I see each situation and encounter, are colored by the wholeness of who I am. I intentionally use the descriptor "colored"; regardless of the identity I may claim, it often seems that the first lens through which others perceive me is race, and gender the second. We often see the terms *race* and *gender* together, and while they are "both forms of discrimination, they are not necessarily evidenced in the same way" (Ladsen-Billings, 1995, p. 67). Unfortunately, women of color—Black women in particular—face both forms of discrimination, regardless of when and where we enter.

I continue to be fascinated by the way socially constructed identities serve as a wedge to segment people even within the same race and among the same gender. For example, among a gathering of well-educated Black heterosexual women who are from Chicago, I am often set apart because I am from the West Side and not the South Side, where the first migration of African Americans from the South settled and gained an economic and social footing before the latter migrants who settled on the West Side. Oprah Winfrey built her television studio on the near-downtown Chicago West Side, an area she described as being inhabited by prostitutes and rats (The Daily OWN, 2011). In my entire professional career, I have not met another Black person who will admit to growing up on the West Side.

As I think back on the impact of socially constructed identities, even as a teen I realized the tax and toll on one's feelings of worth when one is judged by someone else's prejudicial beliefs. For Black women, hair has been one more way to segment and stratify. Because naturally straight hair was the model to achieve, it was impossible for me to use hair as a way to increase my standing or position on the scale of beauty. In my utopian dreams, I would wish that no one would have hair of any kind. I thought the world would be a much less harsh and hard place if we all were born bald and had the option of wearing colorful, decorative skull caps according to one's own sense of style, fashion, and self-image.

INTERSECTION OF SELF AND OTHERS' IDENTITIES

External stimuli and my own perspective about particular identities of others prompt me to highlight one or the other of my many selves. I was in Heathrow Airport in London during the summer of 2011 having a snack when I sensed someone's eyes on me. I looked to my left and noticed a young girl, probably 7 or 8 years old with Scandinavian physical characteristics, had turned completely around in her seat to give me her full and undivided stare. I smiled at her, as I thought she had probably not seen many people with dark skin, and I was a curiosity for her. What might have been my reaction if I had been in the United States and a White child of the same age was staring? Early in my tenure as executive director of NASPA, I was a curiosity for some of the White men who were heads of higher education associations in Washington, D.C. There were few women in such roles, and in meetings, quite the opposite of being stared at, I simply was not seen.

Back when it was rare for women to serve in leadership positions, their ideas and suggestions were often not heard by men, who only heard "irrelevant" questions. I say the men did not hear suggestions and ideas because good ideas from women were invariably repeated by a man and heard by all as if the woman had not voiced the same sentiment. It was apparent that these men were holding women to a standard they did not believe we could achieve:

Conceptualizing research on leadership as a mirror in which women and people of color are expected to be a reflection of White men ultimately marginalizes these two groups because they are viewed as having fewer skills and less power. (Oakes, Joseph, & Muir, 1995, p. 71)

Early in my career, I reacted in two ways when people responded negatively to my race and gender: anger and/or hurt. It took a while before I realized the advantage of low hierarchical expectations. If the expectations are low, a little effort can go a long way to impress.

SHIFTING IDENTITIES

Identities socially constructed, identities acquired over a lifetime of experiences, and identities related to a profession are all integrated and active in how one presents as a professional. In light of the interplay of identities and their impact on how one may be perceived in a professional role, I have found it important to know when and where I allow particular identities to enter.

In representing NASPA, an organization with diverse professional members, I adjust my role depending on the occasion and the expectation. In the larger higher education community, I see the world as my stage in which I play a part in advancing the vision of the association as a worldwide leader in student affairs. However, my identity among the community of NASPA members is completely different. For example, it is the volunteer leaders who take the stage and spotlight (both literally and figuratively) at regional and national conferences. I believe that knowing my place and when to assume different postures has contributed to my success at NASPA.

Similarly, my identity within my family and among long-time friends is different than when I am with other groups. I am a professional with those who are in my outer circle of relationships. Without a conscious effort, when I am with family and close friends, I immediately adopt the vernacular and, as my family often says, I begin to "bust verbs all over the place." Some use the term "code switching" to describe the ease with which Black Americans and others from the lower economic strata revert to who they were before college. The identity I forward as a professional representing

NASPA comes out of a sense of responsibility for my role. The identity I forward among NASPA volunteer leaders and among my family and inner circle comes out of a sense of wanting to be accepted.

For the sake of simplicity, a person might select two or three leading identities from which his or her perspective and self-image emanates. Among these, the person will lead according to the circumstances and environment. My experience indicates that race and gender are two of the identities by which I am judged and, therefore, the ones uppermost in my mind. When I am in a situation where I, as a heterosexual, am in the minority, I do not feel the need to proclaim my difference. I believe this is because I have not experienced injustice or prejudice based on my sexual identity. I firmly believe that the identities from which our perspective emanates are tied closely to those emotional experiences of having been subjected to injustice and prejudice because of these externally socially constructed identities. Some of us resist by proclaiming them and some of us choose to check them at the door as much as practicable because of our professional role.

PROFESSIONAL IDENTITIES

During a meeting in the summer of 2011, I found myself proclaiming identities and checking them all within a short period of time. In a small group setting, the majority of the participants were from academic affairs at four-year colleges and universities. One colleague who had recently been president of a community college failed to mention the community college when introducing himself. He only referenced the four-year institutions where he had worked. When it was time to introduce myself, though I was representing NASPA and need not have mentioned my career in community colleges, I felt the need to claim community colleges even though it had been nearly 20 years since I had worked at a community college. Within all things, there are hierarchies of privilege. Because of my race and gender, I am perceived within a certain place in those hierarchies. Likewise, higher education has its own hierarchies, with the perception that community colleges do not hold a legitimate seat in higher education, and at best are simply a starting point for further attainment at four-year institutions. I think it is important not only to be proud of who you are, but also where you are and where you come from, and so I found myself claiming community colleges.

During this same meeting, when time was running out for discussion, a Black male who was speaking was cut off by the moderator and a White male was given the floor. When this occurred, race was at the forefront of everyone's mind and much follow-up discussion ensued. The Black male was understandably upset and did not participate in the rest of the meeting. I thought about what I would have done in this situation if I had been cut off. I am not sure what else I would have done, but as a representative of NASPA, I would have pushed the race issue to the background to continue participation in the meeting. I have no doubt that my way of responding is based on many experiences over the years where I have had to weigh what battles to fight and what wars to wage. What was more important at that meeting was to stay in the conversation where the opportunity to address race could be gained rather than leaving the scene. Responding to socially constructed identities is a choice, and I do not presume to judge. My reactions are based on my individual experiences and the goals I set for myself in my professional role.

Parsing and wrestling with the prominence of identities among the panoply is the Gordian knot each professional must unwind. My strategy is to mentor and inspire myself to exceed expectations of known identities that might be ascribed to me. I reflect on the slights, hurts, and disrespectful gestures to see what lessons might be learned and used to develop my own character.

One such humiliation occurred during the summer of 2011 when I attempted to check into an exclusive Las Vegas hotel where NASPA was hosting its annual Assessment and Persistence Conference. After standing in line and waiting patiently for a reservation agent to see me, I was pleasantly surprised when the agent directed me to the VIP welcome center to receive the keys to my room. Because I was executive director of the association hosting this conference, the hotel management wanted to show appreciation by holding the keys to my room in an area where I would feel special and to entice me to bring more business to the hotel.

Instead, as I was entering the VIP reception area, a woman behind the counter immediately gestured and told me that I was in the wrong place. I indicated that I had already been to the front desk, where they told me to pick up my room keys from the VIP area. The woman responded as if she did not hear me and said, "I assure you that you are in the wrong place. Please go out to the reservation desk and they will help you." As I left the VIP center, dragging my bags back to the reservation desk, the woman closed the door behind me as if to keep others like me from wandering into that space.

At the reservation desk, the agent could not believe what had happened and with exasperation, she went to the VIP center herself to retrieve my keys. I will never know why the woman in the VIP center thought I was in the wrong place, but because of previous experiences, at hotels in particular, I could guess why. She did not see "executive director" when she saw me. It is in such instances that self-knowledge becomes incredibly important. "Clarity about our identity, our purpose, and our desired legacy can be an important anchor during stable, uncertain, or changing times. . . . Self-knowledge provides a solid foundation on which we can build strong leadership" (Roper, 2011, pp. 123–124). Unlike the affirmation I received at the Georgia reception after the high school boys said I was ugly, in this instance I had to rely on self-knowledge and affirmation to prepare myself mentally to open the NASPA conference.

PROFESSIONAL GOALS

In a professional role, I have found that a person must sometimes endure for the sake of reaching a goal or destination that is beyond his or her feelings as an individual. I see examples of this choice played out often. Leaving the office for a meeting one day, I told a person who had just called me that I had to get to a taxi and I would call back once I was in the car. The radio speakers in the taxi were directly behind my head, so I asked, "Sir, could you please turn the radio down so I can make a phone call?"

I think I struck a chord with the gentleman in the way I asked him to turn the radio down. He opened up, and for the next 20 minutes he told me about indignities he had experienced while driving a taxi in Washington, D.C. He told me that when people who think they are important get into his taxi, they think they are doing him a favor by striking up a conversation beginning with, "Driver, where are you from?"

This question was particularly irksome to him because he did not want to be called "Driver" as if he were a servant. The question about where he was from was based on his skin color and accent and indicated to him that the person asking did not believe he belonged here. He said when he gets fed up with the questions or the way he is referred to, he pulls over to the curb and asks the passenger to leave his car. The passengers are incensed and cannot believe they have been thrown out of the taxi! Interestingly, I understand both the point of view of the gentleman driving the taxi and of the passenger unable to see how the gentleman driving the taxi would think there was any disrespect. The gift I developed as a person with multiple identities that are often the source of disrespect, unknowingly on many occasions, is empathy. As a dark-skinned woman in the United States, coming of age as part of the generation of the 1960s, being the first in my family to graduate from college, and calling student affairs my profession, I know what it is like to walk in the shoes of others whose identities define them before they can introduce themselves as whole and unique human beings who have something of value to offer. The difference between a person like me who must identify as a professional and the gentleman who drove the taxi is that I cannot pull over to the curb and ask the passenger to leave. I have to keep driving until we reach our destination.

REFERENCES

Giddings, P. J. (1984). *When and where I enter: The impact of black women on race and sex in America.* New York, NY: William Morrow.

Ladsen-Billings, G. (1995). New directions in multicultural education: Complexities, boundaries, and critical race theory. In J. A. Banks & C. A. McGee Banks (Eds.), *Handbook of research on multicultural education.* New York, NY: Macmillan.

Oakes, J., Joseph, R., & Muir, K. (1995). Access and achievement in mathematics and science: Inequalities that endure and change. In J. A. Banks & C. A. McGee Banks (Eds.), *Handbook of research on multicultural education.* New York, NY: Macmillan.

Roper, L. D. (2011). The search for authentic leadership. In G. J. Dungy & S. E. Ellis (Eds.), *Exceptional senior student affairs administrators' leadership: Strategies and competencies for success.* Washington, DC: National Association of Student Personnel Administrators.

The Daily Own. (2011, June 6). *Behind the scenes – Oprah with Gayle & the BEST of the BEST of the cast of SNL.* Retrieved from http:// www.thedailyown.com/behind-the-scenes-oprah-with-gayle-the-best-of-the-best-of-the-cast-of-snl

Negotiating Multiple Identities in Academic Leadership

Brian L. Foster

Brian L. Foster is provost and professor of anthropology at the University of Missouri. He was provost at The University of New Mexico, liberal arts dean at the University of Nebraska–Lincoln, and graduate dean at Arizona State University. He also served as chair of the Graduate Record Examinations (GRE) Board and the Council of Academic Affairs for the National Association of State Universities and Land-Grant Colleges, and was a member of the Test of English as a Foreign Language (TOEFL) Board.

T he academic world is complex in many dimensions. Accordingly, academic leadership is complicated and often misunderstood. One constant theme is that effective leadership on both the faculty and administrative sides strongly depends on relationships, many of which are built on and managed by use of personal and professional identities.

TWO CASES IN POINT

Two cases in which I was involved illustrate many identity and relationship issues suggested above. The first case has to do with mentoring a faculty member who aspired to a leadership position. He was a leader in the academic sense: strong publication record and national stature. At the time of our relationship, he had not defined the kind of administrative leadership to which he aspired. I

233

met him when he received an American Council on Education fellowship—a program that prepares fellows for higher-level administrative roles. In this program, fellows generally spend a semester or a year in close relationship with a senior academic administrator.

In this case, the fellow was director of a center at a major university in a field very different from mine. I was provost at The University of New Mexico—a unique environment in many ways, located in a minority/majority state with an Hispanic and Native American environment unlike any other in the United States. As a Caucasian European American from the Midwest, I was clearly an outsider; the fellow, as an African American, was also clearly an outsider in this minority/majority environment. In an ironic way, then, our Midwestern Caucasian and African American identities aligned as outsiders. But there was more. I was from a small town in northern Illinois, while the fellow grew up in the South Side of Chicago. So, we had a common Illinois identity that made sense in this environment, but probably not in any other. Moreover, the fellow's faculty appointment was at a university where I had been several years before. We had not interacted, but this common institutional identity was another link.

The relationship was very positive: there was a high level of trust and virtually no issue for which he did not have total access. He attended all deans' council and other formal meetings and was present in many one-on-one meetings with deans, faculty, other administrators, and external constituents. Accordingly, he gained a great deal of insight into how a large research university works. Our common identities contributed significantly to making a strong personal connection.

A second, very different case concerns my effort to make positive relations with community colleges across the state. I hired a former community college president to help with this effort; his job was to maintain relations with current presidents in the state's community colleges, to facilitate collaborations, and much more. My own position was very much based on my identity as a first-generation student who was passionate about access. It was also based on my identity as provost in another university that had four branch community colleges with which I had strongly engaged. The vice provost for community college partnerships had great recognition as a former president and former employee of the Missouri Department of

Higher Education, an identity that gave him credibility with the community college presidents and on campus. And his academic credentials—he was appointed to a faculty position in education—increased his credibility on campus among faculty and administrators. Thus, I was able to build a strong identity as an advocate for community college partnerships (in securing articulation agreements, launching economic development collaborations, and preparing faculty for community college positions) for access, for serving local communities, and for building productive relations among different sectors of higher education.

ACADEMIC COMPLEXITY, IDENTITIES, AND RELATIONSHIPS

A key source of academic identities is the complexity of higher education. A primary element of complexity is differences among sectors, for example: research universities; regional, four-year institutions; liberal arts colleges (some selective, some not); community colleges; public versus private institutions; nonprofit (public and private) versus for-profit institutions; vocational schools; free-standing professional schools (e.g., law, medicine); and others. Many provide more than education—for example, health care in association with medical education. These sectors relate to each other in complicated, politically sensitive ways and generate strong professional identities.

Individual institutions are also complex. Institutional issues vary dramatically by sector. My discussion will be informed primarily by my public, research university experience; however, many of the issues addressed cut across most sectors, with subtleties that I am unlikely to recognize.

A critical organizational principle of most sectors is that the faculty control academic operations—most important, curriculum. This poses sensitive issues, because the structure of the curriculum has significant impact on finances, facilities, and other aspects of the university's operations. The link between curriculum control and the management of budget, facilities, and other functions often generate conflict. One thing is certain: administration has limited competency for structuring curriculum content or for modes of delivering instruction.

Faculty also control the most important elements of the promotion and tenure process, which ultimately comes down to assessing the quality of the candidate's contributions: teaching, publications, service, and other aspects of faculty performance. As with curriculum, only the faculty can make informed judgments about the substance of teaching, research, and other activities, because such judgment requires sophisticated understanding of each candidate's academic field. As with curriculum, the promotion ad tenure decisions made for individuals in specific units have implications for institutional stature, external funding, quality of instruction, capacity, fiscal viability, and other matters that are essentially administrative. Many identity issues follow—for example, tenured or not, full professor or not.

A somewhat different kind of complexity is that individual institutions and specific parts of institutions have many constituent groups (often with conflicting interests and demands), such as faculty, students, parents, alumni, donors, legislators, athletic fans, corporate partners, employers, staff, academic associations (disciplinary, sector-related, political, academic, etc.), accrediting bodies, and professional associations (e.g., for law, accounting, journalism, medicine, and veterinary medicine). Members of these constituent groups have strong identities and interact in complicated ways—for example, members of professional associations with federal and state legislators, athletic fans with regents and trustees, regents and trustees with legislators, researchers with corporate collaborators, or alumni and donors with regents, the governor, or legislators. These complicated identities and constituent relationships have a strong impact on day-to-day activities of all educational, research, service, and other mission elements.

I could give other examples, but the bottom line is this: there is a strong, principled tension between faculty and administration, captured by professional identities, which shape relationships. A major source of this tension is the fact that for many sectors—especially research universities—creativity is the core value of faculty. Research is a key element of the research institution's activities, but so is educating and socializing students to be creative—perhaps the most important outcome of education in today's highly competitive, global environment. By definition, creativity cannot be structured. In the corporate world, when really creative, new products are under development, it is common to create a so-called "skunkworks" unit, which is separated from the firm's business models and design standards that could limit the creativity needed for conceptualization and design of new products. In an important sense, the academic part of a university is a skunkworks, because its role is to do creative research and train students to be creative and adaptable in a world that is rapidly changing. These issues strongly support the principles of faculty governance and faculty control of curriculum, promotion and tenure, and other "academic" elements of the institution.

Given this kind of fundamental division among administration, faculty, and constituent groups, how does higher education function? A "formal structure" seems to be a contradiction in terms—even a highly negative element, given the focus on creativity in the core education and research missions of universities and colleges. The answer is that much of the "order" in higher education is a "structure" driven by individuals' strategic use of their many personal and professional identities. Much of this "identity manipulation" is "structural" in the sense that it is entirely unconscious. Much is intentional; one might say "political." Most is in-between. Effective faculty and administrative leadership depends on productive relationships, many of which are built on and managed by use of personal and professional identities.

STRUCTURED AND INTENTIONAL IDENTITY MANAGEMENT

The matter of managing relationships by managing identities is much broader than in just higher education. In fact, most of the underlying research on the issue is found in a broad range of sociocultural subject matter. My own research about minority traders in Thailand is a relevant example. It focused on Mon traders who controlled the distribution of utility ceramics, trading from boats on the extensive river and canal system. The Mon were descendants of immigrants from southern Burma, many of whom came from villages that produced utility ceramics, a craft they brought to Thailand.

The theory of the underlying structure that drove the dynamics of the Mon identity is based on the exchange theories of Emile Durkheim (1964) and Marcel Mauss (1967), as extended in my paper "Trade, Social Conflict and Social Integration: Rethinking Some Old Ideas on Exchange"

(Foster, 1977). The argument is that in traditional societies, where there is no strong trader role (or "identity"), trading for profit violates the moral principles of exchange—the strong, deeply held ideals of family and community. Local, informal sanctions come into play when such norms are violated, and consequently, people do not become traders to trade among their own people. But these sanctions do not apply to outsiders, so the natural person to be a trader would have an identity as an outsider, for example, comes from a different ethnic group, speaks a different language, or is otherwise set apart from the community in which the trade occurs (see Gladwell, 2008 for a broader perspective).

The relation of trader status with identity manipulation is clear in several ways. First, the Mon people were Theravada Buddhist, lowland southeast Asians who were culturally very much like the Thai; they spoke a different language, but when I was there, all spoke fluent Thai. The traders remained Mon and continued to speak Mon amongst themselves but spoke Thai with others. This trader identity led to a somewhat negative stereotype for Mon ethnicity (i.e., ethnic identity). Most immigrants (and their descendants) became farmers and their primary identity was Thai; they recognized their Mon ancestry, very much like Americans with German ancestry recognize their German roots. Even more noteworthy, in 1981 I returned to the traders' village I studied in 1970–1971. About half the villagers had left trade and bought barges to haul construction materials, rice, and other cargo on the river. These people had all changed their identity to Thai, but those still in trade remained Mon.

These ethnic identity "decisions" were not really decisions in the sense that the Mons thought about their identity options and made a decision. Rather, the structure led to a more or less unconscious identity "choice." This is very different from the kind of situation described by Circe Sturm (2011) in her book *Becoming Indian: The Struggle over Cherokee Identity in the Twenty-first Century*. "Race shifting," as she calls it, is a process by which a conscious decision is made to "become Cherokee" (pp. 184–188). These decisions may come about from a variety of circumstances, including people who find Native American ancestry when exploring their genealogies and for whatever reason decide to adopt a Cherokee identity (not necessarily their only or their main identity). Others may have known of their Native American ancestry, but for some reason it becomes important to somehow "use" this identity—for example, perhaps having connected with a family member who has a Cherokee identity.

ACADEMIC LEADERSHIP AND IDENTITIES

The range of identities that play into academic leadership is broad. "Leadership" identities interact in complex ways with faculty, disciplinary, and other identities of people in a wide variety of institutional roles. The very idea of "academic leadership" has many definitions, and administrative roles or identities may become either negatively or positively stereotyped, not unlike traders in traditional Thailand. They may carry heavy value judgments including fear of retribution, or perception of inappropriate influence on, for example, curriculum or promotion and tenure decisions. On the other hand, administrative identities may carry admiration, respect, and often puzzlement over administrators' roles. Some of the most critical identities for thinking about academic leadership are the following.

- Academics versus nonacademics. Universities are inherently about the academic enterprise, and many academics believe nonacademics have no place in making decisions about the institution. Many nonacademics see academics as having no sense of the kinds of business issues that must be dealt with and as impractical and haughty people.
- Faculty versus administrators. Faculty often perceive administrators as attempting to exert too much influence on academic matters.
- Disciplinary differences. Different disciplines have very different values, modes of productivity, methods, ways of framing problems, knowledge bases—even very different kinds of research outcomes (some seek applications, some see applications as trivial and want the outcome to be the basis for asking questions that could not have been asked before). People in many disciplines or professions see a strong hierarchy of disciplines.
- Disciplinary alignment. Disciplines generally align with the structure of the organization—for example, with departments, colleges,

schools, other units—and an identity based on membership in a unit is important in institutional politics.

- Faculty status. Status includes such indicators (read "identities") as tenure track versus nontenure track, rank, named professorship, and so on. In addition, those with a primary faculty role—for example, instruction, research, service, extension, clinical, and so forth—have very different status from those with a secondary role. (In research universities, research identity carries more prestige than instructional identity.) Honors, such as being elected to the National Academies or receiving a nationally recognized award, also provide very positive identities.

Every academic has many professional identities; in addition, they have personal identities (e.g., race, ethnicity, language, gender, age) that interact with the academic ones. Moreover, less obvious identities may come into play in special academic situations: place of birth, places one has lived, where one went to school, first-generation college graduate, religion, socioeconomic status (present or past), and much more.

These identities come into play in an endless set of circumstances and situations in which relationships are critical. Much of our use of identities in the academic arena is finding common identities with others in order to strengthen relationships. The situational environment can take an endless number of forms. For instance, when one wishes to collaborate with a prominent scholar; the scholarly "fit" and stature are of course critical, but in addition one finds common identities (being alumni of same schools, hailing from the same city, serving in a post-doctoral position with the same mentor, receiving funding from the same agency, and so on). Or perhaps one is running for a leadership role in faculty governance on campus. Strong faculty identity (as opposed to administrative) would be critical in many cases—for example, identity manipulation may be more to separate from administration than to make positive relationships. But for a faculty member who is competing for an administrative position on campus, the identity management would take a very different form, linking to relevant administrative competencies, experience, professional relationships, and perhaps separating from a faculty identity that would link to a hostile piece of faculty governance. Or, for that matter, a strategy could be that a faculty governance identity would be an asset in dealing with a hostile faculty governance issue.

From an administrator's point of view, leadership issues involve people both inside and outside the university—academics and nonacademics, other administrators and faculty, academic administrators and nonacademic administrators (e.g., budget, human resources, facilities, athletic director, or general counsel), administrators at other institutions (e.g., connections for collaborations), legislators or other political figures, and corporate executives. There is an endless list of relationships that could be managed using personal and professional identities. To use my own case as an example, I have strongly advocated for an international and multilingual campus environment. In doing so, I use my personal identity as a Thai scholar, spouse of a person who is a German native, father of bilingual children, and competent speaker of two non-English languages. In linking with community colleges and making the case for access, I build on my personal identity as a first-generation student who went to undergraduate school in my late 20s after supporting my financially challenged family. With nonacademic administrators, I use my identity as a former business person—owner of an independent insurance agency before I went to college—for credibility in the business side of the university. Clearly, these identities are used in connection with very different kinds of relationships and different situations.

CONCLUSION

The management of professional and personal identities is critical for leadership in higher education. Many such identities are used in highly structured (but not conscious) ways, while others are purposeful, conscious, and decision-based. These issues are complex, but in the end they all come down to relationships—to the symbolic foundations of strong relationships or the separation of people in negative relationships—that are the foundations for successful leadership.

REFERENCES

Durkheim, E. (1964). *The division of labor in society*. New York, NY: Free Press.

Foster, B. L. (1977). Trade, social conflict, and social integration: Rethinking some old ideas on exchange. In *Economic exchange and social interaction in Southeast Asia: Perspectives from prehistory, history, and ethnography* (Michigan Papers on South and Southeast Studies 13). Ann Arbor, MI: University of Michigan, Center for South and Southeast Asian Studies.

Gladwell, M. (2008). *Outliers: The story of success*. New York, NY: Little-Brown.

Mauss, M. (1967). *The gift: Forms and functions of exchange in archaic societies*. New York, NY: Norton.

Sturm, C. (2011). *Becoming Indian: The struggle over Cherokee identity in the twenty-first century*. Santa Fe, NM: School for Advanced Research Press.

Public Service and Politics
Perspectives on Pressure and Influence

Viola E. Florez

Viola E. Florez is a professor and education endowed chair at The University of New Mexico. Her professional career experiences include serving as a P–20 educator and administrator in higher education, as well as holding office as a public executive for higher education.

The best authors of works on leadership, politics, and public service are those who have reflected long and hard on what they experienced as a public servant and have figured out how to share that information with others. Knowing how to pass on the lessons learned to others is difficult; however, I will attempt with this essay to share personal insights and experiences as a public servant in various roles and responsibilities during my career as an educator, administrator, and public servant in a governmental position as secretary for higher education in New Mexico. Hopefully, my experiences will provide useful information to those who are pursuing a career in public administration and public service.

The undertaking of sharing information with others is difficult because of the complexity of various roles as a public servant. Most of my professional career in public service work involved working closely with individuals from various walks of life, especially working directly with K–12 personnel, university faculty, staff, higher education administrators, political leaders, legislators, and public executives. Understanding how to work effectively with other perspectives on multiple or controversial issues creates challenging moments; however, the rewards come when mutual understanding or resolutions to problems occur. This does happen, believe it or not, and understanding how to reflect on what was accomplished and what happens next is important, especially how actions can or will affect others. Through it all, I learned that much of what I did was actually teaching, mostly helping colleagues realize the function and nature of whatever it was we were trying to accomplish together.

PROFESSIONAL JOURNEY AS AN EDUCATOR

I began my teaching career as a middle school teacher on the Hopi and Navajo Reservation teaching reading and language arts to students who functioned in two cultures and tried desperately to maintain their home culture in an ever-changing society with demands that were difficult and often foreign to them. The time I spent teaching Native American students taught me the value of understanding the diverse thinking of others and how to examine my own behaviors of respecting others and accepting what I did not know or understand. Many instructional strategies and approaches I learned in college as I prepared to become a teacher were not very useful to me in a bilingual and bicultural classroom. I soon learned I had to develop new ways of modifying instruction and teaching creatively using cultural pedagogy if they were going to be successful learners and I was going to be an effective teacher. It became obvious to me that understanding the politics and culture of schooling on the reservation was important as an educator, especially a person who wanted to make a difference for someone else's children.

I grew up in the Four Corners area of New Mexico with Navajo children attending the same school as myself, which was during the time of segregated schools and racial tensions in New Mexico and nationally. I was a student who spoke very little English—forced to learn English and assimilate into White culture at school. However, at home, I could maintain my culture and Spanish language—a demand from my grandmother to never lose our language and culture. Attending school was painful for me in my early years, mostly because of the tough times I personally experienced and what I observed happening to other Hispanic and Navajo children. I believe the memories of early schooling helped shape my career as a determined professional to correct the injustices that occurred to children in a place called school. I became very aware of cultural differences, social justice, and how to adapt to any environment. I discovered the value of not taking anything for granted and learning all that I could to understand the culture of the students I taught. I took time to reflect on who I was as a teacher and what type of professional I wanted to become. The school and community experience on the reservation taught me the value of knowing self and how to truly respect others beyond borders of my own culture.

Continuing my education was important, so I moved to Colorado to attend graduate school. I secured an elementary position teaching children in a diverse multicultural school setting, identified as a Title I school—a school that received federal and state funding to support various academic programs, plus offered school lunch and breakfast programs. The children were predominately Hispanic and Black students who came from homes that were similar in some respect to my upbringing, especially the Hispanic students, but very different in many cases. I was raised on a cattle ranch in northwest New Mexico with opportunities to farm the land, which provided various advantages to living in a city. The students came from low-income areas of the community where resources were limited to assist with basic family needs, which affected student learning and success. The high poverty level in the community affected the school in numerous ways, which created challenges for teachers and administrators in the school district and particular schools in the neighborhood.

This teaching experience was very different from teaching on the Hopi and Navajo reservation, mostly because of the culture of the community, school environment, and local politics. The pace and demands of the school environment seemed hurried and city, school, and community politics played a significant role in the education of the children. Public service was more difficult because of other social variables affecting the lives of the children we served, such as hunger, homelessness, health issues, and so forth. I quickly learned how to effectively communicate and work with parents.

They trusted the teachers and wanted their children to have opportunities they never had, which in their minds meant a better life. Learning the value of parental support and involvement with their children's education was important, especially knowing and understanding the politics of working in the community to create change in order to improve educational opportunities for student success. The understanding of community challenges was real to me since I had witnessed my parents struggling with community politics and racial discrimination in a small rural school.

In 1980 I completed a doctorate, which changed my professional career path from K–12 to higher education. Upon completion of doctoral studies, I began my academic career as an assistant professor at the University of Nebraska–Lincoln. This took me into the Midwest, which was very different culturally from any place I had ever been. This was my first introduction to teaching at a university and working with adults in an academic setting. I enjoyed the experience and quickly observed the politics of higher education at local, national, and federal levels. I held a joint teaching appointment between the College of Arts and Sciences and Teachers College, which created a different paradigm for success. Understanding university expectations as a new faculty member was critical to my success as a faculty and researcher. The experience at this particular institution was very different because of the size of the institution, lack of diversity among the faculty, and functioning in two academic colleges. Adapting to a new culture was important and life experiences taught me how to do this well.

Pathways to Leadership

I continued teaching in higher education until 1997, moving into higher education administration at Texas A&M University, which spanned more than 15 years of valuable experience in teaching, research, service, and administration at various levels. In 1993–1994, I received the American Council on Education Fellows award to study leadership at the national level. This experience was beyond anything I had experienced thus far, especially the opportunity to shadow leaders, such as university presidents, provosts, deans, and other executive leaders in higher education internationally and across the country. The opportunity to study and talk with leaders about leadership and discuss important characteristics of an effective leader was exciting and invigorating. This experience opened the door to other administrative positions held at multiple universities, providing rich opportunities for professional growth. Serving in various administrative roles allowed me to observe other interesting styles of leadership, thus helping me establish my own style of problem solving and leading in complex organizations.

As a public administrator, I was very conscious of my loyalty to the institution and personal principles and values, which I refused to compromise. If direct conflict arose, I managed to figure out a way to resolve the issue without compromising my values or principles, which was not always easy to do, especially with some supervisors who had a different set of values or principles. Figuring out a way to create a win-win situation was always my goal. Many times this goal was achievable. Understanding loyalty and the right thing to do was a constant challenge, mostly because of change in leadership at the executive level, which happened frequently. The constant need to get acquainted with behaviors and demands by senior executives affected day-to-day activities in day-to-day demands. Knowing how to treat people in time of transition was important to my success, especially when I started out in my administrative career and wanted to make the right decisions. My grandmother always told us that we should not burn too many bridges because we never knew when we might have to cross them again. This concept was very true, and I tried always to remember her advice, especially because I consistently dealt with people—sometimes very difficult people—to accomplish my goals and maintain my professional integrity and ambitions.

FAMILY INFLUENCE ON LEADERSHIP

Leadership has been defined in numerous ways by many authors who have studied and written about what it means to be a leader. Ashworth (2007) described leadership as an art, not a science or a set of axioms or formulas, despite all the discovered secrets and recorded tapes and miracle manuals available on the market. He explained that leadership is learned by studying and holding the responsibility of a leader. From a personal perspective, I agree that leadership is learned, resulting in the mastery of skills and techniques most likely acquired as an adult or from an early stage in childhood.

I recognize that being the eldest in a family of 12 children gave me experience and practice in leadership that happened naturally as I carried out the responsibilities demanded of me by my parents, especially my mother. A university president to whom I reported once commented that every job he gave me I managed to get done and do well. He attributed this to my experience of being part of a large family. At the time, I laughed; however, I often wonder if perhaps he was correct. My mother was an extremely well-organized person who defined chores for all of us before and after school and demanded high performance in all that we did. Being the eldest, my responsibility was to assist with and supervise my siblings. I guess you could say it was my job to make sure things got done. I observed my mother as she performed her duties every day and learned from watching her demonstrate life skills and techniques regarding family responsibilities that needed to be accomplished in a timely manner. I learned how she managed and treated all of us. We understood the expectations.

Often I reflect on my upbringing and wonder how much of it influenced my behavior as a leader, especially knowing how to interact and work productively with others. I believe early development influences behaviors and the ability to problem solve along the pathway to adulthood. Perhaps family upbringing influenced my leadership style and philosophical beliefs along my professional journey. Some leaders believe that effective leaders decide early in the process of dealing with a crisis or problem how they will resolve the issue. This practice was observed over the course of my experiences and training in leadership. Personal observations have revealed that some leaders gather and study all facts before deciding what to do and before taking any action. My experience tells me that the majority of leaders do gather facts, but often have to move quickly and resolve the issue at hand, therefore not allowing for much time. Taking time to think and reflect on data is great; however, if time is not available, taking action is important. Taking action and worrying about the consequences later was something I had to deal with on many occasions. Following your instincts is probably not the best ingredient for leadership, but I do know that it often worked for me. This, too, I believe comes with personal experience and training as a leader.

Spending time in the trenches and experience is important as you move up the chain of command. I learned through my experiences that leaders have institutional memory and historical context to see more clearly than others which options are available and which path of action stands the best chance of success. In their minds they are assessing the responses of those who will be affected by the decision and weighing positive and negative reactions. Most leaders make connections and measure gains and losses immediately, including acceptance and criticism, and size up the consequences of action and inaction. This I found fascinating as I observed and worked with top executives in higher education as well as government public executives. I tried to learn what to do and not do from observing leadership in multiple and various settings.

The leadership position as cabinet secretary for higher education was an experience that was beyond anything I had ever done or imagined. Working directly with politicians was a new experience for me, and I am not sure I could have prepared for the task. Every day presented new challenges and was full of ambiguity, especially if my schedule included meetings or presentations with state elected officials. Understanding the politics of the issues was critical and knowing the different opinions and positions held by individual politicians and university presidents demanded high-level planning and communication. Every time a legislative bill was introduced, politics quickly took over. I watched as committee chairs convened the conferees for a vote or killed the bill before any one convened to vote. There were so many angles to getting things done, and I often found myself at a loss trying to figure out what I should do. The commonsense approach to understanding definitely did not work with politics, so I decided to join forces with others who had common interests to influence and pressure legislators to move legislation forward. I experienced firsthand how to collectively effect change within a political environment. The ability to work quickly and influence others to change policy based on personal ideas that could make a significant impact on policy issues was exciting to witness.

LESSONS LEARNED

I hope these personal experiences provide insight into public service and reaffirm the necessity of effective leaders and public servants to influence change.

As I reflect on my experiences, I believe effective public service to others can make an incredible difference in their everyday lives. The opportunity to be a change agent in government agency work was the reason I accepted the responsibility in the first place. I tried to give a greater predictability and stability of activities and legislative mandates to postsecondary leaders as they struggled to implement mandates or special projects with no or limited funding. I enjoyed working directly with college and university presidents and other key leaders to improve higher education for students in New Mexico. The issues were complex, but we worked together to surface and address funding issues important to the future of higher education and the students served.

Over the course of more than 20 years, I learned many lessons that made me a better educator, administrator, and public servant. I believe I am a strategic contributor to public service at the university and in the community because of service I engaged in personally and professionally. Awareness of how politics influences individual lives makes a difference in how I approach particular activities in the community. I also approach university administration very differently because of my knowledge of funding mechanisms, political pressures, and responsibilities beyond a leader's control. I feel a stronger commitment to the students I teach and the community engagement and leadership work I do on a daily basis. Working together collectively to impact change is the thrust I take with my work, especially raising awareness among community members that educating students on a continuum of cradle to career is critical to our future. We all own the children, and they are the future of this country. We must work together for the common good, which means being productive citizens and giving back to a community to improve the quality of life for everyone. This is a joint effort, and working collaboratively will achieve greater gains.

REFERENCE

Ashworth, K. (2007). *Caught between the dog and the fireplug, or how to survive public service.* Washington, DC: Georgetown University Press.

Leadership Lessons Learned From Family and Personal Trials

Elizabeth Hoffman

Elizabeth Hoffman has been executive vice president and provost and dean of liberal arts and sciences at Iowa State University; president of the University of Colorado System; provost and vice chancellor for academic affairs at the University of Illinois at Chicago; and director of the Master of Business Administration Program at the University of Arizona.

I n the purest sense, I was born into privilege, and not just simple White privilege. My maternal grandfather was a Russian count, whose mother served as a lady-in-waiting to the last Czarina of Russia. He was descended from a great Cossack chieftain who signed a peace treaty with Peter the Great. My maternal grandmother was descended from Benjamin Rush, signer of the Declaration of Independence and doctor to the American Revolution. My paternal grandmother's maiden name was Wright and she could trace her ancestry back to the Quaker founders of Philadelphia. My family members are all in the Philadelphia Social Register and

Partial support for this essay provided by NSF ADVANCE Institutional Transformation Award: HRD 06-00399. Any opinions, findings, conclusions, or recommendations expressed in this essay are those of the author and do not necessarily reflect the views of the National Science Foundation.

my childhood was much dominated by that fact. My paternal grandfather, who was an alternate on the 1912 Olympic rowing team, an architect, and a graduate of The University of Pennsylvania, made sure that we were members of the "right" summer swimming club and that I attended the "right" dancing schools from seventh grade on. In 1964, when I graduated from high school, I was "presented" to Philadelphia society in a six-month series of "coming out" parties, culminating in the Assembly, an annual Christmastime ball that dates back to the 18th century.

Privilege, Revolution, and Strong-minded Women

What I took from those experiences was an understanding of how to be a gracious hostess, despite a lifetime of extreme shyness. While being a gracious hostess may not seem like an important leadership trait, it means that I am comfortable with fundraising, a very important part of a successful deanship or presidency. I know how to entertain graciously, everything from giving an intimate dinner for a couple I am courting for a gift to a large party to celebrate the beginning or end of a fundraising campaign. I know instinctively how to make people feel comfortable in a small or large gathering and how to ask for a gift without ever seeming to be asking. I often say that fundraising is more about "friend-raising" and about helping people fulfill their dreams than it is about asking for money. I also often say that I spent the first half of my adult life trying to escape my upbringing and the second half capitalizing on it.

More important for my development as a leader were other facts about my family and my childhood. First, while my family was privileged, it was also full of revolutionaries. From my Cossack ancestor, who defied Peter the Great, to Benjamin Rush and his father-in-law, who committed treason by signing the Declaration of Independence and fighting in the Revolutionary War, to my great grandfather, William Redwood Wright, who left his Quaker family to fight in the Civil War because he believed that slavery was so evil it was not enough to "bear witness" against it, to my Russian grandfather, who was imprisoned in the fortress of St. Peter and St. Paul and brought before the firing squad before finally being released, the blood of revolution runs in my veins.

Second, I come from a family dominated by strong women. My maternal grandmother divorced my Russian grandfather in 1938, a time when women did not do such things. She moved my 17-year-old mother and 14-year-old aunt from New York to Philadelphia and started a bakery. Her bakery was legendary on the Philadelphia Main Line until my mother and aunt sold it in the 1980s. My grandmother was a force to be reckoned with. She assembled a unique crew of workers and partners for a woman of her social standing, and she worked—wearing an apron and work dress—side by side with them every day until she died of bone cancer in 1966.

DON'T GET MAD, GET EVEN

The combination of my revolutionary ancestry and the strong women who raised me gave me a belief that I could do anything I set my mind to, regardless of gender stereotypes of the 1950s and 1960s. It never occurred to me that I could not participate in sports or do math and science. I went to a women's college because I wanted to, not because I felt I had to. My first encounter with discrimination was when I applied to graduate school and found that my gender and marital status were suddenly more important than my brains. I was told that women do not finish graduate school. My response was to do a statistical analysis of entering classes in the history PhD program at The University of Pennsylvania. I found that, on average, they admitted 2 women and 28 men a year, and half of those who started finished, men and women. The problem was there were so few women that faculty could remember every woman who left and formed an impression that mostly women did not finish. They forgot about the nameless and faceless numbers of men who left. I vowed to finish early and do well. I completed a PhD in history in 4.5 years, 2.5 of those while teaching economics in Minnesota, a feat few could match today. One of my mottos is "don't get mad, get even." By that I do not mean that I want to get revenge on someone. Rather, I mean, do not waste your time getting mad about a situation when you can get even by showing that an assumption is wrong, by solving a problem, or by doing such a good job that you defy stereotypes.

This motto and the strength I gained from my family generally served me well. When my first husband was not supportive of my need for intellectual independence, I took strength from my grandmother's decision and left him. When my first full-time tenure-track job as an assistant professor of history did not turn out to be in a welcoming environment, I accepted an unusual offer to enter a new PhD program in social science at Caltech University. Both of these decisions turned into two of the best decisions of my life. I earned a second PhD and formally entered the field of economics, which has been remarkably supportive of me as a woman and a scholar my entire working life. And I married one of my classmates. We have been married for 36 years. My husband and I often say, "Life is what happens to you while you're busy making other plans," a quote from one of John Lennon's (1980) last songs, *Beautiful Boy*.

My background and life experiences have not always provided the right guidance, however. Perhaps because I am shy or perhaps because I am too trusting, I am easily hurt. And, when I am hurt, I cry, a very unfortunate trait for a leader! I was not able to understand how to prevent myself from crying until I went through a year of intense therapy following the worst failure of my life, resigning from the presidency of the University of Colorado System.

Moreover, "don't get mad, get even" can also lead to not accepting failure and staying too long in a fight you cannot win. "Failure is impossible" was a motto of one of my heroes, the suffragist Carrie Chapman Catt. I probably stayed at the University of Colorado too long in the face of a fight that I see in hindsight I could never have won. I could have left a hero after 3 years, but I stayed to fight until it became clear that the forces aligned against me would not relent until I resigned. I learned valuable and painful lessons from that experience.

COMING TO TERMS WITH THE POLITICS OF RACE AND GENDER

Third, my family consistently defied the stratified conventions of the 1950s and 1960s, despite our socially privileged position. My grandmother's first partner was a Holocaust survivor and my early memories include visitors to our home who had tattoos on their wrists. Her bakery workforce included a Black head bread baker, whom everyone agreed baked the best bread on the Main Line. The women who kneaded bread were Black and Italian. In many places they would have refused to work together, but my grand-mother established an expectation with words and personal leadership that everyone who worked at her bakery would work hard, put aside their differ-ences, and treat one another with respect. In the late 1950s, she put a Black woman behind the counter selling cakes, pies, and doughnuts. A number of her "friends" were outraged and told her she would ruin the business. They said no one would buy food from the hands of a Black woman. My grand-mother's response was that she did not need the business of people like that! Somehow, her business did not suffer. In keeping with my family's views of civil rights, my mother never said a word when I brought home friends of all races and creeds. I know she cringed a bit, only because of what "others" might say, but she never told me not to be friends with someone because of their race or religion. Moreover, when Marian Anderson, the famous Black opera singer, was denied the right to perform in Constitution Hall by the Daughters of the American Revolution (DAR) in 1939, my mother joined Eleanor Roosevelt and other prominent White members of the DAR and quit the organization in protest.

When my grandmother died in 1966, her loyal workers wanted to have a proper Catholic and Black wake, with an open casket and every-one throwing themselves on the casket and wailing. My aunt, a reserved Episcopalian, was outraged. To her, the correct way to honor the dead was a quiet, closed casket funeral. My mother intervened and said, "We will have both." The night before the funeral, my grandmother was beautifully arranged in her open casket in front of the fireplace in the living room of her home, which was attached to the bakery. Her employees filed past the casket and showed their respect by kissing her, crying, and wailing. The next day, we had our proper Episcopalian closed casket funeral and burial.

My upbringing that defied racial stereotypes left me with both chal-lenges and opportunities. I cannot say that anyone in my family was a conscious crusader for social justice, even though by the standards of their time they lived lives that fostered social justice. When I wanted to go to Selma, Alabama, and the March on Washington in 1963, my mother said, "No." I was too young, and it was too dangerous. When my cousin married a Liberian American it caused a minor stir in the family, but the wedding was held in my aunt and uncle's garden and the couple and their children were quickly absorbed into the family. That was 41 years ago and they are still married. I think it would be more appropriate to say I was brought up with little consciousness about race, except to the extent that it mattered to other people. This lack of consciousness about race (and even gender to a large extent) was beneficial to me in college, graduate school, and as a faculty member and professor, in that I always cared more about a colleague's or a student's performance than their gender or racial/ethnic background. However, when I became a dean at Iowa State University, I had to learn the importance of racial and gender consciousness and the use of gender, racial, and ethnic political strategies the hard way.

FAILURE IS IMPOSSIBLE!

I noted earlier that one of my heroes is Catt, the valedictorian of the class of 1880 at Iowa State and Susan B. Anthony's hand-picked successor to carry on the fight for women's suffrage to the final passage of the 19th Amendment. Along the way to winning the fight for suffrage, she made political compromises with the segregationist South that, to the sensitivities of African American students looking for a cause in 1995, appeared suspect. The students formed the "September 29th" movement, for the date when they discovered documents they considered offensive. They called a meeting to discuss the fact that we were rededicating—within a week—a renovated building named for her, demanding we change the name and calling me a racist for defending Catt. I was devastated and started crying in a public meeting. How could someone call me a racist? I knew it was not fair. I was not a racist. I was shaken to the core by the accusation and by calls for my dismissal for crying in public.

But, these events did not deter me from continuing with the rededication of Carrie Chapman Catt Hall, a name the building still carries today. I met regularly with the student protesters, serving cookies and cocoa to them at the end of their march from the administration building to Catt Hall. I listened and even encouraged them to write about their concerns and put a plaque outside the building commemorating the protest. But, I did not stop raising money for the building nor give in to calls to rename it. I always finish what I start, even if it kills me! As Catt herself would have said, "Failure is Impossible!"

Two years later, I was starting a new job as provost at the University of Illinois at Chicago. At my first meeting of my first day on the job, the Illinois Legislative Black Caucus called on the chancellor to berate him over the poor performance of a few Black medical students on the state medical boards. As we introduced ourselves around the table that morning, I said that this was my first meeting of my first day on the job. The chair of the caucus looked me in the eye, smiled knowingly, and said, "Honey, you are in for a treat!" For the next two hours they hammered the chancellor, called everyone in the university racist, and ceremonially presented him with hundreds of signatures of local residents denouncing the university for racism because the medical students were not becoming doctors.

Understanding that the university was hardly to blame for students not passing their state boards and thinking about the chair's opening comment to me, I realized I was witnessing the highest form of political theater as a method of social activism and that what I had experienced at Iowa State was also political theater as social activism. I think because I could stand on the sideline and witness the action with no personal attack on me implied in the denunciations, it came to me as a revelation and an important education that informs my leadership to this day.

Shortly thereafter, the chancellor enlisted the help of Reverend Jesse Jackson in providing assistance to the students to study for the boards, in helping the university develop better mentoring programs for the students, and in helping the Black Caucus understand the roles the university could and could not play. Jesse Jackson and I formed a personal bond that persists today. He helped me learn how to get to the bottom of an issue and not let political theater get in the way of doing my best to identify and try to solve the real problem that has prompted a group to engage in social activism in the first place. Now I understand that when I am called a racist it is not a personal statement about me, but, rather, a political statement about a general frustration regarding an issue that may or may not be racially motivated, but is easily perceived as such. Now I can enter a highly charged meeting and quickly get everyone to focus on the real issue, temporarily putting aside, to the extent possible, perceptions of discrimination. I do this by recognizing the differences among the individuals, stating the problem to be solved, and asking everyone to temporarily put aside their differences and work on a resolution of the problem. While I am not always successful, my success rate is much higher when I can take my personal feelings out of the picture and focus on the problem to be solved. I have come to understand the importance of race and gender in how others' lives have been shaped and the importance of discrimination in how other women and individuals of color perceive my leadership.

At this point in my career, having conquered my tendency to cry in public, my upbringing that defied both racial and gender stereotypes has been very helpful to me as a leader. Once parties to a dispute understand that calling me a racist or otherwise attacking me personally is not going to get a rise out of me and that I am genuinely interested in trying to understand and address their grievances, if possible, they tend to calm down and get to work on the real problem. Some people may say I am a White woman playing at social justice. To me, I am just doing what I do best— figuring out what the problem is and trying to find a way to solve it. I have learned that race and gender are as important to others as my unique family history is to me. But, I still believe that the best approach is to do the best job you can: "Don't get mad, get even!"

REFERENCE

Lennon, J. (1980). Beautiful boy. On *Double Fantasy* [LP]. Los Angeles, CA: Capitol Records.

How My Life and Values Shape My Presidency

William V. Flores

William V. Flores grew up in San Diego, California. He holds a BA from the University of California, Los Angeles, and an MA and PhD from Stanford University. He served as dean at California State University, Northridge; provost and interim president at New Mexico State University; and deputy secretary for higher education in New Mexico, prior to serving as president of the University of Houston–Downtown.

We do not grow up wanting to be college presidents. At least, I certainly never thought in those terms. Yet, here I am today, as president of a university. I learned my core values from my parents and from my aunt, Francisca, all of whom helped shape and influence my sense of purpose and leadership. Allow me to explain how my parents and my aunt, among others, shaped my views and my actions. I will start with my mother and father.

FAMILY VALUES AND MENTORS

When I think back on why I went to college, I must say that it was because of the encouragement of my mother and father. The turning point for me was third grade. That was the year when my father chose to go back to school. He left high school during World War II and decided after having children to pursue his high school diploma. He worked in the defense industry, as did most of my family. He sought a better life for all of us and understood that he needed a high school diploma to even consider other jobs. He began taking courses, and I studied with him at the dinner table and at the breakfast table. My mother, who graduated from high school, tutored us both.

My mother always made sacrifices to help others. She would put together food packages for needy families in our church. When anyone in our large extended family was sick, she would be there for them with soup or would cook food for their children. She made sacrifices to save money to be sure we had books to read. One of my earliest memories is of her reading the Bible to me and explaining its meaning. She would buy children's books and read them to me and my brothers and encourage us to read, even at the earliest age. As we grew older, she wanted us to have an encyclopedia, but we could not afford to buy an entire set. Then, our local market, Safeway, had a special. If you bought two bags of groceries, you could buy one volume of an encyclopedia each week for less than a dollar. It took us two years, but we got an encyclopedia. Unfortunately, we were on vacation for two weeks and when we returned they did not have the letter R, so I could never look up anything that began with that letter. When I was in high school, we finally bought a complete set of the *World Book Encyclopedia*.

In sixth grade, I learned algebra because that was what my dad was studying at the time. He would watch educational television at 6:00 a.m., and I watched and learned with him. By the seventh grade, we took standardized tests, and I scored the highest in my school. Several of my teachers could not understand, as they had ignored me as "just one other Mexican kid" who would probably drop out. I was placed into honors courses in high school, and counselors began to view me differently. They encouraged me to apply to college. I went to the University of California, Los Angeles, and subsequently to Stanford University.

My dad was an important role model in other ways. For example, when I was in my early teens, he bought a set of new tires at Sears. After a few months, one of the tires blew out, but Sears refused to replace it. My father was incensed that they had falsely advertised the tires with an "unconditional" replacement warranty. That is why he bought them there in the first place. My dad and I stood outside of the store, showing potential customers the tire. He would tell them, "Don't buy tires here. Look at my tires. Sears's tires are no good and they don't honor their warranty." Eventually, he got a whole new set of tires! My dad told me afterward, "Remember, 'No' is just a beginning point in negotiations. Never give up, especially if what they are doing is wrong. Find a different way of getting to 'Yes.'"

My mom and dad were always there for me. When I was associate dean at California State University, Fresno, I was diagnosed and underwent treatments for cancer. The chemotherapy caused a mild stroke that left me partially paralyzed on my left side. My parents drove up from San Diego and stayed with me during my recovery. My mom had suffered a series of strokes and was paralyzed on the right side. There was a time after my stroke when I felt depressed and just stayed in bed. My mom came up to me, stroked my hand, and kissed my forehead. She said, "Bill, let's go for a walk. You may be paralyzed on the left side and I can't walk too well on the right side, but if we hold hands and support each other, we can walk." And, we did. Bit by bit, I recovered. With her support and with the help and prayers of many friends, I found the inner strength and confidence to fully recover. I gained strength from her compassion and courage.

Similarly, one of my aunts, Francisca Flores, was a role model to me. She lived in Los Angeles, but growing up, I was always drawn to her and loved hearing her accounts of politics in L.A. She always encouraged me to pursue a college education. My dad related her personal story to me, something she rarely discussed. At the age of 15, she was diagnosed with tuberculosis. About the same time, her older brother, who was also my dad's brother, Vincent, died when he was 19 years old of the same disease. Francisca had one lung removed and entered a convalescent hospital. At age 26, she was released but placed on permanent disability. Even so, she went on to be a political activist and writer. Francisca founded La Comisión Femeníl Mexicana and served as editor of *Carta Editorial* and *Regenerción*. She later founded and served as director of the Chicana Service Action Center in East Los Angeles. Francisca dedicated her life to creating opportunities for the Mexican American community and fought for social justice, despite her disability.

Francisca once told me, "Having a disability doesn't define or limit me. It's not who I am. It's what I do to make a difference that matters. Remember, Bill, when people say you can't do something, tell them you will, and figure out how you can." She also told me, "Some see the glass as half full, others as half empty. But, if you're in the desert, you grab it and drink. Be a realist and grab that glass of water, but share it with others." She also told me that she did not just want me to go to college, but to "do something that will make me proud." Before she died, she told me that I had made her proud, and she knew someone in the family would continue working for social justice.

I learned very important values from my family. These values inform my everyday actions as a leader. I believe it is not enough to hold a position of administrative leadership; you must do something to make meaningful change—to make the world a better place. I believe in servant leadership and principle-centered leadership. I lead and develop a vision based on strong values and based on the specific needs and aspirations of the communities I work in and serve.

SERVING THE PUBLIC GOOD

Education is vital to democracy and an educated citizenry is its life blood. In 1905, William Rainey Harper described the university as "prophet of democracy—the agency established by heaven itself to proclaim the principles of democracy" (Benson, 2005, p. 187). Universities perform a vital role for the preservation of liberty and democracy by educating future leaders. Simply stated, universities serve the public good.

As my life evolved and my commitment to public service grew through volunteerism and work with community organizations, my views resonated with Robert Greenleaf's (2002) conception of "servant leaders." Servant leadership "begins with the natural feeling that one wants to serve, to serve *first*. Then conscious choice brings one to aspire to lead" (p. 27). I approach my work from a standpoint of trying to better society and build organizational capacity. I believe we gain by giving of ourselves and learn by engaging others. Serving as a volunteer and community service has made me a better person and strengthened my leadership.

My heroes growing up were Abraham Lincoln, John F. Kennedy, Martin Luther King Jr., César Chávez, and Nelson Mandela. All of them shared the same view of what they wanted for posterity, to create a more just society and a better world. Their values guided their actions. Most did not live to see their dreams realized, but each led with firm conviction and passion. Each provided hope and a dream of a better world, enunciated their vision clearly, built organizations to achieve their dreams, and inspired others to take up their causes. Later, I came to know and respect Dolores Huerta; I include her on that list, as I do my own parents and my aunt, Francisca Flores.

Living through the era of the civil rights movement and my participation in the efforts to expand civil rights and social justice taught me many things, such as organizational skills, leadership, and the ability to communicate in front of a variety of audiences, including Spanish-speaking and working-class communities. My work in several Catholic parishes with immigrant communities and my work in health care laid a basis for understanding fundraising, marketing, decision making in constrained environments, and developing and managing efficient operations, as many of these enterprises were run on less than a shoestring budget. For example, while doing volunteer work in immigrant communities, I learned to judge people based on their values and actions, not their title, education, or the way they spoke. I saw individuals grow, taking on considerable responsibility because the person they worked for had confidence in them, encouraged them, mentored them, and inspired their commitment with vision and example.

LEADERSHIP LESSONS

As a Latino, I often felt I had to work harder and be better than others just to be considered as a finalist. Even so, it was not uncommon to get bypassed for positions. Do not be discouraged, if this happens to you. Keep trying. Work twice as hard and achieve results that no one can question or dismiss. Think big and achieve big. Help improve your institution, particularly in how it serves and graduates Latinos. After all, Latinos have become a larger segment of the higher education population and represent the largest group in K–12. In 2009, 37% of students were Latino—the single largest racial and ethnic group (Council of The Great City Schools, 2011, p. 14). One day, I hope soon, there will be more Latino deans, vice presidents, and presidents. But, we have to work at it every day.

When I first arrived at the University of Houston–Downtown (UHD) in 2009, I found it a very strong institution. It had stable leadership and was growing. Upon my arrival, everyone asked, "What changes will you make?" I believe the best leaders, certainly those who most influenced my life, listened to the needs and desires of those people they served. I felt it was essential to better understand the culture and traditions of UHD, but also to meet and engage stakeholders. I held focus groups on campus with faculty, staff, and students and mailed a survey to alumni, donors, employers, and friends of the university. We appointed a committee to summarize the feedback and present the findings to the campus. This process helped me better understand UHD's strengths and weaknesses and forge a leadership team to build a stronger institution.

Near the end of my first semester at UHD, we launched a good-to-great process, inspired by the work of Jim Collins (2001). We held several retreats in which more than 70 faculty, staff, and students participated. Since my arrival, we have developed a strategic plan and launched a number of initiatives to strengthen student retention and increase graduation rates. We have developed a new vision: "That UHD will be a premier city university where all students are engaged in high-impact experiences and graduate with 21st century skills." Our faculty and staff are now involved in developing these high-impact experiences (learning communities, internships, undergraduate research, service-learning, internships, etc.) and integrating them into the curricula (Association of American Colleges and Universities, 2008). We are also examining our degrees to ensure students receive skill sets for a rapidly changing world.

My approach is value-centered. I believe the same is true for UHD faculty and staff leaders. We realize that the main mission of UHD is to provide an opportunity for student success. Because UHD is both a Hispanic-serving institution and a minority-serving institution, we have an opportunity to build close ties with surrounding Latino and African American communities. UHD has been named one of the top producers of Latino and African American graduates and ranks 33rd and 37th, respectively, in the country in granting bachelor's degrees to both groups

(Diverse Issues in Higher Education, 2012). We are strengthening partnerships with community-based organizations and with the schools in nearby neighborhoods. As our students engage more, they learn more. Moreover, what they learn is made more important by its impact on the communities and schools that surround us. UHD has been recognized as an engaged university by the Carnegie Foundation for the Advancement of Teaching (2008), and in 2012 it was named to the President's Honor Roll for Community Service with Distinction, an honor shared by only 110 colleges and universities across the country (Corporation for National and Community Service, 2012). But, it is more than community service. The university serves as a laboratory for teaching, learning, and research. Engaging students inspires their learning and gives meaning to it.

My experience underscores this point. As an undergraduate at the University of California, Los Angeles, I was overwhelmed by the size of the campus. There were more than 30,000 students and very few Latinos. In my first quarter, I almost dropped out. There were about 800 students in my introductory chemistry course, and I never had a chance to even meet the professor. Fortunately, I met a few Chicano students in my residence hall and, through them, met others. I got involved in support efforts for the United Farm Workers and by that service found a new reason for my education. Later, I worked in a recruitment center in East Los Angeles where I tutored students. I was mentored by and in turn mentored others. Community service inspired my learning, and I have been a strong advocate of engaged learning ever since.

As UHD engages more with the community, we will see more students graduate and go on to graduate and professional schools. We have much work to do at UHD, but it will not be done in isolation. Building partnerships with community-based organizations helps them to grow, provides greater opportunity to our students for engagement, internships, and employment, and enriches our teaching. I am confident that UHD will grow and be a stronger university. In the process, I am committed to developing others as the next generation of leaders, not only in the university, but in Houston. I regularly write a blog on educational issues (http://uhdprez.blogspot.com) and describe my lessons and observations on what is occurring at UHD and nationally.

Over the years, I have served on boards and commissions, held positions of increasing responsibility and authority, and had opportunities to help create stronger organizations. I worked in many community-based organizations, some where I was employed, others where I volunteered or served as a consultant. Certainly, these experiences prepared me for administrative leadership positions. However, fundamentally, my values guide my actions. I am grateful to my mentors, to my parents, and to those with whom I have worked over the years, as I have observed their different leadership styles and techniques. I remain committed to servant leadership and to mentoring future leaders, and I encourage them to mentor others. Recently, in a trip to New Mexico, I had an opportunity to meet with an old friend, someone who I mentored. She told me, "Bill, you opened the door for me and for so many like me. Now, I am doing the very same thing." I see it in the campus where she serves as president. She inspires and encourages others to grow, as she builds a strong institution and an even stronger legacy.

Throughout my career, I have been fortunate enough to find good mentors who encouraged my scholarship and prodded me to consider administrative positions. Now, I encourage others to do the same, advising and mentoring them along the way. I have appointed many Latinos, women, African Americans, and Native Americans to positions of administrative leadership. Several of them are now deans, vice presidents, and even presidents. Mentoring the next generation of higher education leaders, particularly those from underrepresented populations, is vital to the future of this country and to ensuring that our universities are inclusive and serve an increasingly diverse population. As the Latino population grows in the United States, it is essential that we mentor and grow a new generation of Latino college and university leaders. America will be stronger for it.

Eleanor Roosevelt once said, "A good leader inspires people to have confidence in the leader, a great leader inspires people to have confidence in themselves" (Eleanor Roosevelt quotes, n.d., para. 1). Let us inspire others and make a better world.

REFERENCES

Association of American Colleges and Universities. (2008). *High impact educational practices.* Retrieved from http://www.aacu.org/leap/documents/hip_tables.pdf

Benson, L., Harkavy, I., & Harley, M. (2005). Integrating a commitment to the public good into the institutional fabric. In A. Kezar, T. Chambers, & J. Burkhardt (Eds.), *Higher education for the public good: Emerging voices from a national movement.* San Francisco, CA: Jossey-Bass.

Carnegie Foundation for the Advancement of Teaching. (2008). *All classified community engagement institutions.* Retrieved from http://classifications.carnegiefoundation.org/descriptions/2006_2008_CE.pdf

Collins, J. (2001). *Good to great.* New York, NY: HarperCollins.

Corporation for National and Community Service. (2012). *Colleges awarded presidential honor for community service.* Retrieved from http://www.nationalservice.gov/about/newsroom/releases_detail.asp?tbl_pr_id=2079

Council of the Great City Schools. (2011). *Today's Promise, Tomorrow's Future: The Social and Educational Factors Contributing to the Outcomes of Hispanics in Urban Schools.* Retrieved from http://www.cgcs.org/cms/lib/DC00001581/Centricity/Domain/4/HispanicStudy2011.pdf

Diverse Issues in Higher Education. (2012). *Top 100 Degree Producers: Baccalaureate.* Retrieved from http://diverseeducation.com/top100

Eleanor Roosevelt quotes. (n.d.). Retrieved from http://thinkexist.com/quotation/a_good_leader_inspires_people_to_have_confidence/169218.html

Greenleaf, R. K. (2002). *The servant-leader within: A transformative path.* Mahwah, NJ: Paulist Press.

PART III

*Going Inward to
Enhance Leadership*

An Introspective Guide to
Identity and Leadership

Alicia Fedelina Chávez

This chapter offers a guide for introspection of identity with leadership and professional practice. I developed processes over time to work with professionals at conferences, retreats, institutes, and other professional development venues. In addition, for more than 17 years at three different universities, I incorporated first a cultural autobiography and later an identity and leadership autobiography assignment into many of my graduate educational leadership courses. Five of the essays in this book were originally developed by authors for this assignment.

In this chapter, I offer a word of caution, a brief history of evolving processes, and several tools to assist with reflection and facilitation in self and others. In addition, I provide the most recent iteration of the identity and leadership assignment I use in both master's and doctoral courses at The University of New Mexico.

A WORD OF CAUTION

Entering your own introspection on identity and leadership and professional practice as well as facilitating it in others is not for the faint of heart. As you can see in this collection of essays, individuals share profound wisdom and insight yet often share incredibly painful experiences. Not everyone is ready to face the discomfort of going inward or offering empathy required to facilitate introspection of identity and professional practice. Many of these authors discussed with me the difficulty of honestly reflecting on identity, delving deeply enough to understand, and facing certain memories. Most of the authors also shared a deep joy, healing, and helpfulness in the process for their leadership, their continual learning, and their humanity.

I continue this work because of the profound, often life-changing influence it has on individuals and my belief that social justice and higher education are better served by introspective professionals with a deep understanding of these intersections. Each time I read essays of this kind or facilitate professional development, I say a prayer for strength, guidance, empathy, and wisdom. I offer thanks for the gift of each individual and the incredible insights they share with me. I never let myself forget that it is a sacred responsibility and honor to facilitate this depth of introspection in others.

A BRIEF HISTORY

At some point around 1995, I attended the annual meeting of the Association of American Colleges and Universities. During the conference, I attended a session by two professors who presented an assignment they were using in their social sciences courses called a cultural autobiography. Their assignment asked undergraduate students to explore some aspect of their identity that had a strong impact on self-awareness. This presentation served as one impetus for my work on facilitating deeper introspection on identity and professional practice in myself and others.

At the time, I was teaching in a graduate higher education and student affairs program and decided to develop a similar assignment: have students apply an anthropological analysis process to one of their identities and take it a step further to consider how aspects of this identity manifest in their professional practice. In this assignment, students choose identities present before the age of 5 because much of our foundational self is formed in this early period of life (Evans, Forney, Guido, Patton, & Renn, 2010). These early identities form influential foundations, worldviews, and paradigms of how we see, judge, experience, and interpret everything in our lives, including our professional practice.

At first, I decided to have students use a framework similar to those proposed by modern educational and organizational anthropologists, including elements of culture (values, beliefs, assumptions, and norms)

(Ott, 1989) and levels of culture (artifacts, perspectives, values, and assumptions) (Kuh, 1993). Over time, I found the cultural elements of values, beliefs, and behaviors to be the most salient in facilitating graduate student and professional introspection of identity and its manifestations in professional practice and later specifically in leadership.

In more recent years, I frequently facilitate introspection on the intersection of identity with leadership and/or professional practice. I published three identity and leadership autobiographies prior to this book. Currently, a colleague and I are facilitating introspection on culture and college teaching among two cohorts of faculty at two southwestern universities. In addition, a number of colleagues in other universities regularly include this assignment in their graduate higher education courses.

TOOLS TO FACILITATE INTROSPECTION OF IDENTITY AND LEADERSHIP

I often use the following tools in professional development sessions and graduate courses to assist individuals with introspection centered on one identity and leadership or professional practice. As I facilitate, I share examples from my own processing of identity and offer stories to illustrate. I ask participants to choose an identity they are willing to share, using the tools provided or creating from their own imagination. I then ask for everyone to move around the room to see what others create. I usually provide newsprint, markers, and/or crayons to encourage this initial exploration. Participants are often inspired by colleagues' ways of making meaning and gather to discuss ideas with peers. I facilitate discussion to enhance the process and assist participants to apply a variety of techniques to their own introspection. Identities of the Self Worksheet (see Appendix B) is a simple visual to provide participants a chance to ascertain multiple identities. I ask them to reflect first using the worksheet, then share at least one identity from their early years, assisting them to make these determinations by posing questions and inviting input from others.

Identities of the Self Example (see Appendix C) offers an illustration from my identities to share with participants before asking them to use the Identities of the Self Worksheet to list some of their identities. This process assists them to understand what I mean as well as to share parts of myself before asking them to do the same. I encourage participants at this point of the introspective process to share only what they are comfortable disclosing with others. It is important to honor individual privacy and safety, and I encourage them to reflect without using the worksheet if they find that more comfortable.

The Identity and Leadership Worksheet (see Appendix D) is designed to facilitate the going inward analysis of participants from identity through values, assumptions, origins, and current reinforcers to leadership behaviors. The worksheet I filled out (see Appendix E) is part of what I used to write my essay for this book. I developed this worksheet years ago to illustrate this process, and then chose this identity for my current essay on being from a military and sheep herding family. Facilitating participants through this process is helpful to getting started on identity and leadership/professional practice introspection. When completing the Identity and Leadership Autobiography Assignment (see Appendix A), some students include the chart in their autobiography, so I provide it in electronic form as well.

The final step of writing an actual identity and leadership autobiography is helpful to individuals by providing an opportunity to journey deeply inward to understand how our own foundational values, beliefs, and assumptions manifest in current professional priorities, behaviors, and principals. I would encourage professionals reading this book to take time to explore your own identities deeply and consider how these identities influence your judgment, interpretations, and interactions with those who are different from you and those who are similar. By doing so, you will be better able to effectively serve and lead, especially those with fundamentally different ways of being and doing.

I hope you will find deep meaning in identity and leadership introspection. It is challenging to take a close look at ourselves professionally and personally, yet I believe it is well worth the journey.

IDENTITY AND LEADERSHIP
AUTOBIOGRAPHY ASSIGNMENT

Many students describe this assignment as a life-changing experience, though a difficult task to go deeply inward and analyze identity. Even years later, I often hear from former students who are still processing and considering how their many identities manifest in their professional practice. In addition, many discuss how the process of exploring their identities caused them to pause and consider the impact of others' identities allowing them to serve and/or work with them more effectively.

In this autobiography assignment, I require a focus on only one identity, though I know we each embody multiple identities. I do this because it helps learners focus and analyze deeply enough to gain the most from this introspective exercise. I also do not permit focus on identities after the age of five. (For example, I usually have at least one person who has survived a major illness as an adult and requests that focus.) A focus on early identities has proven most helpful to graduate student professional development because early identities serve as a foundation for all that comes later in our lives (Evans et al., 2010).

Identities chosen by students over the years include those we often associate with social justice efforts, such as sexuality, race, socioeconomic class, gender, nationality, ethnicity, culture, tribal affiliation, religion, spirituality, and ability or disability. Early on, I was also asked by students to allow focus on identities such as body type, family size or make up, contrasting parental socioeconomic class, survivorship from childhood trauma such as molestation, parental alcoholism, or abuse. I also had a few students offer strong proposal arguments for focusing on a specific personality trait or ability such as being artistic or catastrophically stubborn/persistent or being from a particular professional family such as all engineers. I do allow students to discuss how a chosen identity might be deeply defined by a second identity, for example, if being nurturing as a woman is defined in a certain way within an African American cultural context. In each case, students have delved more deeply than I ever imagined—exploring, analyzing, illustrating, and discussing manifestations in their professional practice and gaining important insights about their leadership.

Grading the Identity and Leadership Autobiography Assignment is a difficult endeavor for me, as someone with strong empathy. Years ago, I began to offer a tentative grade with extensive guiding feedback—usually on going deeper; providing illustrations, stories, and examples; or filling in missing components. I am careful to provide very specific feedback, using questions, asking them to consider how a "reader" might understand (even though the assignment is private), to clarify, or to consider offering a story or illustration. I offer students a choice to keep that grade or take a week to revise and resubmit for additional learning and an improved grade if they receive anything less than an A+. I am no longer surprised when most students turn in revisions even when they earn an A; they often share that this has been so important they want to continue. I also strongly believe in motivating learning and development through multiple incentives. In this assignment, I encourage "creative enhancement" that substantively enriches meaning making of this identity. Almost all students add some type of creative enhancement including poetry, photos, models, flowcharts, drawings, cartoons, quotes, Internet links to video, or ideas from literature. Most offer multiple types of enhancement. These go well beyond decoration toward deep meaning making of the identity itself. To encourage this enhancement, this is one of the few written assignments or projects in any of my courses that is not required to be in American Psychological Association style.

As is typical of my courses, the assignment description is extensive yet leaves many choices up to the learners. My hope is for each to find unique ways to analyze, explore, illustrate, and interpret—and they do. I offer a "how to" presentation and facilitate several activities to assist them in getting started. This assignment is one of the few that is individual and private, including what identity they choose, unless students wish to share.

Last, I offer many samples through internal university course websites of previous students' autobiographies (shared with permission of the authors), excerpts from a number of autoethnographic works, and several of my own identity and leadership essays (Chávez, 2001; Chávez, 2009; Chávez, 2010). Some students find these samples helpful while others choose to read them after completing the assignment so as not to be influenced. Later in the course, I facilitate conversations in class or online for my web-based courses about identity and professional practice as well as ways we can lead across differences and value systems, especially leading outside the boundaries of values we hold most dear.

In the end, deeply guided introspection centered on identity and leadership seems to provide an important influence to personal and professional growth and development. My current iteration of the Identity and Leadership Autobiography Assignment follows in Appendix A.

REFERENCES

Chávez, A. F. (2001). Spirit & nature: Reflections of a Mestiza in higher education. In M. Jablonski (Ed.), *The implications of student spirituality for Student Affairs Practice* (New directions for student services, no. 95, pp. 69–79). San Francisco, CA: Jossey-Bass.

Chávez, A. F. (2009). Leading in the borderlands: Negotiating ethnic patriarchy for the benefit of students. *NASPA Journal About Women in Higher Education, 1,* 39–65.

Chávez, A. F. (2010). Women and minorities encouraged to apply: Challenges and opportunities of critical cultural feminist leadership in academe. In C. C. Robinson & P. Clardy (Eds.), *Tedious journey's: Women of color use autoethnography to explore their experiences in higher education* (pp. 173–194). New York, NY: Peter Lang.

Evans, N. J., Forney, D. S., Guido, F. M., Patton, L., & Renn, K. A. (2010). *Student development in college: Theory research, and practice* (2nd ed.). San Francisco, CA: Jossey-Bass.

Kuh, G. D. (Ed.). (1993). *Cultural perspectives in student affairs work.* Lanham, MD: American College Personnel Association.

Ott, J. S. (1989). *The organizational perspective.* Pacific Grove, CA: Brooks/Cole.

APPENDIX A

Identity and Leadership Autobiography Assignment

I n *Salsa, Soul, and Spirit: Leadership for a Multicultural Age,* Juana Bordas (2007) showed some of the ways cultural identity and epistemologies affect our leadership and the importance of effectively leading across cultures. Identity has a clear impact on our leadership practice in education and on how we interpret those around us. We each have many identities including those we were *born with* (such as gender, sexuality, race/ethnicity, body type, etc.), and those we were *born into and learn* (such as culture, religion or spirituality, socioeconomic class, the norms of where we were raised, etc.).

Each of our identities has within it an "identity culture" made up of *values, assumptions, beliefs,* and *behaviors.* By reflecting deeply and analyzing our own identities, we can get a better sense of how values originating in these identities affect our leadership in education and enhance our ability to see how individual identities impact daily practice. In addition, this type of self-analysis and self-awareness can offer insights and empathy into serving students from similar and different identities and backgrounds. An identity and leadership autobiography is a deep self-analysis of *one* of our many identities and how it manifests in who we are as leaders today.

For this assignment, choose *one* identity that you have had *since birth or prior to age 5.* Analyze, illustrate, and process personal values and/or beliefs originating in this identity, and how each manifests in your leadership practice or how you believe it will manifest in your future leadership practice.

Autobiographical writing is a kind of storytelling or making sense of things through narrative. This identity and leadership autobiography should be a narrative and interpretation about your life and leadership from within this identity culture. *Be sure to go deep with your analysis!* You are encouraged to utilize metaphors, artifacts (e.g., photos, themes), or other creative means to explore this identity, but be sure to stay focused on specifically describing and interpreting elements of *one* identity only.

Identity and leadership autobiography essays will be kept confidential, though students will be asked to discuss what they learn about their own leadership from completing an identity and leadership autobiography in a discussion following the due date. During this class, we will also discuss leading across identities.

ONE PARAGRAPH/ONE PAGE PROPOSAL

- Submit via the course website.
- A one paragraph/page proposal is due for feedback and approval on the date specified. Feel free to e-mail or arrange a phone or in-person appointment should you wish to discuss your ideas or have questions.
- The Identity and Leadership Self-Analysis Tools will facilitate several activities to assist you in getting started on this assignment. These tools and materials will also be available on the course website. *(Note to reader: These tools are the ones illustrated in Appendices B, C, D, and E.)*
- Samples of identity and leadership autobiographical essays are provided on the course website for you to see how other students and published authors have reflected deeply on personal identities in relation to their leadership. *(Note to reader: Essays from this book could be used as samples for this assignment.)*
- In your one paragraph/one page proposal, discuss the identity you would like to focus on in your autobiographical essay and how focusing your analysis on this specific identity will assist you as a leader in education.
  - *Do* propose an identity that is meaningful to you.
  - *Do not* propose more than one identity. This will be turned down because even though identities intersect and are difficult to separate, it is a very useful exercise to concentrate fully on analyzing the impact of one identity on your leadership. Focusing on one identity allows you to journey more deeply into its manifestations.

o   *Do not* propose an identity that you have come into after the age of 5. Even very strong identity influences, such as major illness, are experienced through the lenses of those identities we were born as or born into. (For example, how one might experience breast cancer as an adult is profoundly influenced by gender and expectations of others about gender).

o   Identity self-analysis can be uncomfortable. Discomfort is often present in deep learning experiences and is helpful to our growth and development as human beings and as leaders.

IDENTITY AND LEADERSHIP AUTOBIOGRAPHY ESSAY

The Identity and Leadership Autobiography Essay is a 14–20 page essay with the following components. Keep in mind that *depth of analysis* and *illustration through narrative* are the keys to success in writing this self-reflective paper. Be sure to *complete every step of the analysis* outlined below. To assist you in depth of analysis and in your writing, essays will be reviewed and assigned a grade. You may choose to accept this grade or revise and resubmit by the deadline provided for additional learning and a better grade. Although this may seem like a long paper, inevitably, even the most concise writers tend to want more than this page amount to explore and discuss intersections of identity, life, and leadership.

Autobiographical Steps of Analysis

1. **Introduction**
   - Describe the identity you chose and how analyzing this identity is important to your effectiveness as an educational leader. This identity should be one you were either born as or born into and have lived within for all or most of your life.
     o   Born as: gender, sexuality, ethnicity/race, ability/disability.
     o   Born into and learned (prior to age 5): culture, family size/type, socio-economic class, religion or spirituality, nationality, geographic region or circumstance such as rural or urban upbringing, and so forth. This must be something you have lived with all or most of your life.

Note: For the following components of this assignment, feel free to integrate all components in each theme/value of your chosen identity *or* use the step-by-step section approach shown here. Some individuals think in integrated ways and others in step-by-step ways.

2. **Identify, describe, and illustrate three to five major values or themes from this identity**

   - If you want, use the Identity Self-analysis Worksheet to *analyze each of three to five major values or themes* that originate in your chosen identity. *(Note to reader: This worksheet is illustrated in Appendix D.)* You may also use metaphors to symbolize each value or theme.

     o For example, students have utilized Catholic sacraments or Jewish rituals as themes to explore the effect of religion; relationships as themes to explore sexuality; cultural symbols to explore ethnic/racial culture; family photos to outline themes of being from a large family; and material objects to explore different class distinctions between two parents.

   - For *each* value or theme in your chosen identity:

     o First, describe and illustrate each value or theme—explain each value/theme and tell stories or give examples to illustrate how/why this value/theme is important to you

     o Second, discuss assumptions and beliefs *underlying* this value or theme and their meaning to you. What assumptions and/or beliefs about others or about the world serve as a foundation for this value or theme? (For example, if you come from a culture that interprets most things from an individual—rather than a collective—perspective, then individuality is likely an underlying assumption beneath some of your values, behaviors, and beliefs.)

     o Third, discuss how this value/theme manifests itself in your personal behaviors, priorities, and/or choices. Be sure to provide examples/stories to illustrate each.

3. **How identity values and themes manifest in your leadership**

   - Describe *and* illustrate how these *three to five values* manifest in your *leadership* or emerging leadership by discussing *both* benefits and limitations of your values in each area below:

o   Analyze the effect of this identity on ways you view and judge others in educational environments—interpretations, assumptions, generalizations about others you work with in education (students, colleagues, those you report to, community, parents, etc.). Focus especially on how you view, judge, or interpret those who have values *different* from yours. (For example, if you are a highly competitive or logical person, how do you interpret and judge those who are not competitive or are intuitive or feeling rather than logical?)

o   Analyze the effect of these values/themes on your behavior toward those you lead or wish to lead in the future. (For example, if you value intuitive or emotional decision making, how would you support, lead, and work with those who value logical aspects of decision making? How do you or could you lead in ways that are supportive of others' different values and ways of doing things? How might you harness their unique values, processes, and abilities toward organizational mission?)

o   Discuss the implications of these values on your ability to *lead a diversity* of students, parents, and community members as a leader.

4. **Identity and leadership effectiveness**
   - Based on the analysis above, summarize how you believe this identity is or will be *helpful* to your effectiveness as a leader *and* how it is or will be *limiting* to your effectiveness as a leader.
   - How can you draw on helpful elements and negotiate limiting elements to be effective with others *not* from your identity? Keep in mind that how *others* see and judge us often impacts our leadership—so how can we negotiate this to be effective?
     o   The following essays on negotiating across identities to lead effectively may be helpful examples to review. The course website contains additional samples written by other students and published authors.
       □   Chávez, A. F. (2009). Leading in the borderlands: Negotiating ethnic patriarchy for the benefit of students. *NASPA Journal About Women in Higher Education, 1,* 39–65.
       □   Chávez, A. F. (2010). Women and minorities encouraged to apply: Challenges and opportunities of critical cultural

feminist leadership in academe. In C. C. Robinson & P. Clardy (Eds.), *Tedious journeys: Women of color use autoethnography to explore their experiences in higher education* (pp. 173–194). New York, NY: Peter Lang.

☐ Chávez, A. F. (2001). Spirit & nature: Reflections of a Mestiza in higher education. In M. Jablonski (Ed.), *The implications of student spirituality for Student Affairs Practice* (New directions for student services, no. 95, pp. 69–79). San Francisco, CA: Jossey-Bass.

5. **Discuss three learning goals**
   - For your continuing/future reflection and development toward deeper awareness, understanding, and practice in relation to identity and leadership.

Essay Format

For this paper, you are not required to use outside citations or American Psychological Association Style.

Creative Enhancement

You are encouraged to enhance the identity and leadership autobiography with metaphor, photos, poetry, imagery, visual representations such as models or flowcharts, and so forth. A higher grade is possible for substantive creative enhancement. Be sure creative additions *enhance* the analysis, description, and illustration of your identity—not just decorate the paper.

Reference

Bordas, J. (2007). *Salsa, soul, and spirit: Leadership for a multicultural age.* San Francisco, CA: Berrett-Koehler.

APPENDIX B

Identities of the Self Worksheet

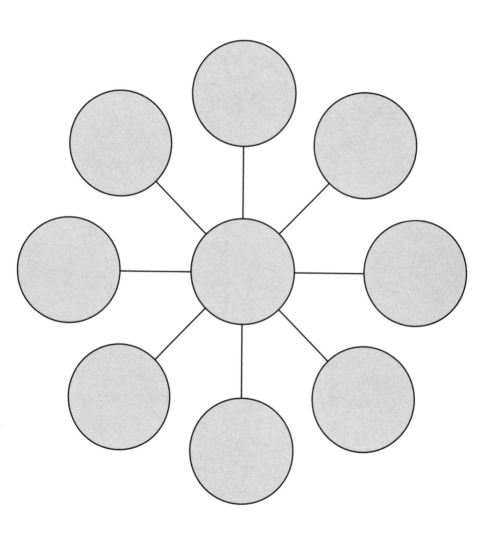

APPENDIX C

Identities of the Self Example

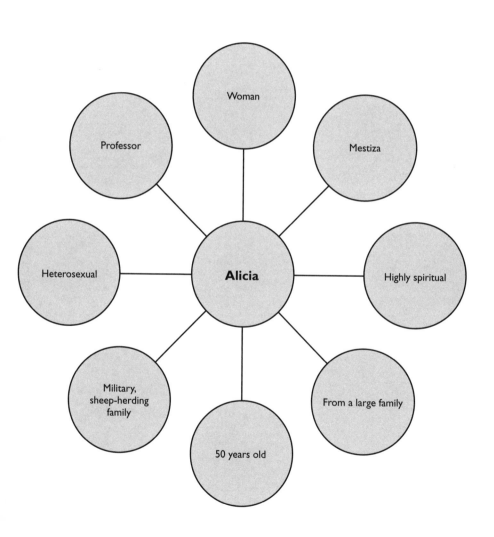

APPENDIX D

Identity and Leadership Worksheet

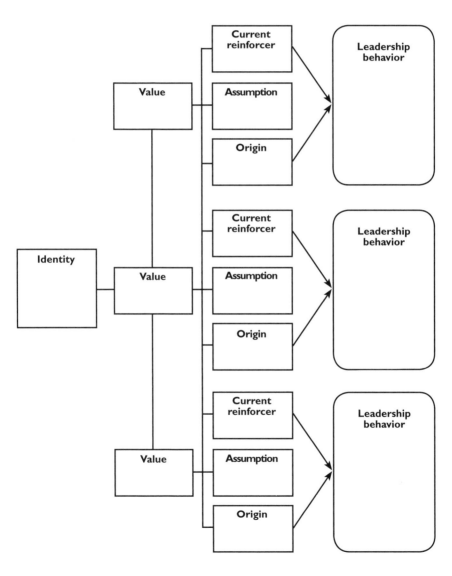

APPENDIX E

Identity and Leadership Worksheet Example

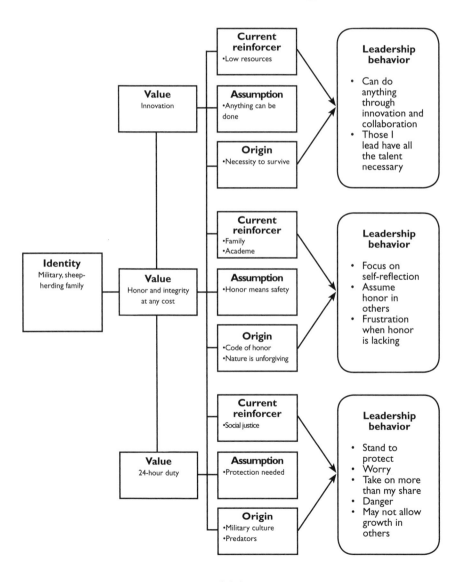

Identity
Military, sheep-
herding family

Value
Innovation

Current reinforcer
•Low resources

Assumption
•Anything can be done

Origin
•Necessity to survive

Leadership behavior
• Can do anything through innovation and collaboration
• Those I lead have all the talent necessary

Value
Honor and integrity at any cost

Current reinforcer
•Family
•Academe

Assumption
•Honor means safety

Origin
•Code of honor
•Nature is unforgiving

Leadership behavior
• Focus on self-reflection
• Assume honor in others
• Frustration when honor is lacking

Value
24-hour duty

Current reinforcer
•Social justice

Assumption
•Protection needed

Origin
•Military culture
•Predators

Leadership behavior
• Stand to protect
• Worry
• Take on more than my share
• Danger
• May not allow growth in others

INDEX

PRAISE FOR
CHASING GREATNESS

"The 1973 U.S. Open had everything: the most terrifying golf course in the land; an aging but still fiercely competitive Arnold Palmer; Jack Nicklaus, Lee Trevino, and Gary Player at the top of their games; a brilliant but troubled golfer named John Schlee making his one bid for immortality; and Johnny Miller's final-round 63 that remains the Everest of major championship lore. Now that tournament has a chronicle worthy of it, *Chasing Greatness*, a prodigiously researched, elegantly written, myth-debunking eagle from the fairway by Adam Lazarus and Steven Schlossman. Fore!"

—Ron Rapoport, author of *The Immortal Bobby: Bobby Jones and the Golden Age of Golf*

"In 1973, Oakmont was the stage for one of the most riveting sports stories of the twentieth century. . . . Adam Lazarus and Steve Schlossman deliver a grand retelling of a U.S. Open finish like no other. . . . Johnny Miller's final turn of 63 shocked the world, denied the hometown hero, Arnold Palmer, a magical punctuation to his prime, and left an impossibly difficult game looking downright vulnerable. This is a must read for fans of golf, and for fans of the human spirit."   —Ian O'Connor, *New York Times* bestselling author of *Arnie & Jack: Palmer, Nicklaus, and Golf's Greatest Rivalry*

"Informative, engaging, and entertaining . . . captures the excitement of the 1973 U.S. Open and explains why it was so special in the history of golf."

—George B. Kirsch, professor of history, Manhattan College, and author of *Golf in America*

"Authors Adam Lazarus and Steve Schlossman re-create the 1973 U.S. Open with a drama worthy of the event itself. . . . Every sentence is rich with detail, all woven into an intimate play-by-play. Four days of golf changed lives and careers, and in this precise account, you understand why."

—Chico Harlan, *Washington Post* staff writer

"If you want the most thorough history of a most memorable championship, this is it."   —Al Barkow, former PGA broadcaster and author of *Golf's Golden Grind* and *Gettin' to the Dance Floor: An Oral History of American Golf*

CHASING GREATNESS

. • • • .

Johnny Miller, Arnold Palmer, and
the Miracle at Oakmont

ADAM LAZARUS

STEVE SCHLOSSMAN

NEW AMERICAN LIBRARY

NEW AMERICAN LIBRARY
Published by New American Library, a division of
Penguin Group (USA) Inc., 375 Hudson Street,
New York, New York 10014, USA
Penguin Group (Canada), 90 Eglinton Avenue East, Suite 700, Toronto,
Ontario M4P 2Y3, Canada (a division of Pearson Penguin Canada Inc.)
Penguin Books Ltd., 80 Strand, London WC2R 0RL, England
Penguin Ireland, 25 St. Stephen's Green, Dublin 2,
Ireland (a division of Penguin Books Ltd.)
Penguin Group (Australia), 250 Camberwell Road, Camberwell, Victoria 3124,
Australia (a division of Pearson Australia Group Pty. Ltd.)
Penguin Books India Pvt. Ltd., 11 Community Centre, Panchsheel Park,
New Delhi - 110 017, India
Penguin Group (NZ), 67 Apollo Drive, Rosedale, North Shore 0632,
New Zealand (a division of Pearson New Zealand Ltd.)
Penguin Books (South Africa) (Pty.) Ltd., 24 Sturdee Avenue,
Rosebank, Johannesburg 2196, South Africa

Penguin Books Ltd., Registered Offices:
80 Strand, London WC2R 0RL, England

Published by New American Library, a division of Penguin Group (USA) Inc. Previously published in a New
American Library hardcover edition.

First New American Library Trade Paperback Printing, April 2011
10 9 8 7 6 5 4 3 2 1

 REGISTERED TRADEMARK—MARCA REGISTRADA

New American Library Trade Paperback ISBN: 978-0-451-23264-9

The Library of Congress has catalogued the hardcover edition of this title as follows:

Lazarus, Adam.
Chasing greatness. Johnny Miller, Arnold Palmer, and the miracle
at Oakmont/Adam Lazarus, Steven Schlossman
    p. cm.
Includes bibliographical references
ISBN 978-0-451-22987-8
1. U.S. Open (Golf Tournament)(1973. Oakmont, Pa.)   2. Golf courses—Pennsylvania—Oakmont
(Allegheny County)—History.   3. Miller, Johnny, 1947–   4. Palmer, Arnold, 1929–
5. Golfers—United States.   I. Schlossman, Steve.   II. Title.
GV970.3.U69L39 2010
796.352'66—dc22   2009052780

Set in Electra
Designed by Ginger Legato

Printed in the United States of America

For Mom and Dad, who helped me to chase greatness.

—AGL

To Stephanie—still my sunshine.

—SS

CONTENTS

CHASING GREATNESS

Talkin' Oakmont

"Since my arrival in this country . . . all the boys in New York are talking Oakmont and what is liable to happen there in the Open," said Sid Brews, South Africa's top golfer, as he debarked in America to compete in the 1935 U.S. Open. From coast to coast—indeed, around the golfing world—everyone was talking Oakmont.

In 1935, the U.S. Open came to the Oakmont Country Club: a field of nightmares planted three decades earlier by iron baron Henry C. Fownes on rolling farmland northeast of Pittsburgh, flanking the Allegheny River. No one expected this contest to be easy: The 1927 U.S. Open, which saw Tommy Armour defeat Harry Cooper in a play-off, was the most exacting test in the history of amateur or professional golf. That week, putting on Oakmont's greens, according to the sportswriter Grantland Rice, was "like a marble skidding across ice."

Armour, the intrepid, shrapnel-filled war hero, admitted that the strain of playing Oakmont in 1927 and 1935 emotionally scarred him. Cooper—whose twenty-foot putt on the fifth green ran into the sand sixty feet beyond the flagstick—insisted that while Oakmont was superbly designed, the slippery greens and uniquely "furrowed" bunkers were simply unfair. Walter Hagen stated his viewpoint concisely: "Oakmont is a duffers' course. It makes duffers out of all of us." And Scotsman MacDonald Smith, briefly Oakmont's head professional before World War I, held his tongue, but spoke clearly enough for his colleagues in 1935: "We canna' say anything, ye ken, but we can think our thoughts."

Not every notable judged Oakmont so harshly in the weeks leading up to the championship. All agreed the course was the toughest in the United States and perhaps "the severest test of golf in the world"—a "real Frankenstein"—but several praised it as rigorously fair and "scientific." Even Bobby Jones, who after winning the 1925 National Amateur at Oakmont criticized the furrowed bunkers as unjust to better players, was on board: "I always regard Oakmont as the finishing school of golf. . . . If you have a weakness, it will be brought to light playing there. It is not tough because it is freakish. The holes are all fair. They are fundamental from an architectural and scientific point of view."

Oakmont's most vocal advocate among the era's great golfers was Gene Sarazen. In 1922, as a twenty-year-old, Sarazen won the PGA at Oakmont; in April 1935, just two months before the U.S. Open, he electrified the golfing world by scoring his famous double eagle at Augusta National to win the Masters. Sarazen became the bookmakers' favorite (6–1 odds) to win his eighth major at Oakmont, and his views naturally received close scrutiny by the partisan Pittsburgh press.

"Wherever you go they ask you about Oakmont," Sarazen told reporters upon his return from playing exhibitions in South America, the South Seas, and Australia. "It is the most talked-of course in the world . . . a masterpiece . . . one of the few scientifically constructed layouts . . . I have come to the conclusion that it is the greatest golf course in the world."

But its being the "greatest" course did not necessarily mean that the greatest golfers won. That was clearly the case in the 1919 National Amateur, won by Davey Herron, the son of an Oakmont member and former collegiate golfer (of no great distinction) at Princeton. Admittedly quirky, Oakmont gave locals like Herron a distinct advantage—most obviously in its lightning-quick, sharply tilted, compulsively undulating greens, and its two hundred–plus "furrowed" bunkers, where the ball lay partially submerged between deep, wide furrows of sand (better fit for growing potatoes, said an irate Brit). The course also stood out for its great length (nearly seven thousand yards), the long carries required off the tee, huge greens, narrow fairways, cross bunkers, thickly grassed mounds, and assorted ditches, pits, and other hazards to harshly penalize the slightest error.

And to add insult to injury in 1935, H.C.'s son, William C. Fownes Jr., and his trusted greenkeeper, Emil Loeffler, had recently stiffened the difficulty of the course. Following a record-setting score of 294 (six over par) by Willie Macfarlane in the Pennsylvania State Open, they added numerous bunkers, expanded existing bunkers, and shifted tees laterally to lengthen holes and prevent "shortcuts." "Yes, you bet this course is tougher than it was in 1927," Armour told reporters. "I would say that it is easily two shots tougher. . . . Those traps and greens are going to make a lot of trouble."

The course setup perfectly embodied the stern philosophy of Fownes and Loeffler: "A shot poorly played should be a shot irrevocably lost."

Given these conditions, Sarazen made a startling prediction. Without downplaying his own chances of victory, he told everyone to watch out for the relatively unknown Sam Parks Jr.

The current teaching professional at nearby South Hills Country Club, Parks had improved his game during the past two seasons on the Florida winter tour; he'd finished thirty-seventh in the 1934 U.S. Open and fifteenth in the recently contested Masters Golf Tournament. Parks had also become an exceptionally straight driver during a two-year stint as the pro at Summit Golf Course near Uniontown, where the penalty for errant shots was a lost ball over a cliff. Parks had been practicing feverishly at Oakmont, working especially on adapting his putting stroke and pitch shots to the exceptional firmness and speed of Oakmont's greens.

"His knowledge of Oakmont and its pitfalls should be a great asset," Sarazen observed of the native Pittsburgher. "Oakmont is a course that needs knowing. This knowledge must be gained long in advance of the championship, to give one a chance to get over the first shock coming from its severity."

In the end, Parks won the 1935 U.S. Open by two shots with a score of 299, largely because he outputted everyone and kept most of his tee shots in the fairways. A few commentators begrudged Parks his triumph. H. B. Martin labeled Parks a "mediocre player," and the long-hitting Jimmy Thomson, who finished second to Parks and toured with him afterward, called him (according to Charles Price) "the most consistent seventy-five player who ever lived."

Still, Parks earned his victory at Oakmont in classic U.S. Open style: straight driving, great lag putting. The top players were mainly furious at the course setup by Fownes and Loeffler that allowed a journeyman with special local knowledge to triumph. Inaccessible pin positions and "spun-glass" greens ("a bit of fuzz atop a rock-hard surface of tiny pebbles," according to Ron Whitten) made three- and four-putts commonplace. The greens came to befuddle, even embarrass, stars like Leo Diegel and Harry Cooper, each among the game's best short-game artists.

Some called the 1935 U.S. Open "Fownes's Folly." In the words of New York golf journalist George Trevor, the championship was transformed into "some strange species of outdoor bagatelle . . . a travesty on golf." Bob Harlow, the PGA Tour manager, called the greens "skating rinks" that presented not "a test of skills, but a roulette wheel, upon which no one could tell what hole the ball would drop into."

Armour especially stung the stewards of Oakmont for making the course itself, rather than the quality of golf, the main show: "the first course I ever saw that was bigger than the player," said the 1927 champion.

W. C. Fownes gave back in kind: "The virility and charm of the game lies in its difficulties. Keep it rugged, baffling, hard to conquer, otherwise we shall soon tire of it and cast it aside. . . . Let the clumsy, the spineless and the alibi artist stand aside!"

The 1935 championship had barely ended when Oakmont's counterparts at Baltusrol—host of the 1936 U.S. Open—let it be known that they would give the players "a sporting chance to recoup the prestige lost on Oakmont's roller-coaster greens." Baltusrol did just that: Tony Manero, already a six-time winner on the tour, won the 1936 U.S. Open with a score of 282, the lowest by four shots in over four decades of U.S. Open history.

Regardless of the murky legacy of the 1935 U.S. Open, no one—including W.C. and Loeffler—wanted to revive the controversies that surrounded Oakmont's extreme penalty. It simply wasn't good for the game; golf wasn't meant to be a public display of self-flagellation.

The 1935 U.S. Open inevitably left club members queasy. How long could Oakmont maintain its fearsome reputation if it produced "fluke" winners? What could Oakmont's stewards do to better enable the course to identify the best golfers in the world?

IN 1973, AS THE U.S. Open returned for the fifth time to Oakmont Country Club, its reputation as the meanest test in American championship golf remained fully intact. And while Fownes and Loeffler were long gone, their penal philosophy—embodied in slick, mystifying greens and endless carpets of sand—

continued to be the course signatures. Oakmont still screamed tough, and not due to a U.S.G.A. makeover. "If they want to see Oakmont when it's really tough," the members liked to say, "they should play in the member-guest." That was when the greens rolled till tomorrow and the fairways were best located by microscope.

Much had changed since the 1930s. Oakmont still set the punitive standard in American championship golf, but it was no longer as brutal. Oakmont officials had cut the number of bunkers nearly in half, and removed just about every cross bunker. More important, furrows no longer striped the bunkers. In 1964, Oakmont substituted a conventional silicon-based sand for the heavy, coarse Allegheny River variety that had made it possible to form furrows in the first place. The bunkers would now have to stand, strategically, on their own.

The one-of-a-kind greens had also been rehabilitated agronomically, following Loeffler's passing in 1947. His frequent low mowing (one-sixteenth of an inch) of the naturally growing Poa annua grass (a weed, in reality), combined with constant topsoiling, no aeration, and incessant rolling—using rollers that weighed around 500, maybe even 750 pounds—had caused irreparable damage. Modern greenkeeping methods eventually brought the putting surfaces back to good health in the 1950s, and while they were definitely slower than in 1927 and 1935, the greens—at the express request of the membership—remained exceptionally "keen" and preserved all of their original undulations. In the postwar era, as earlier, Oakmont's greens still set the standard as the fastest, firmest, trickiest, and truest in the United States—"true to the ultimate wiggle," as Rice described them over a half century earlier.

Oakmont had seen several other changes, as Sam Parks observed when he made an appearance at the 1973 U.S. Open, thirty-eight years removed from his one and only tour triumph. The course played much longer, as the fairways were now irrigated and the grass grew taller (Loeffler had also "rolled" the fairways with his heavy machinery, making three-hundred-yard drives common when conditions were dry). Several fairways in 1973 had been narrowed and the rough grown thicker, partly to compensate for the removal of bunkers (Fownes and Loeffler preferred to see errant shots scamper into the furrows). Overall, Parks contended, the course in 1973 would play around two shots easier than when he won in 1935.

While the changes to Oakmont had evolved gradually, under the club members' careful scrutiny, one question they no longer had to address in 1973 was whether the severity of the course tended to produce quirky champions. Since World War II, Oakmont had hosted three major championships: the PGA in 1951 and the U.S. Opens of 1953 and 1962. And a more stellar, era-defining group of champions was impossible to find.

Sam Snead won his third and final PGA Championship in 1951, struggling in early matches (the PGA was still contested at match play) before winning big against his last two opponents. Rains affected play decisively; one of the longest hitters of his generation, Snead was delighted to see a wet course that played longer, with softer and slower greens as well. (Like most who learned to play on Bermuda grass, Snead preferred slower greens.)

Rain or no rain, Snead broke par in most of his matches, and he shot well under par in both closing matches. Oakmont may still have been the toughest course in the land (that was what the assembled pros said), but with the U.S. Open scheduled for Oakmont in 1953, a four-round total over 300 would no longer be a competitive score.

Unavailable to play the PGA in 1951, Ben Hogan showed up very early to practice at Oakmont in the late spring of 1953, and his scoring improved dramatically with successive practice rounds. His comfort with the Oakmont terrain peaked during the first round, as he shot a record-breaking 67, five under par. Hogan scored even par for the remainder of the championship, enough to easily defeat Snead, who collapsed over the final holes to lose by a large margin (283 to 289).

Hogan and Snead were undeniably the two greatest players of their generation; the post-Fownes, post-Loeffler Oakmont now boasted a superior ability to filter out and crown the era's top players as its champions. And with two other Hall of Famers, Lloyd Mangrum and Jimmy Demaret, finishing in the third and fourth positions in 1953, the renovated course allowed the cream to rise to the top.

The 1962 U.S. Open only confirmed Oakmont's stature as America's best course for bestowing golf greatness (later it would be joined by Augusta National). In one of the most famous championships in history, Arnold Palmer and Jack Nicklaus tied for the lead after four rounds—totaling the same 283 as Hogan had nine years earlier. Nicklaus, the most accomplished "rookie" in tour history, defeated Palmer in a mild upset (a staggering defeat to distraught Pittsburghers, however). As with Hogan and Snead nine years earlier, the 1962 championship marked another indelible moment at Oakmont, when the two top players of their generation separated themselves out from everyone else.

It was hard to deny that the modifications club members introduced to Oakmont in the postwar era—without damaging the course's reputation as quintessentially tough—had produced a better, fairer, and more predictable test of championship golf than during the reign of Fownes and Loeffler.

For the 1973 U.S. Open, several fairways were pinched and a few bunkers were added or removed: a number of holes arguably played slightly tougher than in the previous championship. On the sixteenth, for example, a strategic bunker that Fownes and Loeffler had placed in front of the green for the 1935 U.S. Open—but which had been removed afterward to ease up on amateurs—was now restored, "changing the whole character of this long par-3." On the seventeenth, the members spent $10,000 to build a new tee farther back and farther left than the original, in order to fend off exceptionally long hitters: a guarantee that for everyone, this short, dogleg par-four would require two well-executed shots to set up a birdie opportunity.

Other than that, the course in 1973 remained virtually identical to the course where Snead, Hogan, Nicklaus, and Palmer had finished on top. There was no better place to chase greatness in golf, and to identify the era's greatest golfers, than Oakmont.

· DAY ONE ·

June 14, 1973

· 1 ·

The King Never Left

Arnold Palmer had made the drive dozens of times.

Early Thursday morning, June 14, 1973, he once again hopped into his statement Cadillac and headed west. It was just forty-five minutes from his home in Latrobe to Oakmont Country Club in Oakmont, Pennsylvania.

As he drove, first along U.S. State Route 30, then veering north up the Pennsylvania Turnpike, he passed through the foothills of the Allegheny Mountains and the eastern sections of greater Pittsburgh, the region that for the past decade also went by another name: Arnold Palmer Country.

At the end of the familiar route, he pulled into the nondescript, austere entry of Oakmont Country Club. It had been thirty-two years since Palmer first visited Oakmont as a precocious twelve-year-old golfer—accompanied by Harry Saxman, president of Latrobe Country Club and an Oakmont member—but not all that much had changed.

"I think my first round was about 1941," Palmer said decades after posting what he remembered was a ten-over-par 82. "And I was enthralled with the golf course, with the presence of this place, the locker room, the pro shop, everything here. The wooden floor in the grillroom, all the things that made it feel like a golf club and one that you wanted to be present in. And you wanted to go out and play golf and come back in and have that cool drink, whatever it might be. This was a place that lent itself to golf."

11

A few years later, in August 1945, a fifteen-year-old Arnold Palmer, along with eight thousand other golf fans, crowded Oakmont's fairways to see Gene Sarazen, Sam Snead, Harold "Jug" McSpaden, and Byron Nelson tee off in the Victory Loan golf tournament, a four-day exhibition in which the participants were paid in war bonds. Nelson, nearing the end of the most triumphant season in golf history (eighteen wins, including eleven in a row), recorded the lowest total, three less than Snead. But Oakmont proved the real winner: Nelson, whose 68.33 scoring average that season set a record that would last fifty-five years, finished at seven over par 295. On a daily basis, Oakmont still played as tough as any championship golf course in America.

Soon Palmer became the area's top young star, winning five of six West Penn Amateur tournaments between 1947 and 1952. Given his growing local celebrity, as well as his close friendship with Oakmont pro Lew Worsham's younger brother, Bud, the club's brass happily invited the brawny local kid to play.

"I used to play it a lot in my high school days," Palmer said about Oakmont at the peak of his professional career. "In fact, it almost amounted to a daily diet."

Over the years, Palmer did more than just play the club regularly—to the point where it became his second "home" course. From childhood on, Oakmont served as a main stage for landmark moments that defined his illustrious career. There in 1949, he won his second West Penn Amateur title, trouncing four-time champion Jack Benson, 11 & 10 in the final match. Four years later, still a top-notch amateur, he competed in his first U.S. Open at the then par-seventy-two course, missing the cut while Ben Hogan cruised to his fourth and final national title in 1953. A decade later, Oakmont was the site of Palmer's most painful career disappointment, when his putter betrayed him and the favored King of the PGA Tour lost the 1962 U.S. Open to upstart Jack Nicklaus in an eighteen-hole play-off.

And now, at forty-three years of age, Arnold Palmer—his hair slightly grayed, his body saddled with aches and ailments, yet still hungry as ever for victory— returned to conquer treacherous Oakmont and raise an eighth major championship trophy into the air.

Palmer's march to iconic status in golf history was unprecedented in so many ways. Equal parts sports star and sex symbol—an anomaly for a game as buttoned-down as golf—he somehow blended a plainspoken, aw-shucks celebrity with creative, aggressive entrepreneurship to build an empire. That empire recast modern golf as a business and spawned IMG, the behemoth of modern-day global marketing. And, on the golf course, Palmer flashed the kind of raw energy and transparent emotion that enabled a TV-addicted generation of postwar Americans not merely to share but viscerally feel his joys and disappointments from thousands of miles away.

But it was especially refreshing that a man so well-known across the globe—and so fabulously wealthy—still woke up each summer morning in his tiny, blue-collar hometown of Latrobe, Pennsylvania. In fact, the relatively modest, middle-class home in which he and his wife, Winnie, lived stood just a solid tee shot from the small, undistinguished quarters adjacent to the sixth tee of Latrobe Country Club in which he grew up; on the same fields where, as a boy, Arnold and his father, Milfred "Deacon" Palmer, hunted pheasants and rabbits to supplement the family diet during the depths of the Great Depression.

His choice of residence was no small virtue, and no calculated PR stunt. Even though he dined with movie stars, played golf with presidents, and won recognition in 1970 as *Sports Illustrated*'s Athlete of the Decade for the 1960s—edging out names like Ali, Russell, Mantle, and Unitas—Palmer never became too big for Latrobe. To be sure, he was far shrewder and more downright intelligent than he often let on, and not only about the game of golf. He also craved wealth, fame, and some of their perks; his conservative Republican politics reflected his rapid ascent into the status of the superrich (his father, by contrast, remained a staunch Rooseveltian Democrat). Palmer remained happily secure in his core small-town identity.

And in the spring of 1973, Palmer leaned on his hometown roots more than ever.

DURING THE 1950S AND 1960S, Arnold Palmer won more tournaments, prize money, and public adoration than anyone ever imagined possible in the game of golf. Great sports stars abounded in the postwar era, but not since Babe Ruth in the 1920s had anyone earned the sovereign mantle of "the King."

But, as Shakespeare's King Henry IV observes, "Uneasy lies the head that wears a crown."

For all the miracles that King Arnie performed during his reign—sinking impossible putts, driving undrivable greens, recovering brilliantly from sand

and forest, stealing the 1960 U.S. Open with a final-round 65 for the greatest comeback in history—the public remained fickle. Fed by a gaggle of golf journalists who mingled intimately with the touring pros, the fan bandwagon got lighter at any sign of adversity.

As early as 1965, Palmer's worst year in a decade on tour, the whispers began. He turned thirty-six that fall and had won only one tournament in the previous seventeen months. The "What's wrong with Arnie?" chatter swelled. He rebounded the following season, winning three times and nabbing top-ten finishes in each of the four major championships. But a breathtaking collapse in the final round of the 1966 U.S. Open at the Olympic Club stuck in the minds of fans and writers. Despite a seven-stroke lead with nine holes to play, Palmer lost his concentration and composure down the stretch, and the following day he lost the 1966 National title to Billy Casper in a play-off.

After winning seven major championships in seven seasons (1958–1964), an emotionally draining string of five runner-up finishes in majors plagued Palmer in the late 1960s. Sportswriters who understood the facts were puzzled by the failures: Until the end of the decade, Palmer remained competitive both with Nicklaus and the dozens of can't-miss All American collegians who funneled onto the tour.

"At the age of 39," wrote Dave Anderson of the *New York Times*, Palmer "has not won a tournament on the Professional Golfers' Association tour this year and he has earned only $34,967, hardly enough to keep his Lear jet in fuel. Physically, he hasn't changed much. His neck appears carved out of mahogany. His hands are thick, his stomach flat, and he seems to march, rather than stroll, onto a green. But he isn't winning."

Palmer didn't duck his critics. In fact, he agreed with some popular theories about why he could no longer win the big ones.

"I will admit," he told reporters in June 1969, at the age of thirty-nine, "I've been a bit preoccupied with my business interests. I need to settle down and start concentrating more. I intend to do it. I see no reason why I shouldn't start winning again."

Palmer's collection of dry cleaners, golf resorts, car dealerships, etc., certainly consumed his mental energy and disrupted his practice sessions between tournaments. Three times during the decade he actually passed up the British Open—the event he single-handedly resuscitated by finishing second in 1960 and winning the event the next two years—claiming other business obligations.

But it was a host of medical issues that speared him on the course. Though his muscles still rippled and he appeared virile, even indestructible, on TV and magazine covers, the kid from just outside Pittsburgh was no longer the man of steel.

For one, Palmer's eyesight declined steadily (extreme nearsightedness) during his thirties and he had a hard time addressing the problem on the golf course. He switched back and forth between glasses and contact lenses, sometimes shunning both out of sheer frustration. Palmer wasn't yet ready to accept the early signs of aging. Years later, he tellingly called the situation "the most traumatic thing that happened in my career."

Palmer's back also troubled him. A month before his U.S. Open nightmare at the Olympic Club, Palmer nearly fell to his knees in severe pain after teeing off in the second round of the Greater New Orleans Open. He withdrew from the tournament the next day.

Three years later, an injured hip hampered his entire 1969 season. In March, he took two weeks off to ease a chronic ache in his hip that had actually emerged in the late 1950s, but that he had kept from the public. Unfortunately none of the home remedies sent by his beloved fans—liniments, pads, exercises—brought relief from the considerable stress caused by his unorthodox, whiplash swing (as Sam Snead said, on Palmer's every tee shot he appeared to be trying to drive the green). After losing his exemption to play in the U.S. Open for the first time, and having to compete in a sectional qualifier to earn entry—Palmer didn't say so, but his fans complained to the U.S.G.A. that this was beneath the King's dignity—he gritted through and heroically tied for sixth at the Champions Golf Club in Houston, just three shots behind the surprise winner, Orville Moody.

But the hip never really healed. A woeful 82 at the NCR Country Club in Dayton, Ohio, to begin the PGA Championship in August, followed by numbing pain when he awoke the next morning to play the second round, forced Palmer to withdraw—his first and only withdrawal from a major championship. Doctors suggested that he take a long rest and let the hip heal. While friends like Gary Player and Jack Nicklaus scoffed at the notion that Palmer's career was in jeopardy, others were not as optimistic.

"Arnie had to withdraw from the PGA Tournament the other day with an inflamed hip," golfer Frank Beard wrote in his on-the-tour diary that soon became a bestselling book. "Nobody's got more determination or more spirit, but this time I really think he's finished," Beard dourly concluded after witnessing the agony Palmer was suffering.

Sentiments like these inspired rumors in 1969 that Palmer might leave golf for politics. Widely known as a friend and Augusta golfing partner of former President Dwight D. Eisenhower, Palmer later met privately with President Richard M. Nixon, a closet golfer, to offer his thoughts on ending the Vietnam War. His celebrity, charm, and likability convinced Republican strategists he might be the man to run for governor of Pennsylvania in the fall of 1970 against Democrat Milton Shapp. The idea gained enough momentum that only two weeks after his withdrawal from the PGA, Palmer had to issue a written statement to the press declaring that golf—not politics—was his profession for the foreseeable future.

The following week, *Sports Illustrated* trumpeted the passing of a spent hero into the fading status of a timeless legend. On September 1, nine days before his birthday, Palmer's face, his brow wrinkled, appeared on the cover of the magazine beneath the headline, "Farewell to an Era: Arnold Palmer Turns 40."

Inside the magazine, legendary golf writer Dan Jenkins stated that the issue's goal was "not to signal an end to the Age of Palmer, but to salute it." And salute it Jenkins did, by re-creating the U.S. Open win in 1960, painting with words a picture of Palmer as the masculine, heroic people's champion, even suggesting that Palmer had recently "given a nobility to losing." The "Age of Palmer" sounded like a salute to a retired warrior from the distant past.

Palmer's exit from golf's spotlight in 1969 did not last long. Accustomed to these doomsday appraisals—he had been addressing them for years, and with considerable candor—he simply ignored this latest set. He stayed away from the tour for eight weeks and, begrudgingly, followed his doctor's advice and played sparingly. And perhaps to send a clear signal to pessimists like Beard, while away from the tour and "resting," he shot a career-low score of 60 during a warm-up at Latrobe Country Club, the homestead where he had learned to live the game (and which he purchased two years later, enabling his father to work there forever).

In three autumn events after he returned to the tour, Palmer finished no better than twenty-seventh, but he managed to break par in half of the rounds, was relatively pain-free, and was confident his game was improving each week. Then, beginning on Thanksgiving Day 1969, Palmer boldly reclaimed his place among the game's greats. Over Harbour Town Golf Links in Hilton Head, he nabbed three birdies on the opening seven holes to share the first-round lead at the Heritage Golf Classic. By Sunday afternoon, Palmer had secured his first win in over a year.

"This was as important to me as winning the National Open or the Masters or anything," he told reporters afterward in a euphoric display of a forty-year-old's delight. As he well knew, Ben Hogan had his greatest year on tour in 1953 at age forty-one, and Palmer's longtime competitors Julius Boros and Sam Snead remained long off the tee and were winners well into their forties. After the triumph at Harbour Town, no one could deny that Palmer glory still lay ahead.

Palmer needed only one more week to fully reveal his resurrection. Though eleven under par after three rounds at the Danny Thomas–Diplomat Classic in Miami, he still trailed a red-hot Gay Brewer, former Masters champion, by six strokes. But no one charged a golf course, or a leader board, on the final day like Arnold Palmer. Just before closing out the front nine in only thirty strokes—just as at Cherry Hills, missing a hole in one by inches on the ninth—Palmer reduced Brewer's lead to three. Consecutive birdies on numbers fourteen and fifteen gave Palmer a share of the lead, and he then surged in front for good by two-putting for birdie on the par-five seventeenth. He then put an exclamation point on the comeback win by draining a twenty-foot birdie putt at the home hole.

"Getting it going again is probably the thing I wanted most in my life," he said afterward. "I knew I was going to play again, but I didn't know how successfully. There were some doubts in my own mind."

A bit uncertain, perhaps—as a forty-year-old superstar athlete should rightly be. But three months earlier, Jenkins's *Sports Illustrated* article had reminded everyone that it was Palmer who set the standard for great comeback victories, and on that Sunday in Miami—his last tournament of the 1960s—Palmer did it again with a heroic closing-round 65.

OVER THE NEXT TWO SEASONS, 1970 and 1971, Palmer played superbly. He won five PGA events (four in 1971), finished fifth and third, respectively, on the tour money list, and enjoyed one of the top-five scoring averages on tour (though he, like Nicklaus, did not play in enough tournaments to compete for the

Vardon Trophy). And had it not been for a miraculous final round eagle by Dave Stockton, Palmer might have won the 1970 PGA Championship at Southern Hills. Instead, he settled for second place—his sixth runner-up finish in his previous twenty-three major championships.

Palmer fared even better in the majors in 1972. In what he called "probably the toughest Open I've played in," Palmer battled Jack Nicklaus, Lee Trevino, and an unusually firm and nasty Pebble Beach course for three days. His game was razor-sharp on Friday. As did his Wake Forest protégé, Lanny Wadkins, Palmer carded the tournament's lowest round of 68. When he drained a thirty-footer for a birdie at the windy third hole on Sunday, Palmer tied for the lead. But the back nine was less kind and, unable to make a birdie as the miserable weather deteriorated, he settled for third place.

On the heels of that fine showing, Palmer tied for seventh at the British Open in Muirfield, and knocked in five birdies during the first round of the PGA Championship at Oakland Hills to sit just a stroke off the lead; he finished the tournament tied for sixteenth. In late October, Palmer walked to the seventy-second green at the Sahara Invitational in Las Vegas, twelve feet from forcing a play-off with Wadkins, two decades his junior. He narrowly missed the putt and finished alone in second place.

Though Palmer went winless in 1972 for the first time in his eighteen-year PGA career, he proved himself a serious contender wherever he chose to play, finishing eleventh in scoring average and posting eleven top-ten finishes in only twenty-three starts. Only Nicklaus, Trevino, Grier Jones, and Bruce Crampton scored more top-ten finishes in 1972, and the latter three each played in many more tournaments (Jones played thirty-five, Trevino thirty-two, and Crampton twenty-nine).

After two mediocre performances in California to start the 1973 season, Palmer tied for twenty-second at the Hawaiian Open in early February, where, at the Waialae Country Club, little-known veteran John Schlee won his first event in nearly a decade on tour. Even in the faraway paradise of Honolulu, Palmer was still the main attraction. Immediately following the tournament, along with Jerry Heard and two Japanese golfers, Masashi "Jumbo" Ozaki and Takaaki Kono, he traveled to Maui to compete in a pair of taped matches to be broadcast in Japan.

Monday morning, he awoke at five a.m. and hit the course to practice. In between bantering with the crowd, signing autographs, and posing for photographs, he cruised to a ten-stroke victory over Masashi, Japan's top golfer. After the match, Palmer quickly boarded a plane back to the States and then captained his private jet to Palm Springs, where he would compete in the Bob Hope Desert Classic that week.

On Palmer's schedule the very next day: first, an early morning business meeting; second, eighteen holes of golf to raise funds for a local charity; third, a groundbreaking ceremony at a nearby resort that he was building; fourth, a return appearance to socialize at the charity event; and fifth, an evening banquet.

Just another ordinary day in the life of Arnold Palmer.

When asked why he kept so busy at age forty-three, after achieving so much success in every phase of life, Palmer was unyielding.

"I've got to. . . . It's the way I am. If I quit, I'd be climbing the walls. It's just my nature to keep busy. I'd go nuts if I didn't," he told a sportswriter. "I love to play golf. . . . I don't know what I'd do if I couldn't play. I've been away from the game at times and it's been misery."

With his business for the week completed, Palmer turned his attention toward the five-day, ninety-hole, southern California golf tournament/celebrity extravaganza. During the annual event, touring pros played the first four rounds on four different courses with amateur stars like Frank Sinatra, Dean Martin, astronaut Alan Shepard, and, of course, Bob Hope himself.

Palmer started with a pedestrian 71, but then began to wield a hot putter. A 66 on Thursday at Tamarisk, paired with a 69 at La Quinta, suggested that the eighteen-month victory drought might come to an end.

Many of the more traditional and reserved touring pros despised the pompous amateurs and garish hoopla that shaped Bob Hope's desert circus. But Palmer adored Hope, not only for his decades of sacrifice in entertaining servicemen (including former enlistees like himself during the height of the Korean War), but also because he viewed Hope as second only to President Eisenhower in popularizing the game and elevating the top professionals into bona fide celebrities. And Palmer reveled in the fun-loving, hard-drinking, ultracelebrity setting, dominating the event throughout his career—four wins in the previous fourteen years. When he rolled in lengthy birdie putts on the final two holes at Bermuda Dunes on Saturday, he sat just one in back of Nicklaus and twenty-five-year-old Johnny Miller, the heralded youngster from California who carded a jaw-dropping 63 on Saturday to spring into a tie for the lead.

On Sunday, the pros finally said good-bye to their amateur partners and returned to Bermuda Dunes for a very un–Palm Springs–like final round. The course became a drenched oasis in the desert moonscape, thanks to torrential rains and gale-force winds the night before, but the thirty thousand spectators who braved the elements earned a special treat: Palmer and Nicklaus (along with John Schlee) were paired together in the final group.

"There was a time when Jack and I played each other instead of the course, but not anymore," Palmer assured reporters who strained to hype their head-to-head matchup. "I remember a couple of times we did it and a third man came along and beat us both."

When the celebrated grouping commenced play, Palmer picked up right where he left off the previous day. He birdied number one and excited "Arnie's Army," which was in its "usual form, cheering mistakes by Nicklaus and the other leaders, chatting and running while other players shot and roaring every time Arnie hitched up his pants." As they sloshed through the wet course, Palmer kept Nicklaus and the others at bay early with a birdie on number four. But the rain and the wind intensified, exacerbating the already difficult conditions: Low scores were impossible.

"I kept thinking the round would be rained out," Miller said about his day, which began with a one over thirty-seven on the front nine. "I couldn't concentrate."

Ignoring the soaked greens and the drops of rain that spotted his glasses—this week he chose to wear spectacles—Palmer stayed dialed in all day. He dropped a clutch nine-footer to save par on number one and led Nicklaus by two shots as the final group reached the eighteenth tee.

But the Golden Bear would not let up. On the 501-yard, par-five closing hole, he launched a monster drive high above the soaked Bermuda Dunes turf, then reached the green with his second stroke, leaving an eighteen-foot eagle putt that might steal yet another victory from his rival. Palmer, unable to match Nicklaus's length, was left with a short wedge to set up a birdie putt that looked like it might be necessary to secure the win.

Palmer pitched adroitly to within eight feet of the cup, and when Nicklaus's eagle flirted with the edge but failed to drop, all he had to do was two-putt and the $32,000 first-place prize was his. With vintage Palmer electricity, he rolled in the birdie, spun around in joy, and tossed his visor into the thrilled, rudely partisan, umbrella-toting gallery.

"When you haven't won as long as I hadn't, you start thinking you might never again. But I made up my mind this year that I was going to do some things differently and try my hardest to win."

Afterward, Palmer admitted that the victory was especially rewarding because he had edged out Nicklaus, mano a mano, whom he had tried (in vain) not to compete with directly.

"[I feared] someone else might sneak in and Johnny Miller almost did it," Palmer said. Despite the weather distractions, the spirited young Californian had regained his focus on the back nine and pulled within one shot of Palmer with three holes left. He finished second, tied with Nicklaus.

Sports pages all across the nation ran the photo of the smiling King hurling his visor into the crowd. Vice President Spiro Agnew, a frequent participant in the celebrity-studded tournament, flew in on the final day just to see Palmer close it out, and along with Bob Hope, he awarded Palmer his check and trophy.

"I hope," Palmer told his audience, "it's not as long before my next win."

PALMER'S TRIUMPH IN THE DESERT, especially in such dramatic fashion, helped to quash some of the "Arnie is through" talk that had naturally grown during his winless 1972 season. Two days afterward, famed columnist Jim Murray of the *Los Angeles Times* best captured the joy sports fans everywhere felt in Palmer's rejuvenation:

> Call the florist and tell him to cancel the wreath. Call the stoneyard
> and tell them never mind the headstone, the one which was to read
> "Here Lies the Golf Game of A. Palmer Which Died of Natural Causes
> in the Left Rough of a Par-5 Sometime in 1971. R.I.P."

Cancel the wreath, for sure, but the win unfortunately didn't provide a catalyst for Palmer after the players left the West Coast in mid-February of 1973. He did no better than eighteenth in the next seven events. And while a fifth Bob Hope title had proved he could still win against stiff competition, Palmer still burned for another major championship, starting, of course, with a fifth Green Jacket at Augusta National. An ugly opening round buried his dream from the start.

"I'm not upset, but I'm disgusted. I'm not upset because I'm not surprised. I'm not surprised I shot 77. And that's what upset me," he said afterward. "I think the only thing to do is get away from it, maybe for a month, and just practice. I think I'll do that—just pack it in until I start playing better or . . ."

But Palmer, as the world's most famous golfer, could not retreat from the limelight that easily. With Palmer obligated to play in New Orleans the following week in the Tournament of Champions, his mood stayed sour, after he failed to break par in any of the four rounds.

"I'll play Byron Nelson next week and if I don't do any better than I have been, I might not play again until the U.S. Open. I really don't know, but I might just take the time off and try to get ready for the Open."

Palmer stayed true to his word. A final-round 77 the next week in Dallas hastened his hiatus from the weekly grind in order to revamp his game and prepare his mind for the rigors of the next major championship—the U.S. Open, just six weeks away.

To every touring pro, amateur, or club pro who is fortunate enough to qualify, the National Open brings about a harsh self-reckoning. The U.S.G.A. toughens up each site to the point where it can forever erode the confidence of a player not in command of every aspect of his game. For Palmer, the Open had been the stage for both his greatest triumph—the comeback at Cherry Hills—and several of his greatest disappointments. Since his only U.S. Open win in 1960, he had finished in the top five seven times, without a title to show for it. Most agonizingly, he had three times found himself on the losing end of an eighteen-hole play-off.

But the 1973 U.S. Open meant so much more to the man who hadn't won a major title in nine seasons.

This year, the Open was returning to Oakmont. There he would receive a hero's welcome, the beloved western Pennsylvania son returning to play before his hometown fans. For each of Palmer's sixty individual PGA triumphs, none had come in the Pittsburgh area (twice, Palmer, playing a four-ball tournament with Nicklaus as his partner, had won PGA events at Laurel Valley in Ligonier, Pennsylvania). To win the National Open on his own turf—sacred turf, both he and his dad fervently believed—would culminate a lifelong quest. And the thousands of local soldiers in Arnie's Army—those who knew him well long before he became the King—desperately wanted their idol to win on Pittsburgh soil, rather than among the palm trees of Orlando, his winter home, or the dogwoods of Augusta.

But a U.S. Open win at Oakmont offered an additional incentive that no other venue could match: redemption. It was there on June 17, 1962—Father's Day—that Palmer, the world's most celebrated golfer, lost a U.S. Open play-off to a twenty-two-year-old, winless tour rookie. Of course, that rookie was two-time U.S. Amateur champion Jack Nicklaus, who would soon redefine the boundaries of major championship greatness. Still, Nicklaus's upset of Palmer at Oakmont in 1962 shook the golf world.

That Palmer-Nicklaus play-off became canonized as one of modern sport's most memorable one-on-one showdowns. Just as well remembered was the gallery's unsportsmanlike, blatantly cruel mocking of Nicklaus during the play-off round. The fans also noisily hustled off to chase Palmer's ball or reposition themselves to watch his next shot while Nicklaus was preparing to play. Beyond that, many shouted scurrilous insults at the portly, crew-cut, sloppily dressed Nicklaus in order to undermine his concentration. (Not until the early 1970s did the Golden Bear slim down, grow out his blond locks, and become a crowd and fashion favorite.)

As always, after Palmer lost he showed pure class, smiling for photographers, praising the new champion, and articulating one of the great prophetic sound bites in sports history:

"Now that the big guy is out of the cage, everybody better run for cover."

But the loss stung deeply.

Nicklaus's victory stunned the sports nation, not just because he defeated the game's greatest player, but because of how he did it.

He regularly outdrove the strappingly built Palmer, one of the game's longest hitters, by twenty to thirty yards. And he eradicated Palmer's chief hometown advantage by completely outplaying him on Oakmont's singular greens. The statistic most often used to explain Palmer's defeat was startling: eleven three-putt greens by Palmer, compared to only one by Nicklaus.

"I wanted every putt to drop and when I missed the first try, I was in a daze. That's the only way I can explain those short ones I missed," Palmer concluded. His three three-putts during the play-off (none for Nicklaus) stood out most during Nicklaus's 74-to-71 play-off victory, and reflected more generally what Palmer refused to admit: He never putted great on superfast greens (the speed of Augusta National's typically Southern, Bermuda-grass greens didn't compare with Oakmont's greens during the 1960s).

The putting gloom that week devastated Palmer, especially since he fully understood that no one could succeed by putting Oakmont's keen greens "aggressively." Yet, overlooked in the commentary about *why* he lost was how fantastically he had struck every other club in his bag. In regulation play, Palmer hit an incredible sixty-three of seventy-two greens, and in the play-off his tee-to-green game was equally sharp. To score thirteen bogeys while missing only nine greens in regulation play was the kind of statistic that made a fearless scrambler like Palmer cringe at the possibilities he threw away.

"I can't play any better than I played here and I couldn't win," he told the press.

The 1962 U.S. Open at Oakmont was the stage where Nicklaus began to overtake Palmer as the world's greatest golfer. But the transition took much longer than golf fans and journalists often remember.

For the eight years in the 1960s that Palmer and Nicklaus were both professionals (1962–1969), they shared nearly same the amount of victories: twenty-nine for Palmer and thirty for Nicklaus. And the number of runner-up finishes in major championships was also virtually identical: six for Palmer and seven for Nicklaus. Major *wins* became where Nicklaus overwhelmed Palmer during these eight years: only one for Palmer versus six for Nicklaus.

So, after the finest tee-to-green ball striking of his career, before thousands of die-hard fans on a course he knew better than anyone in the field, Palmer opened the door for the man who would usurp his throne. A win by Palmer in 1973 at Oakmont obviously would not undo Nicklaus's surge to golfing greatness (seven wins in 1972, including two majors). But the thought of redemption had driven Palmer throughout his career—he regularly recycled past defeats in his mind as a spur to future achievement—and in 1973 he wanted to remind the world that, not so long ago, major championships and Arnold Palmer heroics were synonymous.

"Ever since I lost in 1962, I've been waiting for the Open to come back to Oakmont," he admitted two days before the 1973 championship began. "This is my country; I am very eager to redeem myself."

No one was better suited to help Arnold Palmer achieve that lofty goal than the man who had taught him everything he knew about golf: his sixty-eight-year-old father, Deacon Palmer.

• • •

PALMER DID NOT PLAY ANOTHER event in the four weeks following the Byron Nelson tournament at the end of April. He did, however, maintain much of his typically harried, around-the-globe golfing schedule, including a hospital charity exhibition at Hidden Valley Country Club in Reno and the filming of *The Best 18 Holes in America*, a three-part television series featuring courses all over the country. Even when he "took off" from the tour, he didn't shun the obligations (or financial rewards) of celebrity. He happily met public expectations—just as long as the demands centered on golf.

At a press conference to promote the Reno exhibition in early May, a reporter asked Palmer what made him so successful. His answer was simple, his personal identity crystal clear.

"A great amount of desire to play golf," he responded. "It's been a life's ambition since I've been a youngster. It's never fluttered. It never went away. It's still there." In between business ventures, Palmer flew back to Latrobe, parking his private plane barely a mile from his home and playing regularly on the course where he had grown up. In mid-May, the power brokers at Oakmont offered him a nonresident membership (though even he had to pay a $5,000 membership fee). Now eligible to play in the club's intraclub competition known as the SWAT (invented by H. C. Fownes) while tuning up for the Open, Palmer jumped at the opportunity.

Although Oakmont made for a second home as a teenager, Palmer had actually not played the course since losing the 1962 play-off to Nicklaus. There had been only a few changes to the course over the past decade.

In the weeks prior to the Open, Palmer played in the SWAT a handful of times and reinforced his memories of each hole. But his major preparation was back home in Latrobe, hitting practice balls under his father's sharp eye.

Early in the 1973 season, Gardner Dickinson, a tour regular and a Hogan disciple, told Deacon (or "Pap," as Arnold called him) that a bad habit had crept into Arnold's swing and undermined his consistency. Arnold acknowledged the problem and tried various corrections while still on tour, but each piecemeal "fix" not surprisingly generated new difficulties.

Now back in Latrobe for an extended stay, father and son—as only they could—reevaluated every aspect of Arnold's technique. Working more effectively together as adults than their conflicting personalities had allowed during

Arnold's youth, the two concluded that Arnold had become so "out of position" that major swing surgery was necessary. Together, they took apart his swing and rebuilt it.

"[We changed] the whole ball of wax—the address, the swing, everything."

It was no wonder Palmer felt so comfortable in drastically reshaping his technique, even this close to a U.S. Open: Deacon was the only man he'd ever trusted with his homemade swing.

"Almost from the moment he put that cut-down club in my hands, Pap would tell me in no uncertain terms to permit nobody to fool with or change my golf swing."

Even after earning dozens of victories and tens of millions of dollars, Palmer had returned to his father's side during the 1960s and let him toy with his swing. Weeks before the U.S. Open in 1969, in the midst of a terrible slump, Palmer returned to Latrobe to seek his father's advice. The work paid off as Palmer tied for sixth place. Four years later, only a month before his much-anticipated return to Oakmont, they hoped for even greater results.

"I worked pretty hard," Palmer vividly recalled thirty-five years later. "I put a great emphasis on driving, and I practiced my irons a lot. The thing that I should have done was go to Oakmont and putted on the greens more. I didn't do that as much as I should have."

By the end of May, Palmer was ready to test his game on tour. A strong 68 at the Kemper Open in Charlotte put him within a stroke of the lead after day one, but he played the final three rounds at even par to fall out of serious contention.

"I'm discouraged by my scoring, but not my game," Palmer said.

The next day Palmer flew to Ashland, Ohio, and donated his services to help raise money at the Johnny Appleseed Boy Scout Golf Jamboree, where he not only bought a new putter that he liked, but tied the course record before flying back home.

While most tour regulars traveled to Philadelphia for the IVB Classic, Palmer continued his solitary preparation under Pap. Mostly he practiced at Latrobe Country Club, but a week before the Open, he joined former Pittsburgh Pirates stars Dick Groat and Jerry Lynch for a few holes at Oakmont before going off by himself to practice on the course.

Palmer may have gone eleven years without setting foot on Oakmont, but he felt like nothing had changed.

"I feel very much at home here."

In fact, he felt so much at home at Oakmont, so intimately connected to his childhood memories, that he made a surprising decision just before the championship began. He would forgo the use of either eyeglasses or contact lenses during the U.S. Open, aids that he admitted had become critical to him in recent years in order to judge distances, both on the greens and from the fairways.

"I probably should wear them but I'm not," he said. "The fact I know the course as well as I do should make up for not being able to see at a distance."

While that week's tour stop wrapped up on Sunday in Philadelphia, Palmer fired a solid one under 70 at Oakmont in his final practice round before U.S. Open week officially began.

By late morning on Monday, the 150-man field started arriving at Oakmont to register. All of the PGA tour stars were there: Nicklaus; the new "people's champion," Lee Trevino; red-hot Tom Weiskopf, winner of three of his last four tour stops; and Australia's Bruce Crampton, who had already won three times during the 1973 season. Representing the new breed of "young lions" were the former collegiate sensations Lanny Wadkins and Jerry Heard, the current U.S. Amateur champion, Vinny Giles, and the reigning three-time NCAA champion, Ben Crenshaw. Sixty-one-year-old Sam Snead, fifty-three-year-old Julius Boros (a two-time U.S. Open winner), and forty-two-year-old Billy Casper (also a two-time U.S. Open winner) spoke for the previous generation of stars.

But amid all these great players of past and present, Palmer was undeniably *the* star.

During the practice rounds, children and adults alike crowded excitedly beside him wherever he walked, begging for autographs. The enormous galleries that followed the King's every move continuously shouted words of encouragement whenever he hit a shot or simply passed by. More ambitious members of the army even managed to sneak in a quick photograph with Palmer as he made his way around the course or into the clubhouse.

The reporters who gathered at Oakmont acted much like the fans, craving every minute they could spend with the King. While experts agreed that Jack Nicklaus was the greatest golfer who ever lived, many still believed that Palmer had an honest chance to win the 1973 U.S. Open. In light of his victory in the Bob Hope, where he had outlasted a direct challenge from Nicklaus, his close familiarity with Oakmont, and his dead-serious intent to seek vindication for what happened in 1962, Palmer was as much a threat as anyone. And for those who saw him in the flesh, he still conveyed the robust athletic magnetism of a true champion, the same dynamic figure they had admired so often during the past decade and a half on magazine covers and newspaper pages.

"Palmer still is the well-muscled piece of talent he's always been," Bill Nichols of the *Cleveland Plain Dealer* wrote that week. "His bronzed arms still ripple with every swing. He stalks the fairway as though he's trying to beat everyone to the end of the rainbow. And he forever hitches his trousers as he prepares to assault the unprotected flagsticks."

But others viewed Palmer very differently, agonizing that the chiseled hero—a model of athleticism—had unfortunately not been frozen in time. Readers of the *New York Times* opened their morning editions on the first day of the 1973 U.S. Open to find a column by the noted sportswriter Dave Anderson, entitled "The Last Stand." Anderson not only didn't share Nichols's optimistic appraisal; he didn't even see the same Palmer:

"But he's 43 years old. When he crouches over a putt, his jowls thicken. So does his belly. The charisma isn't quite the same. Jack Nicklaus is the most feared golfer now. Lee Trevino is more respected too. And now Tom Weiskopf, with three victories in his last four tournaments, appears to be maturing. But for many people golf still means Arnold Palmer, nobody else. Especially here, where he is Pittsburgh's most exalted sports idol.

"Maybe the electricity will begin to flow in him tomorrow," Anderson continued. "But maybe there is no electricity in him anymore, not even in his last stand."

Remarkably, on the dawn of Oakmont's fifth U.S. Open, all anyone could talk about was the aging King of golf, Latrobe's Arnold Palmer.

· 2 ·

The Big Three Reborn

almer's "last stand" began at 1:52 p.m. Thursday afternoon, as he stepped to the first tee with eighteen-year-old Vince Berlinsky, who drew the honor of carrying his bag that week. (Until the U.S. Open in 1977, local caddies were randomly assigned by the host club; the pros were not allowed to use their regular tour caddies.)

The gallery roared wildly when Palmer's name was called, and for nearly five hours Arnie's Army remained at fever pitch, yelling, jostling, and running ahead for position to catch a glimpse of their hero. Over half the fans that afternoon followed Palmer, unconcerned about being still or silent in fairness to his playing partners, two-time tour winners Johnny Miller and Lou Graham. And, with a vintage-Palmer display of peaks and valleys, the King's opening round consumed the crowd's emotions.

Palmer stumbled on the relatively easy 343-yard, par-four second hole when his short-iron approach to the green landed in a bunker and he two-putted for bogey. He immediately rebounded on the next two holes, sticking a five-iron to inside two feet on the famous Church Pews third hole and then a wedge to two feet on the par-five fourth hole. Landing irons off the tee into bunkers on the par-three sixth and par-three eighth yielded bogeys, canceling out the two early birdies to return to one over par.

A strong drive and a crisp four-wood allowed Palmer to easily birdie the par-five ninth and return to par, only to give the stroke right back by three-putting the perilous tenth green. Ten holes, just three pars; not the ideal way to play a U.S. Open.

But Palmer righted the ship, first with pars over the next five holes, then by lasering a four-wood to within eight feet of the flagstick on the challenging par-three sixteenth. Following pars on numbers seventeen and eighteen, Palmer met with reporters, eager to dissect his first-round score of par 71.

"I was happy with the score but I'm not particularly happy with the way I played," Palmer said. Most distressing was his inability to get down in two from green-side bunkers as well as his "mediocre" driving—most annoying because he and his father had worked so intently on driving during the past month.

Although Palmer was satisfied with his four birdies (all from inside eight feet), the four bogeys were curious. For years, the press and fans had chalked up Palmer's major championship failures to mediocre putting. And the enormous tally of three putts during the 1962 U.S. Open was well documented. On day one in 1973, however, Palmer three-putted only once, on the infamously difficult tenth, and that had come from fifty feet: Three-putts from that distance, on that green, were nothing worse than a draw.

Overall, an even-par start to the Open encouraged Palmer, and the Army. By the time he signed his scorecard, nearly every group had completed their rounds, yet only four men broke par. The course—though toughened up only slightly since 1962—was playing as difficult as the vigilant members had hoped (the average first-round score of 76.8 was actually a half stroke higher than in 1962). And Palmer's 71 matched his opening-round score in 1962. Eleven years older, the field stronger, and his career having been to hell and back, Palmer remained in the hunt after one round.

The man who had dethroned Palmer as the world's greatest golfer, Jack Nicklaus, was far less pleased by his start—at least through the first sixteen holes.

Nicklaus had been the talk of the sporting world during the spring and summer of 1972, when he won the first two legs of the Grand Slam. Though he came up just short in the British Open, losing by way of Lee Trevino's miraculous chip-in on the seventeenth hole at Muirfield, Nicklaus, at age thirty-two, had reached his peak. He took the scoring title, the money title, and a second PGA Player of the Year award in 1972, in addition to winning seven tournaments. Eclipsing that spectacular season seemed impossible, but when Nicklaus arrived at Oakmont in June 1973, he was on his way to doing just that.

As his family and business ventures grew exponentially during the late 1960s, Nicklaus scaled back his playing schedule: He vowed never to be away from his four children and college-sweetheart wife, Barbara (whom he'd married at age twenty) for more than two weeks. (Barbara was currently pregnant with their fifth child.) While many touring pros played in over thirty PGA events a year to make ends meet, Nicklaus now appeared in less than two dozen, yet still regularly finished at the top or near the top of the annual money list. And 1973 was no exception. Prior to the Masters in early April, Nicklaus won twice and finished sixth or better in three of the other five events he competed in.

Only a terrible stretch during the second round of the Masters—three bogeys, then a double bogey on the front nine—kept Nicklaus from winning a fifth Green Jacket. He shot a final-round 66 and finished tied for fourth.

But fourth was not nearly good enough for Nicklaus at this dominating stage of his career. As he later explained, in a logic uniquely his: "Through that period of time, when I didn't win [at] Augusta, I sort of thought the year was over. It was . . . I suppose, an immature way to look at it, but . . . the Grand Slam is what I was really after. I did not achieve it. But that's what I was really after, so, if I didn't win the first leg, then I sort of felt like, Let's wait till next year."

Still, Nicklaus—arguably the most insatiable competitor in golf history—battled ferociously throughout the entire season.

"Even in 1973 I still won a lot of golf tournaments [seven]," he acknowledged. But: "I think I probably won those in spite of myself."

While the psychology of Nicklaus's 1973 season remains elusive, he did stay home in Orlando for most of the two months following his disappointment at Augusta. He practiced, tended to the family, and actively oversaw his diversifying business empire (including the creation of Muirfield Village, the bold new golf course and housing development that broke ground months earlier in his hometown of Columbus, Ohio). To the chagrin of PGA Tournament sponsors, who knew that Nicklaus's presence boosted gate and TV revenues, he played in only two events during the next eight weeks: He won both of them, each with a stellar field.

First, at the Tournament of Champions the week following the Masters, Nicklaus outlasted his rival Lee Trevino by a shot. Then, in another single-stroke win, he defeated his heir apparent, Tom Weiskopf, in May's Atlanta Golf Classic for his fourth victory of the season (he also won in January in the Bing Crosby Pro-Am National Golf Tournament and in late March in the Greater New Orleans Open).

With the U.S. Open at Oakmont only two weeks away, Nicklaus's game showed no signs of rust. Since he'd already demonstrated that he did not need as much practice or tournament hardening as other top professionals to remain at peak readiness, everyone assumed Nicklaus would, as usual, spend time before the Open preparing on-site for another major. And, predictably, in the two weeks leading up to the 1973 U.S. Open, he visited Oakmont to relearn the course that had jump-started his professional career.

In early June, from his base in Columbus (the Muirfield Village project had entered a key financial stage), Nicklaus awoke early in the morning and flew in his private jet to nearby Greater Pittsburgh International Airport. He then rented a helicopter that, ten minutes later, dropped him off adjacent to Oakmont's first tee. Even Jack Nicklaus couldn't switch on his game instantaneously: He cold-topped his opening drive.

Nicklaus shook off the faux pas and played the course at a leisurely pace, with several balls. He also putted from various locations on each green to begin the mental and physical process of adapting to their exceptional speed and mystifying contours. Then the multimillion-dollar entrepreneur jumped back into the helicopter and flew home for a business meeting in Columbus later in the afternoon. Arnold Palmer and Mark McCormack, the founder of IMG, had invented this frantic blend of golf/business multitasking. But Nicklaus practiced it at least as avidly as Palmer, and added several novel twists so that he could remain intimately involved in the daily lives of his children.

Curiously, even though he had just won at Atlanta and felt confident about his practice session at Oakmont, Nicklaus concluded that for him to successfully defend his U.S. Open crown, his game required additional work under the strain of tournament competition.

He broke his long-standing practice of foregoing the PGA event the week before a major championship. To the delight of its sponsors, Nicklaus registered at the last second to play in the IVB Philadelphia Golf Classic at Whitemarsh Valley, a classic course built in 1907, just four years after Oakmont.

"The Whitemarsh course has small greens and narrow fairways and is similar to Oakmont," Nicklaus told the press in explaining his surprise decision.

Nicklaus's observation set off a minor war of words between him and Palmer.

The sharply contrasting personalities of the two giants of modern golf created a gnawing friction between them, defining their relationship for decades. The discord even extended to an arcane disagreement about whether playing Whitemarsh was good preparation for playing a U.S. Open at Oakmont.

"There's no similarity," Palmer stated. "I won't be at Whitemarsh. . . . Whitemarsh is a good course, but Oakmont was designed as a links similar to a Scottish course. It has few trees compared with Whitemarsh. Its bunkers are famous, although they are no longer furrowed. It has magnificent greens and it has no water holes, while Whitemarsh has creeks and ditches. I just don't agree with Jack at all."

Nicklaus played erratically at Whitemarsh, especially from tee to green. Still, after three mediocre rounds, he carded a masterful 67, the lowest Sunday score. Six shots behind the winner, Tom Weiskopf, he tied for fifth place. Nicklaus now had only three days left for practice prior to the start of the U.S. Open, but he had a clearer idea (whatever Palmer might think) about which parts of his game needed work before he was Oakmont-ready.

Naturally, Nicklaus stood out as the clear-cut favorite to defend the title he had won at Pebble Beach. He could also become the first man in seventy years to win two U.S. Opens on the same course (Scotsman Willie Anderson won his first and fourth U.S. Open titles at the Myopia Hunt Club in Massachusetts in 1901 and 1905).

Unlike the year before, the Grand Slam was not in Nicklaus's sights in 1973: He had not won the Masters in April. But never before had he won four tournaments (out of eleven entered) prior to the U.S. Open. Las Vegas oddsmakers set Nicklaus as a four-to-one favorite. So, too, did famed sports prognosticator Jimmy "the Greek" Snyder, who predicted that the winner would set a new record score of 279, four below the 283s that Hogan had shot in 1953 and Nicklaus and Palmer had matched in 1962.

Still, by the early 1970s, both the experts and journalists dubbed Nicklaus the favorite in just about every tournament. Since he'd recovered from a minor "slump" in the late 1960s, and especially since his father's death in 1970, no one (save perhaps Lee Trevino) possessed both the shots and the intestinal fortitude to go toe-to-toe with Nicklaus in the final round of a tournament.

Internally, Nicklaus had a personal, revenge-driven incentive to triumph again at Oakmont. From the moment he arrived in town in June 1973, sports-writers rehashed Pittsburgh fans' heckling of Nicklaus eleven years earlier. They also stressed how much had changed in his public persona since then.

"He returns now as the game's premier player, acknowledged the world's best and eyeing a plateau of performance and accomplishment unattained by any other man to play this old game," wrote Bob Greene of the Associated Press. "He returns no longer fat, no longer a kid, no longer uncertain. He's a trim 185 pounds. He's a mature 33, quietly confident, self-contained, self-assured, unfailingly courteous. His drab garb of the early '60s is gone, replaced by quiet, subdued colors. His blond mane is at modish length."

Winning tournament after tournament, major title after major title, helped make Nicklaus more appealing to serious golf fans. And once he consciously remodeled his image in the late 1960s—losing weight, lengthening his hair, and modifying his wardrobe to follow the style of the day—Nicklaus transitioned from a spectacularly talented golfer to admire from afar, into a beloved fan favorite. "Jack's Pack" now crowded the fairways with an intensity that, on occasion, almost rivaled Arnie's Army.

Nicklaus sternly brushed aside any hint of animosity toward the Palmer-faithful for their unkind behavior in 1962. The crowd's scorn for Nicklaus may actually have motivated the Golden Bear, as he birdied the first three holes in round one.

"Honestly, I don't remember the gallery; all I thought about was golf," he said. "I played with blinders on, I suppose."

Still, no one could deny that a second triumph at Oakmont, in Palmer's backyard, would be payback to fans who had so harassed the rookie in 1962 that his father had to be restrained from physically lashing out—restrained by, of all people, Ohio State football coach and Nicklaus family friend Woody Hayes.

In 1973, Nicklaus was the marquee name in a threesome that included reigning U.S. Amateur champion Vinny Giles and former Masters champion Bob Goalby. Teeing off at 10:04 a.m., Nicklaus did not get off to the same blistering start as he had eleven years earlier. He carded three bogeys and a lone birdie over the first thirteen holes. Still, that wasn't as disturbing as *how* he racked up strokes. Not only did he fail to birdie the par-five fourth hole, which he had played superbly in 1962; he ended up with a six after hooking his drive into the Church Pew bunkers and then hitting wildly before finally reaching the green.

One over par through eight holes, Nicklaus felt his spirits buoyed when he crossed the bridge that connected the two halves of the Oakmont course. (After completing the first hole, players walk across a bridge above the Pennsylvania Turnpike, play numbers two through eight on that side of the course, then travel back across the bridge to complete the round. Oakmont is the only venue in the world where an interstate highway actually runs *through* the golf course.) There, Jack spotted his ten-year-old son, Jack Jr., after he crossed the bridge and arrived on the ninth tee.

"Did you play golf yesterday?" Nicklaus asked.

The boy nodded.

"How many holes, thirty-six?"

Again, the answer was yes.

"Did you win?"

Negative. Nicklaus grinned and proceeded to the ninth.

Nicklaus then blasted two enormous shots that placed him on the par-five green in two, and barely rimmed out his eighteen-foot eagle putt. His birdie returned him to one over par for the front nine.

But Jack Jr. wasn't in sight to energize his dad on the next hole; following a mediocre iron shot, Jack three-putted the tenth green for another bogey. On the par-three thirteenth, his four-iron landed in the rough and a poor chip left him a tricky fifteen-footer to save par. He fortunately rolled it in to keep from ballooning to three over par.

Nicklaus canceled out a terrific birdie on the fourteenth with a bogey on the difficult par-four fifteenth, falling back to two over. After a routine par, he walked down the grassy slope and up to the new tee box on Oakmont's seventeenth hole, a classic teaser par-four of only 322 yards.

For decades, Oakmont's next-to-last hole had morphed players' great hopes into great anguish. Before the Open returned in 1973, the seventeenth measured only 290 yards, an uphill, slight dogleg left with small pin oaks and deep rough that blocked a direct route to the green. Often—in search of an eagle or at worst a birdie—pros chose to cut the dogleg with a single blast of the driver, fly their ball over the trees, and land it just in front of the green. If they were successful, their main concern was avoiding the exceedingly deep sand pit—known affectionately as Big Mouth—that blocked the right entry to the green.

Anyone who arrived at Oakmont in 1973 could recite in detail the maddening series of events that had occurred to Phil Rodgers on the seventeenth hole in the first round of the 1962 Open. Rodgers, a former marine from San Diego, was putting the finishing touches on a stellar opening round. One under par with two holes to play, he aimed for the green in hopes of a birdie that would give him at least a share of the lead.

Rodgers's drive initially looked good but then smacked right into a branch of a pine tree, four feet off the ground, and stayed there. After surveying the situation, he chose to play the shot rather than remove the ball and take a one-stroke penalty ("unplayable lie"). In order to get his best angle to hit the ball, Rodgers dropped to his knees and swiped at it. The ball fell and became ensconced in the next-lowest branch. At this point, pride grabbed hold of Rodgers, and he took two more stabs before the ball finally dropped to the ground in a miserable lie, from which he still could not play to the green.

When he finally holed out, Rodgers had used eight strokes, a quadruple bogey, on the par-four hole. His search for an easy birdie had ended in a "snowman." Instead of the opening-round lead, Rodgers saw twenty-nine names ahead of his on the scoreboard.

Over the next three rounds, Rodgers fought back valiantly. He tied for the lead at one under par with a birdie on the fourteenth hole of the final round, but then bogeyed the fifteenth and sixteenth and ultimately tied for third place, two behind the leaders. Had it not been for Rodgers's pine tree adventure on Thursday, the classic Palmer-Nicklaus play-off might never have happened.

The seventeenth hole was just as tantalizing to Arnold Palmer in 1962. He grabbed birdies there in the opening two rounds; then, on the morning of the final day (the third and fourth rounds of the U.S. Open were still played on Saturday), he nailed the green with his drive and dropped an uphill eighteen-footer for an eagle. The army gave Palmer a two-minute standing ovation, as he regained the lead despite frittering away shots earlier in the round.

As Palmer had shown, great drama (he was four under through three rounds) regularly unfolded on the seventeenth. Unfortunately, following another thunderous whack onto the fringe of the green in the afternoon round, he missed a short birdie putt that would have avoided the play-off against Nicklaus.

The Fowneses had designed the seventeenth to encourage a bold try for the green across the dogleg. To make the alternate, "safe" route difficult, they tilted the fairway sharply and protected the green with Big Mouth. They also tilted the green from right to left so that when it was firm, even a perfectly struck high-iron might not hold the putting surface. Even W.C., one of the nation's premier amateurs, but never a long hitter, regularly tried to drive the green on number seventeen. He felt that cutting the dogleg provided him a better chance to score a par or birdie than playing conventionally through the fairway.

But Palmer's eagle in 1962 prompted the modern-day Oakmont members to rethink the design of number seventeen. They delighted in the course's in-your-face toughness, premised on straight-ahead, pinpoint accuracy off the tee. Apart from the two par fives on the front nine, Oakmont offered no clear-cut birdie opportunities for even great players to redeem themselves. If a player made mistakes along the way, he should, as the Fowneses had put it, "irrevo-cably" suffer the consequences in his final score. Oakmonters did not want their course vulnerable to a dramatic comeback at the tail end of a major championship—even at the hands of their hometown son. Thus, the club mem-bers, following the 1962 U.S. Open, questioned whether the original design of the seventeenth still fit with Oakmont's punitive philosophy.

Shortly after Oakmont hosted the 1969 U.S. Amateur, the club spent $10,000 redesigning the hole. The pine trees that had so frustrated Phil Rod-gers were removed and a series of punishing bunkers took their place. But the most money went toward building a new tee box thirty yards farther back and to the left of the old tee, thereby sharpening the dogleg and making the hole play completely blind. Members confidently believed that direct access to the green was now impossible except from the fairway.

"A man would be a fool to try to drive seventeen now," said Oakmont's longtime head pro and former U.S. Open champion Lew Worsham.

During his practice round two weeks before the Open, Nicklaus initially heeded the advice of Worsham: "It wouldn't be worth the gamble," Nicklaus said before he hit a three-wood safely onto the fairway. But, as he walked toward the green, Nicklaus reconsidered the strategy when he realized that the pine trees—the same pine trees that ensnared Rodgers—had been removed.

"Maybe you can go for it. You're not much worse off in the sand than you are on the fairway," Nicklaus reasoned. "The fairway is not a very good place to approach from the green—it's too tough a shot. My thinking is to put it over in the bunker or in the rough."

When U.S. Open week began, Nicklaus remained leery of playing the seventeenth aggressively because of his recent troubles in driving the ball straight. After his final practice round on Wednesday, he went to the driving range and toyed with his grip.

Nicklaus had practiced incessantly as a youth. At the driving range the young boy hit thousands of balls, running up huge bills, which his father gladly paid. But as a pro, he had become much more efficient in his tournament preparations. He never practiced for practice's sake, à la Ben Hogan. Instead, he drilled with specific, technical goals in mind that had been instilled by his teacher, Jack Grout. Once satisfied, Nicklaus might require only a dozen or two perfectly struck shots to complete a practice session.

Thus Nicklaus needed very little time to experiment with his grip before he felt ready to return to the course. With the sun setting and the course abandoned by everyone else, Nicklaus walked onto Oakmont's fifteenth, a tee box near the driving range.

"I didn't want to start playing [Thursday] using a new grip," he said. "So I went out and replayed the last four holes."

With the wind at his back, Nicklaus knocked his ball onto the seventeenth green. Regardless of what Worsham and the Oakmont faithful thought, Nicklaus now knew what he needed to know: Under the right wind conditions, and especially if his chance to win the championship hung in the balance, he would not hesitate to drive the "undriveable" green.

As he ascended the seventeenth tee box on late Thursday afternoon, a disappointing two over par for the round, the wind was again at Nicklaus's back. Going for the green and scoring an easy birdie would help take the sting out of a mediocre performance. It would also send a message to the field: Nothing was impossible for Nicklaus, and he would attempt the unthinkable to defend his title.

Nicklaus motioned for the driver to his caddie, Joe Stoner Jr.—the son of Oakmont's caddie master, who had suspiciously won Nicklaus in the "random" drawing for bags. Stoner eagerly handed the club to Nicklaus; he alone had witnessed Nicklaus drive the green less than twenty-four hours ago, so why not again? This could be the shot that put Nicklaus back in the hunt for the $35,000 first prize, of which Stoner stood to earn a hefty payday.

Bob Goalby, a member of Nicklaus's threesome, hardly shared young Stoner's enthusiasm.

"When I saw him point his driver at the trees on the dogleg, I knew he was going to try and cut the dogleg," Goalby said. "I turned to a marshal and said, 'That's a stupid shot. He'll wind up in a tree. Or he'll hit a bunker. Or he'll hit weeds so deep we'll never find the ball.'"

Nicklaus remained unmoved by the criticism that would come his way if Goalby's prediction came true.

"I needed to keep [it] close," he quietly said afterward, revealing the supreme confidence of a player whose only goal was victory.

Nicklaus tattooed the tee shot, on his trademark high trajectory, a hundred feet above the hazards that blocked its pathway. In the words of columnist Jim Murray, the ball seemed "to be in the air longer than *Skylab I*." (America's first space station had been launched one month earlier.)

"That one's on the green," Nicklaus said casually.

"How the hell do you know," asked Goalby, who, like Nicklaus, could not see the green from the tee box.

"I know because I came out here and practiced it last night."

Indeed, the ball dropped from orbit ten yards shy of its target, rolled up a modest incline, and came to rest twelve feet from the flagstick.

"When we got down the fairway and I saw the ball on the green, I said, 'Jack, that will teach me to keep my mouth shut,'" Goalby told reporters after the round. "I also told Jack, 'I think that shot will win the Open for you.'"

Goalby, who five years earlier had won the infamous Masters Tournament in which Roberto De Vicenzo signed an incorrect scorecard, continued his praise of Nicklaus.

"You watch now," Goalby said to the third member of their threesome, Vinny Giles. "Jack will work harder on this twelve-foot putt than he has on any other today. When the course gives Jack something, he always takes advantage of it."

Nicklaus did exactly that. The Golden Bear sank the eagle putt and returned to even par for the day.

"That got him all pumped up," added Goalby. "Now watch him go on and win it. I don't care what anybody else shoots."

• • •

ON A COURSE LIKE OAKMONT, Goalby's prediction sounded reasonable. When the world's best player can make up two shots with a single swing, other legitimate contenders begin to seem irrelevant. There was, however, one very special man in the field, in addition to Arnold Palmer, who possessed the temerity and grit to topple Nicklaus. Even though visibly gaunt due to a recent battle with cancer, Gary Player did not tremble before Oakmont, Nicklaus, or anyone else.

For fifteen years Player, the indomitable, five-foot-seven South African—a brash-talking health addict who dressed in black, supposedly to absorb maximum energies from the sun—conquered golf tournaments across the world. The son of a miner who worked twelve hundred feet under the earth's crust, Player grew up in Johannesburg yearning for a life in the great outdoors. He dropped out of school at age fifteen, turned pro two years later, and adopted the grueling Hogan ethic of endless practice to tame a lashing, homemade swing.

Like Hogan, Player fought a crippling hook during his early career; established British players who observed gave him no chance for success. But Player improved with astonishing rapidity and, helped financially by his future father-in-law, traveled the world in search of fame and lucre. By the age of twenty-three, he had won sixteen tournaments in England, Australia, the United States, Egypt, and South Africa, including the 1959 British Open at Muirfield. He was also a runner-up to Tommy Bolt at the 1958 U.S. Open in Tulsa.

Although Player mainly competed abroad, wins in the Masters and the PGA Championship in 1961 and 1962 made him a bona fide superstar in America as well. In 1965, he won the U.S. Open at Bellerive Country Club in St. Louis and became the youngest man, at age twenty-nine, to capture the "Career Grand Slam." (Gene Sarazen and Ben Hogan were the only others to have won each of the four major championships; Nicklaus would do so in 1966 at age twenty-five, and Tiger Woods in 2000 at age twenty-four.)

Player saved his best golf for the grandest stage: critical moments of major championships. He fought off Palmer in a classic final-round duel at Augusta in 1961 to win his first Green Jacket. The next year, late in the third round of the 1962 PGA Championship, he nearly gave away a two-stroke lead. With his tee shot buried in deep rough on the eighteen at Donald Ross's Aronimink Golf Club, Player grabbed a two-iron and hit "the best iron shot of my life" under a tree and onto the green. He two-putted from sixty feet to save par and, the next day, holed a string of clutch par putts to win the title. And during the final round of the 1968 British Open, paired with Jack Nicklaus, Player edged out the Golden Bear, Billy Casper, and Bob Charles to take his second British Open title.

By the middle of the decade, Palmer, Player, and Nicklaus had established themselves as the most dominant golfers in the world. From 1960 to 1966, the Masters title went solely to one of these three men; they combined to win eight of the other major championships during that stretch. Boosted by the catalytic role of television in popularizing golf, they hosted their own TV show as golf's "Big Three," replacing the Big Three of the preceding era, Hogan, Nelson, and Snead. Sports fans across the country knew each member of the trio by first name alone.

Each man had his own distinct public image within the Big Three. Nicklaus's quiet, cold demeanor, combined with his consistently dominant play, rendered him robotic: respected, not beloved. Nicklaus was the perfect adversary for Palmer; warm, approachable, and with a knack for the sensational (or horrendous) shot, Palmer took fans on a roller coaster of emotions. Crowds—young and old, male and female, die-hards and casual observers—worshiped Palmer.

Player was more mysterious. Nicklaus was hefty, Palmer the brawny one, but Player was the most physically impressive. A fitness fiend of the Jack LaLanne ilk, he jogged obsessively, lifted weights, and earned the admiration of every ex-military man by knocking out fingertip push-ups on Ed Sullivan's popular variety show. Just 150 pounds in his prime and all muscle, Player never hesitated to single out his peers who could stand to lose weight and exercise (including Nicklaus, his closest American friend on tour).

But Player did not live in the United States and, for practical reasons, could not compete in as many PGA tour stops as Palmer and Nicklaus. Besides the major championships and a handful of other featured PGA events, Player took his game worldwide and—like Gene Sarazen before him—portrayed himself as the sport's international ambassador. With his large family occasionally in tow (six children, plus nanny and tutor as well as his wife) and at great personal expense, he logged more miles competing worldwide than any golfer in history. "The Americans have no idea how tough it is for me. No one does. I can't fly home for a day or two to see the family. It's 8,000 miles."

As a result, Player rarely finished a season near the top of the PGA money list, and never won more than three PGA events in a season (he did win seventy-three South African titles in a twenty-five-year stretch). To many golf fans, by the early 1970s, Player's role in the Big Three seemed outdated. Lee Trevino had unmistakably emerged as a bona fide American star on tour. He tapped into the blue-collar, ethnic American crowd that never warmed to a man like Player, who spoke with a distinct British accent.

In August 1972, at the halfway point of the PGA Championship at Detroit's famed Oakland Hills Country Club, a reporter asked Player if he agreed that Trevino had usurped his spot among the Big Three.

"The record speaks for itself," Player said before storming out of the press tent.

"The record" that Player referred to was dozens of worldwide victories as well as five major titles and sixteen PGA tour wins. The reporter's question further irritated Player because it dismissed his chances for victory in the current championship: After two rounds, he was just two shots behind the leader (and well ahead of Trevino). Apparently, Player's record did *not* speak for itself, and he set out with extra determination during the final two rounds of the PGA Championship to prove he was far from over-the-hill at age thirty-six.

Ben Hogan had dubbed the remodeled Oakland Hills "the Monster" upon winning the U.S. Open there in 1951. And earlier during the week of the 1972 PGA, Player had echoed Hogan, calling Oakland Hills the toughest golf course in America and claiming that the dramatic pitch of its greens presented the toughest putting challenge he had ever faced. But less than twenty-four hours after his unhappy encounter with the dismissive reporter, Player slew the "Monster" with a brilliant string of long, curling putts, rolling in four birdies from over twenty-five feet on his way to grabbing the lead with a 67.

"I think it will be a very exciting day tomorrow," was all that Player would say afterward. "The tournament doesn't really start until the tenth hole tomorrow."

Fulfilling his own prophecy, Player faltered early, shooting a two-over-par front nine on Sunday. But he then righted the ship, parred his way in, and claimed a second PGA Championship by two strokes. Throughout the remarkably competitive final round—at one moment, a single shot separated the top ten golfers—Player never flinched. He outlasted them all, finishing with a one over 281 and besting his "heir apparent," Trevino, by five shots (and besting Nicklaus and Palmer by several strokes more).

A month later, Player fortified his reputation as one of the world's premier players. He edged out both Nicklaus and Trevino in the annual World Series of Golf (the tournament contested by the winners of that year's majors; there were only three players in 1972 because Nicklaus had won both the Masters and the U.S. Open). Player then won in Brazil that November, and two weeks later he took a third consecutive South African Masters title.

Given Player's devotion to physical training and his stellar close to the 1972 season, what happened to him at the beginning of 1973 stunned the golf world. In January, doctors urged him to have an emergency operation to remove a blockage between his kidneys and bladder. The team of surgeons also removed a cyst on the back of his left knee. The successful procedure relieved the large family clan, which was about to get larger: His wife, Vivienne, was eight months pregnant.

"Still, the big question that blocked out everything in my mind was: What will this do to my professional golf career . . . ? I certainly didn't know, and at that point neither did anyone else."

Player remained bedridden for twelve days after the surgery, and doctors forbade him to touch a golf club for an additional six weeks. He lost considerable weight and muscle and was crushed that, for the first time in fifteen years (and the only time between 1959 and 2008), he did not compete in the Masters.

By the end of April, Player's doctors deemed him sufficiently recovered to return to competitive golf, although he chose to play closer to home in Asia (and spend time with his newborn) before tackling the longer trip to America. He took fifth place at the Chunichi Crown golf tournament in Japan, thanks to a closing-round 65. In May, Player withdrew from the Houston Open, but finally made the trip to America two weeks later for the Atlanta Golf Classic—his first appearance on the PGA tour in more than eight months.

Although he surprised himself by winning the pro-am the day before the tournament, Player got off to a rocky start in Thursday's opening round. Fortunate to make the cut, he then held his own and tied for nineteenth. Player rested the following week and then, to his chagrin, missed the cut by a single stroke at the Kemper Open in Charlotte. He decided to skip the IVB Classic in Philadelphia and instead headed to Pittsburgh to prepare for the U.S. Open. He also hoped to spend time on and off the course with Arnold and Winnie Palmer.

At Oakmont, Player repeated the same mantra each time reporters and well-wishers asked him about his health.

"I'm fit as a fiddle, laddie. I'm fine now. No aftereffects."

His golf game, he believed, was still on the mend.

"I'm playing worse than I ever have since I've been a professional," he said days before the Open.

Although his fellow pros considered Player among the most affable men on tour, some felt he regularly embroidered the truth for dramatic effect, and occasionally indulged in gamesmanship. But his recent surgeries, frail physique, and obvious fatigue created sympathy from fans and peers alike, while also dampening expectations that he could seriously contend.

Certainly Oakmont, in the middle of a hot, humid June, did not seem the best place for Player to return to top golfing form. George Blumberg, a South African businessman who followed Player for years, predicted he "cannot yet be mentally strong enough to come back in an event of this toughness." A *London Times* reporter reinforced Blumberg's point when he spied Player yawning on the sixth tee during a practice round.

Player's memories of Oakmont during the 1962 U.S. Open also did little to put him in a positive frame of mind. Indeed, several of the comments that Player made at the time seemed downright mean, and were considered insults by the club's devout Fowneseans.

"I still say this is the worst course that the Open has ever been held on," Player told reporters in 1962. "The bunkers are unfair. Other than that I like this course. But the traps make it awful."

Player's conciliatory double-talk afterward hardly undid the damage.

"Still I don't throw any clubs and get mad. Because it was a wonderful tournament. I never saw such tremendous crowds before. It was a great moment. I was privileged to play in the Open."

However Player felt about the course, he competed splendidly: With a little luck, he could have delayed Nicklaus's launch toward golf immortality. Player matched Nicklaus stroke for stroke at the thirty-six- and fifty-four-hole marks, two behind the front-running Palmer. He even held the lead at one point during the third round. Only a disappointing final round of 74 prevented a magical Sunday play-off that would have pitted the emerging Big Three against one another.

Then again, Player may have been acting coy in the lead up to the 1973 championship. Palmer knew his longtime friend and competitor well.

"I played a practice round with Gary on Wednesday," he told reporters as the tournament got under way. "And he was putting awfully well. He had a lot of confidence in his putting."

Palmer, the resident Oakmont expert that week, was again dead-on. From Player's first stroke of the tournament, he looked brilliant. A long, straight drive and a crisp seven-iron, followed by a delicate fifteen-footer, gave Player a birdie on the especially difficult first hole. He rolled in another fifteen-footer on the second, bolting to two under par. With back-to-back drivers (testimony to Oakmont's immaculate turf), Player reached the par-five fourth hole in two shots and carded a two-putt birdie. An hour into the championship, Player glistened at three under par.

Thus far, Player showed no signs of his winter illness or recent fatigue. Never a long hitter, he still had the length to attack the course when it played fast and firm, as it did on Thursday. Player's fourth birdie came on the par-five ninth, where his fairway wood landed in the sand and he exploded close enough to the pin to roll in a short putt for a breathtaking thirty-two on the front side.

Player was widely recognized as one of the world's great bunker artists, so his fine recovery on number nine was no surprise; but his command of the greens was. He had played just twelve rounds of competitive golf in six months, and none on courses whose greens even approached Oakmont's in difficulty. Yet he putted flawlessly. Twice he needed just two strokes from over sixty-plus feet to save par, and he continued his attack by sinking a twenty-foot birdie putt on the tenth hole.

"I putted as well as I could. It was fantastic. It would be impossible for me to putt any better," Player said. "This course is a pleasure to play."

When he dropped a three-foot birdie on number eleven, Player's scorecard not only amazed; it was historic. In the eight previous major championships at Oakmont—where revered players like Sarazen, Jones, Armour, Turnesa, Snead, Hogan, and Nicklaus had won major championships—no one had ever reached six under par in a medal-play round. Ben Hogan in 1953 and Deane Beman in 1962 shared the course record of 67, and Hogan had to birdie the final two holes to achieve his mark.

If Player could shoot par over the final seven holes, his 65 would establish a course record that might last forever. More immediately, he would surge into a huge lead; no one even approached Player's mastery of Oakmont that day.

Unfortunately, Player's torrid pace cooled on the par-five twelfth, where he made bogey by driving into the thick rough; he also bogeyed the par-three sixteenth, bunkering his three-wood. Nevertheless, pars everywhere else completed a tremendous, record-tying round of 67 that was almost ten shots under the average score for the day—a true anomaly.

When the last man on the course finished up, Player owned a three-stroke lead.

"Someday you'll realize what a good round it was," Player proclaimed with his customary bravado. "I'd like to have three seventy-twos and not even play. That's how tough the course is."

Although the weather for the first day of the 1973 U.S. Open was ideal—low seventies, no wind, sunny—Oakmont kept most of the world's greatest golfers at bay. Besides 70s by Lee Trevino, Raymond Floyd, and Jim Colbert, no one else besides Player scored a subpar round.

Given that Player was not expected to be a factor prior to Thursday, the three-stroke difference at the top of the leaderboard startled everyone except, fittingly, Arnold Palmer.

"What surprises me is not that Gary shot sixty-seven. It's that no one else could shoot better than seventy," Palmer candidly observed. "There shouldn't be so big a gap in there."

Player also knew the strength of the field, and to expect that anything could happen during the world's toughest championship.

"I remember one U.S. Open in which Arnold Palmer had a seven-stroke lead with nine holes left to play and lost," Player recalled.

"You never know what's in store for you, but the only thing you can do when you're in this position is go out and try your best. This is the type of golf course [where] it doesn't matter whether you're six in front or six behind; you've got to keep going. In fact, anybody six behind with one round to go honestly could win it quite easily."

· 3 ·

A View from the Parking Lot

H is whole life, Lee Trevino felt like an outsider.

As a poor Mexican-American boy, Trevino grew up during the 1940s in the small farm town of Rowlett, northeast of Dallas. He lived with his mother, Juanita, grandfather Joe, and two sisters in a tiny unpainted shack in a desolate hayfield.

Living without plumbing, electricity, windows, or wallpaper, Lee and his two sisters bathed together twice a week in a metal tub over a wood-burning stove filled with lake water. Joe worked as a gravedigger at Hillcrest Cemetery while Juanita cleaned houses for families in north Dallas. Usually left on his own, young Lee entertained himself when he wasn't harvesting cotton or sporadically attending school.

"It was a lonely life," Trevino recalled. "I was never around anybody. I was all by myself, no one to talk to. I'd just go hunt rabbits and fish."

Golf eventually found him. By chance, the Dallas Athletic Club golf course lay just across the street from the dilapidated Trevino home. Though he knew nothing of the rules, Lee learned he could make money off the game. The right side of the seventh fairway caught many wayward tee shots and Lee collected balls, then sold them back to their original owners.

In that same hayfield, he also found a discarded old club.

"In those days, if you could afford to play golf, you could afford to throw away clubs," Trevino said.

Though the club was left-handed, Lee made do by turning it around and hitting balls with the blade's tip. Eventually, a second disgruntled Texas golfer tossed another iron—this time a righty—into Trevino's front lawn, and Lee was on his way.

The club's caddie master, "Cryin' Jesse" Holdman, noticed the enterprising kid hanging around the course selling balls to players and offered him a caddie job.

"I feel like I helped raise Lee," Holdman said years later. "Lots of nights when we finished at the club, I'd take a package of cold cuts over to Lee's old house and have dinner with his family."

With nothing but time on his hands as he ditched school and waited for loops across the street, Trevino fashioned a makeshift course out of a nearby pasture and taught himself the game.

Despite his small size, Trevino showed considerable athleticism in Little League and, when he actually attended school, on the playground. Quickly his raw talent produced easy money.

"I caddied for one little old man real late on Sundays, and as soon as we got out of sight from the clubhouse he'd let me play him for my caddie fee, double or nothing. I beat him every time."

The extra dollars went a long way toward helping to feed his family, so when Lee chose golf over school, Joe and Juanita (neither could read nor write) did not object. Although Lee had mastered the art of ditching the local truant officer, Juanita went before a judge to legalize his absences and received a work permit for her thirteen-year-old son.

Lee persuaded the superintendent of the golf course (today known as Glen Lakes) to hire him and he earned $1,250 during that first year—a substantial sum for a young kid in 1952. In the daily company of older caddies and club members, most of whom were twice his age, he grew up fast.

"I went from a country kid to a cool kitty from the city. I was smoking when I was ten, something I picked up from older caddies, just like the foul language. I was a little boy thrown in with men," he remembered. "Some of them were dangerous people who carried knives and guns. Hardly a day passed that I didn't watch a knife fight. We were shooting dice and playing cards and there always were arguments. It was an education of hard knocks."

Despite earning a livelihood and being surrounded by the golf culture, Trevino did not play his first complete round in a golf tournament until age fifteen, when he qualified for the *Dallas Times Herald* tournament by shooting a 77 at the Stevens Park municipal course. That first competitive appearance turned out to be short-lived, however, when he lost 2 & 1 in the second round of his age bracket.

Trevino had entered the event only on the suggestion of a local driving range owner, Hardy Greenwood, who had seen him pounding balls endlessly as a skinny eight-year-old. The driving range was just a few miles from Trevino's home, and Greenwood gave Lee a job, clubs, shoes, and entered him in the Dallas tournament.

With extra money in his pocket and dressed like most teenagers of the day—jeans, leather motorcycle jacket, wide-collared shirts, and boots—Trevino drove around the city courting girls and trouble with the law. One night in 1956, he and a friend stole a set of hubcaps from a member of River Hills Country Club, where he now worked (he had quit the driving range after a falling-out with Greenwood). A policeman managed to crack the case—Trevino put sparkling new hubcaps on his beat-up, 1949 Ford—but let the two boys go after they returned the goods to the rightful owner.

"Confused, unsettled, and almost seventeen," Trevino turned to the military for guidance (and to avoid an appearance in court). On his birthday, he walked into the local marines recruiting office, passed the enlistment test, and, despite little formal education, was inducted within three weeks. A few days before Christmas 1956, he left Dallas for boot camp in California.

After a rocky start during basic training—"I got hit in the stomach and slapped in the head so many times I lost count"—Trevino trained hard and was deployed as a machine gunner in the southwest Pacific. He reenlisted after his initial two-year hitch and, shortly afterward—to make up for an error that assigned him to kitchen duty—a captain in Okinawa offered Trevino a place in Special Services based on his golfing talents. Not surprisingly, spots on the team were highly prized and hotly contested—it was a heck of a way to satisfy one's military obligation. Trevino earned his spot but only after he thumped a superior officer who challenged him to a match.

"I didn't do anything but play golf with the colonels. That's when I really learned to play. I started out as a private, but after beating the colonels a few times, I rose to sergeant."

Twenty-year-old Buck Sergeant Lee Trevino returned to Dallas after his discharge in 1960, having realized that golf could rescue him from both a life of poverty and a long-term military career. He patched things up with Hardy Greenwood and returned to work at the driving range. The next spring, he joined the north Texas chapter of the PGA. He soon won several pro-ams at local Dallas and Fort Worth courses.

Though Trevino continued to spend the bulk of his days and nights with a club in his hand, he found time to date a seventeen-year-old North Dallas High senior. Within months, the couple married—they doctored her birth certificate to avoid needing parental consent—and by November 1962 Trevino's first child was born. His wife was only eighteen.

But Trevino spent much more time on the links than he did with his new family, and one course in particular became his most popular mistress. Just ten minutes from Hardy's driving range, Tenison Park Golf Club in east Dallas—with its rolling hills, pecan trees, and multiethnic clientele—became Trevino's home away from home. He eventually moved his young family to an apartment just across the street from Tenison. Trevino insisted he never "hustled" anyone at Tenison, but he had no trouble finding matches and money games there. When he wasn't working and hitting balls at the driving range, he was playing against anyone who would take up his challenge at Tenison.

Within two years of their marriage, his wife, fed up with her husband's absenteeism, offered the twenty-three-year-old Trevino an ultimatum. "Either it's going to be golf or it's going to be Ricky and me. We don't know you. You never take us anyplace. Why don't you get an eight-to-five job like everyone else?"

Trevino remained wedded to Tenison Park and in late 1963 his wife packed up their year-old son and moved out. Trevino spiraled into "a savage uninhibited tear—drinking to excess, eating, in his own words, 'trash' foods, sleeping irregularly and seldom in the same place. He lost fifty pounds."

Given sage advice from his grandfather—"the only way you forget a woman is to find another one"—Trevino soon married another seventeen-year-old high school student, Claudia Fenley. Although Greenwood felt Lee wasn't mature enough for domesticity (he'd felt the same way about Lee's previous hasty marriage), Trevino made time one Monday afternoon—his day off—to fit in a wedding after a late-morning eighteen holes.

The groom returned to work the next morning and Greenwood continued to ready Trevino for life on tour. He took his pupil to the 1963 PGA Championship at the Dallas Athletic Club (now relocated in the posh Mesquite suburbs), where Lee had his first chance to see all the tour regulars: Palmer,

Nicklaus, Player, and Snead. He also sent Trevino to PGA business school for two weeks to earn credits toward a tour card.

Meanwhile, Trevino slowly bolstered his local reputation, reaching the sectional qualifier for the 1963 U.S. Open and placing fifteenth in October's Lake Charles Invitational in Louisiana. Greenwood's friends also arranged an exemption for Lee to play in the 1964 Dallas Open, where he made the cut and impressed, among others, his Saturday playing partner, two-time U.S. Open champion Julius Boros.

Within months, Trevino came to dominate the region and rack up local press ink. In November, he won the Northern Texas PGA Assistants tournament, then won the Northern Texas PGA Championship two weeks later. He now felt he was ready, at age twenty-four, for the tour. Having completed the necessary requirements—four years as a club pro, plus the credits earned at the PGA business school—he should have been eligible for a Class A membership as a golf professional and ready access to play on tour (PGA Q School did not begin until 1965 as the standard route onto the tour). All that remained was for Greenwood to verify his four years of work.

"Hardy wouldn't sign it," Trevino later said. "He believed I wasn't ready, that I was too wild and immature to handle the responsibility of traveling all over the country and playing professional golf."

That fear rested on solid logic. Before the Lake Charles Invitational, Greenwood gave Trevino $600, telling him to keep a record of his expenses. "Instead, I stayed drunk for six days," Lee admitted.

Furious at Greenwood, Trevino quit his job at the driving range and, bolstered by minimal savings, set out to prove he was tour-ready. In fall 1965, he birdied the first hole of a play-off to win the Texas State Open in Houston, an event that included notable touring pros such as Miller Barber and rookie Homero Blancas. Two months later, he finished second to Blancas at the Mexican Open in Mexico City, earning $2,100.

Trevino's play grabbed the attention of several Texas businessmen who looked past the rough edges and saw dollar signs in Trevino's consistent swing. Some set up money matches or sponsored Trevino in events as far away as Panama. In early 1966, Martin Lettunich, a wealthy cotton field landowner and obsessive gambler, who had arranged hustles for Lee before, convinced Trevino to move Claudia and their young daughter, Lesley, to El Paso. Lettunich introduced Trevino to Jesse Whittenton, part owner of Horizon Hills, a club for a hard-drinking, brawling, gun-toting crowd among El Paso's nouveau riche. Whittenton hired Trevino as the club's jack-of-all-trades so that he could practice with few interruptions while continuing to work toward getting his tour card.

"We discovered Lee quite by accident," said Whittenton, a former defensive back for the Green Bay Packers who had retired early to pursue his own golfing dreams. "He came to me looking for a job. We put him to work shining shoes, and his golfing prowess became apparent, so we financed him for the pro tour."

Trevino's hardscrabble nature fit perfectly with the crowd at Horizon Hills, which managed to attract some high-profile names. In between breaking up fights among club members, Trevino fashioned a legendary reputation on the course. Twice, with dozens of local farmers betting from pickup trucks lined along the fairways, he outplayed young tour sensation Raymond Floyd, who was initially told he had come to El Paso for a high-stakes match against the "clubhouse boy."

These mano-a-mano matches honed Trevino's mental toughness and proved invaluable in shaping his later public image. His facade as an unpolished player depended on projecting an image that he didn't belong on the same course as touring pros or elite country clubbers, most of whom had sharpened their skills in high-profile amateur or collegiate events.

Trevino proved to be a capable tournament player in the Southwest, but no one outside the region knew him. He came up short when trying to qualify in Texas for the 1963 U.S. Open at The Country Club in Brookline, Massachusetts, but made it through both the local and sectional qualifiers in 1966, at age twenty-six, when the national championship came to the Olympic Club in San Francisco.

Trevino had never played a course as hilly, contoured, or quick as Olympic, or one set to the U.S.G.A.'s challenging specifications for the National Open. But after a few practice rounds, despite his shoddy bag and mismatched clubs, he felt confident and ready. Paired initially with Harry Toscano and a nineteen-year-old Brigham Young University sophomore named John Miller, Trevino shot 74-73, ten strokes behind the halfway leaders, Arnold Palmer and Billy Casper. Back-to-back 78s over the weekend dropped Trevino into a tie for fifty-fourth place with Johnny Bulla and Long Island club pro Gene Borek.

A mediocre finish in his first U.S. Open hardly discouraged Trevino, who resumed dominating his niche in the Southwest golfing scene. In late September, he won the New Mexico Open with a closing two-under-par 69, then successfully defended his Texas State Open crown with a win over future tour pros Marty Fleckman and Butch Baird at Sharpstown Golf Club in Houston.

In May 1967, Trevino was finally granted his Class A card. Shortly afterward, in the local U.S. Open qualifier, he fired the lowest score in the nation (134 over two rounds). He then took second in the Dallas sectional qualifier to earn a return trip to the U.S. Open, this time at Baltusrol Golf Club in New Jersey. That first visit east of the Mississippi River was major culture shock.

"You had to wear a coat nearly everywhere you went to eat," Trevino remembered. "Baltusrol is one of the famous old clubs in the East, with one of those big brick Tudor clubhouses sitting up on a hillside. I'd never seen anything like it and I was nervous about just going inside. The first morning I had to borrow a jacket to enter the dining room. After that I said to hell with breakfast and did without."

Trevino felt uneasy every time he had to mingle with the stodgy, club-member elite; he also felt awkward about hitting several balls in front of U.S.G.A. marshals during practice rounds. But he needed to learn a lot in a short time in order to compete more effectively at Baltusrol than he had at Olympic, and his game—remarkably for a Texas boy bred on Bermuda grass and without prior golf experience in the northeast—felt right at home on the tricky, Tillinghast masterpiece. Trevino kept score during his four practice rounds and shot even-par 280, helping to bolster his confidence.

Trevino played the opening two rounds at even-par 140, and a 71 on Saturday put him just four shots behind the leader, amateur Marty Fleckman. With his name on the leaderboard throughout the final round, just below names like Palmer, Casper, and Nicklaus, Trevino shot another 70 on the final day. No doubt feeling more pressure than he'd ever experienced, Trevino three-putted the fourteenth and fifteenth greens, but a closing trio of pars led to a 283 and sole possession of fifth place. He earned $6,000, far more than he'd earned in any of his previous tournament victories.

From start to finish, Trevino demonstrated he could adapt his Texas game to the radically different demands of a classic Eastern golf links. Still, the national press was more interested in his colorful background than his golf. His habit of wearing "scuba goggles because of West Texas desert winds," the (erroneous) label as a "son of a Mexican gravedigger," and his sheer joy at receiving "more money than I've ever seen" as a paycheck overshadowed the media's interest in his stellar golf. But even that brief moment of celebrity passed quickly.

"And that night [the night after the final round], just like all week, no one spoke to me or asked me for my autograph," Trevino remembered. "That just shows you how much I was known."

The New York metropolitan area fans may not have wanted his autograph, but savvy tournament directors had no trouble recognizing a new media favorite and invited him to join their fields. The following week, Trevino was persuaded to fly to Ohio for the Cleveland Open, a regular PGA tour event. Trevino's nomadic golfing existence had begun.

Over the next six months, Trevino quietly pieced together an impressive résumé for any newcomer to the tour. In half of the 1967 season, he earned $26,472 in prize money, won *Golf Digest*'s Rookie-of-the-Year award, and—the ultimate symbol he had "arrived"—was invited to play in the Masters the following April.

In years to come, Trevino would be remembered for several controversies he stirred at Augusta National, but the future discord was nowhere evident (not publicly, at least) during his first appearance in 1968. Despite "a humble background that would startle the staid old Augusta National Golf Club's members," the galleries at the Masters warmly welcomed Trevino from the start.

"The 28-year-old Trevino, whose father was Mexican, has captured the fans with his carefree approach to the game," noted an admiring reporter. "He tips his hat, waves his arms and laughs with the fans. And, he's been skipping down the long slopes of Augusta like a kid."

It wasn't just his attitude or upbringing that intrigued the elite Augusta fans. Trevino scored par or better in his first three rounds and trailed the leader, Gary Player, by just two shots. Touting a forty-year-old Tommy Armour putter he'd bought a week earlier at Tenison Park, he sank four birdies during a six-hole stretch on Saturday for a three under 69.

Trevino's hopes of slipping on a Green Jacket died the next day, Easter Sunday, thanks to an eight over 80, but he was clearly a burgeoning star. He narrowly missed out on victories in two PGA events in May and June.

When Trevino arrived in Rochester, New York, for the 1968 U.S. Open at Oak Hill Country Club, he may still have felt like a long shot, but he could no longer sneak up on the golfing world. Tom Weiskopf, another rising star, predicted before the tournament that with the nasty rough along the fairways, the favorites had to be Billy Casper and the upstart Trevino, whom one reporter called "the swarthy Mexican-American from Dallas." Oddsmakers concurred, establishing Trevino as a ten-to-one favorite.

After three superb rounds, the twenty-eight-year-old Trevino trailed front-runner Bert Yancey by just one stroke. Though he was, in fact, an insider's choice to win, Trevino still stood out among the field, and not just because of his colorful background. His swing was embarrassingly homemade, and while he was paired during the last two rounds with Yancey, a tall, svelte, former captain of the West Point golf team, the contrast was startling.

Sportswriters and members of the gallery marveled at Yancey's smooth, long, elegantly powerful motion. Trevino's swing, on the other hand, was short, herky-jerky, and offplane.

"In purely technical terms," as *Sports Illustrated*'s Curry Kirkpatrick explained, "Trevino's swing is all wrong. He takes the club back on an extremely flat plane from an open stance that is aiming left. To avoid the danger of duck hooking, he blocks out solidly with his left leg firm as he comes into the shot. At that moment he corrects whatever else is negative by the use of his hands."

"If he ever gets up high with [his shoulder]," fellow pro Dave Hill observed, "he's got to go back to eating tacos. His right side stays so low he never has to worry about getting over the ball too much. Lee doesn't know it, but he plays with his right arm and right shoulder almost exclusively. He's the best I've ever seen at coming through with the right hand and wrist."

That week—and well into the next decade—Trevino perplexed golf traditionalists with his unorthodox yet remarkably consistent swing. During the opening fifty-four holes at Oak Hill, Trevino carded only four bogeys and stood at four under par.

Even though Yancey and Trevino were the only men under par for the tournament—in fact, Trevino was half a dozen strokes ahead of the man immediately below him on the leaderboard—they knew the fourth round would not be a two-man race; Jack Nicklaus was lurking in third place.

"Lee said, 'I'm not that worried about Bert [Yancey],'" recalled John Kircher, one of the children who lived in the suburban Rochester house where Trevino lodged that week. "'But I am worried about that big bear [Nicklaus].' It kind of scared the little kids. We're thinking, There's a bear on the course?"

The following afternoon, while Yancey faded with a four-bogey binge in little over an hour, Nicklaus charged up the leaderboard. Experts wondered whether Trevino could stand up to the challenge.

Dressed in red socks, a red shirt, and black slacks—colors that would soon become his famous Sunday "payday" trademark—Trevino boldly responded on the back nine, largely due to deft putting. He followed a thirty-five-foot birdie on the eleventh with a twenty-two-footer on the twelfth for another birdie to take a commanding four-stroke lead over Yancey, five better than Nicklaus. Trevino parred his way in, taking his only risk of the week on the finishing hole.

"On eighteen, I missed the fairway to the left, and when I wanted to get it out of the rough and back into the fairway with a sand wedge, my caddie wouldn't let me."

"You don't want to be remembered as the U.S. Open champion who laid up on the last hole," said his caddie, Kevin Quinn, an eighteen-year-old Cornell student.

Unfortunately, Trevino's swing was not built for six-iron heroics from dense rough. He was lucky to move the ball forty yards ahead—still in the tall grass, but now with a sand wedge in his hand and seeking only to avert further embarrassment. Attempting just to strike the ball cleanly and put it somewhere on the green, he thrilled the gallery with the best shot of his young career.

"The pin was set right by the bunker and I was aiming at the right of the center of the green just to get it on the green. The ball came out of that tall grass, went straight at the flag and stopped two feet from the hole. Then I realized if I made the putt I'd be the first man in history to shoot four rounds in the 60s in the U.S. Open. I made it. I had another 69 and won by four shots over Nicklaus."

The press simply loved Trevino.

"What Lee Trevino really did, when he won the Open championship last Sunday," *Sports Illustrated*'s Dan Jenkins wrote, "was shoot more life into the game of golf than it has had since Arnold Palmer, whoever that is, came along."

Practically overnight, Trevino morphed into a tour superstar. With guidance from his visionary, superambitious agent, Bucky Woy, soon there were endorsement contracts for clothes, clubs, balls, cars, soft drinks, and very lucrative exhibition appearances.

"I was his traveling companion for the better part of a year," Woy recalled, "[and] it was like living with a cyclone corked in a bottle."

Everyone wanted a piece of Trevino. And most everything he did was soon scrutinized. When he won at Rochester, a reporter asked him what he would do with his $30,000 paycheck.

"I'm so happy I'm gonna buy the Alamo back and give it to Mexico," he said.

That raised a few eyebrows, but most wrote it off as a comment made in jest by a mercurial jokester. He had quickly developed a reputation for rapid-fire comedy with his gallery, constantly talking during his backswing, and beguiling the press with his self-deprecating humor.

But as Trevino's celebrity grew, so too did the scrutiny. After his initial three fine rounds at the Masters in 1968, Trevino never again fared that well at Augusta National. In 1969, while Trevino was talking with Charlie Sifford inside the locker room of Carlsbad's La Costa Country Club a week after the Masters, Sifford complained that none of the past Masters champions would help him in his bid to break Augusta's color barrier. (Every year, the former winners granted one player an exemption to the tournament.)

Attempting to reassure Sifford, Trevino offered his blasphemous opinion about the sanctity of the Masters.

"I said I didn't like it, that I didn't think I'd ever have a chance of winning there, and that I didn't think I'd ever play there again. I thought I was just letting off steam in the locker room. What I didn't know was that Bob Greene, the Associated Press golf writer, was nearby and heard what I said. The next day my comments about the Masters were carried on the wire all over the world."

Bucky Woy urged Trevino to own up to the remark and say it was simply not meant for public consumption. Trevino elected to insist that Greene, a highly respected reporter, had misquoted him. Though the remark stuck to Trevino's profile for many years, he was still invited to the Masters in 1970 and in subsequent years as well.

"I should have just swallowed my pride and gone on and played. But I felt everyone was wondering if I was as good as my word, so I had to stick by my guns."

He refused Masters invitations in the spring of 1970 and 1971 before finally returning the next year, but he never truly contended for the title: Never slipping on a Green Jacket didn't surprise Trevino, because Augusta's great length and wide-open spaces weren't "conducive to my style of play."

"That was the greatest mistake I've made in my career," he later admitted.

Part of Trevino's appeal—both to fans and to corporate sponsors, whether Wrangler jeans or Dodge Motor Cars—was that he was the real deal, an authentic everyman. A decade earlier, Arnold Palmer had fit this image: the Steeltown kid who *worked* at an exclusive country club rather than belonging to one as a member. After more than a decade of raking in the millions, Palmer obviously could no longer pass as everyman. He drove and endorsed Cadillacs, owned (and flew) a private jet, built condominiums and golf resorts, and dressed impeccably sharp.

Many Americans could no longer relate to that aspect of the new Palmer persona.

"You look at my galleries. You'll see tattoos. Plain dresses," Trevino observed. "I represent the guy who goes to the driving range, the municipal player, the truck driver, the union man, the guy who grinds it out. To them, I am someone who worked hard, kept at it, and made it. Sure, I go out of my way to talk to them. They're my people."

Trevino's genuine proletarian image—undersized, paunchy, a homegrown swing, all traits the Sunday duffer could relate to—fostered a lucrative marketing strategy of its own. When Bucky Woy set out to sell his client to the Blue Bell clothes company, his "sales pitch would be: 'If Lee Trevino, with his short, dumpy figure, looks good in Blue Bell jeans, just think how good you'll look.' Blue Bell bought it, handed Lee a lucrative, six-figure contract, and began producing and marketing a Trevino line of pants, shirts, and hats."

With Woy's encouragement, details of Trevino's personality and home life also became part of his appeal to the press, consumers, and corporations. He fed off his ethnic and class heritage, Archie Bunker style, cracking politically incorrect jokes about himself and his family. Poor Hispanics like himself were known in Texas as "Mexicans," he quipped, but once he became rich he became a "Spaniard." After his 1968 U.S. Open victory, he joked, "Yeah, I been married before, but I get rid of 'em when they turn twenty-one." And on more than one occasion at tournaments he told galleries and reporters, "Naw, I didn't bring my wife here. Do you take a hamburger to a banquet? I didn't take a six-pack to Milwaukee, did I?"

Trevino may have fed one-liners to captivate a crowd and merchandise a brand image, but for all his financial success, his private life was a mess, especially compared to that of other elite golfers. While Palmer, Player, Nicklaus, and Billy Casper exemplified steady domestic bliss, Trevino described his marriage as "shaky" and his jokes about his wife only made it worse. In truth, he hardly saw Claudia enough to escalate the frictions between them. He shared a roof more often with his business manager than with his family, and he never really let go of the marine R&R lifestyle: drinking, carousing, flirting with young girls, and staying out late with his buddies.

Trevino could win every tournament imaginable, but he would still never fit in with the family-focused, politely prosperous country-club image projected by the Big Three.

Even Trevino's most pedestrian personal habits reflected an erratic, unhealthy lifestyle.

"You'll seldom see Trevino eating bacon and eggs for breakfast, a sandwich and soup for lunch, steak and a salad for dinner," Woy observed. "Here's the kind of food Lee might eat on any given day: two pounds of grapes, a gallon of ice cream, and six dozen cookies—all things he wanted and couldn't enjoy as a boy."

With his cadre of endorsement deals and his "regular guy" image, Trevino had branched out of the sports world and into popular culture. While on the East Coast to play in the Westchester Classic in 1970, he was invited to appear on Johnny Carson's *Tonight Show*, which still taped in New York City. Though he often told reporters he was not a hard drinker, he downed more than a few Scotches at a nearby bar before heading to the green room at NBC Studios. Once there, for the first time in his life, he drank cognac . . . a lot of cognac. To the dismay of the usually unflappable Carson, an inebriated Trevino wandered onstage before the live studio audience.

"I was stumbling, falling-down drunk on national television," Trevino remembered. "Elaine Stritch, the actress, was on the show with me and she didn't have one of her all-time-great performances either. She got off on me pretty good, saying she liked little Mexican guys because they made wonderful elevator operators. To show her she couldn't outwit me, I propositioned her before millions of people."

Afterward, an embarrassed Trevino headed south on the New Jersey Turnpike to get as far away as possible from Westchester, finally stopping at a hotel when he could stay awake no longer. He missed his opening tee time Thursday morning; the press simply reported that he overslept. Recognizing that her husband was burned out and possibly on the verge of a breakdown, Claudia scheduled an immediate vacation for them in Acapulco.

Though the *Tonight Show* debacle was the closest Trevino ever came to "crashing and burning," his heavy drinking continued without interruption during the early 1970s and became, by his own admission, a way of life. Having five Scotches during a rain delay at the tail end of a round in the Atlanta Golf Classic was typical of his professional conduct, as was showing up to a tournament hungover or still drunk.

Whether he was sober or not, the most remarkable feature of Lee Trevino, Class A professional golfer, was that his exceptionally steady game rarely suffered from his off-the-course implosions. He struggled in the second half of the 1969 season due to a knee injury and was unable to win after January. But in 1970, he received the Vardon Trophy for the lowest stroke average on tour, and in 1971, he recorded one of the finest seasons in the history of modern golf.

Trevino started the 1971 season slowly, dropping out of three early-season tournaments (another increasingly common feature of his whirlwind personal life). But he won two spring tournaments and posted three runner-up and three additional top-five finishes in a ninety-day stretch. Heading into the seventy-first U.S. Open at Merion Golf Club outside Philadelphia, Trevino—with $135,110.10—ranked second only to Nicklaus in earnings.

At Merion, where Bobby Jones clinched the Grand Slam in 1930, Trevino was as consistent as he had been three years earlier at Oak Hill. Had it not been for an ugly triple bogey at the sixth hole on Friday, the "Happy Hombre" would have again fired par or better in all four rounds of a U.S. Open. Trevino and Nicklaus finished in a tie after seventy-two holes, but Trevino stared down Nicklaus in a Monday-afternoon, eighteen-hole play-off to decide the championship. Trevino saved his best for last, cruising through Merion's back nine to shoot a 68 and a three-stroke victory in one of the most memorable U.S. Opens in history.

"Yes, this one is more rewarding," he told the press. "Someone, Mr. Walter Hagen, I think, once said that anyone can win the Open once, but only a great player can win it twice."

It was fitting that Trevino would show such reverence for Hagen. Half a century earlier, Hagen, also a two-time U.S. Open champion, had boldly challenged the sharp line of class distinction at elite, private country clubs in both the United States and Great Britain. He, too, enjoyed an excessive lifestyle that didn't seem to faze his game. And Trevino, who earlier in his career had relied on mind games to gain an edge in high-stakes gambling matches, complimented Hagen as "a helluva psych artist" for his dramatic displays of confidence before every match.

Trevino's brilliance did not end in Philadelphia. Nine days after his victory at Merion, he headed north of the border for the 1971 Canadian Open. Trevino began the final round two strokes behind former Masters champion Art Wall Jr. Playing one group ahead of Wall, Super Mex immediately made up the deficit by holing out a wedge for an eagle on the first hole. Trevino—who would score a five under 67—and Wall spent the rest of the July Fourth Independence Day battling neck and neck across Montreal's Richelieu Valley Golf Club. With a sudden-death play-off needed to determine the winner, Trevino dropped an eighteen-foot, left-to-right sidehill putt on the first play-off hole to take his second national championship in as many weeks.

The next day, he left Montreal for Southport, England, and Royal Birkdale, the site of the one hundredth British Open championship. Trevino probably felt more comfortable at Birkdale than at the aristocratic American settings of Baltusrol, Merion, and Augusta National, and not simply because he had played Birkdale so well during the Ryder Cup two years earlier. During the long week leading up to the final round, the British press educated their American associates about the intersection of golf and social class.

In comparison to the other six British courses that rotate the Open championship, Birkdale, said one English reporter, "is the worst of the lot . . . Not in terms of space, cordiality, clubhouse access, hotel rooms and the things that helped produce the record crowds, but in terms of enchantment, charm, playing quality and tradition. 'Birkdale is what you might call nouveau riche,' said one journalist, referring to the fact that the course only got started in 1889.'" When Arnold Palmer—the son of a greenkeeper from blue-collar America— won his first British Open title there, he fit the Birkdale profile.

While Trevino's transition from indigent kid to Horizon Hills upstart blended perfectly with Birkdale, his celebrity was beginning to weigh him down. A six-to-one favorite (defending champion Nicklaus was four-to-one), Trevino became slightly annoyed by catcalls from a few rude spectators who cheered when he missed putts during round two. He also grew more than "a little testy" when the curious British fans crowded him as he tried to sharpen his stroke on the practice green.

But Trevino played through the annoyances at Birkdale, shot 70 or better each day, and won his third National Open championship in four weeks.

"This is the most fantastic day of my life," he told the press. "To be established as a world-class player you have to win one of the big ones staged outside the United States. I think from now on that I must be regarded as world-class."

Trevino was world-class, and not just on the golf course. The $13,200 check he earned pushed his winnings over $200,000 in prize money for the season, breaking Billy Casper's all-time earnings record in 1968, with more than four months remaining in the 1971 season. How Trevino *spent* that money soon earned more attention than how he won it. He donated more than one-third of the paycheck ($4,800) to an orphanage in Formby, the small Merseyside town in northwest England.

"When I win a championship of this stature, I have the feeling that the man upstairs is looking after me and I want to give something back," Trevino said. "I wanted to do something for the kids like me who had a difficult start in life."

This was not the first time, nor the last, that Trevino flashed his philanthropic side. He visited sick children in hospitals and competed in numerous charity pro-ams, including several in Puerto Rico, with his outgoing Hispanic friend Juan "Chi Chi" Rodriguez. Trevino had also donated $5,000 of his winning paycheck from May's Memphis Open to the local St. Jude hospital, and even handed over his entire purse from his 1969 World Cup team victory (with Orville Moody) to a Singapore caddie scholarship. Years later, on the Senior Tour, Trevino earned $1 million for a hole in one at an event and promptly gave half to the St. Jude Children's Hospital.

Perhaps his most memorable gesture came in February 1968. With a heavy heart, Trevino won the 1968 Hawaiian Open—just his second PGA tour win—two months after his close friend and frequent motel mate on tour, Hawaii's Ted Makalena, drowned in a freak swimming accident in Waikiki Beach. Trevino set aside $10,000 of his $25,000 payday to create a trust fund for Makalena's children.

"It was such a tragedy—a fine young man with a wife and three kids wiped out in a matter of minutes," Trevino said. "I had to figure it simply was his time to go. The Lord wanted him and there is nothing more you can say."

Trevino often spoke like a golf mercenary, perpetually chasing prize money and endorsement deals. He was also notorious for being a spendthrift ("I could give him $15,000," Claudia told the Pittsburgh sportswriter Myron Cope in 1968, "and he'd blow it in a week. Money means nothing to him"). So it was not surprising that his public obsession about making a million dollars overshadowed his low-key philanthropy. Professional golf's version of Robin Hood, Trevino not only instilled pride in poor and minority communities as a sporting hero; he looked after those who had once been poor children like him.

"The world's a funny place . . ." he said with trenchant irony. "When you have no money, no one will do anything for you. If you become successful and pile up enough money to buy anything you want, people deluge you with gifts you don't need and try to do all kinds of things for you."

WHEN HE RETURNED TO AMERICA, Trevino's star radiated nationwide. He was on the cover of *Newsweek* and *Time* magazines and both Dallas and El Paso honored him with "Lee Trevino Day." In addition to collecting a second straight Vardon Trophy and PGA Player-of-the-Year awards, he was named *Sports Illustrated*'s "Sportsman of the Year," edging out, among others, boxer Joe Frazier, who that March had handed Muhammad Ali his first loss to become heavyweight champion of the world.

Trevino was arguably as good in 1972, winning three PGA events and successfully defending his British Open crown by holding off Nicklaus with a memorable downhill chip on the seventeenth green at Muirfield. Even more heroic was his play a month earlier in the 1972 U.S. Open at Pebble Beach. A serious bout with tracheobronchitis, an infection of the windpipe and bronchial tubes, could not keep him from competing, even though he spent several days in the hospital immediately beforehand, and his doctor urged him not to play. Loaded up with painkillers and antibiotics, Trevino pulled within one of the leader after three rounds but ran out of stamina during the cold, windswept playing conditions of the final day.

Trevino had been tremendous on the course that year. But off the course, personal melodramas drained his time, energy, and peace of mind.

Trevino broke his two-year Masters boycott in April, but a ticket mishap prompted tournament police to attempt to throw his caddie, Neal Harvey, off the course during a pretournament practice session. Trevino confronted the police and threatened to withdraw if Harvey was not allowed to caddie. This embarrassing public controversy only fueled the behind-the-scenes drama, as Trevino was already on thin ice with Masters chairman Clifford Roberts after refusing Roberts's invitation for coffee one morning by saying, "Just tell Mr. Roberts I don't drink coffee."

Later that August, Trevino arrived in Boston only the night before the U.S. Industries Classic began at Pleasant Valley Country Club, and didn't have time to play a practice round. With Nicklaus absent, a high finish by Trevino would spring him back into the race for the 1972 money title. But after shooting a first-round 74, he had to be helped by marshals to a waiting car, with a high fever and a virus infection. Trevino returned to the course the next day, fought through the pain and blur, and finally recovered well enough to shoot a closing round 68, the second-lowest of the tournament. He finished in a tie for nineteenth.

More health problems festered in late October, as Trevino broke a blood vessel jogging near his home in El Paso. Again, the incident did not stop him from competing the following week and placing second in the Texas State Open. What did prevent him from finishing another autumn event, however, was his increasingly volatile temper. At the Sahara Open in Las Vegas, Trevino became so angered by slow play on the tenth hole that he marched off the course and withdrew from the tournament. Almost immediately, he regretted his decision, and he actually asked tournament officials to impose disciplinary action. He was fined $850.

"The damage has been done so the apologies [he telegrammed Sahara tournament officials to apologize] don't do any good," Trevino told reporters. "But I know that one hour after I had done this, I would have given $5,000 if I could have walked back out there and resumed play."

A strong end to the 1972 season helped Nicklaus distance himself from Trevino and everyone else in earnings and victories. With second place in earnings all but locked up, Trevino, who had competed in thirty-one PGA tournaments during the year (compared to Nicklaus's nineteen), stunned the family with a decision late in November.

After wrapping up a golf instructional television series, he returned to El Paso to spend Thanksgiving at home.

"I'm usually on the road playing tournaments this time of year. I decided it was time for a break, time to relax with my family and kind of get to know my wife and kids again," he told a local reporter. "I just hope no one asks me to carve the turkey. It's been so long since I've done it, I hardly remember how. For the past five years I've been eating bologna sandwiches for Thanksgiving."

As Trevino settled down a bit with his family, he tried rededicating himself to golf. He vowed to give up drinking and jogged all winter. He dropped twenty pounds. Though he liked what he saw in the mirror, he didn't like what he saw on his scorecards.

"[Losing the weight] ruined my swing, and I got moody," he said. "Now I'm going back to enjoying the game and enjoying myself. If I put a big score on the board, well, I'm just not going to worry about it."

The "ruined" swing manifested itself in his missing his first cut in over a year at Riviera in January's Los Angeles Open. Although at first Trevino remained unconcerned by his struggles, the press and his beloved fans, dubbed "Lee's Fleas"—two groups that had usually shown him unconditional support—speculated about the decline in his performance. That did not sit well with Trevino.

"They said I have not won since September [1972] and I'm in a slump. You just can't win 'em all. No one can," he responded gruffly. "If my fleas (his fans) don't like it, well, I guess they'll just have to go over to Jack [Nicklaus]." Trevino's disarming candor remained intact, even if his cheery exterior was clearly eroding.

But Trevino's change in public persona during early 1973 ran deeper. His fun-loving, devil-may-care reputation was mainly a facade. Trevino lived in constant fear that as quickly as he had become a star, it could all vanish in an instant.

"No matter how he clowns it up for the gallery, deep down inside he is insecure," Bucky Woy observed. "It's just that he never had anything in his life and has become superdetermined to succeed. . . . Miss the shot, and Lee Trevino fears he might slip back into his former life as a nobody."

On the fairway at a VIP outing a few months after winning the U.S. Open at Oak Hill, Trevino had walked down the gallery signing autographs for fans, yelling out, "Tacos, get your red-hot tacos! Never know . . . when my game will go and I'll be out hustling in the streets again. Gotta keep my voice in practice."

It was no wonder, then, why Trevino feverishly chased dollar bills, not trophies. As a child of poverty and the first superstar of Mexican descent in professional golf, he carried a burden of personal and professional insecurity that he could never shake.

But Trevino's disdain for his detractors vanished once the tour left the West Coast in February and moved to the warmer, more familiar climes of the southeast, where his game responded to the change in playing conditions. With dramatic one-stroke victories at both Florida venues (Jackie Gleason and the Doral Open), Trevino proclaimed that "spring training now is over," and he sprang to the top of the tour money list.

The return of his familiar exuberant mood was short-lived, however. During a fishing trip in mid-March, Trevino overdid it trying to yank a bass into his boat, and pulled muscles in his neck and chest. For the former marine who, the previous summer, had spent a week in a Texas hospital, then days later flourished in the U.S. Open at Pebble Beach, a minor muscle strain was not necessarily cause for concern. But the injury seriously hampered his performances for the next several weeks, thus rekindling his touchiness with both fans and the media.

In late April 1973, Trevino flew to Dallas for the Byron Nelson Golf Classic. Though he had finished second to Nicklaus the week before in the Tournament of Champions, the injury and his inconsistent play troubled Trevino as he returned to his hometown. The last thing his delicate temperament needed was a slew of people wanting a piece of the local kid and looking for a handshake, a photograph, or a courtesy appearance at a local event. (Around this time, Trevino was also fending off another distraction: a much ballyhooed challenge from daredevil Evel Knievel, who claimed that the pressures faced by golfers paled in comparison to those he faced.)

Trevino vowed to his wife to stay clear of the parties and hard drinking that were central to Texas country club hospitality, and to focus solely on his game. But the chest/shoulder/neck injury sustained a few weeks earlier—which he now told the press was the result of hitting the punching bag too hard during a spa workout—prevented him from finishing his swing. He played so poorly during the first round of the Byron Nelson that even his hometown fans deserted him: At any given tour event, Trevino's gallery usually numbered over a thousand, but in Dallas there were less than a hundred people watching him by the end of the day.

Whether it was the injury, the humiliating nine over 79 that he posted, or a combination of both, Trevino immediately withdrew from the tournament after signing his scorecard, claiming he needed to see a doctor. The next day, he had to be "carried" into the St. Paul Hospital emergency room, where X-rays revealed he simply had strained muscles. Nonetheless, Trevino decided to rest for two weeks before returning to the tour—against his manager's advice—to play in the Colonial Invitational in Fort Worth in early May.

"Man, I've got to play," he said. "I can't stand another week off, because I need the money."

Trevino certainly did not *need* the money. By gutting his way through the injury to a second-place finish three weeks later at the Danny Thomas Memphis Classic, Trevino passed the million-dollar career earnings mark. And he left Tennessee with more than just the $16,000 in prize money.

In typical spendthrift Trevino fashion, he purchased a $30,000 Dodge motor home he believed would solve all of his personal problems. Pregnant with their third child, Claudia could not fly around the country to see her husband, and with Lee booked practically every day for tournaments and appearances, he hardly saw his family. The RV, equipped with a full kitchen, showers, toilets, stereo, and a color television to entice his daughter and four-year-old son (later that year, Trevino estimated he'd seen him "about sixty days since he's been born"), was spun as a way for the family to enjoy much-needed quality time.

But Trevino had other intentions for the conspicuous motor home.

"I don't sleep and live in this vehicle but it's where I go after a round to relax and get away from the crowds. I guess I have lost some of my effervescence or my enthusiasm for showing it. I feel like I am hiding seven days a week. The demands on me have become so numerous that I just can't put up with all of it. I realize the image I have made but it's been very tough lately to maintain it."

In early June, Trevino drove his locker-room-on-wheels north to Pennsylvania. With the IVB Philadelphia Golf Classic scheduled the week before the Open and only a five-hour drive from Oakmont, Trevino headed to Whitemarsh Valley Country Club to sharpen his game.

Though he made sure to joke and smile for photographers and reporters, Trevino's patience for the burdens of celebrity continued to wear thin, despite his mobile home/hideout. After a very poor opening round in Philadelphia, he posted a strong 68 on Friday, but he could no longer conceal his mounting frustration before the enormous gallery that came to watch him. Though he occasionally bantered with the crowd, he kept to himself far more than usual, and when he jerked his drive far into the left rough on the eighth hole, he lost it. He bolted over a hill to locate his ball, leaving his caddie in his wake.

"Where you going?" asked his caddie, to which Trevino responded for the crowd to hear, "I'm playing about eleven more holes; then I'm getting the hell out of here."

The people who heard Trevino's comment held their breath for a moment—then smiled and laughed. Later, in a moment of less ambiguous disgust, Lee slammed the head of his putter into the turf.

"I'm wasting a whole week," he said. This time there were no laughs from the fans.

The following afternoon, after opening his third round with four bogeys that produced a dismal 77 and left him fifteen strokes behind the leader, Trevino walked into the scorer's tent and, without offering any excuses, announced he was withdrawing from the tournament.

"Mentally, I wasn't here [in Philadelphia]," he said. "I wasn't playing good and there didn't seem to be any point in keeping on with it."

The next day, Sunday, Trevino left Philadelphia and drove west toward Pittsburgh to become acquainted with Oakmont Country Club. He had never seen the fabled course, and if he wanted to get his game back on track and win a remarkable third U.S. Open in six years, he would need time to prepare.

Of course, getting out of town fast was also wise to escape the wrath of the Philadelphia press. Still, Trevino could not hide from his fans.

"We were going on the Pennsylvania Turnpike, and the guy handing out the ticket at the booth says, 'Thanks, Lee. Good luck next week.' And I'm in the backseat of the car."

The price of celebrity only mounted after Trevino arrived in Pittsburgh. The people of Pittsburgh—an unusually friendly and folksy group for a major city—immediately recognized him and acted as if they were best buddies. When he went into a small grocery store to pick up a few essentials, he was mobbed by well-wishers and never even got a chance to shop. He constantly felt backed into a corner.

"I can't go into a restaurant and enjoy a dinner. I eat two meals in my motel room most every day. I'd like to go into a bar now and then with my friends and just sit down and have a quiet drink, but I can't. Privacy is getting harder to get. I just don't have any privacy, really."

To remedy that problem, Trevino sought and got permission to park his motor home in a partially secluded area near Oakmont's driving range for the duration of the Open. Before beginning his practice round on Monday, he met with reporters and detailed the continuing headaches caused by his fans' persistent adulation.

He was most fond of telling reporters a story about how he sat in the back of a movie theater to escape notice, yet was still approached by the theater manager, who asked for an autograph and urgently sent the usher to fetch Trevino a Scotch on the rocks. "Look, I love to have fun, tell jokes, but then I'll go and hide. You'll never see me in the evening."

The only real privacy Trevino could find was inside the ropes on the golf course.

After his first practice round, finally relieved to be addressing questions about golf, Trevino discussed his thoughts about Oakmont. Considering that this Open was being played in Arnold Palmer's backyard, Trevino graciously deferred to him, even when King Arnie suggested that Trevino's style of low, left-to-right shot making might not be optimal for low scoring at Oakmont.

But when another aging tour legend offered his opinion about Trevino's chances of winning the 1973 U.S. Open, the "Not-so-happy Hombre" immediately reappeared, and with attitude.

Billy Casper, whom Trevino had admired early in his career, told the press that big hitters such as Nicklaus and Weiskopf had a ten-stroke advantage at Oakmont due to their length off the tee. Trevino, who was known more for consistency and accuracy than prodigious distance, fired back.

"I thought that was a cute quote in the paper the other day, what Casper said. . . . He wasn't talking for me. He wasn't talking for the Mex. He was talkin' for himself. As for me, I'm ready to win. I'm not going to run off and hide, no matter what happens on the golf course."

Not everyone shared Casper's concerns. In fact, Weiskopf—the longest straight hitter in golf, said Sam Snead—regarded Oakmont as a fairly short course for a U.S. Open. And even after his poor performance in Philadelphia, the oddsmakers still regarded Trevino as a six-to-one favorite to win, second only to Nicklaus.

But Oakmont's most demanding test, everyone agreed, had nothing to do with the need for power. The course's greatest challenge lay in the slickness and confounding curves of its putting surfaces.

"This thing will be won or lost at the greens," said Trevino. "They'll eat you alive. But they're not going to chase me away from this place. No, sir, I'm not going to get mad. . . . There is only one U.S. Open and they can't kick me off this place, because somebody's gonna win and it might be me."

THURSDAY MORNING, SPIKES ON AND dressed in black from head to toe, Trevino opened the door of his motor home and headed for the practice tee. During the opening two rounds, Trevino would be dwarfed in size and strength by the other members of his threesome, six-foot-two-inch J. C. Snead and six-foot-three-inch Jerry Heard. But the Merry Mex's career achievements towered over both of theirs, and over all but a half dozen or so of the remaining men in the field. No one, not even Nicklaus, had won more major championships in the previous five years.

Trevino scored a conventional par on Oakmont's troublesome starting hole and made another easy par on the second. Cautious with a two-iron off the tee, followed by a precise five-iron from the fairway, he reached red numbers with a twelve-foot birdie on the fifth. Trevino moved to two under par at the turn with a fabulous bunker recovery to three feet on the par-five ninth.

The momentum of that second birdie faded halfway into the back nine. He three-putted on the short eleventh to lose a stroke, but quickly gained it back with a brilliant iron on the lengthy, par-five twelfth, which he had decided to play rather creatively by hitting two consecutive six-irons following his drive. Two holes later, a missed green followed by a poor chip gave another shot back to the course.

"[Trevino] fell victim to the easy-looking par-4 14th," wrote a future chronicler of Oakmont's history, Marino Parascenzo, for the *Pittsburgh Post-Gazette*. "The pin was in a depressingly deceptive little swale. Coming from behind there, one inch wide meant four feet too long and Trevino was both, for a bogey 5."

What angered Trevino most about the two strokes he squandered was not how, but where they happened.

"I bogeyed the two easiest holes," he remarked, speaking about his bogeys on the eleventh and fourteenth.

As much interest as reporters showed in Trevino's performance, many wanted his take on how Nicklaus had negotiated the beguiling seventeenth a little earlier by driving the green for an easy eagle.

For decades, Trevino's approach to life had been anything but conservative. He drank, gambled, stayed out late, occasionally associated with seedy characters, and frivolously spent his income—whether it was a few dollars or a few thousand. But his risk-taking lifestyle bore no resemblance to his golf game, which was meticulous in its sobriety and advance planning.

"I think about what I should make on a hole in every tournament," he said at the height of his dominance in the early 1970s. "For instance, if I've got a par-three, two-hundred-and-twenty-yard hole I'll hope to play the thing in one over par for four rounds. I won't go for the pin, just the green, and I almost never gamble."

Oakmont was no exception. After one round he believed "[you] don't have to make a lot of birdies to win, but you have to avoid the bogeys."

Predictably, Trevino found fault with Nicklaus's game plan to attack the seventeenth green with a driver.

"I hope he does it every day. Because if he [pushes] one he's over on the driving range and he's got to reload and fire away again," Trevino proclaimed. "I won't do it unless I'm two shots behind on Sunday and I have to make up some ground. I have a game plan and I stick to it. That's not in my game plan.

"I used a three-iron and I was only eighty-seven yards from the hole. I measure that hole as three hundred and sixteen yards to the front of the green. But there was no point in my gambling today with a driver," he insisted.

That game plan centered on a belief that the championship would be won on the greens. And after the first round, he was pleased with his one-under score of 70. Trevino faced nine forty-foot putts and two-putted each time, including a snake from seventy feet. "My round couldn't have been better. I two-putted from here to El Paso," he told Bill Nichols of the *Cleveland Press*.

Remarkably, Trevino hit sixteen greens in regulation and missed only one fairway in round one (he had missed only one fairway during forty-five practice holes). But Trevino was still annoyed by his inability to position approach shots near the flagsticks, and by his overall timidity in playing the course.

"I want to shoot a decent round, not blow it all. I didn't go for the flag. I didn't want to take a chance of knocking it over the greens," he added. "The longer you stay in there, the more you get to know the course. I played very scared all day but tomorrow I'm going to start going for the flag."

Save for Jack Nicklaus, Lee Trevino understood course management as well as any golfer of his time. He'd played every type of course imaginable, in every type of climate: Texas, California, Florida, Panama, Japan, Britain, Singapore. Oakmont, as Palmer had said, was built loosely in the style of the Scottish links courses, and on Thursday it played hard and fast in the British tradition. A two-time British Open champion, Trevino had certainly proved he could master those speedy tracks.

But that week in western Pennsylvania, there was only one authority on Oakmont toward whom everyone deferred: Arnold Palmer. And when reporters relayed Trevino's comment that he intended to play much more aggressively on Friday, the King smiled.

"This is a course which requires conservative play," he said. "Going for the pin can cause you a lot of trouble."

Trevino had made a meteoric career of defying the odds and showing up the "experts." After his opening round, he walked briskly through the crowds and across the parking lot before encasing himself in his fortress motor home— lonely, but never alone.

· 4 ·

Carnage

Geoff Hensley wanted to make a good first impression. Making his debut in the U.S. Open, the pro from Quail Hollow Golf Club, thirty miles northeast of Tampa, was given a tall order.

Hensley had captained the University of Cincinnati golf team in the early 1970s and, as a sophomore, became just the second Bearcat to compete in the NCAA individual championships. Two months after graduating in 1971, at the Western Amateur in Benton Harbor, Michigan, Hensley fired an opening-round 68, which tied the course record.

In early June 1973, he took fifth at a Cincinnati sectional qualifier for the U.S. Open, and was rewarded with the daunting task of teeing off first in Thursday's opening round.

"I was thrilled," Hensley remembered, "being with the best players in the world at one of the top clubs in the country."

That club was Oakmont, the course that Tommy Armour called "the final degree in the college of golf." The very first hole set the tone: a 459-yard, downhill par four, widely accepted as the most challenging starting hole in all of championship golf.

Eager to get off to a strong start, Hensley left the locker room a half hour before his tee time to warm up with a few balls at the driving range and stroke a few practice putts to get a feel for how the greens were rolling in the morning dew. He planned to calmly ascend the first tee minutes before his 7:29 a.m. start time and block everything from his mind, except striping a drive down the heart of the tight fairway.

Typical for a young pro in his first U.S. Open, Hensley's game plan went right out the window. While he was still on the range, a member of the grounds crew charged up in a golf cart and anxiously yelled to him:

"Hey, you're on the tee!"

"What time you got?" Hensley asked his caddie.

"Seven twelve."

"Hop on; I'll ride you up," the grounds crewman said. Some 340 yards separated Oakmont's practice range from the first tee.

Startled and panicky, Hensley got in the cart while his caddie trailed behind.

"The caddie's running with the bag," Hensley remembered years later, "the clubs are falling out, jingling all over the place."

When they finally reached the tee box, Hensley discovered that he had actually been summoned to participate in the U.S.G.A.'s traditional opening ceremony, which began roughly ten minutes before the first scheduled tee time. With that completed, the championship formally began.

"Good morning, ladies and gentlemen, welcome to the seventy-third U.S. Open," cried out Jack Crist, the starter. "First off the tee this morning are Geoff Hensley, from Zephyrhills, Florida; Bob Gilder, an amateur from Tempe, Arizona; and Roland Stafford of Verona, Pennsylvania. Mr. Hensley has the honor. . . . Mr. Hensley, first tee, please."

Frantically, Hensley put on a glove, teed up a ball, and swung away with his driver.

The ball sailed into the deep, dew-laden rough on the right side—dead. He double-bogeyed the hole.

Given his jarring start, Hensley gathered himself pretty well and played the next seventeen holes in six over par, finishing with a 79. He got some extra sleep with his 11:17 a.m. tee time the next day and fired a solid 72; unfortunately, he missed the cut by a single stroke.

Hensley was not the only golfer Oakmont exasperated that week. Days before the first round, volatile Dave Hill had played four practice holes at Oakmont, walked off the course, and withdrawn from the tournament.

"I don't have the equipment to play this thing," said the thirty-six-year-old who had been performing superbly in the first half of 1973. In fact, he had scored his tenth tour victory four weeks earlier in Memphis at the Danny Thomas Memphis Classic.

Hill was infamous for bashing U.S. Open courses, as he did in 1970 at Hazeltine in Minnesota, calling the course a "cow pasture." Three years later, at Oakmont, he focused his criticism more on the U.S.G.A. officials.

"In the Super Bowl, they don't move the goalposts into the stands. In basketball, they don't grease the floor for the play-offs. In the World Series they don't flood the outfield. So why does the United States Golf Association have to take a course and make it impossible? That's like digging chuckholes at the Indianapolis 500. I guess they want to embarrass pro golfers."

Hill withdrew Tuesday afternoon and was content to play cards at his home club outside Denver while the U.S. Open (which would have been his ninth) proceeded without him. He'd finally had enough of the U.S.G.A. "taking a good course and making it zero fun to play."

The only man who seemed to have less fun on a U.S. Open golf course than Hill was Australia's Bruce Crampton. But then again, Crampton never seemed to enjoy himself, not even in the middle of the 1973 season, which was by far his finest in sixteen years on tour.

Crampton had developed a solid résumé since first being invited to play in the Masters in 1957, three years after winning the New Zealand PGA Championship at age nineteen. Between 1961 and 1971, he accumulated nine PGA tour victories, topped $100,000 in earnings for five consecutive years (starting in 1968), and in 1972 twice finished as runner-up to Jack Nicklaus when the Golden Bear won the first two legs of the Grand Slam at Augusta National and Pebble Beach.

Once the 1973 season began, Crampton only got better, winning the Phoenix and Tucson opens on consecutive Sundays in January. And in the spring, he nearly won consecutive tournaments again, escaping the Houston Open with a one-stroke victory in May, then holding the lead after seventy-one holes the following week at the Colonial in Fort Worth. A horrific double bogey on the final hole cost Crampton his thirteenth tour win, and gave Tom Weiskopf the honor of donning the tournament's traditional Scottish plaid jacket.

Weiskopf's victory—which would set off a hot streak of his own in the weeks leading up to the U.S. Open—had its ironic side. Even the quarrelsome Weiskopf found Crampton insufferable: "He's just not any fun."

Several other notables on tour also couldn't bear Crampton's melancholy.

Dow Finsterwald and Gardner Dickinson openly proclaimed they didn't want to play with him, and on more than one occasion, even placid Julius Boros chewed him out for offensive behavior toward fans, marshals, and photographers.

"We all have double bogeys; we all blow tournaments," Boros said. "His kind of conduct is totally unnecessary."

Crampton's three wins early in the 1973 season inevitably brought his behavior under greater scrutiny. But even though *Sports Illustrated*—in an article entitled "Golf's Jekyll and Hyde"—acknowledged that Crampton was *occasionally* kind and thoughtful and was consciously seeking to become more polite and "affectionate," he hadn't yet changed many of his colleagues' minds.

"[You're] asking a leopard to change its spots. That's a tall order," Dickinson said. "He's winning now. It's easy to act in a socially acceptable manner when you're winning. I'll reserve my judgment until he loses a few, the kind that really hurt. It happens. We all lose. Let's see what he does then."

That spring, Crampton confided to a friend/physician that he was "desperately unhappy," and admitted that though his life goals were success, health, and happiness, achieving the first two were "not worth a thing without the third." Years later, Crampton would reveal he had been fighting a lifelong battle with depression.

For all the pros, journalists, and fans who were repelled by Crampton's mean streak and holier-than-thou attitude toward the rules of golf (he harbored no regrets about turning players in for minor violations), his most outspoken critic was also his complete opposite.

Arnold Palmer hated to be paired with Crampton, and often reached "near rage" when he learned of another nasty Crampton episode. In a 1971 four-ball tournament at Laurel Valley Golf Club, not far from Palmer's hometown of Latrobe, Crampton complained to a reporter about the behavior of the gallery, presumably Arnie's Army.

Palmer's response upon hearing the quote: "Why doesn't he quit bitching and play golf!"

For his part, the raucous galleries were not the only reason Crampton wasn't a fan of the King. In more than a decade of coexisting with him on the PGA tour, Crampton claimed that Palmer "never gave me the opportunity to putt out, never told me I had a nice round."

Although the two men did play together in the third round of April's Byron Nelson Golf Classic, and were even seen talking and laughing together—"[I] never had such a congenial round with Arnold"—Palmer wasn't likely to share a drink with Crampton during U.S. Open week at Oakmont. And not just because most experts considered Crampton—the tour's second-leading money winner—more likely to contend for the title than Palmer. After the tremendous first half of his 1973 season, Crampton appeared ready to shed *Golf Monthly's* recent tag as "the most successful journeyman golf professional the world has ever known." Likewise, said *Golf Magazine*, "His steady play and new winning habit make him the most serious foreign contender."

But Crampton shot an opening-round 76. The next afternoon, a 75 left him one stroke over the cut line. At Arnie Palmer's U.S. Open, Bruce Crampton made a quick exit.

So did Billy Casper, Palmer's old nemesis from the 1966 U.S. Open at Olympic. Casper's loud claim that because of their great length, Jack Nicklaus and Tom Weiskopf held a ten-stroke edge over the field—the claim that so irritated Lee Trevino—didn't seem to ring true when neither booming hitter broke par during round one.

"Nicklaus and Weiskopf, they can use a six-iron or seven-iron on eighteen," Casper noted of the 456-yard, par-four finishing hole. "The rest of us, we're going to be hitting from much farther back. I'll tell you, if they move the flag back on that hole, I'll be using a four-wood. . . . I would say my chances are very slim here."

Casper's defeatist attitude in 1973 stemmed from more than bad memories of having played Oakmont during the 1962 U.S. Open, when he missed the cut with a pair of 77s. In 1972, for the first time since 1955, the forty-one-year-old didn't win a single event during the entire season. And though he came close a couple of times—losing a play-off in April at the Byron Nelson, and finishing fourth at the PGA—he hardly resembled the same man who, not long ago, had twice won the PGA Player of the Year award (1966, 1970) and become the first man in golf history to own five Vardon Trophies.

"I've been doing a lot of traveling around the world in the last few years, and I don't feel I've given myself a chance to recuperate from it. Jet lag, that sort of thing. As you get older, it tells on you a little more. You're never at ease on the golf course; you're stirred up from the tension; you lose your keenness to perform," Casper said in March 1973. "Because of my travel and a lot of things I was doing, I haven't really watched my diet. I was not only playing golf but had a lot of speaking engagements and appearances. The banquet circuit. I eat and enjoy everything now. When you're being the guest of someone, it's pretty hard to turn them down."

Having given up his famed, exotic buffalo-meat diet several years earlier, by spring 1973 Casper weighed at least thirty pounds more than during his mid-1960s prime.

Aboard airplanes as often as he was on the golf course, no longer in peak physical shape in his early forties, and fresh off his first season on tour without a victory, Casper appeared ill equipped to contend in the 1973 U.S. Open. And he wasn't. He shot a 79 on Thursday, matched that horrid score on Friday, and missed the cut by eight shots. No other elite player performed so poorly at Oakmont, a course where Casper—the man many considered the greatest putter of his time—should have shone. His awful play seemed to mark a sad, final U.S. Open hurrah for the world's then-greatest Mormon golfer.

IN HIS ENCOUNTER WITH OAKMONT'S maddening greens, seasoned pro Charlie Sifford struggled more than anyone: He six-putted the par-four seventh (five of his putts were within five feet). The PGA tour's first great African-American pro was already in bad shape before reaching the seventh green, however: He had double-bogeyed the first hole and triple-bogeyed the third.

"It wasn't the greens; it was me. I just putted like hell," said Sifford while chomping his trademark cigar. "Dave Hill told the truth. People didn't believe him. This golf course is too tough. You just can't play it."

Several other veterans, those who had seen just about every type of nasty lie and slick green, also couldn't do anything right on day one. Ed Merrins, the renowned teaching pro at such classic courses as Merion, Westchester, and Bel-Air, shot an 86 that featured a pair of eights. The 1964 U.S. Amateur Champion, Bill Campbell, had a similarly tough afternoon.

Campbell arrived at Oakmont the night before the Open began—after hosting his stepdaughter's wedding in Huntington, West Virginia—only to shoot an 84. Besides landing his tee shot in mud on the par-three sixth, the honest-to-a-fault career amateur called a penalty stroke on himself for hitting the ball twice with one stroke. (Incredibly, the next day, he would call two more penalty strokes on himself, both on the eighteenth.) If anyone could get away with missing a few practice rounds at Oakmont, it was Campbell, who had competed there in two U.S. amateurs and now three U.S. Opens. He took his awful first round in good humor.

"I shot an 86 my first time here in 1938, so I've improved two strokes in thirty-five years."

Even a supremely gifted putter like Dave Stockton was flustered by the course setup on Thursday. He needed thirty-six strokes on the greens just to card a 77. "I'm an aggressive putter. A U.S. Open course just doesn't fit my game," Stockton said. "I don't like to be made to look foolish. It's a humbling week."

Oakmont—the Hades of Hulton—was living up to its nickname.

Anyone named Snead (or Sneed) who walked off the course that afternoon was inclined to agree with Sifford and Stockton. A member of Ohio State's golf team during the early 1960s, Ed Sneed had been overshadowed by teammates Nicklaus and Weiskopf. Sneed's career got off to a poor start after he turned professional in 1967, but his game improved dramatically in 1973 and he scored his first tour victory later that year. Tee-to-green, Sneed played superbly during the opening round at Oakmont, as he hit sixteen of eighteen greens. But he could still manage only a 76, mainly due to mishaps on the greens.

The first hole was typical. After driving into the wet rough (he teed off early, shortly after Hensley), Sneed was fortunate to draw a good lie, and landed his second shot only twenty feet from the flagstick. "[But] then I three-putted. I had three three-putts today, all of them on relatively good first putts."

Sneed had joined Nicklaus and Weiskopf in a practice round on Wednesday. With former NCAA champion Hale Irwin joining the three Buckeyes, thousands of fans crowded the fairways to see the high-profile foursome. The participants were unusually eager to play that day: A terrible rainstorm on Tuesday, which knocked down trees and the press tent, had washed away vital practice time. Since most players—including Sneed, Irwin, and Weiskopf—had never played Oakmont before, studying the course's idiosyncrasies firsthand was essential.

Tuesday's afternoon downpour bothered more than just the golfers. Over eighty-three hundred fans had bought cheaper tickets and traveled to Oakmont to see their favorite pros play in a more relaxed environment. Most swarmed around Palmer's foursome, only to be disappointed when lightning and rain chased the King off the course after he had played just a few holes.

A uniformly older group of fans was at least as disappointed as Arnie's Army.

The indomitable Samuel Jackson Snead, at age sixty-one, had qualified for his twenty-ninth U.S. Open. Hitting the ball as long as ever, and increasingly proficient in his sidesaddle putting stroke, Sam genuinely expected to contend with players less than half his age.

Sam had planned to practice and offer some pointers on Tuesday to his nephew, Jesse Carlyle (or J. C.) Snead, a three-time PGA tour winner, who had never seen Oakmont. J.C. was quite sour on how the U.S.G.A. "tricked up" courses for the Open, seemingly with the goal of humbling the best players in the world and occasionally making them look foolish. J.C. still had lots to learn about what the U.S.G.A. had in store for him at Oakmont, so Tuesday's storms set back his preparations considerably.

"Uncle Sam" was not nearly as concerned about losing practice time. While Jerry McGee and other youngsters peered out the locker room window, praying that the storms would cease, Sam—his trademark straw hat balancing on the slight bulge of his belly while exposing his bald head—lay down on a bench and slept peacefully through the loud blasts of thunder. Snead already knew Oakmont and how the U.S.G.A. would set it up for a major championship.

Four times Snead had narrowly missed out in the National Open, and two of those failures had Oakmont ties. In addition to his collapse against Hogan on Oakmont's back nine in 1953, Snead had squandered a late lead in the 1947 Open in St. Louis, then lost in a play-off to Lew Worsham, Oakmont's recently appointed head professional. Twenty-six years later, Worsham was still the man in charge of Oakmont's pro shop.

Snead owned a Claret Jug, three Green Jackets, three PGA Championships (including the 1951 installment at Oakmont), and more PGA tournaments (eighty-two) than any man in history. He also won his seventeenth West Virginia Open in 1973, nearly four decades after winning his first in 1936. But for all his record-breaking achievements and the continuing stellar quality of his game, Snead's string of second-place finishes in the U.S. Open—he never won the championship in twenty-eight tries—hung sadly over his head.

"Why does the Open mean so much?" was his evasive reply to the predictable questions about whether or not he could finally win one.

"I'm playing the same fellows I beat each week. There's just too much emphasis and prestige put on it. It's like Mickey Mantle hitting three home runs in the last game of the World Series and winning the batting title for that. In 1950 I won twice as many tournaments as anybody else, I had [the] low average,

I won the Vardon [Trophy]. [Ben] Hogan wins the Open and he's player of the year. Sentiment is fine and Hogan did a helluva thing by coming back, but are they going to let sentiment go by the record? Heck, I beat Hogan that year in a playoff at Los Angeles. A man doesn't just have to play well to win the Open; he has to have a hell of a lot of luck. . . . I guess the Open is rated so highly because it's the daddy of them all. They've been playing it since the year one."

Snead happily put his gripes on hold in 1973; after two years of failing to qualify, he returned to the event by tying for first place in the nation's largest sectional U.S. Open qualifier in Charlotte. Well rested and anxious to resume his lifelong quest, Snead joined two of the most flamboyant young stars in the field, twenty-three-year-old Lanny Wadkins and twenty-one-year-old Ben Crenshaw, for an early Thursday morning start.

"Hey, Sam," a member of the gallery called to him after the round, "you're older than those two guys you played with combined!"

"Hell," Snead replied, "you could throw a third one in."

By sticking his approach to within eighteen inches on the fifth green, Snead found himself one under par early in the round. But he mangled the last three par-threes, bogeying the eighth and sixteenth and double-bogeying the shortest hole of all, the thirteenth. As usual, Snead mainly blamed his handiwork on the greens; he just couldn't turn brilliant approach shots into birdies.

"I missed only two fairways," he said after shooting a 75. "And I only had one long putt. Just one putt over twenty feet. I was putting awful. Kept missing 'em to the right. I had no three-putt greens, but had thirty-three putts. Should have had a seventy."

"Sam is a better putter than he gives himself credit for," Wadkins observed after the round. "He might do better if he were more positive about it. Sometimes he finds ways to miss putts."

Snead (like his nephew) also couldn't help but continue his diatribe about U.S. Open golf, complaining especially about the long rough along the fairways.

"I know everybody's got to play the same course, but it sure ain't fun playing this course. But maybe the U.S. Open ain't meant to be fun."

Aside from a few golfers—the rejuvenated Player, a plucky youngster like Wadkins, or the unflappable Nicklaus—it was hard for anyone to stay positive, much less have "fun," that afternoon at Oakmont.

"I think this course is unfair," said Ben Crenshaw, after wrapping up his round of 80 with Snead and Wadkins. Nine days later, the University of Texas superstar would win his third consecutive NCAA title (he was the first ever to do that), turn pro that August, and take the San Antonio Open in just his fourth start. But in the opening round at Oakmont, Crenshaw hit only two fairways and seemed content that he'd three-putted only three times on what he would later call "maybe the strongest greens on the face of the earth."

Another hotshot twentysomething came to Oakmont Thursday morning with very high hopes, but left bewildered by his disintegration on the course. As a psychology major at Stanford, Thomas Sturges Watson had taken fourth place in the 1969 U.S. Amateur at Oakmont (won by Steve Melnyk). Originally from Kansas City, the twenty-three-year-old, four-time Missouri Amateur champion had even carded a hole-in-one with a three-iron on the long eighth hole (shortened a bit for the Amateur, as was the entire course). Watson turned pro two years later, and although still winless in 1973 when he arrived at Oakmont for his second U.S. Open, he had nearly won his first tournament in February's Hawaiian Open, but squandered a four-stroke lead to tour nomad John Schlee.

Watson had reason to feel that his past familiarity with Oakmont would play to his advantage. Unfortunately, it didn't, as he shot 81 on the first day, and a 73 on Friday was not enough to make the cut. The legendary Tom Watson had not yet emerged.

Pittsburgh's most promising young golfer, Jim Simons, who teed off in the group after Watson, also couldn't catch a break during his first round at Oakmont. A two-time Pennsylvania Amateur champion, Simons had seen his national golfing reputation soar in the 1972 U.S. Open, where he tied for fifteenth and was low amateur. Soon afterward, he turned professional, became a club pro in nearby Butler, Pennsylvania, and sought to atone for having played so poorly before his hometown fans during the 1969 U.S. Amateur: he shot 81-77 and failed to make the cut.

It didn't get any easier for Simons four years later, with Oakmont stiffened to U.S. Open specifications. Suffering from a sore shoulder, he bogeyed three of the first four holes. Three over par and his spirits fading, Simons was thankful to see a familiar face, his father's, on the fifth tee.

As a marshal on the 379-yard par-four, Ralph Simons had an inside-the-ropes view of his son's tee shot, and Jim responded positively to his dad's words of encouragement by birdying the hole. Unfortunately, that proved to be the only bright spot for the Simons family that afternoon; Jim didn't make another birdie and added eight more over-par scores to finish with an 81, the same embarrassing number he had posted in the first round in 1969.

"Everything went bad," Simons said. "My putting was terrible, but I missed a lot of fairways and got myself into trouble. All I can do is go home and forget this round."

Although Watson and Simons teed off just eight minutes apart, and each man finished ten strokes over par, they were not the only golfers that afternoon to post nightmare scores. Dean May, Bill Rogers, Richard Lee, Dean Refram, Bobby Mitchell, and Ron Cerrudo all failed to break 80, each a postnoon starter. And only an injured hand saved Robert Barbarossa—once a fine junior player who won the 1964 Minnesota State Amateur Championship at age sixteen—from a terrible afternoon round. He withdrew after forty-four strokes on the front nine.

Still, as bad as some of the afternoon scorecards looked, the morning starters did not exactly tear up the course either: Of everyone to tee off before noon (there were ninety), only one, Raymond Floyd, broke par.

Floyd was a powerful, fierce competitor from North Carolina who showed enormous promise early, joining the tour in 1963 and winning the St. Petersburg Open four months later. He rose to stardom with three wins in 1969, including the PGA Championship, only to go winless over the next three seasons. In 1972, he fell to seventieth in the performance rankings, his lowest position since turning professional.

By 1973, Floyd was better known for his reckless antics off than on the course, especially his drinking and alleged womanizing. At the Masters one year, a pack of young women dressed in hip-huggers paraded through the stodgy Augusta crowd (before being asked to leave) with buttons reading, MRS. RAYMOND FLOYD, attached to their see-through tops. One Pittsburgh columnist that week referred to him as "a rogue in spiked shoes, a Romeo with a niblick, Valentino in a Ban-lon."

"I haven't lived the straightest life," he acknowledged to the press, "but I think the playboy tag is overrated. When you're a bachelor on the tour, you're seen different places with different girls. After a while, everybody assumes you're a playboy."

In preparation for the U.S. Open, Floyd did not exactly show steadfast devotion to his craft. As he was relaxing in his adopted hometown of Chicago, his tournament preparation consisted mainly of traveling to Wrigley Field to watch his beloved Cubs. He even took batting practice with the team.

Floyd's practice with the second-place Cubbies may well have been inspiring; after completing his round of 70 in the early afternoon, he held sole possession of the lead. As he tried to make clear to a disbelieving media, he had taken time away from the tour not to indulge his "playboy" lifestyle, but to regroup mentally.

"I played in four consecutive tournaments and was playing well but not scoring," he said. "That's one of the biggest burdens out here—that's when you get tired of golf—so I just decided to get away from it for a while."

Refreshed by the layoff, Floyd played remarkably steady golf on Thursday: Aside from a birdie-bogey-birdie stretch between the ninth and eleventh holes, he scored easy pars the rest of the way. Thankful for sinking a twenty-five-footer on the eleventh, he genuflected before Oakmont's greens.

"These are the fastest greens I've ever putted on, and I've been playing golf for twenty-seven years."

Floyd was among only ten players who navigated Oakmont in par or less on opening day. The 1961 U.S. Open champion, Gene Littler—a smooth-swinging San Diegan known affectionately as "Gene the Machine"—posted a solid 71. Two three-putts scarred his excellent play from tee to green, but he was fortunate to drop a monster putt on the seventh hole, and also to birdie both par-fives on the front nine without reaching either green in two. Everyone came to expect this sort of unflashy brilliance from Littler, especially on a U.S. Open venue.

Though overshadowed by Gary Player's inspiring story of return from illness, Littler's saga during the past year was no less a showcase of resiliency.

Littler and Player shared more than just a spare, 150-pound frame. The previous summer, a diagnosis of lymphatic cancer had halted Littler's sterling nineteen-year career.

"At the time, I wasn't thinking about playing golf; I was just hoping to stick around."

He not only "stuck around"; Littler made a quick, full recovery and went on to win five more PGA events in his mid-forties (including his twenty-fifth tour victory over an elite field in the St. Louis Children's Hospital Classic a month after the Open at Oakmont).

But after the opening round, instead of his being recognized for high-caliber golf despite his age, the first thing that concerned everyone was Littler's health and long-term prognosis.

"People are bound to talk about it. They wanted to honor me in a testimonial. I am grateful, but this isn't something I deserve credit for. I'd rather be honored for doing something positive," he told the media. "I may be doing some good. People watch me on TV and they know about my illness. There is a glad kind of forgetting in golf. And it may be that it did me good in a way. Now petty things don't bother me; nothing angers me."

Even Oakmont's greens didn't dampen Littler's spirits. In fact, he pretty much picked up in 1973 where he had left off in 1962, when he was the defending U.S. Open champion. He had then rammed in three birdie putts of more than twenty-five feet *and* sunk a hundred-foot eagle to grab the first-round lead with a 69. Littler stayed strong throughout the 1962 Open, taking eighth place behind Nicklaus and Palmer.

Asked rather cruelly by a reporter in 1973 if his recent bout with cancer might lead to another strong start, mediocre finish, Littler responded, "It's not the operation. It's just that I'm [almost] 43."

Arnold Palmer.

· DAY TWO ·

June 15, 1973

· 5 ·

The Prince and the King

"Whoever in the long ago said a prophet is without honor in his own back-yard never thought an Arnold Palmer would come along a few hundred years later."

—AL ABRAMS, JUNE 16, 1973, *PITTSBURGH POST-GAZETTE*

"Oh, oh, [I'd] better get out of here," Johnny Miller joked. The twenty-six-year-old San Franciscan stood up from his seat at the dais in the press tent, almost finished recapping his just-completed second round.

"Here comes the King," Miller announced.

Shielded by a police escort to buffer the autograph hounds, Arnold Palmer walked into the sportswriters' big top.

Five hours of grueling U.S. Open golf and the rugged tour veteran still had enough energy to exchange banter with the rail-thin California kid, who could pass as the sixth member of the Beach Boys.

"Take your time, Johnny. But please limit your remarks to ten seconds," Palmer joked.

Miller knew the drill. He had just completed a third consecutive U.S. Open round alongside golf's King (they were also paired in the final round a year earlier at Pebble Beach).

"If I start playing the way I'm putting, I'll be in business," added Miller, wrapping up the summary of his two under 69 in Friday's second round. "This is the best I have ever putted."

Coming from Johnny Miller, that was quite a statement.

Born April 29, 1947, John Laurence Miller epitomized the modern-day golf prodigy. His father, Laurence Otto, married Ida Meldrum in 1942, and their first child, Ronald, was born a year later. Laurence had been a communications specialist in Manila during the Second World War, a post that led afterward to a long career with the Radio Corporation of America (RCA).

In his spare time, Laurence joined the burgeoning group of middle-class Americans during the Eisenhower years to become enchanted with the game of golf. He competed regularly on the local amateur circuit, winning the Roos Brothers' San Francisco golf championship and the sportsman's flight of the San Francisco City Amateur in 1956. But his greatest golf legacy would be his second-youngest boy, John.

By his fifth birthday, John had already become an avid golfer—of the indoor variety.

Under Laurence's eye, John smacked a cut-down iron into a green canvas tarp in the family basement. To strengthen his grip, Laurence taught John to constantly squeeze a rubber ball, and, under his father's guidance, the boy studied the game's finer points by reading the three leading prophets of the postwar era: Byron Nelson, Ben Hogan, and Sam Snead. From the start, John would learn to chase greatness along the proven path of the modern masters.

Although he would eventually become famous as a touring professional with a casual attitude toward practice—"I don't deserve to be the best player. I just don't put the time in," he said in his midthirties—as a child, he resembled a young Hogan.

"Johnny just loved the game," his father remembered. "Dinner would get cold, and his mother would get mad, but Johnny kept hitting shots into the canvas. He was very dedicated."

Laurence complemented the physical regimen with his variant of Norman Vincent Peale's credo in *The Power of Positive Thinking*, which became a best-seller the same year (1952) that John took up the game.

"His number one rule was to always be positive," Miller later wrote. "Dad had a saying: 'Four parts praise, one part pruning.' He knew that children who are complimented constantly bloom like flowers, whereas those who are criticized and chided develop all sorts of problems with self-esteem."

To his father, John was known as "Champ."

"He treated me as though I were something special."

So special, in fact, that after John began his formal training for the game, his father decided to shelter him from it.

"For the next three years, I never set foot on a golf course," Miller later explained. "I just hammered away at balls in that basement, memorizing the correct grip, stance, and posture, and matching my swing positions to the ones I saw in the book."

After John served his time in golf purgatory, Laurence declared him ready for outdoor training. At San Francisco's Harding Park course, the eight-year-old boy was finally allowed to exercise the skills he'd learned in solitary. And by summer—standing "about knee-high to his pop"—John won his first event, the Roos-Atkins Father and Son tournament, played on the par-three Golden Gate Park course.

Three years into John's happy, golf-filled childhood, tragedy struck the Miller family. In October 1958, while fishing with his father and a friend at Lands End—the windiest, rockiest stretch of San Francisco's cliff-lined coast—fifteen-year-old Ronald reached into the ocean to haul in a striped bass. A wave crashed down and swept him under; after fighting valiantly to survive, Ronald drowned.

The Millers, who had formally converted to Mormonism in 1956 at the famous Los Angeles temple in Westwood, relied heavily on their faith to cope with Ronald's death. Laurence also hoped that golf could serve as an additional distraction for his grieving eleven-year-old son. Three years earlier, Laurence had tabbed fellow Mormon John Geertsen, the head professional at San Francisco Golf Club, to mentor John's budding golf skills. Coach and pupil became closer after Ronald's death (indeed, Geertsen later claimed that he first met John at church after his brother's accident), and Miller's skills blossomed with the onset of adolescence.

"He was the smallest guy I've ever seen, but he loved to work. He'd do almost everything you asked," Geertsen remembered. "Johnny didn't pick up golf right off; it was a slow process. But when he started to come, he seemed to have all the strokes to be a great one."

By age eleven, Miller showed enough potential for the prestigious Olympic Club—the site of the 1955 U.S. Open—to grant him a junior membership. As a frequent caddie at the seaside course along with his pal, Steve Gregoire—whose father, Leon, happened to be a member—Miller learned the course inside out. No challenge seemed to faze the cocky youngster, and both Laurence and Geertsen encouraged their prodigy to cultivate a fearless mind-set.

Miller was especially gifted as a putter; he routinely one-putted the greens at Harding Park, and once needed only sixteen putts there to complete an eighteen-hole round. Miller's smooth stroke and sure nerves often won him twenty-five-cent bets on the practice greens. His father and John Geertsen overlooked the moral transgression.

"If there were a better putter in the world than me when I was twelve years old, I'd like to have seen him," Miller wrote.

If, on occasion, the undersized, preteen Miller coaxed both friends and unwitting marks into putting contests, by the time he entered Lincoln High School his hustling days were over. He grew ten inches between his freshman and junior years (he grew three additional inches in his twenties), went undefeated in three years of interscholastic matches, and won the 1963 San Francisco City Championship.

And teenagers were not John's only golf victims.

In June 1963, at age sixteen, Miller reached the second round of the California State Amateur championship at Pebble Beach. There he faced a forty-two-year-old petroleum engineer named John Richardson. Miller won two of the three opening holes against the former champion before his caddie, high school teammate Steve Gregoire, saw an unfamiliar club in the bag: a one-iron Miller had used to warm up. Realizing that this was the fifteenth club (one more than the rules allow), Gregoire handed the club to Miller's mother, who was trailing her son throughout the match. Miller also immediately admitted the mistake to Richardson, on the fourth tee.

Although Richardson chose not to invoke the appropriate penalty stipulated by California's rules of golf (forfeit each hole to that point or a total of three holes), "[D]iscussion of it spread around the course via the grapevine and by the time Miller reached 18, a 2-up winner, almost every galleryite on the course, and the officials as well, knew about it."

Technically, the issue was simple: Miller should have forfeited the first three holes of the match instead of holding a two-up lead.

But Richardson—the father of a teenage boy—saw that Miller was in tears because of the ordeal and refused to formally protest. "If I can't beat him (Miller) on the golf course, I don't want to do it on a technicality," he said.

After a lengthy conference, according to a local reporter, "The committee ruled that Richardson lost the case when he refused to squeal," and Miller walked away with a victory. California's rules of golf left enough leeway for the committee to reach this decision, and the rules, in any case, took a backseat to Richardson's paternal instincts. The press also treated Miller kindly.

"John Miller, a quiet, bright young man who minds his manners and obeys his conscience, won a golf match Thursday and learned, the hard way, a few facts of life."

Losing in the following round did nothing to diminish Miller's superb performance in America's most prominent state amateur tournament. And local reporters still printed the label assigned to Miller by his swing coach, John Geertsen: "a cinch for future golf greatness."

The next summer, he not only proved himself the best young golfer in his state by winning the California Junior Amateur; he vaulted onto the national stage.

Prominent local golf icon Bill Powers convinced Miller to travel to Oregon to enter the National Junior Amateur Championship. In July 1964, the Eugene Country Club hosted the seventeenth-annual showdown of the world's top players under age eighteen, and from the outset Miller dominated. At the qualifier on July 28–29 (the top 150 qualifiers advanced to match-play competition), Miller earned medalist honors with a two-under-par 140—a record that lasted for over four decades.

During three days of match play, Miller cruised through the field. His only challenge came in the quarterfinals, when he drove wildly and hit numerous trees as well as a member of the gallery. But he still won the match when his opponent, sixteen-year-old Minnesota State Amateur champion Robert Barbarossa, three-putted the eighteenth green.

In the finals, Miller jumped out to a quick lead against Mexico's Enrique Sterling, but the match remained close throughout. One up at the turn, Miller traded blows with Sterling until the par-three seventeenth, where a win meant the championship. Miller just missed dropping a hole-in-one and took the title.

"I like [Arnold] Palmer because he's so bold," he told the press. "I think I pattern my play after him quite a bit."

The triumph in Eugene made Miller a minor celebrity in the world of golf. The August 24, 1964, issue of Sports Illustrated featured a fresh-faced Miller as one of the "Faces in the Crowd" (the publication's recognition of athletes not in mainstream or "big-time" sports). The brief entry celebrated Miller's victory in the junior amateur, boasting about his second-round 68 in the qualifier as well as the almost hole in one on the seventeenth during the final match. The article also referenced the adoring Miller's quote about Arnold Palmer.

Sports Illustrated was not alone in marking the promise of greatness in John Miller. The University of Houston, the nation's dominant college golf program, offered him a full scholarship (they also, according to Miller's book *I Call the Shots*, offered Laurence a Mustang convertible!). Miller elected to stay closer to his family, both geographically and religiously, by choosing Brigham Young University in Provo, Utah, the nation's leading Mormon institution of higher learning.

The University of Houston and BYU shared the same team nickname, the Cougars, but the comparisons ended there. While Houston had won twelve Division I national championships between 1956 and 1970, Miller chose a program that had yet to produce a conference champion or a prominent golf professional.

That changed with the star-studded class that Coach Karl Tucker recruited in 1965. During the next two years, four Cougars competed for the team's top spot, but reigning Mississippi State Amateur champion Mike Taylor—not John Miller—was the team's best player.

"Mike was the first player I saw who looked like he could lead us out of the wilderness," Coach Tucker recalled. Taylor's teammates Jack Chapman and Bud Allin also regularly shot scores equal to or better than Miller's in college matches.

Led by Taylor and the strong supporting cast, almost overnight the Cougar program sparkled in the Western Athletic Conference. An 8–0 record during the 1966 spring season, followed by superb performances by the team's top four players, brought the championship title to Provo for the first time in school history. Miller finished seven shots behind Utah's Bruce Summerhays in the individual championship, and several strokes behind Taylor, Allin, and Chapman.

Thus, the BYU legend that "Johnny came in and gave the program a face-lift" isn't quite accurate; Miller was not *the* savior of the school's golf program. Instead, similar to his development under Geertsen, Miller's game progressed gradually during his college years, and saw a series of streaky up-and-down moments.

As a notable collegiate golfer and former national junior champion, Miller was already an emerging star. But it took a serendipitous return to his roots for millions of Americans to learn his name.

In the summer of 1966, the U.S. Open returned to San Francisco's Olympic Club. Eleven years earlier, Jack Fleck had stunned the sports world by catching Ben Hogan in the final round and then beating him in a play-off—along with Sam Parks's victory at Oakmont in 1935, one of the greatest upsets in golf history. Now, an even stronger field fought to an even more dramatic conclusion. Although no dark horse like Fleck shockingly claimed victory, the 1966 U.S. Open at Olympic was the birthplace of an international golf legend.

Seven years of seasoning at the Olympic Club had taught Miller every idiosyncrasy of the hilly, 6,727-yard terrain (the Olympic Club then featured two courses; the Open was played on the Lake Course, founded in 1927 and remodeled by Robert Trent Jones in 1953). Home from BYU for the summer, he signed up to caddie when the Open commenced in the middle of June. John would have been a huge asset to any professional or amateur lucky enough to have him tote their bag. But the sophomore did not want to squander his inherent advantage at Olympic on someone else; he chose to compete in the early June sectional qualifier to try to make the field.

Playing his other "home course" (the San Francisco Golf Club) in the sectional qualifier—another stroke of good fortune—Miller shot 143 over two rounds. That was the third-lowest total in a field that included such notables as Harvie Ward, George Bayer, and Bob Lunn to earn a spot in the Open. Miller gladly turned over his caddie slot to BYU sophomore Mike Reasor, who—perhaps even luckier than his Cougar teammate—drew Arnold Palmer's bag.

Paired with Jack Nicklaus for two practice rounds, Miller tasted the stardom of a U.S. Open even before the championship began. Still described as "burly," Nicklaus casually went about his round with Miller on Wednesday snapping off wisecracks for the hordes of fans and writers.

The Golden Bear's serenity must have rubbed off on Miller: He dozed off at ten p.m. on Wednesday evening and nearly slept through his opening-round tee time. Although Miller showed little sign of nerves, his father was on pins and needles.

"I'm the only nervous one in the family," said Laurence after the first round. "I was up at six a.m. and I figured Johnny would be too. But I kept looking in and he was sleeping after nine o'clock; I figured it was time he got up."

The well-rested Miller joined Harry Toscano and another U.S. Open first-timer named Lee Trevino on the tee at 10:51 a.m.

"I guess I was a little bit nervous on the first hole, but after I sank my par putt there, I relaxed. My father and my pro, John Geertsen, were pretty nervous, I guess. I just hope they made it around okay."

Armed with a five-wood that rescued him from the rough several times, Miller fired an even-par 70 to grab a share of fifth place—one stroke better than Nicklaus and Palmer. The only blemish on the round, according to Miller, was a blown eighteen-inch putt on the sixteenth, which resulted in a bogey six.

"I wouldn't take this round over, except for that putt on the sixteenth," he told the press upon sinking a lengthy birdie putt on the eighteenth. "It was funny, but I wasn't really worried about playing in the Open. In fact, I was worried because I wasn't worried."

Miller slept easily again at home that night—another twelve hours—and he kept pace with the leaders by firing a solid 72. At two over par by the halfway point, Miller had matched Nicklaus, whom he would be paired with for Saturday's third round.

"[Nicklaus] won't bother me," Miller confidently said, "but the crowd will."

Enveloped, for the first time, in a gallery of thousands, Miller's performance tailed off during the third round with a 74. Though Miller was nine strokes behind the front-running Palmer and no longer in contention to win, the *San Francisco Chronicle* still praised him for "refusing to crack under the pressure of being paired with the long-hitting Nicklaus," as well as the large crowds that followed them. And Miller still held a four-stroke edge over the next-closest amateur, the reigning U.S. Amateur champion and University of Florida ace Bob Murphy.

"They billed this one as the kid and the veteran," Nicklaus said. "It's the first time I ever played in this tournament with anyone that young. Usually I'm the youngest player."

As a onetime child prodigy himself, the Golden Bear looked past his teenage partner's years and saw promise.

"I thought Miller was quite impressive," Nicklaus said. "I played two practice rounds with him before the tournament but he hit the ball better today than he did then. He'll fill out, become stronger, and hit the ball even longer than he does now. I think he has quite a future ahead of him."

Miller not only impressed the nation's top golfer; he wowed viewers across America. With the television cameras following his partner, Miller stole a share of the spotlight. Millions of viewers saw him "put on quite a show" when he sank a chip shot from the rough for par on the fifteenth; not long after he dropped a fifteen-foot putt for a birdie on the thirteenth. He even closed out the round dramatically by holing a slippery twelve-footer for par on the treacherous eighteenth green.

Still, following five bogeys, frequent detours from the fairway, and the burden of sharing a tee with Nicklaus, Miller felt totally drained.

"I was never at ease," he said. "It seemed like every time I wanted to hit a green, I missed the shot."

Nicklaus outdid his playing partner by five strokes—only Dave Marr bested his one under 69—to move into third place. But even with the Golden Bear only four strokes behind, the story at Olympic centered on Arnold Palmer.

OPENING WITH A BIRDIE ON the first hole, Palmer outplayed his partner and fellow midtournament leader, Billy Casper. He even weathered a terrible back-nine stretch (double bogey, bogey) to build a three-shot lead over Casper going into the final round. Still, Palmer's past preyed on his mind when he spoke to the press immediately after the round.

"I've lost some in this position," he said, "the Masters, for one, although I won it in the play-off. But I did let it slip away the final day."

His apprehension seemed unwarranted early Sunday afternoon. A fantastic 32 on the front nine extended Palmer's lead over second-place Casper to seven strokes. (Nicklaus and other close contenders all failed to break par that day.) With an enormous cushion, Palmer had history, as well as a second U.S. Open title, on his mind.

"I was feeling pretty good about the lead. I'd never lost with seven shots and nine holes [to go]," Palmer said. "Yes, I am well aware of Ben Hogan's 276 Open record. I was thinking about it at the turn—thinking if I could beat it."

While British reporters cabled news of Palmer's victory across the Atlantic, Casper hadn't yet given up. No one paid attention when Palmer drove into the bunker on the tenth for a bogey, or lost another stroke by failing to make par on the thirteenth. After both men made pars on the fourteenth, Palmer still owned a five-stroke edge with only four holes to play.

But, starting on the fifteenth, the man who had set the standard for miraculous U.S. Open comebacks at Cherry Hills was soon fed a taste of his own medicine. His seven-iron off the par-three tee landed in a bunker and, after a good recovery, he could not save par from eight feet. Casper's successful twenty-footer for birdie meant a two-stroke swing; the lead was now three shots with three holes to play.

Palmer's charge in reverse worsened on the sixteenth, Olympic's signature 604-yard par-five. His drive grazed a tree branch and dropped into high rough, and his attempt to escape with a three-iron simply "didn't get airborne." He needed another stab with a nine-iron just to reach the fairway.

"My first three shots at this hole didn't go more than three hundred and fifty yards."

With his fourth shot—a three-wood—dropping into a green-side bunker, Palmer was lucky to salvage a bogey. Casper's birdie four cut the difference to a single stroke with two holes remaining.

Palmer's errant ball striking continued on the seventeenth: driver into the left rough, six-iron into the right rough. He then struck a fine wedge to within seven feet, but when his par putt missed for a third consecutive bogey, the insurmountable seven-stroke lead had entirely disappeared.

Even "Arnie's Army" lost its cool watching the horror unfold.

"My caddie told me he was kicked in the shins and almost knocked down," Palmer said, "but I can't really blame the crowd. I suppose I'd push and shove if I wanted to get a look at a match, too."

The rowdy members of the army weren't alone. Millions more at home turned on their sets just as Palmer's nightmare began at four p.m. on the East Coast. The American Broadcasting Company employed seventeen cameras—the most ever for televising a golf tournament—to cover the final five holes at Olympic.

Viewers who tuned in for the eighteenth hole feared it was all over for their hero. Wild off the tee again, Palmer hooked a one-iron into the rough. From the same (now thinner) patch of fairway rough that had sealed Hogan's play-off loss in 1955, the King muscled the ball onto the green and managed to two-putt for par. When Casper's downhill, sidehill birdie putt missed, an additional eighteen holes on Monday were needed to determine a champion.

As he had done four years earlier at Oakmont, prior to his play-off with Nicklaus, a smiling, whimsical Palmer posed for photographs with the man who, minutes earlier, had crushed his hopes for a second U.S. Open title.

"I'll be eating buffalo meat pretty soon too. It might help me make a couple of birdies," Palmer joked in front of the cameramen. Casper's exotic diet, which also included bear and elk meat, had become legendary; he ate bear meatloaf the night before the final round.

In his third U.S. Open play-off in five summers, Palmer seemed poised to break a cycle of poor starts: In both losses, to Nicklaus in 1962 and Julius Boros (at The Country Club in Brookline) in 1963, he immediately fell behind with bogeys at the opening hole, and trailed by three strokes at the turn. This time, Palmer cruised during the early holes, and took a two-stroke edge over Casper at the midway point.

But, for a second straight afternoon, Palmer collapsed on Olympic's back nine. Casper's birdie and Palmer's bogey on the eleventh evened the score. Casper then outplayed his partner by a stroke on each of the next three holes, and the tournament was essentially over by the time Palmer ran into another catastrophe on the seventeenth; he needed five shots to reach the green. With a one under 69, Billy Casper, not Palmer, won his second U.S. Open.

Immediately after the championship, reporters huddled around Palmer to ask how this play-off measured up to the others.

"It was pretty damn similar."

LESS THAN AN HOUR BEFORE Palmer's fourth-round meltdown ended, John Miller walked off Olympic's eighteenth green. A closing-round 74 had put him into a tie for eighth place. Though not even BYU's top golfer, he had just become the first teenager in more than half a century to finish in the top ten of a U.S. Open.

"I wanted to play so good in that Open," Miller said years later, "that when I came in eighth I was almost upset."

Not too upset; the entire Miller family—not just John—had enjoyed Casper's unprecedented rally.

In addition to the novelty of shrimp-and-avocado breakfasts or buffalo-steak dinners, Casper, too, belonged to the Mormon Church. Similar to Laurence Miller, Casper and his wife had joined the Church of Jesus Christ of Latter-day Saints long after starting a family. In fact, Casper was baptized just six months before his win at Olympic.

"Golf isn't the most important thing in my life now as it used to be," Casper said after Olympic.

Miller and Casper—both converted Mormons, California born and raised (Casper was from San Diego)—never crossed paths at Olympic. But Miller, as the top amateur, earned an invitation to play in the following spring's Masters Tournament, and, starting that week at Augusta National, a close bond and mentorship between the two formed.

"Billy told me to wait it out: that there would be good days and bad ones, but never look back on the bad ones. He could see I was a little on the frustrated side when I had a bad round. He leveled me off and was a steadying factor in my first golf play. I learned from Bill that when you have that bad day, which I have had many times, the next one might be brighter—and bright enough to win." Miller made the cut in his first Masters Tournament, finishing fifty-third to Casper's twenty-fourth.

But—especially on the intercollegiate front—Miller was not regarded as *the* dominant player of his era. Contemporaries such as Hale Irwin, Grier Jones, Marty Fleckman, Bob Murphy, Bob Dickson, and Ron Cerrudo earned All American acclaim largely for great performances in the major national collegiate and amateur events, especially the U.S. Amateur and the NCAA Individual National Championship. By contrast, Miller's greatest achievements came *outside* the collegiate sphere: the eighth-place finish in the 1966 U.S. Open, and the impressive showing at Augusta National the following spring.

Miller's greatest moment while representing BYU came in the fall of 1967. In October, he and his Cougar teammates headed south to Albuquerque, New Mexico, to compete in the William H. Tucker Invitational, a prestigious event featuring several of the region's top programs. Colorado, Texas Tech, New Mexico, Louisiana State, Arizona, and Arizona State were all there. So was the University of Houston, the nation's best golf program and the school Miller had turned down for BYU.

Miller shook off bad memories of the University of New Mexico South Course—the previous May he had shot an 82 to detonate any chance of winning the Western Athletic Conference individual title—and turned in a four under 68 to take the second-round lead in both the individual and team standings. Over the last two rounds, Miller played the course at one under par to win the individual title (over such notable Houston stars as Hal Underwood and Bob Barbarossa), and to lead his team to perhaps the most important victory in the history of BYU's golf program.

Even before turning twenty-one, John Miller was a U.S. Open hero, a weekend qualifier at the Masters, and a first-team All American (an honor announced by Arnold Palmer, chairman of the selection committee) the previous year. And in May 1968, at a dinner inducting Casper into the California Golf Hall of Fame, Miller accepted the Northern California Amateur of the Year Award. Ultimately, the evening turned into a celebration of Mormon golfers: Miller's former mentor, John Geertsen, was also presented with the state's Golf Professional of the Year award.

Miller proved to be the best amateur in all of California later that summer by winning the California State Amateur championship. Sparked by a new putter and a new putting stance (he took only thirty-seven putts in twenty-six holes), Miller cruised to a 12 & 10 victory in the thirty-six-hole final round at Pebble Beach. The candid 160-pound senior proclaimed, "[Every] iron in my bag was great."

Miller's sparkling amateur résumé naturally fostered visions of future greatness.

"Gene Littler and Ken Venturi both sprang from the California State Amateur Golf Championship to capture the United States Open," the *Oakland Tribune* observed. "Johnny Miller is destined to follow in their footsteps."

Like those two fine amateurs who quickly became great professionals, Miller did not return to Brigham Young in the fall of 1968. He never received his college degree and never undertook a Mormon "mission" at home or abroad (usually for two years), as did most Mormon male students at BYU.

"A college degree," he said, "is not going to help you sink those two-footers."

During the summer and fall of 1968, Miller competed in a few amateur tournaments and prepared for the tour qualifying school in Palm Beach Gardens in April. He experienced tour life in January 1969, qualifying for the Kaiser International Open Invitational at the Silverado Country Club and Resort in Napa. Playing just an hour from his home, Miller held his own among a field that included Trevino, Palmer, and Littler. His two under 70 on the first day was even more impressive because he lost a ball in a pond on the eighteenth. Terrible rains over the next two days—both Friday's and Saturday's rounds were washed out—did nothing to interrupt Miller. When he finally returned to the course on Sunday, he shot five birdies on the front nine, only to have the score erased due to more rain. The following morning, with the course drenched in water, Tournament officials declared Miller Barber the thirty-six-hole winner; John tied for forty-second.

Miller received his tour credentials in April 1969, finishing in the top fifteen at Q School along with fellow Californians Rodney Curl and Bob Eastwood. With representation by Ed Barner, a fellow Mormon and Billy Casper's agent, and initial financial backing from a San Francisco–based group of businessmen, Miller ventured onto the PGA tour in May 1969.

Just like when he learned the game under John Geertsen, or his steady rise to first-team All American status at BYU—he received only honorable mention status, along with teammate Mike Taylor, following his brilliant performance at Olympic—there would be a few growing pains for Miller. After he quickly bagged $770 for a twenty-fourth-place finish in his first event, the Texas Open, he reached the top twenty-five only twice the remainder of the year.

Life on tour changed quickly for Miller in 1970. Playing desert golf in January at the Phoenix Country Club, he carded 72-71 and just made the cut. Forty-year-old Paul Harney's 65 was the talk of the tournament, as the long-hitting tour journeyman led by one shot after two rounds. But the next day, Miller grabbed all the headlines and revealed for the first time a unique talent that would become his signature as a touring pro: The young man could "go low."

Miller got off to a fast start on Saturday morning: birdies on the first three holes. Three more birdies on the front nine made for a stellar six under 30. Shooting par on the back nine would yield a 65, two off the course record of 63. Miller seemed headed for exactly that number over holes ten to fifteen. But he then rolled in lengthy birdie putts on the sixteenth and seventeenth; another par would tie the course record and spring Miller back into contention.

Miller's Saturday was shaping up to be the mirror opposite of the day before.

"My putting was real bad," he said about his Friday round. On Friday night, Miller had vented to Karsten Solheim, the innovative golf-club maker who, at the time, still personally hawked his controversial PING putters and new perimeter-weighted irons at tour events. Later that evening, Solheim helped Miller regrip and recalibrate his clubs.

"But while he was there," Solheim recalled, "I started brainwashing him about my putters."

Curiously, Solheim was just continuing a conversation he had started years earlier with Laurence Miller. In 1956, nine-year-old John and his father had participated in a hole-in-one contest at Lincoln Park, near the family's San Francisco home. Solheim—then an engineer for General Electric—approached Laurence and tried rather aggressively to sell him on his inventions. But even a demonstration back at Solheim's garage/workshop couldn't convince Laurence to buy any of his oddly designed putters.

Skeptical at first, just like his father fourteen years earlier, John warmed to the rogue designs that Solheim handed him and selected a PING Cushin number four putter.

"[When] I rolled in about thirty straight putts on the rug, I started getting excited."

With the new putter in hand, Miller exuded confidence on the greens during his Saturday dream round, especially around noon when he reached the 535-yard par-five eighteenth in two shots. A conventional two-putt birdie from forty feet meant the course record. Instead, Miller boldly stroked the putt, which dropped dead center for an eagle and a mind-numbing score of 61, one shy of the PGA tour record.

"[It] worked like magic," he said of Solheim's oddly shaped flat stick.

Miller's 61 jumped him to within two shots of the leader, Gene Littler, and close to his first tour victory.

"It was just one of those days. It's got to be the greatest round I ever played," he told the press. "Golf is a game of ups and downs—and sometimes they come very quickly."

Nashville, Tennessee's Lou Graham drew the esteemed honor—or sad misfortune—of playing consecutive rounds of a U.S. Open at Oakmont with Arnold Palmer. And though the former military guard of the Tomb of the Unknown Soldier would eventually overshadow everyone at a U.S. Open, with a shocking play-off victory at Medinah two years later, few noticed him at all during the second round at Oakmont in 1973.

As Graham hovered near the cut line all Friday afternoon (he would miss by a single stroke), his playing partners—Palmer, golf's graying King, and Miller, the golden-maned young lion—provided more than enough excitement for the gallery. Like Palmer, Miller shot 71 on Thursday and was confident he could win the title.

Dressed in a powder blue shirt, houndstooth slacks, and no hat to cover his flowing mop top, Miller joined the man whose bold style of play had inspired him since childhood. The threesome teed off at 10:04 a.m., and although news of a serious sprinkler malfunction (see chapter six) had not yet fully surfaced to the press, gallery, and players waiting to begin, visual evidence blanketed the course.

"There was casual water on the sixth green," Miller joked. One putt Miller stroked actually left "a rooster tail."

"You could see water around your shoes," Palmer added. "Even with soft greens, it's not all that easy."

Had reporters spoken to Palmer as he made the turn, they might have heard a different response. With the greens considerably slower than usual in the late-morning haze, Palmer cruised through the front nine almost flawlessly.

Following a routine par on number one, he crossed the bridge and nailed a birdie from fifteen feet on the short second hole. On the par-five fourth, he rolled in a putt from eight feet for a second birdie. On the eighth, the 244-yard par-three that he bogeyed the day before, Palmer stuck his tee shot onto the back edge of the green, twenty-five feet away.

He rolled the right-to-left slider into the center of the cup, and doffed his white visor to an army in uproar. At three under par for the day and for the tournament, Palmer had begun his charge. And with the ninth hole up next—a par-five he'd birdied four times in his last six rounds at Oakmont—he hoped to close out the front side within one stroke of the leader.

Grabbing the tournament's lead was not on Johnny Miller's mind Friday afternoon; maintaining even par was challenge enough. He found trouble on the third hole when his approach from the fairway fell into a green-side bunker, leading to a bogey. On the next hole, he squandered an easy opportunity to regain the lost stroke.

"I missed a two-and-a-half-footer for a birdie on the fourth hole," he said, "and I got a little down."

Miller now trailed his regal playing partner by three strokes after only four holes, and with the more boisterous members of Arnie's Army stirring, he faced an uphill battle just to remain competitive.

"[Palmer] doesn't bother me any more or less than any other player. I've matured. I've gained confidence. Playing with Arnie or Jack would have shaken me up a few years ago, but not now," he said. "Those guys used to make me nervous. I can remember stealing glances at them, trying to copy what they were doing and watching to see if they were watching me. If they weren't I thought I was doing something wrong. If they were, boy, did that make me jittery."

Any hint of those butterflies quickly vanished late Friday morning. Two poor iron shots on the par-four fifth left Miller a difficult fifteen-footer to save par. Staring down another bogey, he rolled in the putt to spark a spirited turn-around.

"As mute testimony that I don't get tight anymore in that sort of company, I had the best putting round of my life from the fifth hole on."

Following a solid iron from the seventh fairway that left him twenty feet from the flagstick, the confident Miller—he now used an Acushnet Bullseye putter, not the PING that had secured his 61 in Phoenix—converted the birdie putt to pull back to even par.

Neither Palmer nor Miller could shave another stroke off par on the inviting uphill ninth or the difficult tenth holes. Palmer remained three under and Miller even par for the day.

Everything began to change on the eleventh green.

Reminiscent of his brilliant ball striking in 1962, Palmer had hit every fairway and every green in regulation on Oakmont's first ten holes. The streak of straight hitting continued on the eleventh, where he was pleased with par. But Miller matched not only Palmer's excellent shot making; he nailed a twenty-five-footer for birdie.

Putting magic produced another birdie for Miller on the twelfth. Again twenty feet from the hole—this time facing a severely breaking downhill putt over the rapidly drying green—he rammed it home to move to two under par.

Palmer, who also had a twenty-footer on the par-five twelfth, couldn't cash in the birdie and, worse yet, missed his comebacker. The three-putt bogey dropped Palmer into a tie with Miller, whom he had led by three shots just two holes earlier; eleven-year-old memories of Oakmont three-putts festered.

"The three-putt green put me off a little and seemed to cause my other problems," he said.

Problems such as hooking his iron to the par-three thirteenth, just shy of a steep bunker. Palmer's recovery shot sailed thirty feet above the hole and, luckily, he escaped with a bogey.

Palmer's previously superb driving broke down on the fifteenth. Bogged down in the rough, he missed another green and could do no better than a third back-nine bogey.

Despite three consecutive bogeys, Palmer's friendly demeanor did not change. On the sixteenth fairway, he paused for several moments to chat with a few friends in the gallery, including harness-racing legend Del Miller, and Bobby Cruickshank, the seventy-nine-year-old, two-time U.S. Open runner-up who still gave lessons at nearby Chartiers Country Club. In front of his friends, Palmer stopped the bleeding and made a par.

Palmer's bandwagon, nevertheless, fretted over his errors. Near the seventeenth green, someone asked Deacon Palmer how he felt.

"I felt good, until Arnie came up with those three bogeys."

In front of the eighteenth green, surrounded by anxious spectators, Palmer stroked a bold chip shot that bounded past the hole. He then sank the six-foot comebacker to remain even par at the halfway point of the championship.

"It seemed like every time I missed a green, I would get a bogey. If I can cut down the mistakes, I will be there in the end," he said. "I drove it numerous times in trouble. I had only one three-putt green, but a lot of putts I hit were bad putts."

Miller seemed incapable of stroking a bad putt. After the beautiful pair of birdies at numbers eleven and twelve, he again saved par from twelve feet on the thirteenth. Pars all the way into the clubhouse gave Miller a two under 69 for the day. Playing numbers eleven to fifteen five shots better than Palmer catapulted Miller into a tie for third place, just three behind Player.

Commenting on Miller's putting display, Palmer called it, "[The] greatest I've ever seen. It got to the point where he finally missed a twenty-footer at number sixteen—and was mad."

Miller oozed confidence in the press tent.

"You need to do three things in a major championship. You have to be a good driver—keep the ball in the fairways—hit the ball high to hold the hard greens, and be a fast green putter. I'm all three," he said. "I grew up playing an Open course, Olympic, and I like tough courses. I can't play easy courses. I like courses where you shoot a seventy-three and you're still in competition.

"I can win," he added. "But I can't try to win. I've got to play well and maybe some of the leaders will make some bogeys."

That was the fate that befell Palmer during his second round; he let his emotions get the better of him.

"The old Palmer wouldn't have let a little three-putt bother him," one veteran reporter reflected. "He would have eagled the next hole with a chip shot or something. He is not the old Palmer, though, and one of his playing partners, Johnny Miller, agreed that it is partly mental."

"Palmer is playing well," said Miller. "He will be near the top . . . if he doesn't try too hard."

Trying too hard: That didn't seem to fit Johnny Miller's laid-back, California image.

· 6 ·

A Watered-down Open

Neither Player's six birdies nor Nicklaus's eagle on the seventeenth—not even unheralded Tom Shaw's sixty-foot birdie putt on the roller-coaster eighteenth green—could diminish Oakmont's reputation for unrelenting toughness after Thursday's opening round. Intermittent heroics could not nullify the body-dragging weariness that Oakmont induced in the world's best golfers.

And that was the way Oakmont's members and the U.S.G.A. wanted it.

Thursday evening, after tying the course record of 67, Player proclaimed that shooting 72s the rest of the way would please him greatly and result in his second U.S. Open championship. As the course continued to dry out after Tuesday's storm, it would play even firmer and faster and "become more difficult and I expect the scores to rise."

Player had no idea that on Friday morning, under the same heat, humidity, and blue skies as the day before, the playing conditions at Oakmont would change radically.

He did not get off to the same hot start on Friday, scrambling for pars on two of the first three holes. One of the game's top sand players, he chipped softly out of a green-side bunker on number four to set up another birdie. He bogeyed number seven, the result of driving into a bunker and failing to negotiate a six-footer to save par. Player then atoned with two fine woods and a two-putt on the dicey ninth green for a birdie four.

"I was pretty fortunate to do the front nine in one under par," he said after missing five greens and one-putting four times to save par. "[My] short game today was about as good as it could be."

Player's short-game wizardry continued on the back side, as he managed nine knee-rattling pars to close out his second subpar performance (70). He walked into the press tent still on top of the field at 137, the lowest score for the first two rounds in Oakmont's U.S. Open history.

"I've been putting very well here, and I credit that to hours and hours of practice. If practice and putting mean perfection, then maybe, just maybe, that's my fate here," Player said. "Next to Ben Hogan, I probably practice more than any player in the game."

For all that bravado, Player was not quite ready to claim victory at the half-way point.

"The leader very seldom wins the tournament. Any tournament. The leader wins about two out of ten times at most," he said. "Sure, there'll be quite a few low rounds, but when you come to the last nine holes of the [U.S. Open] tournament, you suddenly get a bad case of tonsillitis."

Though he finished by early afternoon, Player had already changed his tune from a day before, when he predicted that scores would rise on Friday. In fact, within his own threesome, only Player's score rose: Tom Weiskopf's 69 and Tommy Aaron's 71 were, respectively, four and seven strokes better than their scores the previous day. While Player had to scramble, several golfers near the top of the leaderboard began chasing him down.

Like Player, Bob Charles of New Zealand pioneered international golf in the early 1960s, but because he competed in Asia and Europe as much as the U.S., the American media excluded him from the "elite player" debates. His fellow pros knew better. The tall, thin left-hander's refined skills and mental agility produced a 1963 British Open Championship and four PGA tour victories. And during a five-week stretch in 1968, he won the Canadian Open, then took second place in both the British Open and PGA Championship. Arnold Palmer called Charles the greatest putter he ever saw.

Charles, however, was never blessed with great length off the tee, and by 1973 he had become discouraged about his future on the PGA tour.

"This is my last tournament on the American tour this year, no matter what happens. It's too tough here. I must be getting old. There are too many young kids who can beat the ball three hundred yards and putt like hell," Charles told reporters. "I have a farm in New Zealand and another in South Africa. I plan to become a gentleman farmer. I may come back to America for two or three tournaments a year, but no more."

Charles's candid disinterest in American golf reached a new low that week at Oakmont. As he brazenly told reporters, the "U.S. Open really doesn't mean anything to a foreign player."

Although Charles shot a solid 71 on Thursday, he began his second round like someone with retirement on his mind. Teeing off at 8:04 a.m. with Al Geiberger and Chi Chi Rodriguez, Charles blew a three-footer for par on the first green, then missed the third green for another bogey, dropping to two over. But a brilliant short game always gave a player a chance at Oakmont, and at the next hole, Charles began one of the most remarkable scoring stretches in Oakmont's history.

Matching the length of those "young kids," the thirty-seven-year-old reached the 549-yard, par-five fourth in two shots and registered an easy birdie. A perfect four-iron off the sixth tee that died three feet from the flagstick led to another birdie that returned him to even par. Two holes later, at the long par-three eighth, Charles ran his four-wood onto the green and demonstrated his putting prowess by dropping a thirty-footer for birdie.

And he was far from finished.

On number eleven, he split the fairway with a solid drive and, from 130 yards, stroked a nine-iron directly into the cup for an eagle.

"It was just a lucky shot."

Lucky or not, Charles's precision carried over to the 603-yard, par-five twelfth. Still a long way from the green in two, he nearly sank his next shot to score consecutive eagles. When he tapped in for birdie, he had made up six strokes over nine holes and, at four under, was back in contention.

Although Charles's hot streak cooled during the final holes (he bogeyed numbers fourteen and eighteen), he stood at two under par for the championship and only one behind the leader, Gary Player. Now that he was a contender halfway through a championship that "doesn't mean anything" to him, reporters relayed Charles's indifference toward the U.S. Open to his fellow pros.

"I can't believe Bob said it; that's absolutely horse crap," said Player, who a decade earlier had hosted Charles's wedding in Johannesburg (Charles married a high school friend of Player's wife). "Let me say only that if somebody offered me a million dollars in one hand and the U.S. Open title in the other, I'd take the Open title."

To Charles's playing partner, Chi Chi Rodriguez, who had grown up in poverty in Puerto Rico and served in the American military, the U.S. Open Championship also meant far more than a million dollars. To him, just having a *chance* to win stirred patriotic fervor.

"No matter who wins or loses," he said, "it's beautiful to get up in the morning, look out the window, and realize not only are you in the best country in the world, but also you're a citizen of it. To me, that is worth more than winning 100,000 U.S. Opens."

Just nine days older than Player and of similar small stature, Rodriguez was also a marvel of physical fitness. Despite his size, not many on the tour hit the ball longer. And in the spring of 1973—while Player lay in bed recovering from his dual illnesses—Rodriguez flourished. He won April's Greater Greensboro Open, followed that up with a tenth-place finish a week later at the Masters, then, two weeks afterward, took fourth place at the Tournament of Champions. By early June, he ranked seventh on the PGA money list, the highest in his career. And having placed ninth in the brutal U.S. Open the year before at Pebble Beach, Rodriguez proved that—despite a herky-jerky, whiplash swing—he possessed enough game to compete at an unyielding venue like Oakmont.

Prior to the first round, reporters had crowded around the fast-talking Puerto Rican to hear his prediction of the favorites.

"Nicklaus, Weiskopf, Palmer, Trevino, Player," he immediately spat out. "With all the heat and humidity here, this is no fat man's weather. Notice those I mentioned? Which of the ones I named is fat?"

"What about you? You're skinny," a listener responded.

"I never pick myself. Besides, in Puerto Rico, I'm a giant."

By the early 1970s, Rodriguez had become a hero in his native land, even though golf on the island was mainly reserved for the superrich. But the most beloved Puerto Rican athlete of all time was Roberto Clemente, the star right fielder for the Pittsburgh Pirates. Sports fans in western Pennsylvania had come to bond with Clemente almost as closely as native Puerto Ricans. Those fans and Clemente's countrymen also now shared the same grief.

On New Year's Eve, 1972, Clemente had hastily boarded a plane filled with relief supplies destined for Central America. An earthquake had brought death and suffering to thousands of impoverished Nicaraguans, and Clemente, a proud Latin American, vowed to lend his own hand in the relief effort. Badly overloaded with supplies, his plane crashed into the Atlantic Ocean within minutes of takeoff. Rescue teams never found his body.

Americans of all nationalities mourned Clemente, whose devotion as a humanitarian had cost him his life. But to those from his homeland, Clemente was more than just a great ballplayer, or a great man. He was a symbol that no matter where they came from, they too could rise out of poverty and achieve the "American dream."

"Every time I strike a ball, I will be thinking of Roberto Clemente," Chi Chi said on the eve of the U.S. Open.

An inspired Rodriguez got off to a slow start on Thursday afternoon, shooting three over par on the front side, but playing better on the back nine to shoot a respectable 75. On Friday, playing with the *un*inspired Bob Charles, Rodriguez carded a smooth 71 and was thrilled that he'd easily made the cut for the third consecutive June.

But Rodriguez wasn't the only contestant geared up for the high stakes of the U.S. Open. Regardless of what Snead or Charles had said, or the criticisms that several veterans and newcomers had levied at Oakmont and the U.S.G.A., most players considered qualifying for a U.S. Open the defining moment of their professional or amateur careers.

"I look forward to the Open. Sure, the pressure is there, but if you're going to measure up, you have to accept the demands of the Open. It demands things of you no other tournament does. You have to play all the shots or go home," said Jim Colbert, a thirty-two-year-old Kansas State product who attended college on a football scholarship.

"I've been playing in tournaments for the last two weeks, but my heart has been up here."

He also couldn't wait for another trip to Oakmont. He'd been fortunate to play the course several years earlier because his sister, a Pittsburgh-area resident, belonged to a nearby club and arranged for him to play with a friend who belonged to Oakmont.

Colbert certainly was not a tour superstar. In eight years, he claimed three wins and one top-ten finish in a major championship (the 1971 U.S. Open at Merion). But he had moved up in the performance rankings from fifty-ninth to twenty-third between 1971 and 1972. Early in 1973, he won the Greater Jacksonville Open in March, and took third at the Tournament of Champions in April. Still, inconsistency plagued him in the first half of the season: He finished no better than twenty-third in any other event, and missed the cut in nearly half of his nineteen tournament starts.

A grind-it-out competitor who never lacked confidence, Colbert stitched all facets of his game together just in time for Oakmont. After dropping two strokes to par early on the front nine, he carded four birdies during a seven-hole stretch and shot 70, joining Player, Floyd, and Trevino as the only players under par.

Colbert's excellent play continued into the second round. With only his wife and three children, plus his sister and her three children, watching him, Colbert teed off just before nine a.m. on Friday. He birdied number two by sinking a tricky fifteen-footer, and grabbed another birdie on number seven thanks to a perfectly lofted nine-iron that stopped seven feet from the flagstick.

Two holes later, on the strength of a once-in-a-lifetime shot, Colbert pulled within a single stroke of Player.

In his bag that week, Colbert carried clubs the *New York Times* referred to as "Golf's Magic Wand—Maybe." Colbert was one of the first touring pros to experiment with graphite-shafted woods in order to hit the ball farther. Not a long hitter, he would especially need a boost to compete on par-five holes (like Oakmont's fourth and ninth), where power players enjoyed a considerable advantage: They could easily reach the green in two shots.

In the early days of graphite technology, most pros considered the experimental shafts too whippy, too unpredictable, too fragile, or all of the above. In their view, the tradeoff between greater distance versus less control or predictability was simply not worth it. Indeed, most power players went in the opposite direction, preferring superstiff or X shafts (at least on their drivers) to restrict the bend of the club, and thereby achieve maximum strength without sacrificing control. And this, of course, held especially true on tight U.S. Open venues, where slightly off-line shots yielded steep penalties.

But Colbert would try anything to neutralize the advantage the longer hitters held over him. And at Oakmont, the gamble worked. Despite one sharp hook on the third hole that landed him in the Church Pews, he was driving the ball longer than usual, and down the middle. He approached number nine confident he could get home in two shots.

Again, however, Colbert badly hooked his tee shot, which brought into play one of the Fowneses' more terrifying hazards: the deep, narrow ditch. Ten minutes of studying his awful lie forced him to remove his ball from the ditch, take a one-stroke penalty, and drop the ball no more than two club lengths away. "I was tempted to hit the ball out of the ditch," he said, "but Homero Blancas was playing in my threesome and it took him three swings to get a similar shot out of it."

Even after the drop, Colbert's ball lay in deep, gnarly rough: virtually invisible. Still 225 yards from the green, he decided, to his caddie's astonishment, to go for broke and hit his graphite-shafted fairway wood from the buried lie.

Miraculously, Colbert "fractured" the shot, and his ball came to rest eighteen inches from the cup. "My three-wood came so close that it should have been a gimme."

"Jim made the greatest shot I've ever seen in my life at No. 9," recalled Rusty Guy, Colbert's seventeen-year-old caddie, and an Oakmont member to whom Colbert attributed much of his success that week.

Following his miracle birdie, Colbert promptly dropped a stroke when he drove into a bunker on the tenth, only to gain it back on number eleven, where he stuck his short-iron approach to six feet. A birdie and four consecutive pars over the next five-hole stretch put Colbert at four under for the championship, just one shot behind Player.

On the tee at the long, par-three sixteenth, Rusty Guy handed Colbert two more pieces of golf equipment not usually carried by an American touring pro: a Skyway Ball from Japan, and an iron made by Karsten Solheim, the golf guru/engineer now in the early stages of reinventing the shape and composition of "iron" clubs.

Colbert smacked the Japanese ball crisply with his PING one-iron, and with Oakmont's greens holding like never before—especially on the punchbowl–shaped sixteenth green—it came to rest fifteen feet from the flag. Colbert rammed in the birdie putt to pull even with Player at five under par.

Unfortunately, an errant drive into a bunker on number eighteen cost Colbert a share of the lead. Alone in second place, one behind Player, he earned a spot in the last pairing for Saturday's round. As spirited as ever, Colbert brushed aside questions about impending weekend nerves.

"After I got to be starting quarterback in high school, I eloped with my girlfriend. We had to come back to tell our parents. That's pressure."

• • •

ANOTHER EARLY MORNING STARTER ON Friday was Lee Trevino, who carded eight pars over eight holes. He then thrilled the crowd of several hundred on-lookers as he nearly carded an eagle on the ninth; his fifty-foot putt rolled directly over the hole, and he had to settle for a birdie that dropped him to two under par.

Trevino's play was nothing short of brilliant; astonishingly, he hit every fairway and green over the first twenty-seven holes. At the turn, he stood just three shots off the lead. But two hours later, when he returned to Oakmont's unofficial hub—the spot where the clubhouse, the ninth, and the eighteenth greens triangulate—Trevino fumed. Not only did he miss an eight-foot birdie opportunity at number twelve, he three-putted and became noticeably "testy" afterward.

Having nailed every fairway that afternoon, Trevino continued his textbook golf on the home hole. From the eighteenth fairway, his approach shot landed comfortably on the green but a long distance from the hole. The large gallery, eager to see Trevino's first birdie on the back side, crowded the green, only to be disappointed when the ball died inches from the hole. Forced to settle for a one over 72, Trevino sighed and then stuck out his tongue in frustration.

The events on the eighteenth summed up Trevino's round, and his entire tournament so far: perfect tee shot, adequate but slightly misjudged approach, followed by a birdie-miss that petered out on the lip. Trevino's hometown paper, the *El Paso Herald-Post*, reported he "had at least five birdie putts stop short by as little as a quarter or half an inch."

In typical Trevino fashion, his postround antics made news. U.S.G.A. protocol paved a short path from the eighteenth green to the scorer's tent so that players could sign their cards. From there, several players were ushered into the press tent so reporters could speak to the leaders or perennial stars. Although Trevino was both a leader and a star, he walked right past the press tent and onto the practice green. His head down, a somber look on his face, he spoke to no one, stroked putts for a full hour, then retreated hurriedly toward his motor home.

One of America's most popular sports figures, Trevino could not get away with skirting the press.

"There's nothing merry about the Super Mex when things aren't going his way," wrote a Richmond columnist. "After his one-over-par-72 Friday, Trevino refused to come to the press tent to be interviewed. Instead he went to the practice green, where he remained in the middle of the big green to avoid questioning. His complaints about his lack of privacy are fast becoming boring."

The unshakable fear that Trevino had long masked with humor and a grin—that he would soon wear out his welcome in the elite game—felt legit without his "Happy Hombre" facade.

That evening, Trevino's grumpiness diminished when he learned his third-round playing partner would be Jack Nicklaus. Trevino always seemed at his best when dueling with the Golden Bear. In fact, of his four major title victories, three had ended with Nicklaus the runner-up. The pairing was less encouraging to Nicklaus.

"Trevino had beaten me in majors, not to mention the other defeats he had handed out," Nicklaus observed about their fierce rivalry. "I had played close to my best every time, which always helps you feel a little better about yourself than when you've tossed a tournament away. But there could be no question by now that Lee Trevino was the player who had given me the most trouble up to this point in my career."

As an angry Trevino stormed off the eighteenth green early Friday afternoon, Nicklaus stepped to the first tee. His start was inauspicious: He drove into the rough, launched a six-iron over the green, and chipped poorly to score a bogey. Fifteen minutes later, he missed a very makeable birdie putt from five feet.

Nicklaus grabbed a stroke back with a birdie on number five; a missed green on the short, par-four eleventh produced an annoying bogey, and he fell back to one over par. Six shots behind Player, Nicklaus headed to the twelfth tee. The 603-yard behemoth—once the longest hole in U.S. Open history—*should* have been ideal for a player of Nicklaus's power to regain control of his round. But Nicklaus had never birdied the twelfth in six prior rounds of U.S. Open competition (including his play-off with Palmer). And a few swings into his seventh stab at the long hole, he seemed destined to come up birdieless again.

After a good drive, his three-wood drifted into deep rough, and when his nine-iron flew the green into a bunker, even a par appeared unlikely.

For years, the only knock on Nicklaus was his mediocrity out of green-side bunkers.

"The good Lord gave Nicklaus everything—and I mean everything—except a wedge," Trevino once said. "If he had given him that, the rest of us might never have won any tournaments."

At least on this day, Nicklaus proved his detractors dead wrong: He blasted his ball out of the sand and into the cup for an incredible birdie four.

"That shot was the turning point of my round," Nicklaus said—for the second straight day.

Buoyed by his good fortune, Nicklaus took advantage, as he promptly knocked a six-iron stiff on the thirteenth to grab another birdie. He expected to gain another stroke back on the seventeenth, where a repeat of his marvelous eagle the day before might challenge Player for the thirty-six-hole lead.

But the U.S.G.A. had other thoughts.

The $10,000 that Oakmont's members spent to lengthen the hole had failed to achieve its goal on Thursday, so the next morning the U.S.G.A. took one last stab at Nicklaus-proofing the hole.

"They had the tees so far back on seventeen that I had to watch that I didn't hit some trees on my backswing."

The additional yardage worked. Still defiant and determined to have his way, Nicklaus again selected the driver and launched another majestic shot. This time, however, the ball faded a bit to the right, carried through the fairway, and stopped just short of an out-of-bounds fence that separated the course from the driving range. After nearly fulfilling Trevino's pretournament prediction about how dangerous it was to "go for the green" on the seventeenth, Nicklaus retained his customary nonchalance and managed to save par. And, to cap his performance, he struck two fantastic shots at the home hole that left only a four-foot birdie putt, which he stroked into the center of the cup for a back-nine score of 33. His 69 moved him into a three-way tie for third place, just three behind Player. But a seemingly crestfallen Nicklaus walked into the press tent early Friday evening, annoyed that he hadn't knocked more strokes off par.

"The greens were much softer than I expected they'd be," he said. "The rough was there, and the course is longer than in the past, but the greens weren't as fast."

FIRING A THREE UNDER PAR 68 on Friday put Jim Colbert in some elite company. Along with Ben Hogan, Deane Beman, and Gary Player, only Arnold Palmer, in the second round of the 1962 Open, had ever shot as low as 68 prior to Friday. Colbert's 68 had tied the fourth-best championship score in course history: At Oakmont, "going low" essentially meant breaking 70.

Colbert chalked up his fine round to more than solid ball striking, brilliant putting, or the shrewd guidance of his young caddie.

"The greens are soft, men," he observed early in the afternoon after completing his morning start. "If you drive well you've got a lot of short irons and the ball's coming back when you hit the greens—they definitely were softer today than yesterday. That's why you'll be seeing some low scores today."

Colbert was right. For the first time in seven decades of Oakmont golf, breaking par, even shooting in the 60s, was not particularly exceptional, especially for those who teed off in the morning. And, naturally, the greens told the story.

Ever since W. C. Fownes and Emil Loeffler had reconfigured Oakmont's putting surfaces in the early 1920s, the greens had intimidated, irritated, and occasionally humiliated just about every great golfer in the world. Except Jack Nicklaus.

"I would prefer to see the greens as hard as a table and just as fast," he told reporters. "Then I don't think many players would be able to handle them."

No one shared the view of the man who, in 1962, had miraculously carded just one three-putt in ninety holes at Oakmont. But even Nicklaus admitted that near eighty-degree temperatures during round one—and the possibility of three more days of midsummer sun—meant that the greens needed to drink. Without *some* water, players would be putting on char by the end of the championship.

U.S.G.A. and club officials, along with members of the grounds crew, met Thursday evening. Ultimately, U.S.G..A. executive director P. J. Boatwright authorized a five-minute watering of the greens.

Oakmont's course superintendent was Lou Scalzo, who started at the course in 1930, left seventeen years later, then returned the following decade to fill a vacant superintendent post. In 1971, the club installed a new automatic sprinkler system, and he was delighted to use it.

"Scalzo punches some buttons and the sprinklers go on at night," the *Pittsburgh Press* noted prior to the start of the championship. "[And] he seems almost smug that he will have the course in prime condition by the first round on Thursday. 'Rain won't bother it too much anymore,' he said."

Scalzo nurtured each hole at Oakmont like a family of prize Thoroughbreds; he especially rejoiced in exasperating professional golfers.

"I don't have a favorite [hole], but the most stubborn is the eighth. The easiest to take care of is the twelfth, and the undulations on the fifth make it the one with the best sense of humor. But they're all fast. I like to have 'em fast so golfers in the Open can't break par." With the Fownesean arrogance that made Oakmont notorious, Scalzo concluded: "I know there'll be a lot of golfers complaining about the greens. But I don't listen to anything they say."

Those prayers of dissenting golfers seemed to be answered that morning. Something went terribly wrong after Scalzo punched the buttons late Thursday evening. Unbeknownst to anyone, the five-minute watering cascaded into a deluge.

In the wee hours before dawn on Friday, first Boatwright and U.S.G.A. executive committee vice president Frank "Sandy" Tatum, then Scalzo and the others recoiled when they walked the course and the turf squished underneath them. Whether the sprinklers were simply left on too long, or the system malfunctioned and then restarted after it shut down, or some other unknown mishap, no one knows for certain. One explanation passed on since that day seems most unlikely: The act-of-God scenario that claimed a bolt of lightning struck the sprinklers and restarted the water flow after the system had properly shut down.

Regardless of how it happened, the putting surfaces were saturated.

When the players gathered on the course early Friday morning, no one informed them of the problem or its source. A few assumed several sprinkler heads had broken, while another joked that he saw "casual water" on the greens.

The situation was not funny to everyone.

"Let's just say the greens are softer than I'd like to see them. They won't be watered tonight," said Boatwright.

Boatwright tried to hide his frustration, but apart from the unaesthetic look—a few greens looked like mush—the wet greens infuriated U.S.G.A. officials. But not nearly as much as they drove Oakmont's proud members insane. Some even accused the U.S.G.A. of surrendering to players who complained about Thursday's high scoring.

Green speed is relative. The sprinkler-induced flood slowed down the surfaces early in Friday's round, but—as Oakmont claimed the fastest greens known to man—they were still "keener" than most other putting surfaces on tour. Oakmont was tamer—just by a hair—not tame.

Oakmont's greens had earned their infamous reputation not simply because they were fast but because, under normal conditions, they refused to hold all but the most perfectly struck approach shots. Many seemingly excellent irons landed on the green, then rolled and rolled and rolled before finally sliding into trouble. Only the course's unique variants of Poa annua—so fine and without grain—could explain how this happened time and time again.

On a typical day like Thursday, a golfer might try to carry a ball onto the center of Oakmont's slanted sixth green, then watch in horror as it darted through the putting surface and into a bushy plot of rough or one of several deep bunkers. Before the second round, anyone who shot "for the flagstick" at Oakmont was plain foolish. On Friday morning, by contrast, players encountered much softer and more inviting greens than the day before or, perhaps, at any time in Oakmont's prior U.S. Open history.

Significantly slower *and* receptive greens invariably altered how the course played. The 150-man field on Friday quickly figured out that approach shots would actually stick close to where they landed or—an incredible sight at Oakmont—spin backward after impact. Even players who teed off in the afternoon, after the course started to dry out, could be aggressive in attacking the flagstick. Iron shots and even fairway woods settled only ten or fifteen feet from where they landed; on Thursday, those same shots would have bounded another twenty or thirty feet.

In Friday's predawn hours before the first group teed off at seven thirty a.m., Lou Scalzo, his grounds crew, and several frantic U.S.G.A. officials scurried around the course tamping down towels or raking squeegees over the greens. With so many rounds to complete before cutting the field to less than half, a delay in the start time was not an option. The damage had been done: Oakmont's greatest defense against subpar golf was vulnerable, and a record number of golfers took advantage.

First to do so was Larry Wood, a thirty-three-year-old former club pro, whose only tour triumph had come in November 1970. Teeing off at 7:38 a.m., Wood shaved eight strokes off his Thursday round to shoot par 71. For decades, even par at Oakmont during a major championship was an extraordinary feat. But by sundown on Friday, twenty-six more golfers—better than one-sixth of the field—would match or break Oakmont's hallowed par. Nearby—so the legend says—Emil Loeffler and the Fowneses were rolling over in their graves.

Forrest Fezler, a twenty-three-year-old tour rookie, quickly eclipsed Wood. Back in February, Fezler had torn through the field at the Jackie Gleason Inverrary Classic, leading at the end of rounds one, two, and three. He continued to lead through fourteen holes on the final Sunday, before Lee Trevino overtook him late on the back nine.

Fezler contended on a few more weekends throughout the season, and later would win the PGA's Rookie of the Year honors for 1973. But the highlight of his season came Friday morning at Oakmont. Minutes after Wood surprised everyone in the scorer's tent with his even-par 71, Fezler wowed them again with his two under 69. The U.S. Open newcomer shaved eleven strokes off his opening-round 80, a radical reversal in fortune at traditionally bulletproof Oakmont.

It was only the beginning. Each with early morning tee times, Bert Yancey, Tom Joyce, and young Jerry Heard all shot 70, and Tom Shaw, another early riser, netted an even-par 71.

As the day wore on, the field continued to assault Oakmont's sacred identity. Journeyman John Schlee broke par by a stroke, as did fellow former Memphis State Tiger Greg Powers, a young, winless pro who had bounced back and forth between club jobs and the tour. But Powers's 70 wasn't even the best round in his threesome. Another winless twentysomething only three years removed from collegiate golf, Billy Ziobro, sank a twisting fifteen-foot birdie putt on the closing hole to post a 69.

Collectively, Ziobro and Powers shot seventeen strokes lower on Friday than on Thursday. On any other day, that remarkable combined effort would have put their picture on the front page of the weekend sports section: "Unknown Duo Scores Revenge on Mean Old Oakmont." Except that by the time Powers and Ziobro finished their rounds, they had been completely upstaged by another resurgent pairing.

At twenty-nine years old, Brian "Bud" Allin was already one of the tour's most well-traveled golfers. Born in Washington State, Allin, along with Mike Taylor and Johnny Miller, led Brigham Young to the school's first Western Athletic Conference title in 1966. But the following year, at the height of the Vietnam War, he left Provo to join the army. An artillery lieutenant, the 135-pound, baby-faced Allin earned two bronze stars in eighteen months of service before returning to America to start a career as a professional golfer.

In his first season on tour, Allin won just $355, but he somehow survived and his career truly took off early in 1973. At the Citrus Open in March, he shot 66-65-67-67 to take an eight-stroke victory, the second of his career. With more than $61,000 earned by mid-June, Allin held down the fifteenth spot on the tour's money list. And after finishing late Thursday afternoon with a 78, Allin returned to Oakmont Friday morning and stunned the U.S.G.A. by matching Gary Player's record-tying 67.

Twenty-four hours earlier, Player had labeled his 67 his "finest Open round" ever. Coming from a former champion with five previous top-ten finishes, that statement carried much weight. On Friday, by the time the sun set over Oakmont's soggy terrain, even 67 had lost its luster.

ALLIN'S PLAYING PARTNERS IN THE first two rounds were originally Kermit Zarley and Dave Hill. Hill's pretournament outburst and subsequent withdrawal had left an opening in the field. John Frillman, a club pro from Omaha, was the U.S.G.A.'s first alternate and would have taken Hill's place, except he was already filling a spot vacated by Don January, who that very week abruptly abandoned the tour to focus on course design. The U.S.G.A. then turned to its second alternate, thirty-six-year-old Gene Borek, to join Zarley and Allin.

For ten years, Eugene Edward Borek had been the head golf professional at Pine Hollow Country Club in East Norwich, Long Island. Although elite players viewed the job of club pro as a backup for those who could not survive on tour, Borek—who married young and raised four children—had *chosen* the more stable, family-centered life over that of a touring pro.

Born to a Polish-American family in Yonkers, New York, Borek had first learned golf by caddying at nearby Dunwoodie Golf Course. As a teenager at Saunders High School, he captained the golf team and won consecutive Yonkers Scholastic Golf Championships. Enrolled at Oswego State the following summer, Borek quickly decided that college wasn't the place for a blue-collar kid with seven older siblings.

"If my family had had the money, I probably would have been able to take a scholarship and go to college. But we were basically a poor family, and none of us went to college. My father was a machinist, but he had heart problems early in life and didn't work much during the time I was growing up. My mother carried the load during the Depression. She worked very hard. I got all of my drive from her."

Instead, the seventeen-year-old Borek briefly took a job at the Upper Montclair Country Club in New Jersey, then returned to work closer to home as an assistant to the pro at Scarsdale's Sunningdale Country Club, Elmer Voight. During his apprenticeship, Borek befriended his boss's son, Jon, and in August 1954 the two made their first trip to the Midwest for the National Caddie Championship at the Scarlet Course of Ohio State University.

Jon lost in the quarterfinals; he would find more success as a Hollywood movie star than as a tournament golfer. Borek took third place and realized how good he might become . . . and the financial constraints that would limit his horizons.

"When we got home on the train in Grand Central we had eleven cents between us," said Borek, who also won the Westchester caddie tournament that year. "I had the penny."

When he wasn't performing the mundane chores of an assistant golf professional at Sunningdale—the club closed down for the winter, so he also worked during those months at the Estate Carlton House and Resort in St. Croix—Borek scraped up enough money to compete on two of the PGA's minor-league winter circuits in the Caribbean and the Southern states.

"In 1959, I played the Caribbean tour from St. Croix. I remember bringing back a lot of Panama hats and Mrs. Voigt sold them for me," Borek recalled. "The club gave me some money the first year to play during the winter. Otherwise, I played as far as the money went. It was hard to make money. You didn't make money just because you made the cut. If you didn't finish in the top twenty-five, you didn't make expenses."

By 1963—on the same day President Kennedy was shot and killed in Dallas—Pine Hollow Country Club offered Borek the head golf professional job, an unusually high position for a twenty-six-year-old.

"Most of the guys didn't get their first jobs until age thirty-five or so, only after they had been on tour awhile."

Excellent tournament performances during 1963 helped Borek land the plum job. He played in thirteen professional tournaments that season, won a (team) Metropolitan PGA event in October, and qualified for both his first United States Open and PGA Championships.

Over the next decade, Borek remained at Pine Hollow while he and his wife, Joan, stayed in Long Island, raising two girls and two boys. He decided not to pursue the temptation of a touring pro's fortune, but that didn't stop him from amassing perhaps the most impressive competitive record of any club professional since Winged Foot's Claude Harmon. Between 1963 and 1972, Borek qualified for seven U.S. Opens and three PGA Championships, and made the cut in six of those events.

Like Lee Trevino—another golfer whose game matured without junior tournaments, amateur championships, or the college circuit—Borek's finest season came in 1971. Since he never really enjoyed an "off-season," Borek's game stayed sharp all year round. So when the PGA held its championship in February (instead of the normal summer date), Borek was ready.

After two days of play at the PGA's National Golf Club in Palm Beach Gardens, Jack Nicklaus set the pace with consecutive three under 69s. The *unfamiliar* name near the top of the leaderboard was Borek, who, at two under, held a share of fourth place going into the weekend. He maintained that spot the next day, despite a one over 73, and while Nicklaus left the course Sunday afternoon with his ninth major championship, Borek left Florida knowing he could compete with the world's best (a tired final round of 77 dropped him to a twenty-second-place tie).

That May, Borek overcame a four-stroke deficit in the final round to win his second Long Island Open. Four weeks later at Merion, while Trevino and Nicklaus battled for another U.S. Open championship, Borek made the cut thanks to a one over par 71 on Friday: a lower round than either Trevino or Nicklaus that day. And if he hadn't already done enough to shore up a second consecutive Metropolitan (New York) Golf Writers Player of the Year Award, he grabbed more headlines in October.

In the Metropolitan PGA at Sunningdale, Borek took the opening-round lead with a course-record-tying 67. The return to the club where he had spent nine years was a wonderful stroke of good fortune . . . and hazardous to his health.

In between rounds, he caught a virus and his second-round 75 dropped him out of the lead. During the thirty-six-hole final, Borek was so weak officials allowed him to use an electric cart. Despite chilly New York October weather, he shot a one under 70 in the morning, then "in the gusty cold wind that swept the Sunningdale Country Club," shot a 73 to finish alone in third place, two behind the winner, Tom Nieporte. (Borek and Nieporte—a former Bob Hope Desert Classic champion—were the two best club pros in the New York area during the era.)

Despite his illness, Borek returned to the tee a few days later at Pinehurst's grueling number two course, site of the National PGA Club Pro Championship. While ageless Sam Snead took the lead (and eventually won), Borek posted consecutive 69s to tie for sixth place at the halfway point. He remained in the top ten after three rounds, then dragged to the finish with a 76, which dropped him into a tie for seventeenth place; he still outscored Nieporte by four strokes.

Over the next year and a half, Borek padded his résumé: In February 1972, he took second and third, respectively, at the Caracas Open and the International Open in Columbia. High finishes in several New York State tournaments, and a victory in the Long Island PGA Championship in July, earned Borek another Metropolitan Pro of the Year award. The next January, he won a $10,000 stroke-play championship at the PGA National and, in late spring, took runner-up to Nieporte in the 1973 Long Island Open. In June, he felt confident he would earn one of the New York Metropolitan District's nine qualifying spots for the U.S. Open.

Borek shot 72 in the morning round at the North Hills Country Club in Manhasset, then made the short drive on the Long Island Expressway to the Fresh Meadow Country Club for the final eighteen holes. There he shot another round of even par. Tied with four other players at 144, he returned to Fresh Meadow's difficult opening hole to compete in a play-off for the remaining two slots.

Peter Kern, the lowest-scoring amateur, effectively bowed out when he launched a shot into a pond; Nashawtuc Country Club pro Charles Volpone Jr.'s double bogey also eliminated him. When former Masters champion Doug Ford sank a thirty-five-foot birdie putt, and Middle Bay Country Club's Craig Shankland made a conventional par, Borek needed to sink his par putt to remain in contention. He missed and had to settle for first alternate.

Nevertheless, later that week, Borek was headed to Oakmont. A Pine Hollow member in the steel industry, Gil Merrill (the brother of Metropolitan Opera star Robert Merrill), was on his way to Pittsburgh on business and had been invited to play at Oakmont. He asked Borek to come along.

"I said, 'What?' but then quickly agreed to fly out with him on his plane."

Borek arrived at Oakmont the same afternoon that Palmer and Player were prepping for the Open. Early in his career, Borek had jumped at the chance to practice alongside tour stars; by age thirty-six, he had decided against it.

"In the past, whenever I'd play with a 'name player,' there was a lot of conversation and the emphasis was inevitably on him. As a result, I found that I would not pay sufficient attention to learning the course itself. Moreover, unlike me, the 'name players' usually liked to hit a lot of balls. So, as nice as it was to come back after the Open and say that I'd played with a star, I generally tried to avoid it."

Instead, Borek focused on the course. He found the greens simply nightmarish; never had he encountered greens so fast and so nuanced in their undulations. He decided to spend every free minute on the practice green, trying to store in his mind and his fingers—just in case an alternate spot opened up—the delicate touch needed to cope with Oakmont's greens.

Several days later, back in Long Island, still no luck. "I called [U.S.G.A. officials] Tuesday morning and the answer was still no," said Borek. "I was told it might happen once in twenty years."

That was until Dave Hill's outburst.

"John Frillman—we've been buddies for a long time—he was the guy who encouraged Dave Hill to withdraw, knowing that I was next, telling Dave that he just couldn't putt Oakmont's greens!" Borek quipped many years later.

Hill withdrew Tuesday afternoon and the U.S.G.A. officials immediately called Borek, whose wife transferred the call to him in the pro shop. He drove hurriedly to LaGuardia Airport for a flight to Pittsburgh, only to see it canceled just before departure. He finally boarded a plane later that evening and didn't arrive in Pittsburgh until three a.m. on Wednesday.

With no motel rooms available near the overstuffed township, Borek headed directly to the course for another practice round. Eventually an Oakmont member, Willie Robertson, who lived only a hundred yards from the course, offered him a place to stay.

"I feel right at home," Borek said about the six-child Robertson household.

Fortunate after his hectic U.S. Open travel odyssey to have a late tee time (1:35 p.m.), Borek rested Thursday morning. Not long into his round, however, he looked every bit a last-minute substitute who had never equaled par in seven prior U.S. Open championships by shooting 41 on the front side. He "scrambled [his] way back" on the second nine to match the field average of 77.

"I felt that I'd played very well . . . the birdies just didn't convert, and two or three poor shots led to bogeys and double bogeys. You can't force the game, only play it one shot at a time. I wasn't discouraged by my first-round score."

The next morning, during the second round, Borek scrambled again—this time into the record books.

To "scramble" meant to snub the Fownesean tradition that Oakmont embodied. Thirty-foot par saves and heroic recovery shots might thrill the gallery, but they were the antithesis of U.S. Open golf. The U.S.G.A.'s ideal winner would split the fairway with his tee shot, find the best spot on the green to place his approach, and two-putt for par. On Friday, June 15, 1973, Gene Borek mocked seven-plus decades of U.S. Open tradition.

Borek did not get off to a good start. His approach shot on the first hole missed the green and he scrambled to save par. A nice up-and-down on number two, where he drove into the rough, saved another par.

On the next green, faced with a tricky twenty-five-footer, the well-traveled veteran read the landscape.

"I remember thinking to myself that if I didn't start making some putts very soon, I'd be going home. I knew that you really couldn't try to make putts at Oakmont; if they go in, they go in. But that was a key moment for my psychology because I really wanted to make the cut. I made the twenty-five-footer."

The long birdie sparked Borek's confidence. He reached the right greenside bunker in two shots on the par-five fourth, blasted out beautifully two feet from the flagstick, and tapped in for birdie. Despite his poor start on Thursday, Borek's scorecard was impressive (one under par in his last thirteen holes), and he was just getting started.

Borek scored easy pars on numbers five to seven, barely lipping out a twenty-footer for birdie on the seventh. But after he snap-hooked a three-wood into the hundred-yard-long Sahara bunker that guards the left side of the eighth, bogey or worse seemed inevitable. With the ball buried forty yards short of the flagstick, Borek took a chance.

"I took a lot of time thinking through my options on the shot and was very undecided. Basically, I didn't think I could hit it high enough over the lip to get to the flag. I was therefore thinking of playing sideways to the front of the green, chipping it up, and trying for bogey that way. I was also concerned about catching the ball too solidly and going fifty yards over the green and possibly out-of-bounds. . . . I had a good round going and didn't want to ruin it."

As his playing partners, Bud Allin and Kermit Zarley, waited, Borek abandoned any rational decision: He needed to hit his shot or be penalized for delay.

"Finally, on an impulse, I just decided to place the ball off of my right foot and beat on it as hard as I could.

"All I can remember about the actual shot is that when I looked up the ball was very high in the air. I recall saying to myself, How the heck did the ball get so high in the air? I couldn't believe it. I must have hit an inch or two behind the ball, no more than that. Because of the lip in the bunker, I couldn't see the shot land. But Allin and Zarley shouted excitedly after the shot and told me that I'd sunk it; the ball had landed well beyond the flag and then spun back into the hole. I couldn't hit that shot again in a thousand balls. Here was a score of five or six in the making, and I ended up with two. If I'd played smart, I would have been lucky to make bogey."

Unexpectedly three under par through eight holes, Borek began to sizzle. With his adrenaline flowing, he crushed a three-wood on the par-five ninth that carried well beyond the flagstick—"almost in the clubhouse"—and scattered the pros gathered on the attached practice green.

Marshals cleared all the players off the practice green for Borek to stare down a terrifying putt from a hundred feet away. Downhill across the enormous, heaving green, he knew that if he hit the putt a touch too hard it might slide fifty feet beyond the cup and off the green; hit it a touch too softly, and the ball might veer thirty feet off-line. Borek had never seen a putt quite like this; with a throng of fellow pros and members gathered on the clubhouse veranda observing his misery, he simply tried not to embarrass himself.

Of all the fears on Borek's mind as he prepared to putt, the sprinkler malfunction earlier that morning was not one of them. Certainly the greens were holding unusually well—his sand shot on the eighth, after all, had *backed* into the hole—but they had started to dry out, and this was still Oakmont.

"[The putt] was incredibly fast. I hit the putt like a twelve-footer," Borek recalled. "The greens weren't slow at all."

On this once-in-a-lifetime day, his touch was golden.

"The ball kept looking like it was going to stop. But it just kept rolling toward the pin at the corner where the green went up." The long, brisk putt rolled slowly enough for Borek to walk alongside most of the way, before it stopped a mere six inches from the cup.

Left with a "gimme," Borek rolled in his fourth birdie for a 32. In Oakmont's entire U.S. Open history, only Gary Player, less than twenty-four hours earlier, had ever put together as fine a front nine. And unlike Player—who had scrambled the day before to card an even-par 35 on the back nine—Borek's magic continued after the turn.

For a moment, the great round appeared to disintegrate when Borek mishit his tee shot on the tenth into the first fairway bunker on the right. Still 180 yards from the green and left with an uphill lie, the ball sat close to the front lip. The "smart" play would be to pitch out sideways and set up a clear third shot with a midiron into the green.

But Borek, unsure that he could play safely back into the fairway from his uphill lie in the bunker, decided to rely again on his strength and instinct. He planted his feet on the bunker slope, lined the ball off his left toe, and swung viciously, hoping to clear the lip and move the ball forward far enough to leave a short pitch to the green. The shot was risky—the ball could easily bury under the bunker lip, or rebound and strike him in the face—but the string of front-nine miracles convinced Borek to take another big chance.

Somehow he held his balance and launched the ball toward the green, with unreal hang time. Immediately he knew he had just struck the greatest shot of his life—and one that (because of the force of the awkward blow) injured his right shoulder permanently.

"The ball went incredibly high," he recalled. "It landed on the green thirty [to] forty feet short of the hole. Remarkably for an Oakmont green that was like linoleum, the ball almost plugged."

Borek two-putted for a memorable par four. He had played numbers eight, nine, and ten in 2-4-4, when he wouldn't have been surprised to score 6-6-6.

On the eleventh green—near the clubhouse, the press tent, and the growing gallery that had heard about his round—Borek rolled in a twenty-footer for another birdie. He was now five under par through eleven holes, and eleven shots better than the day before over the same stretch. The question, "Who the hell is Gene Borek?" reverberated throughout the press tent, as writers hurriedly rewrote their main leads for the evening papers.

Only one over par for the championship, Borek now fully expected to make the cut and compete in weekend play at a fifth U.S. Open. But he did not rest on his laurels.

Orthodox pars at the next two stops followed before Borek made his way back to even par for the championship on the fourteenth, where he dropped a high iron to four feet and rolled in the birdie to reach six under par. He then played the next three holes superbly, including a near-miss for birdie on the seventeenth.

The now intrepid Borek smacked another fine tee shot and an excellent approach to the final green, leaving a chance to tie the U.S. Open single-round low of 64. As he walked up the eighteenth fairway, a large crowd near the clubhouse—now fully aware of his stellar round—stood and applauded. And though his birdie putt missed a few inches to the left, he had earned a special place in Oakmont history, eclipsing not only the 67s by Hogan, Beman, and Player, but also the competitive course record of 66 that former marine Jimmy Clark had set in the U.S. Open sectional qualifier at Oakmont in 1953.

"First, I'd like to thank Dave Hill," Borek joked with reporters afterward. "It's always a privilege and pleasure to play in the U.S. Open, especially on a great course such as this."

As brilliant as his round was, the originality of his tale—unknown club pro, last-minute substitute, breaks the course record—along with his personality, captivated the press.

"Borek did it as easily as a stroll through Schenley Park in downtown Pittsburgh," reported the *Detroit Free Press*. "He is 36 years old and has a nice, warm smile, even if there are gaps between all of his teeth. He has a wife and four kids. He stands 6-1 and weighs 200 pounds. He looks like the guy who runs the corner hardware store."

Borek was used to such anonymity.

"[When] I called home a few weeks ago to tell my wife I won the Long Island Open, all she said was, 'Don't forget the milk.'"

THE STARS OF ROUND ONE had all been men whom the public knew on a first-name basis: Gary, Jack, Arnie, Lee. A watered-down Oakmont—the greens slower and much, much softer than usual—opened the door in round two for a largely overlooked group of golfers to charge onto center stage.

While Borek's record-breaking round stood out, Friday was also a triumph for several other club professionals who didn't, under normal circumstances, have the game to shoot par at Oakmont. In addition to Tom Joyce, Billy Ziobro, Greg Powers (all club pros), Lloyd Monroe, the top qualifier from New Jersey and the head pro at Upper Montclair Country Club, finished up a two over 73, twelve strokes better than he did the day before. And, aided by a birdie on the ninth (he was inches from an eagle with a wedge approach shot), Niagara Falls Country Club pro Denny Lyons posted a 74 and made the cut for the first time in a U.S. Open. His two-day total of 146 was five strokes better than his father, Toby Lyons, had shot halfway through the 1953 U.S. Open at Oakmont.

But for all the surprises of obscure club pros climbing their way up the leaderboard to mingle with tour celebrities, that afternoon no one provided more astonishing golf than career amateur Marvin "Vinny" Giles.

Giles was a throwback to the great Bobby Jones. Although born and raised in Lynchburg, Virginia, in much more modest circumstances than Jones— officials at the nearby fancy country club his parents couldn't afford threatened to notify the police if the teenage Giles didn't stop sneaking onto their course— Giles played his college golf at the University of Georgia. Under his leadership, the Bulldogs won three consecutive Southeastern Conference titles from 1965 to 1967, and Giles earned All American honors each of those seasons, rising to first-team All American in his senior year.

And, like Jones, Giles was never lured to join the pro tour.

"I was planning on getting married and my fiancée made it very clear she didn't want to spend the rest of her life going from one Holiday Inn to another while I played on tour. The purses also were too small to guarantee us financial security."

Instead, Giles enrolled at the University of Virginia School of Law, but still matched his game against the nation's top amateurs. Granted a week off from the firm where he was interning during the summer of 1967, he won the prestigious Southern Amateur. During Labor Day weekend, he headed west to the Broadmoor Hotel in Colorado Springs to compete in the United States Amateur Championship.

Despite his sterling golf résumé—Giles also took second in the 1966 NCAA championship, and had previously competed in three U.S. Amateurs—he still felt like an unknown.

"Most of the players in the field [Bob Murphy, Marty Fleckman, Bill Campbell, Grier Jones, Johnny Miller] had much more decorated careers up to that point. It was a very prestigious field and my name didn't stand out, at least not at the outset."

Giles rebounded after an opening-day 76 to shoot even par for the final three rounds (from 1966 to 1974, the U.S. Amateur was contested at stroke play, not match play). A birdie on the seventy-first brought the twenty-four-year-old within one shot of the leader, Bob Dickson. Granted a free drop following an errant drive into the woods on the final hole, Dickson won the championship, and Giles took second.

As runner-up, Giles won a spot in the following spring's Masters tournament, where he made quite an impression on its founder, Bobby Jones. Shaking off the preround jitters—"I was scared to death before I teed off"—Giles nailed a thirty-foot birdie putt on the first green. He knocked in two more birdies on the front side, and finished his round one under par and tied for a top-ten spot. Giles battled tough throughout the weekend and finished the tournament at even par, the best finish by an amateur in six years.

Although he was clearly one of amateur golf's major stars, more final-round hard luck befell Giles the next summer in the 1968 U.S. Amateur. After three rounds in which he failed to match par at Scioto Country Club—the site of Jones's second U.S. Open triumph four decades earlier—Giles found himself six shots behind the leader, with six golfers ahead of him. A herculean effort in the final round vaulted him up the leaderboard. Three under on the front nine, Giles made two more birdies on the twelfth and seventeenth that cut his deficit to only one shot behind college sophomore Bruce Fleisher. Sparked by a magnificent par save on the sixteenth, Fleisher hung on and escaped with the win. Giles's record-setting 65 was rendered merely a courageous round of golf by the runner-up.

Giles returned to the U.S. Amateur in August 1969, dubbed the "sentimental choice" in a packed field. Now twenty-six, he was practically aged next to Fleisher, collegians Tom Watson, Tom Kite, and John Mahaffey; Western Amateur champion Steve Melnyk; and a nineteen-year-old Virginia rival named Jerry "Lanny" Wadkins. Still, the most daunting obstacle for Giles and every golfer in the field remained the punishing course that confronted them.

"Only Ben Hogan could take this course day after day," one collegian said. They were playing Oakmont.

As the final round began, Melnyk held a three-stroke edge over Giles and Allen Miller, the current golf team captain at the University of Georgia. Although the husky Melnyk "appeared to be sweltering from the humidity," it was his partner in the last pairing, Giles, who spent the afternoon buried in sand.

Melnyk was a natural enemy to both Miller and Giles; that May, his University of Florida Gators had lost the SEC title to the Georgia Bulldogs. After opening with a bogey, Melnyk overpowered both Bulldogs and, at the turn, was eight strokes ahead, largely because Giles bunkered shots on the second, third, fourth, and fifth holes. Giles narrowed the gap late, but Melnyk still emerged with a five-stroke victory.

A third consecutive runner-up in the world's premier amateur event did nothing to discourage Giles. Neither did the steady growth of first-class collegiate talent, including the emergence of the all-world prodigy, Ben Crenshaw. In 1970, Giles took sixth in the U.S. Amateur behind his fellow Virginian Lanny Wadkins. And for those who believed he could no longer claim the state of Virginia's top amateur billing, Giles beat his younger counterpart twice the next season: in May during the semifinals of the North & South Amateur, and again on Independence Day in the Virginia State Amateur. He then took third in the 1971 U.S. Amateur. Over the eight years in which he competed at medal play, Giles averaged better than eighth place, easily the best of his era.

Giles returned to the U.S. Amateur at Charlotte Country Club in 1972 for a ninth try at the championship. He opened with a 73, then fired "one of the best rounds I've ever played"—a bogey-free 68—to grab the lead. Despite an erratic third round (four birdies, five bogeys), Giles retained his one-stroke advantage heading into the last day. He promptly squandered the lead and seemed to be doomed for another U.S. Amateur heartbreak: a three-putt bogey on number two pulled him even with his playing partner, Mark Hayes. Birdies by Hayes on the third and seventh dropped Giles two strokes behind the twenty-three-year-old soldier, who was stationed at nearby Fort Jackson in South Carolina.

But on the eighth, Giles redirected his round . . . and his golf career. At what he called the "key hole," Giles saved par from ten feet and, with Hayes bunkered, pulled to within a stroke. Another par for Giles and a bogey for Hayes on the tenth evened the score before Giles laced a four-iron to three feet on number thirteen. Two strokes ahead of Hayes, Giles soon drained birdie putts from five and twenty feet. And despite a double bogey on number sixteen, followed by a bogey on number seventeen, Giles still closed the championship out with a three-stroke win.

"I always felt I was destined to win this tournament," Giles told the press. (In 2009, at age 66, Giles won the U.S. Senior Amateur; the thirty-seven-year gap between his U.S.G.A. titles is the largest in men's amateur golf history.)

The 1972 U.S.G.A. Amateur title came with several perks. For one, Giles garnered exemptions to play that year in several PGA tour events. And in April

1973, he received his third invitation to play in the Masters. Paired with Nicklaus on the first two days and Trevino in the third round, he tied for thirty-fifth place.

During the first half of the 1973 season, Giles accepted invitations to play in the Colonial Invitational and the Kemper Open. Although he was cut from both events, mingling with the tour professionals accelerated his new business. In February, Giles and his friend C. Vernon Spratley announced the formation of a sports management firm. Over the next three decades, Giles would go on to represent several PGA stars (including Davis Love III, Tom Kite, Justin Leonard, and, eventually, Lanny Wadkins); he arguably became the best-known agent not named Mark McCormack.

As the reigning U.S. Amateur champion, Giles also earned a return trip to Oakmont to play in the 1973 U.S. Open, a major bonus, since he had failed to qualify for the U.S. Open the previous two summers. Giles headed to Oakmont a few days early to reacquaint himself with the course, and despite the rain that cut short Tuesday's practice round, he understood the course's idiosyncrasies better than most contestants.

Giles already knew one of his Thursday playing partners fairly well; Jack Nicklaus and he had been paired together in both the 1969 and 1973 Masters. Giles's uneventful 74 on Thursday lacked the spark of Nicklaus's great eagle on the seventeenth, but it still left him inside the top twenty going into Friday's second round.

Late into the afternoon—both notoriously slow players, Giles and Nicklaus would not finish until nearly seven p.m.—Giles stood at a respectable two over par through number fourteen. Because so many low scores were being shot that day, he would not be a shoo-in to make the cut unless he played the finishing holes close to par.

Even on a day when several anonymous pros posted outrageously low scores, Giles's final four holes stunned U.S.G.A. die-hards.

It all began on Oakmont's treacherous, 453-yard, par-four fifteenth. The hole opens with a blind tee shot onto a sharply left-to-right-sloping fairway, guarded on both sides by bunkers. Giles's perfect drive left him 180 yards downhill to the pin, which stood on the left front corner of the green. With the greens fairly dried out by this late in the afternoon, he knew that trying to carry his iron to the flagstick would only invite disaster.

"I drew back a six-iron and hit it perfect," Giles remembered. "It took a couple of hops before the green and rolled into the left center or left front cup."

Upon the sight of his ball dropping into the cup, Giles hurled his six-iron into the air and was then bear-hugged by his caddie, long-term professional looper "Stormin'" Norman Smith. The huge crowd that had gathered to watch Nicklaus exploded in excitement.

Even the normally tunnel-visioned Nicklaus broke character for a moment.

"After it went in, Jack was standing near me on the fairway," Giles remembered years later. "He took out his seven-iron, held it up to the hole; he pretended to plumb-bob his shot! That was pretty funny and the gallery thought so too. It was really the first time he'd acknowledged my presence all day. Jack was all business on the course. He stayed focused on his game."

Giles picked up a conventional par-three on the sixteenth, then struck a conservative iron shot into the heart of the fairway on the seventeenth (by contrast, Nicklaus again attempted to cut the dogleg and drive the green in a single stroke). With a wedge from a hundred yards, Giles hit his approach shot a bit thin, but it held the softened green and stopped thirty feet from the cup.

"Everyone talks about how soft those greens were," Giles said. "Sure, they were holding better than usual—that's why the thin wedge I hit didn't skid off the back of the green—but they were still incredibly fast. Somehow, I was lucky enough to roll in the birdie."

Safely two over par for the championship and well under the cut line, Giles played the eighteenth aggressively. He nailed a great drive, then again took the magical six-iron from Stormin' Norman. This time, the ball didn't fall into the cup, but it did stop pin-high on the green's back tier, fifteen feet away and on a reasonably flat plateau. Giles struck home the putt for a second straight birdie, almost running directly through Nicklaus's line in his great excitement.

On a day of record-low scoring, Giles's two under 69 earned few headlines. He was, after all, the reigning U.S. Amateur champion and already knew Oakmont well from the 1969 Amateur championship. But completing Oakmont's finishing holes in 2-3-3-3—eagle-par-birdie-birdie—was mind-boggling.

"[I was just trying] to make the cut [which came at 150]. I was trying to shoot seventy-four or better. It's funny how it happens sometimes. I'm still shell-shocked. I'm not supposed to make all these good numbers in a row. [I don't] expect to beat all these guys. I just go out and play and see what develops."

• • •

NINETEEN MEN BROKE PAR ON Friday, and twelve shot in the 60s, besting the old U.S. Open record for low scoring set in 1960 during the second round at Cherry Hills. The average score of the entire field was nearly a stroke and a half lower than on Thursday.

The score needed to make the cut was 150, the same as in 1962, despite the sprinkler debacle. Besides Giles, the only amateur to qualify was University of Florida junior Gary Koch. There must have been a strange connection between Gainesville, Florida, and Oakmont, Pennsylvania: Apart from Melnyk's win four years earlier, former Gators Frank Beard, Tommy Aaron, and Bob Murphy (one of the nineteen to best par) all qualified for the weekend.

The long list of surprise names posting low scores on Friday left several of the "usual suspects" on the outside looking in. In addition to Crenshaw, whose game never rebounded from his first-round 80, tour money leader Bruce Crampton—already a three-time winner that season—missed the cut. So did Orville Moody and Billy Casper, both recent U.S. Open champions. No wonder the *Los Angeles Times* used a double entendre in its headline, calling the event a "watered-down Open."

But in a golf world centered around the belief that Oakmont's impenetrable par was as much a certainty as death and taxes, the *cause* of the low scores hardly mattered. For better or worse, a new day had dawned in Oakmont's history. The Fownes/Loeffler era was now officially over.

"The legend had grown like the pin oaks, the legend of a golf course with massive greens of shaved turf that wouldn't yield to iron shots or birdie putts, of a course where the scores climbed faster than the price of gold," Art Spander wrote in the *San Francisco Chronicle*. "It was Oakmont, that green monster in the suburbs of Pittsburgh, where people had three-putted into oblivion tournament after tournament for more than half a century. But yesterday, during the second round of the 1973 U.S. Open, the legend came to an end."

· DAY THREE ·

June 16, 1973

• 7 •

"He's Longer Than Nicklaus. . . . Go Watch This Boy."

Tom Weiskopf could be smarmy or charming, pensive or funny, and quite often cantankerous, especially with photographers who clicked during his backswing. After experiencing his moodiness for several years, sportswriters assigned the nicknames "Temperamental Tommy" and "the Towering Inferno" to the gifted, yet often disappointing young pro. Still, it was not his emotional outbursts, but his fragile self-confidence and wavering commitment that would determine whether he could ever channel his superabundant talent into a Hall of Fame career.

In 1973, at the age of thirty, Weiskopf began to display a new level of confidence and his professional commitment reached an all-time high. And to no one's surprise, after three rounds in the U.S. Open at Oakmont, he found himself in a familiar spot: the doorstep of greatness.

Weiskopf had been there before, especially at the Masters. Augusta National suited the special strengths of his game, notably his explosive power off the tee and his brilliant command of the long irons. Three of the past five Masters tournaments had featured Weiskopf in the last or second-to-last pairing during the final round. But by the end of each of those April Sundays, he had come up just short of donning the Green Jacket—an honor that his hero, rival, and fellow Buckeye Jack Nicklaus had already earned four times.

Nineteen seventy-three was to be a completely different year. While Weiskopf again failed to win the Masters, he blossomed in May to become the tour's hottest player, posting three wins and a runner-up in the four weeks leading up to the U.S. Open.

As he went about his business at Oakmont, there was no sign of the emotional tempest that usually flashed for all to see. Weiskopf was customarily cocky, but also subdued that week in western Pennsylvania; clearly he was playing for more than money and glory, trying to seize the moment to honor the memory of his father, Thomas Mannix Weiskopf, a local Pennsylvania boy who had died less than three months earlier.

To get to the second tee box at Oakmont, players cross a concrete bridge erected thirty feet above the Pennsylvania Turnpike. Just beside the turnpike lies a line of railroad tracks that connects Ohio to Pennsylvania: two once-great industrial states whose lifeblood had been the steel and rail industries.

Long before he climbed his way up to railroad middle management, Thomas Mannix Weiskopf, a teenager during the Great Depression, had worked part-time as a steel worker in western Pennsylvania. He and his work gang helped lay the railroad tracks that bisected Oakmont's first and second holes.

"My dad worked on those tracks," Tom proudly said to all in earshot. "He was from Beaver Falls and that was one of his first jobs." And, added a local reporter, "Every time Tom Weiskopf saw the railroad tracks he thought of why he had to win the U.S. Open."

As Weiskopf set out to win the U.S. Open—an achievement that Nicklaus told the press Weiskopf needed to validate his decade-long career—his dad was with him every step of the way.

"He sacrificed his vacation and bonus money to keep me on the tour. He was Tom Weiskopf's number one fan. He walked the course with me; he read the papers for news about me when he couldn't see me play. He told me, 'You can be the best golfer in the world.' I feel I let him down a little. I felt I never proved my capabilities in front of him."

Thomas Daniel Weiskopf (the Tom Weiskopf who rose to golf stardom) began his prodigal golf odyssey in modest, middle-class circumstances, first in central and then in northeast Ohio. Thomas Mannix had grown up in the blue-collar steel town of Beaver Falls, and *his* father (i.e., Tom's grandfather—also named Thomas) had done well enough as a mill superintendent at Union Drawn Steel to move his family to the "Heights," less than a five-minute walk from the town's only golf club. Thomas Mannix learned to play golf there and, at age eighteen, enrolled in nearby Geneva College, where he was instrumental in founding the small school's golf team.

Thomas Mannix taught intramural golf at Geneva, and as a competitor he never lost a match in two years of intercollegiate play (all within western Pennsylvania). Upon graduation with an economics degree in 1936, he joined his parents in Massillon, Ohio (Union Drawn's corporate headquarters), to begin work with the Newburgh and South Shore Railway.

It was there he met Eva Shorb—appropriately, on a golf course. Shorb was the sixth of seven daughters of Elmer Shorb, an electrician and one of America's many recent converts to golf. Although he chose not to teach his daughters the sport, at age fourteen the independently minded Eva picked up the game on her own and proved to be a natural. She received instruction from notable local pros such as Al Espinosa and Wilson Crane, and at Massillon's Washington High School she became the first girl in Ohio to earn a (male) varsity letter for her play on the golf team. She dominated the local amateur scene, taking the Stark County and Akron District women's championships, and soon showcased her skill as a "powerful hitter" on a national stage. In the Women's Western Golf Association Championship in Cleveland, a seventeen-year-old Shorb narrowly missed breaking the course record when she missed a short putt on the final hole.

The next summer, as a freshman geology major and first woman member of the men's varsity team at the College of Wooster in Ohio, she again drew national headlines. With a demeanor described by a *New York Times* reporter as "imperturbable," Shorb valiantly battled nineteen-year-old Patty Berg—the 1935 runner-up, and one of the world's finest female golfers—in the first round of the U.S. Women's Amateur at Canoe Brook Country Club in New Jersey. Though she eventually lost one-down to Berg, her unshakable confidence won high praise in the national golf press.

When one reporter asked Shorb if she was nervous while walking down the final fairway in a tie with Berg, she replied, "Why, no; why should I be nervous?" She and Berg were actually close friends from previous golf competitions, and even Berg's father was a fan of young Eva. Having arrived a virtual unknown, Eva left Canoe Brook a minor celebrity: a spirited dark horse who nearly toppled one of the game's emerging giants.

"Now Miss Shorb is calm and composed and charmingly natural," wrote an admiring observer. "She had the gallery behind her solidly, but it never bothered her. She played her own golf game from start to finish."

As her college game progressed, Shorb continued to attract the attention of national reporters, but not entirely for her play *on* the golf course. After a year at Wooster, she was dismissed from the varsity golf team (in a major setback to women in sports, female athletes were increasingly confined to intramural clubs and "play days" on college campuses in the 1930s). Newspapers from coast to coast chastised her banishment and ran photos of Shorb under the banner, "Poor Little Eva."

Eventually, a partial compromise was reached: Shorb was allowed to compete, unofficially, against another precocious woman golfer, Janet Shock, from nearby Denison College. And although Shorb continued to succeed on the national stage (in 1938, she again lost a close match to Berg in the semifinals of the Women's Amateur), she wanted to compete more frequently than she was allowed to do at Wooster. She therefore transferred to Mount Union College in Alliance, Ohio, and was allowed to play on the men's varsity team. Reporters referred to her as "another feminine star who has wavered on the brink of greatness several times."

At some point during college, Eva met Thomas Mannix on a golf course in Massillon, and the two quickly became a golfing couple. Thomas, the district amateur champion of nearby Canton, and Eva competed regularly (sometimes as a duo) at summer tournaments in central Ohio, once scoring the low gross of 74 in a mixed-foursomes event at the Scioto Country Club. Whether Eva left college to be with Thomas is unclear, but she quit Mount Union during the spring 1940 semester to return to Massillon, and within a year the couple was married at St. Mary's (Catholic) Church.

Though still regarded as one of the "top-flight clouters" when he competed in 1941's Ohio State Amateur championship, Thomas now faced several new responsibilities—on the job, as his widowed mother's caretaker, and as a young parent (Tom, the professional golfer, was born in November 1942; two more children soon followed). These left little time for golf during the war years. Shortly after Thomas's mother's death in 1947, his employer transferred him to Cleveland, and while he continued to hold several midlevel administrative posts, career setbacks—plus the expense of Catholic schooling and a growing dependence on alcohol—further eroded his high-level golf.

Eva's game also took a backseat to parenthood, but her natural swing and fierce competitiveness led her to the final round of the Cleveland Women's Golf Association Championship. She lost on the final hole. While the family did not have enough money to join a private club, with excellent public golf facilities available in the Cleveland area, Thomas Mannix and Eva Weiskopf regularly hit the links. Their eldest son, however, didn't care much for golf. In fact, Tom—skinny and still only five-nine at graduation, despite a huge high school growth spurt—never excelled on the athletic fields.

"In high school, I competed in football, basketball, baseball, wrestling, and track and wasn't any good at any of them," Weiskopf candidly admitted at the height of his professional career.

Even golf, his birthright, did not come naturally. Tom's parents would take him out to local courses and try to persuade him to play, but he refused to do so. "When they played they took me out on the course with them when I was a boy eight to ten," Weiskopf recalled shortly after he turned pro. "I never liked the game then." Instead, he hung around the clubhouse with other kids whose parents forced them to remain there.

"He was a very impetuous boy," Eva later remembered. "He could never sit still. In fact, there were times when I wished I didn't have him."

It was not until father and son attended the 1957 U.S. Open at Inverness Country Club in Toledo that golf grabbed fourteen-year-old Tom Weiskopf's imagination. At his father's urging, he watched close-up and was transfixed by the smoothest, most perfect golf swing since Bobby Jones's.

"After we walked through the gate, he took me straight to the practice range and pointed out Sam Snead. The sound of Sam's iron shots, the flight of the ball, thrilled me. I was hooked even before I started playing."

That summer, Tom caddied and played golf for the first time. He immediately set about learning the game—putting, hitting buckets of balls for hours, occasionally under his parents' grateful eyes. Although he made rapid progress, he remained a relatively small child and did not make Benedictine High School's golf team on the first try. He did qualify as a sophomore, and throughout the season competed on equal terms with most of his teammates, all of whom were considerably bigger and stronger.

Weiskopf's game blossomed during his junior year, and the team won the Cleveland city championship in 1959. Shortly afterward, Tom placed eighth in the Ohio Junior Chamber of Commerce tournament in Mansfield, his first sanctioned tournament appearance outside of high school.

As a senior, aided by his continued growth spurt, Tom moved his game to another level. He led Benedictine to another city title and won the individual championship as well. Shortly afterward, he slaughtered the field by six strokes in the Ohio Jaycee Junior Championship, held at the Lost Creek Country Club in Lima, Ohio.

The steep learning curve that Weiskopf displayed over a short time period was enough to convince Ohio State's golf coach, Bob Kepler, to grant Weiskopf a scholarship for the fall of 1960. The Buckeyes already featured golf's greatest amateur sensation since Bobby Jones in Nicklaus, and hopes were that Tom might—if his game kept improving, and his new body filled out—eventually replace Nicklaus as the team's superstar.

As a freshman, Weiskopf had the extraordinary good fortune to practice regularly with Nicklaus (contrary to myth, Weiskopf did not caddie for the upperclassman). But it was largely coach Bob Kepler—who was delighted with Weiskopf's additional six-inch growth spurt that year, taking him to his adult height of six-three—who turned the raw, bony kid into a full-bore athlete.

"Bob put forty yards on my tee shots," Weiskopf said in 1965. "He changed my swing, made it more upright. It made my arc bigger." Weiskopf could not hit his tee shots as far as Nicklaus when the two were briefly teammates at Ohio State, but as a result of Kepler's teaching, he was definitely on his way.

Due to NCAA regulations at the time, Weiskopf could not compete in intercollegiate matches during his freshman season (spring 1961). By his sophomore year—with Nicklaus now on tour—Weiskopf made a push to fill the enormous void. He seemed ready to ascend to Nicklaus's throne when, a month before the start of his sophomore year, he overcame a two-stroke deficit to edge out a thirty-one-year-old former prizefighter, Lalu Sabotin, and win the Ohio Public Links Championship. As a sophomore, Weiskopf led the Buckeyes to the Ohio Intercollegiate Championship and posted the individual low score, 72-76. Two weeks later, he took third place in the Big Ten championship.

Tom's dedication to golf continued to grow, and during the summer of 1962, following his sophomore year, he finished second in the Ohio State Junior Championship, reached the quarterfinals in the Ohio State Amateur, and successfully defended his Ohio Public Links Championship in August. He also finished fourth in local qualifying for the U.S. Amateur, one spot too low for a chance to compete in the championship at Pinehurst.

But it was a tournament where Weiskopf was merely a spectator that jump-started his ambition to chase greatness at the professional level.

The father-son trip on which Snead's sweet swing had captured young Tom was the first of several annual pilgrimages that the two of them made to the world's grandest golf stage, the U.S. Open. Despite the cost of traveling to far-away courses in Missouri, Colorado, and California, Weiskopf did not miss an Open championship after he experienced the Snead revelation at Inverness.

There was never a doubt Tom and his father would drive two hours from Cleveland to the 1962 U.S. Open at Oakmont, not only to seek inspiration from the game's established stars, but also to cheer his friend and former teammate Nicklaus, who was playing in his first Open championship as a professional. Watching Palmer and Nicklaus compete head-to-head transfixed young Tom.

"Jack's ball just disappeared into the sky. I ran down the fairway to get ahead of them. Arnold took off fast, as always, but as he approached his own ball he continued to look down the fairway. He looked and looked and his neck seemed to get longer, like an ostrich. Then his step slowed. He saw Jack's ball, a full twenty-five yards ahead of his. I could see it in Arnold's face. Jack had arrived."

Observing Nicklaus's arrival firsthand on the national golfing stage was pivotal for Weiskopf. He too came from Ohio. He too played at Ohio State, and could smash the ball out of sight. He now was ready for bigger stages than amateur championships and intercollegiate team matches.

Weiskopf decided not to return to Ohio State for the fall semester. He had begun to chant the mantra that would drive him throughout his career:

"If Jack can do it, I can do it."

ASIDE FROM HIS READY ACCESS to Ohio State's superb Scarlet Course (argu-ably the best collegiate facility in the nation), Tom Weiskopf had shown very little interest in college. Golf clearly trumped his studies.

Tom made a regular practice of sneaking out of an afternoon class—after roll call, and with the professor's back turned—and hopping aboard the wom-en's physical education bus headed in the direction of the Scarlet Course.

"It was really funny. I never got caught—but I failed the course."

In the early 1960s, the PGA closely regulated who could join the tour.

Among other requirements, an applicant needed to have $5,000 saved in the bank. Tom didn't have nearly that amount of savings, and his father never earned enough money to fully subsidize Tom's play in his amateur days.

Nobly stubborn on this point, Weiskopf insisted on earning his own way onto the tour, and turned down a number of sponsors' offers to pay his way. Having dropped out of college and looking for ways to save money, he left Columbus and returned to live with his parents in Cleveland. While retaining his amateur status, he worked as an assistant to a club professional in Cleveland, which provided both a steady paycheck and free access to a first-class golf facility to develop his game.

During the summer of 1963, Weiskopf competed regularly in many prominent local events. The highlight of his postcollegiate amateur play came in August. After a disappointing first-round loss in the Ohio State Amateur that July, he passed up defense of his Ohio Public Links title to prepare for the Western Amateur, a high-profile, national match-play event, conveniently being held that year in nearby Benton Harbor, Michigan.

Despite posting the second-lowest score in the stroke-play qualifier, Tom was not among the favorites at the 6,943-yard Point O' Woods Country Club. The reigning U.S. Amateur and NCAA champions, Labron Harris Jr. and R. H. Sikes—both former Walker Cup players as well—highlighted the field. Weiskopf's credentials as an accomplished state-level amateur didn't measure up.

He survived the second-cut qualifier for match play by shooting 76-73. With the field now reduced to sixteen, Weiskopf toppled Cliff Taylor of Spring Lake, Michigan, 6 & 5, to advance to the quarterfinals, where he faced Sikes.

Not in the least intimidated by his much-decorated opponent, Weiskopf won four of the first six holes on the way to a 3 & 2 victory. In the semifinals match, he defeated another hotshot with a solid record in his home state, two-time Kansas champion Johnny Stevens, to reach the finals. There he faced the only golfer with better credentials than Sikes's. The son of a fine public links player (and legendary golf coach at Oklahoma State University), Labron Harris Jr. won the 1962 U.S. Amateur at Pinehurst. Despite a close call in the quarterfinals, Harris was expected to eliminate the upstart Weiskopf at the Western Amateur with little difficulty.

The crowd for the final match turned out to be the largest in the long history of the tournament. With Tom's mother and his two siblings among the record-setting twenty-five hundred spectators, the twenty-year-old bolted out of the gate quickly, taking the first two holes from the "bespectacled Oklahoman." Lights-out putting helped Weiskopf maintain a two-hole lead after the turn (although he did miss a three-footer that cost him the ninth hole). Then Weiskopf surged ahead, one-putting the next five greens, to take the title on the fourteenth.

Everything seemed to go Weiskopf's way that late-summer afternoon. On the par-five thirteenth, he missed the green in the left-side bunker. His thin blast appeared headed well off the green, but it caromed hard off the pin and came to rest six feet away. He nailed the birdie to take another hole from Harris.

On the fourteenth, after his booming drive split the fairway, Weiskopf socked an iron to fifteen feet and holed yet another birdie to close out Harris. He finished the fourteen holes at one under, the only player that week to break par for a full round at the difficult Benton Harbor course.

"I'm glad it's all over," Weiskopf told reporters. "I never did like match play . . . although this tournament may change my mind.

"All I can say is . . . I don't know. . . . Everything has been just wonderful," an exuberant Tom said at the trophy presentation. "This has been the greatest thrill I've ever had."

Almost overnight, Weiskopf became a prominent figure on the national golfing stage. A week after the Western, he played in a one-day event in his childhood home of Massillon that was a warm-up for the Akron Golf Classic at famously difficult Firestone Country Club. He took the top amateur spot in Massillon and then showcased his game at Firestone, finishing fifty-third in a stellar field to earn the low amateur prize—a shiny silver tray—after a one-hole play-off with the current Ohio State Amateur champion, Bob Bourne.

Shortly afterward, Weiskopf qualified for the first time for the U.S. Amateur at the Wakonda Club in Des Moines, Iowa. Disappointingly, he lost one-down in the first round of match play. But he soon grabbed another top-amateur spot in a mixed field at the prestigious Ohio State Open (where Nicklaus had startled the golfing world in 1956 by winning at age sixteen), finishing four strokes behind the professional winner, Bob Shave.

It didn't take long for the national press to jump on the fast-charging Weiskopf bandwagon. In January 1964, *Golf Digest* ranked him tenth on its list of top-ten male amateurs in the country.

That April, Weiskopf broke his finger playing basketball with a group of grammar school kids, and was unable to defend his Western Amateur title the following month. Once the hand healed, he made a bold decision. Now—with an impressive amateur résumé, $2,100 saved in the bank, and endorsement-deal offers from both a clothing company and a Cincinnati golf firm—he chose to turn pro on May 1, 1964.

Those first three months on the PGA tour, Weiskopf lived on $325 a week to cover all expenses, until earning his first paycheck. At the Western Open in Chicago in early August, he followed two marginal rounds with a stellar Saturday 68; only Palmer (67) and Nicklaus (65) posted better scores that day. An even-par 71 the next day pushed Weiskopf into a tie for twenty-ninth place, and he left the Tam O'Shanter Golf Course with a check for $487.50. Weiskopf never forgot those first dollars he earned, and every year afterward he wrote a check for that same amount to the Western Golf Association's Evans Caddie Scholarship fund.

As the 1965 season began, Weiskopf raised his game to the next level. In February at the Tucson Open, he tied for tenth and earned $1,170 as a result of two excellent weekend rounds. A few months later, after years of attending the U.S. Open as a spectator, Weiskopf qualified for and competed in the world's toughest golf test. Though never a threat to win at the Bellerive Country Club in St. Louis, and somewhat thrown by the enormous stage—"I'm so nervous right now I can hardly see," he said at the first tee—Weiskopf performed admirably. On the first day, he outshot Nicklaus by two strokes before finishing in fortieth place. A week later, in the St. Paul Open, he carded an opening 65 before falling out of contention.

Both the media and his fellow pros took notice.

"Tom Weiskopf. Now, there's a boy who hits it a ton," Sam Snead told a writer in the locker room during the U.S. Open. "He's longer than Nicklaus. Go watch this boy."

Weiskopf's confidence grew notably during the autumn season. At an unofficial PGA event, he repeated another Nicklaus feat when he shot all subpar rounds to earn an impressive nine-stroke victory in the Ohio State Open at the Walnut Hill Country Club in Columbus.

Nicklaus not only provided motivation for Weiskopf's first professional win; he served as transportation. Five days before winning in Ohio, Tom had missed the cut in the Seattle Open, but decided to remain in town and hit the practice range. The Golden Bear—who had already earned enough on tour to afford his own plane—offered to fly Weiskopf from Seattle to the Columbus event. Immediately after Nicklaus completed his final round (he finished ninth), the former Buckeye teammates, along with Youngstown pro and future PGA tour official Ed Griffiths, made the grueling trek back to the Midwest.

"We left Seattle at six p.m.," Weiskopf told reporters following his victory. "We had to stop in Salt Lake City and Omaha for refueling and landed in Columbus at nine thirty a.m. It was a little bumpy so we didn't get too much sleep."

That first full season on tour in 1965, Weiskopf banked just under $12,000—good enough to reach the top seventy-five on the money list and second among rookies. The praise he received from his peers meant much more to him.

"Actually, it gives me confidence to know that other players think that much of me," he said. "They come and congratulate you, and you know they're the best, and it makes you feel good. It flatters you. Ken Venturi has called me the longest, most consistent driver on tour. I think Jack is."

Not long before dying in a tragic plane accident, "Champagne" Tony Lema told Weiskopf, "I'd like to have what you're going to make in the next ten years."

And Tom took fierce pride in *how* he had built himself up.

"Everything I've gained in golf I've done it by myself," he said in the summer of 1965. "I feel I might try harder on my own. It would be more personal pride if I make it. I'm about even for the five months I've been on tour this year."

Several great chances for a first PGA victory slipped through Weiskopf's hands in early 1966. He finished in the top five four times during the spring, including a heartbreaking loss to Doug Sanders on the second hole of a play-off at the Greensboro Open.

"I hadn't had much experience in big amateur tournaments because I couldn't afford it," Weiskopf recalled a few years later, "and I didn't have the patience and concentration to win out here."

But that summer, Weiskopf did win the heart of a nineteen-year-old beauty queen. Jeanne Marie Ruth, Miss Minnesota of 1965, fell for Tom while handing out invitations to the Minnesota Golf Classic in St. Paul in July.

"I had seen Tom and thought he was quite handsome, and I was hoping to be introduced to him and maybe be asked for a date," Jeanne remembered. "Well, I handed him his invitation, and he thanked me and just walked away!

I was crestfallen. But we ran into one another on the course later in the week, and he asked me if I'd like to do something that evening.

"He seemed so lonesome," she added. "I was sure he didn't like me. I decided I would be like a sister to him—write him letters while he was traveling to cheer him up. We didn't see each other much until we were engaged later that summer; then Tom started commuting from the tour to St. Paul—I think he was pleading nonexistent illnesses and deliberately missing the cut sometimes—and we were married in October, three months after we met."

Along with several young tour couples, Jeanne joined her husband on the road, enjoying (at least for a time) the glamorous perks of each tour stop: the travel, interviews, fashion shows, and luncheons, as well as the pride of walking beside her husband on every hole.

"Watching Tom improve is thrilling," she said.

But Jeanne's first impression of Weiskopf never truly changed.

"Tom is basically a lonely person. He thinks most of the time. Now he thinks about the difference between being good and great."

Like Jeanne, Weiskopf himself noticed how his mood affected his performance.

"I'm so darn moody. I can feel great one minute and sluggish the next. Gee whiz, it used to take me three holes to get over a poor shot. I got discouraged too quick," Tom said. "Jeanne's wonderful. She doesn't know golf, but she knows me. She's witty and has a little streak of sarcasm in her. She can jar me out of my bad moods. She'll come up to me on the course and tell me how silly I look pouting."

Jeanne also helped Tom mend a growing *physical* ailment that may have been tied to his self-destructive moods. During the 1966 season, Weiskopf reportedly lost twenty pounds when the lining of his stomach started to deteriorate. As his health improved, he attributed much of the recovery to Jeanne. In fact, when Tom assumed the fifty-four-hole lead at the Bob Hope Desert Classic in February 1967, he pointed to Jeanne's presence in his gallery—and her newly acquired culinary skills—to explain his success.

Although he enjoyed moderate financial success on tour, Weiskopf remained sullen and dour, both on and off the course. His was more an inner than an outer boil, manifesting itself in these periodic stomach ailments (he regularly hinted at having ulcers) and self-destructive play rather than emotional venting.

Nonetheless, through all the physical and emotional ailments, Weiskopf's game became more consistent over the next two years, even though he rarely put himself in a position to win. At the U.S. Open at Baltusrol in 1967, he shot four steady rounds and finished fifteenth, twelve shots behind Nicklaus's record-setting performance. He reached thirtieth place on the earnings list at the end of his third full year on tour.

In February 1968, Weiskopf finally broke through and won his first PGA event, the Andy Williams San Diego Open. After an opening-round 66 at Torrey Pines, he braved unusually cold weather to take the thirty-six-hole lead by one stroke over Dave Hill. Nicklaus and Al Geiberger caught him the following day, but on Sunday, the "likable young fellow from Bedford, Ohio," shot a final-round 68 to earn $30,000 in first-place prize money. Tom saved the tournament's best drama for the seventy-second hole.

Thirteen under par for the tournament and tied with Geiberger and a late-charging Raymond Floyd, Weiskopf stroked a bold second shot that carried over the water and stopped just shy of the green on the dramatic par-five finishing hole.

"I was trying to get it close and make four," Weiskopf said. "Then [Geiberger would] have to sink his putt to tie me."

But to Weiskopf's delight, his putt off the apron curved, curled, and found the cup for a brilliant eagle three to close out Geiberger.

"I played real well all the way. It's probably the best four rounds I've put together. I only made five bogeys in the tournament and I didn't three-putt a green in seventy-two holes," Weiskopf noted.

"It's probably the biggest day of my career."

Handsome, awesomely powerful, married to a charming, down-to-earth beauty queen, and moving steadily toward the top of his profession, Tom Weiskopf had seemingly arrived. As Nicklaus, Snead, Venturi, and Lema had predicted, his promise looked boundless.

That was until the spring.

In March 1968, Weiskopf received the greatest thrill that young pros on tour ever experience: his first invitation to the Masters. Besides an admirable sixteenth-place finish, Weiskopf thrilled the Augusta National gallery as the only competitor who could consistently match Nicklaus in distance. At the famed par-five fifteenth—fronted entirely by water that guards a wickedly shallow green—the two Ohio State products were the only golfers who hit the ball far enough and high enough to hold the firm green in two. Both reached with two-irons and scored easy birdies, a feat Weiskopf replicated in each of his four rounds.

But the Tuesday before the Masters began, Weiskopf had been summoned to Columbus by his draft board to take an army physical. With the Vietnam War at its peak, the goal was to determine whether he was fit for military induction. Granted a week's deferment to play in the Masters, he darted back to Columbus immediately afterward at the behest of Uncle Sam, an excursion that would soon become routine for him.

Still holding down second place on the money list by mid-June, Weiskopf played very well in the U.S. Open at Rochester's Oak Hill Country Club, finishing twenty-fourth. A month later, he became a two-time PGA winner with a swarm of Sunday back-nine birdies at the Buick Open in Grand Blanc, Michigan. Despite a bogey on the eighteenth, he closed with a 69 to outlast tour rookie Mike Hill, add $25,000 to his yearly tally, and reclaim the top spot on the PGA money list.

Unfortunately, a rash of poor performances during the next three months, most notably missing the cut at the last major championship, the PGA, had Weiskopf ending the season on a disappointing note and dropped him far behind in the money race.

But this was hardly Tom's biggest career concern. On October 26, he headed south to Fort Polk, Louisiana, to begin active military duty: his mandatory eight weeks of basic training followed by MOS (specialty) training—in Tom's case, the rather sweet assignment of learning to be a clerk in his army reserve unit. As a high-profile tour professional among golf-crazy generals and other high-ranking officers, Weiskopf soon spent as much time on military golf courses as he did at a desk. After completing active duty, Weiskopf admitted that the only aspect of his game that actually suffered at Fort Polk was his putting. And while he claimed not to resent the four-month disruption to his career, he later admitted that the next five years of "dumb meetings" in Columbus (which he estimated cost him $6,000 a year in extra travel expenses) bordered on the absurd.

"I guard the United States," he said sarcastically, several years after beginning reserve duties. "I sit there every Monday night and play tiddledy winks for four hours. It's something I look forward to, flying back all the time to the reserves."

Weiskopf would qualify those remarks—"It hasn't helped me, but it's an obligation everybody has. I'm grateful to the country that allows me to make such a good living"—but some bitterness on his part was probably warranted. Unquestionably, Weiskopf got special treatment shaped around his career needs; he was allowed to fill his reserve obligation by four-hour stints every Monday night, rather than a full weekend each month, which would have seriously hampered his career. Still, even during the height of the draft and the Vietnam War, very few young tour members had their careers impeded by military duty of any kind. Weiskopf's service in the reserves, no matter how casual, was in fact *not* an "obligation" most young professional golfers in the 1960s were compelled to fulfill.

Weiskopf's active duty ended in late February 1969, and he immediately returned to the tour. In the opening round of the Doral in Miami—where he had finished second the previous spring—he carded a one under 71 and finished twenty-sixth in his first event in nearly five months. A week later, he continued to show no effects of his tour hiatus. Shooting a brilliant 32 on the back nine to share the first-round lead, he ultimately finished tied for sixth in the Florida Citrus Open. And, on the eve of his second Masters appearance, he fought his way into a tie for the final-round lead in the Greensboro Open before losing to Gene Littler in a play-off.

Weiskopf then reclaimed his spot as the tour's most promising young star at Augusta National. Playing beside Nicklaus during the opening two rounds, he scored back-to-back 71s that kept him within five strokes of front-running Billy Casper. A bogey-free Saturday moved "the tall and stately Columbuson by way of Cleveland" to within three strokes heading into the final eighteen holes. His confidence soared.

"I'm looking forward to winning it, just like everybody else," he said. "I just hope I play well. If I can putt a little better tomorrow, I'll be right there." And Tom was indeed "right there" on Sunday, until an errant tee shot on the seventeenth (compounded by an unfavorable bounce off a television cart) dropped him into a tie for second place.

"Sure, I'm disappointed. I must have played better from tee to green than anybody in the field," Weiskopf said. "It's great to finish second, but there are only so many major tournaments, and how many times do you have the chance to win?"

Over the next four years, that candid question would come to haunt Tom Weiskopf.

• • •

FOLLOWING HIS RUNNER-UP FINISH IN the Masters in 1969, Weiskopf finished the season strong: posting eight top-ten finishes, making the cut in both the U.S. Open and the PGA Championship, and earning nearly $100,000. And in November, at Pete Dye's new Harbour Town Golf Links in Hilton Head, he again made a run at a title. He entered the weekend tied with Palmer for the lead, but consecutive rounds over par dropped him into a four-way tie for ninth.

But for the next three seasons, Weiskopf's career began to stall; no matter how well he played, he just couldn't win tournaments. He would periodically climb to the top of the leaderboards, only to falter in the later rounds. In 1970, despite playing consistently well, he again went winless on tour, coming very close to victories in Atlanta, Memphis, and Massachusetts, only to suffer final-round letdowns.

Still, Weiskopf's steady improvement validated his enormous hype—the same hype that had led to a June 1968 *Golf Digest* cover story tabbing him "The Man to Succeed Arnold Palmer." Even though he didn't win in 1970, he posted the lowest scoring average and should have edged out Lee Trevino for the Vardon Trophy. (Under stringent tour rules, Weiskopf had filed his application for a Class A PGA membership two days too late to be granted a full membership, and was therefore ineligible for the Vardon until the following year.)

When he returned to Augusta National in 1971 for a fourth try at a Green Jacket, Weiskopf again played his way to the top of the early leaderboard. Late in the second round, he grabbed the lead at five under par before a bogey on the eighteenth, combined with strong finishes by others later in the day, knocked him two shots off the pace.

"There's no doubt in my mind, I think I'm going to win this tournament. I'm so confident I can play this golf course. I'm going to play great the rest of the week," Weiskopf proclaimed. "I'm hitting it as good as I've ever hit it in my life. I don't feel I've misplayed a shot in the last thirty holes, an iron shot anyway."

Some of that confidence evaporated the following afternoon when bogeys on numbers fifteen and sixteen forced Weiskopf to admit he was "not feeling too swift." An even-par 72 on Sunday gave him another excellent finish (tied for sixth), but, as was all too frequently the case throughout his career, even in his hometown he was relegated to "Columbus's other hope," as Nicklaus chased Charles Coody for the Masters title.

In June 1971, Weiskopf finally returned to the winner's circle. In a tense four-man play-off at the Kemper Open in Charlotte, he rolled in a birdie putt on the first extra hole to edge out Gary Player, Lee Trevino, and Dale Douglass.

"I was so nervous at the extra hole after the other fellows had missed their birdie putts that I was shaking," he told reporters shortly after exploding with joy when his fifth consecutive birdie dropped (he made four birdies to close out the round, then another to win the play-off). "I had to back away from the ball. Then I stepped up and it was a straight putt and it went in. I really don't know how long it was, but Gary said it was seven or eight feet."

The sweet taste of his first victory in nearly three years quickly soured; in Weiskopf's worst U.S. Open performance, he missed the cut the next week at Merion with a nightmare second round of 83. "[I] lost my concentration and my desire to keep playing," he said about his horrendous start (triple bogey followed by bogey) to start the day.

Things only got worse during the summer, including a lackluster performance in the British Open at Royal Birkdale. But Weiskopf's hopes for another victory rose considerably when he headed in mid-August to Sutton, Massachusetts, and Pleasant Valley Country Club, where he looked to take advantage of a depleted field, i.e., no Nicklaus, Palmer, or Trevino.

Weiskopf made his case quickly as the top star when only one other golfer, journeyman John Schlee, bested him by a single stroke on the first day. During the next two rounds, despite missing several makeable birdie putts, Weiskopf kept within two strokes of the lead. But everything fell apart on Sunday. Though unable to keep pace with the leaders, Weiskopf still came to the seventeenth in line for another top finish. That was until he totally lost his concentration and followed a double bogey on the seventeenth with a triple bogey on the eighteenth to shoot 78, dropping him from a share of fifth place to an eight-way tie for thirty-sixth and a meager check of $710.

Weiskopf erupted in the locker room. "I'm withdrawing from every tournament for the remainder of the year," he told reporters. "I mean it. I've taken time off from the tour and I'm going to do it again."

This was the type of whining that led the media increasingly to tag him as the "Towering Inferno." And it was no idle threat. After a second-place finish to Billy Casper the previous August (1970) at the same Pleasant Valley course,

Weiskopf had complained to reporters, "[If] I could putt, I'd beat everyone out here." That frustration had prompted Weiskopf to withdraw from the tour for nearly four months at the end of the 1970 season, taking a prolonged hunting "vacation."

Bucky Woy—the agent who managed Lee Trevino and who also had an agreement to manage Weiskopf until Weiskopf "remembered," six months later, that he already had representation—knew the impact that a poor round could have on his would-be client.

"He couldn't stand being bugged [by the media] after an unfortunate round," wrote Woy, who, despite their business mishap, considered Tom and Jeanne Weiskopf close friends. "One of his detracting points is a high-pitched voice, which sounds babyish when he complains. He often sulked, pouted, and was curt with writers because he was disappointed with his own performance." A few years later, at the height of his career, Weiskopf admitted he nearly left the game at several stages of his young career.

"Sometimes I used to get so down on myself that it was terrible. I got so upset when I didn't hit every shot perfectly and win every tournament that I thought seriously about quitting the tour."

Perhaps Jeanne intervened to end to her husband's latest public pouting, but in any event, Weiskopf headed to the Whitemarsh Valley Country Club for the Philadelphia Classic. The "City of Brotherly Love" was, in fact, well-known in the sports world for its harsh spectators and ultracritical press, so Weiskopf's decision to resume playing there carried risks. Not only was his embarrassing blowup in Massachusetts fresh in everyone's mind, but his prior record in Philadelphia earned him few friends.

In 1970, Weiskopf had stormed out of the scorer's tent at the Philadelphia Classic after an opening-round 77 (which featured a quadruple bogey on the par-three ninth) without signing his card, essentially withdrawing from the tournament. He was convinced shortly afterward by a sympathetic tour official to sign his card, but two days later, his first-round card was declared invalid because he had not submitted it "as soon as possible" following the round. Only seven shots behind the leaders following a great comeback on Friday and Saturday, Weiskopf ultimately decided to withdraw before the final round on Sunday because he did not "feel that he could rightfully compete and accept prize money when he had in fact violated a rule."

Nevertheless, Weiskopf returned to Philadelphia in 1971, and after three superlative rounds he led by three strokes. In Sunday's finale, "Weiskopf, the introvert, and [Dave] Hill, the extrovert," stood tied at the turn, with Hill playing one group ahead. Several clutch, one-putt par saves put Weiskopf ahead, and when he sank a long putt for birdie on the sixteenth, he grabbed a two-stroke lead over the fiery Hill. Then, on the short par-five seventeenth, Weiskopf answered Hill's eagle with an eagle of his own. Even though his drive found the rough, he smoked a seven-iron to twelve feet and, anxiously aware of what was at stake, made the putt.

"When I walked up to the creek [in front of the green] I wasn't really checking anything," he said about that critical putt to maintain a two-shot lead. "I was nervous and I was just trying to slow myself up."

With the cushion provided by his third eagle of the week, Weiskopf bogeyed the eighteenth (after missing another fairway), but still held off Hill for his fourth PGA victory.

"I proved something to myself . . . I won this more on desire and determination than good golf. . . . I talked myself into winning this tournament, and I'm a better man . . . and I think a better golfer, for it."

The win sparked Weiskopf to a strong finish in the 1971 season. The next week, at the lucrative $200,000 national match-play championship at Pinehurst, he toppled Raymond Floyd in the quarterfinals, then barely missed advancing to the finals that afternoon by losing on the second play-off hole. He closed out the season with eighth, twentieth, and thirty-first place finishes before missing the cut at his final tour stop in early December.

In a season of highs and lows, Weiskopf managed to top the $100,000 mark for the second time; he also topped the half-million-dollar mark in total earnings for his eight-year career. Two victories and his solid recovery from the debacle in Massachusetts reassured many golf pundits that despite his temperamental outbursts, Weiskopf belonged among the tour's elite. Once the 1972 season began, the New York Times's Arthur Daley and Golf Digest's Nick Seitz— believing that he was "now mature"—predicted Weiskopf would finally break through and win his first major championship.

And that season, Weiskopf darted out quickly, scoring his fifth career win by edging out Nicklaus in the Jackie Gleason Inverrary Classic to win $52,000— the largest single payday in golf history. During the summer, he came closer to fulfilling the prophecies of greatness than at any previous time in his career. At the U.S. Open in Pebble Beach, he took eighth place for his best finish in seven

Open tries. A month later at Muirfield, he again reached the top ten of a major championship with a sparkling final round of 69 in the British Open.

But it was another Masters letdown earlier in the 1972 season that continued to haunt Weiskopf. During a practice round at Augusta, he shot a 67 and oozed confidence.

"I'm playing as well as I was when I won at Inverrary," the number two man on the money list reported.

After a slow start left him five strokes off the lead, Weiskopf surged ahead with precise iron play in the second and third rounds, and climbed into a tie for third with eighteen holes to play. Had a few short putts fallen—he missed five from inside ten feet, including two four-footers—Weiskopf could well have led the tournament.

"I turned a sixty-four into a seventy," he complained. "The back nine was probably as fine a nine holes as I've ever played."

In what was becoming a painful stigma, Tom could not wrestle away a major championship from the Golden Bear on a final Sunday. The implosion occurred early: Three bogeys over the opening four holes cost him dearly, and by the turn he trailed his playing partner, Nicklaus, by five shots. Though Weiskopf gained three strokes on Nicklaus during the back nine, every potential challenger eventually faltered; as usual, Nicklaus did exactly what it took to preserve his lead and win his fourth Masters title.

"I tried my darnedest out there today, and that's the best I could do," Weiskopf said about his second-place finish in the Masters (despite a closing round of 74). "He's the greatest golfer there is in the game. I was three strokes behind. That's a pretty big task—to come from three strokes behind and beat him."

Reporters scrutinized every moment as the game's biggest bombers were paired together during a major-championship Sunday. And on the eighteenth fairway, the former college teammates stopped briefly to share a moment of reflection.

"I said, 'I wish I could have given you a better fight. . . . I'll get you next time.'"

WEISKOPF CLOSED OUT 1972 WITH another victory as a professional, albeit not an official PGA triumph. Lashing towering drives that "turned the 6,997-yard Wentworth course into a toy," Weiskopf won October's Piccadilly World

Match Play Championship in England, 4 & 3, over Lee Trevino. In a thirty-three-hole finale, he carded two eagles and six birdies to topple the crowd and pretournament favorite.

At his opening tournament in 1973, Weiskopf broke par during each round of the Los Angeles Open at Riviera; he tied for second, by far his best performance at that high-profile event. More good news came that week when he learned that Jeanne, pregnant with their second child, was about to give birth. Weiskopf left preparations for the Phoenix Open and flew home to Columbus, where their son joined his two-year-old sister shortly afterward.

Sadly, the Weiskopfs' jubilation surrounding their second child's safe arrival soon gave way to profound sadness.

As a late Christmas present to his father, who had recently been diagnosed with brain cancer, Weiskopf gave his parents a trip to the Bing Crosby Pro-Am Tournament at Pebble Beach. With Tom just a few strokes behind after two rounds, his father's condition worsened and he was taken to a nearby hospital. The next day, Weiskopf shot an understandably distracted 84 (he missed the fifty-four-hole cut), and the entire family returned to Cleveland, where his father's prognosis was poor.

Although Weiskopf soon returned to competition, the stress and pressures of dealing with both a newborn and a dying father proved more than he could handle. In his first start since learning of his father's illness, he withdrew following the second round of the Andy Williams San Diego Open—after he and fellow pro Bob Goalby nearly came to blows during a locker-room shouting match.

"While my father was ill, I just couldn't seem to get with it," Weiskopf said later.

Nonetheless, Weiskopf steadied himself after the Goalby imbroglio and made the cut in consecutive weeks at Inverrary and the Citrus Open. The following Sunday at Doral, he pushed Trevino to the end with a closing-round 67, capped by a twenty-five-foot birdie on the legendary fountain hole. Tom took runner-up honors and just under $14,000 in prize money to show his dying father.

The following Wednesday, on March 14, with his eldest son playing in a pro-am event prior to the Jacksonville Open, Thomas Mannix Weiskopf died at age sixty. Tom immediately withdrew and returned to Cleveland, where a service was held that Friday morning at St. Pius X Church.

Weiskopf took two weeks off to grieve with family before returning to the tour, first at the Greensboro Open and then, in mid-April, at the Masters. He played valiantly in both, finishing twenty-ninth in North Carolina and thirty-fourth at Augusta.

"My father told me he lived and died for my golf. He told me if I set my goals higher I could be as good as the rest of them," he said two months later. "I was upset at the Masters, naturally. It got down to the point [i.e., before the Masters, when he knew that his father was dying] where I didn't spend time practicing. My father was being put back in the hospital before then, but it was not a mental thing. It was just no time for practicing.

"Two weeks after the Masters I started thinking to myself, 'Things have got to change. I've got to start working on my game.'"

With his father's expectations weighing on him, that was exactly what Weiskopf did.

He started drilling daily on putting—easily the facet of his game that had plagued him most in crucial moments.

"When I used to have a week off," he told a Columbus reporter at the couple's lovely Tudor home in Upper Arlington, "I wouldn't do anything and I wasn't sharp when I got back on the tour. I'd play halfway good, but I wouldn't really get it back until the second week."

Inevitably, it all came back to Nicklaus.

"Jack's the only guy who can virtually turn it on when he wants to, but I think even he plays or practices a little more between tournaments. But he's so great he can play bad and still win."

A month under the new training regimen yielded results. Near the end of April, Weiskopf flew to Dallas for the Byron Nelson Classic, where, despite a disappointing final round of 73, he earned a share of eighth place. And he capped off the tour's three-week Texas swing (after the Byron Nelson, he missed the cut at the Houston Open) with a brilliant victory—the sixth official win of his ten-year PGA career—at the Colonial Invitational in Fort Worth.

Although some writers downgraded Weiskopf's triumph by emphasizing Bruce Crampton's collapse in the tournament's final moments, it took four straight rounds of par or better to earn Tom the win. He put pressure on Crampton by rolling in a thirty-foot birdie on the sixteenth from just off the green—his fourth long birdie putt of the afternoon—but a bogey on the seventeenth seemingly cost him a chance at a play-off. Crampton, the hottest player on tour, needed only a par on the final hole for his fourth victory of the early 1973 season. But he played the hole "like a duffer," duck-hooking his drive and breaking his sand wedge en route, and scoring a double bogey to lose to Weiskopf by one shot.

"It's a heck of a way to win a golf tournament," Weiskopf admitted. "I know how Bruce felt. I've done it. I'm happy, but it's sort of a sick feeling. Oh, it's a happy win, but not exciting. But like Jack Nicklaus says, you've got to play all seventy-two holes to the end."

Within two weeks, Tom tested that sentiment in an exciting second-place finish to Nicklaus at the Atlanta Golf Classic. Starting in second place and six strokes behind, Weiskopf seemingly shot himself out of the tournament. His second shot on the opening hole smacked a female spectator on the head, leading to a bogey. He followed that with a disastrous approach shot on the fourth that landed in a pond and resulted in a double bogey. Weiskopf now trailed the leader, Nicklaus, by ten strokes after six holes.

"I really didn't think I could win after I got ten down. [But after teeing off], I was so charged up, I wasn't thinking. I was just charged out there trying to catch up too quick. It always happens to me; I get too aggressive and take silly shots," he admitted.

But the "new" Weiskopf—the confident, fully committed, more emotionally mature Weiskopf—emerged on number seven. There he rolled in the first of five birdies to close out the day and shoot his eighth consecutive round of par or better.

"Up to then I was trying to score as low as possible; then my thought became to win . . . a different attitude. I had to watch it and not make dumb mistakes. I had no intention of trying to reach eighteen in two shots. I played very well the last six holes."

Nicklaus, on the other hand, could make no birdies down the stretch and posted bogeys on the ninth, tenth, and twelfth holes. Weiskopf's third consecutive birdie on number fifteen cut the Golden Bear's lead to three shots.

Still, nothing—not even a dachshund that moseyed in front of him as he prepared to hit his drive off the final tee, or a thunderstorm minutes later—could unnerve Nicklaus enough to throw away a double-digit, final-round lead. Weiskopf finished two strokes behind Nicklaus in second place.

"I'm glad I made it a tournament," he told the crowd at the awards presentation, "interesting for you folks."

On the heels of the best back-to-back finishes of his career, Weiskopf moved just north to the familiar Quail Hollow course in North Carolina, the site of his play-off victory at the Kemper Open two years earlier. As in 1971, the Nicklaus-less field hosted the rest of the tour's big names—Palmer, Trevino, Player, top-money-earner Crampton, and the flashiest of the young lions, Lanny Wadkins. Weiskopf had earned more money playing the Kemper Open than any other man in the field, so his confidence was high.

Weiskopf picked up right where he left off in Atlanta. Four birdies on the first seven holes yielded a 65 and a one-stroke lead over Wadkins, who was nearly as hot. But a few weeks of outstanding play were not enough to erase the media's long-standing doubts about how dedicated Weiskopf really was to joining the game's all-time greats.

"A lot of skeptics find it hard to believe that Tom Weiskopf is serious about his golf game," noted a local reporter. "They keep seeing him reeling off rounds like his seven under par 65 in the first round of the Kemper Open Thursday and they wonder when the other Tom Weiskopf—the one with the fiery temper and foreboding looks and the one who went off on a hunting trip when things were going bad on the golf tour—will emerge."

Weiskopf did not dodge the skeptics. Indeed, he seemed eager to explain his sudden turnaround in his own terms.

"Let's face it . . . I'm not getting smarter. Things that happen on the course don't upset me now like they used to. Then, too, I've decided that discipline is the key to the entire thing." With that wonderful touch of Weiskopf hubris that perhaps sought to camouflage self-doubt, he continued. "Take the other day when I was home and played a round with some friends at the Ohio State course. It took us almost five hours to play; then I went out and hit balls for three more hours. I was hitting the ball so good at the end I almost wanted to applaud. . . . The only thing I've been doing different is that I'm devoting more of my spare time to practice. When I have a poor putting round now, I'll go out and work on my putting, where before I probably would have said to hell with it."

During Saturday afternoon's third round, Weiskopf surged ahead and built a two-stroke lead, thanks to four back-nine birdies that inspired his third consecutive round of 68.

"I won't play it conservative; I'm an aggressive player," he insisted when talking about his strategy for the final round.

Paired with Wadkins in the last round, Weiskopf started spectacularly, posting a four under 32 on the front nine that was sparked by three consecutive birdies. The last birdie signaled that no one was going to stop him from taking the top prize that week. When his tee shot on the 548-yard, par-five ninth landed so close to a tree that he couldn't take a full swing, Tom boldly smacked a one-iron into the adjacent fairway. He then pitched to three feet and made his birdie to push his lead to four strokes. From there he coasted with an even-par back nine for the victory.

"I've always considered myself a good putter, but I can't imagine anybody putting better for three weeks in a row than I [was] putting at the Colonial, Atlanta, and here. I'm not saying it's easy. But it's almost easy for me. I just feel so good," he told reporters. "I wanted to win so badly last night I didn't sleep well at all. The way I looked at it is if I didn't win, it would be a shame because I'm playing so well. I felt the pressure on me to win. That's why this win means so much to me."

The triumph at Kemper gave Tom the first repeat victory of his career—a feat he set out to duplicate the very next week when the tour returned to Whitemarsh Valley Country Club for the IVB Philadelphia Open. And this time, the field included Jack Nicklaus.

Weiskopf made an early statement to his doubters, following up an even-par front nine with a breathtaking five under 31 on the back. He stumbled a bit on Friday (though he posted five birdies, he also ran into a string of bogeys), and trailed an unknown twenty-three-year-old pro, Jim Barber, by six strokes after the weekend cut.

"Who is Jim Barber? I never heard of him," Weiskopf wondered aloud in an unintended display of arrogance that delighted reporters but upset his tour colleagues. "That's a great score, but I'm not out of this yet."

Weiskopf certainly was not out of it, and to back up his remarks he fired eight birdies against just one bogey on Saturday. Unshaken by frequent wildness off the tee, he relied on precision putting to scramble brilliantly, one-putting eight greens. After the round, he led by three shots.

"My attitude is always positive, no more negative thoughts," he said. "I think I finally know what makes me tick. I set some high goals after the Masters and now I'm setting higher ones. I have no new shots, but I'm making all the makeable putts, and I'm not making any silly mistakes. Maybe it's maturity . . . or experience . . . or confidence."

Unlike the raw nerves he had experienced at the Kemper Open, Weiskopf slept soundly the night before the final round in Philadelphia, and he was not shy about predicting the outcome.

"I was driving out to the course before the final round and told my wife, Jeanne, 'They're not going to beat me.' Someone would have to shoot an exceptional round to catch me, because I knew I wasn't going to shoot over par. It may sound cocky but that's the way I felt."

Again, Weiskopf drove wildly during the final round, missing seven fairways; he also lost his putting touch and three-putted three greens. But no one in the stellar field seriously challenged him—though Nicklaus did match the day's low, 67—and Weiskopf calmly closed out with a par on the eighteenth for his third victory of the young, topsy-turvy season. He not only had his seventeenth consecutive par-or-better round; he set a PGA tour record by winning $117,145 in just four weeks. The three wins and one runner-up finish meant more to him than the dollars.

"Winning is the hardest thing to do," he stated. "There's always pressure on you, whether you win by one or six. If I don't get an ulcer in the next month it will be an amazing thing. Someone, I don't remember who, said that we all create our own pressures. I think that's true. If you stand there and think about water to the right and trap to the left and the trouble and all the things that can go wrong, you're creating your own pressure. But if you stand over the shot and say, 'I have the ability to execute this shot,' then commit yourself to it, well, that's something else."

In a matter of weeks, Weiskopf had at last begun to demonstrate that he fit securely among the tour's elite. He blew away the field. He won with less-than-stellar play. He came from behind to win. He won with fine putting. He won with his trademark booming drives. He even outplayed the tour's undisputed master at Philadelphia.

But, fittingly, it was Nicklaus who pointed out the gaping hole that remained on Weiskopf's résumé.

"I've always said that Tom has more talent than anybody in the game," Nicklaus told a hometown reporter from Columbus just before the start of the 1973 U.S. Open. "But he's been slow to use it. He's finally taking advantage of what he's always had. The big test for Tom is a major championship. He needs one of those wins to set him off. So far, he's been his own worst enemy."

The Golden Bear was not alone in believing that before Weiskopf could authentically wear the crown of greatness, he needed to triumph on the game's most grueling battlefields, the major championships. A close pal, former British Open champion Tony Jacklin, echoed Nicklaus's sentiment.

"It should have happened five years ago," Jacklin said. "He has better temperament because he is maturing. I'm not surprised at all the way he has been playing. I wouldn't be surprised if he won seven in a row. He's the only man who could beat Nicklaus. He can hit the ball farther and his swing is as good as Jack's, but Nicklaus has the perfect temperament. But Weiskopf can't be regarded as a great player until he wins a major tournament."

Weiskopf himself readily conceded what a victory in one of the big-four major championships would mean for his career and self-esteem.

"I feel I'm an awful good player but the great players win the major tournaments. The U.S. Open is the premier tournament because of the shots it requires . . . every facet requires a premium," he told reporters on the eve of the seventy-third U.S. Open at Oakmont.

"I can't put myself in the class of Nicklaus or Trevino or Palmer—can't call myself great—unless I win a major championship."

Weiskopf left no doubt: At Oakmont, he would be chasing greatness.

BILLY CASPER'S CONCESSION THAT WEISKOPF'S extraordinary length provided a decided advantage at Oakmont only bolstered Weiskopf's belief that this was his moment to win a major.

"I've driven well the last three tournaments. Why should I lay up now?" he asked. "I think these fairways are the widest I've ever seen for the Open—I may eat my words later in the week—but they almost have to be because of the greens. They're what it really boils down to. Once you get to the green, your work is cut out for you."

A bit overshadowed on opening day—he was paired with Gary Player during the South African's record-tying 67—Weiskopf was unable to extend his par-or-better streak when he shot a two-over-par 73.

"But I'm not discouraged. It could have easily been a seventy, by making a few putts. I missed five putts between eight and twelve feet for birdies.

"[It] was those greens that did it. But I'll be back tomorrow."

Alert to the unspoken, yet obvious Nicklaus-Weiskopf rivalry regarding who was longer off the tee, reporters probed the younger Buckeye for commentary on Nicklaus's first-round eagle two on number seventeen.

"The wind wasn't behind my back," he said. "But if Jack can drive it on the green, I can drive it on the green."

Weiskopf shot "a very easy sixty-nine" on Friday to climb back into the hunt. Though experiencing some trouble off the tee that sent him scurrying afterward to the driving range—"I'm trying to drive it right to left, but I'm hitting the ball straight"—Weiskopf maintained a solid position at the halfway point, locked in a tie for sixth. His total of even-par 142 meant that only five players owned better scores.

"I feel I'm in excellent position to win this tournament," he said afterward. "Five strokes in an Open is nothing, and quite truthfully, I feel lean and mean."

Gene Borek, the Long Island club professional who broke the course record with a second-round 65, was Weiskopf's unlikely partner on Saturday. And not surprisingly, the understated career club professional and the rich, brash touring pro had little in common.

"Weiskopf mainly kept to himself," Borek remembered years later. "He came across as a somewhat aloof kind of guy; you felt that when he walked into the locker room, he could see right through you. Most guys say hello and give you some kind of acknowledgment when they pass by you in the locker room. With Weiskopf on some days, it was like you didn't exist."

Weiskopf drove the ball exceptionally well on Saturday, missing only a single fairway. He overcame an early bogey by sinking midlength birdie putts on numbers three and five, only to have a three-putt on the eighth drop him back to even par for the tournament, and more than a half dozen strokes behind the leaders. He also was unable to gain a stroke on the par-five ninth, an essential birdie hole for one of the game's longest hitters.

Weiskopf gained ground by sinking a tricky twelve-footer for birdie on the eleventh, but he not only failed to birdie the twelfth but bogeyed the par-five. Comfortably on the green in three, he stared down a slippery, twenty-five-foot birdie putt. Even after Borek—on the same line, a little farther away—showed how slick the green was by putting well past the hole, Weiskopf also stroked too firmly, and the ball galloped beyond Borek's. Weiskopf flailed at the comeback putt, and was lucky to escape with a bogey six.

One over for the last two par-fives, Weiskopf gave vital strokes back to the field precisely where he had to catch up. Tellingly, however, even after botching the twelfth, the Tom Weiskopf of 1973 did not implode; instead, he put his failings in perspective and moved on.

"I knocked my first putt past so hard that I had almost an impossible putt coming back. I was actually afraid I could four-putt," he said. "I was so hot, really steaming. But I said to myself, 'This is ridiculous. You made the mental error, but don't let it ruin your day. Put it behind you.' A couple years ago, a thing like that would have destroyed me. But I'm more patient now."

On number fifteen, Weiskopf's newfound patience paid off. He mishit a four-iron that sailed left and struck a spectator, settling into deep green-side rough. He was left with an unpredictable chip to a green that ran sharply away from him, with a huge, deep bunker looming beyond. Facing another possible disaster, he calmly chopped the ball to within twelve feet of the flagstick, after which he deftly sank the putt.

"It was like an eagle," he acknowledged afterward.

After a solid par on number sixteen, Weiskopf approached the short, par-four seventeenth knowing that this was a birdie opportunity he simply couldn't miss if he wanted to contend for the championship. A well-placed long iron off the tee put him seventy yards from the pin, and after a decent pitch, he rolled in the slick, downhill eighteen-foot birdie to go one under par for the day and the tournament.

At the final hole, Weiskopf again tattooed his drive and stroked a towering high iron onto the green. From twelve feet—still using the vintage Tommy Armour putter he had received earlier that year as a gift—he sank the putt and received "some of the birdie roars from the crowd that had accompanied home-town favorite Arnold [Palmer] most of the day." Weiskopf finished two under par, a second straight 69 that left him only one shot behind the leaders after three rounds.

"After those two birdies on the last two holes, I feel like I'd like to go out and play another eighteen holes," he told reporters. "I don't feel like I'm one stroke behind. My concentration has improved each day of this tournament.

"Somebody's going to have to shoot a heckuva round tomorrow to beat me."

· 8 ·

A Day for All Ages

The marquee matchup for Saturday's round was no doubt the third-to-last: Lee Trevino and Jack Nicklaus. Together, the 2:16 p.m. pairing had won four of the previous six U.S. Open championships. During the early 1970s, no matter where or what the tournament, Nicklaus and Trevino had to be considered the favorites.

Certainly their most famous duel had come two years earlier when, in a Monday-afternoon play-off, Trevino outlasted Nicklaus at Merion for his second U.S. Open title. Nearly as memorable as Trevino's three-stroke victory was his preround icebreaker of tossing a rubber snake at Nicklaus's feet just before they teed off. One female spectator, thinking the snake was real, shrieked so loudly that it broke Nicklaus's normally stoic intensity.

Though the most celebrated, the Merion showdown was not the only time that Trevino got the better of his friend. With one swing the following summer, he stole from Nicklaus both the British Open crown and a realistic shot at the Holy Grail of prizes, modern golf's Grand Slam.

Heading into the final round of the 1972 British Open at Muirfield, the "Happy Hombre" enjoyed a one-stroke lead over former Open champion Tony Jacklin. Nicklaus was six strokes behind Trevino, and it seemed highly unlikely that—following his victories earlier that year at the Masters and the U.S. Open—he could still challenge for the Claret Jug. Six birdies by Nicklaus on the first eleven holes—mainly the result of a decision to boldly use a driver on tees where he'd previously used a long-iron—resurrected hopes of victory. He held the outright lead after a birdie on the long tenth hole, then after Trevino spectacularly eagled the ninth, the Golden Bear tied the Merry Mex by birdying number eleven. Trevino maintained his trademark consistency, despite Nicklaus's charge, and when Nicklaus bogeyed the par-three sixteenth after missing the green, Trevino re-took the lead by a single stroke.

Then apparent disaster struck. On the par-five seventy-first hole, Trevino drove into deep rough, hacked into a bunker, sailed his next shot back into the rough, then buried his fourth stroke into "three inches of heather and thistle," thirty feet above the hole on a lightning-slick green. A double bogey appeared inevitable, opening the door for Nicklaus or Jacklin to overtake Trevino.

Somehow, Trevino popped the ball gently out of the thick clump and—before millions of startled TV viewers and the record-breaking crowd—watched it trickle into the cup. Trevino sheepishly stepped toward the hole and retrieved his ball, having made a par for the ages—never once hitting fairway or green, with the British Open championship on the line. Trevino defeated Nicklaus by a single stroke and Jacklin by two.

In addition to his triumphs at Merion and Muirfield, a four-stroke victory in the 1968 U.S. Open at Oak Hill, and a PGA Championship that would come in 1974, Trevino rendered Nicklaus a runner-up in four major championships during the Golden Bear's golden age. And he again showed up Nicklaus at Oakmont in the third round of the 1973 U.S. Open, beginning on the starting hole.

Trevino—not surprisingly, for he had missed just one of each to this point—nailed both fairway and green on number one, and narrowly failed to convert a long birdie putt that would have placed him within four shots of the leader, Gary Player. While Trevino easily tapped in for par, Nicklaus, whose six-iron approach bounded well over the green, opened to a bogey five.

Each gave up a stroke to par on the remainder of the front nine, with Trevino finishing at 37 and Nicklaus at 38. Nicklaus's score could have been much worse; he rarely hit the fairways and his putting blew hot and cold. A three-putt from forty feet on number nine—where he reached the green in two—already tripled the number of three-putt greens he'd suffered during the entire 1962 U.S. Open championship.

More un-Nicklaus-like play followed on the back nine. He three-putted the tenth green and then found bunkers with two different shots to bogey the "easy" eleventh. "So, I should have been four-four-four and instead I was five-five-five," Nicklaus told his hometown newspaper, "and that was the difference in my round right there."

As Nicklaus stumbled, Trevino's steady tee-to-green excellence gained additional shots on his rival. Two successful birdie putts from short distances on the eleventh and sixteenth gave him a 33 for the back side and a 70 for the day—his second under-par round for the championship. If only he could find the cup, he'd run away with his third U.S. Open championship in six years.

"I've played fifty-four holes and missed only two fairways and two greens; that means I'm not happy with my putting."

He also wasn't happy with his choice of equipment: "I've tried fifteen putters this week," he half joked. And the disadvantage of drawing an inexperienced, shaggy-haired thirteen-year-old caddie didn't help either.

But amidst this flurry of complaints, Trevino stewed most about the absence of privacy.

"People bug me everywhere I go. I know that this is supposed to be the price of fame but it starts to get you after a while. I can't go to a bar and relax over a beer without some guy wanting to put the crushing handshake on me to prove how strong he is . . . My wife is so annoyed that we can't go out to dinner in public that she stays home now. What fun is there sitting around a motel all day by yourself while your husband is out playing golf? . . . The way it's going, I'm looking forward to retiring in a few years and do all the things I like to do—in public as well as in private."

Though not as somber, Nicklaus was similarly frustrated. He had drained a twelve-footer for birdie on the short thirteenth to make up ground, but his three over 74 was his worst score ever at Oakmont. Uncharacteristically, he moved quickly past the press tent and onto the practice tee.

"I won't bore you with my round," he explained as he hurried away.

After an intense practice session, Nicklaus returned to regale writers with his customary wit. Ironically—he was notorious for reducing the speed of a round to a crawl—he even suggested how to reduce slow play. He had apparently resolved the swing flaw that hampered his consistency throughout round three, and remained optimistic he could come from behind on Sunday to defend the U.S. Open crown he'd won the year before at Pebble Beach.

"I've been four strokes behind before, and I can make it up. Things didn't go as I'd planned today, and I caught quite a few sand traps along the way. But as someone else has said, four strokes is nothing on a course like this and in the U.S. Open."

Of course, on a terrain like Oakmont in the U.S. Open, four strokes were just as easy to lose—a lesson that front-running Gary Player learned very quickly that Saturday.

THERE WAS NO SPRINKLER MALFUNCTION on Saturday morning. Instead, natural water resoaked Oakmont, as a stiff rain fell between six and ten a.m., leaving the *entire* course soggier than the day before. Rain continued intermittently throughout the day, and then let up enough by midmorning for U.S.G.A. officials to authorize New Zealand's John Lister to tee off, alone, at 10:21 a.m. (an odd number of golfers made the cut, and with the groupings now pairs instead of threesomes, one man was forced to play without a partner).

Paired with Jim Colbert (a stroke behind), Player drew the final tee time at two thirty p.m. A light drizzle had resumed once the thirty-six-year-old began his round—a fitting scene for the gloom he was about to experience. Player opened with a bogey and then was fortunate to string together four pars. Beginning on number five, his remarkable comeback story wilted as he bogeyed five of the next seven holes.

"His tee shots were flying every which way," a Pittsburgh reporter noted. "His irons were erratic; his putter failed him. A complete and total collapse."

Player's sorrows started to become evident on the sixth tee, as his fans scampered from the fifth green to watch his shot into the par-three hole. The noise from the mass of shuffling spectators in plastic slickers and ponchos so irritated Player that he stepped away from the tee and waited impatiently for everyone to settle down. Still obviously annoyed, at himself as much as his fans, he promptly drove into a bunker and bogeyed the hole. Over the next two holes, poor putting led to two more bogeys, and he made the turn with a score of 40. He took twenty putts, compared to only thirteen for the same stretch on Thursday.

"Player had it the hardest," Jerry Heard noted afterward. "He was playing defensive golf. He was way ahead and all he had to do was make pars."

Everyone in Player's rapidly vanishing gallery also felt his pain. "I feel so sorry for him," said a disappointed female follower. Upon missing a short par saver on the eleventh green, Player smashed the head of his putter into the ground and stared angrily into the distance. He was now six *over* par for the first eleven holes Saturday, whereas he had been six *under* par for the first eleven on Thursday.

Player scored an impressive birdie on the long, par-three sixteenth (his first in twenty-six holes), only to give it back immediately with a bogey on the seventeenth. After completing his round, the normally chatty Player gave no excuses and refused to give interviews to the press. A 77 had left him in no mood for conversation. He ended the day four shots behind the leaders and tied with his old Big Three comrade Nicklaus.

Player's partner in the third round, Jim Colbert, didn't fare much better, and certainly not at the outset. On his way to a three over 74, Colbert opened with bogeys on the first three holes. Fortunate to make consecutive birdies at the close of his round, he remained in the picture tied with Trevino at one under par, two shots behind the leaders.

No one expected a repeat, record-setting performance from Gene Borek on Saturday afternoon. By the end of the day, he returned to club pro anonymity by shooting an 80. Unbeknownst to others, Borek's right shoulder still throbbed following Friday's heroic four-iron from the fairway bunker on number ten. He aggravated the injury on Saturday when he tried, unsuccessfully, to execute a long explosion shot from a wet green-side bunker on number nine.

The greens gnawed at him even more than the shoulder. Wet, arguably even slower on Saturday than on Friday, the putting surfaces still remained precariously slick downhill. Regardless of the level of saturation, the speed and contours of Oakmont's greens still confounded Borek.

"When I shot eighty in the third round, I played pretty well but I three-putted six times. . . . I could have three-putted another six times in that round except I made several good comeback putts."

Once the championship ended, Borek would leave Oakmont with a career-best thirty-sixth-place finish, clutching a piece of U.S. Open history and the battle scars (his shoulder) to prove it.

On Friday, Borek and his playing partner, Bud Allin, together shot the two lowest scores of the day, 65 and 67. While no one on Saturday could match Borek's 65, the two lowest scores of the day, 66 and 67, again came from a single pairing: veteran long shot John Schlee and his hungry young lion playing partner, Jerry Heard.

After a frustrating start to the Open, the congenial Heard left Oakmont Saturday evening tied for the lead.

Blessed with abundant athleticism, the six-foot-three twenty-six-year-old from Visalia, California, had played tackle for Redwood High School's varsity football team, and in a Central Yosemite League track meet even ran the hundred-yard dash in 10.1 seconds.

But Heard was most gifted as a golfer. By age twelve, he had already shot 70 in the Fresno Bee Junior City Golf championship, an event he won four of the following five years. In August 1964—the same month his friend and northern California rival John Miller won the National Junior Amateur—Heard nabbed the California Junior title. He moved on to Fresno State College, where, as a junior, he set the school record for low scoring average in a single season. He then left college without a degree and earned his pro credentials by taking sixth place in the PGA's Q School in October 1968.

Despite a great résumé and a classic golf swing—he channeled great natural power into a rhythmic, seemingly effortless flow—Heard struggled early on the tour. He missed most cuts and could barely make expenses; even in 1970, when he moved up to fifty-fourth on the tour performance chart and earned nearly $45,000, he left his supporters in the red.

"I wasn't doing too well when I first came out here," he later said. "[My] dad told me I had the game and that I just had to have some fun playing."

Heard listened to his father's advice and soon began having more fun. In 1971, he took thirteenth in the U.S. Open, nailed second- and third-place finishes in two other tournaments, nearly tripled his earnings, and burst through for his first victory in the prestigious American Golf Classic at the Firestone Country Club. Suddenly among the tour's top ten in earnings, Heard blew past his California pal John Miller, who also enjoyed his first victory the same year.

The next year, Heard began to make his case as the tour's "next great star." Early in the season at the Bob Hope Desert Classic, he held the lead going into the final round, and ultimately finished third in the star-studded field. His fast start foreshadowed a tremendous stretch over the next three months. In between his second and third tour wins at the Florida Citrus Open in March and the Colonial in May, Heard made a run for the Green Jacket at Augusta National. Two early birdies in the final round pulled him into second place behind Nicklaus; he ultimately finished tied for fifth. After competing well at the U.S. and British Opens, Heard assumed sole possession of the halfway lead in the 1972 PGA Championship, and eventually tied for seventh place.

No other member of the tour's young lions blossomed in 1972 as fully as

Heard: fifth on the money list, and only Nicklaus and Trevino won more tournaments. Heard expected to shine as the new season began.

But during the early months of 1973, Heard just could not take the next steps toward greatness. While he put up a strong fight in trying to defend his title at the Colonial, he finished no higher than sixth in his first nineteen events. And he scored a miserable 80 during the final round of the Masters, to finish second-to-last: Only John Schlee closed out the day and the tournament with worse totals. By May, Heard ranked only thirty-first in earnings.

In Heard's next stab at a major championship, the U.S. Open at Oakmont, the slump seemed to get worse. Heard was partnered with Lee Trevino and J. C. Snead; his opening-round 74 did not reflect how inconsistently he played from tee to green, nor how badly his confidence sagged. Only a marvelous short game saved many pars.

"I had been playing poorly," said Heard, who reminded everyone that two years earlier, during the U.S. Open at Merion, Trevino had taught him how to fade the ball. "Lee Trevino suggested I alter the weights of my irons and switch to a new driver. I dumped the contents of the bag, weighted the irons, and bought a driver in the Oakmont pro shop. That's the first new driver I've used in ten years."

With his new equipment, Heard shaved off four strokes the next afternoon to finish with a two-round score of 144, in a tie for sixteenth place. And while several of the preround leaders—Player, Colbert, Borek, Nicklaus—finished well over par on Saturday, Heard thrashed the already subdued Oakmont ego with the best round of his career.

Every part of Heard's game clicked on Saturday. Splendid from tee to green, he scored easy pars to open the round, then sank a fifteen-footer for a birdie on number three. When his three-wood second shot into the par-five ninth ended up sixty feet from the flagstick, a three putt seemed more than likely. Instead, he drained the monumental putt for an eagle.

"I had to go over two terraces," he said. "It was the best putt I've ever made."

Now one under par for the championship and back in the race, Heard climbed up the leaderboard. On numbers eleven and fourteen, he landed short irons inside of ten feet and one-putted for birdies.

Heard rebounded from a bogey on number fifteen to strike his finest shot of the day from the sixteenth tee. With the course still soft from intermittent rains, he floated a four-wood to within eighteen feet of the cup and rolled in yet another sizable putt.

"I had a couple putts that if there hadn't been any rain I would have gone way past the cup," he said after the round. "Rain is great for a player who misses fairways; he knows he can throw his ball to the green and can make it stop . . . it's just like throwing darts."

And when Heard stuck another shot onto the green on the eighteenth, a chance to tie Gene Borek's 65 came with it. His long birdie putt on the home hole died inches shy of the cup, but the five-under score marked the second-lowest round in Oakmont's history. Although few members of the field broke par that day, Heard believed Oakmont was in "the easiest condition we'll ever find it."

Heard wasn't the only member of his twosome to have a career day on Saturday, or to blister his way into the U.S. Open lead.

John Schlee, a well-traveled thirty-four-year-old in his eighth year on tour, had also experienced a strange opening round. A long hitter, Schlee tallied unpardonable numbers (bogey, double bogey) on Oakmont's two front-side par fives. A pair of birdies on the back nine salvaged his day, for a respectable 73.

The following afternoon, "sprinkler Friday," Schlee started red-hot, birdying three of the opening four holes. His final score of 70 pushed him up the leaderboard into a tie for eleventh place, only six strokes off the lead. Still, Schlee's underdog-makes-good story was lost in the headline-making achievements of Borek, Giles, Ziobro, and Fezler on Friday. In fact, the *Pittsburgh Post-Gazette* added insult to injury by leaving Schlee's name entirely off the list of players. Even during his finest season on tour, Schlee could not sidestep obscurity.

Four months before the U.S. Open, Schlee had won the prestigious Hawaiian Open—the $40,000 payday was more than he'd earned during his first three seasons on tour. And in the months that followed, Schlee twice contended during the final round of notable tournaments. A week after his Hawaii victory, he was the also-ran at the Bob Hope in a final Sunday threesome with Palmer and Nicklaus, ultimately finishing sixth. And just days before traveling across the state from Philadelphia to Pittsburgh, Schlee scored well enough to earn fifth place behind Tom Weiskopf at the IVB Classic.

Several high finishes helped Schlee pay his bills easily—no small achievement for a man who'd barely scraped out a living for much of the past decade. In 1973, Schlee redirected his goals toward the major championships: In four previous majors, two National Opens and two Masters, he had never finished higher than thirty-sixth.

Schlee built on his consistently excellent 1973 play to take top medal honors in the U.S. Open sectional qualifying event at Las Colinas Country Club in his hometown of Dallas, and signed a new lease on golf life.

"In the past, I've put too much emphasis on the major tournaments. I've always practiced too much and too hard. I've never done any good in a major event, I feel, for this reason. So I'm going to go at it different. . . . I'm going to treat it just like another tour tournament. You know, that's the way Ben Hogan did it. I don't know if he and I have much in common, though."

The gangly, garrulous Schlee—though a onetime student of Hogan—could *never* be mistaken for the somber "Wee Ice Mon," as the Scots dubbed him. Neither could his golf game. While Hogan's strategic brilliance and consistent ball striking were legendary, Schlee's swing was quirky; he rarely played an uneventful round. But Schlee posted a magnificent score at Oakmont on Saturday that was once synonymous with Hogan.

Lucky to escape the second hole with a bogey—his tee shot sailed far off-line and lodged in a tree, forcing him to declare an "unplayable lie" and take a penalty stroke—Schlee seemed headed for a typical afternoon of clawing and scratching just to stay near par. He had posted five bogeys, a double bogey, and six birdies during the first two rounds, and had played the six par-five holes miserably in two over par. And even on Saturday, Schlee's erratic play continued: "He was under trees, in the rough, and buried in traps most of the day." Much like his playing partner Heard, however, Schlee's scorecard shimmered.

A birdie on number five returned Schlee to even par. He also birdied the par-five ninth despite landing his approach in thick, green-side rough. And on the fourteenth, he drove into a fairway bunker but recovered to within fifteen feet of the flagstick, then rammed in the putt for another wacky birdie. Seemingly the only "bad break" that befell Schlee on Saturday occurred when his nine-iron into the eleventh green rolled in, then out, of the cup to prevent an electrifying eagle. A very un-Schlee-like birdie on number seventeen—a three-iron off the tee, followed by a wedge to within five feet—knocked another stroke off par. By the end of the day, Schlee's four under 67 (32 on the more difficult back nine) matched Hogan's course record from 1953.

Even more than his swashbuckling style of play, Schlee intrigued the press with his eccentric personality. In the late 1960s, he became curious about his horoscope, and as his career developed, so did his formal study of astrology.

"This is a good week for Gemini," said the June-born Schlee, who persuaded a Pittsburgh reporter's wife to lend him three astrology books so he could stay up-to-date. "Mars is in conjunction with my natal moon. My information was fed to a computer, which didn't know I was a golfer, and it said: 'This is an exceptional month. You will do good in athletic events outside.'"

Schlee had horoscopes printed for all of the tour regulars; whether they wanted them or not, he occasionally placed them in his fellow pros' lockers. Not surprisingly, Schlee did not dare to convey his astrological musings to his mentor. The quintessential "old-school" Hogan had already chastised Schlee for wearing gaudy, expensive alpaca sweaters on the course, and surely scoffed at his experimentation with triangular-headed woods, an adjustable system of weights for his driver, and a cross-handed putting style. From the cast of colorful characters who comprised the early 1970s professional golf scene, no one seemed more *unlike* Hogan than his self-proclaimed disciple, John Schlee.

IN CASE THE YOUNG LION Jerry Heard or the New Age John Schlee hinted at a shift away from the tour's old guard, two veteran heroes stepped up on Saturday to speak for the prior generation.

The great Walter Hagen, winner of the U.S. Open in 1914 and 1919, once proclaimed that "Anybody can win one Open but the man who can win again is quite a golfer indeed." Billy Casper's failure to make Friday's cut left just three such men to play over the weekend. Two of them—Nicklaus and Trevino— battled side by side and had long been accustomed to the spotlight. The third member of that elite U.S. Open fraternity was Julius Boros, one of the most underrated players in PGA tour history.

Born in 1920 to an immigrant Hungarian family, Boros came of age during the Great Depression. During World War II, he served in the Air Force Medical Corps but spent all four years stateside at a base in Biloxi, Mississippi. The former captain of his high school golf team, Boros routinely played at a course near the base, and upon his discharge, he returned to his native Connecticut and took a job as an accountant.

Again Boros didn't stray far from golf: He worked for the Rockledge Country Club in West Hartford. In 1948, he finished second in the Connecticut Open, and recorded the lowest U.S. Amateur qualifying score in the New York metropolitan area. That year, he also played in the prestigious North & South Open in Pinehurst, North Carolina, an event that changed his life.

Boros finished second in the tournament and deeply impressed his fellow runner-up, Sam Snead, who urged him to turn pro. He also met a young woman from Massachusetts named Judith "Buttons" Cosgrove, who soon became Mrs. Boros.

Boros and Cosgrove shared more than just a New England background. Soon Buttons would win several women's golf championships, including the Charlotte Open in 1949 and, the following year, the Massachusetts state championship and the Silver Falls tournament, also at Pinehurst. Her father, Frank Cosgrove, owned the Mid Pines Golf Club in North Carolina; after Boros turned professional, Frank promptly hired him as Mid Pines's club pro.

Only six months into his career, Boros made the cut in the 1950 Masters tournament and, showcasing a fondness for the tight course setups favored by the U.S.G.A., finished ninth behind Ben Hogan in the 1950 U.S. Open at Merion. Even better, in 1951 Boros won the Massachusetts State Open two weeks after finishing fourth—again behind Hogan—in the U.S. Open at Oakland Hills.

That September, Judith gave birth to the couple's first child, and Julius rushed home midway through the Empire State Open in Albany to meet his new son, Jay Nicholas. Unfortunately, three days after the delivery, Judith suffered a cerebral hemorrhage and died at the age of twenty-three.

"For a while, Julius never wanted to play again," said Peggy Kirk Bell, a competitor and friend of Buttons. "But then he kept on, because he knew that she would have wanted it that way."

Boros returned to the tour two months later, and the following summer, at the Northwood Club in Dallas, he stunned the golf world by stealing the U.S. Open from Hogan, who appeared to have his hands on a third consecutive national title. Trailing Hogan by four strokes entering Saturday's double-round final, Boros was the only man to break par over the final thirty-six holes. Never known as an outstanding putter, Boros sneaked up on the game's greatest player and snatched victory with just forty putts over the final twenty-seven holes.

Eleven years later, at age forty-three, Boros again chased down a U.S. Open crown. At The Country Club in Brookline, experts considered Boros one of the few players equipped to overtake the four-to-one favorite, Arnold Palmer. A winner of two events during the previous five weeks, Boros stayed hot in an Open that saw scores inflate dramatically as a result of blustering winds and a course battered by a harsh New England winter.

Boros hung within a few strokes of Palmer and the leader, Jacky Cupit, prior to the start of the final round. By keeping his ball underneath the near-gale-force gusts (no golfer matched par in either round on the final Saturday), Boros stayed in contention all day. He then fired birdies on the seventieth and seventy-first holes to pull even with Cupit and Palmer, forcing a play-off the next day. Boros smashed both his challengers in Sunday's play-off: Cupit by three strokes, Palmer by six.

Boros dealt Palmer another bout of major-championship heartbreak by shooting a closing-round 69 to eke out a one-stroke victory in the 1968 PGA Championship. Just as he had done in 1952 in Dallas, the forty-eight-year-old Boros won that week at San Antonio's Pecan Valley Golf Club and shocked the Texas gallery. He was the oldest man to win a Grand Slam event, and the image he cast on the fairways reflected his age.

"His [swing] is like molasses falling over hot biscuits. Sometimes it looks as if he might fall asleep on the backswing," Associated Press writer Will Grimsley observed. "He is a middle-sized man who you can tell likes to eat. A better than adequate bread basket hangs over his belt buckle."

Complementing his relaxed but deceptively powerful swing were Boros's simple philosophy and humble approach to the game.

"Play a round of golf with me and I hope you will relax and enjoy yourself. That's what I plan to do. People worry so much about their games. You can see them out there on any weekend, fidgeting over every shot as if the U.S. Open depended on it. Wind direction, downhill lie, trapped green—is this the right club, maybe a six-iron would have been better, spread the stance a little wider, recheck the grip . . . endless worry," he once wrote for *Sports Illustrated*. "Your life doesn't depend on it. Not even your living. Now, mine does, but when I find that playing golf is work and that I'm beginning to worry about it I'll switch to something else. No game is worth the agony that some golfers go through, and that includes a few of my fellow pros on the tour."

To reinforce his low-key, easygoing attitude, Boros played a relatively casual tour schedule. After Judith's death, he married Armen Boyle in 1954 and the couple had six children. Aside from traveling the world to play in exhibition matches and sightsee, he loved to fish and hunt. Sportswriters and family members alike lovingly described Boros with one adjective: placid.

"He'd come home from a tournament," one of his brothers recalled, "and we'd all jump up and ask him how he did. If we were lucky he'd say, ' won,' or, 'I lost.' Usually he'd say, 'It'll be in the papers tomorrow.'"

Braced by that tranquil perspective, Boros competed well into his "twilight" years and remained a strong threat to win wherever he showed up. Besides cruising to a Senior PGA title in 1971 (he also posted runner-up finishes the next two years), Boros won nearly $100,000 in prize money during his first two seasons after turning fifty.

Boros kicked off the 1973 PGA tour season in grand fashion, sinking consecutive fifteen-foot birdie putts to start the first round of the season's initial event. At the Glen Campbell Los Angeles Open, a bogey-free round (he missed just two greens) gave him a share of the first-round lead; he finished the tournament tied for tenth. And during the early spring months, he tied for ninth in the Byron Nelson in Dallas and then, two weeks later, finished fifth in the Colonial at Fort Worth.

After once again brandishing his Texas mettle, Boros played only two rounds of competitive golf from mid-May to mid-June. The aptly nicknamed "Moose" spent more time fishing, traveling, and hosting a television show funded by his sponsors (*Outdoors with Liberty Mutual*) that shot scenes in Hawaii, Ireland, Hungary, and India. Although he avoided tigers—"I'm not shooting at anything that can bite or that I can't outrun"—Boros bagged more stags and geese in the lead-up to the U.S. Open than birdies or eagles.

In June—a few weeks after attending his firstborn son's college graduation— the fifty-three-year-old Boros made a return appearance to Oakmont. He had last played there in 1953, as the defending U.S. Open champion, and finished nineteenth. (He did not play in 1962 because he missed the cut in the sectional qualifier.) In his twenty-third U.S. Open attempt, his back was a bit sore from fishing more than golfing during the past weeks; he candidly admitted, "My game hasn't been good."

Two over par in Thursday's opening round (the damage came mainly on the first hole, as an errant tee shot into deep rough produced a double bogey), Boros joined the large under-par club on "sprinkler Friday," posting a 69. Sinking midrange birdie putts on the first and second holes on Saturday brought Boros onto the leaderboard in another major championship. Solid putting also bailed him out on number eight, where he drove into a bunker but managed to save par by rolling in a clutch putt.

While he was best-known for accuracy and the elegance of his swing, most tour pros recognized that Boros had one of the best short games of his generation. A high school basketball player, he used powerful hands to master the "soft wedge shot"—a skill of special value on a U.S.G.A. course setup—to save par and score birdies from heavy rough around the greens.

Just before he made the turn on Saturday, Boros's long-iron approach to the ninth drew too far left and landed in a patch of thick, short grass just off the fringe, forty feet above the cup. Unable to put backspin on the ball from the tight lie, he softly popped it forward a tiny distance, barely onto the green. From there—in classic Oakmont fashion—the ball rolled and rolled and rolled, before settling six inches from the hole. His tap-in birdie gave him a 33 on the front side and—as Gary Player imploded behind him over the same stretch of holes—a tie for the tournament lead at three under par.

Boros—either a cigarette or strand of grass in his mouth practically the entire round—promptly squandered a stroke on number ten, only to gain it back on the eleventh by holing a twelve-footer for birdie.

"I played the first fourteen holes as well as ever in my life," he said afterward.

At number fifteen, Boros's fountain of youth looked to have dried up when he pushed his tee shot into a drainage hole in the deep rough off the right side of the fairway.

"That happens once in a while when you get to be fifty-three," he joked later in describing the most critical moment of his round, as a double bogey or worse loomed.

Following a lengthy deliberation, U.S.G.A. officials ruled that the area in which Boros's ball had come to rest was "ground under repair." After two unsuccessful drops, they allowed him to place the ball. Using a self-described base-ball swing with his three-iron, he caught enough of the ball to drive it twenty-five yards shy of the green. A chip to twelve feet and the subsequent one putt produced what Boros's distinguished partner called "one of the greatest pars in the history of golf."

Two more thrilling pars followed. On the par-three sixteenth, he nailed his three-wood onto the green and smacked his birdie putt seven past the cup and considerably off-line. The unflappable Boros then smoothly rolled in the difficult par save. On the 322-yard seventeenth, Boros's iron off the tee left an ideal approach to the pin, located on the right side of the green. But from an uneven stance, he pulled his wedge badly; the ball touched down on the green's left edge and, three hops later, found a green-side bunker.

"So it was perhaps that uphill stance that he had to assume, and from that you get a natural pull," ABC's Keith Jackson said about Boros's horrific shot, to which lead analyst Byron Nelson added, "Yes, that's very easy to do. But I'm surprised that at this point, the way that Julius has been playing, that he let the ball do that."

A mediocre blast out of the bunker left Boros a tricky, right-to-left-breaking sixteen-footer that he gently caressed toward the hole, where it dropped in for another terrific par save.

Boros played the fifty-fourth hole equally on the edge, as his approach shot stopped on the outermost perimeter of the multitiered green, fifty feet from the cup. But he nimbly two-putted for a closing par and a three under 68, the third-lowest score of the day. Boros's outstanding play may have surprised many writers and fans—Hogan never broke 70 as a pentagenarian in two U.S. Opens—but not Boros himself.

"I sure don't feel fifty-three," he said after downing a few beers with Lew Worsham in the pro shop. "I'm not tired and the only thing that bothered me out there today was I heard some guy call me an old man."

Impressed by Boros's wizardry on the greens, slightly graying partner—Arnold Palmer—lauded the old man's sparkling revival:

"Some of the damnedest putting I've ever seen."

ALTHOUGH PITTSBURGH WAS HIS "HOMETOWN" and Oakmont "his course," Arnold Palmer, swarmed all week with his die-hard fans, had a lot working against him before the start of the third round.

For one, the thirty-nine-mile commute from Latrobe to Oakmont wasn't made any easier by Saturday morning's lengthy rainstorm. And once he finally reached the course, changed in the clubhouse locker room, and readied himself for practice on the nearby driving range, the downpour continued.

In rounds one and two, an eighteen-year-old named Vince Berlinsky served as Palmer's caddie. For a man who had played Oakmont dozens, perhaps hundreds of times, a teenage caddie was more a bag toter than a source of special wisdom or practical guidance. But the combination of Palmer's slightly diminished vision, plus his insistence that he knew the course so well he could do without glasses or contact lenses, meant that the King could probably have benefited from an extra pair of educated eyes.

To all appearances, Berlinsky had handled his caddying tasks adequately on Thursday and Friday. Even-par scores on both days gave Palmer a leg up on most of the field. But Berlinsky never showed up to caddie during the third round. Later that day, a reporter implied that there was some sort of disagreement between the boy and the King, to which Palmer declined comment.

"Vince was nervous," said a fellow caddie. "It was too much caddying for a prominent player like Palmer."

While Oakmont's caddie master, Joe Stoner, sought a replacement for Berlinsky, Palmer spoke to both reporters and himself—"Arnold Palmer, go out there, get off your dead [ass], and do something"—then answered a series of inconsiderate questions with his customary grace and good humor.

"Who's the greatest golfer you've ever seen?"

"Jack Nicklaus . . . when he's right," Palmer replied.

"If you had to pattern your entire career after one golfer, who would it be?"

"Sam Snead," he said immediately. "I mean, here's a man still playing golf at sixty-one. How can you beat that? It's sure something I'd like to be doing when I get to be his age."

Nicklaus, Snead, and Ben Hogan, "although not necessarily in that order," was his answer when asked to name the best three golfers he'd ever seen. "I never saw Walter Hagen play. I never saw Bobby Jones either, although I have seen movies of him. I did see [Byron] Nelson play in 1942 and he had one of the finest swings I've ever seen."

After a string of similar questions—best putter, best sand player, longest driver, etc.—Palmer responded to speculation that he might sponsor a younger, rising tour pro who needed backing.

"Not while I'm still playing. I might after I'm all through. You know, some people thought I would sponsor Lanny Wadkins, or that I had been. That wasn't so at all. How would it be if I was sponsoring him and the both of us came to the last hole together needing it to win? . . . You couldn't do a thing like that."

Palmer politely continued speaking as he dressed for the round. Given that each day that week he walked past a parade of ARNIE FOR GOVERNOR signs, perhaps this wasn't the best moment to pump him for self-reflection.

Palmer's last-minute replacement caddie was twenty-two-year-old Tom Tihey, the assigned looper that week for Bobby Mitchell (who missed the cut by five strokes). Tihey had been a caddie at Oakmont since age twelve and knew the course well, though he played most of his golf at Oakmont East, the adjacent public facility, where he boasted a scratch handicap. Shortly before being assigned to Palmer, Tihey had finished up a quick breakfast at the nearby

Howard Johnson, and was hanging out on the pro shop veranda before deciding which players to watch. He was both shocked and elated when Stoner singled him out to work for Palmer—as soon as he could locate an extra orange jumpsuit (Tihey had left his at home), the garish, one-piece garb that caddies were required to wear that week.

After Tihey nervously introduced himself, Palmer asked whether he was nearsighted or farsighted.

"One of each," the bespectacled youngster replied.

Unable to catch a break, even in his own backyard, Palmer burst into laughter.

With the caddie crisis resolved, trouble still followed Palmer onto the course. From the first fairway, he missed the green with an eight-iron. After an overly aggressive chip barely stayed on the green, he two-putted for a bogey. Palmer made a conventional par on the second hole, while Boros sank his second consecutive birdie putt.

Losing an early stroke to par was hardly catastrophic. But falling three behind so quickly to his playing partner, that hurt. A decade after Boros had thumped Palmer in a play-off to win the U.S. Open in Brookline, and five years after he had edged out Palmer to win the PGA Championship, the two veterans were together again at this critical moment in a major championship.

But—as he had done so many times over the years—Palmer quickly reminded everyone never to count out the King. He started his climb back into contention at a familiar location, Oakmont's fourth hole. This was Palmer's tenth visit to the 549-yard par five under U.S.G.A. auspices—twice as an amateur in 1953, five times in 1962 (including the play-off), and twice this week. He owned the hole: six birdies, three pars.

Driver, then a booming three-wood put Palmer to the base of the fourth green, where he stroked an immaculate chip to leave an easy three-footer for another birdie. He then landed a five-iron eight feet from the flagstick on the par-three sixth, rolled in the tricky birdie putt, and moved to one under par. Driving into a green-side bunker on number eight—and subsequently needing two strokes to escape the damp sand—could have been a lot worse if Palmer had not made a clutch putt for a bogey four.

By the time Palmer arrived on the ninth tee, again at even par for the day and for the tournament, he was still in the thick of the race. Then began a revival of the Palmer "charge," the kind that, a decade earlier, had stolen America's heart and made him the most riveting performer the game had ever known.

Palmer's eagle chip from the fringe on number nine bobbled in and out of the cup; an easy tap in clinched his third birdie on the front side. At his own personal hell—Oakmont's tenth, which in nine U.S. Open rounds he had played at nine over par—Palmer followed a strong drive with a brilliant six-iron that stopped dead on the softened green. He nailed the ten-footer, improving to two under par.

Palmer had one more miracle for the army of thousands who marched in stride with him to the eleventh tee. A marginal drive left him under a tree on the fairway's right side that seriously hampered his swing. Somehow, he hit a low eight-iron punch that just carried the front bunker, leaving him forty-five feet from the flagstick. Birdie seemed out of the question. But Palmer's new approach to mastering Oakmont's greens—he slowed his stroke in order to strike the ball more solidly—and a new putter (purchased two weeks earlier during an exhibition in Ashland, Ohio) kept the magic going.

Palmer lined up the putt, sent the ball "over the swales and valleys of Oakmont's undulating green," then exploded, charging his fist into the ground when the ball roared into the hole.

Pars the rest of the way did not lack Palmer's trademark electricity. His gallery cheered so loudly after his successful par putt on the twelfth that the group ahead of him—Bert Yancey and his partner, Raymond Floyd—could barely hear their own thoughts as Floyd lined up his birdie putt on number thirteen.

"Yancey turned around and held his arms up to try and quiet the crowd, but it was useless."

Floyd blew the putt far beyond the hole.

"The gallery following me helped a lot as well," Palmer acknowledged. "It was large and got excited, but hell, I know most of them."

Palmer's own "damnedest putting" continued on number sixteen, where he two-putted from sixty feet. On the seventeenth—as all golfers within earshot waited until he putted out before playing their own shots—an eight-footer for birdie and sole possession of the lead barely missed.

Minutes later, standing on the eighteenth green with Boros, Palmer joked with the crowd about the heroic play of a twosome measuring ninety-six years in combined age.

"One thing about it, when you get older, you learn to putt," he wryly stated. And whether he meant it or not, Palmer *had* putted damn well: His 68 marked the lowest score he ever registered in a championship at Oakmont. Longtime Associated Press golf reporter Will Grimsley—along with several members of the media—delighted in calling the pairing of giants of the previous generation "the Arnie and Julie Show."

"It was a great day for the paunchy and middle-aged and also for Arnie's Army," Grimsley wrote. "Where did those blokes come from, anyway? We thought they were dead."

Boros's and Palmer's matching 68s; the 66 and 67 shot, respectively, by Heard and Schlee; combined with the nightmarish afternoons of the leaders behind them (Player, Colbert, Nicklaus, Borek), created a four-way tie at the top of the leaderboard on Saturday evening: the biggest logjam in U.S. Open history. Although the twentysomething Heard, thirtysomething Schlee, fortysomething Palmer, and fiftysomething Boros were all tied at three under par 210, the players' (as well as the fans') favorite was self-evident.

"I think Arnold's going to be the man to beat," Lee Trevino predicted, "because he knows the course so well."

Palmer, who admitted he was "charged up" by the birdie binge in the middle of the round, tried in vain to shield his glee with cautious optimism.

"When I got my round going I felt like it was ten years ago. I've had opportunities to win major championships in recent years, and it's bothered me that I haven't done it," he said.

"I have nothing to get excited about yet. There are ten or twelve guys in position to win this thing."

Or maybe even thirteen.

molished a year earlier. The "nerveless kid," as one reporter called him, made the turn with three birdies and no bogeys to pull within two strokes of the lead. A pair of birdies on numbers eleven and twelve—where he holed out from a bunker, seventy feet away—gave him a share of the lead.

When Miller sank a six-foot birdie on the fourteenth, the Augusta crowd went wild, and not just because the blond-maned youngster had grabbed the lead.

"[It] seemed that every teenager on the premises was screeching and yelling for him," wrote Lincoln Werden of the *New York Times*. "Clad in a light green shirt and mod slacks of blue, green, black and white stripes, he seemed to personify the younger element on tour and in the gallery."

Another *Times* reporter claimed that Miller's heroics evoked the play of another famed Masters hero, as Miller's three birdies in four holes "brought the tournament alive with a charge that recalled Arnold Palmer in his heyday."

Miller's friend and mentor, Billy Casper, loved his "protégé's" approach.

"He has no fear," the reigning Masters champion said about Miller's birdie barrage. "John said early this week that these Masters greens are easy to putt. Now he's proving it."

Minutes after Miller so easily nailed his birdie, Coody three-putted the fourteenth to fall two behind. With Nicklaus's bogey on the twelfth a little earlier, and then, surprisingly, no more birdies in his arsenal, Miller held sole possession of the lead and seemed destined to win.

"I had a great mental attitude those first fourteen holes," he said. "I was at ease all day. I kept telling myself this was just a practice round, a lot of fun, and everything was going like crazy. . . . When I started walking down the fifteenth fairway I started thinking to myself that my dad will really love to see me win this thing."

In a flash, Miller fell apart. He played the fifteenth (often a birdie hole) poorly from tee to green and luckily saved par, then found the right-side bunker on the par-three sixteenth. When his par putt rattled out of the cup, the lead vanished. Although Coody promptly birdied the sixteenth, Miller was not out of it until his horrid play at the final hole, where his tee shot hooked left, hit a spectator, and bounded into an area once used as practice grounds. With no chance to get the birdie he needed, Miller bogeyed number eighteen and finished as runner-up to the anonymous Coody.

"On that day, I lost my cool," he later wrote.

Not surprisingly, in light of his recent run at the Masters and his earlier top-ten finish at Olympic, the press now considered Miller a gambler's bet to win the next major championship: June's U.S. Open at Merion. In his final start before the Open, Miller fully displayed his dare-the-gods "go low" talent by shooting a seven under 65, the lowest opening round in the history of the Atlanta Golf Classic, before finishing respectably in fifth place behind Gardner Dickinson.

Miller did not quite see himself as a "dark horse."

"I can hit the ball with anybody," he said before the Open. "I always feel I play better in the U.S. Open. I feel a lot of guys choke, but my game isn't affected by pressure."

Whether or not Miller's blow-up at the Masters contradicted his brash claim that everyone choked but him, those who had seen him "go low" expected him to perform as well at Merion as he had at Augusta National. Merion's hilly terrain and numerous small, treacherously slick and contoured greens placed a premium on pinpoint approach shots, and no one hit his irons straighter, higher, or controlled his distance better than Miller. His game clearly "fit" the course, and Miller wondered aloud if that week in Pennsylvania, something grand might happen at the stately, turn-of-the-century venue.

"This is a wonderful course," he said, "but I believe if it's wet there are going to be a lot of low scores—maybe they'll even break the course record."

In his fourth U.S. Open, Miller stared down Merion like an old veteran, finishing fifth behind Trevino after his historic play-off triumph over Nicklaus. Attesting to how well he could play the nation's toughest courses, Miller matched par in three of his four rounds, a feat equaled only by Trevino.

Miller finally reached the winner's circle later in the 1971 season, but he received considerably less praise for his triumph than for his top-five finishes at the Masters and the U.S. Open. After Merion, Miller made the cut in seven consecutive starts, but he felt his game was going stale: Only once did he finish in the top ten, a tie for ninth at Akron's American Golf Classic. Deciding he needed a rest from the tour grind, he and his California junior golf pal, Jerry Heard, planned a fishing trip to Montana.

But John Montgomery, tournament director of the recently established Southern Open, convinced Miller to skip the vacation and compete in September's PGA event in Columbus, Georgia.

"He begged me to go," Miller said. "He said I had done so well previously in Georgia [i.e., April's Masters], I should come back down here again."

Montgomery may have been desperate for *any* name—winless young lion or not—to join the rather lackluster field. Without Nicklaus, Trevino, Player, Palmer, Weiskopf, Casper, or even the hotshot Heard—now eighth on the tour money list—the *Atlanta Constitution* proclaimed lawyer Dan Sikes and defending champion Mason Rudolph the top contenders. Local native Tommy Aaron, Chi Chi Rodriguez, Gay Brewer, Grier Jones, and a few other young-sters provided the remaining "star" power at the Southern Open.

Miller slashed the Green Island Country Club with an opening-round low of 65, then shot a three under 67 to keep pace with Brewer for the halfway lead. A 68 on Saturday put him one stroke on top, heading into the final round. Wearing "a navy blue shirt, red-white-and-blue Uncle Sam pants, no cap and a winning grin," the twenty-four-year-old "Mod Miller" ran away from the field and coasted to a five-stroke victory, his first as a professional.

Tunnel vision, Miller believed, kept him focused throughout the round.

"I'm not going to look at the leaderboards," said Miller, narrating his final round for the press. "I know a lot of people do it, even Arnold Palmer, but I don't want to know what anybody else is doing. A lot of times you'll see what some other guy is doing and you start figuring that you've got to do this.

"I may have been destined to win this one; I had no intention of being here," Miller frankly told the crowd afterward, before handing over the $20,000 winner's check to Linda as a gift (the couple's two-year anniversary would be later that week).

"It was getting a little old being introduced as an 'outstanding young golfer.' Honestly, the money didn't mean that much to me because I've had a [pretty] good year money-wise. I just wanted to win. It means that I will be paired with the tournament winners in the future, guys like Palmer, Nicklaus, Casper, etc., instead of nonwinners.

"Winning this one will give me a big lift."

In truth, Miller did *not* experience any "lift" for the remainder of the 1971 season; he finished no higher than seventeenth, and averaged a thirty-fifth-place finish in four straight late-season events. Still, the win at the Southern Open and his stellar performances in the first two majors earned Miller the seventeenth spot on the tour's annual earnings list, far higher than his fortieth-place finish a year earlier.

Nineteen seventy-two opened with great expectations for the three-year vet-eran, but early in the season he mainly experienced heartache.

Miller eagerly awaited January's Bing Crosby Pro-Am, which was spread over the breathtaking courses of the Monterey Peninsula—Cypress Point, Spyglass Hill, and Pebble Beach—only two hours south of his childhood home. After an ugly first-round 75 at Cypress Point dropped him nine strokes behind the front-running Nicklaus, Miller pulled within three of the leader the next day, thanks to a sparkling 68 at Spyglass. On a calm and peaceful winter Saturday along the rocky shore of Carmel Bay, Miller shot a 67 at Pebble Beach—the same course where he'd won the California Amateur five years earlier, and the site of his controversial extra-club match-play win in 1963—to grab a one-stroke lead.

Naturally, Crosby's Pro-Am—the crooning legend was golf-obsessed—drew Hollywood's most renowned celebrities. With stars like Clint Eastwood and Jack Lemmon doing their best to act like golfers, the tournament was made for television, and NBC invested heavily in the broadcast of the final round.

Before a rapt gallery and a national TV audience, Miller fended off his playing partner, Nicklaus, for most of Sunday, despite three straight bogeys midway through his round. In reality, though, no one was playing well.

"Everyone laid [*sic*] down and died out there. Everyone was chopping so bad out there, it was amazing," Miller admitted. "I don't think there was one good score from the guys who started in the top ten. Maybe that's what this course does to you. It jumps up and grabs you."

Nicklaus took the lead by ramming in a thirty-foot birdie on the fourteenth, but Miller pulled even with Nicklaus, as the TV cameras began to roll, by making a twenty-five-footer of his own on the next hole.

On the short par-four fourteenth, Miller faced a relatively simple second shot from a side-hill lie. After Nicklaus's eight-iron came up short, Miller chose to "leap on a seven-iron."

Leap on it he did: "Instead of hitting it with a solid left side, I went down into the shot with my knee and it threw my swing out into the shank. It was a pretty swing. It probably looked nice on TV. It wasn't jerky or choky." The ball flew laterally right and hit a spectator before stopping behind a tree.

"It was a beauty. I haven't shanked a ball since I was twelve years old. Then I remember if you shank one, you're apt to shank eight in a row."

As shocking as it was for fans to watch a top professional cold shank a short iron, Miller kept his composure. He then amazed viewers by pairing two wonderful recovery shots with a one-putt green to escape the sixteenth with just a bogey. And when Nicklaus could do no better than a bogey on the par-three seventeenth, the two were again tied.

Miller's shank itself did not actually sabotage his chance at victory; at the same time, he could not—and never would—let it go.

"But I had the same iron into eighteen," Miller told reporters later that day, "and I said to myself, 'Don't shank it out-of-bounds.'"

Both men parred the eighteenth, and when Miller missed a lengthy putt on the first play-off hole (the fifteenth), Nicklaus snatched the victory by draining an eighteen-footer for birdie.

The Crosby was not a major, but with the marriage of Pebble Beach and Hollywood—beautiful people embracing golf's Eden—the tournament was made for television. A second-place finish behind Nicklaus again put Miller in the national limelight, and the $16,000 runner-up paycheck was the third-highest he'd earned as a professional.

But Miller did not leave Pebble Beach unscathed.

"From that day forward, I would never be in contention on the back nine on Sunday without thinking, 'Am I going to shank this again?'" Miller wrote. "That's what choking is—having thoughts go through your mind that wouldn't be there during a casual round with your buddies. The shank at Pebble Beach wasn't a choke, but it led to some unnerving, choking thoughts. I contended in tournaments probably fifty times and every time after that, I was worried about shanking. I never did shank again, but you can bet it was dancing around in my head."

Although Miller "never did shank again," tournaments continued to slip out of his hands at the worst possible moments. Winning didn't become any easier in 1972 following his triumph at the Southern Open.

A month after the infamous shank, Miller squandered the lead late on Sunday in another of the tour's star-studded, pro-am extravaganzas. In February's Bob Hope Desert Classic, played on four courses over five days, Miller birdied four of the opening six holes during the final round to grab a share of the lead. After Miller made a birdie on number eleven and an eagle on number fourteen, the tournament was his to lose. And he did.

On the fifteenth, Miller's nine-footer for birdie rolled past the cup; he then blew the two-foot comebacker for par. On number seventeen, a five-footer for par lipped out. Needing an eagle on the par-five final hole to force a play-off, Miller reached the fringe in two shots, only to see his putt come up two feet shy. The suddenly bored twenty-four-year-old then flubbed another two-footer, his second in the final four holes, and both on national TV.

"I lost interest after missing the eagle. It's just not the same playing for second or third place. I want to win."

His spirits didn't pick up after leaving Palm Springs, especially when he missed the cut at the Masters in April. Luckily, Miller's next appearance on the big stage, the 1972 U.S. Open, would come at a familiar place: Pebble Beach.

Once again, the Carmel-by-the-Sea masterpiece—now toughened to U.S.G.A. standards, and played in frightful June weather—confounded the world's best golfers. A two-over-par total after three rounds was good enough to earn Miller a late-afternoon Sunday tee time with Arnold Palmer. Miller shot a 79, but the winds swirling off the Pacific Ocean inflated everyone's score. Miller's score actually matched the average that day, and he finished seventh.

A month later at the British Open in Muirfield, Miller set a new course record with a five under 66 in the second round, mostly thanks to one remarkable shot. Frustrated by an opening-round 76, especially his meltdown on number eighteen—he plugged a three-wood into a bunker, leading to a triple bogey—Miller needed an early spark to rekindle his desire and avoid missing the cut. Using the same unlucky three-wood from the day before, he smashed a tremendous long second shot onto the par-five fifth green.

"I knew it was online. And I heard a polite patter of applause. When I walked up there, the ball was in the hole. Shoot! You don't hole two-hundred-and-ninety-yard shots often."

Miller promptly birdied the next hole, and cruised through the rest of his day to finish tied for second at the halfway point.

"That shot did wonders," Miller said about the double eagle ("albatross" to the Scottish gallery). "I knew I could free-wheel. In my last tournament, the Western Open, I had a seventy-six and then a sixty-six." Miller could not only "go low"; he was most dangerous bearing a wounded ego.

Miller returned to over-par scores in the final two rounds of the British Open and took fifteenth place—eleven shots behind Lee Trevino. And, for the most part, Miller freewheeled his way through the rest of the season. In the next eight individual events, he averaged twenty-eighth place; after a miserable start, he also withdrew one round into August's U.S. Industries Classic.

In early November, Miller found himself outside the top twenty-five in tour earnings.

By that time, Jerry Heard—four days younger than Miller and in his shadow throughout high school, college, and spotlight amateur events—had become the tour's most heralded young lion. A two-time winner that season, Heard topped $100,000 for the second straight year. And the $61,700 that separated the two northern Californians told only part of the story: Heard regularly eclipsed Miller when they competed on the same stage. Heard posted top-ten finishes that summer in the American Golf Classic and the Sahara Invitational, and tied for fourth in the PGA Championship. Miller took forty-ninth, twentieth, and thirty-third in those events.

A year earlier, feeling tired and in need of a vacation, Miller had turned around a frustrating season with one great week by winning the Southern Open. Now again, in 1972, he rebounded at the end of the season. This time, instead of a trip to Columbus, Georgia, Miller flew to Auckland, New Zealand, to play in the Otago Charity Classic. Jerry Heard was there, but Lu Liang-Huan, Taiwan's famous "Mr. Lu," pushed Miller the hardest. Trailing Mr. Lu by a stroke on the seventy-second green, Miller sank an eighteen-foot birdie putt to force a play-off, then drained a forty-footer for another birdie on the first play-off hole to win.

Miller's second ("unofficial") victory seemed finally to produce the "big lift" he had anticipated after his first win; it was just a year late. Three days after the arduous trip home from New Zealand, Miller returned to PGA tour competition, playing at the Heritage Golf Classic in Hilton Head. The touring professional at nearby Palmetto Dunes—a club just five miles away—Miller was already quite familiar with the Harbour Town Golf Links and knew that it fit his game perfectly because of its small greens. Despite admitted fatigue, he shot 65 on the easier Ocean Course to tie for the second-round lead.

Cold winds and rain delayed the third round by a day and also hampered everyone once the event resumed. Miller overcame a front-nine 40 to card 35 on the back side and take a one-stroke lead over Forrest Fezler.

"It's hard to believe I'm leading after a seventy-five," he said. "It's hard enough to shoot par here in perfect weather."

The conditions finally tamed for Monday's final round—still, many women in the gallery wore fur coats—and Miller refused to give up the lead. On the eighteenth, still nursing a meager one-stroke advantage (over Tom Weiskopf), he needed only to sink an eighteen-inch par putt to secure his second PGA tour win.

"All sorts of things went through my mind when I stood over that last putt," he said afterward. "I thought to myself, 'You can't miss this.'"

He didn't. "A week ago I won a tournament in New Zealand and right now I have lots of confidence," Miller said at the post-tournament press conference. "Jerry Heard has given me lots of good advice. He told me to take a deep breath and not get pumped up and excited."

Still, the victory in Hilton Head didn't launch Miller to tour stardom. "Absence of Names Aid to Miller," blared the Associated Press headline, as skeptical reporters pointed out the less than stellar field at the Heritage. And the victorious Miller even agreed with them.

"Coming into the last couple holes, you know, anything can happen. But I felt I could handle those guys around me (the challengers) except maybe Tom Weiskopf. You know, most of them are young guys and I figured I could beat them. But it would be something else if you're coming into the last few holes and Arnold or Jack or Lee is there. Those guys—they're the best players in the world—they put the pressure on you. Maybe you put pressure on yourself. When they're playing, it's something else."

In the first event of 1973, the Los Angeles Open, Miller got his chance to compete against the "best players" on one of the nation's most revered courses, the Riviera Country Club, where Hogan, Snead, Mangrum, Demaret, Littler, Nelson, Palmer, and Casper had previously won. Miller was outstanding on day one, carding a four under 67, and he finished respectably in seventeenth place—below Nicklaus, who took sixth, but higher than Palmer (twenty-fourth) and Trevino (who missed his first cut in nearly two seasons).

Miller left Los Angeles to compete in the Phoenix Open, where he had famously "gone low" three years earlier, but withdrew before the final round to return to the Bay Area and be with his soon-to-give-birth wife. The father of two returned to the tour in early February and nabbed an impressive string of top finishes in high-profile tournaments. He placed seventh or higher in seven of twelve events, including sixth at the Masters. And two days before he headed to Oakmont for the U.S. Open, he continued to shine by taking third in the Philadelphia Classic (behind Tom Weiskopf, who posted his third win in four weeks).

In the months following his second child's birth, the excellence—and more important, the consistency—of Miller's game soared to a new level. He hadn't yet won against the "best players," as he called them, but was battling them almost every week. And on the eve of the U.S. Open, he held down seventh position on the money list, despite not padding his totals with one huge winner's paycheck.

Still, Miller's case as one of the tour's truly elite players remained murky. *Golf Magazine* gave him his due, naming Miller one of its six favorites to win the U.S. Open: "He has the shots for Oakmont and could be a hunch-player's bet." There was, however, one caveat.

"The lanky, blond style-setter was in hot pursuit of the title at Pebble Beach last year, before he ran into a final-round 79. He finished seventh. The year before, at Merion, he closed out with a fine 70, but it was only good enough for fifth place. Some observers are ready to give him the almost-but-not-quite mantle recently cast aside by Tommy Aaron [who won the 1973 Masters]. The 26-year-old Californian has the habit of roaring into contention with brilliant shot-making only to stumble with one weak round."

And his fellow touring pros also noticed the repercussions of Miller's Jekyll-and-Hyde golf game.

As one tour veteran recalled, "If Miller doesn't birdie a couple of the first four holes, he really doesn't even care; he can't shoot sixty-three anymore. I mean, that's the kind of thinking he had.

"He had this belief," the pro added, "that 'if I can't shoot nothing [i.e., an extremely low round], then I'm just out here filling up the day. . . .' And he shot nothin' a lot."

As much as Miller's "stumbles" shaped experts' persistent skepticism, it was his disappointing finish in one tournament earlier that season that he couldn't shake: Arnold Palmer's February victory in the Bob Hope Desert Classic.

A year removed from his collapse at the 1972 Bob Hope, Miller again had a strong chance to win the event in 1973. Tied for seventh after three days in "golf's answer to the Boston Marathon," Miller pounded Tamarisk Country Club in round four with a course-record 63, tying him with—who else— Nicklaus going into the fifth and final round. Earlier that week, the Golden Bear had inspired Miller to believe that if you can't beat 'em, join 'em.

"I don't force birdies anymore," Miller said. "I just hit the greens and let the birds come. My new stroke is like Nicklaus. I address the ball in the same manner he does."

In yet another limelight battle against a "best player," Miller wilted. On a rainy, gloomy desert Sunday, Palmer, not Johnny Miller, triumphed.

Playing one group ahead of the Palmer-Nicklaus-Schlee threesome, Miller lost the lead with mediocre golf on the front side, then charged on the back. Birdies on numbers thirteen and fifteen narrowed the gap to one stroke, a deficit he nearly overcame when his ten-foot birdie putt on the sixteenth just missed. But he then played the seventeenth poorly, and when he failed to drop a lengthy putt for par, he became just a side note to the confrontation between golf's top two heroes.

Afterward, Miller unintentionally confirmed suspicions that he lacked the inner strength of a champion; he just could not keep his head in the game.

"I kept thinking they would rain out the round and we'd play tomorrow. The result was that I didn't concentrate. But that shows my inexperience. It was damned wet out there, but I should have been playing like I meant business."

Despite the abysmal weather, none of the *other* pros obsessed about the conditions. Although Palmer admitted to thinking that the round might be suspended, he stayed focused on winning. Miller's Sunday failure at the Bob Hope only reinforced his fragile self-confidence.

"I was getting a tag like Tommy Aaron. I had heard them down in Augusta, last April. They were calling me another Tommy Aaron because I could never win any of the big ones," Miller acknowledged.

"That hurt. I wanted to do something about it."

Miller's mind-set on the eve of the seventy-third U.S. Open was curious: Though nurtured by a Mormon father who praised him constantly and preached, "Never allow yourself to think negatively," John was actually prone to crippling self-doubt. But this was no paradox to those who knew him well.

"I think Johnny's personality really was a personality that was either very positive and very confident or very negative," Nicklaus explained years later. "I don't think there was much in between for Johnny."

JUST AFTER TWO P.M. ON Saturday afternoon, Miller joined Bob Charles on Oakmont's opening hole to begin the third round, just three shots off the lead.

In the press tent following the second-round 69 that had wowed his partner, Arnold Palmer, Miller had been asked to gauge his prospects of winning the Open, under the inevitably tremendous late-round pressure.

"If it's somebody like Jim Colbert, I feel I'm as good [as] or better than he is, so there'll be no problem. If it's Jack Nicklaus, well . . . it's like a Volkswagen and a Corvette in a race. The VW doesn't win unless the Corvette breaks down."

From the first tee box, Miller could see Nicklaus strike an approach from the rain-soaked fairway that sailed far beyond the green—the first of several "nondescript shots" that led to a 74 and frustrated the usually unflappable defending U.S. Open champion.

Miller's afternoon would be far more maddening—starting when he reached into his pants pockets, then into his golf bag, for the yardage book he had relied on heavily during the first two rounds.

"I got to the first tee and I went through the first zipper and second zipper and third zipper, and then I started panicking," he remembered. "I got Linda. I said, 'You've got to go, my yardage [book] must be back at the house! You've got to go back and get it!' So she had to go back to the car and drive all the way there and back.

"Talk about stupidity!" he once said. "The biggest tournament in the world, and I don't even double-check. I tried to play by guesswork Saturday, not knowing if I was a hundred and fifty yards or a hundred and sixty yards from the flag."

Miller bogeyed the first hole. Then he bogeyed the second. After a pair of pars, he bogeyed the fifth and followed that with a disastrous double bogey on the sixth. He was five over par after six holes; his hopes of winning the U.S. Open seemed over.

Blindly making club selections, Miller launched his approach to the seventh green into a bunker, setting up another likely bogey. A blast from the fluffy sand ran twenty feet beyond the cup and nearly against the fringe; two putts would place him six over par after seven holes and seal his fate. But Miller stroked a perfect, par-saving putt and breathed a sigh of relief as the ball disappeared from sight; still drowning, but not officially dead.

As Linda fought traffic on her way back to Oakmont, Johnny hit a superb tee shot on the par-three eighth and sank his first birdie of the day. And on the par-five ninth, Miller—still without his precious yardage book—launched a high two-iron toward the front right "sucker" pin; it barely carried a bunker and settled seventeen feet from the hole. Exuberantly rolling in the eagle putt, Miller closed out the front side with a roller-coaster 38, two over par. The birdie-eagle momentum from numbers eight and nine helped ease Miller's mind almost as much as Linda's appearance on the tenth tee, yardage book in hand.

As it turned out, the yardage book was no panacea. Just as his round had begun, Miller started the back nine by bogeying the tenth and eleventh holes with wild shot making. He was lucky to score only a bogey on the par-four eleventh after he drove into the deep rough and bunkered his second shot.

The zaniness of Miller's third round continued with a birdie on the par-five twelfth, but any illusion that he had returned to top form died with bogeys on numbers fourteen and sixteen. In total, Miller's strokes added up to 76: seven bogeys, one double bogey, two birdies, and an eagle. So much for the steady golf necessary to win a U.S. Open.

"The round was a nightmare."

When Miller awoke, he trailed the four-way conglomerate of leaders (Palmer, Boros, Heard, Schlee) by six strokes. Even if he believed Gary Player's first-day prognostication that "anybody six behind with one round to go honestly could win it quite easily," the problem for Miller was *who* stood in front of him. Twelve golfers, including the four greatest of his time, and seven major championship winners in all: Nicklaus, Palmer, Trevino, Player, Boros, Gene Littler, and Bob Charles. The list also included the tour's hottest player, Tom Weiskopf, and its top young lion, Miller's fishing buddy, Jerry Heard.

"I was really down [Sunday] morning. I had almost no desire," Miller recalled. "I went out there . . . and I didn't have the faintest idea of what to do."

What followed was the greatest round ever played.

· 10 ·

Chasing a Living,
Chasing Trouble

"When I got to the course [Sunday] morning, I was like a Thoroughbred itching to run, but I had to wait and then wait some more," John Schlee recalled about his 2:23 p.m. tee time as a coleader of the 1973 U.S. Open.

Schlee's main anxiety, however, was not his start time but his final-round partner. Playing alongside western Pennsylvania hero Arnold Palmer was a fate that one reporter likened to "facing a firing squad without the blindfold." Whereas Palmer received a lengthy introduction and a rapt ovation from his army lining the first fairway, few noticed Schlee, even though he had notched his first PGA tour victory a few months earlier at the Hawaiian Open, and ranked twelfth on the 1973 earnings list.

Nevertheless, Schlee found some comfort in being paired with the King. Sunday would be the twelfth time the two had played together, and, according to Schlee, "I beat him every time except Palm Springs." That February, following his victory in Hawaii, Schlee had battled valiantly alongside the world's *two* most intimidating golfers—in a threesome with both Palmer and Nicklaus— during the last round of the 1973 Bob Hope Desert Classic. Over the drenched Bermuda Dunes course, he shot a one under 71 (one better than Nicklaus, two higher than Palmer) and took sixth place.

Still, Palm Springs was not Oakmont, home of the raucous enlistees of

Arnie's Army. "It's like a two-shot penalty playing with Arnie. It's so hard to concentrate with people yelling, 'Arnie, Arnie,'" Schlee told reporters.

Schlee was not bad-mouthing golf's superhero—far from it.

"Don't get me wrong; thank God for Arnold Palmer. . . . We wouldn't be here without him. I'm one of his biggest fans."

Schlee's affection probably diminished a few moments later when, amidst the noise and chaos, his opening drive flared high and right toward the out-of-bounds fence. But no one standing guard along the first fairway, except Schlee's wife and caddie, really cared.

John Schlee was born John Harold Tabor, in the small mining town of Kremmling, Colorado. Founded in 1881 during the Colorado Silver Boom, Kremmling was home to Cecil Harold Tabor and Mary Ethel Jones, who gave birth to John on June 2, 1939. With her son, Mary Jones left both Cecil and Colorado in 1945 and moved to Oregon. She soon married Carl "Lucky" Schlee, a Navy man based at Tongue Point, located in Oregon's northwest corner.

Lucky and Mary raised their only child in Seaside, the small coastal town formed after railroad tycoon Ben Holladay built a vacation home there in the 1870s. (Even today it remains a popular summer resort area.) Middle-class vacationers from Portland helped pay the family's bills, as Mary managed a modest, six-unit motel adjacent to their small house. Portland's "old money" vacationed just north of Seaside on the beaches of Gearhart. Each town supported a public golf course: nine holes in Seaside, eighteen in Gearhart.

While John was in the sixth grade, Lucky's navy buddy, Bill Otto, gave the boy a set of golf clubs. He quickly put the gift to good use and within two years, John became a staple at Seaside Golf Course, located barely a hundred yards from his home.

Schlee was already a fine player by the eighth grade, when he befriended Jim Cartwright, the son of Seaside Golf Course's laid-back owner, Charlie Cartwright. Jim played on the high school golf team as a freshman and he realized that Schlee's game far exceeded that of the team's current ace. Exceptional power and a fearless mind-set stood out most, and Cartwright could hardly wait for Schlee to join the squad.

Cartwright soon became Schlee's best friend. Still, even he didn't know about Schlee's past in Colorado, although Schlee did not legally change his name from John Tabor to John Schlee until 1955 (age fifteen). Perhaps further disguising his roots, Schlee went by the name of "Jack" throughout his entire upbringing in Seaside.

At the start of high school, Schlee played as Seaside High's number two golfer, then quickly took over the top spot during his freshman year. As he matured and reached his adult height and weight (six-three, 185 pounds), Schlee's golf astonished both peers and a small network of Seaside adults who attended the school's matches. The town had a statewide reputation for producing star athletes in football and baseball, but no one had ever seen a high schooler play golf like Jack Schlee.

More than even how *far* he hit a golf ball was how *hard* he hit it that awed the small high school galleries. With wrists that seemed five inches longer than the average person's, Schlee "popped those wrists . . . and just killed it," remembered Seaside's star football player Neal Maine, also a member of the Seagulls links team.

Even adults who watched the professionals each year at Portland's PGA tour event believed that no one—not even Arnold Palmer—hit the ball harder than the teenage Schlee. Some observers of Schlee at the Seaside Golf Course concluded that his low trajectory resulted from how hard he hit it: The dimples on 1950s golf balls were simply not designed to be struck with such force, and the ball could not get fully airborne as a result.

True or not, an aura of mystery surrounded Schlee's power, intriguing every golfer in town. That aura earned him more "free passes" than other Seaside youth.

And Schlee was not simply a power player. He drilled religiously at chipping and putting on the practice green adjacent to the Cartwright home. Charlie Cartwright allowed all the high school golfers to play for free, and when the course was not in use, he let them "hunt" for lost balls to keep or use or sell. Charlie loved kids, wanted them to have fun, and he became especially close to Jack, his oldest son's best friend.

Charlie knew that Jack and his mother quarreled often, and that Lucky hesitated to assert himself as the family disciplinarian. Throughout high school, Jack practically lived with the Cartwrights, eating many of his meals in their house or in the golf club's restaurant for free.

No one was surprised to learn that once Jim Cartwright graduated and left Seaside for military reserve duty, Jack moved into the Cartwright home, sharing the bedroom with Jim's twelve-year-old brother. For the better part of four years, Jack Schlee could be found either on the Seaside Golf Course or in the home of its owner, Charlie Cartwright.

Apart from Schlee's raw power, his imagination, self-confidence, and capacity to live entirely in the moment inspired locals to predict PGA stardom for him. Schlee delighted in achieving the impossible, or at least trying shots that no one else dared. Not only did he hit the ball a ton, he regularly scrambled pars with nerves of steel and shaped shots high and low, left and right, like a seasoned pro. For every golfer in Seaside, a round with Schlee was a grand adventure.

Seasiders also noticed that Schlee never displayed anger or threw clubs when he failed, or gloated upon pulling off an unthinkable shot. As Maine recalled, "you always had this feeling that even the ultimate end wasn't all that important. . . . Every shot was an event unto itself: 'Forget the before and the after; this shot stands on its own for what I can do with the ball at this point in time, period.'"

At a junior tournament in Portland, several boys stepped up to the first tee (a dogleg par-four) and took ferocious practice swings, pretending to drive the green before playing the hole safely down the middle. When Schlee's turn came, he took no practice swings, aimed directly across the dogleg, and smashed the ball onto the green, within eagle putt range. He then walked unassumingly off the tee without acknowledging the applause of the gallery. Six under par at one point during the round, Schlee refused to coast, and his go-for-broke spirit ultimately yielded several large numbers that cost him the tournament.

Erratic, up-and-down rounds like this defined the teenage Schlee. He would put together a hot streak and fearlessly pursue it, seemingly headed for a record score. Then, as Maine recalled, "the whole thing would go sky-high." Even when Schlee shattered Seaside's course record by shooting a 58 (twelve under par), he bogeyed the last two holes, a product of his unceasingly aggressive style of play.

Because he concerned himself only with preparing for a future on tour—not helping his team's chances for victory—Schlee practiced high-risk shots in every match, posting a good, not great, high school record. Still, during his junior year, the Seaside Gulls won the North Coast league championship and Schlee earned medalist honors with a 74. That summer, he totaled the lowest score in the thirty-six-hole medal qualifier for the Oregon Junior Golf Tournament, and finished sixth in the event.

The next year (1957) Schlee only got better, taking medalist honors in nearly all of the Gulls' matches. At the state championship in May, Seaside finished thirteenth in a field of thirty-one teams; Schlee closed out his high school career with the Gulls' best score, a four over 152, nine strokes behind the medalist winner. Schlee's play during the 1957 season impressed Oregon State University enough to dispatch two of its best players to meet with him and see if he might consider attending OSU on a golf scholarship.

OREGON GOLF COURSES WERE NOT the only place where Schlee flashed his athletic gift. Not just tall but with a sculpted physique and muscled legs, he could "leap like a kangaroo." One year, Lucky surprised his stepson with an expensive racing bicycle, and Schlee further built up his legs by riding to and from the Washington state line on weekends, before returning for a late round of golf.

Schlee occasionally ran hurdles for the track team, and started for the football team during his senior season. As a defensive end, he earned a place in Seaside sports history by securing a championship game victory, thanks to his solo, open-field tackle of the opposition's star running back.

The Seagulls basketball team was where Schlee stood out most. Although not a good shooter, he dominated the paint because of his leaping ability and penchant for diving for loose balls and sacrificing his body. Overly aggressive (without starting fights or getting thrown out of the game), he inspired teammates with his all-out effort. "[It was] just the same way he played golf . . . going way too hard and oftentimes out of control," Maine recalled.

Many of his teammates loved Schlee for his fiery spirit. Teachers, town officials, and many Seaside High students detested him for that same reason.

Often arrogant, he delighted in "putting down" and verbally abusing others, especially those who were not good athletes or simply got in his way. He claimed to be dyslexic, but he certainly had a sharp wit. "He didn't do much kiddin'," recalled Ray Sigurdson, a tough-skinned acquaintance who joined the marines after high school. Once, when Schlee finally defeated an older archnemesis, Ralph Diechter, in northern Oregon's premier match-play tournament, Schlee publicly taunted and humiliated him.

There was more to Schlee than the simple immaturity of his arrogance; most people around town knew him as a troublemaker, a liar, and a petty thief.

He threw stones and broke all of the streetlamps on one of the town's main streets, and even tried to kill a rare, protected bird with a string of golf shots. A disrespectful wiseass in school, he taunted fellow students and generally made life miserable for teachers and coaches.

Never suspended, Schlee banked on school officials to cut him slack because he contributed so much to the varsity sports teams. And he was smart and devious enough to know the limits of what he could get away with.

But not always. On one occasion, the school principal, fed up with Schlee's classroom antics and tired of hearing complaints from teachers, persuaded a group of school toughs to grab Schlee, blindfold him, and force him to fish banana peels out of a toilet with his mouth. (Fifty years later, former and current school officials still successfully campaign to keep Schlee out of the high school's sports hall of fame.)

Schlee was most infamous around town as a thief. He would shake down the paperboy when he was short of cash, and regularly siphon gas from lumber trucks to fuel the souped-up hot rod he raced late at night, James Dean style. Seaside's police chief knew of Schlee's transgressions and stashed officers in various locations to catch him in the act. They never caught him, a source of great embarrassment to the town's police chief: Schlee was dating his daughter at the time.

Schlee mostly stole golf equipment, both on and off the Seaside course. He swiped golf balls from the bags of those he caddied for, and from the shed where Charlie Cartwright stored thousands of them. He used them to sharpen his game, sell them to Seaside duffers, or sell them to nearby Gearhart's pro shop.

Charlie suspected his de facto son, but never caught him in the act. And Charlie's easygoing nature, his personal sympathy for Schlee, and his hopes that the troubled teen might have a golf future caused him to overlook the thefts. Even when Schlee's excuses were obvious lies, he received no more than a slight reprimand. In the end, Schlee came to believe he could get away with anything. "I was a pretty bad actor as a kid," he admitted years later.

Although he made a few bucks from selling his stolen merchandise—and like many juvenile delinquents, enjoyed the thrill of the crime—Schlee needed an endless supply of balls to prepare for his imminent career as a professional golfer. He loved to close out summer days at Seaside by driving balls down the fairways and into the brush at twilight, with no intention of retrieving them.

Anything not tied down, including clubs and other golf equipment, was not safe around Schlee. If he saw a club he felt would improve his game, he simply took it. Visits to fancier clubs than Seaside and Gearhart (usually to play in sanctioned junior or amateur tournaments) meant a prime opportunity to steal. After making his way into the bag room, he took whatever he wanted and was never caught in the act. He did the same in the pro shop. Years later, Seasiders who heard tour professional Johnny Pott's complaint that Schlee stole his shoes knew the tale was no joke.

John Schlee's charmed life as a petty thief ended abruptly during the summer of 1957, a few months after his high school graduation. Despite scouting from Oregon State, Schlee did not intend to go to college. He made no plans for the future and played golf endlessly. With his game steadily improving, he set his sights on the PGA tour; a high-profile amateur win might entice sponsors or convince a prominent club to make him an assistant professional. Schlee had tried for several years but failed to win the state's second-most-prestigious match-play tournament, the Oregon Coast Open, in nearby Astoria. As the summer came to an end, he and one of his former teammates set out to win the state's leading match-play tournament, the Southern Oregon Open, several hundred miles away in Medford.

Needing money to pay for travel and housing during both practice rounds and the event, Schlee sneaked into Charlie Cartwright's shed and stole hundreds of brand-new golf balls. He then drove to the Gearhart golf course and somehow persuaded the skeptical pro to buy them. With cash in his pocket and more than enough golf balls to play with, Schlee and his friend drove to Medford for the open—at the aptly named Rogue Valley Country Club—and began preparing for their first-round matches.

Charlie Cartwright discovered the heist the next morning. He didn't suspect Schlee (only because so many balls were stolen) and reported the theft to the Seaside police chief, who conferred with his counterpart in Gearhart. Questioning of the Gearhart pro made it clear that Schlee had stolen the balls.

The state police were dispatched to Medford, where they found Schlee practicing on the course. They promptly arrested him, snapped on handcuffs, and marched him off the course, befuddling the other contestants. Schlee spent the night in Seaside's jail. The next morning, the police chief asked Charlie Cartwright to come down to the station and make out a formal complaint.

When he learned that Schlee was the culprit, Cartwright would not file the complaint. This infuriated the Seaside police chief, especially since Schlee had recently broken up with his daughter. Although Charlie was disappointed that Schlee had so blatantly betrayed his trust, he knew that the grand-theft charge would mean substantial jail time. In an informal arrangement (not uncommon during the 1950s), Schlee escaped incarceration by agreeing to join the military.

SEASIDERS—THOSE WHO WEREN'T OVERJOYED BY his departure from their community—could hardly believe the news of Schlee's enlistment.

"A whole lot of people were saying, like, 'What, Jack in the military? Good luck!'" Neal Maine recalled. "He was a plenty bright guy; it wasn't like he got in trouble because he wasn't smart enough to figure it out."

Whether by choice or because his drill sergeants noticed his outstanding leaping ability, Schlee was assigned to paratrooper school after basic training. Although paratroopers were among the army's elite, the schooling requirement was relatively short. Schlee, however, spent most of his time at Fort Bragg playing golf at the base's two excellent courses. Several months in the military did little to soften the conceited, impish, occasionally malicious ways that had defined him in Seaside.

On the golf course, the long-driving Schlee wouldn't bother to wait for the group ahead to complete holes, and he swung away regardless. He hardly cared that the groups he sprayed were often comprised of the wives of Fort Bragg's flag officers, including the wife of the base's top general. And rather than show remorse on one occasion when he nearly beaned the general's wife, Schlee chastised her for getting in his way! Very soon, those in charge of Schlee's destiny again decided it was time for him to leave town, as rapidly as possible.

Still, with military golf more popular than ever, thanks to a golf-obsessed commander in chief, Schlee's fairway transgressions may have impressed as many as they upset. No one could deny Schlee's disciplined power and overall talent. At a time when golfer/soldiers were at a premium—like Lee Trevino and Orville Moody, who dominated the armed services' golf teams in the Pacific theater—Fort Bragg's officers knew that Schlee would be a great asset to the army's golf team.

By the spring of 1958, after spending just a few months with the paratroopers, Schlee was transferred to West Point. Officially, Private John Schlee's role was to work as an assistant mail clerk; he would also serve as a part-time life-guard, golf instructor, and member of the "honor guard." But his primary mission at West Point—which boasted arguably the finest military golf course in the nation—was to help the army golf team win. As he wrote to his parents, "I don't know how I was lucky enough to be picked for this."

"[Except] for being in uniform, he would hardly know he's in the army," reported the Seaside newspaper. "Accommodations are several cuts above the army barracks he has encountered before, and he has time enough in the evenings to keep up with his golf game."

Schlee certainly earned his cushy quarters and easy military assignment. In August 1958, he won the West Point Golf Championship and later that month won the first United States Army Golf Tournament, for which West Point's detachment commander personally presented him an award. During the winter months, making creative use of his brief paratrooper training, Schlee kept limber by hanging an open parachute in the barracks and driving balls into it.

As Schlee's discharge date approached, West Point's golf coach, Walt Browne, persuaded Memphis State University's athletic department to offer Schlee a golf scholarship, funded largely by profits from the Memphis Open, a prestigious PGA tour stop. Schlee—less than two years removed from evading a grand-theft jail sentence, and having spent an eighteen-month military golf vacation—was now a full-time college student, handed four years of subsidy to prepare for a career in professional golf.

During his freshman season at Memphis State, Schlee made the varsity and more than carried his weight on the team. He told few people about his military career—apart from acknowledging the thrill of jumping out of airplanes—and said nothing about his forced departure from Seaside or about his parents. And even when a few Seaside residents visited his dorm to see how their hometown prodigy's career was shaping up, Schlee refused to take their calls or see them.

Despite trying hard to hide his past, Schlee did little to change his ways. Every day at Memphis State was "wrapped around golf." He showed little respect to authority figures and flaunted his Seaside sense of entitlement as a star athlete.

Unlike Fort Bragg and West Point, however, Memphis State did not have its own golf course. The team did have year-round free access, in the afternoons, to different country club courses on specific weekdays. When the Tigers finished their practice, the coaches usually convinced a club member to spring for a hot dog and Coke for everyone. Naturally the boys were expected to follow a few courtesies: No hitting several balls into a green or off the tee, no extended bunker practice, no playing too slowly, and, of course, no hitting into the group in front. Most important, the players could practice only as a team, not as individuals, and they could show up to play each course only on the team's designated day.

John Schlee didn't believe these rules applied to him.

"When I was at Memphis State, we had five country clubs at our disposal [for practice], and at one time or another during my career I got us kicked off all of them," he said later.

Schlee refused to let anyone stand in the way of his tour destiny. He had only one dream, and he fiercely felt a right to pursue it.

"He was probably the most self-centered, goal-directed person I've known in any walk of life. He was a total loner," a college teammate observed. "I was as close to him as anybody, and you couldn't get that close. Nothing else mattered but being the best golfer in the world."

Schlee's favorite of the five available courses was the Memphis Country Club, a challenging layout only a few miles from campus. When the team practiced there, the two-time U.S. Open champion and Tennessee native Cary Middlecoff would often walk around with a club in hand, hitting an occasional shot and regularly talking with and advising the players. The club was formally closed on Mondays, but members were allowed to play if they carried their own bags.

Although Monday was not the team's designated day to play the Memphis Country Club, Schlee had an uncontrollable urge to do so, and one day he convinced himself it would do no one any harm if he did. He sneaked on at a distant hole location, far from the clubhouse, prepared to scam his way out of trouble if he got caught.

Before long, Schlee was spotted on the course and called back to the clubhouse to explain what he was doing there. As a former teammate, Ken Lindsay, recounted, Schlee "was not very gracious in being caught," trying to make his case by saying things like, "Well, hell, there's nobody out there and I need to practice. . . . You got the best course out here and you ought to open your heart and let us come out here and play a little bit more often." Not surprisingly, that explanation didn't impress club members, who promptly revoked the team's playing privileges for the entire school year.

"I was there to play golf, not socialize," Schlee said with little remorse.

Neither was Schlee at Memphis State to study anything but golf. During his junior year, he struggled all semester in his accounting course, and one day during class he quietly asked a teammate if he would bring his books back to the dorm. The teammate couldn't understand what Schlee meant, until he noticed that Schlee's hands were clasped tightly over a pencil, in a golf grip. "I've just found something; I've got to go try this," he said.

Schlee stood up, sidled to the aisle, and started walking toward the back door of the large classroom. The instructor asked, "Mr. Schlee, are you going somewhere?" To which Schlee responded, without breaking stride, "Hell, Professor, I've been waiting to get this grip for a long time, and now that I've got it I'm not letting up until I can try it out." By that time, Schlee had reached the door and just kept going.

Unlike in high school, Schlee wasn't openly disruptive at Memphis State; he was just indifferent to academics as his mind drifted toward golf. To his teammates he could be enjoyable, telling jokes, easing the mood.

"He was a good person to be around," said Lindsay, his regular senior-year golfing partner. "I have no bad memories whatsoever about John."

Schlee also became close friends with a young couple who lived near the athletic dormitory in married-student housing. They entrusted Schlee with babysitting their infant son. Schlee treated their home as his, regularly eating meals there and sneaking in when they were away (once removing the air conditioner to gain entry) in order to sleep with a flock of coeds.

Some shared less fond memories of John Schlee. One day during lunch in the cafeteria, he was eating a hamburger and fries when one of the football players reached over periodically to grab a few fries. Schlee already had a tumultuous relationship with the football team: He liked to hit balls dangerously close to the team's practice facility. Schlee told the fry snatcher to stop and buy his own, but the player persisted. Finally, one last warning was issued to the player, who ignored him and attempted to snatch another fry. Schlee took a sharp fork and "absolutely stabbed him" on the back of the hand. No matter where he moved—Seaside, Fort Bragg, West Point, Memphis—Schlee's whatever-it-takes attitude came with him.

Still, Schlee impressed and fascinated his golf buddies. No one practiced longer or harder, both on and off the course, than Schlee. And with his physical strength, he hit "some of the longest drives that I had ever seen in my life," Lindsay recalled. "John's forearms reminded me of Arnold Palmer's. He just had tremendous hand-arm strength."

Just as in high school, Schlee still hit all of his clubs very low, which gave him a tremendous advantage: The cold and wind of spring in Memphis were similar to the weather he'd experienced nine months a year while learning the game on the Oregon coast.

For all his talent and confidence, Schlee knew that as a member of the unheralded Memphis State program, joining the PGA tour would not be easy.

"In my first year at Memphis," Schlee recalled, "I asked Dub Fondren [a well-known Memphis-area professional] to take a look at my swing. He let me practice six straight hours with every club in my bag before he said a single word. I was so tired I was ready to collapse. Finally he said, 'John, if you want to be a good player, it's going to take a long time.'"

Instead of studying accounting or British literature, Schlee meticulously analyzed the basic elements of the golf swing, as defined by Ben Hogan in his 1957 classic, *Five Lessons: The Modern Fundamentals of Golf.* Hogan's popular but exhaustively technical book became Schlee's bible. He regularly quoted it verbatim at Memphis State as he sought to emulate Hogan's swing positions, and encouraged his teammates to do the same.

For Schlee, a better swing guru than Hogan did not exist. But Schlee took many Hoganisms too literally, such as, "Reverse every natural instinct and do the opposite of what you are inclined to do, and you will probably come very close to having a perfect golf swing." Other, relatively simple ideas, Schlee morphed into extreme concepts.

SINCE CHILDHOOD, SCHLEE HAD EMPLOYED a strong left-hand grip (i.e., the V formed by the thumb and forefinger were pointed to the right shoulder); this made him prone to hitting sharp hooks. In his book, Hogan recommended as a remedy a weaker left-hand grip, with the left thumb on top of the shaft and the V aimed at the right ear or perhaps even the chin. This grip—which produced a predictable, soft fade that he could control without sacrificing power—helped transform Hogan into a nine-time major championship winner.

Schlee obsessively tried to implement Hogan's grip advice, but he just could not achieve the results he hoped for. Out of frustration, he broke off the butt end of a golf club (the grip and upper part of the shaft) and asked a Memphis State athletic trainer to tape his left hand to the club in the extreme weak grip position. Although he kept his hand taped for a full month, Schlee still tended to draw the ball from right to left, despite his weak left grip.

Five Lessons made Schlee the golf team's technical authority and a convert to Hogan's "fundamentals." A chance, outside-the-ropes personal encounter following Schlee's freshman year clinched his conversion to the Hogan gospel.

In June 1960, Ben Hogan arrived in Tennessee to warm up for the U.S. Open, just two weeks away. Forty-eight years old and semiretired, Hogan played in only the Masters, the U.S. Open, and a few other American tournaments; the Memphis Open would be just his fifth appearance of the season.

The site of the event, the Colonial Country Club, was only a short distance from Memphis State's campus, and Schlee—a summer lifeguard at the club's pool—managed to find a ticket to the third round. He even received VIP treatment, as an official brought him and a few friends to the door of the players' locker room. There Schlee spotted Hogan, and the excitement of seeing golf's swing guru in the flesh led Schlee to blurt out, "I would love to learn how to play golf from you someday."

As Schlee's friend and future pupil Tom Bertrand later wrote, the stoic, four-time U.S. Open Champion didn't quite know what to make of the tall, gangly collegian.

"Their eyes locked," Bertrand wrote, "and the room instantly fell silent. John could feel the intensity of Hogan's gaze boring straight through his eyeballs. Everyone knew that Hogan hated to give lessons.

"Before Hogan had a chance to reply to this impertinent outburst, John's official escort grabbed his arm and whisked him away. The official cast an apologetic glance toward Hogan as they marched out the doorway."

However awkward, this brisk encounter with golf's "Wee Ice Mon" seemed to elevate Schlee's game. Three days later at the nearby Fox Meadows Golf Course, he scored a 70-72 (the second-lowest total) in the qualifier to earn a spot in the National Public Links Championship. A few weeks later, in July 1960, he flew to Hawaii for his first appearance in a national event. Although he failed to qualify for the match-play portion of the championship, the experience on the big stage paid off. On his return to the mainland, he finally won the Oregon coast match-play championship in Astoria that had eluded him in high school.

The following summer, in 1961, Schlee scored the nation's third-lowest qualifying score (138), and then reached the semifinals of the national Public Links Championship, contested in Detroit. There he lost 2 & 1 to the eventual winner and future NCAA individual champion, R. H. Sikes.

Schlee's tournament play only improved and he performed well in several high-profile Southern events, including the Tennessee State Amateur and two Arkansas-based invitational tournaments. That reputation blossomed with consecutive strong showings in the National Public Links in 1962 and 1963. He even had a shot at revenge against Sikes in the 1963 championship.

"You are darned right I've been waiting to play him," Schlee told a reporter on the eve of a 3 & 2 loss to Sikes in the third round.

By then, Schlee had already left Memphis State, without earning his degree. He had begun to prepare for a professional golf career.

"I needed a couple of dumb courses like British literature to get my degree in marketing and I couldn't see how they would help my backswing, so I left."

With a few sponsors behind him, Schlee turned pro and joined the tour in 1964. Poor showings in his first three events convinced his backers to pull their support. He found work as an assistant pro at Woodmont Country Club in Nashville and competed in local events, winning the 1964 Capital City Open with a record score.

But an ugly scuffle with a member of a new group of sponsors in Nashville—just days after he won the Capital City Open—forced Schlee out of town once again. He soon landed a club job in Phoenix, and within a few months found support from several Moon Valley Country Club members, who agreed to cover all his expenses ($13,500) on tour for a year, in exchange for a substantial share of his eventual earnings. He also secured an additional $200 per month from Arizonan Del Webb, who paid him to represent the Sun City retirement community.

By late August, Schlee's game was sharp (he took third in the Wyoming Invitational) and he headed for Florida in October. There he was set to compete in a brand-new event that, to some, meant far more than a U.S. Open trophy or a Green Jacket at Augusta National.

In 1965, the PGA established a new avenue to the tour: a grueling event in which fifty-one players certified by their local PGA section competed to earn their "tour card." The commencement of the first "Q School" (officially, the PGA Tour Qualifying Tournament; the players also studied business, rules, and public relations, and attended lectures to pass a 150-question examination) took place at PGA National Golf Club in Palm Beach Gardens.

Before the advent of Q School, prospective touring pros could get into the field for PGA events only if they finished among the top sixty money earners the year before, or if they made the cut in the previous week's tournament. They could also receive special invitations to play in select events. After the creation of Q School, the seventeen top finishers became eligible to play in each week's tournament, but only by qualifying on Mondays for one of the limited entry spots.

Still, a "tour card" provided a regular opportunity to compete for purses, and the PGA had created this new path explicitly so that fervid dreamers, like Schlee, might chase golfing greatness. "If we all realized how much it meant to everybody," said one member of the pioneer Q School class, "we probably all would have fainted."

Schlee—who found short-term sponsorship from a Valley Dodge, Californian named Bill Smith—made the most of the opportunity, emerging as the school's prize pupil. He bested the course's par 71 during the opening two rounds, then hung on to his lead through the next ninety holes, finishing three strokes better than the runner-up, John Josephson. His tour card in hand, Schlee wasted no time in beginning his career. He Monday-qualified to play at the Cajun Classic in Lafayette, Louisiana, the PGA's last event of the 1965 season. In his first round as a tour professional, he shot a 69, matching the same score as Jack Nicklaus. Schlee tied for eleventh and earned $850.

But during the opening months of his official rookie season in 1966, Schlee's game deteriorated and he made the cut just twice in his first thirteen starts.

"[Out] here on the tour is something else. That's been one of the biggest problems . . . adjusting to losing," he told the *Dallas Morning News* in April. "I have $1,000 a month to spend, but I try to send some of it home to my wife. She works. It's hard to get by for less than $200 a week. I have made it for $175 on occasion . . . you know, when a (club) member takes you to lunch, maybe. A couple bucks here and a couple of more there add up."

Because Schlee had to qualify on Mondays before events began, *and* play in the Wednesday pro-ams, he sometimes played six formal rounds per week, and the grind wore him down.

"I seem to get it going and then have a bad round," he said. "But I don't intend to stay out here that long if I'm not doing any good. I figure I'll have the answer after twenty tournaments."

Schlee's mental toughness was his strongest asset, recalled Curt Siegel, a fellow Q School student whom Schlee traveled and roomed with during their first season on tour. From the start, Schlee exuded a confidence that eclipsed every other rookie.

"[He] had that instinct, 'Nobody's gonna beat us,'" said Siegel.

Schlee validated his self-assured psyche by July. At the Minnesota Golf Classic (the same event where Tom Weiskopf met his future wife, Jeanne Marie Ruth), he shot a closing-round 66 to finish in second place, only one behind Bobby Nichols.

"It was only my fifth [pay]check. I figured I had a chance to do something big on those last few holes and I was shaking like a leaf," Schlee said after accepting the $12,000 runner-up prize. "I look back at a double-bogey seven I had on the twelfth hole Friday and think maybe. . . . But I have no regrets. This is the biggest day for me. It's a super day."

Another "super day" followed just two weeks later, as he fired nine birdies and a 66 in the opening round of the Indianapolis "500" Festival Open. He tied for twelfth to earn another $2,000, then scored a pair of late-season top-fifteen finishes in Canada and Louisiana. In the end, despite the poor start, he finished forty-eighth on the tour money list—posting an impressive 72.62 stroke average that season—and earned *Golf Digest*'s PGA Rookie of the Year.

The prize money and honors meant less to Schlee than the approval of his peers.

"I enjoy being on tour. The players are a nice bunch of guys. Nicklaus came around to me after I shot an eighty-two and told me not to lose confidence and told me how he shot eighty in the British Open once. Palmer came around and congratulated me once after I had a round in the sixties."

Playing beside the tour's best only bolstered Schlee's confidence.

"I was in a threesome with Arnold Palmer and Mike Souchak. I shot a lousy score but I'm a good driver. Every hole, Palmer is here, Souchak is a little farther, and I'm maybe five yards ahead of him. The gallery can't believe a young guy can outdrive them, although I do it all the time. Now, Palmer hits his ball and the whole gallery takes off. . . . I'm lucky I get to swing. It's a race to keep ahead of the gallery. . . . All I hope is someday, they'll be following me like that."

SCHLEE FREQUENTLY APPEARED IN THE spotlight during his sophomore season on tour. In February 1967, during the final round of the Tucson Open, he was again paired with Palmer (the tournament's eventual winner), and even had a few chances during the weekend to catch the King. Schlee's hitting into a lake on the last hole on Saturday, coupled with a wild tee shot out-of-bounds at the fifteenth on Sunday, widened the gap between him and Palmer to four strokes. Despite besting Palmer by two in the final round, Schlee had to be content with finishing fourth in the Arizona desert.

Just four weeks later, Schlee shot a course-record final round of 63 in the Greater Greensboro Open (trumping the record shared by Byron Nelson, Sam Snead, and George Archer) to tie for eighth. Some believed him to be the tour's next big star.

Then it all fell apart. His game probably didn't benefit from his constantly experimenting with different putting methods and a variety of innovative golf clubs, including the Shakespeare Company's fiberglass Wonder Shaft, and the bizarrely shaped, reconfigurable driver head with removable weights invented by Steve Biltz of Phoenix. (Schlee claimed that at the 1966 Sahara Invitational, Jack Nicklaus was curious enough to ask Schlee to order him two of the triangular-headed drivers.)

A collapse in Schlee's personal life probably also triggered his professional decline.

Schlee's wife had given birth to a daughter around the time he triumphed at Q School. His absence while on tour, coupled with financial hardships during his initial fallow months, badly damaged the marriage. And when Schlee happened to meet a woman he had briefly known and corresponded with several years earlier in Oregon, his first marriage effectively ended.

"It's something I had to do. It's a lonely life," he tried to explain later.

Schlee divorced quickly and remarried in mid-1967. He chose to have nothing to do with his daughter (his new wife had a child from a previous marriage). In the meantime, as his wife and stepchild accompanied him on tour, his game continued to deteriorate. Although he competed in his first U.S. Open that June at Baltusrol (he missed the cut by six strokes), the remainder of the season was a disaster: He earned less than $5,000 in the final eight months. When the 1967 season ended, Schlee had fallen from forty-eighth on the money list a year earlier to seventy-fourth.

The slump turned out to be more than just a sophomore jinx. Aside from two fine individual rounds that led to top-fifteen finishes in 1968—a third-round 65 in January's Los Angeles Open, and another in August on the tough Firestone course at the American Golf Classic—Schlee turned in a second consecutive terrible season. Few reporters or sponsors noticed him any longer, other than to poke fun at his triangle-shaped driver and the odd putter he was then using (the head came from a discontinued model that had spent the past decade as a secretary's paperweight). The media that did cover him mostly just commented on how the twenty-nine-year-old was "graying prematurely at the temples."

By March 1969, Schlee was ready to give up the tour. "I was materially, not spiritually, in bad shape," Schlee recalled. Having been dropped by his Arizona sponsors, Schlee and his family moved to Texas. There he paid his own way on tour for the next few months and returned to using the more standard Wilson clubs with which he had learned the game.

"There are a lot of young kids who can play good, but their sponsors don't give them enough money. They have to eat hamburgers and hot dogs, sleep in cheap motels, and then go out and try to play against the millionaires. It's hard to do. You have no idea how hard it is to play golf without money."

The whole Schlee family struggled to endure financial hardships.

"Christmastimes were the worst for us," his wife remembered a few years later. "We have an eleven-year-old daughter and twice in recent years sponsors have called us just before Christmas to tell us they were dropping us. It was awful always to be broke around that time of year. However, John never stayed in any flophouses on the road. He always believed in staying in good hotels. He felt if you stayed in cheap places then you played like a cheap person."

Schlee didn't practice at cheap places either.

Regardless of his meager earnings and winless record, he was still a regular member of the PGA circuit and enjoyed a few of the perks that came with tour celebrity. Dallas's Preston Trail Golf Club—a luxurious, Ralph Plummer/Byron Nelson–designed club composed of wealthy businessmen and high-profile athletes—invited Schlee to play their course and use their facilities free of charge. Hitting balls on the Preston Trail driving range in April 1969, Schlee noticed Ben Hogan drive right past him in a cart and hit balls at the opposite end of the range. He hadn't seen the legend—who had now entirely given up tournament golf—since shouting out to him at the Memphis Open nine years earlier. Schlee tried in vain to "look my best and be professional, but I was scattering golf balls everywhere."

Then, a life-changing event—according to Schlee, a "miracle" and one that he likely distorted while retelling—occurred.

"After about twenty minutes, he got into his cart and approached me. I could feel myself freezing with anticipation. Could he possibly remember the fleeting moment when we first met? Would he even know my name? He stopped his cart a few yards away and said simply, 'John, would you like to play?' I put my clubs on his cart and we headed for the first tee. It was the beginning of a journey that would change my life."

The gawky nomad and golf's most revered shot maker were well into playing the back nine at Preston Trail before the two exchanged a single word.

"The first six, I witnessed near perfect golf from tee to green. Ben hit every fairway, every green and never had a birdie putt over fifteen feet. In total contrast, I was spraying the ball all over the course. Also in total contrast, I made every putt. I holed them from sixty-five feet . . . forty-five feet, you name it.

"After five holes, I could sense a turmoil in Ben's mind. . . . Finally, he looked at me with total honesty—the kind a father might show toward a son—and said something like, 'John, you are destroying everything I've worked for in my life. It's so obvious you are confused and have no idea what you need to do to swing a club and play golf. All you can do is putt.'

"He sensed my desire to learn and, in the next six holes, he tried to help me. My mind was so confused, so stuffed with 'try this, try that' golf, I was unable to comprehend what he was telling me. There literally wasn't any place for the information to go."

Hogan soon took Schlee under his wing (how much so remains unclear, although Schlee kept a tape recorder in his car to retain Hogan's advice while it was still fresh in his mind). Over the next few months, the two met periodically and worked on every technical part of his faltering game, from setup to follow-through. Schlee also signed up to play exclusively with Hogan golf equipment.

"He said to me, 'Son, with that left-hand grip, you're going to have to learn how to use the right side—your power side, where you've got most of your athletic and artistic ability. You're going to learn how to load that side to the maximum . . . then let it go to the target,'" Schlee recalled twenty years later. "Ben taught me to look at the left side as the stabilizing side. There is no cup in the back of the left wrist. The bowed-out left wrist allows maximum cupping or leverage in the right wrist."

And Hogan tweaked more than just Schlee's grip on the golf club; he secured his mental grip on the game itself.

"You see, golf is an attitude game," Schlee wrote in his book, *Maximum Golf*, paraphrasing another Hoganism. "It's played one shot at a time with a dream . . . and believing it will come true. When you have the courage to let this concept underly [*sic*] your golf strategy, you'll be a winner."

Schlee's association with the game's greatest technician also strengthened his confidence. More important than any swing advice Schlee drew from Hogan was a focus on the now, not on past failures. "It is a mind that wipes the slate clean with moment-by-moment, minute-by-minute rebirths, one shot at a time. It is a renewed mind, the ultimate clean machine, washed with forgiveness and forgetfulness."

Having absolved himself for all the missed cuts, the dropped sponsorships, and the struggles to provide for his family, Schlee believed he could start again. And there was no better occasion for that rebirth than his thirtieth birthday.

BEYOND ITS BOLD POLITICAL and sexual messages, the 1968 Broadway musical *Hair*—especially its theme song, "The Age of Aquarius"—reflected 1960s Americans' growing fascination with the cosmos.

In March 1969, *Time* magazine's cover—under a banner reading "Astrology and the New Cult of the Occult"—featured a celestial-bound portrait of Carroll Righter, the widely syndicated "astrologer to the stars" (including Grace Kelly and Joan Fontaine) and the de facto leader of the era's popular astrology movement.

"Isn't astrology just a fad, and a rather absurd one at that?" wrote the article's author. "Certainly. But it is also something more. The number of Americans who have found astrology fun, or fascinating, or campy, or worthy of serious study, or a source of substitute faith, have turned the fad into a phenomenon."

In addition to alerting readers about yet another revolution among America's youth, *Time* attempted to profile its followers. "They're interested in astrology because they've found the material things failing them, and they're trying to find their souls. . . . Preposterous as it may be, the astrology cult suggests a deep longing for some order in the universe—an order denied by modern science and philosophy."

He was writing about people like John Schlee.

Schlee boarded the astrology bandwagon earlier than most; by the late 1960s, he was reading his horoscope religiously. Sometimes, Righter's horoscopes seemed personally written to redirect Schlee's self-centered, combative ways.

> *Your Horoscope: Sunday, June 1, 1969:* Show much consideration for persons dwelling with you and clear up any quarrels tactfully. Make harmony the keynote. Take it easy tonight at your own home and have fun.

Whether or not Schlee took this horoscope to heart, he spent that June first preparing for the thirty-six-hole U.S. Open sectional qualifier in Dallas. After his prolonged slump and loss of sponsorship, this qualifier could demonstrate that he still belonged on tour.

Schlee had good reason for optimism. Emotionally, he felt grounded, thanks to both a happy second marriage and his devoted study of the stars. On the golf course, he was buoyed by having the greatest U.S. Open player of all time—Hogan *averaged* better than third place in ten consecutive appearances—enthusiastically in his corner. The brash optimism of Schlee's high school, military, and collegiate days was finally resurfacing.

In one of their early training sessions, when Hogan asked Schlee what his goals were, his response was that he wanted to win five consecutive U.S. Opens and finish among the top-ten all-time money earners. According to Tom Bertrand, Hogan replied, "That's very admirable, John, but let's see if we can get you ready to make the cut at the L.A. Open next week."

In "one of the strongest sectional qualifying fields in Dallas history" assembled that year—including former Masters champion Jack Burke Jr., tour star Doug Sanders, U.S. Open single-round record holder Rives McBee, as well as Texas prodigy Ben Crenshaw—Schlee was the only man to break 70 in the morning round at Dallas Athletic Club's Blue Course, firing a three under 68. Later that day—a few hours after Arnold Palmer, embarrassingly, had been forced to compete in his first U.S. Open qualifier in nearly two decades at the Youghiogheny Country Club in McKeesport, Pennsylvania—Schlee posted another fine round, a two under 69. His five-under total earned him a coveted spot in the U.S. Open, and was the most subpar qualifying score posted throughout the nation. The combination of a great score and the fact that it came on the precise day of his thirtieth birthday earned a headline in several national sports pages, including the *New York Times*.

Schlee was a Gemini. According to the zodiac chart, Geminis enter the world beneath the twin stars Castor and Pollux. These twin sons of Zeus—one mortal, one immortal—are frequently depicted as battling each other; the perpetual conflict is said to render Gemini "maddeningly inconsistent."

Traditionally, a person's birth month is supposed to be fruitful. That year, 1969, it certainly was for John Schlee.

Two weeks after the qualifier, he drove south to Houston for the U.S. Open, held at Champions Golf Club. And while best remembered for the breakthrough performance of another army man (Sergeant Orville Moody), the 1969 Open was also a watershed moment in Schlee's career: He made his first cut in a major championship. That same week, the PGA also approved a new financial sponsor for Schlee. A pair of New Jersey businessmen had read about Schlee's struggles in the *New York Times* and offered him a fabulous arrangement: They would cover his travel, food, and lodging expenses but take only ten percent of his winnings. Castor and Pollux were certainly watching over Schlee that June.

With his game on the upturn and a few more dollars in his pocket, Schlee's rebirth resumed in Cleveland. Wearing red slacks, red patent-leather shoes, and a red shirt, he exuded optimism and projected (or at least sought to project) that he belonged. Although Palmer—in the midst of his own redemptive 1969 season—was the star in late June's Cleveland Open, Schlee again quietly outplayed the King. Teeing off in the first group on Friday morning, Schlee scored a four under 66 to forge ahead at Aurora Country Club. Only a course-record 64 by Charles Coody later that afternoon kept Schlee from leading at the halfway point. Two over par during the weekend was not good enough for him to win his first professional tournament, but Schlee earned $3,960 for fifth place, his best PGA finish in a very long time.

"It's great to play without money worries," he told a Cleveland reporter that week. "I've really studied golf and attitudes and I've found you play well when you are happy, and it's not the other way around—that you are happy when you play well. And I am happy. There aren't many people who get to play this tour. It sure beats working. Sometimes I get up in the morning and count my blessings."

Schlee may not have worn bell-bottoms, tie-dyed shirts, or smoked grass, but the astrology zealot spoke like a hippie. And with the enthusiasm of a cultist, he tried to bring his fellow touring pros to his new church.

"I'm keeping this big book," he told a reporter in early 1971. "I'm charting all the pros on the tour. I've got all their birthdates and I'm working out a chart."

Whether or not his colleagues wanted these charts, Schlee occasionally posted them on their lockers before they were scheduled to tee off.

Schlee may have trusted his ultimate destiny to the stars, but he still put his golf game in Ben Hogan's hands. He worked intensely between tournaments to replicate Hogan's arduous practice routines, and also tried to integrate Hogan's mental and technical tips into his own game. Occasionally, he would drive thirty minutes from his Dallas home to Fort Worth to work with Hogan on the practice tee at Shady Oaks. There was no meteoric rise to stardom after the mentorship with Hogan began, and neither expected Schlee to rebuild his game overnight.

"Mr. Hogan said it would take me three years to groove my swing," Schlee said a few seasons later, "and he was right."

In the three full seasons that followed the "miracle" of 1969, Schlee reclaimed a respectable place on the PGA tour. In 1970, he posted four top tens, including third place in October's Azalea Open Invitational via a final-round, course-record 62. Finishing in seventy-ninth place on the money list that season comforted Schlee: He'd returned to the top one hundred after failing to do so the previous year. And because his generous New Jersey sponsors asked for only one-tenth of the cut, his lifestyle also improved.

Even better the next season, Schlee nearly doubled his money to place fifty-fourth in tour earnings. He earned $47,816 in 1971, over $20,000 more than his career best a year earlier. During the summer months, he and his family could now occasionally fly to tournaments and have his caddie drive the car to meet them. Schlee played best early in the season, posting top tens in three early winter/spring events. Just as important, he received his first invitation to the

Masters that April and made the cut, tying for thirty-sixth place. That June, he also tied for forty-seventh in the U.S. Open at Merion.

But the highlight of Schlee's 1971 season may have come in late April. Schlee's spending so many hours practicing on the Preston Trail range had convinced several club members there to provide additional financial sponsorship.

The Dallas club, founded in 1965 and represented by recent Masters champion Gay Brewer, didn't really need the publicity of having a second touring pro associated with the club. One of the nation's last all-male clubs, Preston Trail was golf-only with a vengeance: no swimming pool, no tennis courts, no elaborate banquet hall. Nor was it lacking in prominent affiliations. Well-known members included the owners of the Dallas Cowboys and Kansas City Chiefs football teams, and the founders of Lay's potato chips and Hagar slacks.

But the most famous member was New York Yankees slugger Mickey Mantle. When Mantle retired from baseball in 1968, he frequently brought his powerful—and dangerously unpredictable—golf swing to Preston Trail. Seeking to satisfy his competitive fire after injuries had forced his early retirement, Mantle joined the sponsoring group. In an act of encouragement and generosity, Preston Trail made Schlee a full member the next year.

In front of Mantle—whom he played with occasionally—and his other backers, Schlee posted an opening-round 69 in May's Byron Nelson Classic, held at Preston Trail. He scored over par the next two rounds, but then revived the faith of his supporters by shooting a Sunday 66, tied for the second-best round of the tournament.

"I'm trying like mad to make the top-sixty list," he said, "but I'm coming into my slump time of year. I won more money than I ever had last year [$27,678], but I still finished seventieth and remained nonexempt for this year's tour [i.e., he still had to play in Monday qualifiers]. The spring and summer did me in. But right now I'm doing better than I ever have."

Just as good in 1972, Schlee nabbed three more top tens and returned to the tour's top-sixty earners for the first time since his 1966 Rookie of the Year season. It had taken six more years than expected, but Schlee's game and personal life appeared better than ever.

Financially secure and well liked by many of his peers—all admired his dogged work ethic—Schlee finally seemed to have put his troubled past behind him. He was no longer just chasing a living but chasing greatness, in the form of Palmer, Nicklaus, Trevino, and Weiskopf.

And, on the surface, John and his second wife looked like the model tour couple, much like Tom and Jeanne Weiskopf, Bert and Cheryl Yancey, and other well-known young marrieds on the tournament trail.

But despite his blossoming career, Schlee could never quell his inner demons or persistent womanizing; his rudeness, belligerence, and lack of concern for others repeatedly seeped through.

His wife had to work full-time to be perfect and please her husband, and only "his way of doing things" would suffice. "You had to be on all the time," always "perfectly dressed, perfectly groomed," in order to sustain the impression of happiness and success that Schlee wanted to convey to his colleagues. His wife dutifully walked most rounds with her husband, including the Wednesday pro-ams, taking time between tournaments only to do the laundry on Mondays.

And Schlee's attention, even when he was away from the course, remained on his game. Golf was all that he truly cared about, talked about, or read about. Other people bored him, and he did his best to avoid them.

"He wasn't a social person," his second wife recalled.

Schlee sometimes stayed with friends while going from event to event. In Miami, during the Doral and Jackie Gleason tournaments, Schlee bunked for two weeks with Julia and Jim Donovan, the couple for whom he'd babysat at Memphis State—running up a huge phone bill. But Schlee and his wife mainly stayed in motels, as John felt he could not be distracted by anyone prior to or during a tournament if he was to play his best. Only during the Masters did they rent a house and socialize informally with other tour members. Apart from Brian Comstock and Rives McBee, Schlee had few close friends on tour.

With painful regularity, John's sharp tongue at required social events embarrassed his wife, to the point where she started avoiding them. Schlee was predictably rude and inappropriate, putting people down at the first sign of disagreement. Even those who admired Schlee professionally admitted he was regularly "over the top" and "outspoken"; he would never "shave the truth even a little bit" just to be kind. His wife constantly served as the family's buffer, always apologizing for her husband's "caustic behavior."

And when Schlee's game suffered, his wife bore the brunt. At one tournament, Schlee did not play well on the final Sunday and, having left the public view, he "slugged" her, knocking her down, leaving her nose and face bloody. On another Sunday, while she was driving the car on the highway following a disappointing final round, she said something that upset him. He punched her hard in the face, which forced her to lose control of the wheel. Luckily, they landed safely in a deep ditch.

Into her second marriage and with a child to protect, his former wife admitted to wearing "blinders" during the good times, even after she understood he could be "a volatile, abusive man." But she kept her fears to herself.

RAISED ON OREGON'S NORTHWEST COAST, a stone's throw from the beach, Schlee was more than comfortable playing in windy, damp, cold weather and instinctively adapted to links-like course conditions. Several high points in his early career had come playing along the ocean, including his win in the 1960 Oregon Coast Open. His greatest victory to date had come in November 1965 at Q School, which was played that year in extremely damp, harsh weather along the south Florida coast.

And the PGA event in which Schlee played most often during his professional career—largely through the influence of his distinguished amateur playing partner, Dick Chapman, a great friend of Bing Crosby—was the invitation-only Bing Crosby Pro-Am in Pebble Beach. Weather during the annual late-January event usually ranged from bad to worse at the Monterey courses.

Fittingly, Schlee's first PGA victory came with palm trees and the Pacific Ocean as the backdrop.

Schlee first played Hawaii golf in the 1960 National Public Links Tournament at the Ala Wai Country Club in Honolulu. In his great 1966 rookie season, he competed in the second Hawaiian Open at the Waialae Country Club, just three miles from Ala Wai. While the local Hawaiian hero (and Lee Trevino's close pal) Ted Makalena took that title, Schlee finished twenty-second. The next year—despite being mired in his two-year slump—he did even better, finishing fifteenth to earn a much-needed $1,750.

Schlee played respectably over the next two editions of the Hawaiian Open, but when the PGA switched the tournament from autumn to February (after discontinuing it for 1970), Schlee flourished at the increasingly prestigious and popular event.

In 1971, Schlee grabbed the lead with a first-round six under 66, one better than the headliner, Palmer. While the "unpredictable trade winds were softer than usual," Schlee nailed all eighteen greens in regulation—a stunning rarity for him, and especially satisfying for a Hogan disciple. He finished eighth and earned $5,000, his largest payday since his runner-up at the Minnesota Golf Classic five years earlier. The following year, February 1972, he took home just under $6,000 for a sixth-place tie.

The tournament returned once again to Waialae on February 1, 1973. With a field featuring Palmer, Trevino, and Bruce Crampton—who already had two wins during the young season—Schlee was by no means a favorite to win. Given his performances the past two years, perhaps he should have been. Aside from knowing the course so well, Schlee thrived, as his combative personality seemed to take a vacation when he traveled to Honolulu.

"There's something about the air here, about the people. You never see anyone getting mad. Everyone seems to be happy. I feel close to people. And that makes me happy," he said that week. "In other places my wife follows me around every course in the country. She's known as one of the great [course] walkers. But she's never been on the Waialae course. Never even been out here. She spends all her time on the beach at Waikiki. And if I didn't have to play golf for a living I'd be there with her."

Schlee continued to play great golf at Waialae. By the close of the third round, only his playing partner, Tom Watson, owned a better score. But Schlee liked his chances on Sunday, despite trailing by four strokes. He didn't hesitate to engage the twenty-three-year-old former psychology major from Stanford in spirited gamesmanship.

"I think I am playing better than Watson is," Schlee said. "He got down those three putts on the fifteenth, sixteenth and seventeenth holes—all over twenty feet. There's no way he can keep that up. Nobody does.

"Second isn't bad, but I'd like to win."

On Sunday, Watson collapsed: A double-bogey seven on the thirteenth hole crushed his chances. Meanwhile, Schlee played the front nine consistently at even par before making a move on the back, scoring birdies on numbers ten, twelve, and fourteen. He came to the eighteenth tee nursing a two-stroke lead over Watson, Orville Moody, and fellow Preston Trail member Gay Brewer. With Waialae's par-five eighteenth measuring 566 yards and a very real eagle possibility for those trailing him, Schlee still had work to do.

From the seventy-second tee, Schlee nailed "his best drive of the day." Caddie Bruce Forsythe stood next to Schlee on the fairway, watching him envision the next shot. In Schlee's mind, a third person stood beside him.

"I got to thinking, 'Now, what would [Hogan] tell me to do in this situation?' If it hadn't been for him, I'd have never pulled it off. I'd have been out on the street somewhere."

"He was walking one step beside me all the way."

Schlee landed a perfect three-iron onto the putting surface. With his wife standing green-side—she made it to the course just in time, thanks to tournament sponsors, who retrieved her from the beach, where she was calmly reading a book—he two-putted for a birdie and a score of 32 on the back nine to win by two strokes. After nine maddeningly erratic years as a professional, John Schlee had finally made his mark on the PGA tour.

Sporting a lei around his neck, he told the crowd after raising the trophy: "I owe this great moment to a lot of people—most of all my wife . . . who encouraged me when the going was the roughest."

His wife, tearful and exultant, repeated over and over, "I can't believe it, I can't believe it." And then she added, "Tonight, I'll know how it feels to sleep with a winner."

The same year when Arnold Palmer desperately hoped to reclaim his throne; the same year when Jack Nicklaus again craved the mythical Grand Slam; the same year when Lee Trevino set the million-dollar milestone in his sights; and the same year that Tom Weiskopf and Johnny Miller each struggled to overcome a festering legacy of unfulfilled greatness, John Schlee's modest, decade-long goal of *survival* was far more poignant.

"Not once over the first ten or twelve holes was I thinking of winning," he said. "I was just trying to make a living."

The $40,000 paycheck that Schlee took home—one of the largest on tour that year—meant that for the foreseeable future, the Schlee family would not have to worry about making ends meet. An official PGA tour victory would lead to new endorsement deals for equipment and clothes, much larger appearance checks for exhibitions, and guaranteed invites to several of the tour's most lucrative stops, like the Masters and the Tournament of Champions, as well as an exemption for the entire 1974 PGA season. But Schlee's most satisfying reward came much sooner.

"Right after I won the Hawaiian Open in 1973, I headed to Palm Springs for the Bob Hope Desert Classic. When I went to the Registration Table at the hotel, there were a lot of press people waiting for me.

"One of the reporters told me that there was a telegram for me from Ben

Hogan. He handed me the telegram and I opened it in front of the people who were gathered around the desk. 'What does it say?' they all asked.

"I read it to them: 'ATTABOY. BEN.'"

Boosted by a lofty "tournament champion" title, the praise of his peerless mentor, and media hype as "one of the favorites" at next week's Bob Hope Desert Classic, Schlee was reborn.

"Now my confidence is up," he told the *Dallas Morning News*, "and really, that's all you need to win out here."

• DAY FOUR •

June 17, 1973

· 11 ·

The Mad Scramble

"What did you do last night, Arnie," one of the many reporters called out Sunday morning in Oakmont's locker room.

"I went to a birthday party," Palmer replied as he changed into his cleats. "My sister and brother celebrated their birthdays. . . . No, they're not twins. They're close together—their birthdays are close together, not their ages."

"Why'd you join Oakmont, Arnold?" another yelled out.

"I like to come in to play, to play in their swats [an intraclub competitive format invented by the Fowneses that remains unique to Oakmont]. I always like to bring friends in, which I couldn't do before."

"Are you thinking of getting in politics, Arnie?" another chimed in, for the umpteenth time that week.

"I'll have to stop playing competitively before I start thinking about it," Palmer answered. "There are times when I think about giving up everything else and playing more competitively. . . . But I've worked too hard just to get things in order." Those "things" included IMG, the multimillion-dollar management company that he built with Mark McCormack—an empire that grew more profitable each day, despite Palmer's inability to win a major since 1964.

Even though he shared a piece of the final-round lead—and less than twenty-four hours after shooting 68, tying his finest performance in three U.S. Opens at Oakmont—the King was still being politely ushered off the throne.

While Palmer sat in the clubhouse, the final round got underway. Long before the big names hit the course, Sunday morning featured several intriguing matchups, or lack thereof. At 10:21 a.m., six-foot-five behemoth George Bayer hit the first tee alone: With an odd number of golfers in the field, Bayer had no partner to play with. The day before, New Zealander John Lister also had to play as a single; he attributed part of the blame for his third-round 80 to the belief that "playing alone disrupts your rhythm. All year you get used to the pace of playing with someone and suddenly you are by yourself. It's nice to relax while you are waiting for someone else to hit a shot."

With no one to pace him, Lister needed just two hours and forty minutes to complete his Saturday round. Bayer actually scored three strokes worse that same day, a twelve over 83; as he entered the final round, his main interest was finishing early enough for brunch.

"I played so badly in the third round that I just wanted to get the last round over with."

He easily achieved his goal, needing just over two hours to shoot a 79 and finish alone in last place. He still earned $800 for his time.

Bud Allin, the Vietnam veteran and former BYU teammate of Johnny Miller, was lucky enough to have a playing partner, and one with whom he shared much in common. Former West Point cadet Bert Yancey joined him for an early afternoon tee time. Sam Snead and Chi Chi Rodriguez formed another intriguing twosome: arguably the most beautiful and the ugliest golf swings in the history of the professional game. The ninety-eight-year-old duo both finished inside the top thirty.

And Ralph Johnston, a Queens-born journeyman pro, turned in a fine appetizer for the main course of Palmer, Nicklaus, Trevino, and the other heavyweights preparing to do battle. The former aeronautical engineer from Texas A&M constructed a scrambling three under 68 to balance a 76 the day before. The $2,300 he won by tying Al Geiberger and Larry Ziegler for thirteenth place marked nearly a quarter of his earnings for the entire season, and ensured him a place in the 1974 U.S. Open.

Of the many inevitable also-rans—those who began Sunday too far behind to contend for the title—Lanny Wadkins was the most defiant: He refused to simply go through the motions. In addition to the Wake Forest connection, Wadkins's brawny, compact physique and emotionally charged, go-for-broke mentality reminded many of the young Arnold Palmer.

Wadkins's boldness accounted for a mercurial performance in his third trip to the U.S. Open. On Thursday, the Richmond native, who tied for eleventh when Oakmont hosted the 1969 U.S. Amateur, outplayed the younger (Ben Crenshaw) and older (Sam Snead) members of his threesome. He played the first ten holes at even par and seemed headed for a top spot on the leaderboard, until four bogeys over the last eight holes sent him reeling. Although he hit every fairway—an exceptional achievement on Thursday's firm, fast track—a three over 74 dropped him outside the top thirty.

"I went for the birdies, and I wound up getting bogeys."

Still, Wadkins had no regrets and stayed true to his aggressive personality. The following day, he missed only two fairways (both produced bogeys) but made four birdies, two via lengthy putts, for a two under 69.

"Two more sixty-nines and I can be a winner," the twenty-three-year-old proclaimed at the halfway point. "That will put me at two eighty-one, and if you can have anything between two eighty and two eighty-four, you can be right in there for those last two or three holes Sunday."

Wadkins's boyish optimism only increased when he learned that his third-round playing partner would be fellow Virginian Vinny Giles. Eight years apart in age, Giles and Wadkins shared impressive résumés, including consecutive Walker Cup appearances in 1969 and 1971, and matching U.S. Amateur trophies.

At age sixteen, Wadkins had reached the semifinals of the 1966 Virginia State Amateur and narrowly lost to Giles—the eventual champion—in a classic match-play battle. At the North & South Amateur in April 1970, Giles lost a morning match but lent his putter to fifty-three-year-old insurance salesman and Pennsylvania golf notable Bill Hyndman. The next afternoon, Hyndman and Giles's putter triumphed over Wadkins. And on July Fourth, 1971, in a state finals match still regarded as the greatest ever played in the Old Dominion State, Giles again defeated Wadkins (the reigning U.S. Amateur champion) 3 & 2.

Even in victory, Giles deferred to his fierce young rival and friend.

"There's no question in my mind at all that Lanny Wadkins is the top amateur in the country."

Not for long; Wadkins left Wake Forest only nine days later. After two years as a college All American and winner of the coveted Byron Nelson Award for combined golf and academic achievement, he joined the PGA tour in 1971 and found immediate success, winning his first tournament and Rookie of the Year honors in 1972.

But when the two again shared a big-time championship stage at Oakmont, both men's performances could best be summed up as, well, amateur.

Giles—fresh off his eagle-par-birdie-birdie finish the day before—got off to a rough start on Saturday, missing the first green for a bogey, one of four that yielded a three over 74. Wadkins was worse, taking a double-bogey six on number one, bogeying the next hole, and finishing with a disappointing 75 instead of the 69 he hoped for.

"I felt I hit the ball better than I did yesterday. I just hit some bad shots. I missed my yardage because I figured today's air was heavy—but it wasn't."

With the two best scores on Saturday coming from the group immediately behind them—Jerry Heard (66) and John Schlee (67)—Giles's and Wadkins's struggles were baffling and, to their wives, even darkly humorous.

"Hey, you guys," Wadkins's wife, Rachel, yelled out to the group. "How about hitting a few in the fairway?"

"Yeah," chimed in Key Giles, "how about hitting it out of the rough?"

"If they keep playing like this," Mrs. Wadkins added, "they'll be lucky to break a hundred."

By a fluke in scheduling, on Sunday afternoon Giles and Wadkins were right back where they were a day earlier: teeing off together at the one-o'clock hour, with Giles one stroke ahead of Wadkins and seven off the pace. And though little changed for Giles in the final round (he shot 73 and finished sixteenth—the top amateur), twenty-four hours made a huge difference for Lanny Wadkins.

At five over par—eight strokes behind the pack of leaders—Wadkins predictably aimed for the flagstick in the final round. After a birdie on number two, he reached the par-five fourth in two shots, rolling his three-wood onto the green for the first time in four days. He then drained a forty-five-footer for an eagle. Roughly an hour later, Wadkins made another spectacular eagle putt on the difficult ninth green, this time from forty feet.

Had it not been for a poor iron shot on the par-three sixth—he made a bogey there by missing the green—Wadkins would have made up all five strokes to par on the front nine. Instead, he settled for one over par at the turn, after a sparkling 32—tying Gary Player and Gene Borek for the best front nine posted during the championship.

Considering that this was the U.S. Open, the tournament that brings out the inner choker in every player, Wadkins felt certain he could stage the greatest final march in championship golf history—an eight-stroke, come-from-behind win. None of his fellow touring pros dared doubt him.

Two weeks before the U.S. Open, a reporter had asked Jack Nicklaus to assess who posed the most serious challenge to defending his Pebble Beach title. With typical candor, Nicklaus voiced veteran players' respect for Wadkins's steely drive.

"Tom Weiskopf has more talent than anyone, but he hasn't learned to harness his insides. Lee Trevino is about as sound as there is in golf," Nicklaus said. "The best young player coming along is Ben Crenshaw. Some say he hits the ball farther than I, but I don't think so. There's Lanny Wadkins, who has more guts than talent. Johnny Miller has all the natural talent and does everything a golfer on tour should. If he had Wadkins' guts . . ."

BY HIS OWN ADMISSION, JOHNNY Miller did not have Lanny Wadkins's guts early Sunday morning at Oakmont. The 76 he shot the day before—whether due to the missing yardage book or not—had drained his hopes and evoked old fears that he didn't have what it took to win a major championship. Now in a four-way tie for thirteenth place and six strokes back, Miller had no illusions of contending for the title. Indeed, Linda Miller was "so unhappy with the way I played yesterday she nearly cried" and decided to stay behind on Sunday morning, packed the car, and waited with their infant to pick Johnny up and head to the next tour stop in Akron. Meanwhile, Johnny hitched a ride to the course with a colleague's wife, mumbling throughout the drive about his miserable play on Saturday.

Miller dragged himself to the practice tee and, with his caddie observing, began warming up for his 1:47 p.m. tee time with tour veteran Miller Barber.

"I was really down [that] morning. I had almost no desire," Miller said that evening.

"Here I had had a chance to win the Open, and I had gagged it."

The third-round 76 may have deflated Miller, but it also liberated him. Freed from the burden of strategizing his round and planning each hole, he relaxed.

But exactly what happened next remains a puzzle. Over the years, accounts have changed greatly, even taken on supernatural overtones, regarding Miller's preparations for Sunday's final round.

While hitting balls on the practice tee, Miller decided to open his stance (i.e., draw back his left foot and point his left toe more in the direction of the target). Later that evening, Miller explained that this was not a radical or new adjustment; during February's Bob Hope, he had made this exact change, with success, to correct a small glitch in his alignment.

"I remembered earlier in the year, when in eight weeks I was seventy under par and I shot a sixty-three in the Hope Classic. I was playing with an open stance. I had let my stance slip closed [since then], allowed my left foot to slide around too far, so I opened it up on the practice tee."

As Miller's "Miracle at Oakmont" has been embellished over the decades, so, too, has his memory of what occurred beforehand. When Miller returned to Oakmont thirty-four years later to broadcast the 2007 U.S. Open, he added a new element to what he had been thinking on the practice tee. His Sunday-morning stance adjustment was no longer just a recollection of a similar change he'd made a few months earlier.

"Well, I was on the practice tee and I had about five balls to go and I just had this clear thought or voice say to me, 'Open your stance way up. Way open.' And I never had that before, and never had it since. I was thinking, 'What was that?' It was like, I don't want to do that, and it just said, 'Open your stance way up,' again. And I thought, 'Well, I'll try it.' I'm always open to trying things."

Miller's caddie, "Sweet" Lou Beaudine, offered a still different account of Miller's swing adjustments.

"On Friday evening [after Miller's second-round 69] he went down on the range and worked on opening his stance. He was hopped up. 'I'm going to win,' he said. He was hitting his five-iron two hundred yards."[1]

---

1 Beaudine's account of the change to Miller's stance appeared in a *Pittsburgh Press* article in July 1978, five years after he caddied for Miller in the 1973 U.S. Open. Miller himself validated Beaudine's account five years later. When the U.S. Open returned to Oakmont in 1983, Ron Rapoport reported as follows on his interview with Miller regarding his play during the first three rounds in 1973: "Miller had scored decently the first two days of the tournament, shooting a 71 and a 69, but he was not happy with his play from tee to green. Only his putting was keeping him in the tournament. So despite the fact that he is not one to practice much during tournaments, he went to the practice

According to Beaudine, Miller's misplaced yardage book wasn't the reason for his roller-coaster round of 76 on Saturday.

"I'm going back to my old stance on Sunday," Beaudine remembered Miller saying. "I shouldn't have changed."

"That's what you get for changing your stance in the middle of a major tournament," Beaudine added. "It didn't matter whether he shot a seventy or an eighty. He had given up."

Of course, blindly endorsing Beaudine's account over Miller's would be foolish. At the same time, Beaudine's account may help explain an overlooked mystery regarding Miller's third-round score.

Without his yardage book on Saturday, Miller shot a 38 on the front nine, two over par. *After* Linda retrieved the book and handed it to him on the tenth tee, Miller shot another 38 on the back side, three over par.

Given how much emphasis Miller, even today, places on the absence of precise yardage measurements to explain his third-round 76, he probably shouldn't have scored *worse* with the yardage information than without it. But that is what actually happened: three over par with the yardage book in hand, two over par without it.

Over the years, as Miller retold the story countless times, the facts became a bit garbled. "I had forgotten my yardage book on Saturday," he claimed years later. "My wife, Linda, went back and got it for me and gave it back to me on the tenth tee. By that time, I was five over par."

In truth, Miller did not shoot a 41 (five over par) on the front nine, as he claimed; he was actually only two shots over par when he reached the tenth tee and his wife gave him the yardage book.

Miller has also exaggerated just how well he played the back nine, with the yardage book in hand. "I played like par on the back nine," he said several decades later. Miller actually played the back nine in three over par: a 38, not an even-par 35.

Whatever the cause, Miller's explanation of his high scoring in Saturday's

tee after his Friday round and did the silliest thing imaginable—he changed his swing. 'I brought my hands four inches forward and opened the club face,' he said. 'I was hitting the ball farther. It was a major swing change, which was really dumb.'" Ron Rapoport, "Johnny Miller Returns to the Scene of His Miracle 63," June 13, 1983, *Los Angeles Times* (*Chicago Sun-Times*).

third round just doesn't add up, or seem solidly grounded in the available facts: neither the front and back nine scores, nor his account of them.

This tangled web of memories remains irresolvable; so, too, the irresistible tendency to embroider a compelling athletic tale. Regardless of when, why, where, or how it occurred, a rejuvenated Johnny Miller stepped onto the first tee Sunday morning: the one-of-a-kind, zoned-in, inspired golfer blessed with an unearthly ability to "go low."

Miller led off his Sunday round with a superb drive down the middle of the damp fairway. He followed that with a high, perfectly clipped three-iron that stuck to five feet, despite the front-to-back-sloping green. The pair of brilliant shots yielded a rare birdie on the daunting first hole.

After crossing the bridge over the turnpike, Miller played for position off the tee on the short, uphill par-four. He then calmly nailed his nine-iron approach to a foot from the flagstick. A pair of birdies from a combined putting distance of six feet: a perfect recipe for conquering two of the most punishing greens in the entire golfing world.

On the third hole, Miller avoided the Church Pews off the tee and reached the green in regulation, but had a long putt for birdie when his five-iron lacked the precision of his two previous approach shots.

"I was just trying to get close from twenty-five feet," he recalled, "but when it went in, I said to myself, 'Well, son of a gun, I'm back to even par.'"

Miller had not played the par-five fourth hole particularly well, scoring no better than par each of the first three days. Still, despite letting his three-wood sail right into the green-side bunker, over a hundred feet from the flagstick, he remained confident about getting his birdie. His sand blast was a beauty, carrying thirty yards in the air before landing gently and skirting the cup's left edge, a mere six inches away.

Four birdies in four holes (three via putts from near tap-in range) unexpectedly made Miller a contender, while the preround leaders continued to stroke putts on the practice green.

"When I get charged up, all I can think about is birdies," he said. "I'm Joe Feast or Famine—I get everything or nothing."

And after the fourth consecutive birdie, clearly Joe Feast was playing Oakmont.

"I was sky-high and said, 'Okay, baby, let's go!'"

Miller fell slightly from his atmospheric high once he walked off the fourth green. Unspectacular on the fifth and sixth—though he did leave both approach shots safely below the hole—his two-putts from around twenty-five feet secured easy pars.

Now two shots behind the leaders, Miller hit a long, straight drive beyond the crest of the hill on the seventh fairway; this left him staring down the unnerving pin located on the green's back right corner. With the afternoon winds picking up, the safe play was to leave the second shot well below the hole to avoid overshooting the green. But Miller was flag-hunting that Sunday afternoon. Just as the last pairing of the day (Julius Boros and Jerry Heard) started their round, Miller flew his nine-iron straight at the flagstick and stopped the ball a mere six feet away.

If he could sink the relatively simple putt on number seven, Miller would be within a stroke of the lead, one step closer to winning his first major championship. But as he lined up his putt, the excitement of what was happening finally caught up with Miller. Not only was he creeping up on the leaders; he seemed yet again on his way to the kind of surreal round that was becoming his tour trademark—much like the 61 he shot at Phoenix three years earlier, or his 63 back in February at the Bob Hope. And just like two years earlier at Augusta National and the following January at Pebble Beach, his mind started to wander.

His short putt for birdie on number seven wasn't even close. "I really got pumped up. I was super nervous . . . my putt at seven was a choke." Still four under through seven holes, but a great opportunity squandered.

Miller regathered himself on the tee at the gigantic, par-three eighth (playing 255 yards that day to the rear pin position), and dropped a four-wood safely onto the green: a fine shot, and close enough to ensure a simple par on Oakmont's flattest putting surface.

But again Miller lost mental focus and stumbled on the green. He misstruck his thirty-footer and it came up well short. He badly missed the remaining five-footer.

"I can honestly say I gagged on those putts on seven and eight," he said afterward. "One thing I kept in my head out there all day. 'Don't shank,' I was thinking. I was thinking that on almost every iron shot. I know that's bad thinking, but I couldn't help it. It was always up there in my mind."

At the most critical moment in his pro career, Johnny Miller seemed to have completely forgotten his father's advice: "Never allow yourself to think negatively."

"I remembered [how] at Augusta in 1971," Miller would say later, "I got so pumped up that I was finger-walking down the fairways and took three straight bogeys."

As he crossed the Pennsylvania Turnpike to play the last ten holes, back to even par for the championship and four shots behind the leaders, Miller couldn't help but fear that history was about to repeat itself.

FOUR STROKES OFF THE LEAD at one over par, Gary Player teed off two groups after Johnny Miller. Sapped of his legendary stamina, Player improved significantly upon Saturday's collapse (77) but never roamed into contention, with a 73 on Sunday. His finishing twelfth at the U.S. Open, just a few months after two major surgeries, let his colleagues know that he was back to stay and a threat in any major championship.

Just minutes after Player teed off, the youngest member of golf's Big Three took the stage. At 2:02 p.m., Jack Nicklaus, also four shots back at one over par, set out to replicate the finest single round of his luminous career.

Six years earlier, at another of America's esteemed golf cathedrals, Baltusrol in New Jersey, Nicklaus began the last round of the Open trailing the leader by a stroke. Playing alongside Arnold Palmer, an inspired Golden Bear shot a faultless five under 65. Four strokes better than his nemesis, Nicklaus won his second U.S. Open, adding another glorious chapter to his major championship legacy—and another heartbreak to Palmer's.

Given Nicklaus's record of final-round brilliance and his 1962 victory at Oakmont, only a fool would count him out. Despite driving the ball inconsistently on Saturday, he scrambled to a 74 and stayed in the hunt. That night, he made an adjustment: not in his strategy or putting stroke, but one he nevertheless hoped would resurrect his chance to win.

Nicklaus concluded that the pillow he'd been sleeping on was cramping his neck and preventing a full turn on his backswing. He switched pillows (he also made this change before the final round of the 1972 British Open, where a 65 nearly edged out Lee Trevino for the Claret Jug) and was pain-free on

Sunday afternoon. From that point forward, Nicklaus traveled with his own pillow to every tournament.

Although he was not quite as keenly motivated as in 1972—when, having won the Masters, he had his sights on the Grand Slam—Nicklaus's competitive fires were still stoked at Oakmont by the roster of men he was competing against: Trevino, admittedly his toughest competitor; Palmer, the man he would always trail in the battle for public adoration; and his heir apparent, Tom Weiskopf, were each playing right behind Nicklaus. A lengthy putt for birdie on number two brought the thirteen-time major championship winner back to even par. Trailing by just three strokes with two reachable par-fives ahead, the Golden Bear believed he could overtake the leaders with a Baltusrol-like final round.

Just as Nicklaus rolled in his birdie putt on number two, a frustrated Lee Trevino shook his head in disgust back on the first green. For a remarkable fifty-third time in fifty-five tries at Oakmont, Trevino had reached the green in regulation figures. And for what must have seemed like the hundredth time that week, he could not capitalize on the opportunity. He promptly three-putted the first green and dropped to even par for the championship, tied with Nicklaus.

Missed birdie putts that teased the hole, along with the bad luck of drawing a thirteen-year-old caddie who knew nothing about Oakmont's harrowing greens, were only minor sources of frustration that week for Trevino. What most drained the once "Happy Hombre" was the weight of his celebrity and the resulting lack of privacy, which he let everyone at Oakmont know about. Each day he retreated as quickly as possible from the golf course to the seclusion of his motor home, parked near the practice range in Oakmont's members-only parking lot.

Yet however much he complained, Trevino's greatest strength as a golfer was his ability to compartmentalize: to separate his professional performance from his turbulent personal life.

Trevino shook off the slipup on the first hole and rebounded by sinking a quick, curling putt on number two that matched Nicklaus's birdie a few moments earlier. That success enticed America's most gifted golf writer, Herbert Warren Wind, to believe that Trevino's putter might arrive just in time.

"Trevino's putt was the first one of any length he had made all week," wrote

Wind, who saw Trevino as Hogan's true successor. "I remember wondering if that might set the little Texan off."

It did stir Trevino up. He grabbed another birdie on the fourth hole to move to two under, then reached the par-five ninth green in two shots, settled for a birdie, and reached three under par for the championship.

Sunday morning, three under par had been good enough for a share of the lead, and—typical of a U.S. Open—not much had changed by midafternoon. Trevino's ball striking at Oakmont remained second to none, and if Wind's prophecy proved true, a third U.S. Open championship in six years might soon be his.

Tall Tom Weiskopf teed up at the starting hole immediately after Trevino. With Weiskopf only one shot behind the leaders, a quick birdie would earn him a share of the top spot, and bring him within reach of that Father's Day present he so dearly wanted to give to the late Thomas Mannix Weiskopf.

He parred number one, then crossed the bridge above his father's railroad tracks and boldly smacked a driver on the 343-yard par-four hole—an option available only to the game's longest hitters. Weiskopf's towering drive carried to the upslope in front of the green. From there, he took dead aim at the devilishly placed flagstick on the green's back right corner, and pitched his ball seven feet above the hole. The putt was as slick as any on the golf course, but Weiskopf knocked in the birdie and, for the moment, grabbed a share of the lead.

Although Weiskopf's birdie pushed him to three under, the logjam at the top remained four deep; Palmer, Boros, and Heard made it through the first hole unscathed. John Schlee did not.

Schlee's "lunar point" may have been sky-high, thanks to the alignment of his natal moon, but after his great 67 on Saturday, he quickly descended back to earth. Being paired on Sunday with Palmer likely hastened the fall: "Gary Player told me last night to just not listen to those people, but there's just so much you can't avoid listening to. It wasn't an anti-Schlee element; the people were well mannered but I just couldn't settle down with them always chanting, 'Arnie! Arnie!'" On Sunday morning, Schlee wore an enormous white visor on his head that, he insisted, was "the same as wearing blinders."

Neither "blinders" nor his consistent success in playing with Palmer in the past helped calm Schlee on the eve of the biggest moment in his professional career.

"[You] should have seen me. Normally, I like to stay up late when I have a late tee time the following day, so I can stay in bed longer. That way, I don't worry about finding things to do for six hours or more before I tee off.

"I think I stared at the ceiling all night Saturday."

Observing on the first tee that afternoon—and just as eager as Schlee—was Bob Ford. A nineteen-year-old from the University of Tampa, Ford had come to Oakmont in early June 1973. The club's famed head professional, Lew Worsham, gave the polite, somewhat intimidated young man a three-week job before, during, and after the Open, selling hats, shirts, and periscopes. At the time, compensation was not discussed, but in the end, Worsham asked what to pay Ford for his work: $300 or a set of Ben Hogan irons. Ford took the irons.

With Worsham's permission, Ford left his cashier's post on Sunday to see the main attraction play the first hole.

"It was all about Arnold Palmer," Ford remembered, admitting to being a bit "brainwashed" because Worsham was so insistent that Palmer was "going to win to get revenge for the loss in 1962."

Having shucked his duties to see the game's greatest star, a thrilled Ford had to endure a most exasperating sight: the journeyman John Schlee alongside Arnold Palmer on the tee at number one.

"I couldn't believe he was in the position he was in," Ford remembered. Even though Schlee had won a tournament earlier that year, he stood out equally, in Ford's mind, for the "goofy Hawaiian shirt" he wore. "He didn't belong with Nicklaus and Trevino and Player and Palmer, my idols, you know."

Dressed in a powder blue shirt with white slacks, and sporting a visor of his own, Palmer mounted the tee as the boisterous crowd cheered in support; they exploded with joy when his opening drive split the fairway.

As several thousand enlistees of the undisciplined army raced down the first fairway, noisily competing for a spot to view Palmer's approach to the green, a practically invisible Schlee lined up his tee shot. The lanky, six-foot-three Dallas pro looked anything but graceful next to the shorter, broader Palmer, and not only due to his tacky wardrobe. Unusually long arms, an elastic upper torso, and an overly weighted left side at address (an extreme interpretation of Hogan's advice) made Schlee seem awkward. Try though he did, his flat, three-quarter swing looked nothing like his mentor's, and unlike Hogan, who was always in perfect balance, Schlee sometimes fell backward after lashing his driver and long irons.

"So many people were packed around the first tee," Schlee remembered. "I tried not to notice, to stay focused on my shot at hand."

Unfortunately, he couldn't do that, as Arnie's fans paraded loudly down the fairway. Schlee unleashed a quick, sloppy swipe at the ball and lurched backward.

"When I made contact, I knew I'd blocked it, and wouldn't like the result."

The ball jumped sharply to the right, a severe block, and headed toward Hulton Road—the busy thoroughfare that guards Oakmont's northern perimeter.

Assuming that the ball was out-of-bounds, Schlee now had to play a provisional, having already given away two shots and still hitting his driver on this demanding opening hole.

Schlee overcompensated for the previous blocked drive; he pulled his second tee shot to the left, into a treacherous fairway bunker. Laying three, he knew that he'd have no choice but to recover safely to the fairway from the bunker, and would be lucky to escape the hole with a triple bogey.

But maybe Schlee's "natal moon" *was* aligned. An alert U.S.G.A. official stationed to locate balls in the deep right rough caught sight of Schlee's first drive before a thick hedge stopped it from going out-of-bounds. As a result, Schlee's "provisional" ball—the second drive he'd hit into the left-side bunker—no longer counted. For official scoring purposes, it had never happened.

With the ball under the hedge and clearly unplayable, Schlee now had two options. He could drop the ball two club lengths from the hedge, no nearer to the hole, add a penalty stroke, and hit his third shot from there. Or he could return to the tee and hit his third shot from where the debacle began.

Schlee chose to return to the tee. "[The relief] wouldn't have done any good because I still would have been two inches short of the outside hedge. I could have spent all day out there."

Even if the two-club relief had taken him beyond the hedge, Schlee would still have been mired in dense, untrammeled rough. Instead, he accepted the two-shot penalty and returned to the first tee to hit what was essentially, in duffer's parlance, a "do-over." With one drive pushed badly right and the second hooked badly left, the odds seemed good that Schlee might finally hit one down the middle. He did.

Though U.S.G.A. video footage clearly shows Heard, Boros, and a huge gallery of spectators looking on in horror while Schlee walked back to the first tee to hit his third drive, Schlee had never felt more alone.

Johnny Miller reacts to a putt during his record-breaking final round of 63, June 17, 1973.
AP IMAGES

Johnny Miller acknowledges the applause of a small crowd around the fifteenth green, following his ninth birdie of the day. This putt gave him the lead, which he never relinquished, June 17, 1973.
AP IMAGES

Johnny Miller and John Schlee, the second-place finisher, are all smiles following the 1973 U.S. Open, June 17, 1973.

Johnny Miller, with his wife and child, after Miller's historic final round. [*Pittsburgh Post-Gazette* June 18, 1973]

Johnny Miller dressed up in the mod style of the early 1970s during clubhouse festivities following the U.S. Open.

Johnny Miller speaking at a trophy ceremony after winning the 1964 U.S. Junior Amateur Championship. COURTESY U.S.G.A. MUSEUM

Arnold Palmer marches with determination after shooting a 68 during the third round, June 16, 1973. AP IMAGES

Arnold Palmer signs autographs for children attending a practice round at Oakmont. [*Pittsburgh Post-Gazette*, June 13, 1973.] COPYRIGHT © *PITTSBURGH POST-GAZETTE*, 2010, ALL RIGHTS RESERVED. REPRINTED WITH PERMISSION.

Arnold Palmer with John K. Mahaffey, Oakmont's chairman of the 1973 U.S. Open Championship.

Arnold Palmer and Jack Nicklaus at Augusta National Golf Club, April 4, 1973.

Arnold Palmer's father, Milfred "Deacon" Palmer, watches the action under inclement weather during Saturday's third round, June 16, 1973.
AP IMAGES

Hired short-term by Lew Worsham to sell merchandise during the 1973 U.S. Open, Bob Ford returned to Oakmont a couple of years later as assistant golf professional, and he eventually succeeded Worsham as Oakmont's head golf professional. He remains in that post as of 2010.
REPRINTED WITH PERMISSION OF BOB FORD

John Schlee in the clubhouse talking to reporters after taking the second round lead of the Kaiser International Open in Napa, California, October 20, 1973.   AP IMAGES

John Schlee driving golf balls into a lake behind the home of friends with whom he stayed while competing in Southern Florida golf tournaments in the 1970s.

John Schlee putting during the United States Industries Classic in Sutton, Massachusetts, where his 67 tied him for the opening round lead, August 16, 1972.
AP IMAGES

Lee Trevino and Gary Player on Oakmont's practice green, June 12, 1973. Player stormed to a three-shot lead by shooting 67 in the opening round.

With Oakmont's clubhouse in the background, Jack Nicklaus sinks a putt on the huge ninth green, where the entire back half serves as the course's practice green.

With trademark intensity, Jack Nicklaus finishes his swing and stares down a drive at Oakmont, June 13, 1973.

Lee Trevino crouches in anguish as his birdie putt fails to drop in the Memphis Classic on May 20, 1973.
AP IMAGES

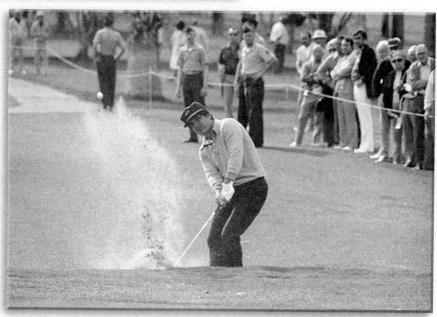

Lee Trevino nearly sinks his explosion from the sand on the tenth hole of Indian Wells Country Club in the Bob Hope Desert Classic, February 7, 1973.   AP IMAGES

Tom Weiskopf chips onto the green of the eighteenth hole at Quail Hollow Country Club in Charlotte, North Carolina, en route to an opening round 65 in the Kemper Open, May 31, 1973.
AP IMAGES

Despite nearly missing a twelve-inch putt, Tom Weiskopf held his composure to win the Kemper Open for the second time in his career, June 2, 1973.
AP IMAGES

Lanny Wadkins follows his fairway wood shot in the Kemper Open, where he finished second behind Tom Weiskopf, June 3, 1973. Wadkins's 65 in the final round of the 1973 U.S. Open is often forgotten in the shadow of Miller's 63.
AP IMAGES

Vinny Giles, the top amateur in the 1973 U.S. Open, lines up a putt during the 1973 U.S. Amateur Championship, where he was the defending champion, September 1, 1973.
AP IMAGES

Julius Boros—the fifty-three-year old, two-time U.S. Open champion who would hold a share of the third-round lead—ponders a drive off of Oakmont's first tee, June 13, 1973.

The sweet follow-through of "young lion" Jerry Heard during the 1974 U.S. Open at Winged Foot Golf Club, June 19, 1974. Heard shared the third-round lead at Oakmont in 1973 with Palmer, Boros, and Schlee.

Jim Colbert had a great deal to smile about after finishing Friday's second round just one behind the leader, Gary Player.

AP IMAGES

Raymond Floyd, whose great career faltered in the early 1970s, rebounded in the opening round of the 1973 U.S. Open to shoot 70 and finish tied for second place. He eventually finished sixteenth.

Gene Borek, the Long Island club professional who shot 65 in round two to break Ben Hogan's U.S. Open scoring record at Oakmont, dries off following his round, June 15, 1973.
AP Image

The classic follow-through of Ralph Johnston, pictured here during a golf tournament in summer 1974. The former aeronautical engineer was one of only four players to break 70 during the final round.
Reprinted with permission of Ralph Johnston

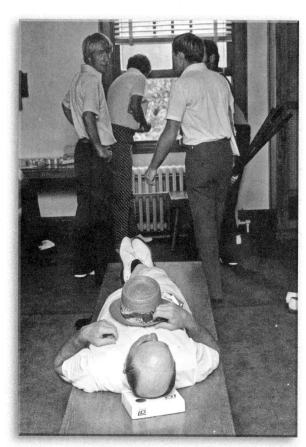

Sixty-one-year-old Sam Snead takes a nap on a bench in the locker room of Oakmont Country Club after torrential rain and wind canceled a practice round, June 12, 1973.

AP Images

The unique promotional logo of Oakmont Country Club for the 1973 U.S. Open.

Reprinted with permission of
Oakmont Country Club Archives

"It was so strange going back to the first tee," he later misremembered. "Hundreds of people were watching us tee off only moments ago, but now the only person in sight was an older gentleman in coveralls. He was holding a bag and a pole with a nail in the end, poking around picking up discarded cups and wrappers.

"When the old man saw me walk up, he stopped poking and stared at me with a questioning look on his face. Then he said, 'Not so good, huh?'

"'No, not so good,' I said as I teed up a new ball. 'But wait'll you see this next shot.'"

That next shot landed safely in the fairway. Still, he was laying three and more than 150 yards away from completing the most difficult starting hole in all of championship golf.

"That verified the fact that he didn't belong," Bob Ford recalled thinking. "I was kind of glad, you know, because I was rooting for Palmer. I wanted everybody out of the way as fast as they could get out of the way."

But Schlee was not ready to move out of Palmer's or anyone else's way—not after the tortuous path he'd traveled from Seaside to the precipice of winning a major championship at Oakmont. Preparing to play his fourth shot into the number one green, "All I could think was, I'd blown the Open with my very first shot," Schlee recalled. "But all the time consumed gave me a chance to talk to myself. I just told myself, 'Okay, you've got to spot these guys two strokes to win; now go out and play.'"

AFTER EACH MEMBER OF THE field had completed at least one hole, three under par still meant a spot at the top of the leaderboard. The first man to break the deadlock was Jerry Heard.

Saturday evening, reporters had asked Heard, the greenest of the final-round leaders, how he planned to deal with the daunting new pressure of leading a major championship.

"I think everybody chokes, except maybe Jack Nicklaus," he said.

By Sunday afternoon, with reporters still badgering the leaders in the locker room, Heard could no longer control his excitement.

"If I win this one I'll get so drunk tonight, I'll be able to fly home without a plane."

Through two holes, Heard could taste the champagne. Like Weiskopf, Nicklaus, Trevino, Wadkins, and his pal Johnny Miller before him, Heard grabbed a birdie on number two to stand alone in the top spot at four under par.

Heard seemed still to be riding high from the momentum of his brilliant third-round 66, an effort he attributed in good part to the levity provided by his playing partner, John Schlee. Chatting about "horses, fishing, girls. . . . everything," Heard and Schlee together had shot Saturday's two lowest scores.

"I hope I get paired with someone who likes to talk," Heard said Saturday evening. "This relaxes me out there. John and I had a great time."

Heard didn't get his wish. For the most part, the only things coming out of the mouth of his Sunday partner, Julius Boros—nearly thirty years his senior— were Kent cigarette butts. With Boros virtually silent on the course and the bulk of the gallery trailing Palmer in the twosome ahead, at least Heard's afternoon was comparatively quiet and mellow.

Not so for John Schlee, whose carefree Saturday became a distant memory the moment he nearly blocked his first drive onto Hulton Road. But somehow Schlee—this interloper trying to fend off a pride of heralded young lions, beneath the shadow of major championship icons—refused to buckle.

Following the double bogey on number one, Schlee strung together a pair of conventional pars on the next two holes, then matched a great drive with an even better four-wood on the par-five fourth. His ball snuggled just inside the fringe on the back left corner of the green and from twenty feet, he stared down an eagle putt that could essentially erase his opening-hole catastrophe. Perched over his homemade putter, he firmly struck the ball into the bottom of the cup.

Schlee removed his visor and doffed it to the gigantic gallery circling the green; they clapped and acknowledged Schlee's remarkable recovery from his first-hole disaster. But the applause was one of respect, not love. Schlee's outstanding eagle putt—like each of his strokes that afternoon—was simply the undercard to the main event: Arnold Palmer's long overdue reunion with U.S. Open victory.

Unlike his playing partner, Palmer did not reach the fourth green in two shots on Sunday. He left his second shot just short of the green, splitting the bunkers that guard the green's entry left and right. From there, he was in position to stroke a long but unencumbered chip to the flagstick from a perfect fairway lie. This strategy for playing the fourth hole worked brilliantly for Palmer, as he was the only leader to birdie the hole the first three rounds.

He made it four straight on Sunday by chipping five feet below the cup and converting the short putt. Now at four under par, he shared the lead with Jerry Heard. With shrill whistles and loud shouts of "Go!" the army's noise momentarily halted all play in the area. And those Palmer faithful who stayed near the fourth green—and didn't rudely hurry ahead, trying to follow the King to the next tee—were rewarded with the sight of Heard botching his long approach to the par-five.

Heard sliced his approach to the fourth green so badly that he was actually pleased with the outcome.

"Hit that right-hand bunker, baby; I'd rather be in the bunker if I'm not on the green."

Heard's wish was granted and the ball landed in a bunker twenty-five yards right of the green. Unfortunately, he couldn't quite execute the game plan of a simple up-and-down. His blast landed on the front edge of the green and rolled only a few feet. Missing that lengthy putt for birdie didn't bother the confident Californian; his failure to save par on his next putt did, and he lost his share of the lead.

Now—for the first time since he had stood on the Olympic Club's seventeenth green late Sunday afternoon in June 1966—Arnold Palmer held sole possession of the final-round U.S. Open lead. And for the fans gathered on this side of the Pennsylvania Turnpike, nothing else taking place on the course really mattered.

Then it got messy.

ABC's FINAL-ROUND BROADCAST OF THE seventy-third U.S. Open began Sunday afternoon at three thirty p.m. on the East Coast. With Palmer tied for the lead and Nicklaus, Trevino, Weiskopf, Boros, and 1972's top young lion Jerry Heard in the hunt, network executives hoped viewership would equal the previous year's dramatic final round at Pebble Beach, when Nicklaus outlasted the field in blustery Monterey weather.

With more color cameras in place to capture the action than ever before at a golf tournament, ABC's producers were excited to use their state-of-the-art technology. And with eleven men separated by only three shots, the producers were forced to move rapidly from one image to another. This occasionally confused the announcers about which players and holes were on-screen.

Versatile baritone Chris Schenkel anchored the nine-announcer ABC crew. Best-known for broadcasting football, the Olympics, and bowling, the forty-nine-year-old offered viewers a reasonably solid knowledge of golf. But to provide expert commentary, the legendary Byron Nelson sat beside Schenkel, microphone in hand. The sixty-one-year-old, five-time major champion remained one of the most respected names in golf, even though he had retired from tournament competition nearly three decades earlier. His slow Southern twang and relaxed style were the perfect antidotes to the natural chaos of a live golf tournament broadcast.

Former PGA champion Dave Marr and distinguished British columnist (and former German Amateur champion) Henry Longhurst provided supplemental expertise as roving commentators, while the lively Jim McKay, Bill Fleming, and Keith Jackson brought their customary enthusiasm to the broadcast.

ABC also utilized the first woman announcer at a men's golfing event, the recently retired LPGA star Marilynn Smith. Along with the suave, former New York Giants halfback Frank Gifford, Smith covered holes eight and thirteen, but was admittedly nervous in her new role. Schenkel's labored chivalry probably did little to help.

"Yes, and we even have a woman, a lady in the group," Schenkel told viewers, "and we welcome Marilynn Smith and we hope she doesn't feel too uncomfortable. The ratio for her is very good, Byron."

Quintessentially the Southern gentleman, Byron Nelson knew that Smith—a feisty, two-time major champion and brave cofounder of the LPGA—was not to be messed with.

"She can take care of herself, on or off the golf course," Nelson responded.

Out on the golf course, birdies were, not surprisingly, scarce for the leaders. Even after Friday's sprinkler malfunction on the greens, followed by Saturday's hard rains, the field was shooting no lower scores than it had on Thursday, when the course played traditionally brutally. So far, no one had matched Gary Player's score of five under that he posted at the end of round two. Oakmont had bent, but not broken.

ABC's telecast began on the downhill, 195-yard, par-three sixth hole, which Schenkel accurately deemed "one of the [most] sensational par-three holes that we've ever seen." While the tee shot required only a mid-iron, bunkers encircled a green that tilted sharply from right to left. Several moguls and countless subtle undulations made for many three putts, even from short distances. And even though the green was relatively soft, stopping the ball on the putting surface was still impossible from the deep right-side bunker. An off-line tee shot to the right could easily lead to a double bogey.

With Sunday's flagstick placed on the center right of the green, landing the ball close required a high fade. But that was a daring shot, because it brought the right-hand bunker into play. Most men felt more comfortable hitting to the left of the flagstick to set up a manageable two putt for par.

Naturally, ABC hoped to open its broadcast with a heroic portrait of Palmer standing beneath the copious trees that shaded the sixth tee. Unfortunately, the Palmer-Schlee twosome had fallen a bit behind schedule. Instead, Tom Weiskopf and Bob Charles were the first golfers to come into view on the sixth, where both men had missed the green to the left. Buried in a nasty, fried-egg lie, Charles could move the ball only a few feet and barely carried it into the green-side rough. From there, the great short-game artist chipped close enough for a bogey.

Weiskopf faced an equally difficult recovery shot, as his ball rested on a downhill slope in thick grass behind a pot bunker. He gently pitched onto the green and—benefiting from the soft conditions—the ball stopped six feet past the hole. He sank the putt to save par.

Within a few minutes, Palmer, still in sole possession of the lead, reached the sixth tee.

"The pin cut where it is today is not an easy shot for Arnie," Nelson informed the TV audience, "because he doesn't fade the ball very well."

As the wind began to pick up, Palmer fretted over what kind of shot to play. Just as he prepared to hit, he paused, stepped back, and asked his young caddie, Tom Tihey, to bring the bag so he could change clubs. He then opened his stance, having made the decision to attack the flag with a fade, and aggressively swiped at the ball.

Long before the ball reached its apex, both the gallery around the tee and the TV audience at home knew that Palmer didn't like the stroke. Immediately, he yelled out, "Oh, no," indicating that he'd double-crossed the shot: aiming left of the flagstick to produce a fade, but accidentally hooking the ball farther left instead. The shot crashed near the end wall of a bunker, accessible but buried near the lip. Palmer would have to stand above and outside the bunker just to reach the ball.

Once the groans of the gallery died down, John Schlee set up on the far right side of the tee box. Noticeably calmer and in much better balance than on his opening tee shot, Schlee arched his ball gracefully from left to right, and it stopped only ten feet from the cup.

Palmer played his difficult bunker shot well, softly exploding the ball to a hair outside of Schlee's. He left his par-saving putt short and settled for bogey. Within seconds, Schlee's left-to-right breaker curled into the cup's left edge, moving him into a five-way tie for the lead at three under with Palmer, Schlee, Weiskopf, Boros, and Heard.

"We may be here for a week," joked Nelson.

SUNDAY'S LEADERS CONTINUED TO JOCKEY for position on the remaining holes of the front nine, with little change. Though Trevino caught up with everyone at three under par, Oakmont's greens continued to perplex him, and his anger burned through the TV cameras. Americans had never seen the "Merry Mex" so glum. On both the fairways and the greens, he constantly fiddled with his putting grip and stroke, hoping to coax his fingers into striking each putt the proper distance. The brilliance of his play from tee to green could not outweigh his irritation at seeing so many putts die just short of the cup.

Nicklaus's difficulties on the front nine were entirely different, as he struggled to drive the ball in the fairway. His neck may have been pain-free, but he couldn't climb the leaderboard after his early birdie on number two. He bogeyed the par-three eighth hole after a poor tee shot, and when his makeable eagle putt at the ninth failed to drop, he remained at even par, several strokes behind.

John Schlee seemed the least likely of the contenders to remain atop the leaderboard. His topsy-turvy start—double bogey, par, par, eagle, bogey, birdie—continued throughout the rest of the front nine. After a conventional par on number seven, he sliced his three-wood weakly into the right bunker on the par-three eighth, over thirty yards from the flagstick. From there he made bogey, which dropped him a stroke behind Palmer and two behind the front-runner, Julius Boros.

Schlee and Palmer then moved on to the ninth, where both men paired long drives with solid approach shots to reach the par-five in two.

In the shadow of the clubhouse, the ninth green is multitiered and, at twenty-two thousand square feet, is one of the largest putting surfaces in American golf (the ninth green and the practice green are actually connected, divided only by a dotted chalk line). The ninth had historically been a source of great angst for Arnold Palmer.

During the fourth round of the 1962 U.S. Open, Palmer stood at three under for the championship, nursing a two-stroke lead over Nicklaus, who was playing one hole ahead. Thinking that a birdie might seal the championship, Palmer brandished his customary boldness.

"I don't suppose it surprised anyone that I went for the green, pounding a three-wood right on the screws," he recalled years later. "The ball drifted a little too much, though, and settled in the heavy rough just off the green, about pin high."

Birdie was still a definite possibility, especially for the man who specialized in the unconventionally extraordinary.

"I was used to playing out of the longer grass, where careful players seldom ventured," he said. "I took my stance and aimed at the pin and drew back my wedge. The unimaginable happened. I stubbed the shot. The ball popped up and settled in the rough mere inches from where it had been. The gallery around the green groaned and then grew so eerily quiet I swear you could hear the blood pumping angrily through my veins. I glared at the ball and tried again, producing another poor effort that left the ball eight feet from the cup. Instead of an excellent shot at birdie I now had to scramble like crazy for par. I missed the putt, grazing the right edge of the hole. I'd turned a surefire birdie into a bogey, which under the circumstances felt like a double bogey. Even worse, it gave Nicklaus just the opening he needed."

Eleven years later, Palmer could now regain a measure of revenge, if not against Nicklaus, at least on Oakmont's ninth. Sinking the forty-foot eagle putt would leapfrog Palmer from one behind the leaders to one ahead.

Sweat soaked through Palmer's shirt as he looked over the putt; the mid-day sun had peaked, firming up the greens. Throughout the championship, no putting surface was faster than the ninth. Palmer sent the severely right-to-left putt downhill across the green before it descended one terrace, climbed another, and finally slid speedily toward the hole. The crowd held its breath in anticipation as the ball neared the cup, curving ever more sharply as it slowed. Gasps turned to *aws* as it died two feet from what would have been a deafening eagle three.

To their dismay, the Palmer faithful had to wait a few minutes to see their general hole out for a share of the lead; Palmer was not playing alone, and John Schlee's turn to putt was next. After Schlee holed out for a birdie, Palmer hitched his pants, replaced his ball, and delicately tapped it into the hole. The five-deep crowd surrounding the green and those watching from the bleachers exploded.

"The hills are rocking!" Schenkel declared. "Now at eighteen it goes up on the scoreboard. Listen to 'em! Well, in the past week Secretariat and Arnold Palmer have received the most applause I've ever heard."

Unlike eleven years earlier, the 1973 U.S. Open was no head-to-head showdown, pitting golf's iconic star against his younger, ascending equal. Instead, Oakmont's fifth Open still remained a mad scramble among nearly a dozen contestants.

Palmer's birdie on number nine returned him to the top of the mountain, and from his perspective, only wily Julius Boros—who twice in the previous decade had stolen major championships from Palmer—posed a serious threat to his victory. And having shot a sparkling 33 on the back nine the day before, Palmer strode to the tenth tee confident that by Sunday evening, when he and "Deke" Palmer hopped into his Cadillac to make the long drive back to Latrobe, the U.S. Open trophy would be sitting between them.

JERRY HEARD'S SUNDAY WAS A struggle all afternoon. From tee to green, he had been brilliant in the third round, but he was far less predictable in round four. Only a good dose of luck and youthful exuberance kept him in contention.

His birdie on number two had been canceled out by the bogey on number four, and he dropped another stroke with a bogey on number six. His prospects dimmed further when—having underestimated the increasing wind—he overshot the eighth green. Fortunately for Heard (less so for the patron), his iron struck a spectator behind the green and died just before entering a series of bushy pine trees. Instead of a certain bogey or worse, Heard rebounded with a superb chip, and the par save kept him just two shots behind the leaders.

If that stroke of dumb luck didn't convince Heard that this might be his day, his odyssey at the next hole certainly did.

Of the several young lions who made headlines in the early 1970s, Heard had impressed tour veterans the most. Byron Nelson liked Heard so much, he took him on as an informal protégé. And ageless Chi Chi Rodriguez loved that Heard possessed one of the most cherished skills of the "old-timers." According to Rodriguez, Heard was the only youngster who could, at will, "hit the ball two ways" (i.e., hit a draw or fade as dictated solely by the shape of a hole or the location of a flagstick). Even golf's ultimate throwback, Lee Trevino—with whom Heard would soon share a near-fatal encounter with a lightning bolt near the thirteenth green of Butler National in the 1975 Western Open—singled out Heard as one of the game's premier ball strikers.

But Heard's celebrated control was spotty throughout the final round. On the ninth tee, trying to fade his drive and stay clear of the punishing bunkers and drainage ditch on the left, he hit a duck hook. The shot strayed so far off-line that, remarkably, it crossed over all the trouble and landed cleanly in the parallel first fairway.

After playing an excellent, long recovery shot safely back into the ninth fairway—no small feat, given the massive cross bunker that loomed before him—Heard flew a pitching wedge straight at the flag, which drew back several feet on the softened green. Faced with an uphill thirteen-footer, Heard knew that his championship prospects were now on the line. Just about every contender had birdied the ninth, and he would fall dangerously behind if he could not make a birdie four.

Heard rose to the challenge, sinking the coiling left-to-right putt and staying in the mix. He joined the large group of contenders who finished the front nine at three under par.

As invigorated as Heard was by his unlikely birdie, Julius Boros, his playing partner, could not have been more deflated when the final twosome left the ninth green. Having birdied the sixth, Boros arrived on the ninth tee at four under. He smacked a perfect drive and seemed guaranteed a third birdie on the front side, which would give him sole possession of the lead. Then a string of events torpedoed Boros's momentum.

As calm and serene as he appeared, Boros was impatient with slow play. He took only seconds to plan each shot, and barely bothered to survey greens or line up his putts. When the two-time U.S. Open champion reached his tee shot in the ninth fairway, he eagerly prepared to hit his approach, make his birdie, slam the door on all the youngsters chasing him, and take the title back to Miami for a week of fly-fishing.

Tom Weiskopf ruined Boros's idyllic dream. The usually imperturbable Boros was irritated to see that there was a delay on the ninth green: Some kind of ruling was in progress. The holdup had already taken so long that Palmer and Schlee had played through (i.e., skipped ahead of) Weiskopf and his playing partner, Bob Charles.

In this type of situation, once Palmer and Schlee sank their putts, Boros probably should have waited so that officials could determine who should hit next. If a ruling had already been rendered, then Weiskopf and Charles would be asked to complete the hole, and Boros and Heard would play behind them for the rest of the round.

Boros didn't wait. Before Schlee and Palmer had even left the green—and with Charles only a few feet from the flagstick, planning his next shot from green-side—Boros addressed his ball and stroked a long iron toward the green.

The shot was well off-line. Boros hooked his two-iron thirty yards left, nearly missing all twenty-two thousand square feet of the ninth green before settling on its far edge. With the pin located on the right, Boros had to traverse countless heaving valleys of Oakmont Poa annua.

Regarded as "an indifferent putter," Boros had already missed a short birdie putt on number seven that would have dropped him to five under par. Afterward, he gently kicked his putter in disgust for blowing the opportunity. But none of the leaders had birdied number seven, whereas everyone—Nicklaus, Trevino, Schlee, Palmer, his partner, Heard—was birdying number nine. Failing to match the rest of the leaders would be costly.

Boros's patience was then stretched even thinner after he hit his second shot: U.S.G.A. officials were busy trying to resolve Tom Weiskopf's green-side conundrum. Worse yet, when a ruling was *finally* issued, officials asked Weiskopf and Charles to finish the hole before allowing Heard to hit onto the green. All the while, a restless Boros had no choice but to wait in the fairway and contemplate his terrifying putt.

Boros nonetheless produced an outstanding eagle effort. His travelogue putt rolled up and down, left and right, over and over again, before halting six feet below the hole. The remaining putt for birdie would break sharply left to right, as Heard's had done. At first, Boros's putt looked dead-on, but he hit it too softly and the ball skirted off the cup's right edge.

Tapping in for par—after witnessing Heard's unlikely birdie—appeared to take a lot out of the fifty-three-year-old, even though he still held a share of the lead. Saturday afternoon's "Arnie and Julie Show" now felt like a solo act.

THE COMMOTION, DELAY, AND RESHUFFLING surrounding the ninth green were entirely Tom Weiskopf's fault.

Weiskopf—the only man among the leaders to escape the front side bogey-free—pushed his tee shot on number nine into the right rough, between two trees; this was one of the few spots at Oakmont where trees actually affected play. Unshaken by the minor setback, Weiskopf, wearing a lime green top and yellow slacks, arched his body over the ball: Tall and narrow, he looked like a half-ripened banana. Daring as ever, Weiskopf eschewed the safe play (pitching back onto the fairway) and elected to carry the trees and attack the green with a high five-iron fade. Unfortunately, the tall grass forced the clubface to open wide at impact and launched the ball into a pronounced slice.

"Oh, my God," Weiskopf moaned as soon as he hit the shot, rushing toward the fairway to follow the ball's wayward flight. A marshal shouted, "Fore to the right," at the top of his voice, to alert everyone in the vicinity of the immediate danger.

In the ABC booth, Chris Schenkel and Byron Nelson saw the ball lift off and curve wildly, but neither knew where it landed. Watching from her home on 179 Bexley Drive in Bedford, Ohio, Eva Weiskopf—the recently wid-owed, former teen phenom who still competed regularly in Cleveland amateur circles—had no clue either about where the ball was heading, and wondered if her son's championship hopes had also vanished. Because trees blocked most of the area from camera view, Nelson could describe the area where it was heading only as "dark country over there."

Green-side fans helped officials locate Weiskopf's ball inside a large, green-and-white-striped tent that was still "in bounds," but well beyond the conven-tional field of play. His wayward iron had struck a vendor selling periscopes near the tent, then bounced through an open flap into a concession stand and onto a snack table, where it nearly hit a few startled patrons munching hot dogs. The ball nestled several feet off the ground on a table—between a mustard jar and a loaf of bread.

While Weiskopf and the crowd chuckled over the absurdity of the scene, U.S.G.A. officials faced a complicated rules quandary that required considerable time to resolve. Ten minutes into the confusion, they instructed the twosome behind (Palmer and Schlee) to play through so the officials could continue deliberating.

The rules issue centered on what constituted fair relief for Weiskopf from the concession stand. Though he did not indulge spectators who suggested he enjoy a hot dog while waiting, Weiskopf remained notably relaxed throughout the ordeal. In the end, the long wait was rewarded with a tremendous break that kept alive his championship dream.

"At the back of the shelf was a protective awning shielding the view of the ball from curious spectators," Lincoln Werden of the *New York Times* explained the following day. "Because of the obstruction it was decided that Weiskopf should be given two club lengths' relief from the edge of the snack bar. This would put him in casual water and therefore he received further relief by being permitted to drop without penalty in a dry spot in rough grass."

While Boros and Heard continued to wait in the fairway, officials carved a narrow path through the gallery as Weiskopf paced back and forth from his ball to the green, scouting his options.

"He will have a difficult shot from there to get the ball close to the hole, even if he does have a good lie," counseled Nelson. "The pin is cut close to that side of the green, and there's a bank between it that goes up to the edge of the green."

Through the makeshift alleyway, Weiskopf decided not to loft the ball high, but rather—with the green-side rough fairly well trampled by spectators—to pitch the ball low. He hoped to deaden the force of the shot against the top of the embankment, and slowly roll the ball onto the green. Weiskopf perfectly executed his creative plan: The ball scampered off the embankment and onto the green, six feet past the hole. For a moment, the shot even looked like it might go in.

"Oooooooo!" the normally placid Nelson exclaimed. "Look at that shot. . . . That's a remarkable shot from where he was."

An elated Weiskopf waved to the stunned crowd and walked onto the green.

His understandably anxious playing partner, Bob Charles—it seemed like an hour since he'd played his last shot—putted out, then watched Weiskopf roll in the improbable birdie to join the leaders at four under.

As he walked to the tenth tee, all smiles and peering up at the Father's Day late-afternoon sky, Temperamental Tommy no longer had reason to lament that his father "never saw me play as good as I can."

· 12 ·

The Greatest Nine Ever

A few myths about the final round of the 1973 U.S. Open need to be debunked.

For one, Oakmont's greens were not slowed by a sprinkler malfunction during the wee hours of *Sunday* morning—or Saturday morning, or Thursday morning, or Wednesday morning either, as several respected authorities have claimed. The sprinklers—or perhaps a member of the grounds crew—actually "malfunctioned" sometime between late Thursday evening and early Friday morning (see chapter six). The accidental overwatering led to considerably slower greens during Friday's second round—though how much slower depended on the individual hole and the time of day. And the sprinkler mishap also led to significantly softer greens for the remainder of the championship.

The players' Friday performances reflected the changed conditions: Scores fell by nearly one-and-a-half shots between Thursday's and Friday's rounds. These unique conditions probably aided Long Island club professional Gene Borek in shooting his course-record 65.

But by late Friday afternoon, many greens had dried in the broiling summer heat and they again putted very fast, especially for those who started play in the afternoon. The ninth green remained lightning-quick all day.

Also contrary to a common legend, no biblical rainstorm occurred Saturday night or Sunday morning that turned the greens on day four to dartboard mush. Not unless the U.S. Weather Service and every newspaper in western Pennsylvania completely missed the storm. The only significant rainfall to strike the Pittsburgh region during the 1973 U.S. Open occurred on *Saturday* between six and ten a.m., when over a quarter inch delayed the first tee time less than an hour.

The Saturday-morning downpour affected more than just the greens: It softened the fairways as well. This helped players keep their drives more easily in the short grass over the entire weekend, especially on Oakmont's more steeply inclined fairways (such as the twelfth and fifteenth), without the ball scampering into the rough.

Sunday-afternoon winds did dry out the course a bit. But between the sprinkler mishap on Friday and the rains on Saturday morning, Oakmont simply couldn't regain its legendary "fast" reputation or return to the same slick greens and fairways that prevailed on Thursday, when the scores were actually a half stroke higher than on day one of the 1962 U.S. Open at Oakmont.

But by no means were the greens "slow" during the final round of the 1973 U.S. Open. In fact, they were speedier on Sunday than on Friday, following the sprinkler malfunction, and also faster on Sunday than on Saturday, following the heavy morning rains. As Byron Nelson explained during an instructional segment on Sunday, to putt Oakmont's quick greens, players still needed to allow for huge amounts of break, grip the club lightly in their fingers, and barely let the putter head touch the ground. The greens, said Nelson on Sunday morning, were putting as fast as proud club members claimed to play them on a regular basis—at least as fast as any other American championship course in this era.

Still, the greens on Sunday did show more variation than usual—depending on drainage, sun exposure, and the amount of sprinkler soaking they'd received on Friday. Discovering *where* the moisture lay on each green mattered most.

For some golfers, these uncertainties produced as many problems as if the greens were predictably lightning-fast. Fear of three-putting from short distances continued to dominate players' minds. Even after the greens dried out on Sunday afternoon, players regularly left putts short from ten or twelve feet, worried about turning a birdie opportunity into a bogey. Whether the greens were damp or not, no one seeking to come from behind dared putt Oakmont's greens aggressively in a last-ditch effort to "go low."

Even though softer greens made gauging approach shots easier, the dampness of the course made the round *more* difficult in other ways for Sunday's sixty-five contestants. The heavy, humid air shortened how far the ball would carry, and soaked fairways slowed drives once they hit the ground: Balls could not run as much as on drier, harder surfaces. The wet conditions also made Oakmont's dense, gnarly rough more of a nightmare than usual. But at no time during the 1973 U.S. Open—including Sunday's final round—were "lift-and-clean" (i.e., winter) rules in effect, as one urban legend maintains.

In short, for the players who made the weekend cut, Oakmont did *not* play notably easier on Sunday than it had on Thursday, when the course played traditionally fast and firm. Only four men broke 70 on Sunday, and the average scores (for the players who made the cut) were not statistically different on Thursday compared to Sunday. The median score on both days was 74. The "most difficult" scoring day (although the differences did not reach statistical significance) was actually Saturday—following the heavy morning rains—when the median score was 75, and the mean score was 74.323.

Thus, the myth that scoring conditions on the final Sunday of the 1973 U.S. Open championship were exceptionally easy and ripe for low scoring needs to be debunked once and for all. On Sunday, just as on Thursday and Saturday, missed fairways, missed greens, and misgauged putts continued to be punished by the merciless logic of the Fownes patriarchs: "A shot poorly played should be a shot irrevocably lost."

LAURENCE OTTO MILLER NOT ONLY introduced his son to golf; he did so without ruling via an iron fist. Still, no matter how much Laurence preached the power of positive thinking, by the time his son reached tour stardom, he did not quite abide. Miller's hang-ups on Sunday about gagging on putts at the seventh and eighth holes, or feeling, in his own words, "depressed" before the final round began, hardly echoed his father's teachings. Then again, twenty-five hundred miles west, in San Francisco's Richmond district, Dad didn't exactly follow his own advice.

"We turned on the TV set Sunday afternoon," Laurence Miller said, "and they said something about Johnny Miller making four straight birdies and getting into contention. We thought they made a mistake. Once we came to the realization of what was happening, we got on pins and needles. My wife was shaking. We just didn't want him to lose it."

During all of the excitement that took place on the ninth green—birdies by Palmer and Schlee, Weiskopf's hot-dog stand adventure, Heard's birdie from the first fairway, Boros's exasperation—Miller played Oakmont's second nine. The day before, Miller had made a clutch eagle on number nine to finish the front side at only two over par, despite playing horribly on the first seven holes. On Sunday, he strained a little less as he walked onto the ninth green: He wasn't frantically looking through the crowd to learn whether Linda had returned from their rental quarters with his yardage book.

Lou Beaudine, Miller's caddie, was frantic enough for both of them.

"Break out a package of new balls, caddie," Miller said as he passed the hot-dog tent that would soon be the scene of Tom Weiskopf's ninth-hole high jinks.

"But, but . . . you don't want to do that now, do you?" Beaudine asked. After watching his man score five front-nine birdies, the well-traveled bagman couldn't fathom Miller changing balls midround.

"Sure, I'm not superstitious," Miller said on the tenth tee.

Almost immediately, Miller reflected on what he'd said. After three-putting number eight, he had climbed back to red numbers with a birdie on number nine. Only three shots separated him from the front-runners, his good friend Jerry Heard and Arnold Palmer, the man whom, as a skinny California kid, he'd patterned his game after. In less than two hours, Miller had cut his deficit in half and leapfrogged seven men on the scoreboard with the entire back nine left to play. Even a religious man like Miller probably didn't think it was a good idea to defy the golf gods. Especially not on the tee at Oakmont's legendary tenth hole.

"Uh, give me one of the old balls," Miller told Beaudine, returning to his senses.

To have a chance for par on the downhill tenth, driving the ball into the right half of the fairway—letting the natural slant of the turf kick it left—is a must. Miller did just that. But his five-iron approach barely reached the front of the green, dying around forty feet short and left of the flagstick.

Like its nearby counterpart (Oakmont's first hole), the tenth green slants steeply from front to back and right to left: hardly an easy two-putt. Hit the forty-footer a tad light, and it would break early and end as far from the cup as it began. Strike the putt too hard and it would build speed as it passed the hole, perhaps not stopping until off the green. The tenth green epitomized the Fownes/Loeffler philosophy of using fear to test a golfer's character . . . and to punish hubris.

From the left front portion of the green, the forty-footer was actually uphill rather than downhill, but it broke at least seven feet from right to left. Miller tapped the first putt with appropriate caution; he quickly realized it was short, but the speed was excellent and he left himself a two-and-a-half-footer that, by Oakmont standards, was relatively flat, straight, and below the hole. A minute later, he carefully stroked it in.

Having escaped with a par on the tenth—a hole that putting guru Dave Pelz would later call "the toughest par-four in America"—Miller happily advanced to the short par-four eleventh, which offered a much better chance at birdie.

Success on number eleven depends heavily on producing a fine tee shot. The fairway peaks, slanting sharply left to right, so to have a birdie opportunity the drive needs to travel far enough to reach the crest. But hitting the ball too far means that it will kick into the right rough, or even into a ditch. From the top of the crest, the green—set at around a forty-five-degree angle from the fairway, and tilted sharply back-to-front—is clearly in view. With the pin placed Sunday in an accessible position on the forward left part of the green, the ideal approach would stop just under the hole, leaving an uphill putt.

Miller smashed a terrific drive to the summit on the fairway, then stroked a smooth wedge that died fourteen feet below the hole. He then grabbed his sixth birdie in eleven holes and—just as Arnold Palmer missed an eight-foot par saver on the sixth to create a five-way tie atop the leaderboard—was only one shot behind the pace, at two under par. Next up, the twelfth.

Since its creation, the 603-yard twelfth hole has been one of the epic par-fives in American championship golf. And not simply because of its length; throughout the U.S. Open's first half century (until 1955), it marked the longest hole in the history of the event. With the fairway flowing lazily downhill and no bunkers to guard the green's entry, a handful of long-hitting pre–World War II golfers—before the advent of a fairway sprinkler system—actually reached the green in two shots by rolling the ball along a summer-baked pathway across the last fifty yards.

But few players ever saw a chance to attempt this stunning feat. Numerous deep bunkers narrowed the driving area, and even if the golfer escaped these, keeping a long drive out of the rough was nearly impossible because of the fairway's sharp left-to-right incline. And the green's front-to-back tilt—featuring innumerable undulations as deceptive as any on the course—flustered even the most skilled putters.

But the twelfth played somewhat easier (though longer) over the weekend, as a result of Saturday's rains; the relatively soft fairway increased chances that anyone who struck an accurate drive would be able to keep the ball in the short grass. Then they could hit a fairway wood past a cross bunker, and clip a wedge from a reasonably flat lie onto the green from around a hundred yards. The pin on Sunday stood planted on a knoll on the green's firm front left side.

Fresh off his birdie on number eleven, Miller struck a driver as hard as he could off the twelfth tee. And for the only time all afternoon (aside from the "gag" putts on numbers seven and eight), he stumbled. The ball hooked slightly left and settled in the thick rough along the fairway. It was a shot poorly played, but, miraculously, not a shot irrevocably lost.

"It was horrible stuff, about eight inches high," Miller said of the tall grass.[1] Those in Miller's gallery who associated him only with high-profile collapses— Augusta National, 1971; Pebble Beach, 1972; the Bob Hope, 1973—thought that making par on number twelve was a pipe dream. So did Miller.

"I should have bogeyed the hole," he said.

From an unexpectedly good lie in the rough, Miller didn't have to take his full dose of medicine and wedge back weakly into the fairway. Instead, he was able to strike a fairly solid seven-iron that brought him within long-iron distance of the green, 190 yards away.

In his bloodred collared shirt and another pair of flashy houndstooth slacks, Miller eased into his picture-perfect, rhythmic backswing, then exploded his four-iron through the ball. He wrinkled his nose and, as the ball flew high and straight, spun the club a few times in nervous anticipation, only to be delighted by the result.

---

[1] Five years later, in a newspaper article (Ray Kienzl, "Caddie Hopes to Bag Miller Again," *Pittsburgh Press*, July 23, 1978) that recapped the final round, Miller's caddie, Lou Beaudine, claimed that the ball was actually deeply buried in the grass, so deep, in fact, that it appeared to have been stepped on. According to Beaudine—who passed away in 2006, and *whose claim has not been verified*—Miller asked for a ruling and a U.S.G.A. official concluded that it had been stepped on, probably by a marshal, and the official granted Miller a free lift and drop.

A few hundred miles east, in Stone Harbor, New Jersey, Oakmont member and later club champion Dick Thompson watched too. His wife had finally worn him down, and the family began a summer vacation that day, despite the final round of the world's greatest golf tournament being played at the country club where he had been a member since 1961.

"I'll never forget twelve," Thompson said, recalling his memory of watching the Open on TV in a bar. "He hit a good drive; he hooked it a little bit and was in the rough. He came out with a seven-iron. Then he hit the most incredible shot I've ever seen, because that number twelve green slopes away from you. And they had the pin . . . I'd say it was about near the middle, but over a little rise.

"What was incredible about it was how it stopped."

The shot hit the front of the green, eight feet short of the flag, grew legs, then died fourteen feet away, leaving Miller an uphill putt with a slight left-to-right break. Miller marched toward the green, surveyed the putt from several different angles, then rolled it in for an incredible birdie four.

"Number twelve was the whole turning point for me," Miller said.

Miller's eighth birdie came only a few minutes later, when he dropped a four-iron to within five feet of the flag on the par-three thirteenth.

"I really flagged it," he said about the stroke that took two hops before settling into the only easy position (directly below the hole) on this fast, partially humpbacked green. The putt broke barely an inch as Miller knocked it in. He cracked a smile, acknowledged the applause of the small crowd, and walked quickly off the green.

In Oakmont's pro shop, Bob Ford was stunned. After watching Schlee and Palmer on the first tee, he had returned to selling merchandise. From the shop's big picture window, he could see the scoreboard near the eighteenth green. He had glanced at it periodically, but the posting of Miller's birdie on the thirteenth really caught his attention.

"I said, 'Mr. Worsham, they must have run out of black numbers, because all they are putting up for Mr. Miller are red numbers.'

"'Son, I think those are birdies,' he said.

"No way he's doing that," Ford countered.

"In my mind, I think in the minds of many, Arnold was still going to win. It's only a matter of time. Arnie will find out what Johnny shoots and then he's going to shoot something better."

Miller—unconcerned at this moment about the men behind him—continued to the next hole. He launched a three-wood off the fourteenth tee that veered slightly toward the safe right side of the fairway: technically in the rough, but in a tame patch that left him a perfect angle to the flagstick, about a hundred yards away. He looked primed for a fourth consecutive birdie (for the second time that afternoon), thanks to a picturesque pitching wedge that cleared the hump before the hole and settled twelve feet away. He spoke briefly to his caddie as the two walked side by side toward yet another realistic birdie try. They could see the scoreboard behind the green confirming that Miller's three consecutive birdies had just given him a share of the lead at four under par.

"Coming down fourteen, I was crying," Beaudine remembered. "I was crying all the way around. I was half hopped up, my heart was beating fast, and I had a lump in my throat. I grabbed hold of his hand and he said, 'Hey, let me get hopped up.' I was thinking about what could happen. He could bogey seventeen and double-bogey eighteen."

When his downhill putt found the perfect line—antsy, Miller tapped at the ground with his putter, trying to *will* the ball in—only to stop two inches short, Miller nodded his head in dismay. The Mormon who "doesn't drink, doesn't smoke, and doesn't wink at the blonde in the gallery" probably didn't curse either, prior to his par tap-in. But he did walk back to the spot of the birdie try and regrip the putter, attempting to re-create in his mind and hands the feel that would have been necessary to sink the putt.

As Arnold Palmer lined up his short birdie putt on the ninth to tie Miller and Boros for the lead at four under, Miller tattooed a 280-yard drive down the narrow fifteenth fairway, safely avoiding the mini Church Pews bunkers that line the left side. Only a lengthy, precise, perfectly struck second shot would hold: The fairway slanted harshly left to right, and the green's right side was guarded by "a mammoth bunker that begins twenty yards ahead of the green and runs almost to the back edge." A month earlier, Palmer had played the 463-yard, par-four fifteenth with a camera crew filming, for his three-part television series, *The Best 18 Holes in America*.

With his adrenaline flowing, Miller's prodigious tee shot prompted a moment of brainstorming between him and his caddie. Despite his weak birdie effort on the hole before, he still oozed courage, especially after the wonderful drive.

"[He] had 187 yards to the flag and a little wind in his face," Lou Beaudine remembered.

"'Looks like a three-iron to me,' I said.

"'Naw, I'm going to use a four-iron and hit it a little different,' he said.

"'Uh-oh,' I thought. 'He's going to open up his stance and hit it into the woods.'"

Miller, in fact, did open his stance to fade his trusty four-iron—the third time he'd used it on the last four holes. As Beaudine expected, he carved the shot toward the pin located on the front right side of the green, dangerously close to the mammoth bunker. The wind picked up as his shot soared—it blew Miller's long blond hair back and flapped the collar of his shirt—but still the ball tracked the flag all the way. Striking twenty feet before the hole—and proof that the afternoon sun had started to firm up the greens—the ball bounced nearly as high as the flag before grabbing hold, then skidded ten feet to the right of the cup, along the surface's natural contour.

Miller walked to his ball and addressed the ten-footer—uphill, almost perfectly straight: the easiest putt he could have left himself on the entire green—determined not to come up short again, as he had on number fourteen. Bent at the waist, weight shifted strongly to the left side, putter aligned off the left heel, hands well ahead of the blade and inches from his left knee, he stroked the putt solidly into the bottom of the cup. He had reached eight under par for the day, and became the first man to reach five under for the championship since Gary Player on Friday evening.

"Come on, Johnny," shouted one member of the still-sparse green-side crowd. Miller, unsmiling, waved once, clenched his teeth, and waited for his playing partner, Miller Barber, to close out the hole. By now, his awesome round had electrified even the tranquil PGA veteran.

Known as "Mr. X," Barber more than lived up to his nickname. He earned a solid living on tour (six victories to date), but was content to stay in the background. Sunday at Oakmont was no exception. His donning black pants and dark sunglasses only reinforced his anonymity during the unfolding drama; so did shooting a final-round 78 to drop to twenty-fifth place.

But the forty-two-year-old from Shreveport, Louisiana, wasn't entirely inconspicuous.

"Barber started pulling for me on the back nine and that helped my confidence," Johnny remembered. "We're not good friends, especially, or anything, and I thought it was wonderful that an older fellow like that would keep cheering me on."

Caught up in the excitement that Miller was fashioning on Oakmont's back nine, Barber opted to shed his role as "final-round playing partner" and become an enthusiastic and encouraging coach—much as Laurence Miller might have done.

"Johnny, you're playing very well," he told Miller with each succeeding birdie or par. "Now let's keep on playing this way."

Next, Miller stepped to the par-three, 230-yard sixteenth. He had bogeyed the hole on Saturday, and while the flagstick on Sunday did not rest as treacherously close to the green's right edge as the day before, he knew he must avoid the deep bunker guarding the right front entry, as well as the bunkers left of the green. Miller aimed to the fat left half of the green—the only pin he didn't target the entire round—opening his stance a bit to encourage a fade, as he had on number fifteen. His goal was to let the green's natural left-to-right slant guide the shot toward the flag.

From the moment he struck it, the shot displeased Miller; the ball stayed left and flirted with the bunkers, from which it would be next to impossible to make par because of the green's severe left-to-right pitch. Dropping to a full knee squat to get a better view, he watched anxiously as the ball barely curled onto the left side of the green, more than seventy feet from the flag. As Keith Jackson observed, Miller would "have to go across a big crown in the middle of the green, an extremely difficult putt to get the ball close to the hole."

While not targeting the flagstick, Miller had certainly hoped to be closer; he simply could not afford to lose momentum (and sole possession of the lead) by giving a shot back to the field at this late stage. Getting down in two from seventy feet would be as good as a birdie, and with that goal in mind, Miller lagged his first putt short and to the right—four feet away. As Keith Jackson explained, "Below the hole, where you can take a good firm rap at a flat, level putt and knock it in." This Miller did, and with two holes to play, he remained an astonishing eight under for the day.

"Johnny Miller," Jim McKay told his audience, "could be headed for the greatest round in U.S. Open history."

Miller was less concerned with history, and more concerned about getting through the next two holes.

"Barber told me when I parred sixteen, 'Baby, you got it won,' and I said, 'Wait a minute. . . .'"

Clearly, Miller did not want to assume anything. He still had two holes to go and was well aware of his history of chokes in big tournaments before. Doing so again would reinforce his reputation as a man who possessed "the habit of roaring into contention with brilliant shot making, only to stumble." And the easiest way to "stumble" would be to do too much on any single shot—a choice that fell at Miller's feet on the seventeenth tee.

All afternoon, Miller had pounded his tee shots magnificently; with his customary high trajectory, he could easily carry the trees and bunkers down the left side of the fairway that blocked the direct path to the seventeenth green. A Nicklaus-like, drive-the-green eagle was tempting; his strategy during the past three days—a wood or iron safely to the fairway—had not been particularly successful. He carded only pars on a short par-four that most pros expected to birdie at least once.

But Miller's irons on Sunday were as sharp as ever. The smart, strategic choice was to place his tee shot where he could nuzzle another wedge into easy birdie range, just as he'd done on numbers eleven, twelve, and fourteen. And at eight under for the day, why should he change strategy now?

So Miller played the safest shot possible, a one-iron to the far right side of the seventeenth fairway. He left himself a perfect angle to the pin, where he could take a full, hard swing with a wedge: nothing "cute" at this stage.

"That looks great," Lou Beaudine said as Miller's shot zeroed in on the flagstick. Landing fifteen feet short, the ball rolled another five feet before coming to a halt. Miller waved to the dazzled crowd, suddenly six rows deep, as Keith Jackson observed, "When Lady Fate is holding your hand, I guess you just grip it as much as you can."

Another birdie here would be mind-boggling, but more important, it would inch Miller's lead to two strokes at six under par. Once the leaders behind him saw that score and began running out of holes, that might be too much for any of them to match.

"If Miller makes that putt at seventeen," Dave Marr concluded, "he'll be pretty hard to catch, cause it seems like in a U.S. Open the first man in with a low score is pretty tough to beat once he's already made the scores."

But a tenth birdie didn't fall. Miller struck the ten-footer a bit too firmly, and the ball glided just past the hole's right edge. As he had done on the fourteenth, a disgusted Miller recoiled, double-checked the line from both directions, and tapped in for par. He was still shaking his head as he climbed up toward the final tee box.

Miller channeled his anger into a fabulous 280-yard drive on number eighteen.

Chris Schenkel, Byron Nelson, and the ABC producers were so impressed by Miller's swing that they showed it twice, the second time employing the slow-motion, instant-replay technology that was becoming a staple of American sports broadcasting.

"What a freewheeling swing!" Schenkel exclaimed.

"I've never seen him hit through the ball as well as he has today," Nelson added. "Of course, naturally the score speaks for itself, but as I was saying earlier, Chris, the greens are absolutely perfect. They are holding well in the best test of grass on the green I've ever seen."

In search of one last birdie, Miller charged down the fairway. He found his ball in perfect position, then kept on walking toward the green, all the while measuring distances and studying his yardage book: His drive there had soared a bit farther than on previous days.

Miller tried to remain calm and follow the advice of his friend Jerry Heard, who had recently told him "to stay cool, not to get the adrenaline flowing so I got too high, too pumped up."

But four hours into the round, Miller's nerves were frayed. Instead of following Heard's advice, or the round-long encouragement of Miller Barber, he reverted to negative thoughts and once again relied on fear, doubt, and self-condemnation to steady himself.

"Standing in the middle of the fairway at the last hole, I told myself, 'You crummy dog, don't shank this shot.'"

He didn't shank, lacing a five-iron in perfect alignment with the flagstick. The ball crashed into the ridge before the cup, looked for a moment like it might jump forward, then rolled back just over twenty feet away, with the ridge still to climb on his putt. Standing next to the green, pin high, Lanny Wadkins thought that Miller's shot was so perfect it would leave him only a five- or six-footer for 62.

But Miller could see none of that from below the green. And all that mattered to him was that he hadn't folded under the pressure, and had given himself every opportunity to win by hitting yet another iron stiff.

Miller sent his eighteenth consecutive birdie putt up over the ridge, then down toward the hole, the ball breaking only slightly left to right as it drew nearer and nearer to the left edge of the cup. No way this putt would be short, with a U.S. Open title on the line.

"[I hit] as good a putt as I'll ever hit under pressure like that," he said.

But, as on the seventeenth green, Miller stroked the ball a touch too firmly. It caught the left edge of the cup and lipped out a full 180 degrees, leaving a tricky, right-to-left-breaking two-footer that he painstakingly lined up and sank for his 63.

"Even with only about a foot-and-a-half putt, I was just trying to avoid the yips."

While the gallery erupted in applause, Miller steamed about his two consecutive birdie misses. He underhand-tossed his ball into the gallery, said his pleasantries to Mr. X, and, with a grimace on his face, shook his head as if he were ashamed. Miller quickly lightened up when Wadkins, standing at the entrance to the scorer's tent, greeted him with a smile and a handshake.

As Arnold Palmer played the par-five twelfth, hoping for a birdie that would tie him for the lead, Miller signed his scorecard and walked to the adjacent press tent.

"No, I'm not nervous," Miller told the *Pittsburgh Post-Gazette*'s Marino Parascenzo and other assembled reporters. "But if I hadn't shot this score, those guys would be out there choking among themselves. But now, with my score up there, they know what they've gotta do."

· 13 ·

Chasing Greatness

Lanny Wadkins indeed had guts, just as Jack Nicklaus said. The eagle he made at number nine brought the twenty-three-year-old to one over par for the championship. With the leaders still at three and four under, he hadn't quite roared back into contention, but he had certainly made some noise.

Despite a three-year age difference, Wadkins and Johnny Miller were close friends. They shared the same business manager and often played practice rounds together. And both were known for raw aggressiveness.

Wadkins kept an eye on his friend from the start of Sunday's round, and he knew that Miller had birdied the first four holes. While each played the front side in 32, Wadkins—who had begun the round eight strokes behind the leaders, and two behind Miller—had more ground to make up. No one brandished more confidence on a golf course than Wadkins, and he earnestly believed he could win.

Apart from the sixth hole, he played with his customary accuracy off the tee on the front side, but did not hit his irons very sharply. That changed with the new nine, as Wadkins lasered one iron shot after another to within close range.

He just missed makeable birdie tries on numbers ten and eleven, then holed short birdie putts on numbers twelve and thirteen. A few more birdies and he might sneak up on the leaders—an even more shocking thought than Miller's doing so. On the fourteenth, Wadkins carried a nine-iron to the perfect spot on the green—just beyond the back ridge, eight feet from the cup, slightly downhill—and readied for a third consecutive birdie.

Dressed sharply in powder blue slacks and white shirt—the same colors as his model, Arnold Palmer—the wavy-haired Wadkins played with familiar urgency. He took two practice strokes and two darting peeks at the flag, then fired at the hole.

But he flubbed the putt: opening the blade, abbreviating his follow-through, and pushing the ball right. It never had a chance. Wadkins tapped in with obvious annoyance, cupped the ball in the air twice to vent, and tossed it toward his bag.

Despite hitting five straight approach shots stiff, Wadkins had only two birdies on the back nine to show for it, and with par at a premium on the fifteenth and sixteenth, he had blown a golden opportunity. Making matters worse, Wadkins—a habitual scoreboard watcher—could plainly see that Miller had just birdied the thirteenth to move three strokes ahead of his fast-charging friend.

Wadkins could make only pars on numbers fifteen and sixteen, but he remained confident that two more birdies and a final-round 63 might just be enough to unnerve anyone still chasing him during the last hour. From the seventeenth tee, he nailed the left side of the fairway, leaving only a choked-down three-quarter wedge to a flag placed far back on the left sliver of the narrow green. He opened his stance and placed the ball across from his right heel, trying to carry it to the rear of the putting surface and spin it to a quick stop. His ball bounced eight feet short of the flagstick, took one large hop, and came to a halt—four inches from the cup.

"Look at that, Lanny Wadkins! That's the closest I've seen in four days of golf," ABC's Keith Jackson screamed about the near-eagle. "The way they are slicing this course today you've got to think that the membership will just be suffering all over the place."

The small green-side gallery burst into applause, as Wadkins and Vinny Giles walked side by side. Wadkins certainly benefited by having his rival and friend—who years later would become his agent—provide counsel and encouragement. After the tap-in birdie on number seventeen, Wadkins eyed another on the closing hole: a fifth (along with his two eagles) that would yield Wadkins an outside chance to win the championship, while sitting in the clubhouse and waiting for everyone to choke.

Unfortunately for Wadkins, a final-round 63 to win the U.S. Open was not *his* destiny. Wadkins swung as hard and fast as anyone on tour, in an attempt to generate as much power as possible from his strong, five-foot-nine-inch frame. For whatever reason—perhaps because he was trying to drive the ball farther than normal—Wadkins's right foot slipped during his swing on the eighteenth tee. The ball hooked wickedly and had no place to go but one of several deep bunkers left of the fairway. The unforced error cost him—he had no choice but to pitch to safety—and he suffered a bogey on the home hole.

With Giles, Wadkins walked off the course and into the scorer's tent. Since Johnny Miller had not yet completed number seventeen, Wadkins's effort earned him a fleeting place in Oakmont's history: His six-under 65 matched Gene Borek's record-setting Friday score. "[For] about two minutes," Lanny Wadkins owned a share of the course record.

"At least I finished well. I really felt like I had it going," he told reporters. "If I had made that little putt at fourteen, I could get in and give them something to shoot at. If I could get three or four under. . . ."

JULIUS BOROS NEEDED TO PLAY only even par through Oakmont's back nine to achieve Wadkins's goal. But he couldn't. The three-putt par he made at number nine turned out to be the beginning of the end for the fifty-three-year-old. He promptly pushed his tee shot on number ten and, from the tangled rough, nailed a spectator on the other side of the fairway with his approach—still sixty yards shy of the green, and buried again. A bogey there, along with another on number twelve, and the oldest man ever to win a major championship knew he was out of the race.

Very soon, so too was his partner, Jerry Heard. Heard kept within one stroke of Miller by securing a safe par on number ten. But the same inaccuracy off the tee that landed him in the *first* fairway when he teed off from the ninth tee cost him dearly on the back nine. On numbers eleven and twelve, he carded bogeys to drop three shots behind. Boros and Heard posted matching two-over-par 73s on Sunday to tie with Wadkins for seventh place, one under par for the championship.

• • •

JUST FOUR MEN NOW REMAINED on the course with a real chance to catch Miller: Schlee, Palmer, Weiskopf, and Trevino. And even though his rival, Nicklaus, had essentially dropped from contention—despite a sparkling 33, the Golden Bear just couldn't birdie enough of the back nine to make up the five strokes he needed—Lee Trevino kept fighting.

Fresh off his birdie on number nine, Trevino hit both fairway and green on the challenging tenth. His ball rested on the same terrifying line as Johnny Miller's uphill curler a half hour earlier, but about ten feet closer. Prior to the opening round, Trevino had harped on the importance of leaving uphill rather than downhill putts at Oakmont.

Still, his birdie attempt came up short. And while he couldn't be too upset by missing such a difficult putt, it was yet another one he misjudged. For Trevino, figuring out the speed of Oakmont's greens had become an impossible riddle—one that if he could only solve would earn him that third U.S. Open trophy in six years. He tapped in the par and sulked, head down, over to the eleventh hole, where his mood was not going to change any.

On the green in regulation, Trevino's uphill ten-footer could vault him into a share of the lead at four under. All week long, he had expected to make a birdie here, stating that number eleven, along with number fourteen, were Oakmont's "easiest" holes. From his crouched, tight stance, the stocky Mexican-American in red patent-leather shoes stroked his putt dead center—before it stopped two inches short.

Trevino knew immediately that he'd babied the putt, walking in glaring disgust behind the ball before it was halfway to the hole. Angrily tapping in— head still down, another birdie opportunity frittered away—he toyed with his putting grip numerous times before moving on to the par-five twelfth.

Trevino found the fairway with his drive on number twelve and, from a reasonably flat lie, piped a three-wood to within wedge distance of the green. Anticipating yet another chance to catch the leaders, he walked spryly toward his ball, nodding to a member of the gallery, flashing them a thumbs-up and a quick grin.

"This is Lee," Jim McKay told ABC viewers. "He is a little under a hundred yards from the flagstick, which is on the front of the green. Now remember, this runs away from the golfer."

Trevino daringly directed his approach left of the pin, on his predictable low trajectory, expecting the green's natural slope to redirect the ball to the right. But it skidded a bit, stayed left, and rolled fourteen feet past. Still a fine shot, leaving himself just the kind of uphill putt he wanted.

"I have never in my life seen so many golfers playing so well; in fact, it's never happened in the history of the U.S. Open," McKay observed, filling in the dead air while Trevino lined up the birdie putt. "And it isn't a question of people stumbling to victory, the way [it] sometimes happens. They're all going for it. Trevino started the day one under; he's now three under. This could make him four under."

The reigning two-time British Open champion appeared to hit an ideal putt, but it was a trifle hard and lipped off the cup's right edge. A gutsier putt than he'd hit on number eleven, but another miss despite his playing every shot superbly.

His final-round partner, Jim Colbert, shared Trevino's frustration.

"[Colbert] started one under; he's even, so he's just one over on today's round," McKay noted. "But that's the quality of the play. One over doesn't get you anywhere. You just keep falling back."

Trevino's Sunday round of two under par through twelve holes was better than anyone except Miller and Wadkins. His tee-to-green game remained as sharp as theirs, but with much less reward. No matter how well he played, he couldn't climb the leaderboard without dropping a few short putts.

Trevino was unaccustomed to a final-round U.S. Open where birdies were so prevalent. At Merion in 1971, he'd needed only two birdies in the final round to force a play-off with Nicklaus; at Oak Hill in 1968, he'd also carded two lone birdies and still won by four strokes. Two front-nine birdies and a mob of pars just didn't seem good enough on this Sunday at Oakmont.

Still, Trevino wasn't done yet, and nobody wrote him off.

"And this is Lee Trevino at the par-three thirteenth, a man who can charge; we've seen him," Frank Gifford noted as Trevino prepared to hit. "We saw him reel off five birdies at the Tournament of Champions in a row earlier this year."

Trevino's wonderfully struck four-iron—"he drilled that one in there beautifully," Marilynn Smith chimed in—stopped ten feet below the hole. And once again, Trevino's putt steered clear of the cup, and he had to settle for a maddeningly short tap-in.

On the fourteenth tee (in his mind, the other "easiest" hole on the course), Trevino was one of the few players to select a driver. He found the ideal spot to take dead aim at the flagstick from the fairway's right side, and his approach climbed just over the ridge that protected the pin: in ideal position to card just the fifth birdie on that hole on Sunday.

While the shot was excellent, Lee's body language continued to shout misery. A demonstratively "unhappy Hombre" paused in the fairway to stroke a few imaginary putts: Oakmont's greens had hypnotized him. Not unexpectedly, Trevino missed the fourteen-footer: still two shots behind Miller, with four to go.

Unable to nab birdies on the next two holes, Trevino walked onto the tee at number seventeen. He didn't want to, but he now had no choice but to rely on his emergency plan. Thursday evening, reporters had asked Trevino about Nicklaus's audacious play on the short par-four, reaching the green in one stroke with a driver.

"I won't do it unless I'm two shots behind on Sunday, and I have to make up some ground," Trevino said. "I have a game plan and I stick to it. That's not in my game plan."

Just as he hypothesized, he now found himself two shots behind the leader, with two holes to go. The eighteenth was just too long and hard to contemplate a birdie, so Trevino reasoned that he had to make an eagle of his own to catch Miller.

Trevino smacked his Faultless with all the force his solid frame could summon, but it was an unnatural gesture. A man who made big money spiking every drive down the middle on a low-trajectory fade could not easily improvise a long, high, soft hook to cut the dogleg. Even for a man who had more creative shots in his arsenal than anyone on tour, it was perhaps too great a stretch.

The drive soared farther than usual, but refused to draw. The ball finally settled well off the fairway's right edge, mired in thick rough and with Big Mouth between him and the pin.

"Trevino had to pitch over a cavernous trap and he had little green to play with," wrote El Paso Herald-Post reporter Bob Ingram—the only reporter to record Trevino's Hail Mary attempt. "The pin was in the neck of the green. On the other side of the green from Trevino was another deep trap. The El Paso golfer got the ball on the green but it didn't bite and rolled into [a] trap on the other side. Coming out of it, Trevino hit the ball too hard and it skidded past the hole and close to the fringe near the trap he had to shoot over. It took two putts to get down for a bogey five and it put him out of contention. Using the driver on number seventeen was a desperation gamble for Trevino. It didn't pay off."

Having suffered a bogey on the short seventeenth, thanks to a high-risk shot that conflicted with his normal style of play, Lee Trevino left yet another Oakmont green depressed: a recurring sight that week for the popular, misunderstood champion. He finished up number eighteen—straight drive, solid approach, two putts—and headed back to his mobile home, exactly how he wanted to be: alone.

LEE TREVINO AND TOM WEISKOPF were polar opposites.

Trevino was short, stocky, mentally tough. Weiskopf was the tall, thin "guy with the million-dollar swing and the ten-cent mind."

Trevino might never have become a professional golfer—let alone an international superstar—had it not been for his days as a marine, where both his life and golf game took shape. For Weiskopf, his five-year stint as an army reservist was merely an inconvenience that sidetracked his rise to stardom (and just happened to occur the same summer as Trevino's improbable U.S. Open victory at Oak Hill).

While Trevino—abandoned by his father and left in abject poverty—spent the better part of two decades honing his game in solitude at dusty Texas driving ranges, hunger did not inspire Tom Weiskopf until after his thirtieth birthday, and the unexpected death of his supportive father.

And even though their fortunes seemed to reverse during the summer of 1973—Trevino's bulletproof facade crumbling, as Weiskopf finally blossomed into a winner—both men's U.S. Open ride ended on the seventy-first green.

Weiskopf's Sunday caucus with U.S.G.A. officials didn't end on Oakmont's ninth. In fact, it reconvened on the very next hole.

Slicing his tee shot far into the rough turned out better than Weiskopf had reason to expect. He was allowed a free drop two club lengths from the original position of his ball, which came to rest in an area designated as ground under repair. This time, however, he couldn't follow up the lucky break with another miracle shot, like the one a hole earlier. From the tall grass, his ball came up twenty-five yards short of the green.

Confident he could scramble for par, Weiskopf readied to pitch downhill onto the green, then suddenly backed away: On the parallel fairway, Arnold Palmer had just made an approach shot, and the army bellowed. Weiskopf reset, gently chipped the ball across the downsloping fairway and fringe, and looked satisfied when it came to rest only twelve feet past the cup. The putt looked fairly straight, but in a classically deceptive Oakmont nuance, it broke much more to the right than he expected.

"That's too bad; you hate to see a man start making bogeys at this point," Marr said, empathizing.

Weiskopf couldn't regain a stroke on the eleventh, the spot where he had made the first of three back-nine birdies on Saturday. Walking down the twelfth fairway, he spotted on a nearby scoreboard the red number next to Johnny Miller's name.

PLAYER	SCORE	THROUGH
Miller	-5	COMPLETED
Palmer	-4	11
Trevino	-3	14
Weiskopf	-3	11
Boros	-3	10
Schlee	-3	11
Heard	-3	10

"I couldn't believe it when I read one of the boards out there and saw that Miller was five under. Bob Charles, who I was playing with, couldn't believe it either. He said, 'there must be some mistake.' But I told him they don't make mistakes like that unless Miller's mother came down to keep score for him."

Afterward, Weiskopf told reporters he was not terribly surprised by the 63: All week long, he had downplayed the intrinsic difficulty of Oakmont, saying, "Oakmont is not a long course. Matter of fact, it's rather short. I had only one difficult hole to play, I thought. That was the fifteenth hole."

The identity of the man who shot the 63, that was another story.

"Johnny Miller?" he told the press. "I didn't even know Miller had made the cut."

By the twelfth, Weiskopf knew but remained confident.

"I really still thought I could catch him at twelve."

But the long-hitting Weiskopf, like Nicklaus, failed to birdie the challenging par-five hole. Still, the deficit—he needed to make up two strokes in six holes—didn't seem to bother Weiskopf. Nor did he give up when he three-putted the fourteenth green to fall back to two under par, a trio of strokes behind Miller.

The new Tom Weiskopf—the motivated, mature, patient winner of three tournaments in four weeks—didn't run and hide. He parred number fifteen, the "one difficult hole" he had deigned to recognize, then moved on to the sixteenth, where he absolutely had to make a birdie.

Oakmont's sixteenth was often overlooked as a torturer of golfers. A lengthy, slanted par-three guarded by bunkers front and left and a steep falloff on the green's right side, the tee shot required a long iron or fairway wood to get home. Shaped like an upside-down punch bowl, the putting surface featured a pronounced hump at its center that made any putt from the more inviting left side of the green extremely difficult.

Weiskopf pulled a three-iron from the bag and, with his unique blend of grace and power, stroked a towering shot that landed pin-high near the center of the green, then anchored twelve feet left of the pin. From there, he drained the quick, downhill putt off the hump to reach three under and strode briskly to the next tee; one birdie down, two more to go.

"When I made a twelve-footer for a bird at sixteen, I thought I was back in, playing for the lead."

Then came the seventeenth. Trevino may have failed to reach the green in two, but the Merry Mex was not Nicklaus's heir apparent off the tee; Weiskopf was. Only he possessed the muscle and high ball flight to launch a driver all the way onto the green. And while Thursday evening Trevino criticized Nicklaus for choosing the high-risk, high-reward approach on number seventeen, Weiskopf saw the perfect opportunity to match his rival and friend.

"[If] Jack can drive it on the green, I can drive it on the green."

Weiskopf tried, but the air was heavier than on Thursday, and the increasing wind kept even the long-bombing Weiskopf from reaching the green. His drive perched just right of the fairway's center, less than forty yards from the flagstick; he could easily pitch over Big Mouth and leave himself a short birdie putt. Weiskopf's bold tee shot had paid off well enough for him to keep his dream of victory alive—and among the leaders, only he had birdied number eighteen the day before.

Whether it was because the greens were firming up in the late afternoon sun and wind, or because he couldn't spin the ball effectively from a soggy lie—water splashed when he made contact with the grass—Weiskopf's pitch took a large first hop before rolling farther beyond the cup than he anticipated. He now needed to sink a delicate twelve-footer for birdie to keep within striking distance of Miller.

Weiskopf thought he hit the putt exactly right, and waited for it to disappear. If anything, it appeared to be a right-to-left breaker. But somehow, just as it approached the hole, the ball angled severely right and danced across the front of the cup.

A dejected Weiskopf stood upright, hung his head, and glared first at the ground, then at his putter.

"I felt like I wanted to have my caddie play eighteen," he said. "I felt so deflated. I really felt I could still catch [Miller]."

Having—perhaps more than ever before—spent every ounce of will and determination, Tom Weiskopf finally gave up.

ALTHOUGH WADKINS, BOROS, HEARD, TREVINO, Weiskopf, even long-shot John Schlee each had a realistic chance to chase down Johnny Miller, by five o'clock Sunday afternoon, Arnold Palmer might as well have been the only man playing Oakmont.

Just a few paces from where Weiskopf and U.S.G.A. officials were still huddling inside the hot-dog stand, Palmer found trouble off the tenth tee, where he launched a horrible drive into the right-side rough, thirty yards off-line. He muscled the ball out, and his approach shot initially looked great, landing just short of pin-high. But the shot didn't hold. It bounced, then scooted across the length of the green—covering at least a hundred feet before thick grass fronting a rear bunker swallowed it up. From there, Palmer played a brilliant recovery chip, popping the ball out with a hard, descending stroke and letting it roll gently to within six feet of the flag.

"A very fine shot. If he makes a four here, it'll be some four after the drive that he hit," Dave Marr observed. "The people are just clapping for him every single hole. I never saw so many people out here that all knew him or know him or are pulling for him. You wouldn't think there's anyone else playing."

Having missed both fairway and green, Palmer now had a chance to leave Oakmont's "toughest" hole unscathed. He drained the six-footer, then breathed a huge sigh of relief while twirling his visor over his head as the gallery roared.

"I couldn't have felt better," he explained. "I was four under par, I was in command of myself, and I had some birdie holes left."

Palmer now headed to the eleventh, precisely one of those vital birdie holes. He skillfully landed his tee shot over the fairway crest to within ninety yards of the green. Then—with what Jim McKay called "a Pittsburgh-type smokestack in the background"—Palmer struck a perfect wedge that touched down ten feet below the hole, bounced once, and stuck pin-high, just four feet left of the flag. It was his finest shot of the championship.

"He could easily get [a birdie], and if he does, he'll move into a tie for the lead with Johnny Miller," said Jim McKay, as Arnie's Army cheered in anticipation. "You truly may be watching the greatest U.S. Open in history, and every year it seems to get tighter and tighter and more and more exciting. There is no tournament like this one in the world."

PLAYER	SCORE	THROUGH
Miller	-5	16
Palmer	-4	10
Boros	-4	9
Weiskopf	-4	9
Trevino	-3	12
Schlee	-3	10
Heard	-3	9
Wadkins	-2	17

Hitching his white slacks, Palmer walked briskly across a small bridge toward the eleventh green. He tipped his cap to the crowd, which let loose a loud cacophony of claps, whistles, and rowdy cheers.

"[What] do they think this is," a nearby marshal joked, "a Steelers game?"

Many among the army—including Doc Giffin, Palmer's trusted press agent, who followed him shot by shot—knew where the King stood in relation to Miller, Boros, Weiskopf, and the rest. And the millions at home who saw the leaderboard periodically flash on-screen also knew the scores.

Palmer did not. All he knew was that sinking the short birdie putt would move him to five under par, an unimaginably good score at the Hades of Hulton, and surely good enough to win the U.S. Open. If there was ever an "easy" chance for a birdie at Oakmont, Palmer had set himself up for one by tagging such a great approach.

The day before, Palmer had birdied number eleven by sinking a titanic forty-five-footer and was so charged up that he smashed his fist into the ground, grinning ear-to-ear as he walked over to pick up his ball. By comparison, his Sunday birdie putt looked like a "gimme."

In fact, it wasn't. On this sharply slanted green, Palmer's short putt was actually downhill and contained considerable left-to-right break. Palmer lined up the putt and, from his signature knock-kneed stance, firmly tapped the ball. But he either didn't read enough break or he opened the blade; the putt missed by a couple of inches on the low side.

Frozen, Palmer winced over his failed short putt: a painfully familiar sports-page image over the last decade. The gallery verbalized Palmer's pain, letting out a prolonged "ohhhhh" of angst.

"I made what I thought was a good stroke."

Palmer gathered himself to tap in for par, shook and hung his head, then—revived by the whistles and the cheers of, "Go get 'em, Arnie!"—marched off the green.

As he walked onto the twelfth tee, Palmer—still playing without glasses or contact lenses—squinted at the scoreboard behind the fourteenth green. With some effort, he "could make out" that Miller had dropped to five under par for the championship.

"Where the fuck did he come from?" Palmer wondered aloud. "How much under par is he?"

"I hear he has [nine] birdies," his partner, John Schlee, told him.

As it had everyone else that day, the news stunned Palmer. And not just because he thought he owned a one-stroke edge; equally confusing was the identity of the man he now trailed. During the opening two rounds, Palmer's much younger playing partner hadn't hit the ball spectacularly from tee to green; he'd remained in contention mainly due to sensational putting, which no one could sustain over four rounds at Oakmont. And in Saturday's third round, Miller seemed to get what he deserved in the form of that tournament-burying 76.

"It never entered my mind that Johnny Miller could win this tournament," Palmer admitted that evening.

"Sixty-three . . . that's just unbelievable. That is just about perfect golf on this course."

But Arnold Palmer—the man whose legend was shaped by heart-pounding, last-minute heroics—didn't collapse. He had no reason to. With numbers twelve, fourteen, and seventeen each a realistic birdie opportunity, he could surely make up the single shot he needed to tie Miller, and perhaps even the two necessary to win his second U.S. Open outright.

"Still confident," U.S.G.A. historian Robert Sommers wrote, Palmer "played what he thought was a perfect drive, shading the left side where the ground slants to the right and will kick the ball to center-fairway. He was so confident he had played the shot perfectly, he hitched his pants, and with an assured, tight-lipped smile, he turned away and didn't watch the ball land."

Palmer walked down the fairway, eager to see where his fine drive was sitting. Along the way, now close enough to see Miller's five-under score clearly, he paused and stared glumly at the leaderboard behind the fourteenth green. Finally, he shrugged his shoulders, hitched his pants, and marched toward his ball, which he was confident rested safely in the fairway.

If bad news truly does come in threes, then after squandering a birdie on number eleven and learning that he now trailed a man who began the day six shots back, Palmer should have expected the ensuing catastrophe.

"I struck what I was sure was a terrific drive at twelve, only to discover a few minutes later that the ball lying in the fairway, which I thought was mine, really belonged to Schlee. Much to my surprise, my ball had caromed left instead of right and was in deep grass on the 603-yard hole."

Palmer shed his visor and trekked into the rough. With his cleats buried in the gnarly grass, he took a fierce, short stroke, chopping up a huge divot. Though he advanced the ball far enough down the fairway to reach the green in three, he remained more than two hundred yards away, awkwardly positioned on a downhill, left-to-right slope.

Trying not to slice, Palmer badly pulled a four-wood that carried into deep rough beyond a bunker left of the green. With the pin located just beyond the bunker and the green slanting away, there was no way to stop the pitch anywhere near the hole; Palmer did well just to keep the ball on the green. His fifty-foot par putt stopped short and left of the hole, and a distraught Palmer had to contain his rage before finishing off his numbing bogey six.

Palmer's back-nine demise unfortunately didn't end on number twelve. A mediocre five-iron to the thirteenth hit the green, but so far away from the flagstick that he three-putted for another bogey. And when he three-putted again after a poor approach shot on number fourteen, all hopes for a storybook close to the 1973 U.S. Open died.

Much golf still remained after Palmer—now three behind Miller, with four holes to play—scored his third consecutive bogey on the fourteenth. Fourteen men, including Jack Nicklaus and Gary Player, still hadn't finished their rounds. And Tom Weiskopf and Lee Trevino had yet to attempt their desperation drives on number seventeen.

Palmer—as he had done with great fanfare to catch Nicklaus in 1962—also tried to drive the green on number seventeen and make eagle, believing, "What did I have to lose?" He came up short.

But for his die-hard fans—including Lew Worsham and Bob Ford, who continued to watch the leaderboard through the picture window of the pro shop—the 1973 U.S. Open effectively ended with Palmer's third straight bogey.

"When Arnold made those bogeys," Schlee said, "it was like playing in a morgue."

With the round finally over, Palmer—sitting in the locker room in his underwear with a cigarette in one hand and a beer can in the other—spoke with the swarm of reporters, many just as dispirited by his back-nine collapse as Arnie's Army.

"I won this tournament once when I wasn't really supposed to. And four other times I lost when I should have won. I guess things balance out," Palmer mused to the press.

"What do they say about this game? It gives you a moment of ecstasy and hours of frustration."

Not long afterward, Palmer showered, thanked reporters, volunteers, U.S.G.A. officials, and fellow club members, and then hopped into his Cadillac for the short drive back to Latrobe. As the sun set on Father's Day 1973, Arnold and "Deke" Palmer headed once again onto Hulton Road without a U.S. Open trophy.

"As we left the course, there were signs everywhere saying, 'Palmer for Governor.' There was a cavalcade. Cars pulled up along the public highway. People got out with signs in their hands. It was nice but I didn't take it very seriously."

THE MORBID SILENCE THAT JOHN Schlee observed once Palmer dragged himself off the fourteenth green was not surprising: to the loyal subjects of Steeltown, their King was dead. But patrons who couldn't bear watching the lame-duck, final few holes of Palmer's twosome missed one hell of a show.

John Schlee had already provided great drama that afternoon. His embarrassing three-drive, double-bogey start on the opening hole embodied final-round pressure: Instantaneously, he seemed to crumble under the weight of sharing the lead in the U.S. Open. Somehow, he pulled himself together to make conventional pars on the next two holes and, with his superb eagle on the fourth, returned to even par for the day. But Schlee's resurrection was short-lived; he immediately embarked on a bogey-birdie-par-bogey-birdie roller coaster to close the front nine.

Over the next two hours, as each past, present, and future PGA giant who chased Johnny Miller that day—Palmer, Nicklaus, Boros, Trevino, Weiskopf, Wadkins—wilted at one point or another, Schlee did not. In fact, he played his steadiest golf of the entire championship on the pressure-packed back nine.

Schlee reached the fiendish tenth green in two splendid shots; his mid-iron to within twelve feet was the day's finest approach by any of the leaders. Nevertheless, like Miller and Trevino before him, Schlee left the sharp-breaking birdie putt a fraction short. Flailing his putter in anguish, he paced around the green to calm down before putting out for par.

Not surprisingly, Palmer continued to be the main attraction when the twosome moved to the eleventh. Although Schlee hit a fine wedge that stopped fifteen feet below the hole, Palmer's great approach to four feet sent the crowd into a frenzy. Once again, practically unnoticed, Schlee missed the birdie try, misreading the putt to break left when it actually broke right.

Within moments, however, Schlee, not Palmer, moved to center stage. After sharing the news of Miller's five-under par score with his befuddled partner,

Schlee set up to play his drive from the center of the fairway—the one that Palmer thought belonged to him.

Following a strong three-wood, Schlee dropped a fine wedge to within eight feet of the cup and drained the birdie putt. He was now a stunning four under par for the day on Oakmont's three par-fives, and, more important, four under for the championship.

PLAYER	SCORE	THROUGH
Miller	-5	COMPLETED
Schlee	-4	12
Weiskopf	-3	11
Palmer	-3	12
Trevino	-3	14
Boros	-3	11
Heard	-2	11

The joy proved short-lived. Schlee now trailed Johnny Miller by only a single stroke, and with Miller in the clubhouse, his orders were simple: Make up one stroke over the next six holes to force a play-off; two strokes and he would win the seventy-third U.S. Open.

Schlee, however, never did anything simply. He found the thirteenth green with a five-iron, then three-putted from sixty feet, dropping back to three under par.

Before the deflated army, Schlee parred the fourteenth and tough fifteenth. Now he had to shave two strokes off his total on the final three holes. Although he had done poorly on the long, par-three sixteenth—bogeying it on Thursday and Friday—he regained some confidence with a solid par there during Saturday's third-round 67.

"Your Individual Horoscope, for Sunday, June 17, 1973: GEMINI: A day in which the Geminian's abilities can shine—especially his gift for successfully judging the advantages of a situation which confounds others."

For the most part, all week long, the field had played the sixteenth cautiously, aiming tee shots at the far left side of the green. But the man who used eccentric, often bizarre training methods and regularly experimented with un-orthodox driver heads, shafts, and putters saw an opportunity to play the six-teenth more brazenly than others. He decided to attack the flag.

Caddie Danny Liester handed Schlee a three-iron that he needed to hit on a much higher trajectory than normal to have a chance of holding the green. With a familiar, whirling stroke, he aimed directly at the flagstick. If he suc-ceeded, he would be left with a short, uncomplicated birdie putt; if he was off a hair, the ball would roll down the hillside to the right, and his chance for vic-tory would be all but dead.

Sharply leaning with body language, begging his shot not to drift too far right, Schlee grimaced in anticipation. Fortunately, his Ben Hogan ball fol-lowed Schlee's command and settled in a great position, pin-high, ten feet away. Best of all, the shot landed to the *right* of the flag: He would not have to navigate any part of the "upside-down punch bowl" region of the green.

Undaunted and showing the composure of a veteran professional, Schlee sank the straight birdie putt, returning him again to sole possession of second place—only a single stroke behind Miller, with two holes to play.

Once he heard that his lead was down to a single shot—and that at least one of his pursuers didn't seem to be "choking among themselves"—Johnny Miller left his wife and child in the clubhouse so he could witness the conclusion first-hand. He stood quite conspicuously at the head of the gallery that surrounded the right side of the eighteenth green.

Meanwhile, Schlee moved to the seventeenth, surely the best chance for the long hitter to make the birdie he needed (he made a birdie three there on Sat-urday), or perhaps even an eagle. But Schlee's unusually low ball flight with his driver was not ideally suited to carrying the distant bunkers on the fairway's left side. Instead, he chose the safe play—leaving his driver in the bag—and hit a long iron into the center of the fairway, which set up a full wedge to the narrow, slightly elevated green.

By the time Schlee played the seventeenth, the afternoon breeze had picked up considerably and Schlee didn't adequately account for this in his second-shot club selection. His wedge stopped a disappointing fifty feet short of the pin. Now he would have to struggle to two-putt for par and keep alive any chance of tying Miller.

His long, burly arms awkwardly bent, Schlee lined up the desperate birdie try. With perfect speed, the ball headed across the green and flirted with the left edge of the cup, missing by only an inch.

Schlee settled for par. The lofty, almost absurd dream of reclaiming his mentor's U.S. Open crown—twenty years after Ben Hogan won it on this very course—would require all seventy-two holes.

"Who wouldn't love to be in an eighteen-hole play-off for the U.S. Open with a guy who shot sixty-three the day before?"

Standing just outside the ropes, Schlee's wife—enveloped by deflated members of the Palmer faithful—watched her husband nail a terrific drive down the center of the fairway on number eighteen, leaving him 188 yards to the pin. As was her custom, she strolled quickly toward the green to await his approach, as a highly idiosyncratic series of strategic thoughts consumed her husband.

"When I'm playing an important round," Schlee later explained, "I carry a 'gallery in my mind.' It consists of Ben Hogan, Byron Nelson, Cary Middlecoff, and Dub Fondren. These men walk with me every step of the way and I discuss many shots with them.

"As I looked at my approach shot, I told my gallery [i.e., Hogan, Nelson, etc.] I wanted to hit a low, left-to-right four-iron. It would land on the front of the green, then run up the hill, next to the pin. In fact, it might go in. They all agreed it was a good plan."

Just as Schlee readied himself for the crucial swing, however, a U.S.G.A. official called for him to wait, as a ruling was in process on the green. The moment of pause jolted him.

"It was then I realized this was the most important shot of my life. I needed to relax. So I relaxed everything. As a student of hypnosis, I was easily able to do this. I did such a good job, I almost fell asleep. Arnie, who I was paired with, awoke me from my semislumber by saying, 'John, you can play now.'

"I went through my procedure and set up. As the club started back, I knew something was wrong. I wasn't doing it. I thought to myself, 'Hang on and hope for the best!'

"As I moved through impact, my legs straightened and I hit a long, thin shot through the green."

The approach shot didn't *look* terrible. Though a shade left of target and a little lower than his normal trajectory, Schlee's ball hit on the front of the green, precisely as he intended. But because the greens had firmed up and the shot was "thin" (topspin rather than backspin), the ball refused to hold. It took a huge, thirty-foot hop, then bounded across the mammoth green and through the fringe, settling in the thick perimeter rough.

"What had gone wrong? I had choked but didn't know why. I had played that shot thousands of times in practice and in competition," Schlee recalled. "It took me six months of playing it over and over in my mind before I realized what had happened. You see, when I relaxed, I relaxed my entire body, including my respiratory system. I overdid it. I was starved for oxygen and my body could not perform smoothly without it."

In a stroke of good fortune, Schlee's ball did not sink deeply into the rough, as usually happened around Oakmont's greens. Instead, it rested atop the grass, forty feet downhill and a half dozen cruel undulations to the hole.

For the man whose natal moon was at its lunar high point, who interpreted his horoscope to believe "I was destined to do well athletically this week," anything seemed possible. And that included sinking a forty-foot chip from the rough on the seventy-second hole of the U.S. Open to force a Monday play-off.

Golf's greatest championship was now on the line. And no matter what happened, the life of one man—either the nomadic, troubled journeyman who spent a decade barely scraping by on tour, or the handsome, religious golfer/model whose inevitable stardom was long overdue—would forever change.

With an understandably nervous-looking Johnny Miller standing nearby, Schlee studied his lie and the twisting pathway between his ball and the pin. He wiped sweaty palms on his pant legs several times, then set up for the shot of a lifetime.

Schlee's four-iron chip—he always preferred low shots from green-side fringe—popped out cleanly, taking one small hop before descending smoothly toward the hole. Both the speed and the line seemed exactly right. To the eager, anxious gallery, it seemed sure to drop.

But just a moment from disappearing into the cup, the ball veered slightly left and missed by three inches.

It was over. Miller had survived.

He had endured and overcome everything. The forlorn, confused feelings of earlier in the day. A six-stroke deficit. The toughest golf course in America. The specter of Jack Nicklaus. The colossal shadow of Arnold Palmer and his hometown crowd. The grinding consistency of Lee Trevino. The inspired charge of Tom Weiskopf. And the spirited, dark-horse, upset bid of John Schlee. Johnny Miller was now the United States Open champion.

After he tapped in for par, Schlee, along with Palmer—who had just gloriously dropped a long birdie putt to tie Nicklaus and Trevino for fourth place—headed for the green-side scorer's tent. On the way, Palmer spotted Miller and walked toward the new champion, offering a smile and a hand of congratulations.

Unknowingly, Palmer stepped right in front of Schlee, who was heading in to sign his card. Reporters and cameramen rushed to document the regal scene: an apparent passing of the torch from King to Prince.

John Schlee glanced momentarily to see where Palmer was headed. Giving way to the flock of media, he continued into the scorer's tent, then faded from the spotlight.

MILLER'S 63 PROMPTLY CHANGED HIS travel arrangements. No longer was the family destined for Akron, Ohio—the trip that Linda Miller stayed behind Sunday morning to pack for. Later that evening, they would leave for Washington, D.C., so that Johnny could make a charity pro-am appearance at Prince Georges Country Club in Landover, Maryland. And the next day, the family would head to the White House; unfortunately, Richard Nixon's meeting with Soviet leader Leonid Brezhnev ran long, so golf-crazed vice president Spiro Agnew personally congratulated Johnny, instead of the president.

But late into Sunday evening, the Millers stayed at Oakmont and soaked up the championship spotlight. Photographers snapped shots of what seemed to be a very relieved Miller hugging the U.S. Open trophy or kissing his wife. Still dressed in his playing outfit, Miller even posed with tournament runner-up John Schlee, who had already showered and changed into a suit. Above a very dated *Pittsburgh Post-Gazette* caption—"Hertz, Avis of '73 Open: Johnny Miller, John Schlee"—the two smiled for the camera.

Considering how much money he had just earned, Miller was glad to stand before the cameras. Aside from the $35,000 first-place paycheck, his manager, Ed Barner—who told reporters he couldn't bear to watch Miller play the final hole because nerves made him "afraid I'd throw up"—bragged to the press what the win would do for his client.

"Just on bonus contracts with various companies, this Open will be worth forty-seven thousand dollars to John the rest of the year," Barner said. "And between now and next year's Open . . . oh, easily two hundred thousand."

And just like Billy Casper had seven years earlier, the Mormon golfer had to explain whether or not he would tithe ten percent of his winnings to the Church.

"No, it's got to be ten percent of the net; otherwise, you'd go broke," Miller said.

Naturally, reporters interrogated Miller for hours after Schlee's desperation chip rolled by the flagstick on number eighteen. He explained his feelings of depression en route to the golf course on Sunday morning, his radical change in stance, the "sky-high" joy that overcame him early in the round, and how he rebounded from "choked" putts on numbers seven and eight to birdie five of the last ten holes.

"I don't know much about Open history, but I don't think too many sixty-threes have ever been shot," he told the press.

Of course, none ever had (see Appendix 1). A few of the game's more distinguished leaders quickly tried to put the round in perspective.

"I still can't believe it," said P.J. Boatwright, the executive director of the U.S.G.A. who had been so angered by the overwatered greens Friday morning.

"I don't know if there has been a greater finish, except perhaps Gene Sarazen's great charge at Fresh Meadow [Long Island] in 1932 when he played the last twenty-eight holes in a hundred shots and won the Open by three," PGA tour commissioner Joe Dey said. "Miller's finish was really unbelievable."

But considering that the first 63 had come at "the Hades of Hulton," the word *fluke* was casually tossed around as a way to explain the inexplicable.

"Without taking anything away from Miller, course conditions contributed to unusually low scoring on the weekend," wrote one reporter who simply stated what many were thinking. "What happened to Oakmont's vaunted ferocity?" asked *New York Times* columnist Arthur Daley. "The members were so proud of that ferocity too. But it was subdued for this Open, by either accident or design or both."

No one wanted to believe such a score was legitimate on the world's toughest golf course, in the world's toughest championship.

"Imagine shooting a 63 in a U.S. Open! That's almost like stoning a church, or painting moustaches on statues of saints," hyperbole-prone *Los Angeles Times* columnist Jim Murray wrote. "You're supposed to win an Open with four 71s or three 69s and a 72. Your swing is supposed to choke up as you get near first money. You're supposed to look up at the leaderboard and say, 'My God! What am I doing leading a U.S. Open! Where do I come off beating Nicklaus and Arnold Palmer and Lee Trevino and Gary Player!' Then you're supposed to go out and faint, or shank and shoot bogey-bogey-bogey-double-bogey."

"Everyone else is griping and worrying so much they don't have a chance," Miller said. "The Open is perfect for me. It humbles everybody else."

Although he certainly feared the worst during his final round, Miller—who always felt destined to win the U.S. Open—didn't succumb to the pressure. He stood up to the world's top players and won.

"No, I don't think I'm a big shot because I won the Open. I'll still dress myself the same way every morning."

But once he had finished narrating the round, Miller's attitude shifted. He became defensive, as if he had to justify his triumph to his fellow pros, the press, and the world. He had craved for some time to separate himself from the cute "young lion" tag, and in the aftermath of victory, he felt a bit slighted and over-looked as someone who "deserved" to win a U.S. Open.

"I've been around and won a little money. I am not out there trying to lag for pars," he assured everyone. "I am no flash in the pan."

Time would tell.

Chasing Greatness, Twenty Years Later

· 14 ·

Arnold Palmer, Jack Nicklaus, and Lee Trevino

True to his word, Arnold Palmer did not run for governor of Pennsylvania and never entered politics—although in 1974, President Richard Nixon did ask for Palmer's opinion on how best to end the war in Vietnam. "Well, if the decision were mine to make," he told Nixon and his national security staff in the president's San Clemente vacation home, "I guess I wouldn't pussyfoot around. Let's get this thing over as quickly as possible, for everyone's sake. Why not go for the green?"

Palmer stuck to golf. The February 1973 Bob Hope Desert Classic proved his last PGA tour triumph, but he remained far more than a sentimental crowd favorite. A year after the heartbreak at Oakmont, he again charged into contention during the Sunday of a U.S. Open. In the famed 1974 "Massacre at Winged Foot," Palmer began the final round once again in the second-to-last pairing, just three strokes behind the lead. Poor putting and a string of front-nine bogeys cost him, and the forty-four-year-old finished tied for fifth.

"I'm not going to quit and give up just because I'm not winning. Physically I feel great. Another eighteen would be no problem right now," he said after his final-round 76. "I hear the players and the fans calling me the 'Old Man,' but I don't feel old. Don't forget, there's Boros and Snead, who are still playing, and they make me feel like a kid.

"There aren't too many things I'd rather do than play golf. It's not the money anymore and, even though I like to win, it might not even be that. Maybe it's just that [the] roar of the crowd is too good to leave behind."

Roars followed Palmer everywhere during the remainder of the 1970s. Finishing ninth in the 1975 U.S. Open tied Palmer with Ben Hogan as the only golfers over age forty to score top tens in four consecutive U.S. Opens. In the 1976 Bob Hope, he one-putted ten greens, two-putted the rest, and shot a second-round 64; sadly, "Deke" Palmer died the next day, and Arnold withdrew to fly back to Orlando. Two years later, a nostalgic final-round charge nearly won Palmer the Phoenix Open at age forty-eight. Five consecutive birdies pulled him into the lead before he ran out of steam and finished tied for fifth.

Palmer turned fifty in September 1979 and was instrumental in the founding of the Senior PGA Tour in 1980. Purses were small (averaging less than $120,000 that inaugural season), and only eleven events were played over the first two years. But he won the Senior PGA Championship in February, and claimed the Senior U.S. Open the following summer. The buzz among fans and corporate sponsors—both groups eager to see Palmer play and win—sparked an explosion of interest in over-fifty professional golf.

By 1985, twenty-four events were on the senior schedule, and the average purse had nearly doubled. Palmer was the main catalyst for the rise in the Senior Tour's popularity and prosperity, just as he had been for the PGA tour three decades earlier.

With a lifetime invitation to the Masters, Palmer continued to appear at Augusta each spring, and he occasionally delighted the European crowds by playing in the British Open. But his exemption for the U.S. Open expired after 1977. The U.S.G.A. issued Palmer special exemptions to play in the 1978, 1980, and 1981 U.S. Opens (winning the 1981 Senior U.S. Open automatically qualified him for 1982). And when the U.S. Open returned to Oakmont in 1983 (which Larry Nelson won), Palmer again received an exemption; he made the cut and tied for sixtieth place, at age fifty-three.

As the 1980s progressed, Palmer scaled back his playing schedule and did not earn any Senior Tour exemptions to play in the U.S. Open. The U.S.G.A. chose not to issue him any more special exemptions . . . until the Open returned to Oakmont in 1994.

Although fans—especially the Pittsburgh crowds—loved the U.S.G.A.'s sentimental move, not everyone believed it was fair for the sixty-four-year-old to earn a free pass into the field.

"There's a school of thought that says golf owes Arnold," wrote former U.S.G.A. executive director Frank Hannigan. "I don't buy it. Arnold most certainly enhanced golf. In return, he became rich and famous. It's a wash."

Hannigan wasn't alone, either.

"I've never needed an invitation before, and I think I deserve one more than Arnold Palmer," said Seve Ballesteros, who eventually earned his trip to Oakmont with a win in early May.

Among others, Lanny Wadkins rushed to defend Palmer.

"I know [Seve's] a big name in golf, but guys like Sam Snead and Arnold Palmer had to go through qualifying, and if Seve thinks he's a bigger name than them, he's sadly mistaken."

Regardless of how he got there, Palmer would be making a record fifth U.S. Open appearance at the same course. He played five Senior Tour events in five consecutive weeks during May and early June of 1994 to sharpen his game, then spent the week before the U.S. Open preparing at Oakmont.

"Yes, this will be my last. I thought that happened long ago, but they want me to play one more," he said after a practice round with a few local amateurs and Oakmont assistant pros. "[My game is] no good. No good. I thought I had the irons for a while but they disappeared again. I'll have to find something pretty soon."

The next day, during an official practice round, Jack Nicklaus joined Palmer (along with the defending U.S. Open champion Lee Janzen and Rocco Mediate) for eighteen holes. Nicklaus and Palmer bantered back and forth, hurling self-deprecating comments and good-natured barbs at each other before closing out the round and meeting with the press.

"I'm sure a lot of people enjoyed it," Nicklaus said. "But I'm sure both of us would have wanted to play better."

"I would like to play respectable golf," Palmer added. "The chance of me doing that on a scale of 1 to 10 is about three or four. I would be happy to play any kind of golf. But I'm just going to enjoy the week."

The last United States Open Championship played without Eldrick "Tiger" Woods began at seven a.m. on Thursday, June 16, 1994. By the early afternoon, 126 golfers had already teed off, including Greg Norman, John Daly, Phil Mickelson, eleven past U.S. Open champions, and Tommy Armour III, grandson of the champion in the 1927 Open. But when Palmer's threesome walked to the first tee at two p.m., no one else mattered.

Despite their vast age differences, Palmer actually had a lot in common with his playing partners. As Palmer did as an amateur in the late 1940s, John Mahaffey had won at Oakmont before; the Texan claimed the 1978 PGA Championship at the Hades of Hulton. And thirty-one-year-old Rocco Mediate, from nearby Greensburg, grew up less than an hour from the Oakmont course. Naturally, he worshiped Arnold Palmer.

"He's responsible for all this," Mediate said that week. "The popularity of golf. The Open. These crowds. The money. We owe him a lot."

Mediate and Mahaffey teed off first. Then Palmer endured an eerie—and presumably comical—moment of déjà vu. His caddie, Royce Nielson, was nowhere in sight. Since Nielson had his clubs, Palmer could only wait. Unlike his young, scared-to-death caddie in 1973, Nielson hadn't abandoned the King; he just couldn't fight his way through the gallery to reach the tee box. After a few minutes, Nielson finally made it through the mass of people and handed the driver to Palmer, who promptly drove into the right rough.

Palmer would go on to make a respectable bogey: In the opening round, more than half of the field failed to par the opening hole. Under a brutal sun, he played the next seven holes in two over par before coming to the par-five ninth tee. Palmer struck a poor wedge for his third shot that left him far from the hole. But he thrilled the next generation of Arnie's Army, massed in front of the clubhouse, by sinking the birdie to finish the front side in thirty-eight strokes. A few hours later, at the home hole, the showman again excited the crowd with a beautiful bunker shot that nearly landed in the cup. From there, he nailed the eight-footer.

"I was pretty darn proud of that shot on eighteen," he told the press after wrapping up a six over 77. "Making the cut was my goal when I started, and it still is. I didn't enhance it, but I have [a] chance. I need a good round [tomorrow]. Then I'll worry about winning the tournament."

Friday morning, Palmer couldn't produce the same heroic bunker saves or long putts. His score ballooned, and standing on the eighteenth tee, he was fifteen over par, well back of the projected cut. Palmer's last U.S. Open was almost over.

He struck a solid, straight drive and headed down the fairway. Two hundred yards ahead, all three grandstands, along with the green-side gallery, stood and cheered. The army momentarily quieted so that Palmer could poke his lengthy approach up the steep bank toward the green. The ball skidded to the green's edge, forty feet from the flagstick. As he walked toward the putting surface, the gallery again roared. Palmer doffed his straw hat to the fans, then flashed a prolonged thumbs-up.

Although everyone wanted to see Palmer close out his U.S. Open career by sinking a long, winding birdie on Oakmont's harrowing eighteenth green—just as he had done in 1973, after John Schlee almost sank his chip to tie Johnny Miller, twenty-one years earlier to the day—it didn't happen. The try rolled six feet past the hole, and he missed the comebacker.

Palmer putted out, and again, the fans exploded.

"When you walk up the eighteenth and you got an ovation like that," he said, fighting back tears, to an ESPN television reporter, "I guess that says it all."

Not long afterward, in the press tent, Palmer sat down to answer more questions. But no one said a word.

"I think you all know pretty much how I feel," he said.

After toweling tears from his face, he haltingly continued. "It's been forty years of fun, work, and enjoyment. . . . The whole experience . . . I haven't won all that much. I won a few tournaments. I won some majors. I suppose the most important thing . . . [*long pause*] . . . is the fact it's been as good as it's been to me."

Palmer apologized to his audience; he just could not continue.

"[Then came] a rare standing ovation from the assembled press," Jim McKay noted. "They know, as do we all, that whatever any future giants may achieve in this game, there will never be another Arnold Palmer."

JACK NICKLAUS TURNED FIFTY-FOUR IN 1994, and that year, unusually, he played a great deal of competitive golf on both the senior and regular PGA tours. Although he won an event in January and accumulated three additional top tens on the Senior Tour, his game was not PGA-tour sharp: in all six of his "regular" tour appearances, including the Masters, he missed the cut.

Still, Nicklaus believed that a miraculous, turn-back-the-clock victory rested inside of him. And there was no better place for that than the 1994 U.S. Open at Oakmont. For inspiration, throughout the tournament Nicklaus even used balls branded with the number five: A win that week would be his fifth U.S. Open Championship.

Aside from playing together in their wistful practice round, Nicklaus largely took a backseat to Arnold Palmer prior to the Open: References to the Golden Bear centered on his heart-rending defeat of the local hero in 1962, not his indisputable place as golf's finest champion of all time. And although Palmer certainly grabbed the headlines on Thursday and Friday, Nicklaus made news.

Barbara Nicklaus had been there in 1962 to suffer the gallery's harsh words when Jack toppled the King. Nevertheless, the morning the 1994 U.S. Open began, she encouraged her husband to flash back to that week.

"Usually, when he leaves, I say, 'Play well,' or, 'Good luck,' or something. But this morning, for some reason [while dangling her fingers in his face to mimic a hypnotist], I told him 'You're twenty-two, you're twenty-two, it's 1962 again.'"

Nicklaus did not repeat that first-round performance; he played better.

In 1962, he had birdied the opening three holes, then fallen apart toward the end of the front nine. Thirty-two years later, again armed with a wooden driver—Nicklaus switched back to persimmon that week—his tee shot on number one sliced into the right rough. He gouged out onto the fairway, then struck a low-running pitch some ninety yards to within par-saving range. He hit the ball well for the next several holes but struggled with his putter, missing makeable birdie putts on numbers two, four, and five before bogeying the sixth and saving par on the seventh.

"And then I started to play golf."

On the par-three eighth, Nicklaus's two-iron landed three feet from the pin. He made birdie there, then sank two birdie putts—a curving twenty-footer on number twelve, and another from twelve feet on number fourteen. Five hours into the round, at two under par, Nicklaus held a share of the U.S. Open lead.

Shaking off a bogey on the sixteenth, Nicklaus parred the seventeenth—he didn't try to repeat his first-round eagle from 1973—then lashed a great drive onto the eighteenth fairway. A mediocre approach left him pin-high, forty feet left of the pin.

"I was just trying to figure some way to get close to two-putt," Nicklaus explained, "and it went in."

The thrilling birdie at the home hole dropped Nicklaus to two under par—the first time he ever broke par in the opening round of a championship at Oakmont. And if Tom Watson had not shot a three under 68 later that day, the Golden Bear would have been tied for the lead.

The next afternoon, Palmer completed his tearful good-bye to the U.S. Open.

"I think Arnie feels he's had enough of it. We've played a lot of golf together for a lot of years, and I think we are all sorry to see anyone finish their career in anyplace, but I think he feels a little bit like I do," Nicklaus said. "There's a time when you sort of pass it on, let the younger players have it. I'm at that point, too. I don't want to be around when I shouldn't."

During Friday's second round, Nicklaus proved he still belonged.

Four front-nine birdies dropped him to five under par. Although he missed six fairways—"the weakest part of my game is off the tee. It used to be my strength"—and carded a trio of bogeys in the late afternoon, Nicklaus reached the halfway point with his trademark confidence on full display.

"I feel very calm about the way I'm hitting the ball. If I get myself in position on Sunday, I think I have a good shot to win."

Friday's 70 put Nicklaus at three under going into the weekend: a better thirty-six-hole total than he'd ever posted at Oakmont. Tied for fifth, he trailed the leader by three strokes.

The magic disappeared over the weekend. A 77 on Saturday and a 76 on Sunday dropped him back into the pack, but for a senior player who hadn't made a PGA tour cut all year, a twenty-eighth-place finish at Oakmont was still impressive. Even for Jack Nicklaus.

FOLLOWING HIS FOURTH-PLACE FINISH BEHIND Johnny Miller in the 1973 U.S. Open, Nicklaus had immediately resumed his quest to become the greatest golfer of the century.

Eight days after shooting a 68 in the final round (only Miller and Wadkins scored lower), Nicklaus served as the unofficial host of the eighth-annual Columbus Invitational Charity Pro-Am. All proceeds from the one-day, Monday event went to the *Columbus Dispatch* Charities and the area's Children's Hospital. Saddled with a well-known hacker named Bob Hope—who managed to birdie the home hole—Nicklaus and three local area pros carded an aggregate 55, the event's lowest score.

Nicklaus played in only seven tournaments the remainder of the season. He posted three wins, a fourth in July's British Open, and three additional top tens.

At age thirty-three, Nicklaus dominated 1973: nineteen tour starts, seventeen top tens, seven wins, first on the money list ($308,362), and the lowest stroke average of his career (69.81). It was another season filled with remarkable highs—arguably equal to his celebrated 1972 season.

His most notable feat came in August. Three closing rounds under 70 at the Canterbury Golf Club in Shaker Heights, Ohio, earned Nicklaus a four-stroke win in the last major of the season, the PGA. That fourteenth major championship (including two U.S. Amateurs) pushed him one past the late Bobby Jones.

"Everything was Bobby Jones," Nicklaus told the press afterward, "and the fact that he had won thirteen major championships, a record, was hammered into my mind."

Nicklaus's excellence in majors only continued after he surpassed his hero. In addition to twenty-one more regular tour victories, he won six additional majors. And he did so in practically every way imaginable.

In perhaps the most exciting Masters of all time, Nicklaus edged out both Tom Weiskopf and Johnny Miller by a single stroke in 1975 to earn a record fifth Green Jacket. In 1978, a year after losing to Tom Watson in Turnberry's famous "Duel in the Sun," Nicklaus overcame a balky putter to win his third British Open—a second straight at his beloved St. Andrews.

But in a career filled with awesome highlights, Nicklaus most enduring victory came in April 1986. He'd turned forty-six three months earlier, and without a victory in nearly two years, chatter pervaded Augusta National the week before that he could no longer compete.

"Nicklaus is gone, done," *Atlanta Journal-Constitution* writer Tom McCollister declared the week of the fiftieth Masters tournament. "He just doesn't have the game anymore. It's rusted from lack of use. He's 46, and nobody that old wins the Masters."

Nicklaus had set the bar so high that even in his mid-forties, he was destined to disappoint if not chasing the Grand Slam or winning six tour events each year.

Rather than ignoring the criticism, Nicklaus used it as motivation, and kept within four shots of the pace entering Sunday's final round. Still trailing Seve Ballesteros, Greg Norman, and Tom Kite by several strokes, Nicklaus scored birdies on numbers nine and ten, then grabbed two more (and a bogey) at Amen Corner to close the gap to two.

With his son Jackie serving as his caddie, Nicklaus eagled the par-five fifteenth after a brilliant long-iron approach, then drained a short birdie putt on number sixteen and a ten-footer on number seventeen to steal the lead. Playing behind Nicklaus, Norman and Kite couldn't catch up, and from the clubhouse, the Golden Bear won at Augusta National for the sixth time. His final-round 65—and an incredible 30 on the back nine—remains the greatest finishing performance in Masters history.

"This may be as fine a round of golf as I ever played, particularly those last ten holes."

Nicklaus never won another PGA event following that indelible scene: the aging, still long-haired champion, in yellow shirt and checkered pants, joyfully raising his putter in triumph. Nicklaus tapered down his already limited playing schedule, spending more time with his large family, refining the Muirfield Village Golf Club and its Memorial Tournament, as well as expanding his architectural firm and other golf-related businesses into a worldwide empire.

Still, as a tournament host and course design magnate, Nicklaus could not completely purge his competitive fire. In early 1990, having turned fifty, he joined the Senior Tour and immediately crushed the familiar field of competitors.

In his Senior Tour debut on the Cochise Course at Desert Mountain in Scottsdale, Arizona—a course he designed—Nicklaus won the season's first major championship, the Tradition. A week later at the Masters, in the best finish ever by a player in his fifties, Nicklaus finished sixth; only three bogeys on the back nine kept him from another Green Jacket miracle. The following Sunday, he tied for third in the Senior PGA Championship. Nicklaus was renowned for competing in tournaments rather sparingly, and his three top tens, in three major championships, in three weeks, reaffirmed his place among the greatest on *any* tour.

With a win at another major, the Senior Players Championship, in June, Nicklaus had won two of the three senior majors in his rookie season. And in sole possession of the lead during the final round of July's United States Senior Open, Nicklaus was all set to claim a third senior major until he was once again stymied by a familiar foe: Lee Trevino.

AS FAR BACK AS 1968—following his improbable U.S. Open win at Oak Hill and subsequent meteoric rise to stardom—Trevino had charmed the press with his fresh enthusiasm for the game.

"My goal is to play as good as I can for as long as I can. I'm going to keep practicing and playing until I get about hundred years old.

"I don't care if it's the Screen Door Open! If the money's out there, I'll tee it up on a gravel road."

That bubbly Trevino had almost disappeared by 1973. During one of many vent sessions to the media at Oakmont, he said, "I don't want to play after I'm forty. That would give me seven more years. I don't have a day off until [December] eighth. Of course, it's my own fault, but I'm scheduled for something every day."

Trevino's frustrations continued well after he pulled his $30,000 mobile home out of Oakmont's parking lot. Putting woes resurfaced the next week at the American Golf Classic; then, at Royal Troon a few weeks later, he couldn't figure out the winds well enough to defend his British Open crown. Still, he finished tenth: his fourth straight year in the top ten in the game's two preeminent national championships (a record only surpassed by Nicklaus).

Regardless of how well he played—he still finished fourth on the 1973 money list, despite not winning another time—Trevino's irritability did not subside. He took a break from the tour in late July and hinted that he might not even play in August's PGA Championship; reporters speculated that he and Claudia were having marital problems.

Trevino eventually decided to play in the PGA, but after shooting 76, then telling a reporter that his desire was not there, he brushed "aside newsmen on his way to his car. A youngster seeking his autograph reached out and grabbed Trevino, and he turned around angrily and told the youth: 'Get your hands off me. Don't touch me again.' Trevino got into his car, slammed his fist against the dashboard, and left."

Once his draining 1973 season came to an end, however, Trevino steadied the ship and the lovable, smiling "Happy Hombre" returned.

In March 1974, he won the Greater New Orleans Open, his first victory in more than a year. By August his revival—in every sense—was complete. "[Twirling] his putter in familiar, fidgety fashion, joking all the while," Trevino grabbed the third-round lead of the PGA Championship at Tanglewood Park. The next afternoon, he held on to win his fifth major championship, defeating, naturally, his playing partner, Jack Nicklaus.

"I was charged up like I always am when I play with Jack and I really hit the ball super."

That week, Trevino confessed that he had tried to bring a measure of stability to his life after years of stealing the last buck from a grueling exhibition and personal-appearance schedule.

"Now I'm learning the way to handle these things. My problem has been scheduling things too far ahead, like making commitments in January for August. Well, the kids are on vacation then, but I forget that in January. I'm figuring out ways of allowing time for my kids. I don't want to raise my family in a hotel room."

But Trevino could never resist the temptation of tournament golf. Not even a bolt of lightning could keep him off the tour for more than a few weeks. While playing the Western Open in June 1975, Trevino, Jerry Heard, and Bobby Nichols were struck by lightning during a rain delay on the thirteenth green at Butler National Golf Club. Trevino had persuaded his friends to wait out the storm.

He suffered a serious back injury that would last for years. Fluid in his spine dissolved from the electrocution, leaving little lubrication between the disks in his vertebrae. Still, Trevino left the hospital early and within two weeks he was at Carnoustie, playing the British Open; he tied for fortieth. By November, he returned to top form and won the Mexican Open. The lightning had sapped some of his strength and endurance, but Trevino's generosity never waned. He donated his $8,000 winner's check to "my good friend Father Wasson, who has an orphans' home in Cuernavaca."

Trevino won one official PGA event per year for the next four seasons, and finished fourth in the 1977 British Open at Turnberry. In 1980, he won a record-tying fifth Vardon Trophy: If being struck by lightning wasn't going to force his retirement, neither was turning forty.

Still, despite some patching up, Trevino's life away from the greens and fairways remained as turbulent as ever. The disintegration of several business deals, and ugly divorces from both his wife and longtime manager, Bucky Woy, left him flat broke in 1977, and then again in the early 1980s.

"It didn't bother me a bit," he said two decades later. "If you've been poor once, being poor again is no big thing. You just look at it as a challenge."

He eventually got back on his feet financially, thanks to his earnings on tour and the endorsements he continued to attract. And in 1984, at age forty-four, Trevino won his second PGA Championship at Shoal Creek. His fifteen-under-par total set a PGA scoring record that would last more than a decade.

There to greet her husband at Shoal Creek was Claudia Trevino, though not the same Claudia Trevino who had stood beside her flawed husband throughout the 1970s. Barely a year after his divorce, Trevino married twenty-four-year-old Claudia Bove, whom he had met at a tournament years earlier when she was just a child. Trevino and "Claudia II" (as the press dubbed her) soon started a family of their own with two young children.

"First, I never used to put anything before or above golf. I can do that now, although it's not easy, because I can still play," he later said.

"To be the best at anything, you have to be a little selfish. Selfishness is the reason I didn't know my first four children. I could have been a better dad, but I would have been an average golfer."

With his home life crawling toward stability, Trevino finally began to reduce his tournament appearances. He joined NBC Sports as an analyst and was often paired with Vin Scully. He still played as often as his body and new wife would allow.

In a year better remembered for Nicklaus's victory at the Masters, and despite playing only four events beforehand, Trevino birdied the opening hole to grab a share of the final-round lead of the 1986 U.S. Open at Shinnecock Hills. A solid 71 to close the championship—won by his former hustling mark at Horizon Hills in El Paso, Raymond Floyd—earned Trevino his fifth top-five U.S. Open finish. He, too, could compete on equal terms at age forty-six with the world's premier golfers.

Born less than eight weeks apart, Nicklaus and Trevino both joined the Senior Tour in 1990. And, as had been the case at Oak Hill in 1968, Merion in 1971, Muirfield in 1972, and Tanglewood Park in 1974, it seemed that only Lee Trevino could foil Jack Nicklaus's major championship conquests.

In July 1990, both men appeared in their first U.S. Senior Open, held at New Jersey's Ridgewood Country Club. In search of his third straight victory in a senior major, Nicklaus posted a Saturday 67 to take the lead with one round to play.

For all of Nicklaus's immediate achievements on the over-fifty circuit (two wins in three tries), Trevino became the Senior Tour's most popular draw. He won five of ten tournaments in 1990, finishing in the top seven all but once. And in the more laid-back environment of the Senior Tour, Trevino's personality flourished.

"I know guys who are hysterically funny in the clubhouse, and when they step to the first tee, they turn stone silent. Then after they're done and back in, they're funny again. But if I had to concentrate every minute, I'd be spastic out there."

Just as at the height of his popularity in the 1970s, Trevino was the same affable showman who clowned around with the galleries, chatted midbackswing, and ribbed his fellow touring pros; and he was also the same fierce competitor.

Nine birdies on the first thirty-six holes gave Trevino a one-stroke lead over Jim Dent at the halfway point. Nicklaus, trailing by six shots, promptly stole the lead on Saturday from Trevino, who shot a one over 73.

"I'll have to play good, 5 or 6 under, to have a shot," Trevino said before the final round. "I know him like a book. Jack will shoot sixty-eight."

Trevino held up his end of the bargain: He played the front nine at four under to forge a four-stroke lead over Nicklaus. But the Golden Bear staged a late charge with birdies at numbers nine, eleven, and thirteen to pull within one. With the lead dwindling, Trevino leaned on the only facet of the game where Nicklaus could never match the Super Mex: his gamesmanship.

"Just when it seemed he might be losing his grip on the tournament, however, Trevino hit an eight-iron to fifteen feet on the 151-yard, par-three fifteenth and drained the putt," the *New York Times* reported. "Then with a vigorous lifting motion of his arms, he urged the crowd to cheer louder.

"'When I made that putt, the cheer wasn't loud enough,' said Trevino.

"'[Nicklaus] might have thought Dent made it, and I wanted to make sure he knew I made that thing.'"

Preparing to chip onto the fourteenth green, Nicklaus heard the roar, didn't hit his shot firmly enough, and promptly missed the par save.

Nicklaus then birdied numbers fifteen and sixteen to narrow the gap, again, to a single stroke. Trevino closed out his round with a trio of pars for a five under 67, then watched Nicklaus from the television booth.

"As Jack was coming up seventeen, I thought back to Merion in 1971. That year I was sitting in the locker room when Jack had a fifteen-foot birdie putt to win. But when I heard the gallery groan, I knew we were in a play-off. This time, I told my wife, Claudia, 'You better call the Hilton and tell 'em we have to stay over for a play-off.'"

Playing the par-five seventeenth in a light drizzle—"If Jack had kept up [with the pace of play], he wouldn't have to play in the rain," Trevino joked—Nicklaus came up short with his eight-iron approach from 128 yards away. A weak chip left him a four-foot putt; if he could save par, he would still have a chance to tie Trevino with a birdie on number eighteen.

"But sometimes Jack has a bad habit of looking up on short putts," Trevino told the press, showing how intimately he knew his great rival's game. "When he moved his head too quick on that putt at seventeen, the ball spun off the lip."

Seeing the surprising bogey six, Trevino claimed victory, shouting, "Gimme the trophy!"

Minutes later, Nicklaus walked into the interview tent to find his beaming, silver-haired rival.

"Well-done," Nicklaus said as the two shook hands.

"Where you playing next?" Trevino asked.

"The British Open."

"I'll see you there."

Three weeks later at St. Andrews, they shot matching final-round 71s.

· 15 ·

Tom Weiskopf

Anew Tom Weiskopf had emerged during the spring and summer of 1973. Although his gutsy third-place finish at Oakmont cemented his place among the tour's elite, Weiskopf's crowning achievement came a month later.

Playing underneath a Scottish rain at Royal Troon on July 15, Weiskopf shot a final-round 70 to win the hundred and second British Open Championship. Not even a closing-round 65 by Nicklaus, a fantastic final round of ball striking (but poor putting) by Johnny Miller, or a valiant six-birdie effort by Britain's Neil Coles could deprive Weiskopf of his first major championship.

"I was in complete control of myself. I was never really worried," he said. "Not that I don't respect the ability of Johnny, or Jack or Neil, but I just knew that no matter what happened, I was gonna win."

Weiskopf spent most of the next day (Sunday) fulfilling the duties of the gracious champion. He posed for pictures—kissing either the Claret Jug or his wife, Jeanne—sent a case of champagne to the writers' tent, and, joined by Nicklaus, even sang songs with Scottish fans at the Marine Hotel.

Fittingly, while her son basked in the joy of undeniably "making it" as a major winner, Eva Shorb Weiskopf was hitting balls down the fairways of a public golf course.

"[The phone] must have been ringing for eight and a half hours straight yesterday," she said. "It finally got to the point where I had to leave for a while."

The fifty-five-year-old widow spent most of Saturday in her home, watching her son win the British Open on television. But the barrage of congratulatory phone calls forced her to drive thirty miles northeast of her Cleveland home to Chardon Lakes Golf Club. She shot 86.

To those who saw her play that day, Eva was beaming.

"I'm just so happy I can't even describe it. I'm very proud of him," she said, "and his father would have felt the same."

Everyone was pleased to see Weiskopf finally win a major. Arnold Palmer's famous prophecy about Nicklaus—"Now that the big guy is out of the cage, everybody better run for cover"—seemed apropos. Prognosticators couldn't help but speculate on the dawn of "the Tom Weiskopf Era."

"[To] compare him right now with a Jack Nicklaus or an Arnold Palmer isn't fair," said Byron Nelson, who witnessed Weiskopf's British Open win as an ABC commentator. "Tom has had a late start winning big, while both Nicklaus and Palmer started winning consistently in their twenties. However, I'm reminded of another golfer who didn't get it all together until he was about thirty-six years old. His name was Ben Hogan."

Comparisons to Hogan would have been absurd just a year earlier. But Weiskopf's newfound ability to keep his composure when in "other years, he has lost his temper and exploded," accounted for his victory far more than his native talents.

"Others had told me of the new, mature Weiskopf," wrote *Cleveland Plain Dealer* columnist Hal Lebovitz. "I had known the younger one. I wondered if the maturity was speculation or real. The Tom I had met before seemed edgy, talked with serious reflection and appeared to put on a confident front in an effort to hide his uncertainty. This time it was a self-assured Weiskopf talking. This one clearly believed in himself."

No longer did anyone question Weiskopf's desire to become the best golfer in the world . . . better than even Jack Nicklaus.

"How bad do I want it? Well, all I can say is, it's one down and thirteen to go."

Weiskopf continued to chase greatness—in the form of major championships *and* Jack Nicklaus—immediately following his British Open triumph. He won the Canadian Open two weeks afterward and, in late July, arrived in Cleveland. He had been to the city several times during the previous weeks—to visit his mother, accept a key to the city, and be honored as chair of the Schmidt's beer company's "Hole in One" program, which sent children to summer camps.

But when he arrived in his hometown again in mid-August, the prodigal son had truly returned. With the PGA Championship being played at Canterbury, a course he knew from his high school days at Benedictine, he was more than just a sentimental favorite.

"I think everybody has his ten best years. I figure the next ten will be my best in golf," he said before the fifty-fifth PGA. "During that period, there will be forty major championships played. I see no reason that I shouldn't win a third of them. That would be thirteen. That's as many as Jack Nicklaus has won."

Weiskopf kept within two strokes of the leaders at the halfway point, but a pair of par 71s on the weekend dropped him to sixth place. Given that Nicklaus won, Weiskopf now had to change his slogan: "One down and fourteen to go."

Still, he did get the best of his mentor later in the year. In September 1973, Weiskopf defeated Nicklaus (along with Tommy Aaron and Johnny Miller) in the World Series of Golf in September—a thirty-six-hole, made-for-television event featuring the season's four major championship winners. Playing at Akron's Firestone Country Club, not far from his birthplace in Massillon, helped inspire Weiskopf, though not as much as being paired with Nicklaus during both days.

"I thought it would be great for me to beat Jack, who's the greatest player in the world. I really wanted to beat him and I think that's what won it for me. You know, this tournament is as much match play as it is medal and you're always aware of Jack."

A changing of the guard now seemed inevitable.

"As Palmer found out a few years ago, there are always footsteps at the door," one Ohio columnist explained. "Nick had best look over his shoulder and listen to the footsteps too . . . the steps of Tom Weiskopf, two years his junior, only one major title to his credit, yet coming on. A transformed man, able to drive tall buildings in a single bound, saying, 'Jack is the greatest, his record proves it, but let's wait until we both retire . . . then maybe we can compare things.'"

Revealing the radical transformation in Weiskopf's reputation, the Golf Writers Association of America chose him as its 1973 "Player of the Year." Nicklaus may have won more money and owned a lower scoring average, but because

Nicklaus and Weiskopf won the same number of tournaments (Weiskopf won the South African PGA in October) and each man won a major championship apiece, some voters felt the tie should go to Weiskopf. And in the fifteen tournaments that featured both men, Weiskopf finished higher than Nicklaus nine times. When he heard that statistic, Weiskopf joked: "I didn't know that. I gotta tell the Bear he's over the hill.

"Everybody said that I ought to have a letdown after the British Open, and my life would get complicated," he said shortly afterward. "I'm playing great. I don't see why I ever have to play bad. And I love attention. Man, so far I think the heat's fun."

Weiskopf didn't exactly handle the pressure that well. He still quarreled with cameramen, both amateur and professional. At several tournaments during 1973—the American Golf Classic, the Westchester Open, the Canadian Open, and even during the U.S. Open at Oakmont—someone snapping photographs enraged Weiskopf and he made a fuss about it.

Weiskopf believed that a foreign photographer, Toshio Yamamoto of Japan's *Asahi Golf Magazine*—who persistently stood in his line of sight—sabotaged his chances in the American Golf Classic at Firestone, and was responsible for his triple bogey on the sixth hole. Yamamoto, who did not speak English, told a translator he was not in the way, but a nearby marshal and a few tour pros backed up Weiskopf; Yamamoto had been a distraction to golfers the week before at Oakmont. Within a few weeks Weiskopf would lead a charge demanding that the PGA ban spectators from having cameras and that marshals better supervise credentialed photographers.

Worse than this impatience with photographers was Weiskopf's casual attitude toward withdrawing or being disqualified from tournaments. Old habits returned in full force.

A betting favorite (with Nicklaus, of course) to win at Augusta National in 1974, Weiskopf tied for second, just two behind the winner, Gary Player. And he performed fairly well at the following two majors: He tied for fifteenth in the Massacre at Winged Foot, and seventh in the British Open. But the man who notched six wins in less than five months the previous summer was winless a year later, including a collapse during the final round of the Pleasant Valley Classic in early August to finish second.

A week later, Weiskopf arrived at Tanglewood Park for the PGA Championship. He had sustained a hairline fracture to his wrist earlier that summer, but assured the press he was healthy before the season's final major. After criticizing the course and its renowned architect, Robert Trent Jones—Weiskopf had already made news that summer by saying of another course, "I feel like I might as well be playing on the women's tour. They set courses up too easy. . . . It's just a putting contest each week"—he stirred up even more controversy in North Carolina.

On the Thursday that President Nixon resigned from office, Weiskopf shot 75, five over par. On Friday, Weiskopf—who for some reason chose a local high school football coach to serve as his caddie—five-putted the sixteenth green. Annoyed by a few rain delays and his thirteen-over-par total, Weiskopf simply walked off the course after posting his nine on the sixteenth, telling an official that his injured wrist had flared up.

"Are you injured?" someone asked in the Tanglewood dining room afterward.

"No . . . I just wanted to quit—I didn't need a reason."

A month later, Weiskopf simply refused to sign his scorecard after finishing the second round of the World Open golf tournament at Pinehurst with consecutive double bogeys. As was the case at Tanglewood, where he was fined, Weiskopf was disciplined by Deane Beman of the PGA tour.

Weiskopf would finish the 1974 season winless, earning less than half of what he made the previous year. Despite the antics, his friend Jack Nicklaus stood by him and refused to replace Weiskopf as his teammate for the season's final event, the Walt Disney World Golf Classic, a $250,000 best-ball competition.

"Tom never pulls stuff like that when I'm around and I think it's about time he reaches the point where he wouldn't want to lose face with the public," Nicklaus said.

Together, the world's two most powerful hitters could finish only in a three-way tie for eleventh, five strokes behind the Hubert Green–Mac McClendon duo.

But at least for a time, his initiation into the fraternity of major champions shielded Weiskopf against sharp barbs from the press.

There was a second consecutive agonizing heartbreak in the 1975 Masters, as Weiskopf and Johnny Miller finished a shot behind Nicklaus; Weiskopf claimed that Nicklaus's forty-foot birdie putt on number sixteen, right after Weiskopf eagled the fifteenth, "broke my concentration." In just seven years, he now had four Masters runner-ups, a record matched by only Hogan and Nicklaus. And Weiskopf also turned in exceptional performances in the PGA in 1975, 1976, and 1978, the last played at Oakmont. At 280, he finished tied for fourth—one stroke lower than in the U.S. Open five years earlier.

During a period in the mid-1970s, Weiskopf even defeated Nicklaus twice, "head-to-head," in prestigious PGA events: A year after his play-off birdie edged out Nicklaus for the 1975 Canadian Open, Weiskopf won the 1976 Doral-Eastern Open Invitational, holding off an incredible charge by the Golden Bear, who birdied number nine and eagled numbers ten and twelve without a single putt.

Despite those triumphs over Nicklaus, one *tournament*—not one player— seemed to bring out the best in Tom Weiskopf. From 1976 to 1979, no one turned in better overall U.S. Open performances than he did. Weiskopf's U.S. Open scoring average was a full stroke lower (71) than Nicklaus's. He also finished inside the top five each of those years. By comparison, neither Nicklaus nor anyone else finished higher than sixth during that stretch.

Fittingly, when the first U.S. Open of the new decade began, the two biggest stars were the pair of Ohio State Buckeyes. In the opening round at Baltusrol, Weiskopf teed off just after noon, and limped out with a bogey on number one. Then he got hot: four birdies on the front, four more on the back. On the par-five closing hole, Weiskopf found himself in easy range of another birdie and a major-championship record 62.

"[But] then I got cute," he said about his wedge approach that landed in a green-side bunker. He still got up and down to save par and close out the day with a 63, tying Johnny Miller's 1973 U.S. Open final round.

"Of course, that was a much easier course than this one," a grinning Weiskopf said afterward.

For all the headlines that he grabbed with his 63, Weiskopf had to share every bit of the spotlight with Nicklaus.

Teeing off just thirty-six minutes after Weiskopf, Nicklaus overcame an early bogey of his own to make the turn at two under.

"I knew Tom had made the turn in four under par and was cruising along," Nicklaus said. "We saw him get another birdie at the fifteenth. That's when Angelo [Nicklaus's caddie] turned to me and said, 'Answer him, answer him.' When I got to the thirteenth I almost knocked my second into the hole."

From there, Nicklaus made an easy birdie, his third in a row, then carded two more, matching Weiskopf at seven under par with one hole to play. Nicklaus nailed the fairway, placed his second shot to the base of the green, then deftly chipped to within three feet of the flag. But he missed the birdie try. A score of 62 in a major championship must have felt—and still feels—like golf's version of the three-minute mile.

"I knew Jack would get charged up when he saw what Tom was doing," Jeanne Weiskopf said. "It's been that way all their lives. They really get their incentives fired up when they are going head-to-head."

Weiskopf usually needed Nicklaus to jump-start his motivation; Nicklaus never needed such a push. Nicklaus's two-day total of 134 at Baltusrol established a new two-round record for the U.S. Open. By Sunday evening, he had defeated Japan's Isao Aoki to claim his fourth U.S. Open trophy by posting the lowest four-day total in the championship's history.

"I've always felt that a large part of winning comes from true desire," Nicklaus said that evening. "If you don't have the desire to spend a lot of time working at it, you're not going to do it. . . . Then you go out and spend six months working your tail off and you wonder if you're doing the right thing. The right thing for the game, the right thing for your family, the right thing for your friends. You wonder if it's right to put them through that."

During the summer of 1973, Tom Weiskopf had proved he could summon Nicklaus's brand of desire to achieve Nicklaus-like results; but he could not sustain it.

So when Weiskopf carded a five over 75 on Friday—he would plummet with a 76-75 weekend performance to finish in thirty-seventh place, seventeen strokes behind Nicklaus—he took the fall gracefully.

"Yesterday was my day," he said after his second-round 75. "Today was not. It's that simple."

There were not many more days on tour that belonged to Weiskopf. He remained a relevant force during the early 1980s: tenth-place finishes in the 1980 PGA and 1982 Masters, along with a pair of tournament wins during a ten-month period in 1981 and 1982.

Neither victory convinced anyone that *these* next ten years would be Weiskopf's best in golf. His September 1981 win in the LeJet Classic in Abilene, Texas, came while all the tour stars, including Nicklaus, were out of the country crushing Europe in the Ryder Cup. His final PGA win came the following Fourth of July. Again, the field that week at the seventy-ninth Western Open was fairly depleted, without Nicklaus, Trevino, Miller, Palmer, Tom Watson, and six of the season's top-ten money earners. But Weiskopf sank a seven-foot birdie on the seventy-second hole of Butler National to edge out Larry Nelson, capping what he called "the best I've ever played from tee to green for four straight days." His sixteenth tour victory also came with a piece of irony: Weiskopf had earned his first paycheck ($487.50) at the Western Open twenty-eight years earlier.

"The press and the fans basically have always kind of pulled for me," he explained. "They don't like to see me do some of the things I do. I guess I don't like to see me do them either. But I'm always trying to improve myself. I don't know if you believe this or not, but I care what people think. I really do."

As much as Weiskopf claimed to have cared what others thought, those who knew him best admired him for the exact opposite.

"[Weiskopf has been] frequently criticized for not being 'more dedicated to golf' or 'true to [his] talent,'" Jack Nicklaus wrote years later. "In my opinion, what [he] really [deserves] is applause for being true to [himself]."

Being true to himself, Weiskopf essentially dropped off the PGA tour in 1984. He joined CBS Sports for a time and, after a tryout in 1981, served as a Masters commentator from 1985 to 1995. Fittingly, Weiskopf was at the microphone to analyze Jack Nicklaus during his memorable victory at Augusta National in 1986.

With Nicklaus standing on the tee at the par-three sixteenth, two strokes behind and in desperate need of a birdie, CBS announcer Jim Nantz asked Weiskopf—on air—what the Golden Bear's mind-set was at this moment.

"If I knew the way he thought," Weiskopf replied, "I would have won this tournament."

Weiskopf still loved to hunt and, as he did on several occasions during his tour days, spent weeks away from everything, secluded in Arizona or Montana cabins while pursuing big game. By the late 1980s, nabbing Alaskan Kodiak and mountain grizzly bears far outweighed birdies and eagles.

But Weiskopf never left the game of golf behind.

To his critics, Weiskopf had "wasted" much of his athletic prime—hunting, fishing, and unwinding while others focused on making themselves great golfers. An ugly dispute with Fred Couples in 1991 highlighted this common belief.

In response to Weiskopf's charge (in a *Golf Digest* article) that Couples had "no goals in life . . . He has great touch and power, but if he had Jack's goals . . ." Couples returned the favor.

"He's a waste product. . . . What did he do, quit at forty? He was supposed to have all that talent. How many majors did he win? . . . I don't think Tom Weiskopf is any Jack Nicklaus, so it goes in one ear and out the other."

Perhaps the most infamous of all Weiskopf indiscretions derived from his refusing a 1977 Ryder Cup invitation in order to go hunting.

"I told them I had applied and had been accepted to go Dall sheep hunting in the Yukon and try to complete my Grand Slam of North American sheep [including bighorn, desert bighorn, and stone]," Weiskopf explained years later. "I told them how I had to book the trip two years in advance, had finally been accepted, and had already put my deposit in. I expressed how much I had enjoyed playing on two Ryder Cup teams, but how I'd rather have someone else have the opportunity."

But all that time in the mountains would eventually make Weiskopf a shining star in another realm of the sport.

"At the end of 1984 I quit the regular tour, because of the way I was handling my temperament," he told the golf journalist and historian Al Barkow. "I was offered an opportunity to work with [famed golf course architect] Jay Morrish in creating Troon North in Scottsdale. I knew I had to get away from the game for at least a year, so I thought I'd see if I liked architecture. I could still go back on tour if I wanted to, but I never did."

While Morrish initially handled the more technical elements of course design, Weiskopf brought to the project a creative imagination, a love of nature and the land, as well as a delight in golf's mental intricacies. By 1986, the duo finished Troon North, which shared the site name of his lone major championship. Eventually, Weiskopf began working more on his own designs (Morrish and Weiskopf parted ways in 1994), and his signature became mountain courses. The Ridge at Castle Pines North in Castle Rock, Colorado, and Loch Lomond Golf Club near Glasgow, Scotland, were among several creations that won him special acclaim.

So dedicated was Weiskopf to making Loch Lomond a gem, he actually spent two summers living in the Garden Cottage near the third tee while he oversaw the project.

"When it's all over, when I'm gone, if people would say, 'You know, I think Tom Weiskopf was a better designer than he was a player,' that would be the best compliment I could ever have."

Weiskopf was now revered as a great course designer and a connoisseur of the game's aesthetics. But—when he wanted to—the man could still play.

In 1993, Weiskopf once again joined the tour . . . the Senior Tour. Like Nicklaus before him, he won his first (unofficial) Senior Tour appearance, shooting 66-67-69 in the Chrysler Cup at the TPC Prestancia Stadium Golf Course in Sarasota.

"There was a lot of anxiety and a lot of fear and a lot of doubt," he said. "It meant so much to play well here. . . . I wanted to show these guys I could still play. I think they know it now."

Weiskopf played exceptionally well during the spring, posting top tens in his next two senior events, and then, at Nicklaus's Cochise Course, placed eighth in the Tradition (one stroke better than the course architect). And a course-record-tying 64 in the PGA National in April gave Weiskopf the lead halfway into the season's second major, the Senior PGA Championship.

Despite a gimpy knee, the familiar 1970s version of Tom Weiskopf—tremendous power, punctuated by laser-perfect long irons—reemerged that week. So, too, did the plainspoken Ohioan who made headlines just by opening his mouth.

Weiskopf's third-round 72 dropped him into a tie for third place, four shots behind the leader, Tom Wargo. A former assembly-line worker at General Motors who began playing the game at age twenty-five, Wargo hadn't cut his teeth on the PGA tour like most of his senior peers.

"Hopefully, it's going to be quite difficult [for Wargo]," Weiskopf said about the final round. "I don't mean that in a nasty way, but it's a little bit different. I don't know what type of player he is—obviously, he's a heck of a player. But has he won out here? That's a big deal. There will be a lot of thoughts going through his head. He'll see names on the scoreboard he knows that are going to put pressure on him. Capable players, accomplished players."

In the end, Wargo hung on and defeated such "capable . . . accomplished" players as Nicklaus, Trevino, Isao Aoki, Bob Charles, and Bruce Crampton, whom he beat in a play-off. Poor play down the stretch crushed Weiskopf's chance to catch Wargo. He finished fourth, tied with his 1973 U.S. Open final-round playing partner, Bob Charles.

Although Weiskopf finished twenty-sixth on the 1993 Senior Tour earnings list, money was not why he had interrupted his semireclusive—and lucrative—course-design career.

"I had one goal in mind as a senior," he said years later, "to win the U.S. Senior Open, because it's the only championship for seniors that is pure. It's on a championship course at around seven thousand yards, has fast greens, rough, tough pins; you have to walk; it has a full field and a cut."

Weiskopf's chance for that first career U.S.G.A. championship came in July.

Although Senior Tour star Chi Chi Rodriguez (five under par) closed out each of the opening two rounds in the lead, Weiskopf played the best of anyone from tee to green. And he still spoke with the swagger of his early days on tour.

"I played perfect today; I have for two days," he said about a 69 on Friday that brought him back to even par. "I hit fifteen greens [Thursday] and never made a putt. I had a lot of opportunities and missed them and got a little frustrated. Situations like that are trying on your patience, and I'm not a patient person, but I stuck with it."

Weiskopf believed he could score at Cherry Hills—"This course suits my game because I'm a good long-iron player and I can use them off the tee"—and he had proven as much by finishing fourth in the U.S. Open there in 1978.

Nevertheless, Nicklaus—not Weiskopf—stepped to the fore on moving day. Nicklaus wanted the 1993 Senior U.S. Open to be the stage for his first tournament win in nearly two years. And a four under 67 on Saturday pushed him within one round of ending the embarrassing streak.

"Saturday is the day you usually get yourself in or out of the tournament," he told the press about his one-stroke lead before the final round. "It's the first Saturday I've gotten myself in the tournament in quite a while."

With another rendition of "Jack is back!" sweeping through the gallery and press tent, Weiskopf's two under par on Saturday went largely unnoticed. Four strokes behind Nicklaus and still unable to turn good shots into birdies, the Towering Inferno bubbled over.

An iron off the tee on the 222-yard, par-three eighth landed on the green and skidded into the rough.

"I guess I just don't have the talent to hit this green," he blurted out.

Carding a bogey there, Weiskopf took his frustration out on nearby U.S.G.A. officials.

"This is ridiculous," Weiskopf shouted for all to hear. "If you're going to keep the greens this hard, move the tees up and give us a chance, let us hit five- or six-irons. Where it is now, I could sit out here all day long and not get the ball close to the hole."

Putting that frustration behind him, Weiskopf played brilliantly on Sunday, birdying five of the first eight holes to tie Nicklaus for the lead. He nearly seized another on the ninth—to card an amazing 29 on the front—but his twelve-foot birdie try died just before the cup.

"I was going under the basic principle that somewhere along the line, things were going to change because I'd putted so poorly in the first three rounds," he said afterward.

"And the only reason I made some [Sunday] was because I was determined that I was going to make these putts. Basically, it's a mind game. You have to be your best cheerleader. You have to just tell yourself you can do these things."

Weiskopf dropped a stroke on the tenth by failing to save par from four feet, then sank a twelve-foot birdie on the thirteenth, to again vault him over Nicklaus. After a three putt on the par-three fifteenth cost him the lead, Weiskopf could still pressure Nicklaus with a birdie or eagle on the 540-yard, par-five seventeenth, reachable in two. But he drove the ball into the rough and settled for par.

Minutes later, Nicklaus sank a twelve-foot birdie on the sixteenth. Although not as dramatic as the forty-footer he drained on Augusta National's sixteenth in 1975, this putt had the same effect: It sealed another major championship for Nicklaus, at the expense of Tom Weiskopf.

Nicklaus preserved his one-stroke lead with a par on number seventeen, and with Weiskopf unable to birdie number eighteen, the toughest hole that week, Nicklaus just needed a par to win. He landed a one-iron safely in the fairway, then took a five-iron from his caddie—once again, his son Jackie—and nailed the middle of the green.

"I knew it was over as soon as he hit his shot on the green," Weiskopf admitted. "Who can tell me when he's three-putted to lose a major championship? The guy is the greatest putter under pressure of all time, bar none."

Weiskopf, watching from behind the eighteenth green, knew his rival well: Nicklaus lagged his thirty-five-footer to less than three feet, then sank his par putt for the victory.

"I gave it the best run I possibly could," Weiskopf said afterward. "I played the best four rounds of golf I have ever played under those types of (major tournament) conditions. I know in my mind no one played better than I did from tee to green.

"The guy is just one stroke better than me all the time, it seems."

· 16 ·

John Schlee

I t could have been John Schlee, the 1973 United States Open Champion. Yet golf never had a prouder second-place finisher than the Seaside, Oregon, native.

His $18,000 paycheck aside, Schlee spoke gleefully upon leaving Oakmont in 1973.

"I'm just fortunate to be where I am," he said Sunday evening. "It's great to be the runner-up.

"No, I'm not let down at all. I only screwed up once in the Open. If circumstances were the same, I'd have been the winner in any of the other seventy-two Opens. But this one I lost because Johnny shot that sixty-three in the final round, something no one has ever done."

Schlee promptly dismissed what reporters and fans naturally assumed: that his one "screwup" (the three-drive start to his final round) would haunt him for the rest of his life.

"No, not at all. After eight years on tour, you develop a short memory. You learn to block things out and go on."

Like each of his fellow top finishers in the U.S. Open—Miller, Weiskopf, Trevino, Nicklaus, and Palmer—Schlee played in the next stop on tour, the American Golf Classic. His poor first round (a five-over 75) did nothing to slow down his great season in the making. Schlee played the next three rounds in one under par on the Firestone course—which, earlier in the week, he declared more "demanding" than Oakmont—and tied with Bobby Cole, J. C. Snead, and Johnny Miller for a spot just outside the top twenty. At three extremely challenging courses during the preceding three weeks, Schlee's stroke average was 70.33; by comparison, Miller's was 70.17.

Schlee's experience in Great Britain's most prestigious tournament, the Open Championship, wasn't nearly as memorable. At Troon in mid-July, where Tom Weiskopf won, he finished dead last, in 153rd place. Schlee's first and only British Open appearance actually ended partway through the second round, when he decided to withdraw.

As "America's Runner-up," Schlee was upset about being required to play in a thirty-six-hole qualifier to enter the Open. The extra rounds, just to earn a spot in the field, reminded Schlee of his harrowing Monday-qualifier days as a pro in the late 1960s. "Players of my caliber," he said, "should not have to qualify. The Royal and Ancient should come up with some rule to avoid this."

Schlee moved past his indignation and finished the 1973 season with a pair of wonderful performances. After a long break from the tour, he returned to compete in November's Kaiser International Open Invitational.

The tournament was played over both courses at the Silverado Country Club, where Johnny Miller owned a three-bedroom condominium, and he was the undisputed favorite to win the Napa Valley event. Not only was there a reduced field (no Nicklaus, Trevino, Crampton, Wadkins, Weiskopf, or Casper), but Miller had just won the Trophée Lancôme, a prominent tournament on the European tour. But by Sunday, Schlee had upstaged the man who bested him at Oakmont by the narrowest of margins.

Despite a modest prophecy from the stars—"[nothing] exciting this month. Perhaps some of the faster-moving planets are in good aspect . . . maybe Mercury and the moon"—Schlee grabbed the Kaiser's top spot by shooting 66-67 in the opening rounds.

"[At] times out there today I felt superhuman," Schlee said at the midway point. "For the first twenty-seven holes of the tournament I was twelve under par—and ten under the last eighteen—and then it was brought to my attention what I was doing and I promptly choked. For a couple of holes I couldn't even breathe."

On Sunday afternoon—while Miller carded zero birdies and six bogeys—

Schlee took command and seemed headed for his second tour win of 1973. But hitting a tee shot out of bounds on the fifth, then posting a double bogey on the seventh, allowed Ed Sneed to catch and tie him by the end of the round.

"Ed and I are pretty good friends," Schlee said, "and when we got to the first tee for the play-off there wasn't much pressure. We knew that one of us would be first and one of us would be second and that was that."

Schlee's Achilles' heel—losing concentration and getting swept up in the excitement—cost him right away. Throughout his career, he was easily distracted or, rather, he easily distracted himself (by the mid-1970s, he was deeply engaged in the study of "biorhythms," in addition to his continuing fascination with astrology). Unlike Nicklaus or Palmer, he could only rarely sustain intensity throughout an entire golf tournament—not in his career year of 1973, and not afterward either. "He always had a tough time staying focused because his mind was so active," recalled someone who knew him well.

At the 439-yard, par-four play-off hole, Schlee sliced into the right rough, then landed his next shot in a fairway bunker. He couldn't make par and Sneed two-putted for the win.

"It was Ed's day and Ed's turn to win, and he beat the hell out of me." Second place again, the third of his career.

At the final tour stop of the 1973 season, the Walt Disney World Open, Schlee broke par each day and finished tied for fourth, just three behind the winner, Jack Nicklaus. A sixth top ten that year yielded another big payday, and he finished the year tenth on the money list.

Schlee earned more money that season ($118,017) than in the last three seasons combined. With additional endorsement perks and higher exhibition fees, the Schlees were suddenly living the high life in Dallas. And the year culminated in a luxurious, all-expenses-paid, six-week sojourn with Gary Player and a few other international stars to give exhibitions, play a few tournaments, and vacation at all of South Africa's top tourist spots.

Schlee backed up his growing reputation in the world of golf in 1974. He followed up a good spring, including another top thirty in the Masters, with a great summer.

A week before his much-anticipated appearance at Winged Foot for the U.S. Open—author Dick Schaap would keep close tabs on the self-proclaimed "National Runner-up" for his book, *The Massacre at Winged Foot*—Schlee grabbed the first-round lead in the IVB Philadelphia Classic. The defending champion,

Tom Weiskopf, grabbed the headlines, however; among other low rounds, it was Schlee's six-under-par effort that prompted Weiskopf to say, "[The courses are] too easy. I feel like I might as well be playing on the women's tour."

Schlee agreed with Weiskopf, but used his latest moment in the spotlight to talk about his second love: astrology.

"June was a good month for me last year, and it will be better for me this year."

When asked if that meant he might win next week's U.S. Open, Schlee proclaimed, "Unless there is somebody else who has a more favorable sign."

Schlee finished tied for eighth at Whitemarsh, only to miss the cut by two shots at Winged Foot with consecutive 78s.

Although he was a Gemini and not a Leo, the stars seemed aligned for Schlee during a stretch from late July to mid-August of 1974. On July 20, with most tour stars playing in the British Open, Schlee shot a tournament-low six under 65 to spring into contention at the B.C. Open in upstate New York (he finished tied for fifth). The following week, in the more prestigious Canadian Open, Schlee collected a runner-up check behind Bobby Nichols. At the home hole, he sank an eighteen-footer to pull into a second-place tie and earn $10,000.

More than fifteen strokes off the pace in the following week's Pleasant Valley Classic, Schlee withdrew during the second round to prepare for the PGA Championship. The tournament sponsors were unhappy, but his decision paid off. At Tanglewood Park in North Carolina, Schlee shot an opening-round 68—five better than his playing partner, Lee Trevino—to tie for the lead in the season's final major.

As always, Schlee was colorful in his recap of the day.

"Man, I wish we were playing this next week," he said. "This is not a bad week but next week's better. In fact, my horoscope the rest of the year is good. When you have a good horoscope, you can relax, have a good time on the course. When you don't, you struggle with your game."

Once again, Schlee's views on astrology captivated his audience in the press tent. In addition to explaining how the current aligning of the stars affected golfers like Sam Snead and Arnold Palmer, he commented on the plight of President Nixon, who had announced his resignation on the same day Schlee shot his first-round 68: "I feel real sorry for him. His sign indicated a bad week for him.

"Since my moon is in Sagittarius and there's a rising sun in Aquarius, this should be a good week for me," he told reporters.

The next afternoon, while Tom Weiskopf "went bananas" on the sixteenth green and withdrew, Schlee shot 67 to maintain a one-stroke lead at the half-way point.

"I think anytime anyone can find anything that gives him a plan to follow—whether it's astrology, religion, anything—it has to help."

"(Kermit) Zarley believes in the Bible, Schlee believes in astrology," Trevino told the press corps that week. "I believe in making more birdies than bogeys."

The Super Mex set about doing just that during the weekend, winning the season's final major on Sunday; Schlee shot a pair of 75s to fall from contention and finish seventeenth.

Schlee finished the 1974 season having made the cut in twenty of the thirty events he entered, earning over $54,000, and retaining his exempt status by finishing in the top sixty. The year culminated in another all-expenses-paid exhibition tour for the entire family, this time to Sweden.

AND THEN, JOHN SCHLEE'S LIFE suddenly fell apart. His back—he'd always claimed to have "an extra vertebrae down there"—bothered him near the end of the season, and he elected to have surgery. Then, abruptly, his second wife opted out of their marriage. For the first time in a decade, Schlee was without a family to soften his personal eccentricities and his career ups and downs.

But Schlee was resilient. In need of money, he returned to the tour just a few weeks after the surgery (much earlier than his doctor advised). He even shot a third-round 65 in the Bob Hope in early February. Given his physical, personal, and financial ailments (the divorce was finalized midyear), Schlee performed well during the 1975 season, carding five top tens in just twenty-five starts (his fewest appearances since 1969). Most important, he finished fifty-eighth on the money list to retain his exempt status for the 1976 season.

Another significant surgery, this time to repair cartilage in his left knee, sidelined Schlee in the early part of 1976: A compulsive fixer-upper, he had fallen through the roof of his house while doing home repairs. Nevertheless, within six weeks, he shot a tournament-record 65 (matched that same day by Lanny Wadkins) in the Pleasant Valley Classic. In fact, he led the tournament after twenty-seven holes, then distracted himself by flirting with a girl who worked in the scorer's tent. He finally had to be called to the tee, rushed his preparation, and quickly double-bogeyed numbers ten and eleven, falling from first to fifteenth place in the span of two holes.

And though the season was similar to the year before—fifty-ninth in tour earnings to barely retain his exempt status—1976 had a notable high point. Shooting impressive scores each round (71-72-70-70), Schlee tied for fourth behind Dave Stockton in the PGA Championship at the Congressional Country Club, where his caddie (for seven events during the summer) was Darryl Donovan, the now sixteen-year-old he'd babysat years earlier at Memphis State.

Schlee continued to hold his own on tour early the following season. Outstanding at the Masters tournament, he was one of only two players to break 70 both Saturday and Sunday. He even endeared himself to the crowd (though probably *not* to the Augusta brass) by snatching a rope barrier that divided the gallery from the players to measure the distance from tee to green on Augusta's famous par-three twelfth; choosing the wrong club off the tee in earlier rounds had convinced Schlee that his caddie's and the official yardage measurement were incorrect. Once the bizarre scene ended, Schlee selected a seven-iron and made a birdie two.

That eighth-place finish at Augusta National was Schlee's only season highlight in 1977. Bothered by a sprained thumb he suffered at the Masters, Schlee missed the cut in the U.S. Open by twelve strokes, then essentially dropped off the tour with a meager $17,397.45 in earnings. For the first time since his "lessons" with Ben Hogan (which he incessantly talked about to reporters, fans, and fellow touring pros), Schlee failed to crack the top one hundred in earnings.

"I was hurting so bad at the Open last year," he said the following spring, "that I quit the tour. I took the golf director's job at Rancho Viejo [in Brownsville, Texas] and didn't intend to play the tour again."

Schlee felt secure in his new career direction, and he invited Darryl Donovan to move in with him for the school year to sharpen his golf game at Rancho Viejo, under Schlee's personal guidance. But Schlee did get one more shot on tour.

With the help of fellow club professional Mike Morley, Schlee altered his extreme weak grip to relieve the pain in his thumb. He then sent Darryl back to Miami and began trying to Monday-qualify for tournaments. At first, he performed fairly well, twice making the cut in early season events, including a nineteenth-place finish in the Players Championship in March. And after one round of the Masters tournament two weeks later—his top-ten finish the previous spring had earned him automatic entry—Schlee looked poised for another career turnaround.

Schlee made the turn at one under, then promptly dropped to even par with a bogey at the start of Amen Corner. From there he birdied the next four holes to shoot 68 and earn sole possession of first place after round one.

Despite Schlee's injuries and his graying temples, his power remained fully intact: He was on the green in two on three of Augusta's par-fives. His great first round placed him in elite company in Masters tournament history: In three consecutive rounds (the closing thirty-six holes in 1977 and the opening round in 1978), Schlee shot below 70 each time, becoming just the fifth man to do so.

"I'm really not surprised that I'm leading," he said. "I've worked real hard on my game lately. Every time I'd hit a practice shot back at my course in Rancho Viejo [Texas], I had the Masters course on my mind."

That opening round proved to be the final "lunar high point" of John Schlee's PGA career. He suffered terrible back pain on Friday morning, and could barely get out of bed to play the second round. Schlee relied on his tremendous physical prowess to finish the tournament with rounds of 75-77-75, tied for forty-second place.

Schlee played in only four more PGA events in 1978, earning just $835, then retired from tour competition. By no means was he embarrassing himself—not once did he score 80 or higher in 1978—but he could no longer earn a living once serious back problems reemerged. Although he had earned $1,850 for his performance at Augusta National, the week cost him more than $2,000: He still insisted on staying in a house complete with a chef and maid, flying first class, and driving a Mercedes.

"How many millionaires do you think are on tour?" he hypothetically asked a reporter. "Maybe three. I mean those whose actual net worth is a million. Palmer, Nicklaus, and Player are about the only ones I can think of offhand."

The thought of living frugally and planning conservatively for the future never crossed John Schlee's mind.

SCHLEE HAD MANY CONCRETE IDEAS about how to swing a golf club. Although he liked to sell himself as Hogan's Oracle, in fact, he was quite a teaching innovator on his own. In the decade following his retirement from the tour, Schlee became a nationally recognized golf instructor, leaving Rancho Viejo in 1979 to establish his own Maximum Golf School, first in Industry Hills, California (just east of Los Angeles), then, starting in 1985, in Carlsbad (north of San Diego).

According to Schlee, he sought Hogan's formal endorsement of his new school, but Hogan gently declined.

"When I retired from competitive golf in 1978, I went to Ben Hogan with a plan for a golf school. I asked him, 'Can I use your name?'

"He fell silent for a long time. Then he said, 'John, my name is all I have. I've worked all my life to develop adjectives that would please me when my name is mentioned. I would like to be involved with your golf school but my duties here at the Ben Hogan Company come first. I think it's time for you to start building your own adjectives.

"'And so, my answer is no. When you want this school in your heart, ten years from now you will understand my answer. Go build your name from your guts out . . . and love doing it!'"

Schlee loved to scientifically narrate and pontificate about golf swing mechanics, but he did not enjoy being a full-time *teacher* of the game. Therefore, the Maximum Golf School featured a group of instructors that carried out much of the nitty-gritty, labor-intensive work with individual students: videotaping their swings and analyzing their faults to death. As Tom Bertrand, one of the school's most devoted instructors, recalled, "John also passed all of the individual lessons my way, which I appreciated as an act of confidence in my abilities, but I knew that, like Hogan, John didn't have the patience or the inclination to deal with students on a one-on-one basis."

Schlee had always struggled to be a patient, nurturing golf instructor. Early and late in his career, he held numerous club positions in Tennessee, Florida, Arizona, Texas, California, and Oregon. But his overtly direct and critical nature frequently discouraged his well-to-do students. Just as in Seaside and Memphis State, Schlee projected a transparent disdain for country clubbers who didn't welcome him as their social equal. He simply wasn't cut out for the full-time job of club professional.

Schlee did feel comfortable lecturing to large groups of "students" about his ideas—as long as they didn't talk back. He would not tolerate opposition, especially from a student who dared point out that some of his ideas were not consistent with Hogan's. Schlee would rather return the money of disbelievers, and tell them to get the hell out of his school. Maximum Golf's three-day weekend seminars were run with such fervor and demand for obedience that a third of the group would often quit the training before Sunday.

Schlee's school remained reasonably successful for a decade, and the staff he hired appreciated his passion, knowledge, and financial generosity. But expanding the school to national prominence just was not in the stars. Golfers struggled to implement (or even understand) Schlee's complex and unorthodox golf ideas, and the overbearing, didactic way he ran the school was really not much fun. Many students didn't get too far beyond the opening injunctions about how to address the ball.

Replicating Schlee's extremely weak grip was often too much for the students; as was Schlee's instruction to load their weight almost entirely on their left side, from the start to the finish of the swing. Completing those two maneuvers—while making sure the right knee didn't "bow out" on the "back turn," and then "laying off" the club, with the right wrist appropriately "cupped" on the downswing—required radical adjustments that many good golfers were loath to make, and that were beyond the capacity of average golfers without injuring themselves.

Many of Schlee's ideas were ahead of their time, and they certainly worked for him. And several of the gadgets Schlee created to help students assume the appropriate swing positions proved quite useful for serious golfers—especially a device to promote a "cupped" right wrist (Greg Norman later acquired the legal rights to and marketed this gadget as the "Greg Norman Secret"). Some experts even consider Schlee the inventor of the modern-day "stack and tilt" approach to the golf swing, used by many of today's top pros.

"I think there will be a lot of changes in equipment in the next few years," Schlee said in 1968, "and I'm doing some pioneering."

In *his* time, however, Schlee failed to popularize his ideas: just too many fundamentals, rules, and procedures for each and every body part for the average golfer to follow. And Schlee's long-term commitment to the enterprise likely diminished when he received a negative response from Hogan, regarding Schlee's request to endorse a book he'd written to spread his ideas.

Hogan's representatives told Schlee he wanted nothing to do with Schlee's book. According to Bertrand, Hogan's representatives punctuated their rejection by saying that Hogan "didn't even remember John Schlee." In actuality, he likely *did* know who John Schlee was: Hogan had gone out of his way to let Byron Nelson know just how displeased he was by Schlee's unauthorized use of his name to market his school.

By the late 1980s, Schlee's enthusiasm for the Maximum Golf School had begun to wane, and his lectures didn't seem as sharp as they had once been. With his *Maximum Golf* book (and the accompanying videotape) clearly not bound for great commercial success, Schlee had to generate alternative financial means. He experimented with a variety of putters (starting with the Taylor Raylor), and, along with other gadgets he invented and marketed, he managed to diversify his sources of income.

And by June 1989, Schlee found another source of income. He turned fifty that month and headed back onto the pro circuit—the senior circuit (because he ranked high enough on the PGA tour career earnings list, he was immediately eligible). Running the Maximum Golf School had kept Schlee from playing regularly—although he could still blast the ball on the driving range and dazzle students by making the ball do whatever he wanted—and his game was nowhere near tournament ready.

Even on the Senior Tour, Schlee remained an ardent preacher of golf theory. In his second Senior Tour stop, the prestigious MONY Syracuse Senior's Pro Golf Classic, Schlee played the Wednesday pro-am with local sports anchor Mike Tirico.

"He's already given me five lessons on nine holes," said Tirico, who would one day be the lead voice for ABC/ESPN's coverage of the NBA Finals, *Monday Night Football*, and the British Open.

During that second half season of 1989, Schlee played in twelve events and earned $7,250: With travel and expenses, he struggled each week to break even. And he posted virtually identical numbers in 1990: twenty-four appearances, just over $14,000. Schlee's days on the Senior Tour were proving to be as unprofitable as his last two years on the PGA Tour. The money he made marketing his long putters and selling equipment and gadgets to his fellow Senior Tour pros rivaled his share of the purses.

Rocky Thompson, who won the Syracuse MONY tournament in 1991, attributed his success largely to the long-shafted putter he bought from Schlee for the extravagant sum of $650. Thompson could afford to help Schlee out, given the $60,000 winner's check he took home; Schlee played in each round and earned only $500.

After just two Senior Tour events in 1991, Schlee's tournament playing career was over. Physical conditioning was a small factor in his retirement: His mental acuity had deteriorated.

For the 1990 Transamerica tournament at Sonoma Golf Club, Darryl Donovan caddied for Schlee for the first time since 1976. Donovan—who a year later would join the pro tour—was now stationed at nearby Fort Ord, following overseas service flying AH-1 Cobra attack helicopters. He was delighted to see Schlee again and, knowing Schlee had not played well in his first year on the Senior Tour, eagerly offered his assistance.

From the start, Donovan saw an enormous decline in Schlee's shot preparation. Donovan knew that, even in his prime, Schlee rarely concentrated on all seventy-two holes. Still, Donovan had always been impressed by Schlee's "orchestrated and regimented" setup routine, which included ample discussion of yardage and strategic goals—the same preparations he had taught at the Maximum Golf School and in his book. There was even a plan for where the caddie should stand before each stroke.

Donovan quickly noticed that Schlee no longer played this way. There was no routine, no mental preparation whatsoever. Everything was done impulsively.

At first, in a practice round, Schlee advised Donovan to "keep it light," so he didn't say anything to Schlee. But on the tenth hole of the opening round, after shooting several over par on the front nine, Schlee reached into his bag while it was still on the ground and pulled a sand wedge for his second shot.

Donovan asked him what he was doing, to which Schlee replied, "Hey, man, I know what I'm going to hit." Donovan then asked what the yardage was, to which Schlee responded, "About a hundred yards." But Donovan had already measured the precise distance, which was 112 yards to the back pin location. For that shot, Donovan knew that Schlee's sand wedge would come up short. When Donovan raised the point, Schlee brashly said, "I can hit this that far."

This time, Donovan could hold his tongue no longer.

"Man, you're not focused," he said in obvious frustration. "You're not concentrating; you're not doing what you've done in the past."

"You're bumming me out," replied Schlee. "I'm out here to have fun."

"No, John, you're out here to make a living and have fun making a living, but making a living comes first, not having fun."

Around this time, Donovan introduced Schlee to Steve Chapman, the head professional at Monterey Peninsula Country Club. Chapman eventually offered Schlee—who had been teaching intermittently on the driving range at Pleasant Valley Golf Club near Portland—a full-time instructional position.

Chapman soon noticed friction between club members and Schlee, who could not recall the names of individuals he'd recently taught. He also wore out his welcome when he played nearby Pebble Beach. Schlee repeatedly tossed cigarette butts onto the ground, and even after apologizing (course officials rightly worried about fires during the dry season), the chain-smoking Schlee continued to do so; he was having difficulty remembering the recent conversations.

At Chapman's urging, Schlee finally saw a doctor. The preliminary diagnosis indicated that Schlee was already far along in Alzheimer's—increasingly forgetful, but still able to function for most everyday purposes.

Schlee's response to the diagnosis was denial. He refused to take additional tests that the doctor advised. Instead, Schlee resigned his position at Monterey Peninsula Country Club, cleared out his house in Carmel (with Donovan's help), and headed south, apparently to Palm Springs, sometime in 1994. Donovan never saw him again.

"People either loved John or didn't care for him. He had that effect on people," recalled Donovan, who eventually regained his amateur status and won the 2001 California State Amateur. "I always looked forward to watching him compress and control a golf ball like only a select few on the planet ever could.

"I loved John and miss him. He was like a second father to me and was always good to me."

A FEW DAYS AFTER SHOOTING 68 in the first round of the 1978 Masters, Schlee spoke to the United Press International's top golf reporter, Milton Richmond, a man who had covered his runner-up finish in the 1973 U.S. Open. In dire back pain, the thirty-eight-year-old Schlee could sense his playing career was coming to a premature end.

"You got to really want it to get it in this business. A lot of guys decide it's not worth the grind. Most outsiders have a misconception of what it's like playing the tour. People don't really know how hard we work, and being on the tour isn't as glamorous as they think it is.

"A lot of the others are broke. That's why so many leave eventually. They just fade away. You hear someone ask, 'Whatever happened to what's-his-name,' and then you get the answer, 'He took a club job someplace in North Overshoe Nowhere.'"

Sometime after he left the Monterey Peninsula, Alzheimer's incapacitated Schlee and he needed institutional care. On June 2, 2000, his sixty-first birthday—unable to speak, less than a hundred pounds, no friends or family nearby—John Schlee passed away at a facility someplace in North Overshoe Nowhere.

· 17 ·

Johnny Miller

Riding the wave of momentum created by his historic U.S. Open triumph, Johnny Miller continued his red-hot play as soon as he stepped back on the pro tour. To start the American Golf Classic in Akron (four days after his victory at Oakmont), Miller sank a twenty-five-footer on number one, birdied number two, then holed a four-wood off the tee on Firestone's 230-yard, par-three fifth. His opening-round 67 earned both a share of the lead and continued praise from his esteemed playing partner.

"Johnny Miller looks like a fine U.S. Open champ," Arnold Palmer told the press, dispelling any whispers that Miller was just another fluke Oakmont champion. "You don't have to worry about that."

A third-round 78 dropped Miller out of contention at Firestone; he tied for twenty-fourth place with, among others, John Schlee. As the season wore on, Miller didn't entirely quash his "feast or famine" reputation.

In July's British Open, he might have topped Weiskopf at Royal Troon had he not missed a pair of very short final-round putts on the fifteenth and sixteenth greens. By year's end, Miller slipped to ninth on the tour money earnings list. In his final seven PGA appearances, not counting the runner-up at Troon, Miller could do no better than eighteenth. (Although, officially, he finished ninth in the U.S. Match Play event, Miller's U.S. Open win exempted him from having to qualify, and he was upset in the first round by an unknown rookie, Artie McNickle.)

But the latter part of 1973 was certainly not a disappointment for Miller. In fact, by late November, he would launch one of the greatest stretches in the history of professional golf. With Jack Nicklaus as his partner, Miller won both the individual and team portions of the World Golf Cup, held in Marbella, Spain. In Miller's mind, he left the Nueva Andalucia course with much more than an unofficial tour victory.

"Before then, I thought there was quite a difference between Jack Nicklaus and Johnny Miller," Miller said. "But I saw I was driving as far as he was, my irons were better and I was putting well. I thought, 'Hey, Miller, you're not too bad.' People will never know how much that World Cup meant to me, matching games with Jack Nicklaus."

Beginning with the kickoff event for 1974, Miller dominated the tour. He won a rain-shortened Bing Crosby Pro-Am at Pebble Beach, then returned to another course he knew quite well. At the Phoenix Country Club, where he had shot a ten under 61 just four years earlier, Miller won the Phoenix Open by a stroke over his friend Lanny Wadkins. Just four days later, he carded a ten under 62 at Tucson National. On Sunday he earned a third consecutive win, over Ben Crenshaw.

"I don't mean to be boastful," he told the press after his first-round course record, "but the game seems easy to me. I was always a streaky player, even in college when I began winning, but I see no reason to hit bad shots. If I were under pressure I wouldn't be able to shoot ten under par."

Miller won a total of eight PGA events in 1974—including another three-in-a-row binge from late August to late September—to take both the tour money title and the PGA Player of the Year Award. And he was almost as dominant in 1975. Again, Miller opened up the PGA season with a pair of victories, first at Phoenix, then at Tucson. Winning a fourth straight event at Arizona-based tour stops, along with a triumph the next month at Bob Hope's desert-based event in Palm Springs, earned Miller the nickname "the Desert Fox."

Even more incredible was the way Miller won. A closing-round 64 in Phoenix yielded a fourteen-stroke victory—the largest in PGA history. The next week, his final-round 61 at Tucson made for a nine-stroke win.

"It was sort of golfing nirvana," Miller said. "I'd say my average iron shot for three months in 1975 was within five feet of my line, and I had the means for controlling distance. I could feel the shot so well."

Amazingly, in 144 holes, Miller missed only two greens in regulation. And during those three early wins (Phoenix, Tucson, Bob Hope), Miller's combined score was seventy strokes under par. Once the major-championship season began in April, Miller came up just a stroke shy of Jack Nicklaus in the Masters, and a stroke shy of Tom Watson and Jack Newton in the British Open at Carnoustie.

"Every time I go out there, I feel sure I'm going to win. The way I'm playing now, I don't believe anyone can beat me," he said. "In the last four years I've shot more low rounds than anyone. I have the potential, the ability, and now for some reason, I'm reaching that potential. I have more experience now; I make fewer mental errors and my choke level is better."

With a third straight Tucson Open victory early in 1976, followed by a successful title defense in the Bob Hope, Miller had become the most electrifying golfer since his childhood hero, Arnold Palmer. And to prove he was more than just "the Desert Fox," Miller finished tenth in June's U.S. Open, and then overcame a two-shot deficit to win the British Open. Yet another masterful final round defeated Nicklaus and Seve Ballesteros by six shots. Miller's 66 at Royal Birkdale sealed his fifteenth victory in less than three seasons.

"When I'm standing over the ball, serenity is knowing that my worst shot is going to be pretty good."

MILLER'S "SERENITY," AT LEAST ON the golf course, dipped considerably over the next few years. Apart from a strong performance defending his British Open title at Turnberry in 1977, and a top-ten finish in the U.S. Open the following summer, the late 1970s were embarrassing for the two-time major winner.

Miller's casual attitude toward practice—"hitting five hundred balls a day wasn't my idea of a good time"—became one explanation for the slump. Another laid blame on new muscles Miller built up via heavy labor on his California ranch; the muscles allegedly interfered with his usual swing. And in the view of a Pittsburgh writer, an issue "ominously echoing the Arnold Palmer of the mid-1960s" was the culprit: Miller's growing business interests.

The forced time away from his large family also hampered Miller. By the late 1970s, Linda was at home with three young children, while the two eldest were in school.

"They can't travel with me now," he said, "and that bothers me."

At the start of 1979, his tenth full season on tour, Miller's woes threatened to end his career. He competed in just sixteen PGA events during the 1978 season and made the cut in only half. His scoring average that season (73.23) was more than a stroke higher than ever before. By season's end, the combination of poor play and minimal appearances had dropped Miller to 114th on the PGA earnings list. Prior to 1978, Miller had never fallen below the top fifty, and he had finished in the top twenty every year from 1971 to 1976.

Famed *Los Angeles Times* columnist Jim Murray chronicled Miller's decline as a sports tragedy. After Murray watched the patron saint of "going low" finish fifty-fifth—eighteen strokes back, and over par for the tournament—at the same event (the Bob Hope) where his subpar scores had christened him the Desert Fox, Murray declared the career of Johnny Miller, age thirty-one, all but over in January 1979.

"The man wearing Johnny Miller's clothes and swinging Johnny Miller's clubs is a clumsy forgery of the artist who used to chase Jack Nicklaus down to the wire at Augusta or who beat back Nicklaus and Seve Ballesteros at Royal Birkdale," wrote Murray.

"Sometimes it can't be cured short of psychiatry. Sometimes it's a simple function of age. In Miller's case, it would seem to be terminal if it doesn't unhand him this year. A man plays his best golf in his thirties, not his worst. Johnny Miller seems in the grip of a giant unseen presence who tilts his clubhead only a millimeter. Just enough to change 62s into 78s.

"If anyone knows the whereabouts of Johnny Miller's golf game, phone or wire collect or go see him personally," Murray concluded. "You'll find him in the rough."

A few years later, Ron Rapoport captured the specifics of Miller's tumble.

"Eventually, Miller's game came apart," Rapoport wrote. "First, his long game deserted him and in trying to get it back, he neglected his irons, which had always been his strongest suit. Even when he was playing well, it seemed he would have three or four bad holes and miss the cut. The man who had led the tour in earnings was now finishing 48th. And 111th and 76th."

The drought did not last for too long. Although his winless streak reached three full seasons in 1979, and he could climb to only seventy-eighth on the tour money list, Miller began the new decade with a win in March 1980 at the Inverrary Classic. His stroke average improved a full shot from the year before, and he jumped to thirty-fourth place in tour earnings.

And by the spring of 1981, Miller was on his way back. He won January's

Tucson Open (his fourth victory there in eight years), and then claimed the prestigious Los Angeles Open a month later.

"I told those who supported me that I thought this would be a good year for me. There were those who dropped me," Miller told the press at the Riviera Country Club. "And for my friends, they can now answer the question, 'What is wrong with your pal?'"

Miller's resurrection seemed complete that April with the annual trip through Magnolia Lane. Employing a "flunky" new putting grip that proved the right antidote for Augusta National's new, wickedly fast, bent-grass greens, Miller grabbed a share of the first-round Masters lead.

"The redeeming factor during the time I wasn't playing well is that I remembered at one point I was maybe the best player in the world," Miller said after his opening 69. "Even when I was playing terrible, I'd tell myself, 'You must have some talent. What you did wasn't all a fluke. Don't get down on yourself.'"

Miller struggled a bit on Friday and Saturday, then soared on Easter Sunday. Five behind front-runner Tom Watson, Miller started the final round in the eighth-to-last pairing—just as he had at Oakmont in 1973—birdied the first two holes, then dropped five more on the afternoon (including three of the final six holes). Three early bogeys, however, left him two short of victory. Sunday evening, Tom Watson claimed his second Green Jacket. When the season ended, Miller had made the cut in seventeen of nineteen events, finished tenth on the money list, and was rewarded with a spot on the 1981 Ryder Cup team.

Over the next two years (1982 and 1983), Miller defeated Jack Nicklaus twice in early season tournaments, and finished among the top twenty money earners. His progress slowed somewhat over the next two seasons, though in both years he shone in the U.S. Open. In 1984, he finished fourth, and in 1985, he played the weekend at "the Monster," Oakland Hills, better than anyone else, at three under par. He finished eighth, three shots behind champion Andy North.

Miller again slipped into a career freefall in 1986, as he dropped to a new low on the tour earnings list (120th), and managed only one top-ten finish in sixteen events. In the 1987 AT&T Pro-Am, however—on his beloved Monterey Peninsula—he overcame a five-stroke deficit in the final round to forge an exciting win over budding tour star Payne Stewart. Four back-nine birdies—including a clutch fifteen-footer for birdie on the home hole—clinched Miller's fourth tour victory at Pebble Beach.

"Most important, maybe the other guys on the tour won't look at me like a dead horse," he said.

But in the spring of 1987 Miller turned forty, leg injuries persisted, and he still craved seeing more of his large family—including a college-age son who the next year would join the San Jose State varsity golf team. Tour fame no longer seemed to drive him. Speaking about his final-round triumph at Pebble Beach, he had curiously stated, "There was no real point in the round when I thought much about winning. I was just trying to have a good time and check out the scenery.

"When I got to the mountaintop," he said later, "I kind of looked at the scenery and wondered, 'Now what?'. . . . When Jack got there, he said, 'Where's the next mountain?'"

A festering problem with his putting expedited Miller's absence from the tour in the late 1980s.

Since his days as a child sinking long putt after long putt at Harding Park, Miller believed that his putting was in constant decline.

"[By] the time I got to college," he later wrote, "my best putting days were well behind me."

Somehow, he managed to overcome the handicap to win twenty-four PGA events, two major championships, and many millions in prize and endorsement money. Miller even came to downplay how good his putting had been during his historic final round at Oakmont in 1973.

"I didn't have that good a putting round. I had twenty-nine putts. That's nothing special. . . . If I'd had a real good putting round, twenty-six or twenty-seven putts, made some of the others coming in, I could have shot sixty. I missed from ten feet and twelve feet coming down the stretch and on the eighteenth hole my putt rimmed the cup."

Such humbleness was lost on his fellow touring pros.

"Someday, maybe after Miller has won a few more championships, he will suddenly wake up with putting problems," Arnold Palmer told Golf Digest just a few weeks after Miller's 63 had crushed the King's U.S. Open dream.

"Every guy who becomes a big winner runs into this thing. . . . You win a few and begin expecting all the crucial putts to drop. When they start missing, you fight it. The thing begins to psyche you out. You fight some more. If you lick it, you're lucky. . . . Young players like Miller and Lanny Wadkins may speak of 'putting problems,' but they don't know the meaning of the term. But someday it'll come. Then is when the real test arises."

For a time, Miller passed the putting "test." He acknowledged a slight case of the "yips" but (at first) combated them with equipment. His win at the 1987 AT&T had come using a forty-eight-inch putter that he kept tucked under his right arm.

Miller also relied on mind games to secure that win: "I knew I couldn't make [the birdie putt at number eighteen]. So I pretended my son was putting it. I figured he could do it. So I'm hanging over the putt saying, 'Come on, young John.'

"So I was sort of a third party to the putt and it went right in the middle," he said later.

Not long after that win, the prophecy by Palmer—who knew plenty about fleeting putting genius—had been realized.

"By 1989, my play on the PGA tour had become so erratic that I considered chucking the whole thing," Miller explained. "From tee to green I was never better, but on the greens I would flinch as though I had some kind of nervous disorder. My yips were so bad I'd feel embarrassed even when I was alone on the putting green. I'd tried every type of putter and technique you could imagine, but nothing worked for long. It wasn't unusual for me to hit fifteen greens in regulation and make only two birdies."

Miller had overcome a career in the doldrums once before in the late 1970s; he didn't want to try again.

"Golf just wasn't much fun anymore, and after twenty years as a tour pro, I'd had enough. I secretly told my wife, Linda, that I was going to retire. I intended to ride off into the sunset and only do a few corporate outings and expand my golf course design business."

Now into his forties, the business-savvy father of six had long ago clipped the lengthy blond locks and flashy wardrobe he'd displayed during the 1970s. But he was still the same man that modeled slacks for Sears and appeared in tomato juice advertisements in Japan: charismatic and photogenic. And he was witty and lucid, especially when it came to clarifying golf's mysteries for the casual fan.

Within weeks of his deciding to retire, NBC Sports approached Miller. The network's current analyst, Lee Trevino, would be eligible for the Senior Tour beginning in 1990, and producer Larry Cirillo needed a replacement. He chose Miller.

As a rookie broadcaster, Miller endured a few growing pains, including feeling "awkward and useless" at the outset. He was chaperoned by sixty-year-old Charlie Jones, an experienced, genuinely passionate broadcaster who steered NBC's expanding golf coverage, and tried his best to serve as Miller's setup man.

Eventually, Miller found his niche. And although it didn't take him nearly as long, "Johnny Miller, the broadcaster" soon blossomed into a boundary-breaking star, just like the upstart who had dared shoot 63 to win the U.S. Open.

Ever since comparing himself to Arnold Palmer in the August 1964 issue of *Sports Illustrated*, Miller had always been self-assured and outspoken. When speaking about his historic win at Oakmont at age twenty-six, he responded, "Some people may have been surprised I won the 1973 U.S. Open. But I wasn't one of them. The surprise in my mind was that I hadn't won the U.S. Open before."

And in early 1975, having just won the Bob Hope to topple the tour's best for the third time in four weeks, he again surprised the golf world with his innocent braggadocio.

"Jack has been on top so long people are beginning to look for someone to beat him. He's been up there, been the best so long, now people are starting to say, 'Maybe, right now, maybe Johnny Miller is better.' Right now I might be."

Rather than suppress Miller's tendency to "go with my gut," NBC Sports executives encouraged it.

"I want to be unpredictable. [NBC Sports Executive Producer Terry O'Neil] has told me to say whatever comes to my mind," Miller said as he warmed to his new vocation.

That directive stirred controversy by the end of his very first assignment. With tour veteran Peter Jacobsen standing on the eighteenth fairway and leading the final round of the 1990 Bob Hope Chrysler Classic, Miller told his viewers exactly what was on *his* mind.

"This is absolutely the easiest shot to choke on I've ever seen in my life," Miller said on air.

The man who, while leading the 1973 U.S. Open, had stood on the seventy-second fairway muttering, "You crummy dog, don't shank this shot," believed his comment to be fairly innocuous. Reporters and fans didn't agree.

"I guess I opened up a can of worms. No analyst had ever mentioned that word [*choke*] before. I'm a loose cannon. It's nice not knowing what a guy is going to say."

Miller would increasingly cultivate an edgy TV persona and shoot from the hip: deeming a bad shot under pressure a "choke," criticizing a club selection, and poking fun at less aesthetically pleasing swings.

Miller was regularly over-the-top, even when he said he wasn't.

"I'll pull a guy's pants down, but I won't pull down his boxers."

During the 1991 Ryder Cup at windswept Kiawah Island, tour star Paul Azinger called Miller "the biggest moron" in the broadcasting booth, after Azinger had finished his match and heard about some of the television commentary. (Azinger later gave a tongue-in-cheek retraction, saying he meant "the biggest *Mormon*.")

Miller, though furious at Azinger's comments, ultimately held his ground and soon expanded his role, as NBC substituted Jim Lampley for Charlie Jones in 1993 to try to climb in the Nielsen ratings. He also began to grow viewers' golf vocabulary, often in humorous ways: He spoke of "muffie" lies to describe shots from fairways or bunkers that players were likely to hit fat; "buggy whip" swings that began and ended much too fast; and "chicken wing" left elbows that condemned duffers to forever slice.

Before long, Miller became as much the attraction to viewers as the golf itself.

"I feel bad when players think I'm an adversary. I'm not. In reality, I'm their best friend. . . . If a player hits a bad shot, I'm not going to make up excuses for him. I might go on the tee and show what happened, how he went underneath, undercut the ball, and left the face open and blocked it to the right. And that player will go, 'I don't like that; why did you say that? You can't talk about me like that.'

"I'm not trying to criticize anyone. I'm trying to report what happened and use the opportunity to maybe help the viewer with his or her game. . . . And while I'm doing it, maybe I can entertain."

Miller didn't completely give up his clubs for an NBC microphone. He made select appearances in the early 1990s at tour stops where he had forged his legacy of dominance two decades earlier. In addition to playing in the 1991 British Open at Royal Birkdale—site of his 1976 win—and tying for sixty-fourth at Tucson a year later, Miller always left a spot in his schedule to play Pebble Beach. He missed the cut in the AT&T in 1992 and 1993, and posted an unremarkable thirty-seventh-place finish at the Pebble Beach–hosted Ben Hogan Invitational, an unofficial event featuring several LPGA and minitour players, including the aspiring young professional Johnny Miller Jr.

So when the PGA tour returned to Pebble Beach in early February 1994, Johnny Sr. was, as always, excited to play, with few expectations.

"I didn't come to win," he said that week. "I just came to have a good time."

One round at Spyglass and another at Poppy Hills in the books, the forty-six-year-old held his own, reaching the halfway point five strokes off the lead, and tied with twelve others for sixteenth place.

Miller was slated to play his third round at Pebble Beach, the course he had been playing since the early 1960s and the scene of some of his most memorable tournaments. Apart from the extra-club, tear-inducing performance in the 1963 California State Amateur, and the embarrassing shank at the tail end of his battle with Jack Nicklaus in 1972, Miller cherished every opportunity to revisit the famed oceanside links.

In a way—even more than Harding Park or Olympic—Pebble Beach Golf Links was his "home" course. He'd won three times there since turning pro and had also posted five top tens at Pebble Beach–hosted PGA events. And in 1994, the Miller family was even building a house in Pacific Grove, just five miles north of the course.

"I've always called Pebble his girlfriend," Linda Miller told a reporter that week.

"Nobody in the field has played more rounds at Pebble Beach than I have. Nobody. Not even Jack Nicklaus," Miller said.

"When I get here to Pebble Beach I just feel like I play young. It's like Nicklaus at the Masters. It's like the seventies again."

Miller's flashback started early in the third round of the 1994 AT&T. Beginning on the second hole, he carded four straight birdies, and added another on the majestic ninth. His superb ball striking that afternoon was evocative of Miller in his prime; he landed several approach shots inside five feet of the flagstick, and also holed out a wedge for a birdie on the thirteenth. By late Saturday, Miller's five under 67 pulled him into sole possession of second place, one shot behind twenty-five-year-old Dudley Hart.

"To be honest, for me to win, it would be a fluke," Miller said that evening.

Fluke or not, with the final round also being played at Pebble Beach, Miller had a chance. Hart eventually dropped out of the race with a series of back-nine bogeys. That left Miller alone in contention with Tom Watson, another forty-something hero of the 1970s.

Like Miller's, Watson's career was punctuated both by Pebble Beach heroics—two victories in the Bing Crosby Pro-Am, plus the unforgettable chip-in to defeat Nicklaus in the 1982 U.S. Open—and recent, notorious putting woes, especially from short distances. Watson had also not won a PGA tour event since 1987.

Playing ahead of Miller, Watson took a two-stroke lead with a birdie on the thirteenth, but Miller soon pulled even. Then, on the fifteenth, Miller made "the biggest club selection blunder of my career" by launching a downwind nine-iron nearly twenty yards past the flag, leading to a bogey.

Miller's stroll down Pebble Beach memory lane was complete on the next hole: His drive on the sixteenth landed in roughly the same spot as where he struck his infamous "shank" twenty-two years earlier, in his final-round battle with Jack Nicklaus.

"I flashed back to that shank," he said. "I had that in my brain. I was thinking, 'Geez, don't shank it.'"

An elder, shorter-haired, more conservatively attired Johnny Miller didn't shank. He parred the sixteenth and, as he waited on the next tee box, assumed the lead when Watson three-putted the seventeenth. From there, Miller sank a pair of clutch par putts to earn an incredible victory at the age of forty-six.

"You want to know the truth? I can't believe I won," Miller said. "It goes to show you that in the right place, at the right time, magic can happen. This is magic."

That magic—and the foresight to try to grow the game's living history—led the U.S.G.A. to issue Miller a special exemption to return to Oakmont and compete in the 1994 U.S. Open.

"No one's going to enjoy this Open more than I," he wrote in *Golf World*. "That's the attitude I play golf with these days. I'm still going to play aggressively—probably too aggressively, I might add—but that's the enjoyment I get from the game now. I'll try to play to win, even though that is a one-in-a-million shot. I'll have fun and shoot for the pins. At least, as many as I can. When I won at Pebble Beach this year, I went for every pin. I had nothing to lose. And that's probably why I won."

In a sentimental pairing, the U.S.G.A. grouped Miller alongside Larry Nelson (winner of the 1983 U.S. Open at Oakmont) and Jack Nicklaus: the last three men to win U.S. Opens at Oakmont.

While Nicklaus fervently believed he would record another major championship victory at Oakmont—and seemed destined to do so on Thursday and Friday—Miller just enjoyed himself, as he intended.

"It's the first time in my life I ever played just for an experience," he said after an opening 81. "Right off the bat I went [double bogey–par–double bogey] and my thinking was that I was going to have a good time regardless of the score.

"I pretended I was two under all day. That's how I approached every shot. I had a good time."

Not everyone was as cheerful about the carefree effort. Miller openly admitted, "I've hardly practiced at all," and, "I never thought of myself as competitive," which only further irritated Seve Ballesteros. As was the case with Arnold Palmer's special exemption, Ballesteros disapproved of Miller's receiving a free pass.

"Why should Palmer keep getting an invitation and why should Miller? He's virtually retired now."

Despite his recent victory at Pebble Beach, Miller was indeed "virtually retired," as Ballesteros said. And he played that way at Oakmont, shooting 81-76 to miss the cut by ten shots. Miller would never again compete in a U.S. Open or any other major championship. And after 1994, he would appear in only four more PGA tour events.

Nevertheless, the very next summer, in June 1995, Johnny Miller again headlined the cast at America's national championship.

Two weeks before Miller's final Oakmont appearance, NBC Sports proudly announced that the network had outbid ABC for the U.S.G.A.'s exclusive television broadcasting rights to the U.S. Open. An impassioned appearance by Miller before the U.S.G.A. helped NBC secure the contract.

"Johnny described what it meant to him and he broke down, remembering what the U.S.G.A. meant for him as a child and a young adult," NBC Sports president Dick Ebersol remembered.

"I thought of all the sacrifices my dad made and how excited he was when I won it," Miller said. "I hold this tournament sacred."

By the late 1990s, Miller had cemented his role as the premier television golf analyst: An NBC Sports golf broadcast featured a distinctive flavor that no other network could match. He proudly stated that his TV persona differed little from his everyday approach to the game. "I was that way before I was on television, saying the same things in my living room watching golf. . . . When I see something, I've got to say it. That's what I'm paid to do. I can't just sugar-coat it, when it's delicious to talk about. I'm not trying to do anything unusual. It's not an act. It's just me. OK?"

Miller was crystal clear about his approach to broadcasting, whether his former colleagues liked it or not. For the growth of the game, he would continue to exercise his "go-for-the-flagstick" mentality on air.

"Golf is on a roll," he said. "It has incredible momentum. . . . There's an opportunity for golf to cross over to the mainstream. . . . The pro tour is really a big, traveling circus. As an announcer, I'm part of it. I'm promoting the traveling circus. The players don't understand that. . . . The sooner more of today's players realize it, the better."

DESPITE MILLER'S ENTHUSIASM FOR THE tour, both golf and his burgeoning television stardom would never be his greatest passion. Minutes after he walked off the Oakmont course and into the press tent, he casually told reporters that "my family and the church are both more important to me than golf. If I had to give up one of the three it would have to be golf."

Miller still kept the game at a distance. He was far more content to spend time at his home in California, see his children (and grandchildren), and devote only an occasional weekend in the spring or summer behind an NBC microphone.

At the peak of his playing career, one that had begun to bring him worldwide acclaim, Miller flew to New York City in May 1975. Linda and their two-and-a-half-year-old daughter with him, Johnny attended an early morning business meeting, then drove through the city to attend the recently finished Church of Jesus Christ of Latter-day Saints. In between a round of golf and an evening flight to Mexico City for an exhibition, Johnny attended a luncheon presented by the National Father's Day Committee.

Standing next to Jim "Catfish" Hunter, Maine senator Edmund Muskie, and a few other prominent figures, Miller received the committee's Father of the Year Award. After the luncheon, he conducted another of the innumerable question-and-answer sessions he'd participated in during the past few years. Amid comments about Jack Nicklaus and his thrilling battle with Nicklaus and Tom Weiskopf a month earlier at Augusta National, a reporter asked, "When you're through with tournament golf, how would you like to be remembered?"

"I'll probably leave as many records broken as anybody who ever played," he said. "I'll never win as many major titles as some others, but I can score. I probably range from sixty-one to seventy-six; Jack Nicklaus would be about sixty-four to seventy-three. His poor is better than mine. My good might be better than his.

"But I'm not driven," he added. "I'm not like Gary Player, who burns to be recognized as the best in the world. Oh, I've got the killer instinct. . . . I never set out to be the best in the world, just to be the best I can be. I was happy with my game in 1974. I had won the National Open, although not the way you would plan it. Six strokes behind starting the last round and shoot a sixty-three to win by one. You wouldn't program the Open that way. Still, I felt good, and last year I did more, leading the money winners. This year has been going well.

"Golf isn't my only goal, though. My goals are eternal."

Of course, Miller was speaking of something spiritual: not about his exploits as a professional athlete. Nevertheless, "the Miracle at Oakmont"—the day when Johnny Miller overwhelmed a legendary course and a Murderer's Row of golf legends to shoot 63 and win the U.S. Open championship—will always hold an eternal place in the game's history.

Appendix I

Johnny Miller's 63:
The Greatest Round Ever?

A Historical and Statistical Perspective[1]

In narrating the final round of the 1973 U.S. Open, we tried to clear up several lingering sources of confusion regarding both the physical conditions at Oakmont, and the overall scoring patterns on the Sunday when Johnny Miller shot his famed 63 to win the championship. The oft-cited sprinkler malfunction, for example, occurred between Thursday and Friday, not between Saturday and Sunday; heavy rains saturated Oakmont on Saturday morning, not Sunday morning; "winter rules" were never invoked, etc.

We have also indicated there was no simple, predictable link between wet conditions and scoring. Despite softer and slower greens due to the major rains that fell on Saturday, the players' scores that day were actually the highest of the entire championship (see boxplot one). Moreover, on the day that Miller shot 63, scoring conditions remained very difficult; only three other players broke 70. As Jack Nicklaus recalled, even though Oakmont was "extra wet," the golf course on Sunday afternoon "played its normal way."[2]

Miller himself has challenged another frequent claim: that it was relatively easy for him to "go low" on Sunday because he was so far behind, and started

---

1 This section was written with Professor Joel Greenhouse, Department of Statistics, Carnegie Mellon University.

2 Quoted in Gerry Dulac, "Johnny Miller: The Best Round Ever," *Pittsburgh Post-Gazette*, June 10, 2007.

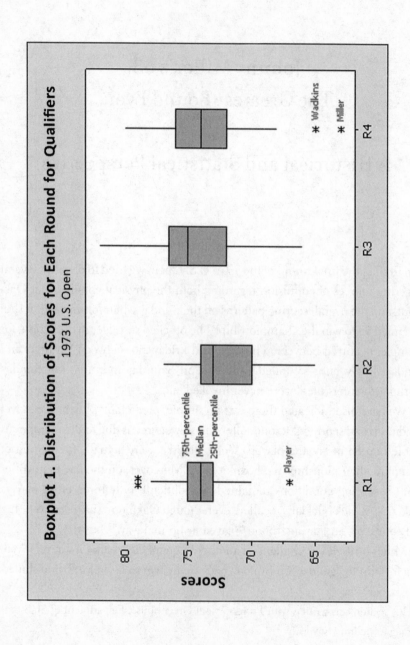

Boxplot 1. Distribution of Scores for Each Round for Qualifiers

1973 U.S. Open

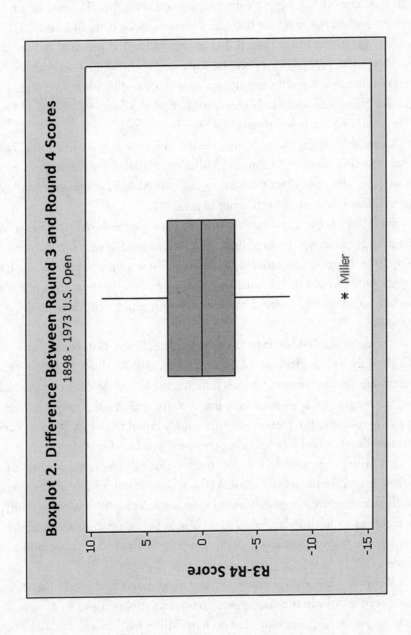

Boxplot 2. Difference Between Round 3 and Round 4 Scores

1898 - 1973 U.S. Open

R3-R4 Score

* Miller

out so far ahead of the leaders, that he felt no pressure; he could shoot at the flagsticks without fear of consequences.

In fact, says Miller, he felt extreme pressure from the fifth hole onward. Once he birdied the first four holes and blew past Nicklaus and Trevino, he knew he was in the hunt. Indeed, he succumbed to the pressure by leaving makeable birdie putts short on numbers five and six, mishitting a short birdie try on number seven, and three-putting a relatively easy thirty-footer on number eight. Just when it looked like his comeback effort was doomed, he birdied five of the remaining ten holes to eke out a one-shot victory.

Claims and counterclaims by participants and observers are one thing; but assessing the historical significance of Miller's final round requires more objective analysis. We employ four criteria to evaluate Miller's performance, all of which confirm its unblemished claim to greatness.

First, Miller broke a golfing threshold by shooting the lowest score ever in a major championship. To do so in the final round, and to win, surely imbued the round with greater historical significance. But setting a new low score for the U.S. Open would have been a tremendous achievement on its own; even if he had failed to win, it would have permanently enshrined Miller in the record books.

Second, Miller shot his record score in the U.S. Open, historically the most difficult of the major championships to "go low." While all of the U.S. Open venues were among the nation's most difficult, the U.S.G.A. always toughened them in consistent ways—narrowing the fairways, growing the rough, hardening and quickening the greens—that inevitably raised scores. "Old Man Par" remained the standard for measuring greatness in a U.S. Open.

That Miller's 63 came on the golf course historically regarded as America's toughest magnified his achievement. A 63 was simply unthinkable at Oakmont. The three consecutive bogeys Palmer made immediately after learning Miller was eight under for the day reflected a blow to his composure so severe that even he, the bravest comeback performer in golf history, simply could not absorb.

A third vital historical marker was how many bona fide great champions Miller overtook to win the championship from six strokes back.

At age twenty-six, after four years on tour, Miller had already won two PGA tournaments, so he certainly knew how to finish strong. But on several prior occasions when he was perfectly positioned to win a major, he had stumbled badly on the back nine—"choked," in the term he would make famous in 1990 as a TV broadcaster. No one had reason to believe that down the stretch in a U.S. Open, Miller could perform at his best. And especially not when the greatest players of the prior generation—Nicklaus, Palmer, Player, Trevino, Boros, Weiskopf, Littler, Charles—were between three and six shots ahead of him.

But that is what Miller did. Too much commentary on Miller's 63 has centered on his dazzling birdie-birdie-birdie-birdie start, but it was his remarkable 31 on the back nine—exactly where he'd sabotaged his previous major championship opportunities—that won him the U.S. Open. Miller knew the well-tested greatness of the players still several shots ahead as he made the back-nine turn, yet he used their greatness as a spur to take their measure and unleash comparable greatness in himself. Remarkably, even though the leaders played quite well by U.S. Open standards, Miller made up the six-shot differential and forged into the lead after birdying number fifteen. And expecting one of the established stars to rise to his challenge, he kept pressing for birdies, missing only by tiny margins on numbers seventeen and eighteen. It truly could have been a 29, even a 28, on the back nine at Oakmont.

Breaking a scoring threshold, conquering a monster venue, and bypassing reigning superstars along the way clearly define a golden path to golf immortality. But Miller's miracle at Oakmont contained a fourth dimension that reinforces the historic significance of his final round and makes it unique in the annals of U.S. Open golf.

After an opening 71, Miller shot a 69 on Friday that was mainly a result of spectacular putting—the best putting Palmer (his playing partner) had ever seen at Oakmont. Even Miller admitted he'd never putted better. Miller's 76 on Saturday allegedly resulted from his missing yardage book on the front nine. But, as we demonstrated earlier, that explanation makes little sense; Miller actually scored worse on the second nine, with yardage book in hand. The plain fact is that from a ball-striking perspective, Miller didn't play particularly well on either Friday or Saturday. A hot putter was all that kept him in sight of the leaders.

On Sunday, Miller obviously turned things around from tee to green. He hit all eighteen putting surfaces in regulation and—vital for good scoring at Oakmont—he kept his ball below the hole each time. Once Miller striped a three-iron and stopped it within five feet of the flagstick on number one—the toughest opening hole in all of championship golf—there was little doubt that this round would yield a very different outcome from the 76 the day before.

But just how different that outcome was is what makes Miller's final round stand out from all other victories in U.S. Open history. Between 1898 and 1973, seventy U.S. Opens were contested over four rounds.[3] Interestingly, there was considerable variation in the winners' scores between rounds three and four. Looking at the difference between the round three and round four scores for the seventy U.S. Open winners, we found that the final-round score for half the winners was within three strokes (plus or minus) of their third-round score (see boxplot two). This is a pretty wide range, especially in a U.S. Open where, the experts tell us, consistent excellence of performance under pressure is essential to victory.

In fact, that's not how it actually worked out for half the winners, whose final-round scores (also captured in boxplot two) were four or more strokes different, plus or minus, from their third-round scores. Perhaps surprisingly, the winners in half the U.S. Opens were thus not very consistent over their final two rounds.

Even more interestingly, one-quarter of the time (25 percent) the winner's final-round score was four or more strokes *higher* than his third-round score; likewise, one-quarter of the time (25 percent) his score was four or more strokes *lower* than his third-round score. A not untypical winner, for example, might shoot 69 in his third round and 75 in his fourth round; similarly, a not untypical winner might finish 75 and 69.

Stated another way, one-quarter of the winners of U.S. Opens did not finish in a blaze of glory; their fourth-round score was considerably higher than their third-round score, yet they still managed to win. And because they won, history will not record them as having "choked." For example, Bobby Jones, in his Grand Slam U.S. Open victory in 1930, shot 68 in his third round and 75 in his fourth round, yet he still won.

Alternatively, one-quarter of U.S. Open winners shot considerably *lower* in their fourth than in their third rounds. Predictably, these victors came from well behind the third-round leaders to win: none more so than Arnold Palmer,

---

3 The first three U.S. Opens, 1895–1897, were only two rounds.

who famously won at Cherry Hills in 1960 from seven shots behind by shooting a record-setting 65 following a 72 in round three.

Johnny Miller obviously fits among that quarter of U.S. Open victors who not only won from well behind (six shots), but scored four or more shots lower in his final than in his third round. But it's the *scale* of Miller's improvement that separates him dramatically from every other winner. Miller had to improve his Sunday score by an incredible thirteen strokes to win (he beat John Schlee by a single shot). That achievement singles him out statistically from all other U.S. Open champions (see boxplot two; only Miller's rate of improvement is statistically different from the rest of the winners).

Not Palmer's dramatic come-from-behind victory in 1960; not Jack Fleck's surprising 75-67 finish at Olympic to tie (and eventually defeat) Hogan in 1955; not twenty-year-old Gene Sarazen's shocking 75-68 finish at Skokie to win in 1922 stand out statistically as unpredictable comebacks. Miller's thirteen-shot improvement in the final round had no counterpart in U.S. Open history.

Whatever his ultimate source of inspiration—an inner voice, a psychic, an anonymous letter from Iowa, or a clear-eyed recall of how to correct a persistent bad habit in alignment—Miller's miracle at Oakmont is sui generis in U.S. Open history. It remains not only the greatest closing round in the history of championship golf, but a personal triumph over previous failure that may match any in all of sport.

Appendix II

Interviews Conducted for *Chasing Greatness*
(in alphabetical order)

Miller Barber

Al Barkow

Andy Bean

Chris Blocker

Gene Borek

Jim Cartwright

Bob Charles

Bill Christine

Jim Colbert

Bob Cooper

Ben Crenshaw

Darryl Donovan

Jim Donovan

Julia Donovan

Dave Eichelberger

John Fitzgerald

Raymond Floyd

Bob Ford

Dick Fuhrer

John Garbo

Bob Gilder

Vinny Giles

Hubert Green

Rusty Guy

Laurie Hammer

Frank Hannigan

Geoff Hensley

Hale Irwin

Ralph Johnston

Tom Joyce

Jason Kunde

Ken Lindsay

Gene Littler

Dave MacDonald

Neal Maine

Dave Marad

Donnie Massengale

Terri McKinney

Bryant Mullen

Bob Murphy

Larry Nelson

Bill Nichols

Jack Nicklaus

Arnold Palmer

Marino Parascenzo

Loren Roberts

Bill Rogers

Sherie Roman

Curt Siegel

Ray Sigurdson

Marilynn Smith

J. C. Snead

Susan Stafford

Dave Stockton

Austin Straub

Sandy Tatum

Dick Thompson

Tom Tihey

Lanny Wadkins

Chick Wagner

Herman Worsham

Rick Worsham

1973 U.S. Open: Scores of the 65 Weekend Qualifiers
June 14-17, 1973

Contestant	R1	R2	R3	R4	Total Score
Miller, Johnny	71	69	76	63	279
Schlee, John	73	70	67	70	280
Weiskopf, Tom	73	69	69	70	281
Nicklaus, Jack	71	69	74	68	282
Palmer, Arnold	71	71	68	72	282
Trevino, Lee	70	72	70	70	282
Boros, Julius	73	69	68	73	283
Heard, Jerry	74	70	66	73	283
Wadkins, Lanny	74	69	75	65	283
Colbert, Jim	70	68	74	72	284
Charles, Bob	71	69	72	74	286
Player, Gary	67	70	77	73	287
Geiberger, Al	73	72	71	72	288
Johnston, Ralph	71	73	76	68	288
Ziegler, Larry	73	74	69	72	288
Floyd, Ray	70	73	75	71	289
Giles, Marvin (amateur)	74	69	74	73	290
Littler, Gene	71	74	70	76	291
Thompson, Rocky	73	71	71	76	291
Funseth, Rod	75	74	70	74	293
Irwin, Hale	73	74	75	71	293
Lyons, Denny	72	74	75	72	293
Murphy, Bob	77	70	75	71	293
Nichols, Bobby	75	71	74	73	293
Barber, Miller	74	71	71	78	294
Beard, Frank	74	75	68	77	294
Shaw, Tom	73	71	74	76	294
Yancey, Bert	73	70	75	76	294
Bies, Don	77	73	73	72	295
Coody, Charles	74	74	73	74	295
Mahaffey, John	74	72	74	75	295

Contestant	R1	R2	R3	R4	Total Score
Rodriguez, Chi Chi	75	71	75	74	295
Snead, Sam	75	74	73	73	295
Allin, Brian	78	67	74	77	296
Archer, George	76	73	74	73	296
Erickson, Bob	73	74	76	73	296
Wise, Larry	74	73	76	73	296
Borek, Gene	77	65	80	75	297
Beman, Dean	73	75	75	75	298
Hunter, Mac	77	73	72	76	298
Moran, Paul Jr.	75	74	76	73	298
Sanudo, Cesar	75	73	76	74	298
Stockton, Dave	77	73	77	71	298
Ziobro, Billy	77	69	77	75	298
Aaron, Tommy	78	71	72	78	299
Campbell, Joe	74	76	74	75	299
Elder, Lee	72	77	78	72	299
Fezler, Forrest	78	69	80	72	299
Ginsberg, Roger	74	75	73	77	299
Jones, Grier	73	76	76	74	299
Wall, Art Jr.	73	77	71	78	299
Baird, Butch	75	74	75	76	300
Jacklin, Tony	75	75	73	77	300
Wood, Larry	79	71	76	74	300
Blocker, Chris	73	76	78	74	301
Glenz, David	76	74	71	80	301
Koch, Gary (amateur)	74	74	79	75	302
Gentile, John	72	74	78	79	303
Goalby, Bob	72	77	79	75	303
Graham, David	73	77	77	76	303
Jamieson, Jim	74	76	79	74	303
Lister, John	76	74	80	73	303
Joyce, Tom	78	70	81	76	305
Powers, Greg	79	70	77	79	305
Bayer, George	72	77	82	79	310

ACKNOWLEDGMENTS

We have benefited from the gracious assistance of many individuals at Oakmont Country Club; their commitment to excellence sustains the vitality of the Fownes vision into the twenty-first century.

Banks Smith, Jim Malone, Bob Wagner, Pat LaRocca, and the late Fred Brand and Bob Hackett (who watched Tommy Armour hole his birdie putt on the eighteenth at Oakmont's first U.S. Open in 1927) provided essential early encouragement.

In recent years, Tom Wallace, John Zimmers, Bryant Mullen, Chick Wagner, Dick Fuhrer, Bob Cooper, Dick Thompson, and Paul Pochan have offered that same heartfelt enthusiasm and readiness to assist. Three former caddies at Oakmont during the 1973 U.S. Open, John Garbo, Rusty Guy, and Tom Tihey, also contributed vital information to our research.

We extend very special thanks to John Fitzgerald, Oakmont's archivist, whose lively intellect, boundless energy, and avid embrace of digital technology provided a model for our own research methods; and to Bob Ford, Oakmont's magnanimous head golf professional, without whose guidance on innumerable occasions this book would not have been possible.

The U.S.G.A. headquarters in Far Hills, New Jersey, has extended vital support to our research, most especially in facilitating use of its archival and film collections. We can't thank Nancy Stulack, Patty Moran, and Shannon Doody enough for making each day at Far Hills a joy, and for tolerating desperate phone call requests as well. Rand Jerris, the U.S.G.A.'s longtime museum director and now its director of communications, not only welcomed our inquiries but also answered them with special insight and meticulous care. Under the spirited leadership and creative vision of David Fay, the U.S.G.A. has pioneered on many fronts during the past two decades, and we are grateful that maintaining a first-class archive for tracking golf's evolution is one of them.

Bernie Loehr, director, amateur status and rules of golf of the U.S.G.A., provided prompt and expert guidance in enabling us to resolve a complex rules deliberation of nearly a half century ago, and we truly appreciate his assistance. And Carol Semple Thompson and the late Phyllis Semple, in their passion for the game of golf, proved more instrumental in launching this project than they probably realized.

We also extend much thanks to Gail Tooks, Jesse Wilson, and the unfailingly helpful staff of the history department at Carnegie Mellon University, and to Joan Stein and Barry Schles of Carnegie Mellon University libraries for enabling us to access an endless stream of print and electronic data.

We were fortunate to interview several outstanding golf journalists who were generous in sharing their time and unique perspectives on golf, notably Al Barkow (a memorable eight hours of nonstop golf talk), Marino Parascenzo, and Bill Nichols. And we gained distinctive insights from several discussions, phone calls, and e-mail exchanges with two legendary U.S.G.A. officials, both of whom were on-site at Oakmont in 1973: former U.S.G.A. executive director Frank Hannigan and former U.S.G.A. president Sandy Tatum.

Stimulated by Bill Fields's pioneering article on John Schlee in *Golf World*, our own research on Schlee (the antihero of *Chasing Greatness*) could not have been completed without candid conversations with various people who knew him well at different life stages. While not everyone will agree with our interpretation, we deeply appreciate the amount of time and energy our informants devoted to helping us shape our own views. Thanks especially to Jim Cartwright, without whose great generosity and personal caring our on-site research in Seaside and Gearhart, Oregon, would not have been possible. Sincere thanks also to Neal Maine, Ray Sigurdson, Dave MacDonald, Jason Kunde, and the wonderfully helpful staff of Seaside Public Library; and to Ken Lindsay, Julia Donovan, Jim Donovan, and Darryl Donovan.

Many players at the 1973 U.S. Open generously took time from their busy schedules to share their recollections of the event, and of Oakmont, with us, and we truly appreciate their courtesy (we list them all in Appendix II).

Thanks especially to Arnold Palmer and Jack Nicklaus, who granted us more time than we had any right to expect. Special thanks also to Vinny Giles, Lanny Wadkins, Jim Colbert, Ralph Johnston, Dave Marad, Doc Giffin, the late Curt Siegel, and the late Gene Borek for sharing their recollections, and to Bob Murphy, Raymond Floyd, Dave Stockton, Bob Ford, and Rick Worsham for educating us about Oakmont in comparison to other great golf venues.

Adam's Thanks

I want to express my never-ending gratitude to my wife, Sarah. *Chasing Greatness* was a part of my life just a few months before I met her, so she has been beside me during nearly every phase of the process. Throughout she has been supportive of me and our vision. Thank you, Sarah, for being an enthusiastic and encouraging cheerleader for this book.

Steve's Thanks

My mother and late father, Ralph R. Schlossman, inspired me to take intellectual and athletic chances on whatever opportunities came my way. That combination has been a precious freedom for which I remain forever grateful.

Many thanks to my good friends, Gary Brant and Jon Schmerling, for sharing their gift of contagious enthusiasm.

ENDNOTES

PROLOGUE

1 "Since my arrival"—*Pittsburgh Post-Gazette*, May 16, 1935, Bert P. Taggart, "Brews Here for Practice at Oakmont."

1 "like a marble"—*Pittsburgh Sun*, June 18, 1927, Grantland Rice, "Armour Worthy Successor to Jones."

1 "Oakmont is a duffer's"—*Pittsburgh Press*, May 14, 1935, "Sports Stew—Served Hot."

1 "We canna' say"—*New York Sun*, June 11, 1935, George Trevor, "Oakmont Terrain Is Freakish."

2 "the severest test"—*Pittsburgh Press*, June 1, 1935, Art Krenz, "296 Score Will Win National Open, Krenz Predicts; Oakmont's Length and Traps Will Be Real Hazards."

2 "Real Frankenstein"—*Pittsburgh Press*, June 6, 1935, Joe Williams, "Real Frankenstein!"

2 "I always regard"—*Pittsburgh Press*, May 12, 1935, Joe Huhn, "Oakmont Pays Dividends to No Golfer Unless His Game's Near Perfect."

2 "Wherever you go"—*Pittsburgh Press*, May 15, 1935, Joe Huhn, "National Open Championship Gives City International Fame—without Cost."

2 "it is the most talked-of"—*Pittsburgh Post-Gazette*, June 1, 1935, Gene Sarazen, "Sarazen Says Oakmont Troubles His Slumbers."

3   "Yes, you bet"—*Pittsburgh Post-Gazette*, June 3, 1935, "300 Score Will Win Open."

3   "A shot poorly"—*Golf Course Management*, May 1983, Ronald E. Whitten, "Mighty Oakmont Rumbles Again."

3   "His knowledge of"— Sarazen, "Sarazen Says."

3   "mediocre player"— Martin, H. B., *Fifty Years of American Golf* (New York: Dodd, Mead & Company, 1936), p. 339.

3   "the most consistent"—Price, Charles, *The World of Golf* (New York: Random House, 1962), p.218.

3   "spun-glass"—*New York Sun*, June 11, 1935, George Trevor, "Oakmont Terrain Is Freakish."

3   "a bit of fuzz"—*Golf World*, June 8, 2007, Ron Whitten, "Putting the 'Oh' in Oakmont."

4   "Fownes' Folly"—*Frederick News*, September 7, 1938, Art Krenz, "Goodman and Yates Seek Double in U.S. Amateur."

4   "some strange species"— Trevor, "Oakmont Terrain."

4   "skating rinks"— Whitten, "Putting the 'Oh.'"

4   "the first course"— Trevor, "Oakmont Terrain."

4   "The virility"— Whitten, "Putting the 'Oh.'"

4   "a sporting chance"— Trevor, "Oakmont Terrain."

5   "If they want"—*Golf World*, June 10, 1995, Geoff Russell, "U.S. Open."

5   "true to the ultimate"—*New York Tribune*, August 15, 1919, Grantland Rice, "Marston Leads Stars in Trial Round with 77."

7   "changing the whole"—*U.S. Open Championship Program*, 1973 *Edition*, "Oakmont's Championship Course," p. 66.

CHAPTER 1
The King Never Left

11   "I think my first"—United States Golf Association, 1994 U.S. Open: *Who Els?* New York: Trans World International, 1994.

12   "I used to play"—*New York Times*, June 8, 1962, Arthur Daley, "Sports of the Times: The Palmer System."

13   "uneasy lies"—Shakespeare, William, *Henry IV, Part 2*, Act III, scene I, line 31.

14   "At the age of 39"—*New York Times*, June 11, 1969, Dave Anderson, "Sports of the Times: Arnie's Army Is Back Following Old Soldier."

14   "I will admit"—*New York Times*, June 8, 1969, (AP), "Palmer, Swamped by Remedies from His Army, Has Own Plan to Cure Slump."

15   "the most traumatic"—D'Antonio, Michael, *Tour '72: Nicklaus, Palmer, Player, Trevino: The Story of One Great Season* (New York: Hyperion, 2002), p. 139.

15   "Arnie had to withdraw"—Beard, Frank, *Pro: Frank Beard on the Golf Tour*, edited by Dick Schaap (New York and Cleveland: The World Publishing Company, 1970), p. 319.

16   "not to signal"—*Sports Illustrated*, September 1, 1969, Dan Jenkins, "Thanks for the Memories."

16   "given a nobility"—ibid.

17   "This was as important"—*Moberly (MO) Monitor Index*, (AP), December 1, 1969, Bob Green, "Palmer Wins in Heritage Classic."

17   "Getting it going"—*Jefferson City (MO) Post-Tribune*, (AP), December 8, 1969, "Crowd Yells 'Charge, Arnie!' and grinning Palmer Does."

18   "probably the toughest"—*Tucson Daily Citizen*, (AP), June 19, 1972, "Arnie Calls It 'Toughest Open.'"

19   "I've got to"—*Honolulu Star-Bulletin*, February 8, 1973, Jim Hackleman, "'If I Quit, I'd Be Climbing the Walls . . .'"

20   "There was a time"—*Long Beach (CA) Independent Press-Telegram*, February 11, 1973, Doug Ives, "A Nicklaus-Palmer Showdown."

20   "usual form"—*Los Angeles Times*, February 12, 1973, Shav Glick, "Arnie Marches Troops Through Mud, Wins Day."

20   "I kept thinking"—*New York Times*, February 12, 1973, Lincoln A. Werden, "Palmer's Closing 69 Wins Hope Golf by Two Shots."

21   "When you haven't"—*Eureka (CA) Times-Standard*, (UPI), February 12, 1973, "Palmer Ends Long Struggle."

21   "[I feared] someone"—*Nevada State Journal*, (UPI), February 12, 1973, "Nicklaus, Johnny Miller 2nd."

21   "I hope"— Glick, "Arnie Marches."

21   "Call the florist"—*Los Angeles Times*, February 13, 1973, Jim Murray, "The Star Is Reborn."

22   "I'm not upset"—*Victoria (TX) Advocate*, (AP), April 6, 1973, "77 'Disgusting' to Arnie."

22   "I'll play the Byron Nelson"—*Albuquerque Journal*, (AP), April 22, 1973, "Nicklaus, Trevino 1–2 in Champs Meet."

23   "Now that the big guy"—Palmer, Arnold, with James Dodson, *A Golfer's Life* (New York: Ballantine Books, 1999), p. 211.

23   "I wanted every putt"—*Pittsburgh Press*, June 18, 1962, "Three-Putt Greens Called No. 1 Factor in Palmer's Defeat."

24   "I can't play"—ibid.

24   "Ever since I lost"—*Miami Herald*, June 14, 1973, "Recluse Trevino Likes Chances."

25   "A great amount of desire"—*Reno Evening Gazette*, May 7, 1973, "Palmer, 44, Jokes About Age in Reno."

26   "out of position"—*The Billings Gazette*, (AP), June 13, 1973, Bob Green, "Palmer: Elder Statesman at 43."

26   "[We changed] the whole ball"—ibid.

26   "Almost from the moment"—Palmer, *A Golfer's Life*, p. 19.

26   "I worked pretty hard"— Interview with Arnold Palmer, September 2008.

26   "I'm discouraged"—*New York Times*, June 4, 1973, Lincoln A. Werden, "Weiskopf Gets 68 for 271 and 3-Shot Open Victory."

27   "I feel very much at home"—*Latrobe Bulletin*, (UPI), June 13, 1973, Ira Miller, "Arnold Palmer Plays It Cool."

27   "I probably should"—ibid.

28   "Palmer still is"—*Cleveland Plain Dealer*, June 17, 1973, Bill Nichols, "Tee Time with Bill Nichols."

28   "But he's 43 years old"—*New York Times*, June 14, 1973, Dave Anderson, "The Last Stand."

CHAPTER 2

The Big Three Reborn

30   "I was happy with"—*Philadelphia Inquirer*, June 15, 1973, "'Shell-Shocked' Player Says He'd Settle for 72-72-72 Finish."

31   "Through that period"—Interview with Jack Nicklaus, September 2008.

31   "Even in '73"—ibid.

32 "The Whitemarsh course"—*New York Times*, May 31, 1973, Lincoln Werden, "To Palmer, There's Only One Oakmont."

33 "There's no similarity"—ibid.

34 "He returns now"—*Hamilton (OH) Journal News*, (AP), June 10, 1973, Bob Green, "Nick Could Join Golf's All-time Elite This Week."

34 "Honestly, I don't remember"—*Cleveland Plain Dealer*, June 13, 1973, Bill Nichols, "Oakmont Is Severe Test."

34 "I played with blinders on"—*Golf Digest*, July 2000, Bob Verdi, "I Had My Century."

35 "Did you play golf"—*Chicago Tribune*, June 15, 1973, Cooper Rollow, "Nicklaus 'Stupid Shot' Turns into Eagle Deuce."

37 "A man would be a fool"—*Pittsburgh Press*, June 10, 1973, Ray Kienzl, "Jack Nicklaus Returns to Where It All Began."

37 "It wouldn't be worth"—*Pittsburgh Press*, June 15, 1973, Pat Livingston, "The Scoreboard: Jack's Gamble Pays Off."

38 "Maybe you can"—ibid.

38 "The fairway is not"—*Dallas Morning News*, (UPI), "Driving the Green."

38 "I didn't want to start"—*Atlanta Journal-Constitution*, June 15, 1973, Al Smith, "Jack 'Tickled' with a 71."

39 "When I saw him point"—*Miami Herald*, June 15, 1973, Edwin Pope, "'Stupid' Shot Keeps Jack in Line."

39 "I needed to keep"—*Rochester (NY) Democrat and Chronicle*, June 15, 1973, Tony Destino, "Player Fires 67, Leads by 3."

39 "to be in the air"—*Los Angeles Times*, June 17, 1973, Jim Murray, "The Stuff of Legend."

39 "That one's on the green"— Pope, "'Stupid' Shot."

39 "When we got down the fairway"—ibid.

39 "You watch now"—ibid.

40 "the best iron shot"—*Dallas Morning News*, July 22, 1962, Frank Reece, "Player Snares PGA Lead."

41 "The Americans"—*Toronto Star*, June 15, 1973, Ken McKee, "Three-way Tie for Lead in U.S. Open."

42 "The record speaks"—*Charleston (WV) Sunday Gazette-Mail*, August 6, 1972, Bob Baker, "Down the Fairway."

42   "I think it will be"—*Las Cruces (NM) Sun News* (UPI), August 6, 1972, "Gary Player Only Golfer to Break Par."

43   "Still, the big question"—Player, Gary, with Floyd Thatcher, *Gary Player, World Golfer* (Nashville, TN: W Publishing Group, 1974), p. 142.

44   "I'm fit as a"—*Miami Herald*, (AP), June 15, 1973, Bob Green, "Player's Putter Pays Off in Three-shot Open Lead."

44   "I'm playing worse"—*Columbus (OH) Dispatch*, June 13, 1973, Paul Hornung, "Open Field Waits Sun."

44   "cannot yet be"—*London Times*, June 13, 1973, Peter Ryde, "Great Course Will Find a Champion to Match."

44   "I still say this is"—*Pittsburgh Press*, June 17, 1962, James O'Brien, "Palmer Foes Like Lee at Appomattox."

44   "Still I don't throw"—ibid.

44   "I played a practice round"—*Pittsburgh Press* (Evening Edition), June 15, 1973, "Player's 70 Holds Lead; Borek (Who's He?) Fires 65."

45   "I putted as well as"— Green, "Player's Putter Pays Off."

45   "This course is a pleasure"—*Erie (PA) Morning News*, June 15, 1973, Jack Polancy, "Player Fully Recovered."

46   "Someday you'll realize"— Green, "Player's Putter Pays Off."

46   "What surprises me"—*San Francisco Chronicle*, June 15, 1973, Art Spander, "Player Leads Open by Three."

46   "I remember one U.S. Open"— Green, "Player's Putter Pays Off."

46   "You never know"—United States Golf Association, 1973 U.S. Open: *Miller's Miracle at Oakmont.* New York: Trans World International, 1973.

CHAPTER 3
A View from the Parking Lot

47   "It was a lonely life"—*Sports Illustrated*, December 20, 1971, Curry Kirkpatrick, "A Common Man with an Uncommon Touch."

47   "In those days"—*Sports Illustrated*, June 17, 1968, Myron Cope, "A Firm Hand on a Carefree Cat."

48   "I feel like I helped"—*Dallas Morning News*, June 17, 1995, Sam Blair, "Back in His Old Backyard."

48   "I caddied for one"—Trevino, Lee, and Sam Blair, *They Call Me Super Mex* (New York: Random House, 1982), p. 22.

48   "I went from a country kid"—ibid., p. 23.

49   "Confused, unsettled"—ibid., p. 32.

49   "I got hit in the"—ibid., p. 34.

49   "I didn't do anything but"—*New York Times*, June 17, 1968, "Golf's No. 1 Extrovert."

50   "Either it's going to"—Trevino and Blair, *They Call Me Super Mex*, p. 53.

50   "a savage uninhibited"—Kirkpatrick, "A Common Man."

50   "the only way to forget"—ibid.

51   "Hardy wouldn't"—Trevino and Blair, *They Call Me Super Mex*, p. 58.

51   "Instead, I stayed"—ibid.

52   "We discovered Lee"—*New York Times*, January 5, 1968, (UPI), "PGA Names Trevino Rookie Golfer of 1967."

53   "You had to wear"—Trevino and Blair, *They Call Me Super Mex*, p. 84.

53   "scuba goggles because"—*New York Times*, June 19, 1967, "Finish Is Rosy to Trevino without Scuba Goggles."

54   "And that night"—Trevino and Blair, *They Call Me Super Mex*, p. 87.

54   "a humble background"—*Dallas Morning News*, April 14, 1968, "Trevino Charms Masters Crowd."

54   "The 28-year-old Trevino"—ibid.

55   "the swarthy Mexican-American"—*Dallas Morning News*, (AP), June 11, 1968, "Open Course Favors Casper."

55   "In purely technical terms"—Kirkpatrick, "A Common Man."

55   "If he ever gets up high"—ibid.

55   "Lee said, 'I'm not that worried'"—*Golf Digest*, August 2003, Jaime Diaz, "Finding His Way Home."

56   "On eighteen, I missed"—Trevino and Blair, *They Call Me Super Mex*, p. 102.

56   "The pin was set right"—ibid.

56   "What Lee Trevino really"—*Sports Illustrated*, June 24, 1968, Dan Jenkins, "Eyes Right . . . but Wrong."

57   "I was his traveling"—Woy, Bucky, with James Patterson, *Sign 'Em Up,*

Bucky: The Adventures of a Sports Agent (New York: Hawthorn Books, Inc., 1975), p. 75.

57   "I'm so happy"—*Dallas Morning News*, June 17, 1968, Harless Wade, "Olé! Trevino Finds His Place in Sun."

57   "I said I didn't like it"—Trevino and Blair, *They Call Me Super Mex*, p. 114; *Golf*, April 1971, Al Barkow, "The Masters, An Idea Betrayed?"

57   "I should have just"—Trevino and Blair, *They Call Me Super Mex*, p. 114.

58   "isn't conducive"—*Golf World*, April 20, 1971, "Back in El Paso . . . Trevino Wins $150."

58   "That was the greatest"—Trevino and Blair, *They Call Me Super Mex*, p. 114.

58   "You look at my galleries"—*Time*, July 19, 1971, "Lee Trevino: Cantinflas of the Country Clubs."

58   "Yeah, I been married"—Jenkins, "Eyes Right."

59   "sales pitch would be"—Woy, *Sign 'Em Up Bucky*, pp. 74–75.

59   "Naw, I didn't bring"—Trevino and Blair, *They Call Me Super Mex*, p. 110.

59   "You'll seldom see Trevino"—Woy, *Sign 'Em Up Bucky*, pp. 80–81.

59   "I was stumbling, falling"—Trevino and Blair, *They Call Me Super Mex*, p. 142.

60   "crashing and burning"—ibid., p. 144.

60   "Yes, this one is more"—*Dallas Morning News*, June 22, 1971, Harless Wade, "Trevino's 2d Open 'More Rewarding.'"

61   "a helluva psych artist"—Trevino and Blair, *They Call Me Super Mex*, p. 146.

61   "is the worst of the lot"—*Sports Illustrated*, July 19, 1971, Dan Jenkins, "Now for the Mexican Open."

62   "a little testy"—*Dallas Morning News*, (UPI), July 7, 1971, "No Gags for Trevino."

62   "This is the most fantastic"—*Dallas Morning News*, (AP), July 11, 1971, "In England, It's Olé and Viva Lee Trevino."

62   "To be established"—*Dallas Morning News*, July 11, 1971, Sam Blair, "Longer the Streak, the Easier It Looks."

62   "When I win a championship"—*Corpus Christi (TX) Caller-Times*, (AP), July 11, 1971, "Lee Trevino Makes Another Donation."

62 "I wanted to do something"—Blair, "Longer the Streak."

62 "It was such a tragedy"—Trevino and Blair, *They Call Me Super Mex*, p. 112.

63 "I could give him $15,000"—Cope, "A Firm Hand."

63 "The world's a funny place"—Wind, Herbert Warren, *Following Through* (New York: HarperCollins, 1995), pp. 251–52.

64 "Just tell Mr. Roberts"—D'Antonio, *Tour '72*, p. 111.

64 "The damage has been done"—*Dallas Morning News*, (AP), November 1, 1972, "Trevino Says He Should Be Suspended or Handed Fine."

65 "I'm usually on the road"—*Dallas Morning News*, November 23, 1972, Marilyn Beck, "Love Lights Jack's Fire for England."

65 "[Losing the weight] ruined"—*Golf World*, February 2, 1973, "Bunker to Bunker."

65 "They said I have not won"—*Dallas Morning News*, (AP), February 1, 1973, "Lee Gets Teed-off at Talk of Slump."

65 "No matter how much"—Woy, *Sign 'Em Up, Bucky*, pp. 80, 83.

66 "Tacos, get your red-hot"—ibid., p. 77.

66 "Spring training was over"—*New York Times*, February 23, 1973, Lincoln Werden, "Brewer, Fezler Share Lead in Golf with 67s."

67 "Man, I've got to play"—*Dallas Morning News*, May 9, 1973, Harless Wade, "Will Lee Buck Chest Pains?"

67 "about 60 days"—*New York Times*, August 23, 1973, "People in Sports: Tour Too Long for Trevino."

67 "I don't sleep and live"—*Pittsburgh Post-Gazette*, June 14, 1973, Phil Gundelfinger, "Tee Topics."

68 "'Where you going?'"—*Philadelphia Inquirer*, June 9, 1973, John Bloom, "Fans Don't Care Who's Leading, They Follow Nicklaus, Trevino."

68 "'I'm wasting a whole week'"—Bloom, "Fans Don't Care."

68 "Mentally, I wasn't here"—*Dallas Morning News*, (AP), June 10, 1973, "Weiskopf Holds 3-Stroke Lead."

68 "We were going on"—*Columbus Evening Dispatch*, June 14, 1973, Paul Hornung, "Trevino Loves His Life, But Seeks Privacy."

68 "I can't go into a restaurant"—ibid.

69 "Look, I love to have fun"—*Toronto Star*, June 14, 1973, Ken McKee, "The 'Other' Lee Trevino Shuns Golfing Stage."

69   "I thought that was a cute quote"—*Pittsburgh Press*, June 14, 1973, Pat Livingston, "Don't Count Out the Mex."

70   "This thing will be won"—*Dallas Morning News*, June 14, 1973, "Trevino Posts 'Danger' Signs."

70   "[Trevino] fell victim"—*Pittsburgh Post-Gazette*, June 15, 1973, Marino Parascenzo, "Down 3 but Confident, Lee Trusting Oakmont."

70   "I bogeyed the two easiest"—*Washington Post*, June 15, 1973, Bob Addie, "Player Comes Back to Lead Open by 3."

71   "I think about what I should make"—*Sports Illustrated*, December 20, 1971, Curry Kirkpatrick, "A Common Man with an Uncommon Touch."

71   "you don't have to"—*Chicago Sun Times*, June 15, 1973, "Player Starts Hot, Leads Open with 67."

71   "I hope he does it every day"—*Atlanta Journal-Constitution*, June 15, 1973, Al Smith, "Jack's Shot Not in Plan Trevino Has."

71   "I used a three-iron"—Addie, "Player Comes Back."

71   "My round couldn't have been better"—*Cleveland Plain Dealer*, June 15, 1973, Bill Nichols, "Player's 4-Under 67 Leads Open by 3."

71   "I want to shoot"—*San Francisco Chronicle*, June 15, 1973, Art Spander, "Player Leads Open by 3."

71–72 "The longer you stay"—*Pittsburgh Press* (Evening Edition), June 15, 1973, "Player's 70 Holds Lead; Borek (Who's He?) Fires 65."

72   "This is a course which requires"—*Pittsburgh Press* (Evening Edition), June 15, 1973, Pat Livingston, "Jack's Gamble Pays Off."

CHAPTER 4
Carnage

73   "I was thrilled"—Interview with Geoff Hensley, October 2008.

73   "the final degree"—Liebman, Glenn, *Golf Shorts: Par 2* (New York: McGraw-Hill, 1998), p. 153.

74   "Hey, you're on the tee!"—Interview with Geoff Hensley, October 2008.

74   "Good morning, ladies and gentlemen"—*Pittsburgh Post Gazette*, June 15, 1973, Bill Christine, "Open Opening a Bit Tardy."

74   "I don't have the equipment"—*Dallas Morning News*, June 12, 1973, Harless Wade, "Rain Opens, Top Hazard."

75 "In the Super Bowl"—*Ogden (UT) Standard-Examiner*, (UPI), June 15, 1973, "'Course Zero Fun to Play'—Hill."

75 "taking a good course"—ibid.

75 "He's just not any fun"—*Sports Illustrated*, June 18, 1973, John Underwood, "Golf's Jekyll and Hyde."

76 "We all have double bogeys"—ibid.

76 "[You're] asking a leopard"—ibid.

76 "desperately unhappy"—ibid.

76 "Why doesn't he quit"—*Pittsburgh Post-Gazette*, June 12, 1973, Al Abrams, "Sidelights on Sports: Crampton Didn't Forget."

76 "never gave me the opportunity"— Underwood, "Golf's Jekyll and Hyde."

76–77 "[I] never had such a congenial round"—ibid.

77 "the most successful journeyman"—*Golf Monthly*, March 1973, "Talking Golf."

77 "His steady play"—*Golf Magazine*, June 1973, "Six for the Money."

77 "Nicklaus and Weiskopf"—*Pittsburgh Post Gazette*, June 12, 1973, Bill Christine, "Nicklaus, Weiskopf . . . So Why Show Up?"

77 "I've been doing a lot of traveling"—*Golf Magazine*, March 1973, Lee Mueller, "Will Buffalo Billy Ride Again?"

78 "It wasn't the greens"—*San Francisco Chronicle*, June 15, 1973, Art Spander, "Oakmont Greens a Nightmare."

79 "I shot an 86"—*Charleston Gazette*, June 16, 1973, Bob Baker, "Sam (75) Blames 'Blankety-Blank' Putting."

79 "I'm an aggressive putter"—*Los Angeles Times*, June 15, 1973, Bill Shirley, "Player's 4-under-par 67 leads U.S. Open by Three."

79 "[But] then I three-putted"—*Columbus Evening Dispatch*, June 15, 1973, Paul Hornung, "Area Hopes Trailing, But Still in Race."

80 "Why does the Open"—*Pittsburgh Press*, June 12, 1973, "Just Another Tournament to Sam Snead."

81 "Hey, Sam"—*Pittsburgh Press* (Evening Edition), June 15, 1973, Dan Donovan, "Snead: A Real Iron Man."

81 "I missed only two fairways"—*Richmond Times-Dispatch*, June 15, 1973, Chauncey Durden, "Old Man and the Greens."

81 "Sam is a better putter"—Donovan, "Snead."

81 I know that everybody's"—Durden, "Old Man."

81   "I think this course is unfair"—*Maryland Cumberland News*, (UPI), June 15, 1973, "Ben Crenshaw Puts Rap on Oakmont Club."

82   "maybe the strongest greens"—United States Golf Association, *Who Els?*, 1994.

83   "Everything went bad"—*Pittsburgh Press*, June 15, 1973, "Stafford Hits Bull's-Eye."

83   "a rogue in spiked shoes"—*Pittsburgh Post Gazette*, June 14, 1973, Bill Christine, "The 24-hour Swinger."

84   "I played in four consecutive"—*Chicago Tribune*, June 15, 1973, Tom Tomashek, "Player Leads Open with 67."

84   "These are the fastest greens"—*Chicago Sun Times*, June 15, 1973, Len Ziehm, "Floyd 'prepared by watching Cubs.'"

84   "At the time"—*Atlanta Journal-Constitution*, June 15, 1973, Al Smith, "Cancer-hit Littler Returns."

85   "People are bound to talk"—*Boston Globe*, June 15, 1973, Tom Fitzgerald, "The Little Things Can't Get Me Down Now—Littler."

85   "It's not the operation"—Smith, "Cancer-Hit Littler."

CHAPTER 5

The Prince and the King

89   "Oh, oh, I'd better"—*San Francisco Chronicle*, June 16, 1973, Art Spander, "S.F.'s Miller a Future King?"

89   "Take your time, Johnny"—*Chicago Tribune*, June 16, 1973, Cooper Rollow, "Arnie Loses Touch, but Not Army."

89   "If I start playing"—*Pittsburgh Press*, June 16, 1973, Dan Donovan, "It Was Like the 60s for Arnie—for a While."

90   "I don't deserve to be"—*Los Angeles Times* (*Chicago Sun-Times*), June 13, 1983, Ron Rapoport, "Johnny Miller Returns to the Scene of His Miracle 63."

90   "Johnny just loved the game"—*Golf Magazine*, September 1973, Johnny Miller, "I'm Not Afraid to Go for the Flagstick."

90   "His number one rule"—Miller, Johnny, with Guy Yocom, *I Call The Shots* (New York: Gotham Books, 2004), pp. 222–23.

91   "about knee-high"—*San Francisco Chronicle*, June 22, 1966, Art Rosenbaum, "Casper's Caddy Made a Deal."

91   "He was the smallest guy"—Miller, "I'm Not Afraid."

91   "Johnny didn't pick up"—*Salt Lake City Tribune*, June 18, 1973, "Geertsen Missed Thrills as Protégé Won Open."

92   "If there were a better putter"—Miller, *I Call the Shots*, p. 221.

92   "discussion of it spread"—*Oakland Tribune*, June 28, 1963, Norm Hannon, "Archer Takes Charge."

92   "If I couldn't beat him"—*Hayward (CA) Daily Review*, (AP), June 28, 1963, Sid Hoos, "State Am Favorites Hex Also Hits J. Lotz."

92   "the committee ruled"—*Los Angeles Times*, June 28, 1963, Bill Shirley, "Teenager Breaks Rule, Still Wins Match in State Amateur."

93   "John Miller, a quiet"—ibid.

93   "a cinch for future"—*San Francisco Chronicle*, June 28, 1963, Joe Wilmot, "1961 Champ Out-of-state Golf."

93   "I like [Arnold] Palmer"—*San Mateo Times*, August 3, 1964, "Bay Area Youth Wins Jr. Golf."

94   "Mike was the first player"—http://www.cougarclub.com/hall_of_fame/taylor_m.jsp.

94   "Johnny came in and"—BYU Alumni online magazine, Jeff Call, "Like Father, Like Sons."

95   "I'm the only nervous one"—*San Francisco Chronicle*, June 17, 1966, Art Spander, "Miller's Formula for Par."

96   "I wouldn't take this round"—ibid.

96   "[Nicklaus] won't bother me"—*San Francisco Chronicle*, June 18, 1966, Art Rosenbaum, "Arnie, Casper Tie; Nicklaus Mad."

96   "refusing to crack"—*San Francisco Chronicle*, June 19, 1966, Nelson Cullenward, "Nicklaus Moves up with 69."

96   "They billed this one"—*San Francisco Chronicle*, June 19, 1966, Roger Williams, "Miller Gives TV Show."

96   "I thought Miller was"—ibid.

97   "I was never at ease"—ibid.

97   "I've lost some"—*San Francisco Chronicle*, June 19, 1966, Roger Williams, "Bird on 14th Sparks Arnie."

97   "I was feeling pretty good"—ibid.

98   "didn't get airborne"—*New York Times*, June 20, 1966, Lincoln A. Werden, "Casper Makes Up 7 Strokes in 8 Holes to tie Palmer at 278 in U.S. Open."

98   "My caddie told me"—ibid.

98   "I'll be eating buffalo meat"—*Oakland Tribune*, June 20, 1966, "Buffalo Meat Blues."

99   "It was pretty damn similar"—*New York Times*, June 21, 1966, Lincoln A. Werden, "Californian Wins for Second Time."

99   "I wanted to play so good"—Miller, "I'm Not Afraid."

99   "Golf isn't the most important"—*Moberly (MO) Monitor Index*, (AP), June 21, 1966, Jack Stevenson, "Casper Fires 69 to Win U.S. Golf Open."

100 "Billy told me to wait it out"—Black, William T., *Mormon Athletes: Book 2* (Salt Lake City, UT: Deseret Book Company, 1982), p. 58.

101 "[Every] iron in my bag"—*Oakland Tribune*, July 1, 1968, Ed Schoenfeld, "Great Future for State Golf Winner"

101 "Gene Littler and Ken Venturi"—ibid.

101 "A college degree"—*Time*, July 2, 1973, "Johnny on the Mountain."

102 "My putting was real bad"—*Tucson Daily Citizen*, January 18, 1970, Verne Boatner, "Young John Miller, 'Man of the Hour.'"

103 "It worked like magic"—*Long Beach (CA) Independent Telegram*, (UPI), January 18, 1970, "Rookie Carves 61."

103 "It was just one of those days"—Boatner, "Young John Miller."

104 "There was casual water"—*San Antonio Light*, (UPI), June 16, 1973, "Player Leads Open; Borek Breaks Record."

104 "You could see water"—*Los Angeles Times*, June 16, 1973, Bill Shirley, "Player Leads by One in Watered-down Open."

104 "Even with the soft greens"—ibid.

104 "I missed a two and a half"—*San Francisco Chronicle*, June 16, 1973, Art Spander, "S.F.'s Miller a Future King?"

104 "[Palmer] doesn't bother me"—ibid.

104 "Those guys used to"—*Akron Beacon Journal*, June 16, 1973, John Seaburn, "Calming down Key to Miller's Game."

105 "As mute testimony"—ibid.

105 "The three-putt green"—Shirley, "Player Leads by One."

106 "I felt good, until"—*Pittsburgh Post-Gazette*, June 16, 1973, Al Abrams, "Sidelights on Sports."

106 "It seemed like every time"—Donovan, "It Was Like the 60s."

106 "I drove it numerous times"—*Pittsburgh Press* (Evening Edition), June 15, 1973, Ray Kienzl, "Player Shoots 70 for Two-round 137 in Open."

106 "[The] greatest I've ever seen"—*Toronto Star*, June 16, 1973, Ken McKee, "Roller-coaster Greens Become Putt Paradise as Par Beats U.S. Open."

106 "You need to do three things"—Spander, "S.F.'s Miller."

106 "The old Palmer wouldn't"—Donovan, "It Was Like the 60s."

CHAPTER 6

A Watered-down Open

108 "become more difficult"—*Rochester (NY) Democrat and Chronicle*, June 15, 1973, Tony Destino, "Player Fires 67, Leads by 3."

109 "I was pretty fortunate"—*Columbus Evening Dispatch*, June 16, 1973, Paul Hornung, "Player's Lead in Open Part of 'Buddy System.'"

109 "I've been putting"—*Akron Beacon Journal*, June 16, 1973, John Seaburn, "Player Credits Putting Practice for Open Lead."

109 "The leader very seldom wins"—*Richmond Times-Dispatch*, June 16, 1973, Chauncey Durden, "Sportsview: Work Is in Player's Bag."

109 "This is my last tournament"—*Pittsburgh Press*, June 16, 1973, Ray Kienzl, "Open Field Puts Heat on Oakmont."

110 "I have a farm"—*Dallas Morning News*, (AP), June 16, 1973, "Charles Plans to Quit Tour after Open."

110 "the U.S. Open really doesn't"—*Columbus Citizen-Journal*, June 16, 1973, Kaye Kessler, "Gary Holds Lead; Jack Gains."

110 "It was just a lucky shot"—*Dallas Morning News*, (AP), "Charles Plans to Quit."

110 "I can't believe Bob said it"—Kessler, "Gary Holds Lead."

111 "No matter who wins or loses"—*Fort Lauderdale Sun-Sentinel*, (UPI), June 14, 1973, Milton Richman, "The Open: It Means Everything."

111 "Nicklaus, Weiskopf, Palmer"—ibid.

112 "Every time I strike a ball"—*Cleveland Plain Dealer*, June 13, 1973, Bill Nichols, "Oakmont Is Severe Test."

112 "I look forward to the Open"—*Los Angeles Times*, June 16, 1973, Bill Shirley, "Player Leads by One in Watered-down Open."

112 "I've been playing in tournaments"—Kienzl, "Open Field."

114   "I was tempted"—*Rochester (NY) Democrat and Chronicle*, June 16, 1973, Tony Destino, "Colbert Snaps Slump in 'One I Want to Win.'"

114   "My three-wood came so close"—Destino, "Colbert Snaps Slump."

114   "Jim made the greatest shot"—*Pittsburgh Post-Gazette*, June 16, 1973, Bill Christine, "Rusty's the Guy for Jim Colbert."

114   "After I got to be starting quarterback"—*San Francisco Chronicle*, June 16, 1973, Art Spander, "Oakmont Reversal—19 Sub-Par Rounds, Course Record."

115   "Trevino had at least five"—*El Paso Herald Post*, (UPI), "Five Trevino Birdie Putts Miss by Inches."

115   "There's nothing merry"—*Richmond Times-Dispatch*, June 16, 1973, Chauncey Durden, "Sportsview: Pars and Pickups."

116   "Trevino had beaten me"—Nicklaus, Jack, with Ken Bowden, *My Story* (New York: Simon & Schuster, 1997), p. 322.

116   "The good Lord gave Nicklaus"—Liebman, *Golf Shorts: Par 2*, p. 67.

117   "That shot was the turning point"—*Cleveland Plain Dealer*, June 16, 1973, Bill Nichols, "Player's 137 Leads Colbert by One."

117   "They had the tees so far"—*Akron Beacon Journal*, June 16, 1973, John Seaburn, "Nichols: Open Ruins Egos."

117   "The greens were much softer"—Spander, "Oakmont Reversal."

117   "The greens are soft, men"—*Chicago Tribune*, June 16, 1973, Tom Tomashek, "Player Keeps Lead in Open."

118   "I would prefer"—*Golf World*, June 22, 1973, Ron Coffman, "A Ravishing Round at Oakmont."

118   "Scalzo punches some buttons"—*Pittsburgh Press*, June 11, 1973, "Golfers Happy with Oakmont."

118   "I don't have a favorite"—*New York Times*, June 15, 1973, Dave Anderson, "Greens Rough for Open Golfers."

119   "Let's just say"—Coffman, "A Ravishing Round."

122   "finest Open round"—*Philadelphia Inquirer*, June 15, 1973, Fred Byrod, "Player's 67 Leads Open by 3."

122   "If my family had"—Interview with Gene Borek, July, August 2007.

123   "When we got home"—*New York Times*, June 16, 1973, Dave Anderson, "65 at Oakmont."

123   "In 1959, I played"—Interview with Gene Borek, July, August 2007.

123   "Most of the guys didn't"—ibid.

124   "in the gusty cold wind"—*New York Times*, October 8, 1971, Lincoln A. Werden, "Nieporte Takes Met. Golf by Shot."

125   "I said, 'What?'"—Interview with Gene Borek, July, August 2007.

125   "In the past, whenever"—ibid.

126   "I called [U.S.G.A. officials]"—*Richmond Times-Dispatch*, June 16, 1973, Harold Pearson, "Club Pro Win Open? 'Easier Than on Tour.'"

126   "John Frillman"—Interview with Gene Borek, July, August 2007.

126   "I feel right at home"—*Atlanta Constitution*, June 16, 1973, Al Smith, "Borek, Man Who Came Late, Breaks Open Record."

126   "scrambled [his] way"—*Pittsburgh Post-Gazette*, June 16, 1973, Phil Gundelfinger, "Borek Hot with Cool 65 in Open."

126   "I felt that I'd played very well"—Interview with Gene Borek, July, August 2007.

127   "I remember thinking"—ibid.

127   "I took a lot of time"—ibid.

128   "Finally, on an impulse"—ibid.

128   "[The putt] was incredibly fast"—ibid.

129   "The ball went incredibly high"—ibid.

130   "First, I'd like to thank"—*Rochester (NY) Democrat and Chronicle*, June 16, 1973, Tony Destino, "Player 1st in Open by Stroke."

130   "Borek did it as easily"—*Detroit Free Press*, June 16, 1973, Joe Falls, "A 1-Day Wonder at the Open."

130   "[When] I called home"—Anderson, "65 At Oakmont."

131   "I was planning on"—Interview with Vinny Giles, June 2007.

131   "Most of the players"—ibid.

132   "I was scared to death"—*New York Times*, April 12, 1968, "Giles Starts His First Masters by Sinking 30-foot Birdie Putt."

132   "Only Ben Hogan"—*New York Times*, August 27, 1969, Lincoln A. Werden, "Top Amateur Golfers to Play Sloping and Fast Greens Today."

132   "appeared to be sweltering"—August 31, 1969, *New York Times*, Lincoln A. Werden, "Melnyk's 286 Wins U.S. Amateur By 5."

133   "one of the best rounds"—*New York Times*, (AP), September 1, 1972, "Giles Leads by 1 in Amateur Golf."

133   "I always felt I was"—*Cumberland (MD) Sunday Times*, (UPI), September 3, 1972, Douglas Monroe, "Vinny Giles Finally Wins Amateur."

135 "I drew back a six-iron"—Interview with Vinny Giles, June 2007.

135 "After it went in"—ibid.

135 "Everyone talks about how"—ibid.

135 "[I was just trying to]"—*Richmond Times-Dispatch*, June 16, 1973, "Giles 'Numbers' 2-3-3-3 for a 69."

136 "watered-down Open"—Shirley, "Player Leads by One."

136 "The legend had grown"—Spander, "Oakmont Reversal."

CHAPTER 7

"He's Longer Than Nicklaus. . . . Go Watch This Boy"

140 "My dad worked"—*Pittsburgh Press*, June 17, 1973, Dan Donovan, "Weiskopf on Winning Track."

140 "Every time Tom Weiskopf"—ibid.

140 "He sacrificed his"—*Pittsburgh Press*, June 12, 1973, Ray Kienzl, "Weiskopf Tempers Game."

141 "powerful hitter"—*Coshocton (OH) Tribune*, July 12, 1939, "Ohio Golf Joust Spotlight Lands on Quarter-Final."

141 "imperturbable"—*New York Times*, September 30, 1936, Maribel Y. Vinson, "Superb Play of Young Golf Rivals Fascinates Crowd at Canoe Brook."

141 "Why, no; why should I"—ibid.

141 "Now Miss Shorb is calm"—ibid.

142 "another feminine star"—*Coshocton (OH) Tribune*, "Ohio Golf Joust Spotlight."

142 "top-flight clouters"—*Zanesville (OH) Signal*, (AP), July 15, 1941, "Same Old Story at Ohio Amateur."

143 "In high school, I"—*Time*, August 20, 1973, "Coming of Age at 30."

143 "When they played"—*Pacific Stars & Stripes*, July 30, 1965, Frank Eck, "Snead Says Weiskopf Is Worth Watching."

143 "He was a very impetuous"—*Cleveland Press*, July 16, 1973, Burt Graeff, "Bedford Bubbles over Weiskopf—So Does Mom."

143 "After we walked"—*Golf Digest*, June 2002, Guy Yocom, "My Shot: Tom Weiskopf."

144 "Bob put 40 yards"—Eck, "Snead Says Weiskopf."

145 "Jack's ball just disappeared"—D'Antonio, *Tour '72*, pp. 4–5.

145 "It was really funny"—*Fitchberg Sentinel*, July 29, 1966, Murray Olderman, "Between You 'n' Me."

147 "I'm glad it's all over"—*Benton Harbor (MI) News-Palladium*, August 12, 1963, Jim Deland, "Tom Weiskopf Wins Western Amateur Crown."

147 "All I can say is"—*Benton Harbor (MI) News-Palladium*, August 12, 1963, Jim Deland, "2,500 See Golf Tournament End."

148 "I'm so nervous right now"—Eck, "Snead Says Weiskopf."

148 "Tom Weiskopf. Now there's a"—ibid.

149 "We left Seattle"—*Golf World*, October 15, 1965, Tom Place, "Weiskopf Gets Lift to Ohio Crown."

149 "Actually, it gives me"—Olderman, "Between You 'n' Me."

149 "I'd like to have what"—ibid.

149 "Everything I've gained"—Eck, "Snead Says Weiskopf."

149 "I hadn't had much"—*Golf Digest*, June 1968, Nick Seitz, "Is This the Man to Succeed Arnold Palmer?"

149 "I had seen Tom"—ibid.

150 "I'm so darn moody"—ibid.

151 "likable young fellow"—*Columbus Evening Dispatch*, February 12, 1968, "Weiskopf Collects."

151 "I was trying to get it"—*Columbus Evening Dispatch*, February 13, 1968, Paul Hornung, "Weiskopf Victory Reflects New Attitude, Maturity."

152 "dumb meetings"—*Dallas Morning News*, May 14, 1973, John Anders, "With Slight Service Charge."

152 "I guard the United States"—ibid.

152 "It hasn't helped me"—*Columbus Evening Dispatch*, June 17, 1973, Paul Hornung, "Weiskopf's Confidence Bolstered."

153 "the tall and stately Columbuson"—*Columbus Evening Dispatch*, April 13, 1969, Paul Hornung, "Weiskopf in Position to Challenge."

153 "Sure, I'm disappointed"—*Columbus Evening Dispatch*, April 14, 1969, Paul Hornung, "Weiskopf Pleased, Also Disappointed."

154 "There's no doubt"—*Columbus Evening Dispatch*, April 10, 1971, Paul Hornung, "Weiskopf Confident of Tourney Chances."

154 "not feeling too swift"—*Columbus Evening Dispatch*, April 11, 1971, Paul Hornung, "Columbus Entries in Title Run."

155 "I was so nervous"—*New York Times*, June 14, 1971, Lincoln A. Werden, "Weiskopf Takes 4-man Play-off at Charlotte on 1st-hole Birdie."

155 "[I] lost my concentration"—*Latrobe Bulletin*, (UPI), June 12, 1973, "Tom Weiskopf Arrives at Oakmont."

155 "I'm withdrawing from every"—*New York Times*, August 16, 1971, Lincoln A. Werden, "Stockton Wins by Shot at Sutton on 66 by 275."

156 "[If] I could putt"—*Boston Globe*, August 16, 1971, Joe Concannon, "Weiskopf May Withdraw from Tour Following Disastrous Last-round 78."

156 "He couldn't stand being"—Woy, *Sign 'Em Up Bucky*, pp. 66–67.

156 "Sometimes I used to"—*Akron Beacon Journal*, June 13, 1973, "'Dissatisfaction' Sparks Hot Streak.'"

156 "feel that he could"—*New York Times*, July 19, 1970, Lincoln A. Werden, "Casper Leads by 2; Weiskopf Pulls Out."

157 "Weiskopf, the introvert"—*Philadelphia Inquirer*, August 24, 1971, Fred Byrod, "Proven Formula Brought Weiskopf Victory."

157 "When I walked"—*Philadelphia Inquirer*, August 23, 1971, Fred Byrod, "Weiskopf Wins Classic by One."

157 "I proved something"—ibid.

158 "I'm playing as well"—*Columbus Evening Dispatch*, April 5, 1972, Paul Hornung, "Par Golf Could Win at Augusta."

158 "I turned a 64"—*Columbus Evening Dispatch*, (AP), April 9, 1972, "Nicklaus Falters, But Leads Late By 1; Weiskopf Three Strokes off Pace."

158 "I tried my darnedest"—*Columbus Evening Dispatch*, April 10, 1972, "Rivals Agree Nicklaus Greatest."

158 "turned the 6,997-yard"—*New York Times*, (AP), October 15, 1972, "Weiskopf Upsets Trevino, 4 And 3."

159 "While my father was"—*Columbus Evening Dispatch*, April 4, 1973, Paul Hornung, "Weiskopf Hungry for 'Green Coat.'"

160 "My father told me"—*Charlotte Observer*, June 4, 1973, Richard Sink, "'I Can't Imagine Putting Better.'"

160 "When I used to have"—*Columbus Evening Dispatch*, June 5, 1973, Paul Hornung, "New Attitude Paves Way for Weiskopf."

161 "It's a heck of a"—*Dallas Morning News*, May 14, 1973, Harless Wade, "Gift NIT for Weiskopf."

161 "I really didn't think"—*Atlanta Journal Constitution*, May 28, 1973, Mike McKenzie, "Catch Jack at the Wire? It Was Already Too Late."

161 "I'm glad I made it"—ibid.

162 "A lot of skeptics"—*Charlotte Observer*, June 1, 1973, Whitey Kelley, "New Weiskopf Keeps Critics on the Defensive."

162 "Let's face it"—ibid.

162 "I won't play it"—*Charlotte Observer*, June 3, 1973, Bob Whitley, "Weiskopf Won't Play It Safe, Weiskopf Predicts."

163 "I've always considered"—Sink, "'I Can't Imagine,'"

163 "Who is Jim Barber?"—*Philadelphia Inquirer*, June 9, 1973, Fred Byrod, "Jim Barber Keeps Lead with 67–132."

163 "My attitude is always"—*Philadelphia Inquirer*, June 10, 1973, Fred Byrod, "Weiskopf Fires 65 for 203 to Lead IVB by 3 Strokes."

164 "I was driving out"—*Golf World*, June 15, 1973, Joe Greenday, "Tom on an Awesome Tear."

164 "Winning is the hardest"—*Atlanta Journal-Constitution*, (AP), June 12, 1973, "Next Target: U.S. Open—Weiskopf."

164 "I've always said that"—*Columbus Evening Dispatch*, (AP), June 11, 1973, "It's 3-for-4 for Weiskopf."

165 "It should have happened"—*Pittsburgh Press*, June 13, 1973, "Greens 'Unbelievable.'"

165 "I feel I'm an awful good"—*Pittsburgh Press*, June 12, 1973, Ray Kienzl, "Weiskopf Tempers Game."

165 "I can't put myself"—*San Francisco Chronicle*, June 12, 1973, Art Spander, "The Open Question."

165 "I've driven well"—*Charlotte Observer*, June 14, 1973, Richard Sink, "Open Forecast: Nicklaus, Weiskopf in Buckeye Battle."

165 "But I'm not discouraged"—*Columbus Evening Dispatch*, June 15, 1973, Paul Hornung, "Area Hopes Trailing, But Still in Race."

165 "[It] was those greens"—*Erie (PA) Morning News*, June 15, 1973, Jack Polancy, "Player Fully Recovered."

166 "The wind wasn't at"—*Richmond Times-Dispatch*, June 17, 1973, Chauncey Durden, "Sportsview: Tom Wonder Is Defiant."

166 "I'm trying to drive it"—*Richmond Times-Dispatch*, June 17, 1973, Chauncey Durden, "Sportsview: Lean and Mean Weiskopf."

166 I feel I'm in excellent"—*Rochester Democrat and Chronicle*, June 16, 1973, Tony Destino, "Player 1st In Open by Stroke."

166 "Weiskopf mainly kept"—Interview with Gene Borek, July, August 2007.

167 "I knocked my first putt"—*Columbus Evening Dispatch*, June 17, 1973, Paul Hornung, "Weiskopf's Confidence Bolstered."

167 "It was like an eagle"—*Los Angeles Times*, June 17, 1973, Bill Shirley, "Palmer Puts Open into Focus, Shares Lead."

167 "some of the birdie roars"—Hornung, "Weiskopf's Confidence."

167 "After those two birdies"—ibid.

167 "I don't feel like"—*Chicago Sun Times*, June 17, 1973, Len Ziehm, "Arnie Charges into 4-way Open Tie."

167 "Somebody's going to"—*Columbus Evening Dispatch*, June 18, 1973, Paul Hornung, "'Heckuva Round' Beat Weiskopf as Predicted."

CHAPTER 8
A Day for All Ages

169 "three inches of heather"—*Dallas Morning News*, (AP), July 16, 1972, "Lee's Chip Keeps Open from Jack."

169 "So I should"—*Columbus Evening Dispatch*, June 17, 1973, Paul Hornung, "Weiskopf's Confidence Bolstered."

170 "I've played fifty-four holes"—*Dallas Morning News*, June 17, 1973, Harless Wade, "Four Create Logjam at U.S. Open."

170 "I've tried fifteen"—*Pittsburgh Press*, June 17, 1973, Dan Donovan, "Weiskopf on Winning Track."

170 "People bug me"—*Washington Post*, June 17, 1973, Bob Addie, "Open Season Here for Pros' Expenses."

170 "I won't bore you"—*Pittsburgh Press*, June 17, 1973, "'Oh, Lonesome Me!'"

170 "I've been four strokes"—*Rochester Democrat and Chronicle*, June 17, 1973, Tony Destino, "Palmer, 3 Others Tied in Open."

171 "His tee shots were"—*Pittsburgh Press*, June 17, 1973, Jeff Samuels, "Player: Yesterday He Was a Duffer."

171 "Player had it the hardest"—ibid.

172 "When I shot 80"—Interview with Gene Borek, July, August 2007.

173 "I wasn't doing too well"—*Boston Globe*, June 17, 1973, Tom Fitzgerald, "Boros, 53 Years Young, Says: 'I Never Think about My Age.'"

174 "I had been playing poorly"—*Akron Beacon Journal*, June 17, 1973, John Seaburn, "Four-way Tie in U.S. Open."

174 "I had to go over two"—*Pittsburgh Press*, June 17, 1973, Ray Kienzl, "Palmer, 3 Others in Open Tie."

175 "I had a couple putts"—ibid.

175 "the easiest condition"—*Miami Herald*, June 17, 1973, "Astrologer Schlee's Stars Favorable; Heard Intent on Keeping Composure."

176 "In the past, I've put"—*Dallas Morning News*, June 5, 1973, Harless Wade, "Schlee Tries Once Again."

176 "He was under trees"—Wade, "Four Create Logjam."

176 "This is a good week"—*Wisconsin State Journal*, (AP), June 17, 1973, "Stars Informed Schlee He'd Have Good Week."

177 "Anybody can win one"—*Sports Illustrated*, June 10, 1968, Dan Jenkins, "Back to Baltus Oaks."

178 "For a while, Julius"—*Long Beach (CA) Press-Telegram*, *Parade* magazine, August 3, 1952, Paul Gardner, "He plays for . . . 'Buttons.'"

179 "His swing is like"—*Columbus Evening Dispatch*, June 17, 1973, Will Grimsley, "U.S. Open Fans Loved Julie, Arnie Production."

179 "Play a round of golf"—*Sports Illustrated*, March 25, 1968, Julius Boros and Mark Mulvoy, "My Easygoing Game."

179 "He'd come home from"—*New York Times*, June 24, 1963, "Phlegmatic Champion."

180 "I'm not shooting anything"—*Golf Magazine*, August 1973, "Reports: News and Views of the Golfer's World."

180 "my game hasn't been"—*Fort Lauderdale News Sun-Sentinel*, June 17, 1973, Craig Barnes, "Julius Steals a Bit of Arnie's Thunder."

181 "I played the first fourteen"—*Philadelphia Inquirer*, June 17, 1973, Fred Byrod, "The Wide Open—No Winner in Sight."

181 "That happens once in a"—*Miami Herald*, June 17, 1973, Edwin Pope, "Boros: 'I Think I Can Play as Well as Anybody.'"

181 "one of the greatest pars"—*Los Angeles Times*, June 17, 1973, Bill Shirley, "Palmer Puts Open into Focus, Shares Lead."

181 "So it was perhaps"—All research materials from the television broadcasts of June 16 and June 17, 1973, provided by ABC Sports.

182 "I sure don't feel fifty-three"—*Atlanta Journal-Constitution*, June 17, 1973, Al Smith, "Four 'Unlikelys' Look Good."

182 "Some of the damnedest"—*Richmond Times-Dispatch*, June 17, 1973, "Four Deadlocked for Open Lead."

183 "Vince was nervous"—*Cleveland Plain Dealer*, (AP), June 17, 1973, "Pressure KO's Palmer's Caddie."

183 "Arnold Palmer, go out"—*Miami Herald*, June 17, 1973, "'4-Way Tie Leaves Open for All Ages."

183 "Who's the greatest golfer"—*Pittsburgh Press*, (UPI), June 17, 1973, "Arnie Calls Jack the Greatest."

18 "One of each"—*Des Moines Register*, June 19, 1973, "Majors Talks Pitt Game."

185 "over the swales and valleys"—*Abilene (TX) Reporter-News*, (AP), June 17, 1973, "Charging Palmer in Four-way Tie for Open Lead."

185 "Yancey turned around"—*Rochester Democrat and Chronicle*, June 17, 1973, Tony Destino, "Arnie's Army on March."

185 "The gallery following me"—Destino, "Palmer, 3 Others Tied."

186 "One thing about it"—*Heyward (CA) Daily Review*, (UPI), June 17, 1973, Ira Miller, "Palmer in 4-way Tie for Open Lead."

186 "It was a great day"—Grimsley, "U.S. Open Fans Loved."

186 "I think Arnold's going"—*New York Times*, June 17, 1973, Lincoln A. Werden, "Palmer Is 'Man to Beat.'"

186 "When I got my round going"—*Chicago Sun-Times*, June 17, 1973, Len Ziehm, "Arnie Charges into 4-way Open Tie."

186 "I have nothing to get"—Smith, "Four 'Unlikelys.'"

CHAPTER 9

Joe Feast vs. Joe Famine

187 "I can win"—*San Francisco Chronicle*, June 16, 1973, Art Spander, "S.F.'s Miller a Future King?"

188 "the best round I ever"—*New York Times*, (UPI), March 21, 1971, "Underwood Ties Miller with 210."

188 "It's the worst wind"—*Oakland Tribune*, (AP), March 21, 1971, "Miller Ties Underwood for Lead."

188 "Miller was in tears"—*New York Times*, (AP), March 22, 1971, "Gary Player Triumphs in Golf Play-off, Beating Underwood on Second Hole."

189 "nerveless kid"—*Elyria Chronicle*, April 11, 1971, Hubert Mizell, "Charlie No Longer 'Choker.'"

189   "[It] seemed that every"—*New York Times*, April 12, 1971, Lincoln A. Werden, "Coody's 279 Takes Masters by 2 Strokes."

189   "brought the tournament alive"—*New York Times*, April 12, 1971, John S. Radosta, "Green Slacks and Old Coin Part of Coody's Magic."

189   "He has no fear"—Mizell, "Charlie No Longer."

189   "I had a great mental"—*Salt Lake Tribune*, (UPI), April 12, 1971, "The Thought of Jacket Sinks Miller."

189   "On that day I lost"—*Golf Magazine*, September 1973, Johnny Miller, "I'm Not Afraid to Go for the Flagstick."

190   "I can hit the ball"—*Idaho Falls (ID) Post Register*, (AP), June 16, 1971, "John Miller Named as U.S. Open Dark Horse."

190   "This is a wonderful course"—*Philadelphia Inquirer*, June 16, 1971, Fred Byrod, "Merion Will Take Toll, Open Contenders Agree."

190   "He begged me to go"—*New Mexican*, (AP), September 13, 1971, "Miller Aces Southern."

191   "Wearing a navy blue shirt"—*Atlanta Journal-Constitution*, September 13, 1971, Charlie Roberts, "Miller Rockets to First."

191   "I'm not going to look"—*Columbus (GA) Ledger-Enquirer*, September 12, 1971, Cecil Darby," 'Blinders' Might Help Miller's Final-day Game Plan."

191   "I may have been destined"—Roberts, "Miller Rockets."

191   "It was getting a little"—*Columbus (GA) Ledger-Enquirer*, September 13, 1971, Cecil Darby, "Miller Winner Now—That's Important Thing."

191   "Winning this one"—Roberts, "Miller Rockets."

192   "Everyone laid [*sic*] down"—*Golf World*, January 25, 1972, Art Spander, "Now Cut That Out! You Can't Win Them All."

192   "Everybody out there just"—*Oakland Tribune*, January 17, 1972, Ed Schoenfeld, "Altered Strokes Wins for Jack."

192   "leap on a seven-iron"—*Oakland Tribune*, January 17, 1972, Ed Schoenfeld, "A Shank Costs Miller."

192   "It was a beauty"—*New York Times*, January 17, 1972, Lincoln A. Werden, "Nicklaus Takes Crosby Tourney on Extra Hole."

193   "But I had the same"—Schoenfeld, "A Shank Costs Miller."

193   "From that day forward"—Miller, *I Call the Shots*, pp. 13–14.

194 "I lost interest after missing"—*Long Beach (CA) Independent Press-Telegram*, February 14, 1972, Doug Ives, "Life Begins at 45 for Rosburg."

194 "I knew it was on line"—*New York Times*, July 14, 1972, Fred Tupper, "Trevino, Jacklin Share Lead with 141s."

195 "It's hard to believe"—*New York Times*, November 27, 1972, Lincoln A. Werden, "John Miller, at 211, Gains Shot Edge in Cold, Wind."

196 "All sorts of things went"—*Salt Lake Tribune*, (AP), November 28, 1972, "Miller Wins Links Duel."

196 "A week ago I won a"—*New York Times*, November 28, 1972, Lincoln A. Werden, "Heritage Golf Won by Johnny Miller."

196 "Coming into the last"—*Oakland Tribune*, (AP), November 28, 1972, "Absence of Names Aid to Miller."

197 "He has the shots for"—*Golf Magazine*, June 1973, "Six for the Money."

197 "If Miller doesn't birdie"—Interview with Ralph Johnston, November 2007.

197 "golf's answer to the"—*Oakland Tribune*, February 14, 1972, Jim Murray, "Hope Springs Anew for Dr. One Putt."

198 "I don't force birdies"—*Long Beach (CA) Independent Press-Telegram*, February 11, 1973, Doug Ives, "A Nicklaus-Palmer Showdown."

198 "I kept thinking they"—*Long Beach (CA) Independent Press-Telegram*, February 12, 1973, Doug Ives, "Arnie Ends Drought in Desert Downpour."

198 "I was getting a tag like"—*Detroit Free Press*, June 18, 1973, Joe Falls, "Miller Wins U.S. Open on Record 63."

198 "That hurt"—*Cleveland Press*, June 18, 1973, Burt Graeff, "From 'Choke' Tag to Open Titlist."

198 "Never allow yourself"—*Golf Monthly*, Joe E. Doan, August 1973, "Hogan Was the Miller Hero."

198 "I think Johnny's"—Interview with Jack Nicklaus, September 2008.

199 "If it's somebody like"—*Toronto Star*, June 16, 1973, Ken McKee, "Rollercoaster Greens Become Putt Paradise as Par Beats U.S. Open."

199 "nondescript shots"—*Pittsburgh Press*, June 17, 1973, "'Oh, Lonesome Me!'"

199 "I got to the first tee"— *Golfweek*, June 9, 2007, "Johnny opens up."

200 "The round was a"—*Cleveland Plain Dealer*, June 18, 1973, Bill Nichols, "Miller Shoots Record 63 to Win Open."

200 "I was really down"—*Pittsburgh Post-Gazette*, June 18, 1973, Marino Parascenzo, "Johnny Replaces Gary; A New Player on Board."

CHAPTER 10
Chasing a Living, Chasing Trouble

201 "When I got to the course"— Bertrand, Tom, with Printer Bowler, *The Secret of Hogan's Swing* (New York: John Wiley & Sons, Inc., 2006), p. 83.

201 "facing a firing squad"—*Pittsburgh Press*, June 18, 1973, Ray Kienzl, "It Was in the Stars."

201 "I beat him every"—ibid.

202 "It's like a two-shot penalty"—*Pittsburgh Press*, June 18, 1973, Ray Kienzl, "Miller Gobbles up U.S. Open."

202 "Don't get me wrong"—*Dallas Morning News*, June 18, 1973, "Schlee 'Survives.'"

203 "popped those wrists"—Interview with Neal Maine, February 2008.

204 "you always had this feeling"—ibid.

205 "leap like a kangaroo"—ibid.

205 "He didn't do much"—Interview with Ray Sigurdson, February 2008.

206 "I was a pretty bad actor"—*Golf World*, June 6, 2003, Bill Fields, "The High Life and Hard Times of John Schlee."

208 "A whole lot of people"—Interview with Neal Maine, February 2008.

209 "I don't know how I"—*Seaside (OR) Signal*, May 22, 1958, "West Point Assignment Pleases Seaside Boy."

210 "When I was at Memphis State"—*The Memphis (TN) Commercial Appeal*, July 4, 2000, Bobby Hall, "Former Tiger Star Golfer, Schlee, Dies."

210 "He was probably the most"—Fields, "The High Life."

211 "I was there to play"—Hall, "Former Tiger Star Golfer."

211 "I've just found something"—Interview with Ken Lindsay, March 2008.

211 "He was a good person"—ibid.

212 "some of the longest drives"—ibid.

212 "In my first year at"—*Golf Digest*, February 1967, "Practice Finally Pays Off."

212 "Reverse every natural instinct"—Apfelbaum, Jim, *The Gigantic Book of*

Golf Quotations: Thousands of Notable Quotables from Tommy Armour to Fuzzy Zoeller (New York: Skyhorse Publishing, 2007), p. 329.

213 "I would love to learn"—Bertrand, *The Secret of Hogan's Swing*, p. 10.

214 "You are darned right"—*Adirondack (NY) Daily Enterprise*, July 11, 1963, Dick Barnes, "Golfers Sight on Dick Sikes at Sacramento."

214 "I needed a couple of dumb"—*Dallas Morning News*, May 7, 1971, Sam Blair, "No Place Like It."

215 "If we all realized how much"—Interview with Dave Marad, August 2008.

215 "[Out] here on the tour"—*Dallas Morning News*, April 18, 1966, Frank Reece, "The Ladder Is Tall."

216 "I seem to get it going"—ibid.

216 "[He] had that instinct"—Interview with Dave Marad, August 2008.

216 "It was only my fifth"—*Minnesota Tribune*, July 18, 1966, John Wiebusch, "Bobby Nichols, He Overcame 'the Impossible.'"

216 "I enjoy being on tour"—Reece, "The Ladder."

216 "I was in a threesome with"—*Los Angeles Times*, January 30, 1967, Sid Ziff, "Golf Mine on Fairway."

217 "It's something I had to"—ibid.

218 "graying prematurely"—*Akron Beacon Journal*, August 9, 1968, Scott Bosley, "Par for Course Is Not Good Enough."

218 "I was materially"—*New York Times*, August 13, 1971, Lincoln A. Werden, "Schlee, with 66, Leads by Stroke."

218 "There are a lot of young"—*Cleveland Plain Dealer*, June 28, 1969, Tom Place, "Tee to Green."

218 "Christmastimes were"—*Honolulu Advertiser*, February 5, 1973, Hal Wood, "Schlee: Hogan's Ghost."

219 "look my best and"—Bertrand, *The Secret of Hogan's Swing*, p. 12.

219 "After about twenty minutes"—Schlee, John, with Swing Meyer, *Maximum Golf* (Columbia, SC: Acorn Sports Inc., 1986), p. 2.

219 "The first six"—ibid.

220 "You see, golf is an"—ibid., p. 14.

220 "It's a mind that wipes"—ibid., p. 141.

220 "Isn't astrology just"—*Time*, March 21, 1969, "Astrology: Fad and Phenomenon."

220   "They're interested in astrology" — ibid.

221   "Show much consideration" — *Dallas Morning News*, June 1, 1969, Carroll Righter, "Today's Horoscope."

221   "That's very admirable" — Bertrand, *The Secret of Hogan's Swing*, p. 16.

221   "one of the strongest" — *Dallas Morning News*, June 1, 1969, "64 to Vie for 9 Slots at Open."

222   "maddeningly inconsistent" — Campion, Nicholas, *The Ultimate Astrologer: A Simple Guide to Calculating and Interpreting Birth Charts for Effective Application in Daily Life* (Carlsbad, CA: Hay House, 2003), p. 17.

223   "It's great to play without" — *Cleveland Press*, June 28, 1969, Don Friedman, "Barber: My Nerves Just Can't Stand It."

223   "I'm keeping this big" — *Golf World*, April 6, "Bunker to Bunker."

223   "Mr. Hogan said it would" — *Hawaii Star Bulletin*, February 5, 1973, Bill Glee, "Schlee's 273 Captures Hawaiian Open by Two."

224   "I'm trying like mad" — *Dallas Morning News*, May 7, 1971, Sam Blair, "No Place Like It."

225   "his way of doing" — Interview with Sherie Roman, March 2008.

225   "He wasn't a social" — ibid.

226   "a volatile, abusive man" — ibid.

227   "unpredictable trade winds" — *New York Times*, (UPI), February 5, 1971, "Schlee Leads Hawaiian Golf by Shot With 66."

227   "There's something about" — *Honolulu Star Bulletin*, February 4, 1973, Hal Wood, "'No Way He Can Keep That Up.'"

227   "I think I am playing" — *Honolulu Star-Bulletin*, February 4, 1973, Hal Wood, "Where the Names Are."

227   "Second isn't bad" — *Honolulu Star-Bulletin*, February 4, 1973, Monte Ito, "Watson by Four after Three."

228   "I got to thinking" — *Golf World*, February 9, 1973, "A Jug of Wine and Schlee."

228   "He was walking one" — *New York Times*, February 5, 1973, Lincoln A. Werden, "Schlee Wins Hawaii Golf for First Tour Victory."

228   "I owe this great moment" — Glee, "Schlee's 273."

228   "I can't believe it" — *Honolulu Advertiser*, February 5, 1973, Ben Kalb, "Oh Babe, I Can't Believe You've Won.'"

228   "Not once over the first" — *Golf World*, "A Jug of Wine."

228 "Right after I won"—Schlee, *Maximum Golf*, pp. 142–43.

229 "Now, my confidence"—*Dallas Morning News*, February 6, 1973, "Schlee 'Hoping' for Best."

CHAPTER 11
The Mad Scramble

23 "What did you do last night"—*Pittsburgh Press*, June 18, 1973, Ray Kienzl, "It Was in the Stars."

234 "playing alone disrupts"—*Pittsburgh Press*, June 17, 1973, "'Oh, Lonesome Me!'"

234 "I played so badly"—*Pittsburgh Press*, June 18, 1973, Dan Donovan, "'Sudden Explosion Wrecks Arnie in Open."

235 "I went for the birdies"—*Pittsburgh Press*, June 15, 1973, Dan Donovan, "Snead: A Real Iron Man."

235 "Two more 69s"—*Richmond Times-Dispatch*, June 16, 1973, "Giles 'Numbers' 2-3-3-3 for a 69."

235 "There's no question"—*Danville (VA) Bee*, (AP), July 5, 1971, "Giles: Wadkins Best—But Not Infallible."

236 "I felt I hit the ball better"—*Richmond Times-Herald*, June 17, 1973, Harold Pearson, "Giles-Wadkins Again; The Winner? Oakmont."

236 "Hey, you guys"—ibid.

237 "Tom Weiskopf has more"—*Long Beach (CA) Independent Press-Telegram*, May 31, 1973, Doug Ives, "New Exciting World Opening up for Laura."

237 "so unhappy with the way"—*Chicago Tribune*, June 18, 1973, Cooper Rollow," 'I'm Not a Flash in the Pan'—Miller."

237 "I was really down"—*Pittsburgh Post-Gazette*, June 18, 1973, Marino Parascenzo, "Johnny Replaces Gary; A New Player on Board."

237 "Here I had had a"—*Golf Magazine*, September 1973, Johnny Miller, "I'm Not Afraid to Go for the Flagstick."

238 "I remembered earlier in the"—*San Francisco Chronicle*, June 18, 1973, Art Spander, "Miller Wary until End."

238 "Well, I was on the practice"— *Golfweek*, June 9, 2007, "Johnny opens up."

238 "On Friday evening"—*Pittsburgh Press*, July 23, 1978, Ray Kienzl, "Caddie Hopes to Bag Miller Again."

239   "I had forgotten my yardage"—*Pittsburgh Tribune-Review*, June 10, 2007, Mike Dudurich, "Miller's Dissection of Oakmont Stands the Test of Time."

239   "I played like par"— *Golfweek*, June 9, 2007, "Johnny opens up."

240   "I was just trying to get"—Parascenzo, "Johnny Replaces Gary."

240   "When I get charged up"—*Pittsburgh Post-Gazette*, June 18, 1973, "Miller Prepped—to Lose."

240   "I was sky-high"—*Latrobe Bulletin*, (UPI), June 18, 1973, Frank Berkopec, "Miller Breaks Record in Open."

241   "I really got pumped"—*Philadelphia Inquirer*, June 18, 1973, Fred Byrod, "Record 63 Carries Miller to Open Title."

241   "I can honestly say I"—Berkopec, "Miller Breaks Record."

242   "I remembered [how] at Augusta"—Kienzl, "It Was in the Stars."

243   "Trevino's putt was"—Wind, *Following Through*, p. 166.

244   "Gary Player told me"—*Chicago Sun Times*, June 18, 1973, Len Ziehm, "Schlee Victim of Arnie's Army."

244   "the same as wearing"—*Pittsburgh Post-Gazette*, June 18, 1973, Bill Christine, "Schlee Schleppes Around with 3 Drives on No. 1."

245   "[You] should have seen me"—Bertrand, *The Secret of Hogan's Swing*, p. 82.

245   "It was all about Arnold"—Interview with Bob Ford, June 2008.

245   "I couldn't believe he"—ibid.

246   "So many people were"—Bertrand, *The Secret of Hogan's Swing*, p. 83.

246   "[The relief] wouldn't"—Christine, "Schlee Schleppes."

247   "It was so strange"—Bertrand, *The Secret of Hogan's Swing*, p. 84.

247   "That verified the fact"—Interview with Bob Ford, June 2008.

247   "All I could think was I'd"—*Akron Beacon Journal*, June 20, 1973, Jack Patterson, "Will Schlee Be 'Star' in Classic?"

247   "I think everybody chokes"—*New York Times*, June 17, 1973, "Palmer Is 'Man to Beat.'"

247   "If I win this one"—*Charleston (WV) Daily Mail*, June 18, 1973, Jerry Izenberg, "Miller's Manager off to Money Races."

248   "horses, fishing, girls"—*Philadelphia Inquirer*, June 17, 1973, "John Schlee Thanking His Lucky Stars after Gaining Share of Third-round Lead."

248   "I hope I get paired"—*Atlanta Journal-Constitution*, June 17, 1973, Al Smith, "Four 'Unlikelys' Look Good."

249   "Hit that right-hand"—*Pittsburgh Post-Gazette*, June 18, 1973, Bill Christine, "Playing Games."

253   "I don't suppose it"—Palmer, *A Golfer's Life*, p. 208.

253   "I was used to playing"—ibid., pp. 208–09.

255   "hit the ball two ways"—Gabriel, Mike, *The Professional Golf Association Tour: A History* (Jefferson, NC: McFarland & Company, Inc., 2001), p. 177.

256   "an indifferent putter"—United States Golf Association, 1973 U.S. Open: *Miller's Miracle at Oakmont*.

258   "At the back of the"—*New York Times*, June 18, 1973, Lincoln A. Werden, "Miller's Record 63 for 279 Total Wins U.S. Open Golf Title."

259   "never saw me play"—*Pittsburgh Press*, June 17, 1973, Dan Donovan, "Weiskopf on Winning Track."

CHAPTER 12

The Greatest Nine Ever

262   "A shot poorly played"—*Golf Course Management*, May 1983, Ronald E. Whitten, "Mighty Oakmont Rumbles Again."

262   "We turned on the TV"—*San Francisco Chronicle*, June 19, 1973, Art Spander, "Miller's Nervous Rooting Section."

263   "Break out a package"—*Pittsburgh Press*, July 23, 1978, Ray Kienzl, "Caddie Hopes to Bag Miller Again."

264   "the toughest par-four"—http://www.worldgolf.com/news/pga/us-open-oakmont-notebook-fred-funk-5555.htm, June 2007, Brandon Tucker, "U.S. Open Notebook: With Fred Dunk high on the leaderboard, Is Oakmont 'Funky Town.'"

265   "It was horrible stuff"—*Los Angeles Times*, June 18, 1973, Bill Shirley, "Johnny Miller Wins U.S. Open—Honest!"

265   "I should have bogeyed"—ibid.

266   "I'll never forget twelve"—Interview with Dick Thompson, March 2008.

266   "Number twelve was the whole"—*Pittsburgh Press*, June 18, 1973, Ray Kienzl, "Miller Gobbles up U.S. Open."

266   "I really flagged it"—Shirley, "Johnny Miller Wins."

266　"I said, 'Mr. Worsham'"—Interview with Bob Ford, June 2008.

267　"Coming down fourteen, I was"—Kienzl, "Miller Gobbles Up."

267　"doesn't drink, doesn't smoke"—*New York Times*, February 13, 1975, Dave Anderson, "The Johnny Miller Market Is Soaring."

267　"a mammoth bunker"—Sommers, Robert, *U.S. Open: Golf's Ultimate Challenge*, 2nd ed. (New York: Oxford University Press, 1996), p. 261.

268　"[He] had 187 yards"—Kienzl, "Caddie Hopes to Bag."

268　"Barber started pulling"—Kienzl, "Miller Gobbles Up."

269　"We're not good friends"—*Chicago Tribune*, June 18, 1973, Cooper Rollow, "'I'm Not a Flash in the Pan'—Miller."

269　"Johnny, you're playing"—Interview with Miller Barber, October 2008.

270　"Barber told me when"—Kienzl, "Miller Gobbles up."

271　"to stay cool, not to"—*Golf Magazine*, September 1973, Johnny Miller, "I'm Not Afraid to Go for the Flagstick."

271　"Standing in the middle"—*Dallas Morning News*, June 18, 1973, Harless Wade, "Miller Blazes Way to Open Title."

272　"[I hit] as good a putt"—*Chicago Tribune*, June 18, 1973, Tom Tomashek, "Miller wins U.S. Open on Record 63."

272　"Even with only about"—ibid.

272　"No, I'm not nervous"—*Pittsburgh Post-Gazette*, June 18, 1973, Marino Parascenzo, "Johnny Replaces Gary; A New Player on Board."

CHAPTER 13
Chasing Greatness

275　"[For] about two minutes"—*Richmond Times-Dispatch*, June 18, 1973, Harold Pearson, "Tied Record 'For 2 Minutes.'"

278　"I won't do it unless"—*The Atlanta Constitution*, June 15, 1973, Al Smith, "Jack's Shot Not in Plan Trevino Has."

278　"Trevino had to pitch"—*El Paso Herald Times*, June 18, 1973, Bob Ingram, "'As I was saying . . .'"

279　"guy with the million-dollar"—*Philadelphia Inquirer*, June 11, 1973, Frank Dolson, "Weiskopf Has Everything . . . Well, Almost."

280　"I couldn't believe it"—*The Atlanta Constitution*, June 18, 1973, Al Smith, "Miller's Scorching 63 Wins."

280 "Oakmont is not a"—*Pittsburgh Press*, June 19, 1973, Pat Livingston, "U.S.G.A. Better Get Lead Out."

281 "Johnny Miller?"—*Sports Illustrated*, June 25, 1973, Dan Jenkins, "Battle of the Ages."

281 "I really still thought"—*Chicago Tribune*, June 18, 1973, Tom Tomashek, "Miller Wins U.S. Open on Record 63."

281 "When I made a twelve-footer"—*Pittsburgh Press*, June 18, 1973, Ray Kienzl, "Miller Gobbles up U.S. Open."

281 "[If] Jack can drive it"—*Richmond Times-Dispatch*, June 17, 1973, Chauncey Durden, "The 19th Green."

282 "I felt like I wanted"—*Columbus Evening Dispatch*, June 18, 1973, Paul Hornung," 'Heckuva Round' Beat Weiskopf as Predicted."

283 "I couldn't have felt"—*Los Angeles Times*, June 18, 1973, Bill Shirley, "Johnny Miller Wins U.S. Open—Honest!"

284 "[What] do they think"—Hornung, "'Heckuva Round.'"

284 "I made what I thought"—Palmer, *A Golfer's Life*, p. 227.

284 "Where the fuck did"—O'Connor, Ian, *Arnie & Jack: Palmer, Nicklaus, and Golf's Greatest Rivalry* (Boston: Houghton Mifflin, 2008), p. 202.

284 "I hear he has [nine]"—Shirley, "Johnny Miller Wins."

285 "It never entered my mind"—*San Francisco Chronicle*, June 18, 1973, Art Spander, "Miller Wary until End."

285 "Sixty-three?"—*Toronto Star*, June 18, 1973, Ken McKee, "Dream Ends for Arnold Palmer."

285 "Still confident"—Sommers, *U.S. Open*, p. 262.

285 "I struck what I was sure"—Palmer, *A Golfer's Life*, p. 227.

286 "What did I have to lose?"—*Pittsburgh Press*, June 18, 1973, Dan Donovan, "'Sudden Explosion' Wrecks Arnie in Open."

286 "When Arnold made those"—Shirley, "Johnny Miller Wins."

286 "I won this tournament"—Spander, "Miller Wary."

286 "What do they say"—Donovan, "'Sudden Explosion.'"

287 "As we left the course"—*Pittsburgh Post-Gazette*, (AP), June 18, 1973, Will Grimsley, "Arnie Drive to 'Office' Out of Play."

288 "Your Individual Horoscope"—*Kittanning (PA) Leader-Times*, June 16, 1973, Frances Drake, "Your Individual Horoscope: For Sunday, June 17, 1973."

290 "Who wouldn't love"—Schlee, *Maximum Golf*, p. 38.

290   "When I'm playing an"—ibid.

291   "What had gone wrong?"—ibid.

291   "I was destined to do"—*Danville (VA) Bee*, (AP), June 18, 1973, George Strode, "Schlee Guessed Wrong."

292   "afraid I'd throw up"—*Miami Herald*, June 19, 1973, Edwin Pope, "Agent Couldn't Look as Miller Sank Putts."

293   "No, it's got to be"—*Washington Post*, June 18, 1973, Bob Addie, "Miller Grabs Open with Record 63."

293   "I don't know much about"—*Pittsburgh Press*, June 18, 1973, Jeff Samuels, "Johnny Takes the Spotlight."

293   "I still can't believe it"—*Columbus Ledger*, June 19, 1973, Cecil Darby, "No Big Surprise."

293   "I don't know if there"—ibid.

293   "Without taking anything away"—*Toronto Star*, June 18, 1973, Ken McKee, "Spectacular Comeback Wins U.S. Open."

293   "What happened to Oakmont's"—*New York Times*, June 19, 1973, Arthur Daley, "The Furious Finish of Johnny Miller."

293   "Imagine shooting a 63"—*Los Angeles Times*, June 18, 1973, Jim Murray, "Open Gets No Respect."

294   "Everyone else is griping"—*Pittsburgh Press*, June 18, 1973, Jeff Samuels, "Johnny Takes the Spotlight."

294   "No, I don't think I'm"—*Pittsburgh Post-Gazette*, June 18, 1973, "Miller Prepped—To Lose."

294   "I've been around and"—Shirley, "Johnny Miller Wins."

CHAPTER 14
Arnold Palmer, Jack Nicklaus, and Lee Trevino

297   "Well, if the decision were"—Palmer, A *Golfer's Life*, p.181.

297   "I'm not going to quit"—*Connellsville (PA) Daily Courier*, (UPI), June 17, 1974, "Palmer Will 'Try Again.'"

299   "There's a school of"—*Golf Digest*, June 1994, Frank Hannigan, "Arnie's Open Invite Defiles the Process."

299   "I've never needed an"—*Galveston (TX) Daily News*, (AP), May 5, 1994, "Open May Be Closed to Seve."

299   "I know [Seve's]"—*Pittsburgh Post-Gazette*, June 16, 1994, "Wadkins Raps Ballesteros for His Criticism of U.S.G.A."

299   "Yes, this will be my last"—*Pittsburgh Post-Gazette*, June 13, 1994, Marino Parascenzo, "Shot That Haunts Arnie Still Tough."

299   "I'm sure a lot of people"—*Pittsburgh Post-Gazette*, June 15, 1994, Gerry Dulac, "Arnie, Jack Walk Down Memory Lane."

299   "I would like to play"—*North Hills (PA) News Record*, June 15, 1994, Kevin Smith, "Back to the Future."

300   "He's responsible for all"—*Pittsburgh Post-Gazette*, June 18, 1994, Ron Cook, "Arnie's Era Ends as His Army Roars."

300   "I was pretty darn proud"—*North Hills (PA) News Record*, June 17, 1994, Kevin Roberts, "Palmer Thrills His Army One More Time."

301   "When you walk up"—United States Golf Association, *Who Els?*, 1994.

301   "[Then came] a rare standing"—ibid.

302   "Usually, when he leaves"—*Pittsburgh Post-Gazette*, June 17, 1994, Marino Parascenzo, "Flashback: It's like the Old Days at Oakmont: Nicklaus Battling Watson."

302   "And then I started to"—ibid.

303   "I think Arnie feels he's"—*Pittsburgh Post-Gazette*, June 18, 1994, Phil Axelrod, "Ageless Nicklaus Still in Hunt for Fifth Open Title."

303   "the weakest part of my"—ibid.

304   "Everything was Bobby Jones"—*New York Times*, August 13, 1973, Thomas Rogers, "Champion of Champions: Jack William Nicklaus."

304   "Nicklaus is gone, done"—*Atlanta Journal-Constitution*, April 6, 1986, Tom McCollister, "This Year Should Be a Wide-open Shootout."

305   "This may be as fine"—*New York Times*, April 14, 1986, Gordon S. White Jr., "Nicklaus Wins Sixth Masters."

306   "My goal is to play"—*New York Times*, June 17, 1968, "Golf's No. 1 Extrovert."

306   "I don't care if it's the"—*Dallas Morning News*, August 13, 1974, Sam Blair, "Jack's Words, Lee's Music."

306   "I don't want to play"—*Columbus Evening Dispatch*, June 14, 1973, Paul Hornung, "Trevino Loves His Life, But Seeks Privacy."

306   "aside newsmen on his"—*Dallas Morning News*, (UPI), August 10, 1973, "'Merry Mex' Crumbles."

306　"[Twirling] his putter"—*Dallas Morning News*, (UPI), August 11, 1974, "Lee Clowns Way to Lead."

306　"I was charged up"—*Charlotte Observer*, August 12, 1974, Tom Higgins, "Trevino Changes His Mind, Will Return to Masters."

307　"Now I'm learning"—*New York Times*, August 11, 1974, John S. Radosta, "Trevino's Surge Gains Lead by Stroke."

307　"my good friend Father"—*Dallas Morning News*, November 18, 1975, "Lee Gives Purse."

307　"It didn't bother me"—*Golf Digest*, May 2002, Guy Yocom, "My Shot: Lee Trevino."

307　"Claudia II"—Trevino, Lee, and Sam Blair, *The Snake in the Sandtrap* (New York: Henry Holt & Co., 1985), p. 41.

308　"First, I never used"—Diaz, "Finding His Way Home."

308　"To be the best at"—Yocom, "My Shot."

308　"I know guys who are"—*Sports Illustrated*, December 18, 1989, Kenny Moore, "It's Nifty Being 50."

309　"I'll have to play good"—*Syracuse Herald American*, (AP), July 1, 1990, "Nicklaus Charges Past Field."

309　"Just when it seemed he"—*New York Times*, July 2, 1990, Jaime Diaz, "Trevino Outduels Nicklaus in Stretch."

309　"As Jack was coming up"—*New York Times*, July 2, 1990, Dave Anderson, "The Trevino-Nicklaus Heat."

309　"If Jack had kept up"—*Salina (KS) Journal*, (AP), July 2, 1990, "Trevino Captures Senior Open."

310　"But sometimes Jack"—Anderson, "The Trevino-Nicklaus Heat."

310　"Gimme the trophy"—Diaz, "Trevino Outduels Nicklaus."

310　"Well-done"—Anderson, "The Trevino-Nicklaus Heat."

CHAPTER 15
Tom Weiskopf

311　"I was in complete control"—*Dallas Morning News*, (AP), July 15, 1973, "Weiskopf Prevails."

311　"[The phone] must have"—*Cleveland Press*, July 16, 1973, Burt Graeff, "Bedford Bubbles over Weiskopf—So Does Mom."

312   "I'm just so happy I"—*Cleveland Plain Dealer*, July 15, 1973, Bill Nichols, "Happiest Mom in Town."

312   "[To] compare him right now"—*Dallas Morning News*, July 16, 1973, Tom Williams, "Weiskopf a 'Changed Man.'"

312   "other years, he has lost"—*New York Times*, July 15, 1973, Fred Tupper, "Weiskopf's 276 Wins Open by Three Shots."

312   "Others had told me"—*Cleveland Plain Dealer*, July 29, 1973, Hal Lebovitz, "Hal Asks . . ."

312   "How bad do I want it?"—*Sports Illustrated*, July 23, 1973, Dan Jenkins, "His First Hurrah."

313   "I think everybody has"—*Cleveland Plain Dealer*, (AP), August 8, 1973, Will Grimsley, "'Era of Weiskopf' in Next 10 Years."

313   "I thought it would be great"—*Akron Beacon Journal*, September 10, 1973, Paul Facinelli, "Nicklaus Was Weiskopf's Target."

313   "As Palmer found out"—*Akron Beacon Journal*, September 10, 1973, Jack Patterson, "Tommy's Footsteps Haunt Big Jack."

314   "I didn't know that"—*Sports Illustrated*, January 14, 1974, Dan Jenkins, "Haunted by His Heirs."

314   "Everybody said that I"—ibid.

315   "I feel like I might as well"—*New York Times*, June 7, 1974, Gordon S. White Jr., "Weiskopf: Courses Too Easy."

315   "Are you injured"—*Charlotte Observer*, (AP), August 10, 1974, "Weiskopf: I Just Wanted to Quit."

315   "Tom never pulls stuff"—*Galveston (TX) Daily News*, (UPI), October 31, 1974, "Nicklaus, Weiskopf Teamed in Disney Golf."

315   "broke my concentration"—CBS television broadcast of the Masters, April 12, 1981. Weiskopf, co-announcing the Masters with Jack Whitaker, went on: "I can remember very vividly, Jack, I just said to myself, how can a guy continually do that to me? And he's a nice friend of mine, too." Weiskopf was standing on the sixteenth tee when Nicklaus sank his putt.

316   "[But] then I got cute"—*New York Times*, June 13, 1980, John S. Radosta, "Nicklaus, Weiskopf, with 63s Lead by 3; Tie U.S. Open Mark."

316   "Of course, that was"—*Syracuse Herald Journal* (*Chicago Sun-Times* Service), June 13, 1980, Ron Rapoport, "Buckeyes Light up Jersey Course."

316   "I knew Tom had"—*Frederick (MD) Post*, (AP), June 13, 1980, "Nicklaus Takes Caddie's Advice, Answers Weiskopf."

317 "I knew Jack would"—ibid.

317 "I've always felt"—*Salina (KS) Journal*, (UPI), June 16, 1980, "Nicklaus Claims 4th U.S. Open Crown."

317 "Yesterday was my"—*The New Mexican*, (UPI), June 14, 1980, "Nicklaus Takes 2-shot Lead in U.S. Open."

318 "the best I've ever played"—*Golf World*, May 7, 1993, Chris Millard, "Tom II."

318 "The press and the fans"—*Chicago Daily Herald*, July 5, 1982, Mike Imrem, "Tom Terrific Deserves Praise."

318 "[Weiskopf has been]"—Nicklaus, *My Story*, p. 308.

318 "If I knew the way"—CBS television broadcast of the Masters, April 13, 1986.

319 "no goals in life"—*Golf World*, March 1, 1991, "Tour Talk."

319 "He's a waste product"—ibid.

319 "I told them I had"—*Golf Digest*, April 2000, Jim Moriarty, "Inferno Erupts Again."

319 "At the end of 1984"—*Golf World*, May 27, 2009, Al Barkow, "Being Tom Weiskopf."

320 "When it's all over"—*Cleveland Plain Dealer*, July 3, 1996, George Sweda, "Heart in the Rough: The Fire Inside Weiskopf Has Been His Best Club and His Trickiest Hazard."

320 "There was a lot of"—*Golf World*, March 5, 1993, Tom Spousta, "Too Much Tom."

320 "Hopefully, it's going to"—*Denver Post*, Tom Kensler, July 6, 1993, ". . . But No-name Players Have Made Their Mark, Too."

321 "I played perfect today"—*Denver Post*, July 10, 1993, "Missed Putts Stall Weiskopf's Drives."

321 "This course suits my"—ibid.

321 "Saturday is the day"—*The Capitol* (MD), (AP), July 11, 1993, "Jack Charges Back for Lead in Senior Open."

321 "I guess I just don't have"—*Denver Post*, July 11, 1993, "Easy Does It with a Driver for Nicklaus."

322 "I was going under the"—*Denver Post*, July 12, 1993, Steve McPherson, "Weiskopf Left Again in Shadow."

322 "And the only reason"—*Rocky Mountain News*, July 12, 1993, Adam Schefter, "Weiskopf Comes up a Putt Shy."

322 "I knew it was over"—*Rocky Mountain News*, July 12, 1993, John Meyer, "Golden Bear Bags Another Major; Nicklaus Holds Off Weiskopf to Win U.S. Senior Open."

323 "I gave it the best run"—*Denver Post*, July 12, 1993, Todd Phipers, "Nicklaus Thunders to the Top."

323 "The guy is just one"—*New York Times*, July 12, 1993, Jaime Diaz, "Nicklaus Regains Golden Touch."

CHAPTER 16
John Schlee

324 "I'm just fortunate to"—Danville (VA) Bee, (AP), June 18, 1973, George Strode, "Schlee Guessed Wrong."

324 "No, I'm not let down"—*Akron Beacon Journal*, June 20, 1973, Jack Patterson, "Will Schlee Be 'Star' In Classic?"

324 "No, not at all"—ibid.

325 "Players of my caliber"—*Walla Walla (WA) Union-Bulletin*, (AP), July 8, 1973, "Unhappy Schlee, Edwards Qualify for British Open."

325 "[nothing] exciting this month"—*Napa Valley Register*, October 20, 1973, Jess Duke, "John Schlee Captures Lead at Kaiser's Halfway Point."

325 "[At] times out there"—*Fresno Bee*, (AP), October 20, 1973, "Schlee Swings to Kaiser Lead with 'Super Human' 67 Score."

326 "Ed and I are pretty good"—*Napa Valley Register*, October 22, 1973, Frank Gordon, "Sneed, Not Snead, Wins 7th Kaiser."

326 "He always had a tough"—Interview and e-mail with Darryl Donovan, July, August 2009.

326 "It was Ed's day"—Gordon, "Sneed, Not Snead."

327 "June was a good"—*New York Times*, June 7, 1974, Gordon S. White Jr., "Weiskopf: Courses Too Easy."

327 "Man, I wish we were"—*Charlotte Observer*, August 9, 1974, Richard Sink, "Floyd, Schlee, Green Tie for PGA Lead with 68s."

327 "I feel real sorry"—*Charlotte Observer*, August 9, 1974, Richard Sink, "Schlee Goes by Stars."

328 "Since my moon"—*Burlington (NC) Daily Times-News*, August 9, 1974, Craig Holt, "Stars Light Way for John Schlee."

328 "I think anytime anyone"—*Charlotte Observer*, August 10, 1974, Richard Sink, "Player Shoots Record 64."

328   "an extra vertebrae down"—Schlee, *Maximum Golf*, p. 3.

329   "I was hurting so bad"—*Atlanta Journal-Constitution*, April 7, 1978, Tom McCollister, "Schlee Puts the Big Hurt on Masters."

330   "I'm really not surprised"—*Atlanta Journal-Constitution*, April 7, 1978, Jesse Outlar, "Schlee's Day Was Guided by the Stars."

330   "How many millionaires"—*Tyrone (PA) Daily Herald*, (UPI), April 11, 1978, Milton Richman, "Today's Sports Parade."

331   "When I retired from"—Schlee, *Maximum Golf*, p. 4.

331   "John also passed all of"—Bertrand, *The Secret of Hogan's Swing*, p. 44.

332   "I think there will"—*New York Times*, August 9, 1968, Lincoln A. Werden, "Schlee Takes 2-stroke Lead in American Golf Classic with 5-under-par 65."

332   "I didn't even remember"—ibid., p. 64.

333   "He's already given me"—*Syracuse Herald-Journal*, June 22, 1989, Donna Ditota and Jeff D'Alessio, "Amateurs Pick up Some Tips from Pros."

334   "Hey, man, I know"—Interview and e-mail with Darryl Donovan, July, August 2009.

335   "People either loved John"—ibid.

335   "You got to really want"—Richman, "Today's Sports Parade."

CHAPTER 17
Johnny Miller

337   "Johnny Miller looks like"—*Akron Beacon Journal*, June 22, 1973, Paul Bailey, "Miller Credits Arnie With Assist on Ace."

338   "Before then, I thought"—*Los Angeles Times* (*Chicago Sun-Times*), June 13, 1983, Ron Rapoport, "Johnny Miller Returns to the Scene of His Miracle 63."

338   "I don't mean to be boastful"—*New York Times*, January 18, 1974, Lincoln A. Werden, "Miller's 62 Leads in Golf."

338   "It was sort of golfing"—World Golf Hall of Fame Profile, Johnny Miller, http://www.wgv.com/hof/member.php?member=1082.

339   "Every time I go out"—*New York Times*, January 23, 1975, John S. Radosta, "The Miller Machine Runs on Confidence."

339   "When I'm standing over"—ibid.

339   "hitting five hundred balls a day"—*Pittsburgh Press*, July 31, 1978, "Miller Hunting Lost Spark."

339   "ominously echoing the"—*Pittsburgh Post-Gazette*, July 31, 1978, Marino Parascenzo, "Can Miller Make It Right?"

339   "They can't travel with"—ibid.

340   "The man wearing Johnny"—*Los Angeles Times*, January 12, 1979, Jim Murray, "The Miller Mystery."

340   "Eventually, Miller's game"—*Los Angeles Times* (*Chicago Sun-Times*), June 13, 1983, Ron Rapoport, "Johnny Miller Returns to the Scene of His Miracle 63."

341   "I told those who supported"—*New York Times*, (AP), February 23, 1981, "Miller Triumphs by 2."

341   "flunky"—*New York Times*, April 10, 1981, John S. Radosta, "Miller among 4 Tied at 69."

341   "The redeeming factor"—*Salina (KS) Journal*, (UPI), April 10, 1981, "Slump Over: Miller Set for Big Tourney."

342   "Most important, maybe"—*Aiken Standard*, (SC), (AP), February 2, 1987, Bob Green, "Miller's Word Games Work for Pebble Beach Victory."

342   "There was no real point"—*New York Times*, February 2, 1987, Gordon S. White Jr., "Victory by Miller His First Since '83."

342   "When I got to the mountaintop"—World Golf Hall of Fame Profile, Johnny Miller, http://www.wgv.com/hof/member.php?member=1082.

342   "[By] the time I got"—Miller, *I Call the Shots*, p. 221.

342   "I didn't have that good"—*Golf Magazine*, September 1973, Johnny Miller, "I'm Not Afraid to Go for the Flagstick."

342   "Someday, maybe after"—*Golf Digest*, August 1973, Hubert Mizell, "Arnie Warns Miller of Putting Woes."

343   "I knew I couldn't make"—Green, "Miller's Word Games."

343   "So I was sort of"—*New York Times*, February 4, 1988, Gordon S. White Jr., "Son Helps Miller Fight 'Yips.'"

343   "By 1989, my play"—Miller, *I Call the Shots*, p. 35.

343   "Golf just wasn't much"—ibid., pp. 35–36.

344   "awkward and useless"—ibid., p. 37.

344 "Some people may have"—Miller, "I'm Not Afraid."

344 "Jack has been on top"—*Wisconsin State Journal*, (AP), February 16, 1975, "Question of Supremacy Heads to Masterful End."

344 "go with my gut"—*Daily Herald*, (UPI), March 16, 1990, "Miller Pulls No Punches, but May Invite Some."

344 "I want to be unpredictable"—*Sports Illustrated*, March 26, 1990, Walter Bingham, "Here's Johnny—Giving It to You Straight Off the Tee."

344 "This is absolutely the"—ibid.

345 "I guess I opened"—*Daily Herald*, "Miller Pulls no Punches."

345 "I'll pull a guy's pants"—*New York Times*, June 16, 1995, Richard Sandomir, "Miller's Job Is to Talk a Good Game."

345 "the biggest moron"—October 1, 1991, *Los Angeles Times*, Scott Howard-Cooper, "What Went Around the NBA Came Around for Thomas"; Miller, *I Call the Shots*, p. 57.

345 "I feel bad when"—*Golf World*, April 8, 1994, Johnny Miller, "In My Opinion: That's Entertainment."

346 "I didn't come to win"—*Logansport (IN) Pharos-Tribune*, (AP), February 6, 1994, "Miller Pushing One of Tour's Youngsters."

346 "I've always called Pebble"—*Sports Illustrated*, February 14, 1994, Rick Reilly, "Aged to a Tee."

346 "When I get here"—*New York Times*, February 6, 1994, Larry Dorman, "Miller, on 67, Trails by 1; Watson Is 2 Shots Behind."

346 "To be honest"—ibid.

347 "the biggest club selection"—*Golf World*, February 11, 1994, Gary Van Sickle, "Johnny Be Good."

347 "I flashed back to that"—ibid.

347 "You want to know"—*New York Times*, February 7, 1994, Larry Dorman, "Johnny Miller, a Sand Blast From the Past, Wins."

347 "No one's going to enjoy"—*Golf World*, June 3, 1994, Johnny Miller, "In My Opinion: Back to the Beginning."

348 "It's the first time"—*Pittsburgh Post-Gazette* (Block News Alliance), June 17, 1994, "Miller's 81 a Far Cry from His 63 in 1973."

348 "I've hardly practiced"—ibid.

348 "Why should Palmer keep"—*Galveston (TX) Daily News*, (AP), May 5, 1994, "Open May Be Closed to Seve."

348 "Johnny described what"—Sandomir, "Miller's Job."

349 "I was that way before"—*USA Today*, June 13, 2002, Jill Lieber, "NBC's Miller Keeps Firing Away."

349 "Golf is on a roll"—Miller, "In My Opinion: That's Entertainment."

349 "my family and the church"—*Pittsburgh Press*, June 18, 1973, Jeff Samuels, "Johnny Takes the Spotlight."

350 "When you're through"—*New York Times*, May 23, 1975, Red Smith, "Father of the Year, with 9-Iron."

INDEX

Adam Lazarus has served as a sports free-lancer for the *Atlanta Journal-Constitution.*

Photo courtesy of Patrick Williams

Steve Schlossman is a professor of American social and cultural history at Carnegie Mellon University, where he teaches a course on the history of golf, which is recognized by the USGA as the first of its kind.

Photo courtesy of Steve Schlossman